Power SAS:
A Survival Guide

KIRK PAUL LAFLER

apress™

ER SAS: A Survival Guide

Copyright ©2002 by Kirk Paul Lafler

All rights reserved. No part of this work may be reproduced or transmitted in any form or by any means, electronic or mechanical, including photocopying, recording, or by any information storage or retrieval system, without the prior written permission of the copyright owner and the publisher.

Library of Congress Cataloging-in-Publication Data

Lafler, Kirk Paul, 1956-
  Power SAS : a survival guide / Kirk Paul Lafler.
    p. cm.
  ISBN 1-59059-066-X
  1. SAS (Computer file) I. Title.

QA276.4 .L34 2002
005.3'042--dc21
                                    2002013258

Printed and bound in the United States of America 12345678910

Trademarked names may appear in this book. Rather than use a trademark symbol with every occurrence of a trademarked name, we use the names only in an editorial fashion and to the benefit of the trademark owner, with no intention of infringement of the trademark.

The information in this book is distributed on an "as is" basis, without warranty. Although every precaution has been taken in the preparation of this work, neither the author nor Apress shall have any liability to any person or entity with respect to any loss or damage caused or alleged to be caused directly or indirectly by the information contained in this work.

Technical Reviewers: Charles Shipp, Mike DiGregorio, and Sunil Kumar Gupta

Editorial Directors: Dan Appleman, Gary Cornell, Jason Gilmore, Simon Hayes, Karen Watterson, John Zukowski

Managing Editor: Grace Wong

Project Manager and Development Editor: Tracy Brown Collins

Copy Editor: Corbin Collins

Production Manager: Kari Brooks

Compositor: Diana Van Winkle, Van Winkle Design

Artist: Cara Brunk, Blue Mud Productions

Indexer: Rebecca Plunkett

Cover Designer: Kurt Krames

Manufacturing Manager: Tom Debolski

Marketing Manager: Stephanie Rodriguez

Distributed to the book trade in the United States by Springer-Verlag New York, Inc., 175 Fifth Avenue, New York, NY, 10010 and outside the United States by Springer-Verlag GmbH & Co. KG, Tiergartenstr. 17, 69112 Heidelberg, Germany. In the United States, phone 1-800-SPRINGER, email orders@springer-ny.com, or visit http://www.springer-ny.com.
Outside the United States, fax +49 6221 345229, email orders@springer.de, or visit http://www.springer.de.

For information on translations, please contact Apress directly at 2560 9th Street, Suite 219, Berkeley, CA 94710. Phone 510-549-5930, fax 510-549-5939, email info@apress.com, or visit http://www.apress.com.

The source code for this book is available to readers at http://www.apress.com in the Downloads section. You will need to answer questions pertaining to this book in order to successfully download the code.

To Darlynn and Ryan for your love and support, and for giving me a sense of balance between family, work, and play. I love you both so very much.

Contents at a Glance

Foreword .... *xxiii*
About the Author .... *xxv*
About the Foreword Author .... *xxvi*
About the Technical Reviewers .... *xxvii*
Preface .... *xxix*
Acknowledgments .... *xxxi*
Introduction .... *xxxiii*

Chapter 1   SAS Basics *1*

Chapter 2   Data Access *43*

Chapter 3   DATA Step Programming *83*

Chapter 4   Data Manipulation *133*

Chapter 5   Data Management *165*

Chapter 6   Data Presentation *185*

Chapter 7   Efficiency and Performance *213*

Chapter 8   Configuration and Support *227*

Chapter 9   New Version 9 Features *241*

Appendix   SAS System Options *251*

Index *263*

Contents

Foreword xxiii
About the Author xxv
About the Foreword Author xxvi
About the Technical Reviewers xxvii
Preface xxix
Acknowledgments xxxi
Introduction xxxiii

Chapter 1 SAS Basics 1

Getting Started 1
1. Understanding what the SAS System is 1
2. Equating SAS terminology with other software and database languages 2
3. Visualizing the SAS data set structure 3
4. Naming conventions for data sets and variables 3
5. Understanding the importance of keywords and the semicolon 3
6. Coding SAS statements in a "free format" style 3
7. Understanding the role of the SAS Supervisor 4
8. Creating variables 4
9. Avoiding reserved names when naming data sets and variables 5
10. Creating observations 5
11. Understanding the difference between in-stream versus external input data 5
12. Understanding the storage format used by SAS System files 6
13. Creating observations with a DATA statement 6
14. Creating observations with an OUTPUT statement 6
15. Creating observations with a RETURN statement 6
16. Creating observations with the SQL procedure 6
17. Understanding the difference between interactive and batch mode 7
18. Turning off the SAS Display Manager System 7
19. Understanding the control flow of a standard SAS program 7
20. Understanding the control flow of a Macro program 8
21. Understanding the concept of step boundaries 8
22. Accessing the built-in Help facility 9
23. Exiting the SAS System 9

SAS System Options 9
1. Controlling how a SAS session performs and behaves 10
2. Determining the settings of SAS System options at SAS invocation 10

3	Displaying SAS System option settings	10
4	Changing SAS System option settings	10
5	Specifying frequently used SAS options in the Configuration file	10
6	Controlling SAS System initialization	10
7	Specifying the AUTOEXEC= system option	11
8	Running a SAS program in batch or non-interactive mode	11
9	Executing SAS statements after AUTOEXEC file	11
10	Erasing WORK library files at SAS invocation	11
11	Erasing WORK library files at the end of a SAS session	11
12	Specifying a value for the YEARCUTOFF= system option	11
13	Centering procedure output	12
14	Displaying the date and time at the top of each printed page	12
15	Specifying procedures to use labels	12
16	Specifying the printer line width and number of lines	12
17	Specifying a value to use for printing numeric missing values	12
18	Specifying a value to use for invalid numeric data	13
19	Displaying a page number at the top of each printed page	13
20	Resetting the page number	13
21	Writing SAS source statements to the SAS Log	13
22	Specifying the SOURCE option for problem detection and resolution	13
23	Writing SAS source files included with a %INCLUDE statement to the SAS Log	13
24	Specifying the SOURCE2 option for problem detection and resolution	14
25	Writing a subset of the performance statistics to the SAS Log	14
26	Writing all performance statistics to the SAS Log	14
27	Controlling what observation to begin reading in a data set	14
28	Resetting the FIRSTOBS= system option back to the first observation	14
29	Specifying the most recently created data set to use in a read operation	14
30	Specifying the last observation to process	15
31	Processing a maximum number of observations with OBS=MAX	15
32	Checking syntax in a DATA or PROC step	15
33	Specifying OBS=MAX with WHERE	15
34	Processing one or more observations in the middle of a data set	15
35	Preventing SAS data sets from accidentally being replaced	15
36	Reducing the size of a SAS data set through compression	15
37	Uncompressing a data set's observations	16
38	Tracking and reusing free space in a compressed data set	16
39	Controlling error-message printing associated with data errors	16
40	Terminating a SAS program with an abnormal termination (abend)	16
41	Disabling the SAS Macro language	17
42	Printing multiple output pages on the same page	17
43	Printing output in color	17
44	Specifying the number of copies of output to print	17
45	Opening an application with the X command in a minimized window	18

46	Generating an error message when a format isn't found	*18*
47	Specifying the sort utility to use in sorting data	*18*
48	Specifying a sort utility with the SORTPGM= option	*18*
49	Exploring other SAS System Options	*18*

SAS Display Manager System *18*

1	Using the SAS Program Editor window	*19*
2	Viewing the Log window	*19*
3	Viewing the Output Window	*20*
4	Accessing output in the Results window	*20*
5	Viewing the Output Manager window	*20*
6	Using Output Manager commands	*21*
7	Clicking your way from one window to the next	*22*
8	Autosaving your work	*22*
9	Saving your work	*22*
10	Turning the Enhanced Editor on	*22*
11	Finding what you want	*22*
12	Having windows at your command anytime and anywhere	*23*
13	Getting help in the SAS System	*23*
14	Viewing and changing SAS System options	*23*
15	Browsing, modifying, and saving function key settings	*23*
16	Exploring toolbar buttons	*24*
17	Customizing toolbar button settings	*24*
18	Controlling how many commands are saved	*25*
19	Changing Editor options	*25*
20	Checking program text for spelling errors	*26*
21	Clearing the contents of the Recall buffer	*26*
22	Clearing the contents of the Program Editor window	*26*
23	Clearing the contents of the Log window	*27*
24	Clearing the contents of the Output window	*27*
25	Clearing tab settings	*27*
26	Clearing the contents of the active window	*27*
27	Replacing the command line with the PMENU Facility	*27*
28	Disabling the PMENU Facility	*27*
29	Using Function Key shortcuts	*27*
30	Accessing Display Manager Windows	*28*
31	Using Display Manager commands	*28*
32	Using Editor commands	*28*
33	Using Editor line commands	*28*

SAS Explorer *34*

1	Invoking SAS Explorer	*34*
2	Creating a new library reference	*34*
3	Selecting one or more files	*34*
4	Viewing a file's properties	*34*

ix

5	Copying files from one library to another	35
6	Moving files from one library to another	35
7	Duplicating files	35
8	Renaming files	35
9	Deleting files from a library	35
10	Sorting files	36
11	Refreshing the file order	36
12	Resizing detail columns	37
13	Toggling between Show Tree on and Show Tree off	37
14	Viewing the contents of a catalog with Explorer	37
15	Displaying large icons for each file	38
16	Displaying small icons for each file	39
17	Displaying files in a list	39
18	Displaying files and all their details	40
19	Exploring Explorer keyboard shortcuts	40
20	Exploring Explorer commands	40

Summary *41*

Chapter 2   Data Access *43*

External Data *43*

1	Exploring file types	43
2	Identifying external text data	44
3	Understanding the input buffer	44
4	Coding an INFILE statement with in-stream data	44
5	Reading blank-delimited data with list input	44
6	Reading comma-delimited input files	45
7	Reading comma-delimited input containing missing values	45
8	Reading comma-delimited input containing quoted values	46
9	Reading tab-delimited input	46
10	Reading named-input data	47
11	Mixing other styles of input with named-input data	48
12	Reading comma-delimited data with modified-list-input	48
13	Avoiding truncation when reading varying length records	49
14	Assigning missing values with the MISSOVER option	49
15	Reading data with column-style of input	50
16	Reading data with formatted-style of input	50
17	Specifying the maximum number of input records to read	51
18	Specifying the first input record to read	51
19	Using column pointers with formatted-style of input	52
20	Specifying the number of lines available to the input pointer	52
21	Using line pointers with formatted-style of input	52
22	Holding an input record	53

23	Reading carriage-control characters from an input file	54
24	Assigning an error condition to missing input data values	54
25	Reading the next input record with the FLOWOVER option	54
26	Concatenating and reading multiple input files	55
27	Another example of concatenating and reading multiple input files	55
28	Reading from multiple input files with the EOF option	56
29	Identifying the last record in an input file	56
30	Conditionally executing input files	56
31	Specifying a logical record length	57
32	Reading records padded with blanks	57
33	Sharing input and output buffers	57
34	Reading hierarchical files	57
35	Accessing External File Interface (EFI)	58
36	Importing delimited files with EFI	58
37	Accessing data from other applications with DDE	62
38	Accessing the DDE triplet with Microsoft Excel	62

SAS Data Objects *63*

1	Associating a libref with a SAS library	63
2	Another way of referencing a permanent SAS data set	63
3	Listing librefs currently defined in a session	63
4	Exploring SAS engines	64
5	SAS/ACCESS engines	64
6	Reading SAS data sets sequentially	65
7	Reading from multiple SAS data sets	65
8	Starting at the nth observation	65
9	Stopping at the nth observation	65
10	Setting a range for reading observations	66
11	Understanding the Program Data Vector (PDV)	66
12	Understanding the difference between a subsetting IF and WHERE	66
13	Subsetting observations with WHERE	67
14	Selecting variables	67
15	Renaming variables	68
16	Understanding a WHERE expression's processing order	68
17	Executing WHERE expressions with BY groups	68
18	Creating an end-of-file indicator	69
19	Determining the number of observations in an input data set	69
20	Reading SAS data sets directly	70
21	Reading a SAS data set into real memory	70
22	Specifying the number of buffers	70
23	Specifying a data set's level of access	71
24	Reading a generation data set (GENNUM=)	71
25	Accessing data from a view	71
26	Understanding dictionary views	71

	27	Exploring the types of dictionary views	71
	28	Accessing dictionary views	72
	29	Identifying the number of observations in a data set with VTABLE	73
	30	Reading catalog source files	73

Structured Query Language (SQL) Procedure 73
    1   Programming with SQL 73
    2   Understanding ANSI SQL and PROC SQL extensions 74
    3   Bundling the SQL procedure with the Base-SAS product 74
    4   Remaining active until a QUIT; statement is issued 74
    5   Processing with RUN groups and the handling of errors 74
    6   Storing separate pieces of information in a data set or table 74
    7   Understanding columns and datatypes 75
    8   Understanding SQL statements and clauses 75
    9   Ordering of columns and a column wildcard 75
    10   Specifying criteria to subset and display values 75
    11   Understanding parentheses and order of evaluation in SQL 75
    12   Understanding SELECT clause ordering 76
    13   Using too many wildcards and processing time 76
    14   Using caution in the placement of wildcard characters 77
    15   Inserting a blank line between each row of output 77
    16   Assigning clarity to column names with aliases 77
    17   Removing rows containing duplicate column values 77
    18   Sorting data by multiple columns 78
    19   Sorting data in descending order in SQL 78
    20   Sorting by relative position in the select list 79
    21   Sorting columns not specified in a select list 79
    22   Calculating statistics with summary functions 79
    23   Using SQL to summarize data 79
    24   Summarizing data down rows 79
    25   Summarizing data across columns 80
    26   Exploring summary functions 80

Summary 81

Chapter 3   DATA Step Programming 83

The DATA Step Programming Language 83
    1   Understanding the DATA step language 83
    2   Understanding DATA step features and capabilities 84
    3   DATA step processing begins with the DATA statement 84
    4   Understanding the observation loop 85
    5   Revisiting the Program Data Vector (PDV) 85
    6   Setting variables to missing at the top of an observation loop 85
    7   Implying a RETURN to the top of an observation loop 86

8	Stopping an observation loop	86
9	Aborting a step	86
10	Branching at end-of-file	87
11	Returning to the top of the observation loop	87
12	Retaining values across observation loops	88
13	Preventing missing values from being assigned to a variable	88
14	Assigning a variable's length with a LENGTH statement	88
15	Assigning a variable's attributes with the ATTRIB statement	89
16	Changing the length of an existing character variable	89
17	Executing WHEN conditions in a SELECT statement	90
18	Counting with counters	90
19	Looping inside an observation loop	91
20	Specifying an indexed DO loop	91
21	Specifying a DO WHILE loop	91
22	Specifying a DO UNTIL loop	91
23	Best practices coding standards	91

Date and Time Processing ... 93

1	Storing dates as a numeric value	93
2	Handling valid SAS dates	93
3	Storing time as a numeric value	94
4	Representing dates and time values with formats and informats	94
5	Applying date and time formats	94
6	Applying a date format in a PUT statement	94
7	Applying a date format in a PUT function	95
8	Applying a date format with a FORMAT statement	95
9	Applying a date format with an ATTRIB statement	95
10	Applying a date format in an SQL SELECT statement	96
11	Defining a one-hundred-year period with the YEARCUTOFF= option	96
12	Understanding date formats	97
13	Understanding date informats	99

Operators and Modifiers ... 101

1	Understanding operators and their order of evaluation	101
2	Understanding mathematical operators in SQL	102
3	Combining comparison and logical operators	102
4	Negating a specified condition with the NOT operator	102
5	Using the IN operator to group equality tests	103
6	Subsetting with the percent sign (%) wildcard and the LIKE operator	103
7	Using multiple percent sign (%) wildcards in a search pattern	104
8	Using the underscore (_) wildcard with the LIKE operator	104
9	Truncating and comparing strings with a colon (:) modifier	104
10	Reading input values with the n* informat modifier	105
11	Writing values with the n* format modifier	105

SAS Functions *106*
1. Using functions as part of a SAS statement *106*
2. Searching a character variable for a character string *106*
3. Reversing a character-string value *107*
4. Exploring host operating system functions *107*
5. Exploring arithmetic functions *107*
6. Exploring array functions *107*
7. Exploring character functions *107*
8. Exploring date and time functions *110*
9. Exploring financial functions *110*
10. Exploring random number functions *110*
11. Exploring state and ZIP code functions *110*
12. Exploring statistical functions *110*
13. Exploring trigonometric and hyperbolic functions *110*
14. Exploring truncation functions *117*
15. Exploring Web tool functions *117*

Program Testing *118*
1. Understanding the program testing process *118*
2. Testing participants *119*
3. Programming errors and their causes *119*
4. Understanding the purpose of testing *119*
5. Exploring defects in programs *119*
6. Determining if a program defect will result in a failure *119*
7. Exploring problems related to data *119*
8. Exploring the types of testing a program should endure *120*
9. Understanding test categories *120*
10. Exploring test objectives and test strategies *120*

Program Debugging *122*
1. Reading the SAS Log to aid in error detection *122*
2. Understanding SAS software usage errors *122*
3. Violating syntax *122*
4. Checking for syntax errors *122*
5. Warnings, warnings, and more warnings *123*
6. Using the Enhanced Editor to alert you to coding problems *123*
7. Enabling and Disabling the Enhanced Editor *123*
8. Enabling the Enhanced Editor *123*
9. Checking for coding errors with the Enhanced Editor *123*
10. Opening the Enhanced Editor Options window *124*
11. Customizing Enhanced Editor general options *124*
12. Customizing Enhanced Editor Appearance options *124*
13. Opening Enhanced Editor Keyboard shortcuts *124*
14. Exploring Enhanced Editor navigation keyboard shortcuts *124*
15. Understanding data-related errors *125*

16	Understanding system-related errors	*125*
17	Understanding programming (logic) errors	*125*
18	Getting the SAS interpreter to recognize SAS statements	*125*

Processing Large Files *126*
1	Avoiding problems related to sorting	*126*
2	Reversing the order of a data set without sorting	*127*
3	Creating subsets	*127*
4	Dividing data in BY-groups	*127*
5	Replacing subsetting IFs with WHEREs	*128*
6	Creating summary statistics	*128*

Documentation *130*
1	Documenting a program with comments	*130*
2	Using comments in a program	*131*
3	Understanding that comments are non-executable	*131*
4	Inserting in-stream comments	*131*
5	Saving labels and formats in SAS data sets	*131*

Summary *132*

Chapter 4   Data Manipulation *133*

Subsetting Data *133*
1	Creating new data sets with a subset	*133*
2	Subsetting IF	*134*
3	Subsetting observations with a WHERE= data set option	*134*
4	Subsetting observations with operators	*134*
5	Subsetting observations with a DELETE statement	*136*
6	Subsetting observations with IF-THEN/ELSE and OUTPUT	*136*
7	Subsetting observations with OBS= and FIRSTOBS= data set options	*137*
8	Subsetting external input data with OBS= and FIRSTOBS= options	*138*
9	Subsetting observations with SELECT blocks and OUTPUT	*138*

Reshaping Columns of Data *139*
1	Understanding what reshaping data means	*139*
2	Subsetting variables from external data	*139*
3	Subsetting variables in a DATA step	*139*
4	Subsetting variables in a PROC step	*140*
5	Creating unique variable subsets for individual data sets	*140*
6	Concatenating SAS data sets in the DATA step	*141*
7	Concatenating SAS data sets with the APPEND procedure	*141*
8	Specifying the BASE= option in APPEND procedure	*142*
9	Creating the BASE= data set in the APPEND procedure	*142*
10	Understanding how the BASE= option works	*142*
11	Omitting the BASE= or DATA= option with the APPEND procedure	*142*
12	Using the FORCE option	*142*

- 13 Missing values in the APPEND procedure ... *142*
- 14 Renaming a BASE= data set ... *142*
- 15 Reshaping data with two SET statements ... *143*
- 16 Reshaping data with three SET statements ... *144*
- 17 Interleaving SAS data sets ... *144*
- 18 Overcoming the interleaving threshold ... *145*
- 19 Using FIRST. and LAST. Variables ... *145*
- 20 Outputting the values of FIRST. and LAST. variables to a data set ... *145*
- 21 Combining data with one-to-one merging ... *145*
- 22 Applying caution when using one-to-one merges ... *146*
- 23 Combining data with match merging ... *146*
- 24 Understanding SAS and SQL terminology ... *148*
- 25 Understanding why joining is important ... *148*
- 26 Combining data with an SQL join ... *148*
- 27 Creating a Cartesian Product join ... *148*
- 28 Creating table aliases when joining ... *149*
- 29 Combining three or more tables with an SQL join ... *150*
- 30 Understanding outer joins ... *151*
- 31 Exploring tasks with an outer join ... *151*
- 32 Deciding on a left or right outer join ... *151*
- 33 Combining data with a left outer join ... *151*
- 34 Combining data with a right outer join ... *153*

Sending Output to SAS Data Sets ... *154*
- 1 Sending output to a data set ... *154*
- 2 Creating an output data set with a subsetting IF statement ... *154*
- 3 Creating an output data with an IF-THEN/ELSE statement ... *154*
- 4 Creating an output data set with WHEN conditions ... *155*
- 5 Creating an output data set with the CONTENTS procedure ... *155*
- 6 Exploring an output data set created with the CONTENTS procedure ... *155*
- 7 Creating an output data set with the FREQ procedure ... *156*
- 8 Exploring the available statistics with the FREQ procedure ... *156*
- 9 Sending output to a data set with the MEANS procedure ... *157*
- 10 Exploring the available statistics with the MEANS procedure ... *158*
- 11 Sending output to a data set with the SUMMARY procedure ... *158*
- 12 Sending output to a data set with the UNIVARIATE procedure ... *159*
- 13 Exploring the available statistics with the UNIVARIATE procedure ... *160*
- 14 Tracing output objects with ODS ... *160*
- 15 Sending output to a data set with ODS ... *161*
- 16 Converting observations into variables ... *162*
- 17 Converting variables to observations ... *163*

Summary ... *164*

Chapter 5 Data Management 165

Copying Data 165
1. Copying data files 165
2. Verifying FIRSTOBS= and OBS= System options are assigned 166
3. Copying text files in a DATA step 166
4. Copying part of each record in a text file 166
5. Copying text files starting in a designated record position 167
6. Specifying the LENGTH= and START= options when copying text files 167
7. Making multiple copies of text files 168
8. Copying SAS data sets in a DATA step 168
9. Exploring the advantages of DATA step copying 168
10. Selecting data sets to copy 168
11. Copying SAS files with the COPY procedure 169
12. Copying SAS Data sets – DATASETS Procedure syntax 169
13. Copying SAS data sets with the DATASETS procedure 170

Describing Data 170
1. Exploring the CONTENTS procedure output 170
2. Printing a list of SAS library data sets 171
3. Suppressing the printing of individual files in SAS libraries 172
4. Printing a contents "short" list 173
5. Printing an alphabetical list of variables 174

Sorting Data 175
1. Returning sorted observations to the original SAS data set 175
2. Saving sorted observations to a data set 175
3. Understanding the sort order for numeric variables 175
4. Understanding the sort order for character variables 175
5. Selecting observations to sort 176

Managing Data 176
1. Accessing SAS data libraries 176
2. Exploring SAS Libraries 177
3. Exploring SAS member types 177
4. Storing SAS libraries on disk 177
5. Storing SAS libraries on tape 178
6. Reading data sets from two or more tapes 178
7. Renaming variables 178
8. Modifying a data set's attributes 179
9. Modifying a variable's label 179
10. Updating a SAS data set with the UPDATE statement 180
11. Aging a SAS data set 181
12. Reading a generation data set (GENNUM=) 181
13. Managing SAS data sets with the APPEND procedure 182
14. Specifying the larger data set as the BASE= data set 182

15	Creating the BASE= data set automatically	*182*
16	Using the FORCE option	*182*
17	Exploring single-level data set names	*182*
18	Handling missing values in the APPEND procedure	*182*
19	Concatenating two or more data sets with the APPEND procedure	*183*
20	Renaming a base data set	*183*
21	Concatenating two or more data sets in a DATA step	*183*
22	Removing all SAS files in a library	*183*

Summary *184*

Chapter 6 Data Presentation *185*

Report Writing and PROC PRINT *185*
1	Suppressing the observation number in PROC PRINT output	*185*
2	Writing a blank line between observations in PROC PRINT	*186*
3	Controlling the orientation of column headings in PROC PRINT	*186*
4	Printing labels as column headings in PROC PRINT	*187*
5	Breaking column headings	*187*
6	Printing the number of observations at the end of a report	*188*
7	Printing the number of observations in BY group in a report	*188*
8	Printing output consistently page-by-page	*189*
9	Conserving CPU time with the FULL option	*189*
10	Printing a blank column header	*190*

Custom Report Writing with the DATA Step *190*
1	Understanding the advantages of "custom" report writing	*190*
2	Specifying _NULL_	*190*
3	Printing headings at the top of each page	*190*
4	Suppressing the printing of the default SAS title	*191*
5	Knowing when the end-of-file has occurred	*191*
6	Counting the number of lines left on a page	*191*
7	Creating two reports in a single DATA step	*192*
8	Creating two-column output in the DATA step	*192*
9	Creating three-column output in the DATA step	*193*
10	Creating four-column report output in the DATA step	*193*

Output Delivery System (ODS) *194*
1	Understanding the advantages of the Output Delivery System (ODS)	*194*
2	Using an earlier version of SAS software	*194*
3	Formatting output with global ODS statements	*194*
4	Opening and closing destinations	*195*
5	Managing system resources	*195*
6	Understanding the difference between batch and interactive use	*195*
7	Tracing procedure output	*196*
8	Selecting output with ODS	*197*

9	Selecting desired output objects	*197*
10	Deleting output from the Results window	*197*
11	Creating the standard "monospace" Listing file	*198*
12	Creating output data sets	*198*
13	Creating RTF	*198*
14	Creating PostScript output	*199*
15	Assigning a default name to a PostScript file	*199*
16	Specifying a PostScript name	*199*
17	Integrating ODS into the DATA step	*200*
18	Locating SAS-supplied format templates	*200*

Output Delivery Goes Web *201*

1	Distributing content anywhere and anytime	*201*
2	Understanding HTML	*201*
3	Exploring links and references in ODS	*202*
4	Exploring ODS HTML file types	*202*
5	Deploying output to the Web with ODS	*203*
6	Streaming (continuous) output with a BODY= file	*203*
7	Viewing the frame file	*204*
8	Ignoring pagesize and linesize settings	*204*
9	Locating HTML files (Windows operating system)	*204*
10	Displaying PRINT procedure output in HTML format	*205*
11	Specifying BODY=, CONTENTS=, PAGE=, and FRAME= files	*205*
12	Changing output labels	*206*
13	Combining output results	*206*
14	Creating PDF output	*207*
15	Exploring the drill-down user interface	*208*
16	Building drill-down applications	*209*
17	Coding a drill-down application	*209*
18	Testing Web output	*211*
19	Checking the Web deployment checklist	*211*

Summary *212*

Chapter 7 Efficiency and Performance 213

Planning *213*

1	Planning is everything	*213*
2	Understanding what is meant by efficiency	*214*
3	Exploring the problem of competing resources	*214*
4	Developing a simple plan	*215*
5	Applying simple strategies one at a time	*216*
6	Striving for an "optimal" balance	*216*

CPU Techniques 216
1. Treating CPU and elapsed time as baseline measurements 216
2. Subsetting IF 217
3. Understanding the efficiencies of WHERE processing 217
4. Using IF-THEN/ELSE 217
5. Using the IN operator 217
6. Concatenating SAS data sets 218
7. Turning off the Macro facility 218
8. Avoiding unnecessary sorting 218
9. Controlling the amount of memory used for sorting 219
10. Using a CLASS statement in procedures 219
11. Compressing and uncompressing data sets is CPU intensive 219
12. Creating an index 219
13. Using LIBNAME engines 220
14. Using temporary arrays 220
15. Using the Stored Program Facility 220

I/O Techniques 220
1. Storing data as data sets 220
2. Subsetting observations 220
3. Creating subsets earlier than later 220
4. Reducing the number of steps 220
5. Copying indexes 220
6. Specifying the BASE= option in the APPEND procedure 221
7. Using SQL to consolidate steps 221
8. Sorting only what is needed 221

Memory Techniques 221
1. Reading only data that is needed 221
2. Using KEEP= or DROP= dataset options 221
3. Deleting WORK data sets 222
4. Reducing memory requirements with WHERE processing 222
5. Handling large data sets 222

Storage Techniques 222
1. Using DATA _NULL_ to suppress the creation of a data set 222
2. Using KEEP= or DROP= dataset options 223
3. Assigning lengths to numeric variables 223
4. Compressing data sets 223
5. Creating user-defined formats for coded data 223

Programming Techniques 223
1. Including RUN statements 223
2. Assigning descriptive variable and data set names 223
3. Saving labels and formats in SAS data sets 223
4. Assigning a length to character variables 224
5. Documenting programs and program code 224

6	Storing data set informats, formats, and labels	*224*
7	Creating views	*224*
8	Avoiding FORCE with indexes	*225*
9	Coding for harmful data conditions	*225*
10	Specifying NOREPLACE	*225*
11	Specifying SAS System options to control messaging	*225*

Summary *226*

Chapter 8 Configuration and Support *227*

Installation and Configuration *227*

1	Exploring Release 8.2 system requirements	*227*
2	Installing Internet Explorer 5 in SAS Release 8.2 for Windows	*229*
3	Removing Internet Explorer 5 in SAS Release 8.2 for Windows	*229*
4	Launching the SAS System installation process	*229*
5	Changing SAS System library locations	*229*
6	Choosing between different installation configurations	*230*
7	Invoking the SAS System	*230*
8	Discovering the SAS System's Configuration startup file	*230*
9	Customizing the SAS Configuration file	*230*
10	Listing of System options under the Windows operating system	*231*

The Service & Support Web Site *233*

1	Accessing the Service & Support Web site	*233*
2	Searching techniques	*233*
3	Narrowing your search results with Boolean search operators	*234*
4	Searching by search categories	*234*
5	Contacting SAS technical support	*235*
6	Searching technical notes for programming problems	*235*
7	Accessing Maintenance Bug Fix documentation	*236*
8	Finding Hot Fixes	*236*
9	Upgrading SAS Release 8.1 to 8.2 under Windows and Hot Fixes	*237*
10	Applying the SAS System Version 8 SETINIT under Windows	*237*
11	Handling SETINIT problems during SAS Release 8.2 installation	*237*
12	Applying a SETINIT when the SAS System has expired	*238*
13	Accessing a library of sample SAS programs	*238*
14	Downloading demos and examples	*239*
15	Subscribing to the SAS-L email list	*239*
16	Participating in SAS-L	*239*
17	Unsubscribing from SAS-L	*240*
18	Exploring the world of SAS user groups	*240*
19	Attending SUGI—the event no SAS user should miss	*240*

Summary *240*

Chapter 9 New Version 9 Features 241

The DATA Step 241
1. Performing faster searches and text replacement with Perl Regular Expressions (PRXs)...241
2. Describing PRXs and metacharacters 241
3. Getting started with a simple match 242
4. Performing another simple match with PRX 242
5. Parsing data with regular expressions 242
6. Finding data with regular expressions 243
7. Retrieving text with regular expressions 243
8. Searching and replacing text 243
9. Exploring other PRX functions 243

Output Delivery System (ODS) 243
1. Understanding ODS MARKUP 243
2. Exploring ODS MARKUP file types 244
3. Obtaining a list of tagset names 244
4. Creating HTML output with MARKUP 245
5. Creating XML output with MARKUP 245
6. Understanding Document Type Definitions (DTDs) 246
7. Creating an XML output and DTD with MARKUP 247
8. Combining MARKUP output 247
9. Using ODS to get "page xx of yy" page numbering 247

SAS Macro Facility 248
1. Exploring new Version 9 Macro statements 248
2. Exploring new Version 9 Macro options 248

One More Tip 248
1. Learning made easy with the SAS Learning Edition 248

Summary 249

Appendix SAS System Options 251

Index 263

Foreword

THE YEAR WAS 1984: Ronald Reagan was in the White House, Microsoft was preparing to unveil a new operating system called "Windows," the Detroit Tigers won the World Series, and, *much* lower on the national radar, SAS Institute took the risk of hiring me as an Account Executive. Over nearly the next two decades, I had the good fortune of chatting frequently with Kirk Lafler, a prominent SAS consultant and trainer in my Southern California territory.

A lot has changed in the last twenty years. In the '80s, SAS advertisements proclaimed, "SAS Saves Time." Now SAS software not only saves time, it also gives business users the "Power to Know." As of 2002, Kirk Lafler has written three books and dozens of articles, has attended so many SAS user group meetings that I suspect even he has lost count, and has undertaken consulting assignments all over the United States. Meanwhile, I climbed the ranks through a number of wonderful positions at SAS Institute and continued to interact with Kirk about his use of SAS, his experiences with the software, and the key applications that he was implementing for his clients. I learned a lot from Kirk about the "real world" use of the software and about the impact it has had, from "Saving Time" to giving organizations the "Power to Know."

Power SAS: A Survival Guide is an extraordinary and useful book designed for all levels of SAS user, from novice to advanced. Writing such a comprehensive book for so many levels of users is a daunting task but also an important one. As my good friend at SAS, Paul "Big Truck" Bachteal, used to say, "We want to get every man, woman, and child in America using SAS!"

In this book, Kirk has mined his extensive experience to compile hundreds of useful tips that promise to empower all you SAS users, no matter how experienced you are, to be more productive. From accessing and managing data to presenting information, Kirk covers it all—and he covers it extremely well.

Much as I'd like to take credit for suggesting some of these wonderful tips and techniques to Kirk in numerous phone calls, emails, and meetings, and through user groups, presentations, and seminars over the years, the fact is I really can't. When it comes to the ins and outs of the SAS System, Kirk is light-years ahead of me. (Now, I could probably give Kirk some tips and techniques on singing a Rolling Stones song at a SAS user group "Kick Back" Party—but I'll save that for another book!)

More seriously, reader, you have an excellent book in your hands, and I advise you to keep it handy and use it often. When it gets dog-eared, well, buy another copy (or maybe two—one for your local library), because it will make you more productive as you work with SAS. As Kirk has said, this book "is the next best thing to having an expert by your side 24/7." To increase your productivity with SAS, you have two choices: 1) Let Kirk (and his family, of course) move in with you, or 2) Buy this book.

Now Kirk's a great guy, but I suggest you simply buy the book—and see how SAS continues to save time today.

Barrett Joyner
Chairman of the Board, FullSeven Technologies,
and former President, SAS North America
Cary, North Carolina
July 26, 2002

About the Author

Kirk Paul Lafler is a SAS Consultant and SAS Certified Professional with 25 years of SAS programming experience. He lives and works in San Diego, California and provides SAS consulting services and SAS and JMP training around the world. As founder of Software Intelligence Corporation, an IT services provider and trainer, Kirk has performed SAS contract programming, designed and developed SAS-based application solutions, and provided comprehensive training to Fortune 1000 companies and government installations since 1983. As author of three books, including *Power AOL: A Survival Guide* published by Apress, more than 100 technical articles, and several SAS Tips columns, Kirk shares his knowledge and many technical experiences with other SAS professionals. His expertise as a SAS Institute Alliance Partner for the past six years includes application design and development, training, performance tuning, and programming using base-SAS, SQL, ODS, SAS/GRAPH, SAS/FSP, SAS/AF, SCL, and FRAME software. Kirk can be reached at KirkLafler@cs.com.

About the Foreword Author

Barrett Joyner, Chairman of the Board of FullSeven Technologies, brings over 26 years of leadership and management experience in technology companies. Barrett had an illustrious 16-year career at SAS Institute in several sales, marketing, and executive management roles, from account representative to President of SAS North America, contributing to the extensive growth of SAS in becoming the world's largest privately held software company, with annual revenues of over $1 billion. Barrett served as CEO of FullSeven Technologies, directing the company through the turbulent economic times of late 2001 and early 2002 as FullSeven increased its corporate customer base by more than 1200 percent. Additionally, Barrett served as Executive Vice President at SciQuest, where he was responsible for e-information services, product marketing, and corporate communications. Barrett frequently speaks and consults on the executive's role in building productive and fully aligned work teams with a "results through relationships" philosophy. He holds a BA in Political Science from the University of North Carolina, Chapel Hill.

About the Technical Reviewers

Charles E. Shipp is a programmer, consultant, and author with 25 years experience working with the SAS System. He has co-authored the popular *Books by Users* (BBU) book, *Quick Results with SAS/GRAPH Software* and a self-published book, *The Year 2000 How To Guide for Medical Laboratories*. His expertise includes application design and development, training, and programming using base-SAS, JMP, SQL, ODS, SAS/FSP, SAS/AF, SCL, FRAME, and SAS/GRAPH software. He's authored and presented several award-winning papers at SAS Users Group International (SUGI) and other regional SAS conferences. Mr. Shipp is also an active supporter of local, regional, and international SAS and Macintosh users groups; Web designer, content creator and developer; and technical reviewer.

Mike DiGregorio has been a SAS programmer and system developer for more than 16 years. During his 22-year career in IT, Mike has worked for several Fortune 500 companies (including Exxon, McGraw-Hill, and American Express) and as an independent consultant specializing in SAS application development. Though he considers himself a programmer first, he has also held management and executive positions. He currently does SAS- related consulting through his company MoholraD Ltd. and can be reached at moholrad-ltd@cox.net.

Sunil Gupta is a principal consultant at Gupta Programming. He has been using SAS software for more than ten years and is a SAS Certified Professional V6. He has participated in over six successful FDA submissions. His consulting projects with pharmaceutical companies include the development of a Macro-Based Application for Report Generation and Customized Plots and Charts. He is also the author of a *Books By Users* book on the Output Delivery System and was a SAS Institute Quality Partner for more than five years. In addition, he has presented numerous SAS papers at international, regional, and local SAS User Group conferences.

Preface

SAS INSTITUTE IS THE WORLD'S largest privately owned software company. With more than 38,000 customers, including 90 percent in the Fortune 500, and annual revenues exceeding $1 billion, SAS Institute has achieved unprecedented success and is driven to become even bigger and better. SAS software provides an extensive array of programming and analytical tools and is used by organizations to access large volumes of data, perform analytical modeling, develop business intelligence, implement Web delivery, and investigate other analytical areas to better understand customers, clients, and users. Although the SAS software has been designed to be easy to use, the sheer number of tools and features offered in the Base SAS product alone can become daunting, to say the least. As a result, this book is intended to be useful to SAS users everywhere.

Power SAS is intended to make it easier for SAS users to take full advantage of the many tools and features found in the base-product. I've organized this book to help readers learn something useful about many of SAS Institute's software tools and features in 60 seconds or less. The tips are based on years of experience using SAS software and are tried and proven for accurate results.

While I assume readers have some general familiarity with computers, I don't assume any knowledge of SAS software to get started with this book. As with any book of this type, code examples are an important element of better learning, and this book is filled with step-by-step examples, code examples, as well as tips. By covering the most widely used SAS software tools and features, I am confident that users will have a better and more rewarding programming experience using the SAS software.

I hope you'll find my style of informal, conversational writing easy to follow, especially in a world filled with technical jargon on virtually any subject. I'll be happy to receive corrections, new tips, and other suggestions for future editions of this book. Send your ideas to me here:

Kirk Paul Lafler
P.O. Box 1390
Spring Valley, CA 91979-1390
KirkLafler@cs.com

or contact me through the publisher:

Apress
2560 Ninth Street, Suite 219
Berkeley, CA 94710
http://www.apress.com

Acknowledgments

THIS BOOK WAS MADE POSSIBLE by the support and encouragement of many people. I would like to extend my sincerest thanks to each person who encouraged me to write this book. For as G. B. Stern once said, "Silent gratitude isn't very much use to anyone." So from me to you, thank you to each one of you.

Karen Watterson of Apress for believing that a book of SAS tips would be useful to other SAS users. Her support and encouragement during the writing and editing process, and for answering so many of my questions, meant so much to me. Karen's guidance, support, encouragement, and suggestions not only helped bring *Power SAS* to life but also improved the content and the way each chapter flowed.

Grace Wong of Apress for her leadership, enthusiasm, and assistance with some of the fine points of writing for Apress. Her willingness to support a new imprint and style is greatly appreciated.

Tracy Brown Collins of Apress for her guidance and editorial assistance during the editing process and for allowing me to see the light at the end of the long tunnel. Her encouragement and support during the edit and review process are greatly appreciated.

Corbin Collins for his wonderful editing skills, and for making my prose a whole lot easier to read.

Valerie Perry for her valuable findings and suggestions early in the writing process.

Gary Cornell, Publisher and Editorial Director at Apress, for giving me the opportunity to write *Power SAS*.

Diana Van Winkle for making this book look wonderful. Her design and formatting expertise made this book come to life on paper.

This book was made easier to write because of the hard work of my Technical Reviewers: Charles Shipp, Mike DiGregorio, and Sunil Gupta. They spent countless hours working with me and on their own, researching topics, reviewing and revising chapter tips, verifying and testing code examples, providing expert advice, and much more. Charlie, Mike, and Sunil are trusted friends whose tireless support and many suggestions helped improve the manuscript content and brought *Power SAS* to life. Their friendship throughout the years has meant a great deal.

To the countless people at SAS Institute Inc. with whom I have developed so many friendships. I'd like to express my thanks to James Goodnight, Barrett Joyner, John Boling, Kathy Council, Herb Kirk, Stephanie Townsend, Paul Kent, Julie Platt, Patsy Poole, Judy Whatley, David Baggett, Betty Angell, Loretta Schlatzer, Donna Saintomas, and all the knowledgeable people in SAS Technical Support. Thank you for developing and supporting such a great product and making the last 25 years a rewarding and enjoyable journey.

To SAS user groups and their members throughout the world. You are the greatest group of professionals anywhere.

To the many teachers I have had in my life I thank you, especially my parents, Lawrence Delk (6th grade), Mr. Almeida (12th grade),

Acknowledgments

Professor Carl Kromp (Industrial Engineering), Dr. Joseph J. Moder (Management Science), Dr. Charles Kurucz (Management Science), Dr. John F. Stewart (Computer Information Systems), Dr. Earl Wiener (Management Science), Dr. Howard S. Gitlow (Management Science), and Ulu (Rydacom).

To all the people that I have worked with and the companies I have worked for. The experiences and memories have been lasting and invaluable.

To Clark Roberts of Decision Analytics and Dr. Roger Glaser of San Diego Gas and Electric. Your friendship, support, and encouragement through the years have meant a lot. You are true professionals and great friends.

To my parents and brother. Thank you for your love and support, for all the wonderful experiences and memories, and for fueling my desire to seek opportunities and live life to the fullest.

Thank you all!

~ Kirk ~

Introduction

"Seek the wisdom of the children...For the children are my sisters and my brothers, their laughter and their loveliness would clear a cloudy day...they're a promise of the future and a blessing for today..."

—John Denver,
Rhymes and Reasons, 1969

POWER SAS: A SURVIVAL GUIDE is designed for SAS software users who want to learn all they can about the many tools and features offered by SAS Institute's SAS software. This book is loaded with valuable tips and tricks for getting more from the Base SAS product than ever before. Inside, you'll find quick and simple tips written in plain English on how to use SAS software more effectively. Novice, intermediate, and experienced users alike will learn valuable insights to help make their programming experience more productive and exciting.

My experiences researching other SAS books, while teaching SAS classes, and talking with other SAS users have convinced me that there is a need for a comprehensive and organized collection of SAS tips, much like those written for other software products and tools. But when I looked, I could find no comprehensive SAS book like it anywhere.

Well, now there is such a book. This is a book for novice, intermediate, and advanced SAS users, who want plain-English tips and techniques clearly written and with a logical organization. It's organized so that readers can get faster, easier, and better results without spending inordinate amounts of time reading paragraph after paragraph of text. *Power SAS* is the perfect companion for the legions of SAS users everywhere. It's the next best thing to having an expert by your side 24 hours a day, 7 days a week.

Organization of the Book

Power SAS is organized so that each chapter covers a new group of related features and services. It's written so that each chapter can be read sequentially, or you can open to the index and access the specific information you need right away. The beauty of this presentation is that users will find the answers they're looking for in 60 seconds or less. The tips are numbered, and many of them appear with step-by-step instructions, code examples, sample logs, output, as well as visual aids.

Chapter 1 introduces the basics of Base SAS software's features and tools. Tips cover topics related to the SAS Supervisor; creating observations and variables; DATA and PROC step processing; Macro processing; SAS System options; controlling performance statistics; data set compression; controlling messages to the SAS Log; SAS Display Manager System; managing the SAS environment; Display Manager windows; command-line and line-number commands; and SAS Explorer.

Chapter 2 presents a variety of data-access tips and techniques to help read and process virtually any file type and format. From external non-SAS files to SAS data sets, this chapter offers tools to help make data input and retrieval quick and easy.

Chapter 3 provides details on the DATA step language; reading external data sources and SAS data sets; data set and table access; date and time processing; SAS-supplied and user-defined formats; SAS functions; program testing and debugging; processing large files; and documentation techniques. This chapter offers users plenty of good ideas and techniques for improved DATA step programming and data access.

Chapter 4 presents data manipulation tips including subsetting data and variables; reshaping columns of data; sending output to SAS data sets; combining data; converting observations to variables; converting variables to observations; and a potpourri of tips covering a variety of exciting data-manipulation techniques.

Chapter 5 gives data management–related tips and techniques including data aging and recovery; describing data; managing data; and sorting and indexing data.

Chapter 6 provides data-presentation tips including report writing and procedures; custom reporting with the DATA step; and SAS Output Delivery System (ODS) including output delivery for the Web. This chapter offers numerous ways to improve the delivery of data.

Chapter 7 contains performance-related tips and techniques to help users achieve improved efficiency levels including planning, as well as CPU, I/O, memory, storage, and programming techniques.

Chapter 8 presents a potpourri of tips and techniques to help answer many important SAS System installation and configuration questions; access technical support 24/7 service; and benefit from educational user group resources.

Chapter 9 offers an early look at many new Version 9 features including business intelligence areas in the DATA step, ODS, and the Macro language.

Conventions Used in this Book

The numbered tips presented in this book frequently consist of instructions, code examples, and other useful tools that you can use to perform some action. You'll often be asked to enter one or more commands, code examples, menu choices, drop-down selection lists, radio boxes, or manipulate other options to accomplish what you want to do. Important commands, statements, options, or button clicks are emphasized using boldface type. In many tips throughout the book, I include code examples, sample windows, screens, logs, and output to assist in the learning process.

To emphasize specific tips and their content, the following icons and their descriptions are used throughout this book.

Icon	Description
	This icon identifies useful timesaving tricks or techniques.
	This icon identifies warnings, errors, and other messages that can cause problems if ignored.

CHAPTER 1
SAS Basics

THIS CHAPTER COVERS valuable SAS software basics tips. Whether you're a SAS expert who is comfortable with the many features offered in the Base SAS product or someone just getting started, these tips will make your programming experience a more rewarding one. By taking the time to learn the Base SAS fundamentals—including terminology, library structures, programming concepts, user interface, SAS Explorer, and numerous other aspects—you'll get better results while using this powerful product. You'll learn about useful features step by step and in the simplest of terms to help you become a more knowledgeable SAS user.

In this chapter, you'll learn how to

- Begin using the Base SAS product
- Equate SAS terminology with other software and database languages
- Visualize the concept of a SAS data set
- Use the SAS Display Manager
- Access the built-in Help facility
- Display SAS System options
- Use SAS Explorer to access SAS files
- Access output in the Results window
- Customize toolbar settings
- Copy and move files from one library to another
- Control the size of icons
- Issue keyboard shortcuts

Getting Started

This section includes tips that will help you get acquainted with Base SAS software, how it works, and its various components. You'll learn essential concepts and terminology, what type of role the SAS Supervisor plays in directing processing activities, a brief introduction to important SAS keywords, and how to access the built-in Help facility.

1 Understanding what the SAS System is

In the early years of SAS, the name SAS was synonymous with statistics. It was said to stand for "Statistical Analysis System" for a short period. But over time, as the SAS software evolved into a dynamo of powerful programmer and end-user tools, this moniker was dropped, and references to the suite of products and tools became known simply as the SAS System or SAS software.

Today the SAS System is recognized as the world leader in enterprise and business intelligence software solutions. As an integrated software environment, SAS software provides the tools that every enterprise needs to transform data into meaningful information.

End-users, programmers, statisticians, IT and database specialists, systems analysts, application developers, and other professionals throughout the world use SAS software for data access, data management, data analysis, and data presentation. For example, the Base SAS product, the heart of the SAS software, provides a vast array of tools for data-driven tasks, including

- A powerful fourth-generation DATA step language that promotes structured coding and best practices techniques

- Self-contained "canned" programs known as *procedures* to handle everyday tasks (such as the SORT procedure)

- A self-contained custom report writer

- Output and reporting capabilities to display results in visually appealing formats

- Built-in functions to simplify programming tasks such as arithmetic, array, character, date and time, financial, mathematical, probability, quantile, random number, statistical, state and ZIP code, trigonometric and hyperbolic, and truncation operations

- A Structured Query Language (SQL) processor

- A Macro processor to help minimize keystrokes and automate repetitive tasks

- A SAS viewer to enable viewing of SAS data sets and text-based files

- An enhanced text editor to make writing and modifying program code easy

- Import and Export wizards to make transferring data a snap between different sources including SAS data sets, comma- and tab-delimited files, user-defined formats

- Descriptive statistical and correlation routines

- Database access engines for leading DBMS packages

- Full-screen menus and data-capture capability

- Windowing for ease of use

- A built-in Help facility for 24/7 assistance

- And much more

2 Equating SAS terminology with other software and database languages

The SAS software's base-product consists of several different languages. It boasts a powerful DATA step language, a SQL, and a Macro language. It even has as a part of the Output Delivery System (described in Chapter 6) a Template language for customizing the way output looks. Like SQL, C, PL1, COBOL, BASIC, and other languages, the SAS software terminology that one should become acquainted with. Table 1-1 identifies a number of SAS terms with their corresponding non-SAS terminology.

Table 1-1. SAS and Non-SAS terms

SAS TERMINOLOGY	DATABASE OR NON-SAS TERMINOLOGY
Data set	Table <or> File
Variable	Column <or> Field
Observation	Row <or> Record

Table 1-1. SAS and Non-SAS terms (Continued)

SAS TERMINOLOGY	DATABASE OR NON-SAS TERMINOLOGY
Library	Database
DATA statement	Create
SET statement	Read
OUTPUT statement	Write
Extract	Query
Merge	Join
PROC statement	Canned program, Procedure, or Utility

3   Visualizing the SAS data set structure

A SAS System data set resembles a rectangular structure, similar to a spreadsheet, with one or more rows (observations) and one or more columns (variables). Visually, it looks like a piece of graph paper consisting of "x-y grids," with x representing the rows and y representing the columns in the data set.

4   Naming conventions for data sets and variables

SAS data set and variable naming conventions must conform to certain rules. The following list identifies the rules all SAS users should adhere to when naming SAS data sets and variables:

- The name can be 1–32 positions in length

- The first position must be a letter (A–Z, a–z) or underscore (_)

- The remaining positions, if used, can be letters (A–Z, a–z), underscore (_), or numbers (0–9), but no other special characters

- Provide meaningful and descriptive names to assist in understanding

5   Understanding the importance of keywords and the semicolon

Every SAS statement begins with a keyword and ends with a semicolon. The SAS language is comprised of numerous statements or keywords, each having its own set of options associated with it. A keyword has special meaning in the SAS System. For example, the DATA statement is a keyword that not only creates a data set but also tells the SAS System that this is the beginning of a user-written program or DATA step. User-written programs are distinguished from PROCs, or procedures (another keyword), because they need to be compiled before they can be executed. Each keyword specified must be terminated with a semicolon. A semicolon marks the end of a statement and represents a complete thought. Should a keyword be misspelled, specified out of order, or if a semicolon is omitted, the SAS System will produce a syntax error resulting in program step not being executed. See Chapter 3 for tips related to SAS errors and program debugging.

6   Coding SAS statements in a "free format" style

The Base SAS programming languages are not only powerful—they permit users to write the lines of code using a "free format" or column independent style. This independence from rigid formatting rules enables users to concentrate on the task they are working on rather than time-consuming and tedious code-alignment and positioning matters. So what does this mean for you? It means that, for example, the keyword DATA beginning in column 1 or in column 20 has the same effect and meaning when processed. This gives you the flexibility to write program code using whatever conventions you or your organization prefers. As long as each keyword is spelled and used correctly, is in the correct order, and ends with a semicolon, it should be fine. This style is in direct contrast to many other languages, such as COBOL, FORTRAN, or PL1; in those languages keywords must begin in predetermined column or starting positions. SAS statements, on the other hand, can

- Begin anywhere on a line
- End anywhere on a line
- Continue over several lines
- Have comments appear anywhere in the program code
- Have any number of blanks separating keywords.

7 Understanding the role of the SAS Supervisor

The *SAS Supervisor* is at the heart of the SAS System. It monitors and directs all activities within the SAS System by controlling which program modules (DATA, PROC, or Macro) are accessed according to the program statements used. The Supervisor controls and manages the following activities:

- Log message handling
- External file data management
- Computer hardware requirements
- Communication between the operating system and user requests
- Memory management
- Interpreting and executing program code
- Initiation and termination of program steps
- Global statements and their settings
- The way the SAS Display Manager behaves
- Macro processing and the passing of parameters.

8 Creating variables

The SAS System provides many ways to create a variable, including the following:

- INPUT statement
- LENGTH statement
- Assignment statement
- Counter
- CREATE TABLE statement in SQL

9 Avoiding reserved names when naming data sets and variables

A few reserved names serve a special purpose in the SAS System. Although the SAS System is extremely tolerant and forgiving about the names you can assign to SAS data sets and variables, you should make every attempt to avoid using the following names for your data sets and variables. Avoid using _ALL_, _DATA_, DATA*n* such as DATA1, DATA2, and so on (representing various data set generations), _NULL_, and _LAST_ in naming your data sets. Avoid using _COL_, _FREQ_, _I_, _INFILE_, _LABEL_, _ROW_, _TYPE_, and _WEIGHT_ when naming variables.

10 Creating observations

An *observation* is comprised of one or more variables in a data set or table. A data set can have any number of observations. The various techniques for creating an observation include:

- DATA statement

- OUTPUT statement

- RETURN statement

- FSEDIT procedure

- SQL procedure

11 Understanding the difference between in-stream versus external input data

Data can be read into the SAS System using a variety of input methods. Two very different methods of reading data consist of data included inside a program and data coming from an external text file outside a program. The first instance, known as *in-stream* data, is not frequently used by practitioners but is important for users to be aware of. It is marked with a CARDS or CARDS4 statement at the end of a DATA step, but prior to the data being defined as input. For example, the following code example reads two columns of data as in-stream data. The program step ends when it sees a semicolon (;) on a line by itself.

Code:

```
DATA IN_STREAM;
 INPUT NAME $1-8 GENDER $9;
 CARDS;
Ryan     M
Darlynn  F
Bruce    M
Ronnie   M
AnnaleisF
Charlie  M
Mike     M
Sunil    M
;
RUN;
```

🖉 *When the data being read as in-stream data contains one or more semicolons in the data itself, it is necessary to specify the CARDS4 statement in place of the CARDS statement. To mark the end of in-stream data containing semicolons, four semicolons (;;;;) are specified on a line by itself at the end of the data.*

In contrast to in-stream data where data is part of a program, a more conventional method of reading data is accomplished when data is stored in an external text file. Data stored in this fashion is easily read in a DATA step by specifying an INFILE statement to identify the file and with an INPUT statement to specify how each data line is to be read. The following example illustrates how the same two columns of data, as seen in the previous example, can be read from an external text file.

Code:

```
DATA IN_STREAM;
 INFILE 'c:\acqaintance.dat';
 INPUT NAME $1-8 GENDER $9;
RUN;
```

12 Understanding the storage format used by SAS System files

The SAS System uses its own proprietary storage format for data files and other file formats such as catalogs, formats, indexes, as well as other structures. Because of this unique storage format, users need to use the SAS DATA step language and/or available SAS procedures to access and decipher the stored information.

13 Creating observations with a DATA statement

A DATA statement's purpose is to begin a user-written step, provide a name for the data set being created, and to facilitate writing the current observation to the specified data set. Every DATA step has an implicit OUTPUT statement at the end of the step to write the observation to the specified data set (see next tip).

14 Creating observations with an OUTPUT statement

An OUTPUT statement directs the SAS System to write the current observation to a specified data set. An OUTPUT statement can be specified in logic conditions such as IF-THEN, SELECT, or DO-group statements. When the SAS System sees a coded OUTPUT statement in a program, the implicit OUTPUT statement (see previous tip) at the end of every DATA step is no longer available.

15 Creating observations with a RETURN statement

An implicit RETURN statement is the last executable statement in a DATA step. When present, it can be used to position processing at the beginning of a step. In these circumstances, the SAS System automatically writes the current observation to any specified data set(s).

16 Creating observations with the SQL procedure

The INSERT INTO statement is used to insert one or more new observations (rows) into a table. The VALUES clause is used to insert one or more values into a table. Entering a new row into a table containing an index will automatically add the value to the index. The following example illustrates adding two rows of data to two variables (columns) using the VALUES clause.

Code:

```
PROC SQL;
 INSERT INTO libref.movies
   (TITLE, CATEGORY)
 VALUES
   ('Rocky Giftset', 'Action')
 VALUES
   ('Gladiator', 'Action');
QUIT;
```

17 Understanding the difference between interactive and batch mode

There are two ways to use the SAS System: interactive or batch. The interactive mode of the SAS System uses a powerful windowing environment for developing, editing, and debugging programs. Referred to as the Display Manager System (DMS), it provides users with an enhanced text editor, messaging and output areas, self-contained Help facility, and numerous other features and options for user productivity (discussed in the next section, SAS System Options).

Depending on the operating system, the batch environment uses the same programming statements as the interactive environment, although users communicate specific resource requirements using a set of commands rather than the windowing environment. For example, running batch programs in a mainframe environment requires Job Control Language (JCL) statements to be executed along with SAS program code.

18 Turning off the SAS Display Manager System

Although interactive SAS users have the Display Manager System (DMS) at their disposal automatically when launching the SAS software, the windowing environment can be turned off. The reason for turning it off is basically to make additional resources (such as memory) available during the execution of resource-intensive programs. Users can turn off DMS in either of the following ways:

- At SAS invocation by specifying the NODMS system option

- By changing the SAS configuration file to turn DMS off

19 Understanding the control flow of a standard SAS program

When a program is submitted for execution, the SAS Supervisor interprets each line of code to determine whether a program step is a DATA step or a PROC step. For DATA steps (represented by the keyword DATA), the DATA compiler converts each statement into machine code. If one or more syntax errors are found (violations of the way a statement is used), the compiler stops and displays the appropriate messages on the SAS log. If no syntax error is found, each statement in the step is converted, and then the machine code is executed.

PROC steps are handled differently than DATA steps. Instead of invoking the DATA step compiler, as was the case with a DATA step, the SAS Supervisor invokes the Procedure Parser. Unlike a DATA step, a PROC is already converted into machine code, so the parser only has to process the unique user-supplied parameters that were provided. The control flow of a typical SAS program consisting of at least one DATA and PROC step appears in Figure 1-1.

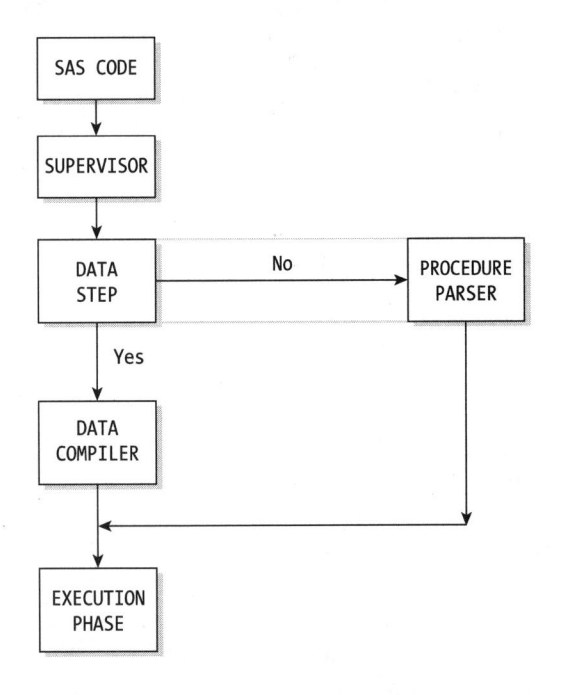

Figure 1-1. SAS program control flow

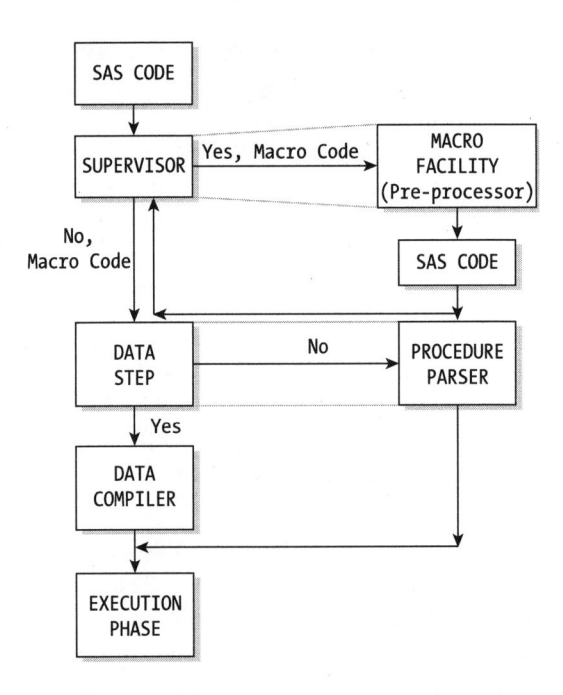

Figure 1-2. SAS Macro control flow

20 Understanding the control flow of a Macro program

When a SAS program contains a Macro reference (such as an ampersand "&", a percent sign "%", symbolic variable, etc.) anywhere in the code, the SAS Supervisor automatically triggers the Macro processor. Because Macro references are evaluated before DATA or PROC steps, the Macro processor must first resolve any and all macro references before the code is sent to the DATA compiler or Procedure Parser. The control flow of a SAS program containing at least one Macro reference appears in Figure 1-2.

21 Understanding the concept of step boundaries

A *step boundary* is the location in a program where one step ends and another step begins. In real estate terms, this would be analogous to the dividing line between one person's property and another person's property. In the SAS world it is the dividing line between one DATA and/or PROC step and the next. Once the SAS System knows where a step boundary occurs it can process the step without the possibility of accidentally processing into another step. Because every SAS program is processed sequentially from top to bottom, a multi-step program can be coded to process data in one step that is then passed and used in a later step.

With the presence of important keywords like RUN or QUIT, the SAS System is able to determine where one or more step boundaries occur in a program. Once a step boundary is known, the execution of that step can proceed until all observations are processed, unless terminated by some adverse event or condition such as a syntax error. Once a step completes, process and control proceeds to the next step, if present.

But occasionally a RUN or QUIT statement is not present in a program. In these cases, the SAS System automatically determines where a step boundary occurs by implicitly searching for keywords such as DATA, PROC, CARDS, CARDS4, and ENDSAS; or conditions such as a semicolon appearing following in-stream data lines or the end of a program. The existence of one or more of these keywords or conditions is often helpful in identifying a step boundary.

Code:

```
DATA EXAMPLE;
  INFILE . . .;
  INPUT . . .;
RUN;          Step Boundary
PROC PRINT
     DATA=EXAMPLE;    Step Boundary
PROC MEANS DATA=EXAMPLE;
RUN;   Step Boundary and End of Program
```

22 Accessing the built-in Help facility

The SAS System Help facility is only a click away. Help guides you step by step through countless topics. Simply click the **Help** button on the Status Line to view the index of Help topics, shown in Figure 1-3. Help is available for use when

- Additional information is needed about SAS statements, procedures, and other SAS software products

- Working in the Display Manager System or any other part of the SAS System (see the next section—"SAS Display Manager" for more details).

Figure 1-3. SAS System Help facility

23 Exiting the SAS System

In SAS DMS, you can exit the SAS System by issuing the **BYE** or **ENDSAS** commands. When running a program in batch mode, the SAS System terminates automatically after it has processed all the statements in the program.

SAS System Options

SAS System *options* convey important information about the way a program operates as well as the conditions in which it operates. Essentially an option is a choice. The SAS System provides numerous options that users can, at their option, modify to affect some response. In the event an option isn't specified or changed, the SAS System applies a default setting. This section includes tips on why options are needed in the first place, how to display and become familiar with default system options, and how to specify one or more options to control SAS System initialization and system behavior.

1 Controlling how a SAS session performs and behaves

System options control the way a SAS session performs, operates, and behaves. Users can accept the default option settings or specify one or more options that affect system initialization, reading and writing data, log and procedure output control, data set control, error handling, Macro facility, product interface, and host-specific options. When a SAS System option is specified, it remains in effect during the entire SAS job or until a new option value is entered.

2 Determining the settings of SAS System options at SAS invocation

At SAS invocation, default settings for all system options are set. To determine what these settings are, the **VERBOSE** system option is specified at SAS invocation. The default settings are then written to the SAS log.

This option must be specified at SAS invocation and cannot be specified as part of an OPTIONS statement during a SAS session.

3 Displaying SAS System option settings

SAS System options are written to the SAS log when invoking the **OPTIONS** procedure. The SAS log list includes options that were set at SAS invocation, options that can be changed during a SAS session, and options that are host specific. The following statement produces the default system options and their values.

Code:

```
PROC OPTIONS;
RUN;
```

4 Changing SAS System option settings

Many SAS System option settings can be changed in the OPTIONS window, by specifying the **OPTIONS** command, during SAS invocation, or in the configuration file. To view settings that can be altered after SAS invocation, enter **OPTIONS** on any command line in Display Manager.

5 Specifying frequently used SAS options in the Configuration file

Each time the SAS System is invoked, it checks for the existence of an external Configuration file (referenced by the **CONFIG=** system option). Any option settings found in this file are used instead of the default SAS System options used during initialization. The nice thing about using this Configuration file is that if you find yourself repeatedly specifying the same option settings often, it may be a time saver to place these option settings in the Configuration file. This way, these settings are automatically set in your SAS session.

6 Controlling SAS System initialization

A number of options affect the way the SAS System is initialized during the current session.

Each option in this category can only be modified at SAS invocation. For example, specifying the **DMS** option (for interactive users) turns the SAS DMS on. If DMS isn't desired to be on, users can specify **NODMS** as an option setting. For a complete listing of other initialization options, users should check the SAS Language Reference manual and specific host documentation.

7 Specifying the AUTOEXEC= system option

The external autoexec file contains statements that are automatically executed at SAS invocation and is specified with the **AUTOEXEC=** option. Any valid SAS statement can be specified in this file. Often one or more LIBNAME statements are specified to make accessing SAS libraries a bit more seamless or transparent. Users should consult their host documentation for specific syntax requirements.

8 Running a SAS program in batch or non-interactive mode

Specifying an external file name with the **SYSIN=** option at SAS invocation causes the SAS System to execute a SAS program in batch mode. This approach is used after a program has been developed and tested and when the Display Manager and other interactive tools are not needed. Users are referred to their host documentation for specific syntax requirements.

9 Executing SAS statements after AUTOEXEC file

Occasionally one or more SAS statements may need to be executed after any statements in the AUTOEXEC file, but before the statements in the SYSIN file. To accomplish this the **INITSTMT=** option is specified. Users are referred to their host documentation for specific syntax requirements.

10 Erasing WORK library files at SAS invocation

Users have the ability to erase preexisting information stored in the WORK library by specifying the **WORKINIT** option at SAS invocation. Alternatively, to prevent the erasure or removal of preexisting information in the WORK library, the **NOWORKINIT** option is specified at SAS invocation. This is automatic when running in batch mode.

11 Erasing WORK library files at the end of a SAS session

Users have the ability to erase information (for example, data sets, etc.) stored in the WORK library at the end of their SAS session by specifying the **WORKTERM** system option during a SAS session. Alternatively, to prevent the erasure or removal of information in the WORK library at the end of a SAS session, the **NOWORKTERM** option is specified during a SAS session. This is automatic when running in batch mode.

12 Specifying a value for the YEARCUTOFF= system option

To control how one- and two-digit years specified in a SAS date should be handled, the first year of a 100-year span (window) is entered as a value in the **YEARCUTOFF=** system option. For example, if 1920 is in effect for a YEARCUTOFF= value, the 100-year window begins with 1920 and ends with 2019. Consequently, any one- or two-digit year such as 02 will assume a century prefix of 20 and produce a result of 2002. Users should use 1920 as the YEARCUTOFF= value for maximum flexibility when dealing two-digit year values. The default in Version 8.2 is 1920.

13 Centering procedure output

By default, procedure output is automatically centered on a page. The system option that controls the centering of all output is aptly named **CENTER**. If desired, the automatic centering feature can be turned off and all output left justified by specifying the **NOCENTER** option. The CENTER or NOCENTER option can be specified in the OPTIONS statement, in the OPTIONS window, at SAS invocation, or in the configuration file.

14 Displaying the date and time at the top of each printed page

The date and time the SAS job began is automatically printed at the top of each SAS log and printed page. The **DATE** option controls whether the date and time are printed. In the event printing the date and time is not desired, it can be suppressed by specifying the **NODATE** option. The DATE or NODATE option can be specified in an OPTIONS statement, in the OPTIONS window, at SAS invocation, or in the configuration file.

15 Specifying procedures to use labels

Certain procedures (such as PRINT) can write a variable's label (if specified) in lieu of the variable's name. In order to take advantage of this feature, a user-defined 40-character maximum label must be defined for a variable, and the **LABEL** system option must be specified. Specifying the **NOLABEL** option (default) results in the SAS System using the variable's names only. The LABEL or NOLABEL options can be specified in an OPTIONS statement, in the OPTIONS window, at SAS invocation, or in the configuration file.

16 Specifying the printer line width and number of lines

Being able to specify the line width and number of lines used for procedure output is an important element in creating custom output. The **LINESIZE=** (alias **LS=**) system option controls the printer line width and can accept a value between 64 and 256. The **PAGESIZE=** (alias PS=) option controls the number of lines on a printed page and can accept a value between 15 and 32,767. Both options can be specified in the OPTIONS statement, in the OPTIONS window, at SAS invocation, or as part of the configuration file.

17 Specifying a value to use for printing numeric missing values

By default, numeric missing values are represented with a dot (.) in the SAS System. In the event another character is desired to represent missing numeric values, users can specify the **MISSING='character'** option. The MISSING= option can be specified in an OPTIONS statement, in the OPTIONS window, at SAS invocation, or in the configuration file.

18 Specifying a value to use for invalid numeric data

When invalid data is encountered in an INPUT statement or INPUT function, the SAS System automatically prints a period (default value). This may be fine for most cases. But occasionally a more discriminating method is needed to distinguish between invalid data derived on input versus a missing value generated as a result of some computation. In these cases, the **INVALIDDATA='some-character'** system option can be specified. The value assigned can be a letter (A–Z, a–z), an underscore (_), or a period (.). The INVALIDDATA='some-character' option can be specified in an OPTIONS statement, in the OPTIONS window, at SAS invocation, or in the configuration file.

19 Displaying a page number at the top of each printed page

A sequential page number is automatically printed at the top of each printed page of output. The **NUMBER** option controls whether the page number is printed. In the event the page number is not desired at the top of every page, it can be suppressed by specifying the **NONUMBER** option. The NUMBER or NONUMBER option can be specified in an OPTIONS statement, in the OPTIONS window, at SAS invocation, or in the configuration file.

20 Resetting the page number

Being able to reset the starting page number to another numeric number comes in handy when printing output. By default, the SAS System starts with a numeric value of 1 incrementing the page counter by 1 for each printed page. The **PAGENO=** option is specified in an OPTIONS statement, in the OPTIONS window, at SAS invocation, or in the configuration file. Refer to host documentation for specific syntax requirements.

21 Writing SAS source statements to the SAS Log

By default, SAS source statements are automatically written to the SAS Log by specifying the **SOURCE** system option. Alternatively, to prevent SAS source statements from being printed to the SAS Log, the **NOSOURCE** option can be specified. Either option can be specified in an OPTIONS statement, in the OPTIONS window, at SAS invocation, or in the configuration file.

22 Specifying the SOURCE option for problem detection and resolution

The **SOURCE** system option must be specified to help in the identification and resolutions of programming problems. Verify that system defaults, program code, configuration option settings, and the OPTIONS window are not suppressing this option prior to debugging a program.

23 Writing SAS source files included with a %INCLUDE statement to the SAS Log

By default, SAS source statements included with a %INCLUDE statement are NOT automatically written to the SAS Log. To print secondary SAS source statements included with %INCLUDE statements, users will need to specify the **SOURCE2** system option. The default setting is **NOSOURCE2**. Either option can be specified in an OPTIONS statement, in the OPTIONS window, at SAS invocation, or in the configuration file.

24 Specifying the SOURCE2 option for problem detection and resolution

The SOURCE2 system option should be specified to help in the identification and resolution of programming problems resulting from SAS source files included with a %INCLUDE statement. Verify that system defaults, program code, configuration option settings, or the OPTIONS window have not turned off this option prior to debugging a program.

25 Writing a subset of the performance statistics to the SAS Log

A subset of computer system performance statistics is written to the SAS Log when the **STIMER** system option is specified. Performance statistics can be suppressed by specifying the **NOSTIMER** option. The STIMER or NOSTIMER option can be specified in the OPTIONS statement, at SAS invocation, or in the configuration file. Refer to this section's tip #26 on the FULLSTIMER option.

26 Writing all performance statistics to the SAS Log

In contrast to writing a subset of the performance statistics with the STIMER system option, the **FULLSTIMER** system option writes a complete list of computer-system performance statistics to the SAS Log. Performance statistics can be suppressed by specifying the **NOFULLSTIMER** option. The FULLSTIMER or NOFULLSTIMER option can be specified in the OPTIONS statement, at SAS invocation, or in the configuration file. Refer to this section's tip #25 on the STIMER option for further comparisons.

27 Controlling what observation to begin reading in a data set

Being able to specify what observation to begin reading in a SAS data set can be a useful feature for greater data set control. By default, the SAS System begins reading with the first observation in a data set.

To override this default behavior, a **FIRSTOBS**=n system option can be specified (where *n* is some positive number) resulting in the observation corresponding to the number specified being read as the first observation in a data set.

When the FIRSTOBS= option is specified, it applies to every input data set used in a program. The FIRSTOBS= option can be specified in an OPTIONS statement, in the OPTIONS window, at SAS invocation, or in the configuration file.

28 Resetting the FIRSTOBS= system option back to the first observation

If the FIRSTOBS= system option was assigned a value other than 1 in a previous step, don't forget to reset it back to 1 to assure that all observations are processed. This will allow the SAS System to begin reading at the first observation for all succeeding data sets.

29 Specifying the most recently created data set to use in a read operation

By default, the _LAST_= system option is set to use the most recently created data set. This automatic feature is commonly found in procedure code when the DATA= option is omitted from a PROC. To override this built-in default, the _LAST_= system option can be defined as any valid temporary or permanent SAS data set name (refer to data-set naming conventions in "Getting Started" section, tip #4). The _LAST_= option can be specified in an OPTIONS statement, in the OPTIONS window, at SAS invocation, or in the configuration file.

30 Specifying the last observation to process

The **OBS=**n system option specifies the last data set observation to read or process in a DATA or PROC step (or in the case of an external data file, the last record to read or write). The OBS= option can be specified in an OPTIONS statement, in the OPTIONS window, at SAS invocation, or in the configuration file.

31 Processing a maximum number of observations with OBS=MAX

By default, the OBS= system option is set at **MAX**. The MAX value is host-specific and is not limitless since it represents the largest signed 4-byte integer available with the host machine.

32 Checking syntax in a DATA or PROC step

By specifying the OBS=0 system option, a program's code (DATA and PROC steps) can be executed and checked for syntax without reading or writing any observations. This is a good way to resolve syntax problems in a program while saving processing time.

33 Specifying OBS=MAX with WHERE

When specifying a WHERE statement, WHERE data set option, or WHERE clause, the OBS= system option must be set to **MAX** or the WHERE will fail.

34 Processing one or more observations in the middle of a data set

By combining the FIRSTOBS= and OBS= system options, one or more observations in the middle of a data set can be processed. For example, to process observations 10 through 20, the following option statement is specified:

Code:

```
OPTIONS FIRSTOBS=10 OBS=20;
```

The order of the two options doesn't matter. The previous example could have been specified as

Code:

```
OPTIONS OBS=20 FIRSTOBS=10;
```

35 Preventing SAS data sets from accidentally being replaced

Users can specify the **NOREPLACE** system option to prevent a permanent SAS data set from being accidentally replaced with another, like-named data set. Conversely, by specifying the **REPLACE** system option, like-named data sets can be overwritten. The REPLACE or NOREPLACE option can be specified in an OPTIONS statement, in the OPTIONS window, at SAS invocation, or in the configuration file.

36 Reducing the size of a SAS data set through compression

A data set's size can be reduced to a smaller size through a process known as compression.

Compression converts repeated consecutive characters to two- or three-byte representations. A compressed data set consists of variable-length records—as opposed to fixed-length records contained in an uncompressed data set. To compress a data set, specify the **COMPRESS=YES** system option. The COMPRESS=YES | NO option can be specified in an OPTIONS statement, in the OPTIONS window, at SAS invocation, or in the configuration file.

37 Uncompressing a data set's observations

To uncompress observations in a data set, users must execute a DATA step that copies the compressed data set specifying the **COMPRESS=NO** system option for the new data set. For example, the following DATA step creates a new uncompressed data set.

Code:

```
OPTIONS COMPRESS=NO;
DATA UNCOMPRESSED;
 SET COMPRESSED;
RUN;
```

38 Tracking and reusing free space in a compressed data set

You can track and reuse free space in a compressed data set by specifying the **REUSE=YES** system option. If specified, new observations are inserted wherever sufficient free space is available—as opposed to at the end of the data set.

*For further information about reusing free space, refer to the COMPRESS= system option. Conversely, by specifying **REUSE=NO** (default setting), free space is not tracked or reused in a compressed data set. The REUSE=YES|NO option can be specified in an OPTIONS statement, in the OPTIONS window, at SAS invocation, or in the configuration file.*

39 Controlling error-message printing associated with data errors

When a data error occurs, the SAS System automatically prints a complete error message for the impacted observation. This can result in rather large and repetitive error messages. To control the number of printed error messages associated with data errors to the SAS Log, the **ERRORS=**n system option is used. The ERRORS=n option can be specified in an OPTIONS statement, in the OPTIONS window, at SAS invocation, or in the configuration file.

40 Terminating a SAS program with an abnormal termination (abend)

By default, when an error message is encountered such as a syntax error, the SAS System writes an error message to the SAS Log, sets OBS=0, and initiates syntax-check mode. For many instances this may be acceptable. But other times the mere thought of setting OBS=0 with the possibility of having a production data set destroyed during a write operation is enough to send you to a therapist for help.

Fortunately, a system option exists to force the SAS System to abend (abnormally terminate before the end of the program) even at the slightest hint of a syntax error. By specifying the **ERRORABEND** system option, your production program will automatically stop running, bringing the error to your immediate attention. Conversely, when the **NOERRORABEND** option (default) is specified, the SAS System handles program errors without abending. The ERRORABEND option can be specified in an OPTIONS statement, in the OPTIONS window, at SAS invocation, or in the configuration file.

41 Disabling the SAS Macro language

When a program contains no Macro statements or Macro variable references, it may be helpful to disable the SAS Macro language. Disabling can help conserve available resources and is accomplished by specifying the **NOMACRO** system option. Conversely, the **MACRO** system option enables programs that contain Macro statements or Macro references to use the Macro language. The MACRO or NOMACRO option can be specified at SAS invocation or in the configuration file.

42 Printing multiple output pages on the same page

If printing multiple output pages on the same page—thereby saving paper by avoiding the start of a new physical page at each page break—sounds like a good idea, then the **FORMDLIM=** system option is worth looking at. By default, the FORMDLIM option is set to a null ('') value causing a new physical page to print whenever a page break occurs. This can be avoided by specifying the following system option:

Code:

```
OPTIONS FORMDLIM='*';
```

The preceding options statement causes the SAS System to skip a single line, write a line of asterisks (*) across the page, and then skip another single line without ejecting to a new page. Whenever the default action of skipping to a new page for each page of output is desired again, simply specify the FORMDLIM= option with a null ('') value. The FORMDLIM= option can be specified in an OPTIONS statement, in the OPTIONS window, at SAS invocation, or in the configuration file.

43 Printing output in color

With the availability of a color printer on practically every desktop, SAS output can be delivered in living color. The **COLORPRINTING** system option supports the printing of output in color, if supported. Of course, if color is not needed, the **NOCOLORPRINTING** option is available. This option can be specified in an OPTIONS statement, in the OPTIONS window, at SAS invocation, or in the configuration file.

44 Specifying the number of copies of output to print

By default, the number of copies of any output that is printed is one copy. But, if more than one copy is needed, the **COPIES=**n system option can be specified, where *n* is any valid numeric value. This option can be specified in an OPTIONS statement, in the OPTIONS window, at SAS invocation, or in the configuration file.

45 Opening an application with the X command in a minimized window

Applications opened with the X command can be displayed in a minimized state by specifying the **XMIN** system option or displayed using the default active state, **NOXMIN**. The XMIN or NOXMIN system option is specified at SAS invocation or in the configuration file.

46 Generating an error message when a format isn't found

Users can control whether an error message is generated when a format associated with a variable isn't found. By specifying the **FMTERR** system option, the SAS System treats the missing format as an error and prints an error message to the SAS Log. It also prevents the replacement of missing formats with the w. or $w. default format as the **NOFMTERR** option does. The FMTERR or NOFMTERR option can be specified in an OPTIONS statement, in the OPTIONS window, at SAS invocation, or in the configuration file.

47 Specifying the sort utility to use in sorting data

Sorting requires a considerable amount of system resources—resources that are occasionally in short supply. To better assist users to manage sorting requirements and control system resource utilizations, the SAS System enables users to select the sort utility of choice (on host systems with multiple sort packages). To specify what sort to use, the **SORTPGM=** system option is specified. The available options are 'sort-utility', BEST, HOST, or SYSTEM. The SORTPGM= option can be specified in an OPTIONS statement, at SAS invocation, or in the configuration file.

48 Specifying a sort utility with the SORTPGM= option

As mentioned in the previous tip, users can do nothing and remain with the default SORTPGM= option setting (see installation settings) or choose from the following list of arguments:

> **'sort-utility'**: Name associated with the desired host system sort utility.
>
> **BEST**: Initiates the sort utility best suited for the data being sorted.
>
> **HOST**: Initiates the available host system sort utility.
>
> **SAS**: Initiates the SAS System's built-in sort utility.

49 Exploring other SAS System Options

See Appendix A for a listing of SAS System options.

SAS Display Manager System

This section includes tips that will help you become familiar with the SAS System interface known as the SAS Display Manager System (DMS). You'll learn the importance of the four primary windows in DMS, how to access and manage output, how to safeguard your work through automatic and selective saves, how to take advantage of time-saving features such as function keys, toolbar buttons, and much more.

1   Using the SAS Program Editor window

The SAS Program Editor is one of the four primary windows of the DMS and the window where program statements are created, tested, and executed. When the display manager is activated, the Program Editor and Log are the two windows displayed by default, shown in Figure 1-4.

2   Viewing the Log window

The SAS Log displays important information about the current SAS session and executed programs. It assists users in solving program-related problems by providing the following information:

- The program statements that were executed

- The SAS data sets that were read and created

- The number of observations and variables that were read and written

- Warning, data, and syntax messages

- The time and memory used by each program step.

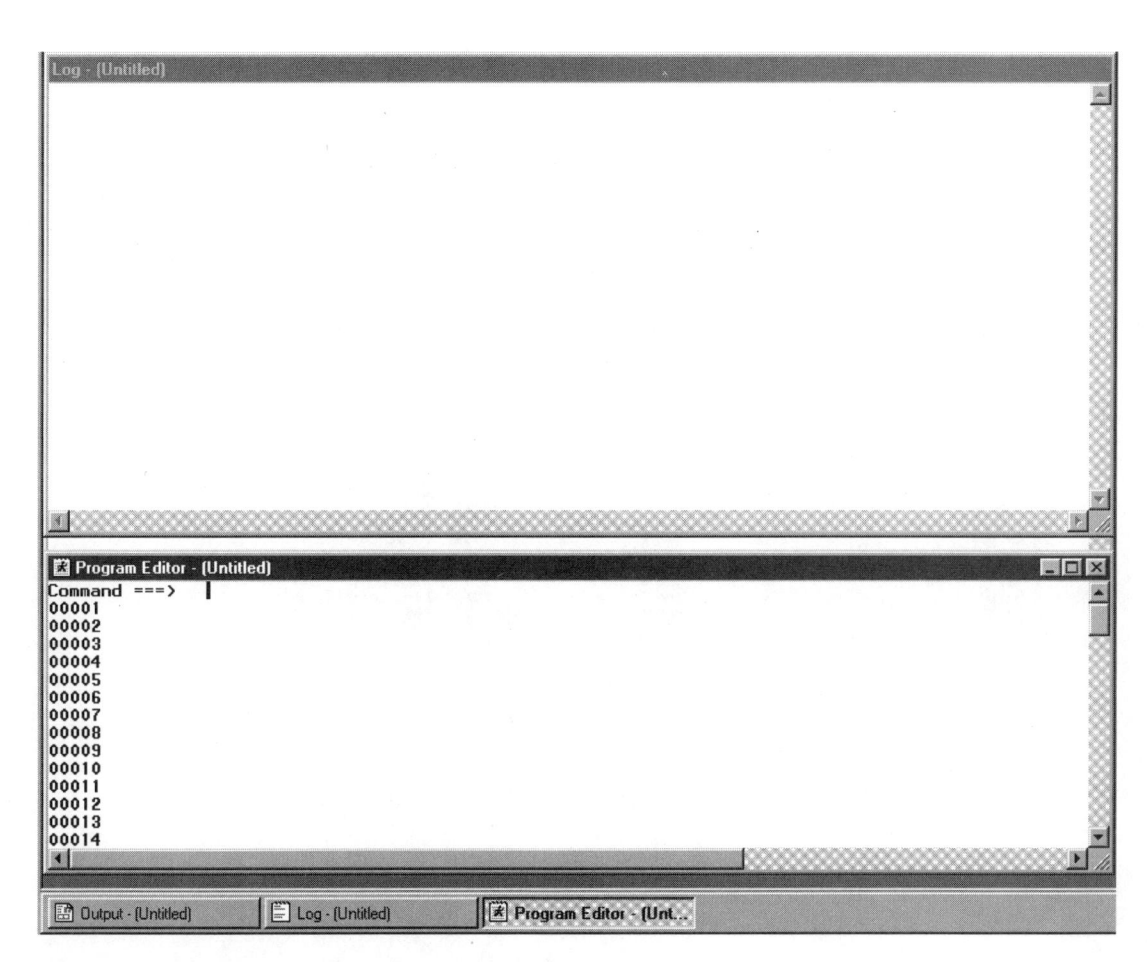

Figure 1-4. The DMS Program Editor and Log windows

3 Viewing the Output Window

The Output window displays output from output-producing SAS procedures and DATA steps unless an alternate destination is specified. In the absence of a **CLEAR** command to erase all output, output is automatically appended to the contents of the Output window, as displayed in Figure 1-5.

4 Accessing output in the Results window

The DMS Results window displays a directory of all output generated during a session. It provides a more efficient way of accessing and displaying output than does the Output Manager (see next tip). Clicking on the **Results** tab located on the left side of DMS and then clicking the desired output displays it, as displayed in Figure 1-6. For example, HTML, PDF, and RTF files can be viewed from within the Results window.

5 Viewing the Output Manager window

The DMS Output Manager window displays a directory of all output that has been generated during a session, or since the last CLEAR command was executed. Typing the command **MANAGER** activates it, as displayed in Figure 1-7. When active, the Output Manager directory displays the following information:

- The name of the procedure that created the output
- The starting page number

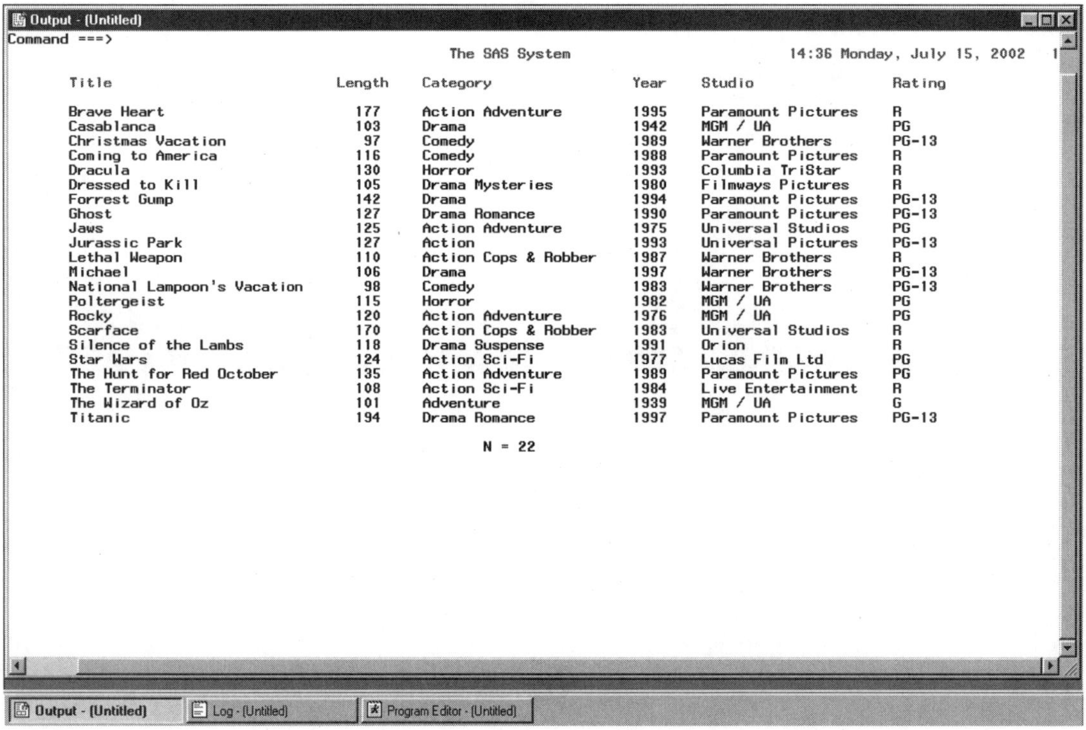

Title	Length	Category	Year	Studio	Rating
Brave Heart	177	Action Adventure	1995	Paramount Pictures	R
Casablanca	103	Drama	1942	MGM / UA	PG
Christmas Vacation	97	Comedy	1989	Warner Brothers	PG-13
Coming to America	116	Comedy	1988	Paramount Pictures	R
Dracula	130	Horror	1993	Columbia TriStar	R
Dressed to Kill	105	Drama Mysteries	1980	Filmways Pictures	R
Forrest Gump	142	Drama	1994	Paramount Pictures	PG-13
Ghost	127	Drama Romance	1990	Paramount Pictures	PG-13
Jaws	125	Action Adventure	1975	Universal Studios	PG
Jurassic Park	127	Action	1993	Universal Pictures	PG-13
Lethal Weapon	110	Action Cops & Robber	1987	Warner Brothers	R
Michael	106	Drama	1997	Warner Brothers	PG-13
National Lampoon's Vacation	98	Comedy	1983	Warner Brothers	PG-13
Poltergeist	115	Horror	1982	MGM / UA	PG
Rocky	120	Action Adventure	1976	MGM / UA	PG
Scarface	170	Action Cops & Robber	1983	Universal Studios	R
Silence of the Lambs	118	Drama Suspense	1991	Orion	R
Star Wars	124	Action Sci-Fi	1977	Lucas Film Ltd	PG
The Hunt for Red October	135	Action Adventure	1989	Paramount Pictures	PG
The Terminator	108	Action Sci-Fi	1984	Live Entertainment	R
The Wizard of Oz	101	Adventure	1939	MGM / UA	G
Titanic	194	Drama Romance	1997	Paramount Pictures	PG-13

N = 22

Figure 1-5. SAS results displayed in the Output window

- The number of pages

- A 40-character description from the title line that's used in the procedure output.

6 Using Output Manager commands

The Output Manager provides access to several menu selections (including Edit, Browse, Select, Rename, Delete, Verify, File, Print, and Save) using single-character commands such as E, B, S, R, D, V, F, P, and ?; or by right-clicking on the desired output to display a selection list of available commands. These commands let you perform a variety of tasks with your selected output. Table 1-2 shows the Output Manager commands and the tasks they perform.

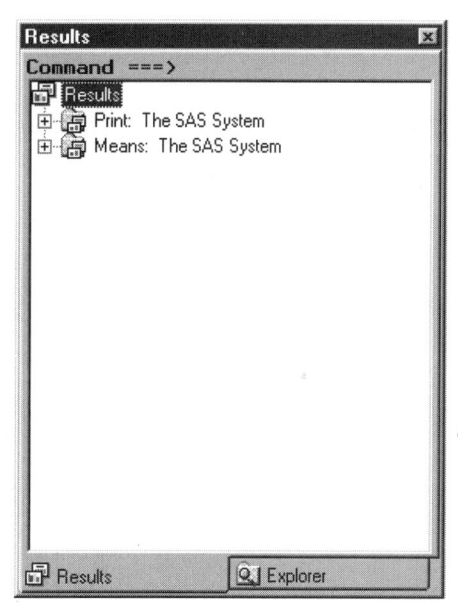

Figure 1-6. SAS results in the Results window

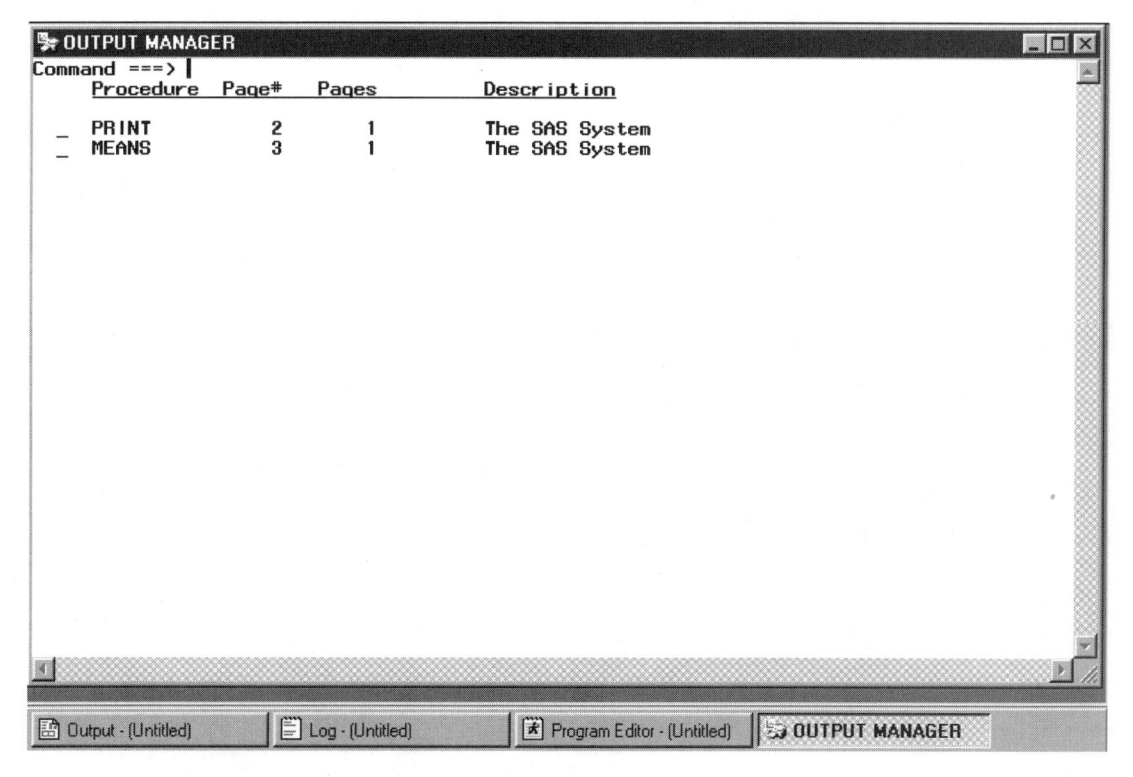

Figure 1-7. Viewing the Ouput Manager window's directory

Table 1-2. Output Manager Commands

COMMAND	TASK
Edit	Open the selected output in edit mode.
Browse	Open the selected output in non-edit (browse) mode.
Select	Open the selected output in non-edit (browse) mode.
Rename	Enable the selected output to be renamed.
Delete	Flag selected output for deletion, and then enter "V" to verify deletion or "C" to cancel.
File	Open the File dialog window to file (save) output.
Print	Open the Print dialog window to send output to a designated printer.
Save	Open the Save dialog window to assign and save output.

7 Clicking your way from one window to the next

Located on the bottom of the DMS is a series of clickable buttons, as shown in Figure 1-8. These buttons are available for quick navigation from one primary DMS window to the next. Just click the desired button, and the window automatically displays.

8 Autosaving your work

Saving your work is easy. Here's an automatic way to have the SAS System save your program code. Select **Tools➤Options➤Preferences**.

Select the **Edit** tab from the Preferences dialog box. Click the **Autosave** box and enter a value (in minutes) corresponding to how frequently you want to save your work.

9 Saving your work

There may be times when you'll want to save your work more frequently than what the Autosave feature is set to do. In these situations, a simple mouseless way is to press the **CTRL+S** keys.

10 Turning the Enhanced Editor on

By default the Enhanced Editor is turned on. If you turn it off or accidentally close the window, you can turn it on again anytime you like by following these steps. Select **Tools➤Options➤Preferences**. Select the Edit tab from the Preferences dialog box and click the Use the Enhanced Editor box. Another way to invoke one or more enhanced editors is to click the View menu and click Enhanced Editor. It's that simple.

11 Finding what you want

To avoid having to scroll up and down in your program to find what you want, you can find it the easy way instead. Press **CTRL+F** to display the Find dialog box. Enter the text you are looking for in the Find text box and click the Find Next button. The default direction for the find is "down" (although either "up" or "down" can be selected) so you may want to position the cursor at the top of your program before beginning a find. You can have SAS match the

Figure 1-8. Ouput Manager's clickable buttons

whole word you've entered by selecting the Match whole word only box. In addition, you can look for the word using the same upper- and lower-case characters entered by selecting the Match case box.

This search feature will work in any window that's selected, such as the Log and Output windows.

12 Having windows at your command anytime and anywhere

Three DMS windows can be invoked anytime and from anywhere within the SAS System: 1) HELP, 2) OPTIONS, and 3) KEYS. Simply type one of these three names on any command line or, for even faster results, define your function key settings so that with the press of a button the requested window displays. Refer to tip #15 in this section to find out how function keys are defined.

13 Getting help in the SAS System

Help is only a command away. Simply type **HELP** on any command line, and a context-sensitive help window will be displayed. The Help window provides comprehensive help information on virtually anything in the SAS System. Four tabs are displayed: 1) Contents, 2) Index, 3) Search, and 4) Favorites.

14 Viewing and changing SAS System options

The options window provides a way to view and change some SAS System options. Options are grouped according to the task or purpose they perform. You'll find system options that control how network and encryption is handled; how display, error handling, files, language control, and initialization and operation behave; how external and SAS files are handled; how data processing options are set; what driver settings are set; how SAS log, procedure output, and printing behave; how SAS macro options are set; what sort procedure options are set; what installation, memory, and performance options are set. By following these simple steps, you can access system options anytime you like:

1. From the SAS Display Manager, click the **Tools** button and select **System** from the **Options** drop-down selection list to display the SAS System Options window, as shown in Figure 1-9.

2. In the SAS System Options window, open the directory corresponding to the option category you'd like to view or change settings for by clicking the plus sign "+". Once open, the available options for that category are displayed in the right-most window.

3. Select the system option you want to reset by double-clicking the name of the option, select the desired value from the window display, and click the **OK** button.

4. Click the **OK** button on the System Options window to save your new settings.

15 Browsing, modifying, and saving function key settings

The function keys window gives users a way to browse, modify, and save function key settings. Simply type **KEYS** on any command line, and

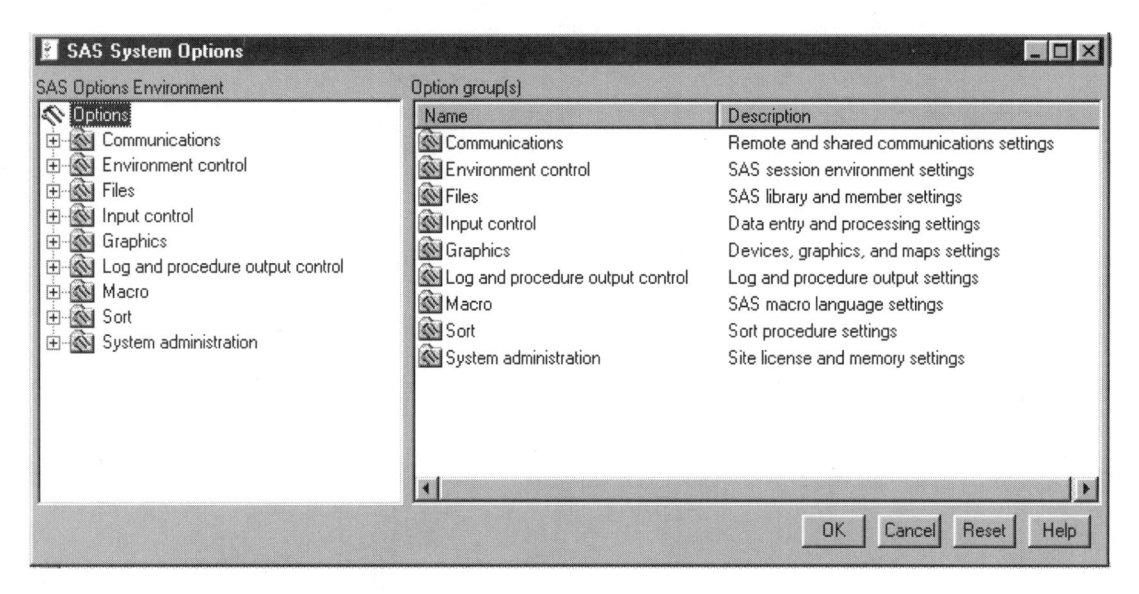

Figure 1-9. SAS System Options window

the function keys window is displayed, shown in Figure 1-10. Function keys may be assigned individually or, if preferred, together to perform multiple actions. Any key with two or more commands joined together must be separated with a semicolon ";". You can take advantage of function keys by saving time and keystrokes.

16 Exploring toolbar buttons

DMS's toolbars and toolbar buttons provide an easy and convenient way to perform window-management tasks. Remembering what the icon on a button represents can sometimes be difficult. To help understand the function of the various buttons, hold the cursor over a button and wait a few seconds for a ToolTip window to reveal the button's name.

17 Customizing toolbar button settings

Display Manager toolbar buttons can be viewed and customized as necessary. You'll be able to add custom controls or change the settings of existing buttons by following a few simple steps:

1. From the SAS Display Manager, click the **Tools** button and select **Customize** from the drop-down selection list.

2. Click the **Customize** tab on the Customize Tools window.

3. Select the icon from the scrollable list to view and/or reset the command.

4. Once you've added or changed a setting in the command field, click the **OK** button.

5. Click the **Yes** button corresponding to the "Do you want to save your changes to SASUSER.PROFILE.TOOLBOX?" dialog window.

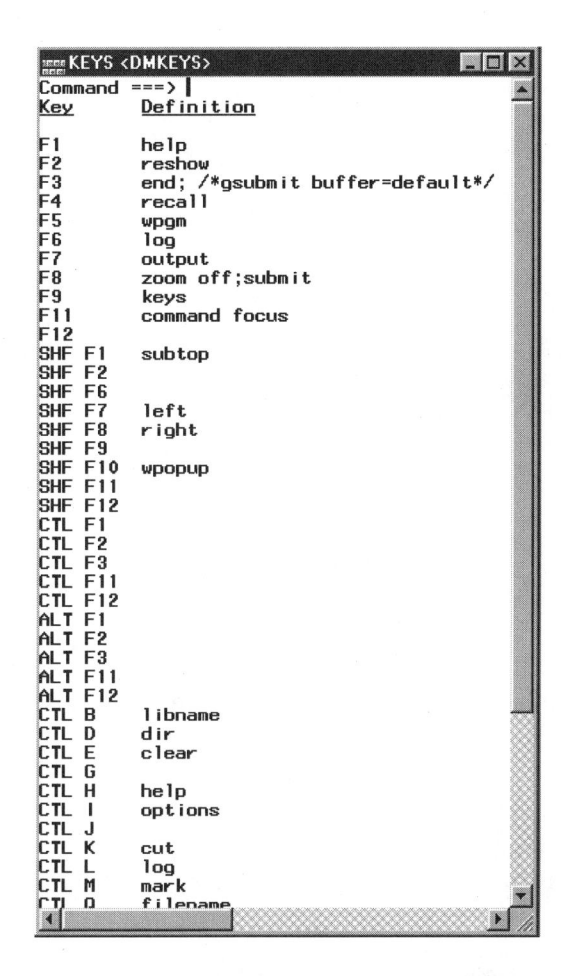

Figure 1-10. SAS System Function Keys window

18 Controlling how many commands are saved

Have you ever issued the **PREVCMD** or "**?**" command to retrieve previously submitted commands that you entered in Display Manager? The SAS System is set to automatically save your most recent 15 commands by default. You can increase or decrease the number of DMS commands that are saved by following these simple steps:

1. From the SAS Display Manager, click the **Tools** button and select **Customize** from the drop-down selection list.

2. Click the **Toolbars** tab on the Customize Tools window.

3. Enter a numeric value corresponding to the number of commands you'd like to save or click on the increase or decrease buttons in the "Number of commands saved:" field.

4. Once the new value is entered, click the **OK** button.

5. Click the **Yes** button corresponding to the "Do you want to save your changes to SASUSER.PROFILE.TOOLBOX?" dialog window.

19 Changing Editor options

DMS lets you control how your Editor operates and behaves. You'll find general option controls that let you specify whether caps are turned on, how the horizontal and vertical scrolling features behave, whether you're prompted to save your work at the end of a session, and whether syntax coloring is turned on. You also have the ability to control the behavior of text editing through a variety of options including automatic text add, automatic text flow, automatic text split, automatic text wrap, text indenting, having numbers turned on, and left and right column boundaries. Adjusting your editor settings is as easy as 1-2-3. Here's how.

1. From the SAS Display Manager, click the **Tools** button and select **Editor** from the **Options** drop-down selection list.

2. In the Editor Options window, select **General Options** located at the top of the Editor Options window. Select the general option you want to reset by double-clicking the name of the option, and select the desired value in the window display. Click the **OK** button.

3. To change one or more text-editing options, select **Text Editing Options** located at the top of the Editor Options window. Select the text-editing options you want to reset by double-clicking the name of the option, and select the desired value. Click the **OK** button.

4. Click the **OK** button on the Editor Options window to save your new settings to SASUSER.PROFILE.TOOLBOX.

20 Checking program text for spelling errors

Have you ever wished there was a way to have the SAS System check your program for spelling errors? Wish no longer. Spelling errors are a thing of the past with the built-in spell-check. In the program editor, enter the command **SPELL ALL** to display a window containing your misspelled program statements, shown in Figure 1-11. Using the "Unrecognized word" and "At line" information displayed in the misspellings list, correct the misspelled keyword(s) in each line in your program. You can also enter the commands **SPELL ALL SUGGEST** and **SPELL SUGGEST** to display Spell windows.

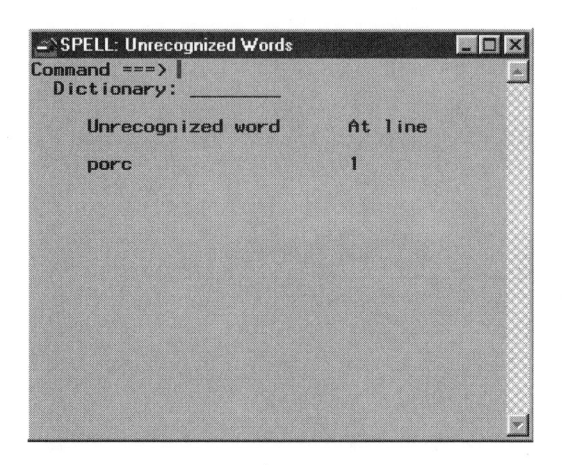

Figure 1-11. Checking program text for spelling errors

21 Clearing the contents of the Recall buffer

Issuing the **CLEAR RECALL** command clears the contents of the Recall buffer area containing submitted SAS statements. You can also clear the contents of the Program Editor, Log, and Output windows—see the appropriate tip to see how each window is cleared.

22 Clearing the contents of the Program Editor window

Issuing the **CLEAR PGM** command clears the contents of the Program Editor window containing SAS program statements and comments. You can also clear the contents of the Log, Output, and Recall buffer—see the appropriate tip to see how each is cleared.

23 Clearing the contents of the Log window

Issuing the **CLEAR LOG** command clears the contents of the Log window containing executed program statements and comments. You can also clear the contents of the Program Editor, Output, and Recall buffer—see the appropriate tip to see how each is cleared.

24 Clearing the contents of the Output window

Issuing the **CLEAR OUTPUT** command clears the contents of the Output window containing output results. You can also clear the contents of the Program Editor, Log, and Recall buffer—see the appropriate tip to see how each is cleared.

25 Clearing tab settings

Issuing the **CLEAR TAB** command clears any and all tab settings. You can also clear the contents of the Program Editor, Log, Output, and Recall buffer—see the appropriate tip to see how each is cleared.

26 Clearing the contents of the active window

Issuing the **CLEAR** command without any arguments clears the contents of the current active window. You can also clear the contents of the Program Editor, Log, Output, Tab, and Recall buffer—see the appropriate tip to see how each is cleared.

27 Replacing the command line with the PMENU Facility

The command line can be replaced with the PMENU Facility by issuing the **PMENU** command on any command line.

28 Disabling the PMENU Facility

The PMENU Facility can be disabled and replaced with the command line by selecting **Preferences** from the Options pop-up menu items in the Tools pull-down menu. In the Preferences window, select **Command** to activate the command line on all windows.

29 Using Function Key shortcuts

Here are a few default Function Key shortcuts that will save you save time and keystrokes.

Function Key shortcuts can be changed to accommodate your specific needs.

Table 1-3 shows the Function Key shortcuts and the tasks they perform.

Table 1-3. Function Key Shortcuts

FUNCTION KEY SHORTCUT	TASK
F1	Help
F2	Reshow
F3	End
F4	Recall
F5	Program Editor
F6	Log
F7	Output
F8	Zoom off; Submit
F9	Keys
F11	Command bar
SHIFT-F1	Subtop
SHIFT-F7	Left
SHIFT-F8	Right
SHIFT-F10	Wpopup
CTRL-B	Libname
CTRL-D	Dir (Directory)
CTRL-E	Clear
CTRL-H	Help
CTRL-I	Options
CTRL-K	Cut
CTRL-L	Log
CTRL-M	Mark
CTRL-Q	Filename
CTRL-R	Rfind (Repeat Find)
CTRL-T	Title
CTRL-U	Unmark
CTRL-W	Access

30 Accessing Display Manager Windows

Here are a number of popular and cool DMS Windows that'll save you time and keystrokes. Table 1-4 shows the Display Manager Windows, the command that invokes them, and a brief description.

31 Using Display Manager commands

Table 1-5 shows a number of DMS commands that'll save you time and keystrokes, along with a brief description of each.

32 Using Editor commands

The SAS Editor has a number of command-line commands that'll give you all the control you need to manage your programs hassle-free. Many of the commands in Table 1-6 can also be defined in your function keys for even greater timesaving opportunities.

33 Using Editor line commands

The SAS Editor lets you perform a variety of operations on the individual lines of your program. You'll be able to change your program line by line or alter a group of lines all at once. Table 1-7 lists editor line commands that provide the ability to alter your program lines quickly and easily.

Table 1-4. Display Manager Windows

WINDOW	COMMAND	DESCRIPTION
AF	AF <arguments>	Activates a user-created SAS/AF application.
APPOINTMENT	APPOINTMENT <libref.dataset<start-weekday>>	Activates a calendar for entering, displaying, and updating daily appointments.
CALCULATOR	CALCULATOR	Activates a calculator for performing mathematical operations.
CATALOG	CATALOG <libref.catalog>	Activates a directory of SAS catalog entries enabling catalog management.
DIR	DIR <libref.type>	Activates a window containing information about SAS files.
FILENAME	FILENAME	Activates a window containing assigned filerefs with their filenames.
FOOTNOTE	FOOTNOTES	Activates a window for entering and modifying up to 10 footnotes for output.
FORM	FSFORM <catalog.form-name>	Activates a window for assigning printer, text format, and destination for output.
HELP	HELP <topic>	Activates available Help information on a SAS topic.
KEYS	KEYS	Activates a window enabling function keys to be displayed, altered, and saved.
LIBNAME	LIBNAME	Activates a window containing assigned librefs with their SAS data libraries and engines.
LOG	LOG	Activates the SAS Log window enabling the display of messages and SAS statements for the current SAS session.
NOTEPAD	NOTEPAD <catalog-entry>	Activates a window for creating and storing text.
OPTIONS	OPTIONS	Activates a window containing SAS options.
OUTPUT	LISTING	Activates the SAS Output window enabling the display of procedure output.
OUTPUT MANAGER	MANAGER | MGR	Activates a directory containing the current session's output.
PROGRAM EDITOR	PROGRAM | PGM	Activates the SAS Program Editor enabling the entry, modification, and submission of SAS statements and programs.

Table 1-4. Display Manager Windows (Continued)

WINDOW	COMMAND	DESCRIPTION
SETINIT	SETINIT	Activates a window containing licensed SAS software and expiration dates.
SITEINFO	SITEINFO	Activates a window containing site-specific SAS information.
TITLE	TITLES	Activates a window for entering and modifying up to 10 titles for output.
VAR	VAR <libref.dataset>	Activates a window containing information about SAS data sets, variables, and attributes.

Table 1-5. Display Manager Commands

COMMAND	DESCRIPTION
**BYE	ENDSAS**	Ends a SAS session.
CLEAR	Removes contents of window.
CLOCK	Turns clock on or off.
END	Removes one of the special windows from the screen. Can't be used with the LOG or OUTPUT windows. In the PGM window the command behaves like SUBMIT.
NEXT {window}	Moves the cursor to the next window and activates that window. Specify a window name for a specific window.
PCLEAR {BUFFER=Pastebuffername}	Clears the contents of a paste buffer.
PLIST	Lists all current paste buffers in the Log window.
PREVCMD	Recalls the last command entered on the command line.
RESHOW	Redisplays the screen.
SIGNOFF	Breaks a link with a remote system.
SIGNON	Establishes a link with a remote system.
SMARK	Identifies an area on a screen to be copied.
STORE {APPEND} {BUFFER=pastebuffername}	Copies marked screen area into a paste buffer.
UNMARK	Returns marked text to the status of regular text.

Table 1-5. Display Manager Commands (Continued)

COMMAND	DESCRIPTION
WDEF srow scol nrows ncols	Redefines the window by moving it to a specified location on the screen.
WGROW	Allows you to enlarge the active window by using the cursor keys. Acts as a toggle switch to turn on and off.
WMOVE	Allows you to move the window using the cursor keys. Acts as a toggle switch to turn on and off.
WSAVE	Saves the window position and background color of the window.
WSHRINK	Decreases the size of the window by using cursor keys. Acts as a toggle switch to turn on and off.
X	Suspends the SAS System and activates operating system mode where system commands can be entered. Enter EXIT to return to the SAS System.
X 'command'	Issues a system command within the SAS System. The command clears the screen before displaying command output. Press ENTER key to return to the SAS System.
ZOOM	Enlarges the active window over the entire screen.

Table 1-6. SAS Editor Commands

COMMAND	DESCRIPTION
**AUTOADD {ON	OFF}**	Allows automatic line addition.
**AUTOFLOW {ON	OFF}**	Allows text to be flowed when included, copied, or pasted.
AUTOSPLIT	Allows text to be split after ENTER is pressed.
**AUTOWRAP {ON	OFF}**	Allows text to be wrapped when it is included, copied, or filed.
**BACKWARD {PAGE	HALF	MAX	n}**	Moves the contents of the text editor backward the amount set by the VSCROLL command or by using one of the options.
BOTTOM	Scrolls to the last line of text.
BOUNDS left right	Left and right boundaries are set when text is flowed.
**CAPS {ON	OFF}**	Changes the default case of text.
**CHANGE 'string1' 'string2' {NEXT	FIRST	LAST	PREV	ALL	WORD	SUFFIX	PREFIX}**	Changes one or more occurrences of string1 to string2 depending on what option is specified.
CLEAR	Removes each and every text line.

Table 1-6. SAS Editor Commands (Continued)

COMMAND	DESCRIPTION
COLOR fieldtype color	The color of selected portions of the window can be changed. Valid fieldtypes are: BACKGROUND, BANNER, BORDER, COMMAND, MESSAGE, NUMBERS, TEXT. Valid colors (machine dependent) are: B{lue}, R{ed}, G{reen}, C{yan}, P{ink}, Y{ellow}, W{hite}, K{black}, M{agenta}, A{gray}, N{brown}, O{range}.
CURSOR	Positions the cursor to the command line.
CUT {APPEND} {BUFFER= pastebuffer} {LAST} {ALL}	Removes the marked text strings in the current window and stores them in a paste buffer.
DICT	Invokes, creates, and maintains an auxiliary dictionary.
FILE {fileref	'filename'} {TABS}	The entire contents of the text editor are written into a file.
FILL {'fillcharacter'} {n}	Inserts fill characters starting at the current cursor location.
FIND 'characterstring' {NEXT	FIRST	LAST	PREV	ALL}	Searches for a specified string of characters.
FORWARD {PAGE	HALF	MAX	n}	Moves the text editor forward as specified by the VSCROLL command or an amount specified by the selection of one of the options.
HSCROLL {PAGE	HALF	MAX	n}	Specifies the default horizontal scroll amount when the right and left scrolling commands are used.
INCLUDE {fileref	'filename'} {NOTABS}	Fetches an external file into the text editor.
INDENT {ON	OFF}	Maintains left-margin indentation as text is flowed.
LEFT {PAGE	HALF	MAX	n}	The program (text) editor will move left corresponding to the amount specified by the HSCROLL command or an amount specified by one of the options.
MARK {CHAR	BLOCK}	Identifies text you want to manipulate.
n	Line n will be scrolled to the top of the window.
NUMBERS {ON	OFF}	Turns line numbers on or off (acts as a toggle).
PASTE {CHAR	BLOCK} {BUFFER=pastebuffer}	Text store in the default paste buffer or in the specified paste buffer will be inserted at the cursor location in the text editor.
PCLEAR {BUFFER= Pastebuffername}	Clears the contents of a paste buffer.
PLIST	A current list of paste buffers are displayed.
RCHANGE	Characters specified in a previously specified CHANGE command are found and changed.
RESET	Removes pending line commands.
RFIND	Characters specified in a previously specified FIND command are searched and found.

Table 1-6. SAS Editor Commands (Continued)

COMMAND	DESCRIPTION
**RIGHT {PAGE	HALF	MAX	n}**	The text editor will move right corresponding to the amount specified by the HSCROLL command or an amount specified by one of the options.
SMARK	Identifies an area on the screen for copying later with the STORE command.
SPELL	Checks text for spelling errors and flags errors.
STORE {APPEND} {BUFFER=pastebuffername}	Copies marked text in the current window into a paste buffer.
TOP	Scrolls to the first line of text in the text editor.
UNDO	Effects of actions are reversed.
UNMARK {ALL}	Marked text is returned to normal status.
**VSCROLL {PAGE	HALF	MAX	n}**	Specifies the default vertical scroll amount when the FORWARD and BACKWARD scrolling commands are used.

Table 1-7. SAS Editor line Commands

LINE COMMANDS	DESCRIPTION
C and CC	Copies one or more lines of text to another location.
CL and CCL	Changes characters in one or more lines of text to lowercase.
COLS	Displays a horizontal line ruler for counting columns.
CU and CCU	Changes characters in one or more lines of text to uppercase.
D and DD	Deletes one or more lines of text.
I	Inserts one or more new lines.
JC and JJC	Centers one or more lines of text.
JL and JJL	Left aligns one or more lines of text.
JR and JJR	Right aligns one or more lines of text.
M and MM	Moves one or more lines of text to another location.
MASK	Assigns the initial contents of a new line.
R and RR	Replicates one or more lines of text.
TC	Joins two lines of text.
TF	Flows text to the first blank line or to the end of text.
TS	Splits line of text at the position of cursor.
) and))	Shifts right one or more lines of text.
> and >>	Shifts right one or more lines of text.
(and ((	Shifts left one or more lines of text.
< and <<	Shifts left one or more lines of text.

Chapter 1

SAS Explorer

This section includes tips that will help you perform essential file-management tasks for program, log, output, and other file types. You'll learn how to view and manipulate SAS files using a Windows-like product called SAS Explorer, how to perform a variety of file-management tasks such as copying, renaming, and deleting files, and how to use SAS Explorer tools to make virtually every programming task much easier.

1 Invoking SAS Explorer

SAS Explorer is similar to Windows Explorer, in that it allows SAS files of all types (including libraries, data sets, catalogs, and host files) to be viewed and manipulated. It is invoked by clicking Explorer from the SAS View menu.

2 Creating a new library reference

You can create a new SAS library reference by pressing the **CTRL+N** keys. Once the New Library window is displayed, as shown in Figure 1-12, you'll need to enter a name consisting of 1 to 8 alphanumeric characters (using valid SAS naming conventions). Then add the requested information in the Library Information area.

*If unsure of the file location, click the **Browse...** button for navigational assistance. Once the required information is entered and complete, click **OK** to create the new library reference.*

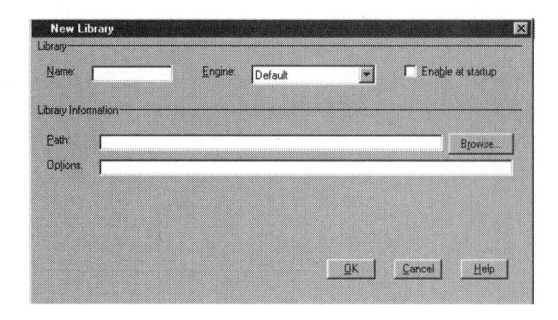

Figure 1-12. New Library window

3 Selecting one or more files

Explorer allows you to select one or more SAS files with a click of your mouse. Simply click the item you want selected with your primary mouse button. To select all files, click the **Edit** pull-down menu and choose **Select All**.

4 Viewing a file's properties

Properties provide pertinent information about a file. Displayed from the Properties window, a detailed image comprised of General Properties, Host/Engine Information, Columns, and Indexes can be viewed.

The properties for a file can be viewed by selecting the file you want with a right-click of your mouse and choosing Properties. With the Properties window opened, specific elements (including General Properties, Host/Engine Information, Columns, and Indexes) can be displayed using a selection list, as shown in Figure 1-13.

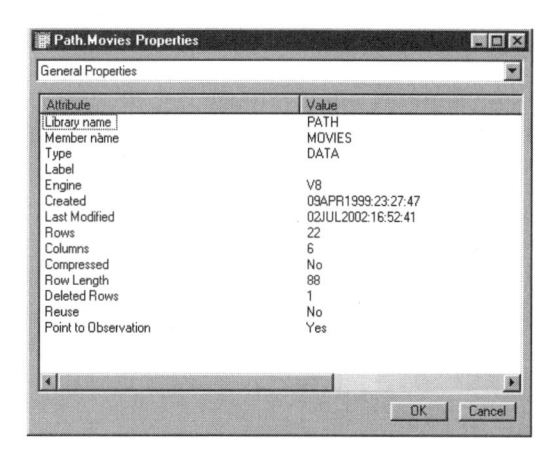

Figure 1-13. General Properties window

5   Copying files from one library to another

To copy a file from one library to another, select the file you want to copy and choose **Copy** from the Edit pull-down menu. Then select the target location where you want the file copied and choose **Paste** from the **Edit** pull-down menu.

6   Moving files from one library to another

To move a file from one library to another, right-click and drag the file you want moved from the current library to the new library. Then select **Move** from the pop-up menu when it appears.

7   Duplicating files

When a file is duplicated it is duplicated in the same library. To begin, select the file you want duplicated and choose **Duplicate** from the **Edit** pull-down menu. The duplicated file will have an assigned name of filename_Copy to differentiate it from the original.

A second way of duplicating a file involves first selecting the desired file with a right-click of your mouse. Then select **Duplicate...** from the pop-up menu. The duplicated file will have an assigned name, as before, of filename_Copy to differentiate it from the original.

8   Renaming files

It is sometimes necessary to rename a file. When this is the case, select the file you want to rename and choose **Rename...** from the **Edit** pull-down menu. When the Rename dialog box appears, simply change the name that is displayed and press the Enter key.

A second way to rename a file is to right-click the file you want to rename. Then select **Rename...** from the pop-up menu that displays. Enter the new name in the dialog box that appears and click **OK**, as displayed in Figure 1-14.

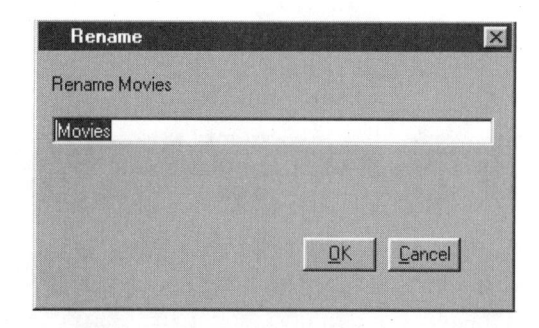

Figure 1-14. Renaming files in the Rename dialog box

9   Deleting files from a library

Performing routine housekeeping, such as deleting one or more files that are no longer needed, is an important part of library management. Use care when applying this tip, because once a file is deleted, it is *permanently*

Chapter 1

removed from its library. As with many of the tips in this section, there is more than one way to delete a file.

The first method requires selecting the file you want to delete and choosing **Delete** from the **Edit** pull-down menu. When the Delete Confirmation dialog box appears, click **OK** to confirm the operation, shown in Figure 1-15. The file is then deleted.

Another way to delete a file is performed by selecting the file you want deleted with a right-click of your mouse. When the pop-up menu appears select **Delete**. The operation is confirmed and completed by clicking **OK** in the Delete Confirmation dialog box.

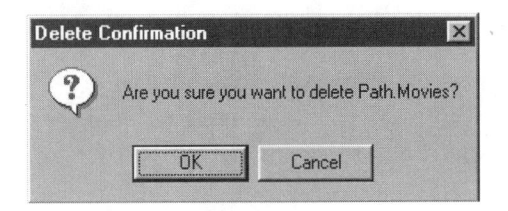

Figure 1-15. Deleting files in the Delete Confirmation dialog box

10 Sorting files

A file's contents can be arranged and displayed in ascending or descending order. Before you can do this, open the desired SAS data set and then select **Edit** mode from the **Edit** menu. To sort the data set, click the desired column header, shown in Figure 1-16. Then click the **A–Z** (ascending order) or **Z–A** (descending order) toolbar button. The data set observations will be arranged accordingly.

A data set and its observations can be sorted this way only if the data set isn't indexed.

11 Refreshing the file order

If you sort or rearrange files in Explorer often, it's important to know that every time you refresh the window, Explorer returns sorted files back to their original order.

	Title	Length	Category	Year	Studio	Rating
1	Brave Heart	177	Action Adventure	1995	Paramount Pictures	R
2	Casablanca	103	Drama	1942	MGM / UA	PG
3	Christmas Vacation	97	Comedy	1989	Warner Brothers	PG-13
4	Coming to America	116	Comedy	1988	Paramount Pictures	R
5	Dracula	130	Horror	1993	Columbia TriStar	R
6	Dressed to Kill	105	Drama Mysteries	1980	Filmways Pictures	R
7	Forrest Gump	142	Drama	1994	Paramount Pictures	PG-13
8	Ghost	127	Drama Romance	1990	Paramount Pictures	PG-13
9	Jaws	125	Action Adventure	1975	Universal Studios	PG
10	Jurassic Park	127	Action	1993	Universal Pictures	PG-13
11	Lethal Weapon	110	Action Cops & Robber	1987	Warner Brothers	R
12	Michael	106	Drama	1997	Warner Brothers	PG-13
13	National Lampoon's Vacation	98	Comedy	1983	Warner Brothers	PG-13
14	Poltergeist	115	Horror	1982	MGM / UA	PG
15	Rocky	120	Action Adventure	1976	MGM / UA	PG
16	Scarface	170	Action Cops & Robber	1983	Universal Studios	R
17	Silence of the Lambs	118	Drama Suspense	1991	Orion	R
18	Star Wars	124	Action Sci-Fi	1977	Lucas Film Ltd	PG
19	The Hunt for Red October	135	Action Adventure	1989	Paramount Pictures	PG
20	The Terminator	108	Action Sci-Fi	1984	Live Entertainment	R
21	The Wizard of Oz	101	Adventure	1939	MGM / UA	G
22	Titanic	194	Drama Romance	1997	Paramount Pictures	PG-13

Figure 1-16. Explorer window and sorting files

12 Resizing detail columns

Detail columns can be resized (increased or decreased) by dragging the column separator between each column.

13 Toggling between Show Tree on and Show Tree off

Showing the hierarchy of SAS and user libraries along with their members can be visually useful. Not only does it convey a common way to visualize a library's structure, it acts as a natural way to navigate between libraries. Explorer allows users to toggle Tree view on or off. To toggle between the "on" and "off" positions, select **Show Tree** from the **View** pull-down menu. If Tree view is off, the next time Show Tree is selected it will toggle to the "on" position. Figure 1-17 illustrates Tree view "on."

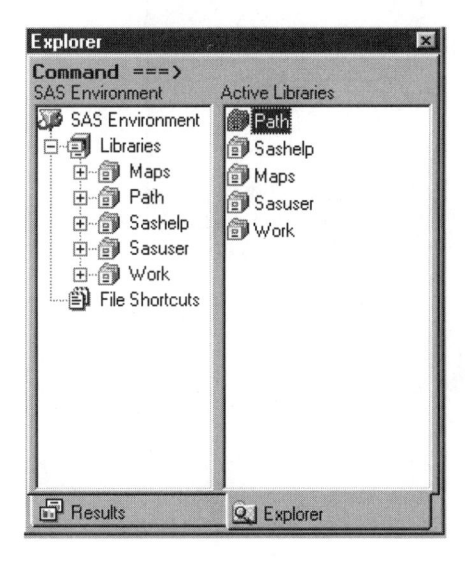

Figure 1-17. Viewing Show Tree

14 Viewing the contents of a catalog with Explorer

You can view the contents of a catalog by selecting the member (file) you want and right-clicking the member. With the pop-up menu displayed, select **Open**, as shown in Figure 1-18.

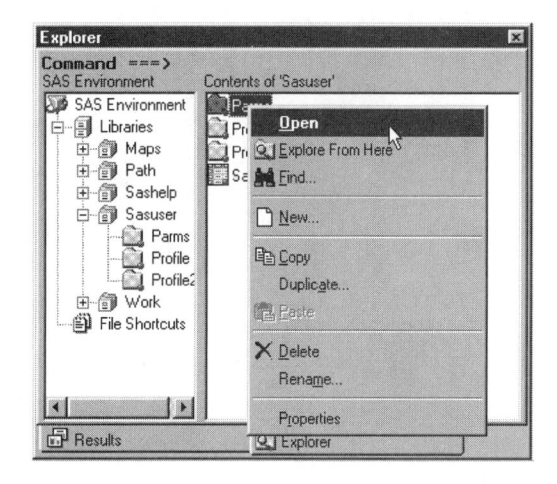

Figure 1-18. Opening the contents of a catalog with Explorer

The Explorer window displays the open catalog, as shown in Figure 1-19.

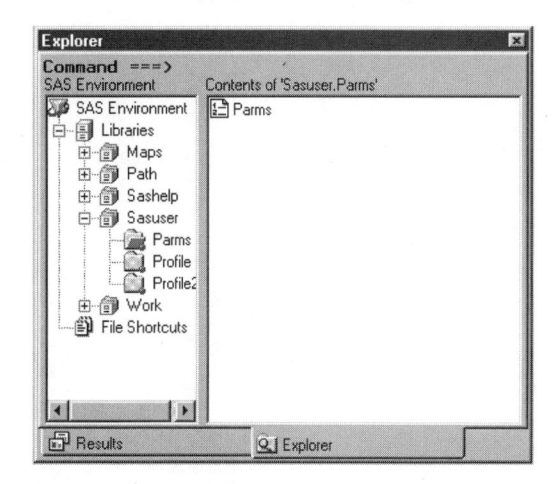

Figure 1-19. Viewing the Explorer window

Chapter 1

Another way to view the contents of a catalog is to select the **Explore From Here** option from the pop-up menu, as shown in Figure 1-20.

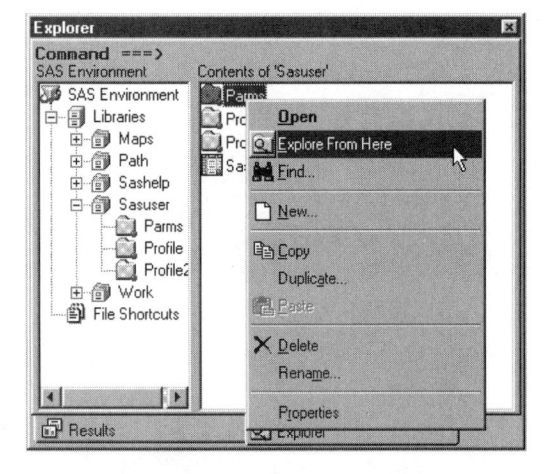

Figure 1-20. Selecting the Explore From Here option to view a catalog's contents

15 Displaying large icons for each file

If you're having a difficult time seeing the icons on your screen, or you're visually impaired, you can display large icons representing each file by clicking **Large Icons** in the **View** pull-down menu, as shown in Figure 1-21.

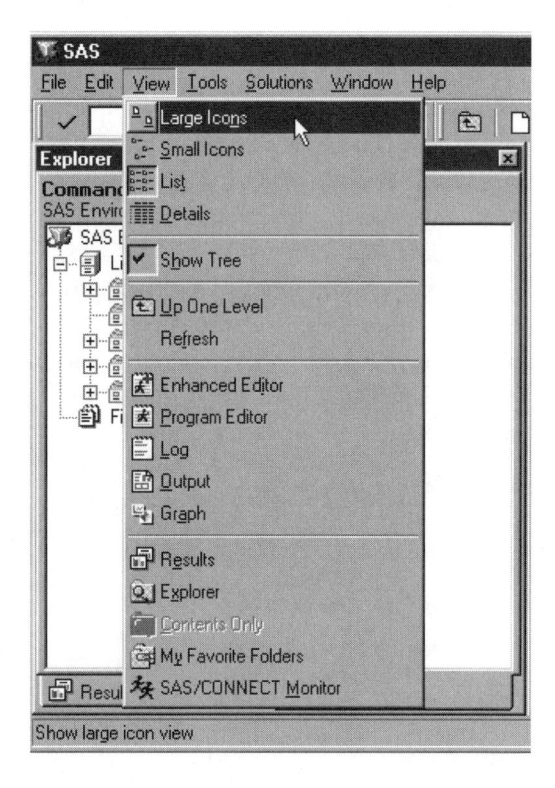

Figure 1-21. Selecting large icons for display with Explorer

SAS Basics

16 Displaying small icons for each file

If you have a large number of files, you can display small icons representing each file by clicking **Small Icons** in the **View** pull-down menu, as shown in Figure 1-22.

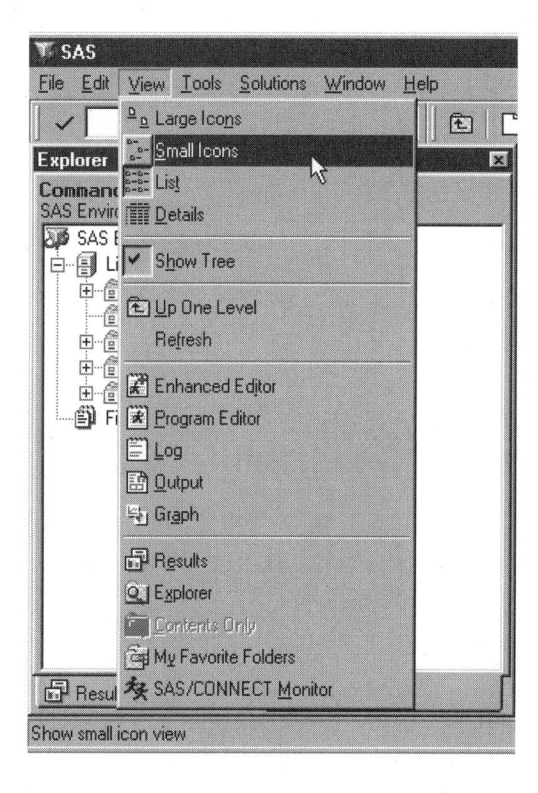

Figure 1-22. Selecting small icons for display with Explorer

17 Displaying files in a list

If you don't like icons representing your files, you can display files in a list by clicking **List** in the **View** pull-down menu, as shown in Figure 1-23.

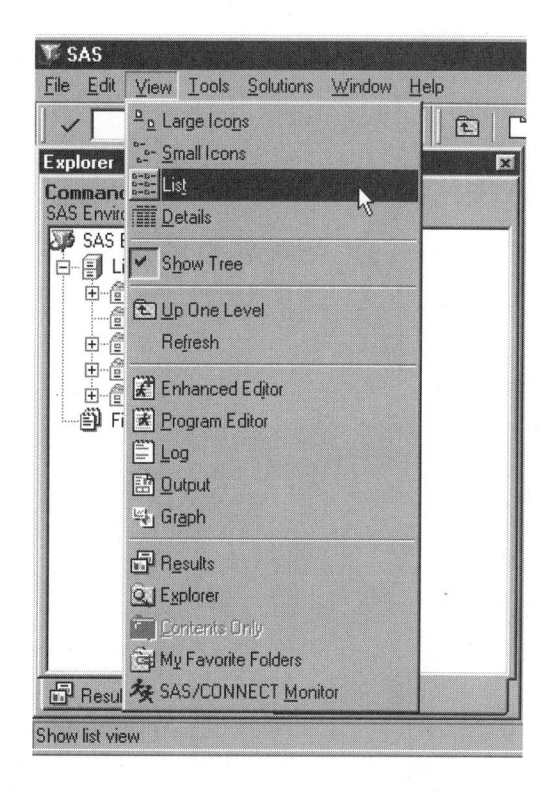

Figure 1-23. Selecting files in a list with Explorer

18 Displaying files and all their details

You can display files and all their details by clicking **Details** in the **View** pull-down menu. File details consist of the following columns: Name, Size, Type, Description, and Modified, as shown in Figure 1-24.

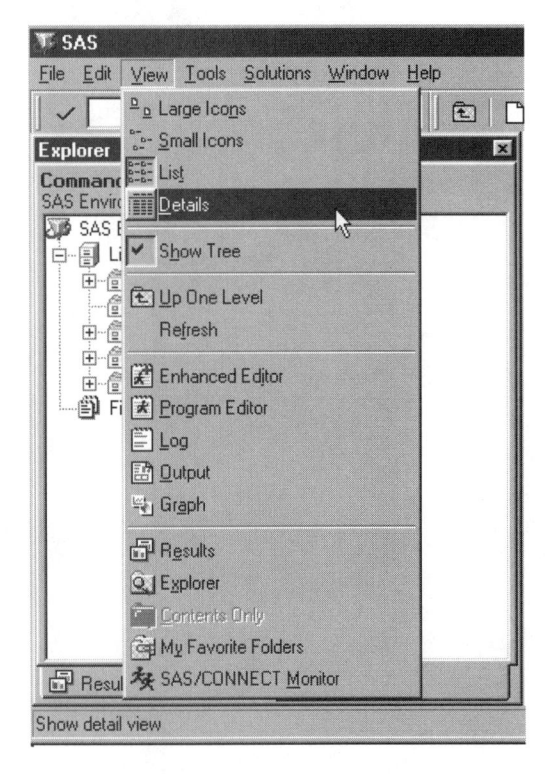

Figure 1-24. Displaying files and their details

19 Exploring Explorer keyboard shortcuts

SAS Explorer provides numerous keyboard shortcuts to help you save time while performing a variety of tasks. With a little practice, you'll be able to issue the following shortcuts quickly and easily just like a pro. Table 1-8 lists the SAS Explorer keyboard shortcuts.

Table 1-8. SAS Explorer keyboard Shortcuts

TASK	SHORTCUT
File	ALT-F
Edit	ALT-E
View	ALT-V
Tools	ALT-T
Solutions	ALT-S
Windows	ALT-W
Help	ALT-H
New	CTRL-N
Print	CTRL-P
Undo	CTRL-Z
Cut	CTRL-X
Copy	CTRL-C
Paste	CTRL-V
Select All	CTRL-A
Cascade	SHIFT-F5
Tile Vertically	SHIFT-F4
Tile Horizontally	SHIFT-F3

20 Exploring Explorer commands

SAS Explorer also provides powerful commands to help you navigate in and out of folders, manage your libraries and files, and gain better control while improving productivity. The following commands can be issued on the Command line—or as an alternative, use the Explorer's pull-down menus to achieve similar results. Table 1-9 lists the SAS Explorer commands.

Table 1-9. SAS Explorer Keyboard Commands

COMMAND	DESCRIPTION
COPYITEM	Copies the selected item from one library or catalog to another.
DELETEITEM	Deletes the specified item from the library or catalog.
DESELECT_ALL	Deselects all selected items from the library or catalog.
DETAILS	Toggles the Details view between on and off.
LARGEVIEW	On some operating systems, icons are changed to large view.
LIBASSIGN	Invokes the New Library window.
MOVEITEM	Moves the selected item from one library or catalog to another.
NEWOBJ	Creates a new item in the selected folder.
REFRESH	Refreshes the window contents.
RENAMEITEM	Renames the selected item in a library or catalog.
SELECT_ALL	Selects all items in the library or catalog.
SMALLVIEW	On some operating systems, icons are changed to small view.
TREE	Toggles the folder list or Tree view between on and off.
UPLEVEL	Moves up one level in the selected folder hierarchy.

Summary

In this chapter, you learned how to use the Base SAS product, communicate with the SAS DMS, access the built-in Help facility to further your learning experience, use SAS Explorer to access SAS files and view your results in the Results window, customize toolbar settings to create a more productive environment for working in, copy and move files from one location to another, and use a variety of keyboard shortcuts, commands, and other useful goodies to make your overall SAS experience a more rewarding one.

In the next chapter, "Data Access," you'll continue learning in a step-by-step approach with an assortment of organized and logical tips. You'll come to know a variety of ways in which SAS can be used to read and process input files. So get ready to learn quick and simple methods to help you access your data.

CHAPTER 2

Data Access

BASE SAS SOFTWARE provides a variety of tools for reading and processing files of virtually any type and format. This chapter presents an assortment of tips that will make your data input and retrieval tasks an easy one. Starting with the basics, you'll learn many useful techniques for accessing input files successfully. Once these techniques are mastered, you'll be ready to move up to the more challenging data-access requirements. You'll learn a variety of techniques that will make your data access requirements fast, easy, and fun.

In this chapter, you'll learn how to

- Read in-stream data that resides inside the program

- Read blank-, comma-, and tab-delimited input files

- Use different styles of the INPUT statement

- Specify what record to begin reading and stop processing in an input file

- Specify column and line pointers when reading an input file

- Handle input files that contains carriage control characters

- Read multiple input files

- Identify the last record in an input file

- Read variable length and hierarchical input files

- Read SAS data sets sequentially and directly

- Subset observations from a SAS data set

- Read and process data using SQL

External Data

This section includes tips that will show you how to process all types of input files. From in-stream data to external input files, you'll learn how to read and process blank-, comma-, and tab-delimited input files, fixed- and variable-length input files, input files containing carriage control characters, multiple (concatenated) and hierarchical input files, and much more.

1 Exploring file types

The Base SAS product, and in particular the DATA step, contains marvelous tools for reading and processing file types of virtually any type and format. Reading raw external input data is a breeze with the SAS software. SAS can read and retrieve input files of all types including fixed- and variable-length, blank-delimited, comma- and tab-delimited, named-input, hierarchical files, hybrid files containing a mixture of file types, XML files, Microsoft Excel, Word, and Access, Lotus 1-2-3, Quattro Pro, Paradox, OLE, and other file types, as well as SAS data sets and views.

2 Identifying external text data

The **INFILE** statement is used to identify and open external non-SAS data residing on storage mediums such as disk, tape, cartridge, and so on. Once identified, an opened external file is prepared for a "read" using an INPUT statement. One or more external files can be opened in a single DATA step.

3 Understanding the input buffer

When a raw data record is read from an external input source, an area of memory is used to store the record. This area of memory, referred to as an *input buffer*, serves as a type of temporary internal storage area (work area) for each raw data record that is read. Its purpose is to construct a logical record in memory that contains data values from one or more input sources.

4 Coding an INFILE statement with in-stream data

You're probably aware that an INFILE statement is used when reading data from an external input file. But did you know you could also use the INFILE statement to read in-stream data? In-stream data is where data records are contained in the program. Using the **CARDS** or **DATALINES** statements specifies the presence of in-stream data.

By being able to specify an INFILE statement with in-stream data, you have greater control over how the INPUT statement reads data, as well as the ability to take advantage of the many options available with the INFILE statement. So, a DATA step could contain an INFILE and CARDS statement in the same step, as the following example shows.

🖉 *DATALINES may be used in place of the CARDS input designation on the INFILE statement and the CARDS statement.*

Code:

```
DATA CARDSDATA;
  INFILE CARDS options;
  INPUT ...;
  Other SAS statements
  CARDS;
. . . .
In-stream data lines
. . . .
;
RUN;
```

5 Reading blank-delimited data with list input

When input data is separated by one or more blank spaces between data values, it's commonly referred to as *blank-delimited data*. Data of this type can be read using a simple list-style of input using the INPUT statement. It should be noted that character variables (denoted with a $ sign) default to a length of 8 bytes. To handle text fields greater than 8 bytes in length, you'll need to specify their lengths in an **INPUT** or **LENGTH** statement. If the data resides in an external file, then an INFILE statement is needed. The following in-stream data is read using a simple list-style of INPUT statement without an INFILE statement.

Code:

```
DATA MOVIES;
 INPUT TITLE $ RATING $;
 CARDS;
Jaws PG
Rocky PG
Titanic PG-13
;
RUN;
PROC PRINT;
RUN;
```

Results:

Obs	TITLE	RATING
1	Jaws	PG
2	Rocky	PG
3	Titanic	PG-13

6 Reading comma-delimited input files

When input data contains a comma separating data values, it's commonly referred to as *comma-delimited data.* The simplest way to read data of this type is to use a simple list-style of input in conjunction with the **DSD** option in the INFILE statement. The DSD option handles consecutive delimiters as missing values. It should be noted that character variables (denoted with a $ sign) default to a length of 8 bytes. To handle text fields greater than 8 bytes in length, you'll need to specify their lengths in an INPUT or LENGTH statement.

The following in-stream data is read using a simple list-style of INPUT statement with the DSD option specified in the INFILE statement.

✎ DATALINES may be substituted for the CARDS input designation on the INFILE statement and the CARDS statement.

Code:

```
DATA MOVIES;
 INFILE CARDS DSD;
 INPUT TITLE $ RATING $;
 CARDS;
Jaws,PG
Rocky,PG
Titanic,PG-13
;
RUN;
PROC PRINT;
RUN;
```

Results:

Obs	TITLE	RATING
1	Jaws	PG
2	Rocky	PG
3	Titanic	PG-13

7 Reading comma-delimited input containing missing values

Reading comma-delimited input data with missing values is relatively easy with list-style of input. Because the presence of missing values in input data can cause misalignment problems with the input pointer, list-style of input should be used in conjunction with the DSD option in the INFILE statement. It should be noted that character variables (denoted with a $ sign) default to a length of 8 bytes. To handle text fields greater than 8 bytes in length, you'll need to specify their lengths in an INPUT or LENGTH statement.

The following in-stream data is read using a list-style of INPUT statement with the DSD option specified in the INFILE statement.

✎ *DATALINES may be substituted for the CARDS input designation on the INFILE statement and the CARDS statement.*

Code:

```
DATA MOVIES;
 INFILE CARDS DSD;
 INPUT TITLE $ RATING $;
 CARDS;
Jaws,PG
Rocky,
,PG-13
;
RUN;
PROC PRINT;
RUN;
```

Results:

Obs	TITLE	RATING
1	Jaws	PG
2	Rocky	
3		PG-13

8 Reading comma-delimited input containing quoted values

When comma-delimited input data contains quotes around data values, list-style input is an effective way to read data. Because quotes surround data values, commas and other special characters contained within quotes are treated as part of the data. To successfully read data stored in this manner, list-style of input should be used in conjunction with the DSD option in the INFILE statement. It should be noted that character variables (denoted with a $ sign) default to a length of 8 bytes. To handle text fields greater than 8 bytes in length, you'll need to specify their lengths in an INPUT or LENGTH statement.

The following in-stream data is read using a list-style of INPUT statement with the DSD option specified in the INFILE statement.

✎ *DATALINES may be substituted for the CARDS input designation on the INFILE statement and the CARDS statement.*

Code:

```
DATA MOVIES;
 INFILE CARDS DSD;
 INPUT TITLE $ RATING $;
 CARDS;
"Jaws","PG"
"Rocky,II", "PG"
"Titanic", "PG-13"
;
RUN;
PROC PRINT;
RUN;
```

Results:

Obs	TITLE	RATING
1	Jaws	PG
2	Rocky,II	PG
3	Titanic	PG-13

9 Reading tab-delimited input

When an input file contains tab characters separating each data value, this is referred to as *tab-delimited data*. Tabs are represented on ASCII (PC, UNIX, VMS, and Mac) as '09'x and on EBCDIC (MVS, VM, and VSE) as '05'x.

Because tab-delimited input can't be read directly, you'll need to specify the **DSD** and **DLM=** options in the INFILE statement to handle data values and missing values.

The DSD option automatically removes quotes around data values while commas and other special characters contained within quotes are treated as part of the data. By specifying the **TRUNCOVER** option, the INPUT statement is able to process varying length records by assigning values when a shorter than expected record is read. It should be noted that character variables (denoted with a $ sign) default to a length of 8 bytes. To handle text fields greater than 8 bytes in length, you'll need to specify their lengths in an INPUT or LENGTH statement.

The following in-stream tab-delimited input is read using a list-style of INPUT statement with the DSD, DLM=, and TRUNCOVER options specified in the INFILE statement.

🖉 *DATALINES may be substituted for the CARDS input designation on the INFILE statement and the CARDS statement.*

Code:

```
DATA MOVIES;
  INFILE CARDS DSD DLM='09'x TRUNCOVER;
  INPUT TITLE $ RATING $;
  CARDS;
Jaws PG
Rocky PG
Titanic PG-13
;
RUN;
PROC PRINT;
RUN;
```

Results:

Obs	TITLE	RATING
1	Jaws	PG
2	Rocky	PG
3	Titanic	PG-13

10 Reading named-input data

When data contains a variable name followed by an equal sign "=" and a value, this is commonly referred to as *named-input data*. To successfully read all or selected data values in each record, list-style of input should be used. It should be noted that character variables (denoted with a $ sign) default to a length of 8 bytes. To handle text fields greater than 8 bytes in length, you'll need to specify their lengths in an INPUT or LENGTH statement.

🖉 *DATALINES may be substituted for the CARDS input designation on the INFILE statement and the CARDS statement.*

Code:

```
DATA MOVIES;
  INPUT TITLE= $ RATING= $;
  CARDS;
TITLE=Jaws RATING=PG
TITLE=Rocky,II RATING=PG
TITLE=Titanic RATING=PG-13
;
RUN;
PROC PRINT;
RUN;
```

Results:

Obs	TITLE	RATING
1	Jaws	PG
2	Rocky,II	PG
3	Titanic	PG-13

Results:

Obs	TITLE	RATING
1	Jaws	PG
2	Rocky,II	PG
3	Titanic	PG-13

11 Mixing other styles of input with named-input data

To add further flexibility when using list-style of input with named-input, other styles of input can be mixed and matched to create a kind of hybrid INPUT statement. When an INPUT statement reads data values constructed with named-input, all remaining values on the INPUT statement must be read using named-input—otherwise, data-related errors may be created. It should be noted that character variables (denoted with a $ sign) default to a length of 8 bytes. To handle text fields greater than 8 bytes in length, you'll need to specify their lengths in an INPUT or LENGTH statement.

DATALINES may be substituted for the CARDS input designation on the INFILE statement and the CARDS statement.

Code:

```
DATA MOVIES;
 INPUT TITLE $ RATING= $;
 CARDS;
Jaws RATING=PG
Rocky,II RATING=PG
Titanic RATING=PG-13
;
RUN;
PROC PRINT;
RUN;
```

12 Reading comma-delimited data with modified-list-input

Occasionally comma-delimited data contains data that must be read using one or more SAS input formats or informats. This approach is referred to as *modified-list-input* because it uses a form of style template to read one or more of the data values using a colon format modifier. The reason why this style of input is useful is to be able to read character data values that are longer than 8 bytes in length, that contain date values that have to be read a certain way, or that contain special numeric values including the use of dollar signs and commas.

As earlier tips suggested, the easiest way to read data of this type is to use a simple list-style of input but modified with the use of one or more informats, in conjunction with the DSD option in the INFILE statement. The following in-stream data is read using a simple list-style of INPUT statement with the DSD option specified in the INFILE statement.

DATALINES may be substituted for the CARDS input designation on the INFILE statement and the CARDS statement.

Code:

```
DATA MOVIES;
 INFILE CARDS DSD;
 INPUT TITLE : $11. RATING $;
 CARDS;
Brave Heart,R
Jaws,PG
Rocky,PG
Titanic,PG-13
;
RUN;
PROC PRINT;
RUN;
```

Results:

Obs	TITLE	RATING
1	Brave Heart	R
2	Jaws	PG
3	Rocky	PG
4	Titanic	PG-13

13 Avoiding truncation when reading varying length records

To avoid truncation problems related to varying length records, the TRUNCOVER option may be specified on the INFILE statement. By specifying TRUNCOVER, the INPUT statement is able to process varying length records by assigning values when a shorter than expected record is read. This prevents the INPUT statement from reading the next record when the current record in the input buffer is shorter than expected. It should be noted that character variables (denoted with a $ sign) default to a length of 8 bytes. To handle text fields greater than 8 bytes in length, you'll need to specify their lengths in an INPUT or LENGTH statement.

🖉 *DATALINES may be substituted for the CARDS input designation on the INFILE statement and the CARDS statement.*

Code:

```
DATA MOVIES;
 INFILE CARDS TRUNCOVER;
 INPUT TITLE $ RATING $;
 CARDS;
Jaws
Rocky,II PG
Titanic PG-13
;
RUN;
PROC PRINT;
RUN;
```

Results:

Obs	TITLE	RATING
1	Jaws	
2	Rocky,II	PG
3	Titanic	PG-13

14 Assigning missing values with the MISSOVER option

When using list input, the **MISSOVER** option is frequently specified as an option with the INFILE statement to prevent the INPUT statement from reading the next data line when it doesn't find values for all the variables specified in the INPUT statement. By specifying the MISSOVER option, values that aren't found in the current input data are assigned missing values.

Code:

```
DATA MOVIES;
 INFILE CARDS MISSOVER;
 INPUT TITLE $ RATING $;
 CARDS;
Jaws
Rocky,II PG
Titanic PG-13
;
RUN;
PROC PRINT;
RUN;
```

Results:

Obs	TITLE	RATING
1	Jaws	
2	Rocky,II	PG
3	Titanic	PG-13

15 Reading data with column-style of input

When an external file contains all input data values in the exact same columns across all records, a different style of input can be used. Data of this type can be read using column-style of input using the INPUT statement. The INPUT statement is constructed so that the starting and ending column position for each data value is defined, hence the name *column-style*.

An important feature with column-style input, unavailable with list-style of input (unless a colon format modifier is specified), is that it allows data values containing embedded blanks to be read. It should be noted that character variables (denoted with a $ sign) could be assigned a length greater than 8 bytes using this style of input. If the data resides in an external file, then an INFILE statement is needed. The example shows in-stream data being read using a column-style of input without an INFILE statement.

Code:

```
DATA MOVIES;
 INPUT TITLE $ 1-11 RATING $ 13-17;
 CARDS;
Brave Heart R
Jaws        PG
Rocky       PG
Titanic     PG-13
;
RUN;
PROC PRINT;
RUN;
```

Results:

Obs	TITLE	RATING
1	Brave Heart	R
2	Jaws	PG
3	Rocky	PG
4	Titanic	PG-13

16 Reading data with formatted-style of input

In the previous tip, you learned how column-style of input could be used to read an external file containing input data values in the exact same columns across all records. Under many circumstances this method of input is satisfactory. But input files may also contain non-standard data such as dates and times, social security numbers, ASCII, binary, EBCDIC, HEX, integer binary, packed decimal, as well as standard types of data that contain commas, percents, and dollar signs. For these special data values, formatted-style of input is the input style of choice to read a file.

The key features of formatted-style of input is that the INPUT statement is constructed using one or more informats to define how SAS should read certain data values, the data type (numeric or character) to use in defining the data value, and the width of the data value. A period "." must be specified as part of the width value to inform the SAS System that this is formatted-style of input. Another important feature is that this style of input allows data values containing embedded blanks to be read. It should be noted that character variables (denoted with a $ sign) could be assigned a length greater than 8 bytes using this style of input. If the data resides in an external file, then an INFILE statement is needed.

In the example, in-stream data is read using a formatted-style of input, specifying an input format of MMDDYY10. to be applied to the RENTED date. In order to display the date values the same way as they were read, a **FORMAT** statement is specified to instruct SAS how the RENTED date should appear.

The period must be specified with a format, otherwise the format would be considered another variable.

Code:

```
DATA MOVIES;
  INPUT TITLE $11.
        RATING $5.
        RENTED MMDDYY10.;
  FORMAT RENTED MMDDYY10.;
  CARDS;
Brave HeartR   07/21/2001
Jaws        PG 02/03/1998
Rocky       PG 11/18/1997
Titanic     PG-1305/14/1998
;
RUN;
PROC PRINT;
RUN;
```

Results:

Obs	TITLE	RATING	RENTED
1	Brave Heart	R	07/21/2001
2	Jaws	PG	02/03/1998
3	Rocky	PG	11/18/1997
4	Titanic	PG-13	05/14/1998

17 Specifying the maximum number of input records to read

You can control how many input records are read as input from an external file by specifying the **OBS=** option in the INFILE statement. The OBS= option specifies the last input record to process from an input source. MAX is the default value for the OBS= option, which means the largest signed, four-byte integer value for the operating system you're running.

18 Specifying the first input record to read

SAS lets you specify the first input record to read from an external file by specifying the **FIRSTOBS=** option in the INFILE statement. The default value for FIRSTOBS is 1, which means processing will begin with the first logical record in the input file.

19 Using column pointers with formatted-style of input

In the previous tip, you learned how formatted-style of input can be used to read an external file containing data values in the exact same columns across all records. Now we'll expand the capabilities of formatted-style of input to include the ability to control where in the input buffer data record to begin reading data. This is important because it gives you complete flexibility to choose where in the input buffer record an input value starts. The available column pointers are described in Table 2-1.

Table 2-1. Column Pointer Controls

POINTER	DESCRIPTION
@n	Positions the pointer to column *n*.
+n	Moves the pointer *n* columns to the right.

In the example, in-stream data is read using a formatted-style of input with column pointer controls. The INPUT statement begins by positioning the pointer to column 1 to read the movie title from the next 11 columns. It then moves the pointer 5 columns to the right in the input buffer record, skipping over the RATING data value, to read the RENTED date in columns 17 through 26 as follows.

Code:

```
DATA MOVIES;
  INPUT @1 TITLE $11. +5 RENTED MMDDYY10.;
  FORMAT RENTED MMDDYY10.;
  CARDS;
Brave HeartR    07/21/2001
Jaws        PG  02/03/1998
Rocky       PG  11/18/1997
Titanic     PG-1305/14/1998
;
RUN;
PROC PRINT;
RUN;
```

Results:

Obs	TITLE	RENTED
1	Brave Heart	07/21/2001
2	Jaws	02/03/1998
3	Rocky	11/18/1997
4	Titanic	05/14/1998

20 Specifying the number of lines available to the input pointer

SAS lets you specify how many lines are available to the input pointer on a read operation. By specifying the **N=** option in the INFILE statement, you can control how many input lines are available to the input pointer to assist in navigating up or down the records in an input file.

✎ *The default number of lines available to the input pointer is 1.*

21 Using line pointers with formatted-style of input

Line pointers can also be used with formatted-style of input to specify which input line to read data from. You use line pointers as a way to move up or down the records in an input file. This is important because it gives complete flexibility to choose which record to read. Combine line pointer with column pointers (see previous tip), and you have complete control over the horizontal and vertical positioning in an input file. The available line pointers are described in Table 2-2.

Table 2-2. Line-pointer Controls

POINTER	DESCRIPTION
#n	Moves the pointer to line *n* in an input file.
/	Positions the pointer to column 1 of the next line in an input file.

In the example, in-stream data is read using a formatted-style of input with line-pointer controls. An INFILE statement is specified to indicate the number of lines available to the line pointer with the N= option. In this case N is set to 2 lines. The INPUT statement begins by positioning the pointer to column 1 of the next line to read the movie title from the next 11 columns. It then moves the line pointer down two records to read the RENTED date in columns 17 through 26 as follows.

Code:

```
DATA MOVIES;
  INFILE CARDS N=2;
  INPUT / TITLE $11. #2
        @17 RENTED MMDDYY10.;
  FORMAT RENTED MMDDYY10.;
  CARDS;
Brave HeartR    07/21/2001
Jaws      PG    02/03/1998
Rocky     PG    11/18/1997
Titanic   PG-1305/14/1998
;
RUN;
PROC PRINT;
RUN;
```

Results

Obs	TITLE	RENTED
1	Jaws	02/03/1998
2	Titanic	05/14/1998

22 Holding an input record

Sometimes it's advantageous to be able to hold an input record in the input buffer. Line-hold controls let you do just that. The normal default is to read a new input record into the input buffer with each INPUT statement or each iteration of the DATA step. But line-holders let you override this default behavior by the INPUT statement and the DATA step to give you powerful record control features. Line-hold controls can be used with list-, column-, and formatted-style of input to allow for powerful data access and control. The available line-hold controls are described in Table 2-3.

Table 2-3. Line-hold Controls

LINE HOLDER	DESCRIPTION
@	Referred to as the trailing @, this line holder holds the current input record to let the next INPUT statement read from the same record.
@@	Referred to as the double trailing @, this line holder holds the current input record for multiple iterations of the DATA step.

In the example, in-stream data is read using a formatted-style of input and a trailing @ line-hold control. The first INPUT statement reads the RATING value into the input buffer and holds it while an evaluation of its contents are assessed. The value of doing this is that the input buffer isn't loaded with a complete input record—just one data value for the purpose of evaluating its value in the IF statement. If the value of RATING is "PG," the second INPUT statement reads the same input record into the input buffer to access the movie title and date rented—otherwise, the current record is deleted, and the next input record is read. The process is repeated until all input records have been read and processed as follows.

Code:

```
DATA MOVIES;
  INPUT @12 RATING $5. @;
  IF RATING = "PG" THEN
     INPUT @1 TITLE $11.
           @17 RENTED MMDDYY10.;
  ELSE DELETE;
  FORMAT RENTED MMDDYY10.;
  CARDS;
Brave HeartR    07/21/2001
Jaws        PG  02/03/1998
Rocky       PG  11/18/1997
Titanic     PG-1305/14/1998
;
RUN;
PROC PRINT;
RUN;
```

Results:

Obs	RATING	TITLE	RENTED
1	PG	Jaws	02/03/1998
2	PG	Rocky	11/18/1997

23 Reading carriage-control characters from an input file

When an input file contains carriage-control characters (identifies line spacing and pagination control when printing), SAS automatically removes them by default by specifying the **NOPRINT** option in the INFILE statement. You can instruct the SAS System to let you use a print file as input without removing carriage-control characters by specifying the PRINT option in the INFILE statement.

24 Assigning an error condition to missing input data values

Another way of handling missing data values from being processed when using list input is to specify the **STOPOVER** option with the INFILE statement. By specifying the STOPOVER option, an input line that doesn't contain the expected number of values as defined on the INPUT statement sets the _ERROR_ system variable to 1, stops processing the DATA step, and prints the offending data line to the SAS Log.

25 Reading the next input record with the FLOWOVER option

When reading variable length records, the **FLOWOVER** option may be specified on the INFILE statement to permit the INPUT statement to continue reading the next input record when the record currently in the input buffer is shorter than expected. Although specifying FLOWOVER results in the INPUT statement behaving the same way as if is it weren't specified, it does help remove any ambiguity as to how variable-length input records are to be handled. Users should use care when specifying this option because data values from a subsequent input record will be applied to the current variables.

DATALINES may be substituted for the CARDS input designation on the INFILE statement and the CARDS statement.

Code:

```
DATA MOVIES;
  INFILE CARDS FLOWOVER;
  INPUT TITLE $ RATING $;
  CARDS;
Jaws
Rocky,II PG
Titanic PG-13
;
RUN;
PROC PRINT;
RUN;
```

Results

```
Obs    TITLE     RATING

1      Jaws      Rocky,II
2      Titanic   PG-13
```

26 Concatenating and reading multiple input files

Reading from multiple input files is easy in the DATA step. When the layout of the input data is the same in all files, you can concatenate the input files together with the **FILENAME** statement. It should be noted that character variables (denoted with a $ sign) default to a length of 8 bytes. To handle text fields greater than 8 bytes in length, you'll need to specify their lengths in an INPUT or LENGTH statement.

The example shows how the FILENAME statement is constructed and specifies the TRUNCOVER option so that the INPUT statement is able to process varying length records by assigning values when a shorter than expected record is read. Each file is successfully read in the order specified in the FILENAME statement.

Code:

```
FILENAME RAWDATA
       ('c:\rawdata\movies-2000.dat',
        'c:\rawdata\movies-2001.dat',
        'c:\rawdata\movies-2002.dat');
DATA MOVIES;
  INFILE RAWDATA TRUNCOVER;
  INPUT TITLE $ RATING $;
RUN;
```

27 Another example of concatenating and reading multiple input files

As you learned in the previous tip, reading from multiple input files is easy. Here's another way of concatenating and reading multiple input files: When the layout of the input data is the same in all files, you can concatenate the input files together directly with the INFILE statement. It should be noted that character variables (denoted with a $ sign) default to a length of 8 bytes. To handle text fields greater than 8 bytes in length, you'll need to specify their lengths in an INPUT or LENGTH statement.

The example shows how the INFILE statement is constructed with three input files as well as specifying the TRUNCOVER option so the INPUT statement is able to process varying length records by assigning values when a shorter than expected record is read. Each file is successfully read in the order specified in the INFILE statement.

Code:

```
DATA MOVIES;
  INFILE "('c:\rawdata\movies-2000.dat',
          'c:\rawdata\movies-2001.dat',
          'c:\rawdata\movies-2002.dat')"
         TRUNCOVER;
  INPUT TITLE $ RATING $;
RUN;
```

28 Reading from multiple input files with the EOF option

Reading from multiple input files is easy in the DATA step. Consider using the **EOF=**label option with the INFILE statement. By specifying the EOF= option, processing is directed to the labeled statement once an end-of-file condition (no more records) is met for the current INFILE statement. This way you can control what input file is read next through the use of a label.

29 Identifying the last record in an input file

Identifying when the current input record is the last record in an input file can be a handy thing to know. By specifying the **END=** option in the INFILE statement, the SAS System sets the variable associated with the END= option to a value of 1 when the current input record is the last record in the file (unless the **UNBUFFERED** option is specified). Otherwise, the value of this user-specified variable has a value of 0.

🖉 *The variable created with the END= option isn't automatically written to a SAS data set. An advantage of knowing when the last record has been processed allows users to define processing conditions to be executed, such as end-of-file calculations or other logic processes.*

30 Conditionally executing input files

Occasionally external files may need to be processed conditionally. By conditionally reading input files, you establish a level of control over data input to safeguard and ensure that data integrity requirements are adhered to.

In the example, data is structured in two different levels: a summary and detail level. By using a formatted-style of input, column-pointer controls, and a trailing @ line-holder control, data can be read and processed correctly. The first INPUT statement reads the TYPE value into the input buffer and holds it while its contents are evaluated. If the value of TYPE is "D," the second INPUT statement reads the same input record to access the TITLE, RATING, and RENTED data values. Otherwise, the held input record is deleted, and the next input record is read, and so on.

🖉 *Summary level records are not read from the input file.*

Code:

```
DATA MOVIES;
  INPUT @1 TYPE $1. @;
  IF TYPE = 'D' THEN DO;
    INPUT @2 TITLE $11.
          @13 RATING $5.
          @18 RENTED MMDDYY10.;
    FORMAT RENTED MMDDYY10.;
  END;
  ELSE DELETE;
  CARDS;
S30002000
DBrave HeartR    07/21/2001
DJaws       PG   02/03/1998
S37002001
DRocky      PG   11/18/1997
```

```
S41002002
DTitanic    PG-1305/14/1998
;
RUN;
PROC PRINT DATA=MOVIES NOOBS N;
RUN;
```

Results:

```
TYPE   TITLE         RATING    RENTED

 D     Brave Heart   R         07/21/2001
 D     Jaws          PG        02/03/1998
 D     Rocky         PG        11/18/1997
 D     Titanic       PG-13     05/14/1998

N = 4
```

31 Specifying a logical record length

When an input data file contains records exceeding 256 bytes in length, consider using the **LRECL=** option in the INFILE statement. Otherwise, the SAS System chooses a length based on the operating system you are using since this value is host dependent. By specifying a logical record length you provide instructions as to how much of an input record to read.

32 Reading records padded with blanks

When an input data file is padded with blanks to the length specified by the LRECL= designation, you may consider specifying the **PAD** option in the INFILE statement. Since the default option is **NOPAD** (not padded with blanks), specifying PAD will ensure that data is handled properly when read.

33 Sharing input and output buffers

When a DATA step program contains INFILE, FILE, and PUT statements, you can instruct SAS to share the same buffer space to enable the update of specific fields in place. By specifying the **SHAREBUFFERS** option in the INFILE statement, CPU cycles are conserved because the record doesn't have to be written to an output buffer. Basically, each record is updated in place.

✎ *This is not the default option.*

34 Reading hierarchical files

Occasionally data is structured in a hierarchical layout, similar to a grandparent-parent-child relationship. When data is structured in this way, formatted-style of input with line- and column-pointer controls can be used to read input data successfully. Best of all, it's relatively easy and fast to do.

In the example, hierarchical data is structured in two different levels: a summary level and a detail level. By using a formatted-style of input, line- and column-pointer controls, and a trailing @ line-hold control, data can be read and processed correctly. The first INPUT statement reads the TYPE value into the input buffer and holds it while its contents are assessed. If the value of TYPE is "S," the second INPUT statement reads the same input record to access the QTY and YEAR data values. If the held record isn't a summary record, the ELSE statement is executed to evaluate whether the value of TYPE is "D." If it's a detail record, the INPUT statement reads the same input record to access the TITLE, RATING, and RENTED data values. Otherwise, the held input record is deleted with the DELETE statement, and the next input record is read.

Code:

```
DATA SUMMARY(KEEP=TYPE QTY YEAR)
  DETAIL(KEEP=TYPE TITLE RATING RENTED);
  INPUT @1 TYPE $1. @;
  IF TYPE = "S" THEN DO;
     INPUT @2 QTY 4. @6 YEAR $4.;
     OUTPUT SUMMARY;
  END;
  ELSE IF TYPE = 'D' THEN DO;
     INPUT @2 TITLE $11.
        @13 RATING $5.
        @18 RENTED MMDDYY10.;
     FORMAT RENTED MMDDYY10.;
     OUTPUT DETAIL;
  END;
  ELSE DELETE;
CARDS;
S30002000
DBrave HeartR   07/21/2001
DJaws       PG  02/03/1998
S37002001
DRocky      PG  11/18/1997
S41002002
DTitanic    PG-1305/14/1998
;
RUN;
PROC PRINT DATA=SUMMARY NOOBS N;
RUN;
PROC PRINT DATA=DETAIL NOOBS N;
RUN;
```

SUMMARY Output Results:

TYPE	QTY	YEAR
S	3000	2000
S	3700	2001
S	4100	2002

N = 3

DETAIL Output Results:

TYPE	TITLE	RATING	RENTED
D	Brave Heart	R	07/21/2001
D	Jaws	PG	02/03/1998
D	Rocky	PG	11/18/1997
D	Titanic	PG-13	05/14/1998

N = 4

35 Accessing External File Interface (EFI)

External File Interface (EFI)—or as it's sometimes referred to, the Import/Export Facility—reads external files (including Microsoft Excel and Access; Lotus 1-2-3; and Quattro Pro and Paradox) and turns them into SAS data sets. EFI provides an easy-to-use interface containing an import wizard to help make your job a little simpler. Follow these steps to access EFI:

1. From the SAS Display Manager, select **File▶Import Data**.

2. The SAS Import/Export Wizard appears, as displayed in Figure 2-1.

36 Importing delimited files with EFI

Importing files with EFI is as easy as 1-2-3. A delimited external file is imported into a SAS data set in the next example.

1. From the SAS Display Manager, select **File▶Import Data** to display the SAS Import/Export Wizard.

2. Select **Delimited File (*.*)** for the type of data you wish to import, shown in Figure 2-2. Click the **Next** button to display the Select File window.

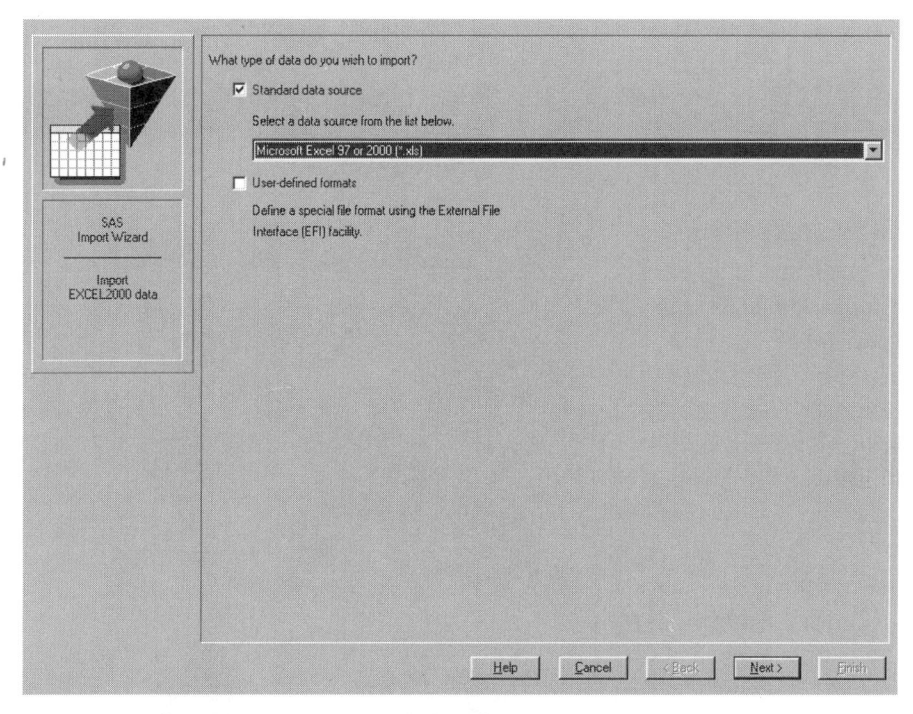

Figure 2-1. The SAS Import/Export Wizard

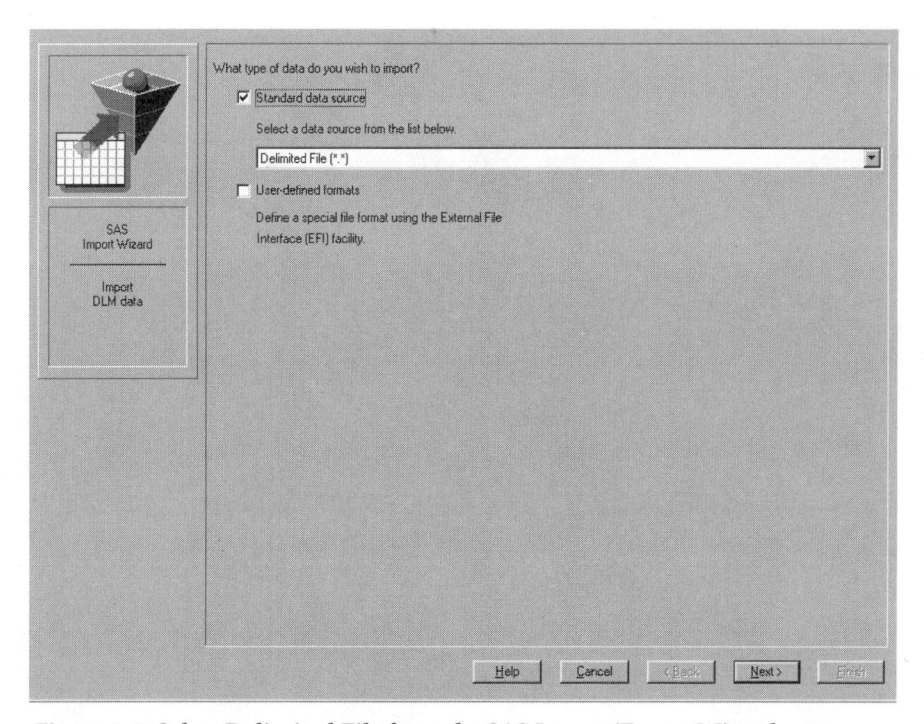

Figure 2-2. Select Delimited File from the SAS Import/Export Wizard

Chapter 2

3. In the Select File window, enter the **filename** and **location** in the "Where is the file located?" field or click the **Browse** button to locate the desired file, shown in Figure 2-3.

4. Click the **Options** button in the Select File window to specify the delimiter found in the external input file (Space, Tab, Character, or Hex Value). Enter a value for the first row of data and click the **OK** button, as shown in Figure 2-4.

5. Click the **Next** button on the Select File window.

6. In the SAS Destination window, select the desired SAS library where you want the newly created data set saved in the **Library** field. Enter a valid SAS data set name in the **Member** field and click the **Next** button, shown in Figure 2-5.

7. In the Select File window, enter the **filename** and **location** of where you want PROC IMPORT statements written to and click the **Finish** button, as shown in Figure 2-6.

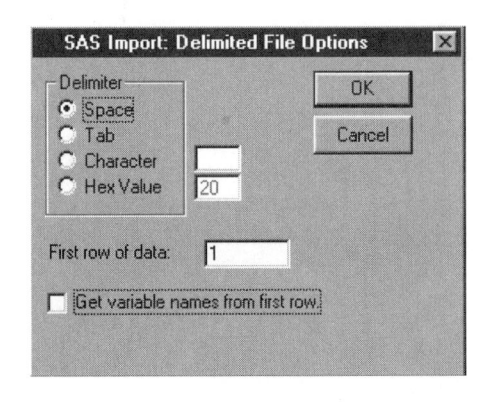

Figure 2-4. Select Delimited File Options dialog box

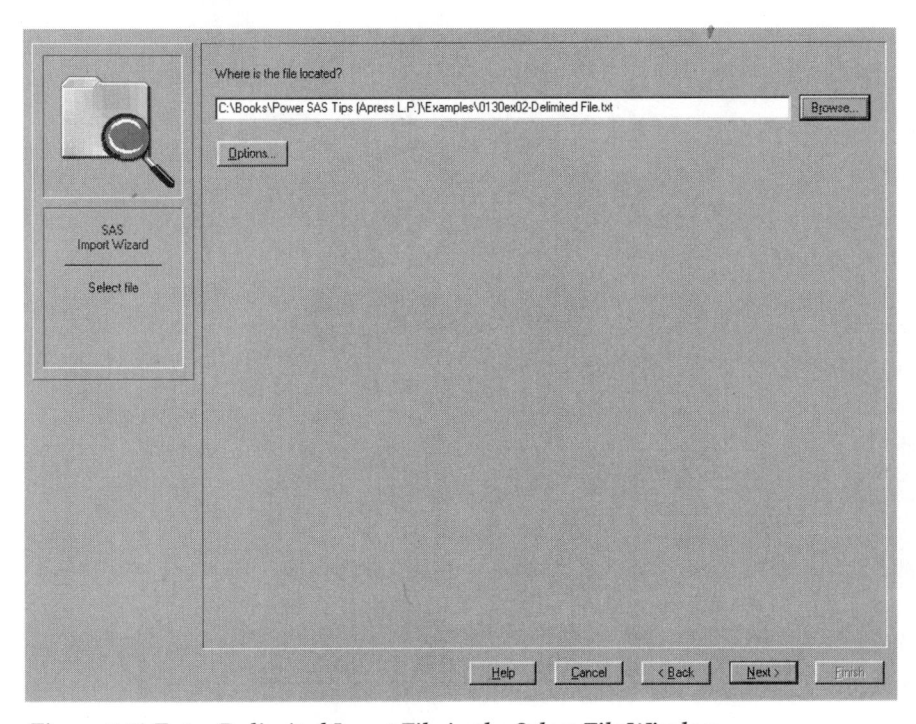

Figure 2-3. Enter Delimited Input File in the Select File Window

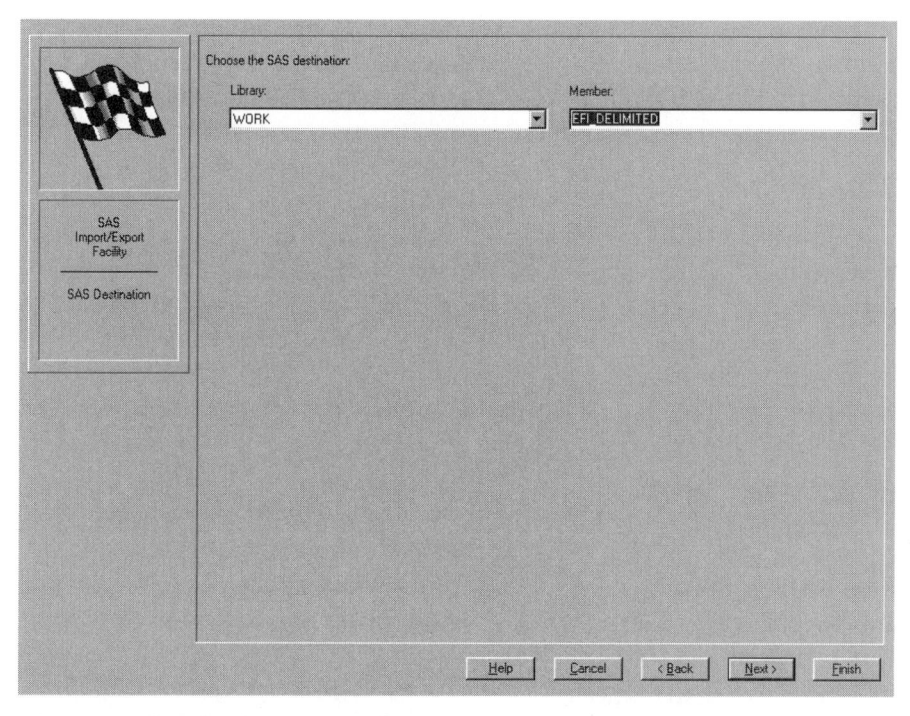

Figure 2-5. SAS Destination Window

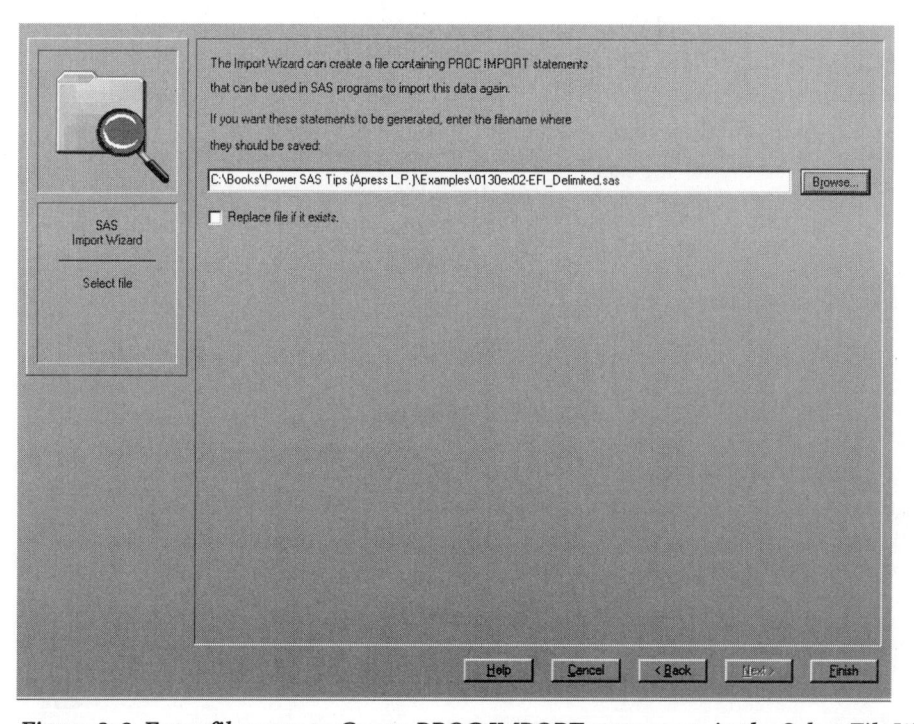

Figure 2-6. Enter filename to Create PROC IMPORT statements in the Select File Window

8. Enter the SAS command "VIEW SAS-data-set-name" to view the imported SAS data set, as shown in Figure 2-7.

	VAR1	VAR2
1	Title	Rating
2	Jaws	PG
3	Rocky	PG
4	Titanic	PG-13

Figure 2-7. View of Imported Data as a SAS Data Set

37 Accessing data from other applications with DDE

Dynamic Data Exchange (DDE) permits data from other applications (including Microsoft Excel, Word, and Access; Lotus 1-2-3; and Quattro Pro and Paradox) to be accessed by the SAS System. By way of server requests and acting as a client, the SAS System and the server application connect using a FILENAME statement with the DDE option specified. Once connected, requests are communicated between the server application and the client in the DATA step using SAS statements such as INFILE and INPUT.

38 Accessing the DDE triplet with Microsoft Excel

You can access the DDE triplet from a Microsoft Excel application in a few simple steps. Before performing these steps, make sure that both the server application (Excel) and the client (SAS) are up and running. Here's how it's done.

1. Highlight the data you want to transfer in Excel.

2. Copy the highlighted data by pressing the CTRL-C keys or by selecting the application's menu item Edit➤Copy.

3. Click Word's menu item Insert➤Bookmark.

4. In the Bookmark dialog box, enter a name for the highlighted text area. This will act as the bookmark

5. Save your Word document by assigning a name to it.

6. Switch over to the SAS System and define the FILENAME statement as follows:
   FILENAME fileref DDE 'winword|document-name!bookmark-name';

7. Create a DATA step including INFILE and INPUT statements to read the highlighted text.

8. Run the SAS program.

The following example uses a bookmark that was created by highlighting text in Microsoft Word, a saved Word document, and a SAS program that is written to read the highlighted text to create a SAS data set.

Code:

```
FILENAME IN DDE
       'winword|dde_word.doc!DDEExample'
       NOTAB;
DATA DDE_WORD;
  LENGTH DDE_TEXT $120.;
  INFILE IN DLM='$' LRECL=120;
  INPUT DDE_TEXT $;
RUN;
PROC PRINT NOOBS;
RUN;
```

Results:

```
DDE_TEXT

DDE and Word Example
This is an example DDE and MS-Word
example. It bookmarks highlighted text
and is used as DDE to the SAS System.
Upon completion of the transfer, the re-

sults are then printed in the SAS System.
```

SAS Data Objects

This section includes tips on how to read and process SAS data objects such as SAS data sets and SAS views. You'll learn how to reference and read data sets sequentially and directly, why concepts like the program data vector (PDV) are important to know, the differences between a subsetting IF and WHERE when subsetting rows of data, and how to read the contents of dictionary views to help monitor and manage your SAS environment.

1 Associating a libref with a SAS library

Permanent SAS data sets and other SAS objects (members) are organized as a collection known as a SAS library. Before a SAS library can be accessed, a **LIBNAME** statement identifies and associates a library with a libref.

2 Another way of referencing a permanent SAS data set

Permanent SAS data sets can be referenced directly without first specifying a libref by using the operating system name in single- or double-quotes. This lets you choose between specifying and using a libref, or simply referring to the operating system's physical storage location and name for the data set. Consult your SAS System Operating System documentation for specific usage. The following example references a permanent SAS data set directly on the Windows operating system without using a libref.

SAS data sets can be referenced this way in any procedure.

Code:

```
PROC PRINT
     DATA='c:\sasdata\movies.sas7bdata';
RUN;
```

3 Listing librefs currently defined in a session

Listing all the current allocated librefs is as easy as 1-2-3. The results are automatically listed on the SAS log. Simply specify the following LIBNAME statement:

Code:

```
LIBNAME _ALL_ LIST;
```

Log Results:

```
1    LIBNAME _ALL_ LIST;
NOTE: Libref=   SASHELP
      Scope=    Kernel
      Levels=   13
       -Level 1-
      Engine=   V8
      Physical Name= C:\Program Files\
```

```
                  SAS Institute\SAS\V8\SASCFG
                      File Name= C:\Program Files\ ↵
                  SAS Institute\SAS\V8\SASCFG
                       -Level 2-
                       Engine=    V8
                       Physical Name= C:\Program Files\ ↵
                  SAS Institute\SAS\V8\core\sashelp
                       File Name= C:\Program Files\ ↵
                  SAS Institute\SAS\V8\core\sashelp
                       -Level 3-
                  . . . . .
                       Engine=    V8
                       Physical Name= C:\Program Files\ ↵
                  SAS Institute\SAS\V8\whouse\sashelp
                       File Name= C:\Program Files\ ↵
                  SAS Institute\SAS\V8\whouse\sashelp
                  NOTE: Libref=   MAPS
                        Scope=    Kernel
                        Engine=   V8
                        Access=   READONLY
                        Physical Name= C:\Program Files\ ↵
                  SAS Institute\SAS\V8\maps
                        File Name= C:\Program Files\ ↵
                  SAS Institute\SAS\V8\maps
                  NOTE: Libref=    SASUSER
                        Scope=    Kernel
                        Engine=   V8
                        Physical Name= C:\My Documents\ ↵
                  My SAS Files\V8
                        File Name= C:\My Documents\ ↵
                  My SAS Files\V8
                  NOTE: Libref=    WORK
                        Scope=    Kernel
                        Engine=   V8
                        Access=   TEMP
                        Physical Name= C:\windows\TEMP\ ↵
                  SAS Temporary Files\_TD01649
                        File Name= C:\windows\TEMP\ ↵

                  SAS Temporary Files\_TD01649
```

4 Exploring SAS engines

SAS specifies the engine name to use for accessing SAS libraries with the ENGINE option. It's specified in the configuration file or at SAS invocation. The available engines for accessing SAS libraries appear in Table 2-4.

Table 2-4. Available SAS Engines under Windows

SAS ENGINE	DESCRIPTION
BASE | V8	SAS engine for Version 8, 8.1, and 8.2.
V7	SAS engine for Version 7 files.
V6	SAS engine for Version 6 files.
V604, V608, V609, V610, V611, v612	SAS engine for Version 6.04, and Version 6.08 through Version 6.12.

5 SAS/ACCESS engines

The engine names for selected database management systems (DBMSs) appear in Table 2-5.

Table 2-5. SAS/ACCESS Engines

SAS ENGINE	DESCRIPTION
INGRES	Specifies the engine name for the CA-OpenIngres interface.
DB2	Specifies the engine name for the DB2 interface.
INFORMIX	Specifies the engine name for the Informix interface.
SQLSVR	Specifies the engine name for the SQL/Server interface.

Table 2-5. SAS/ACCESS Engines (Continued)

SAS ENGINE	DESCRIPTION
ODBC	Specifies the engine name for the ODBC interface.
OLEDB	Specifies the engine name for the OLE DB interface.
ORACLE	Specifies the engine name for the Oracle interface.
RDBORA	Specifies the engine name for the Oracle RDB interface.
SYBASE	Specifies the engine name for the Sybase interface.
TERADATA	Specifies the engine name for the Teradata interface.

6 Reading SAS data sets sequentially

By default every SAS data set is read sequentially. This means that a data set is read starting with the first observation and ends with the last observation (unless FIRSTOBS= and/or OBS= options are specified, or an error occurs to prevent satisfactory completion).

7 Reading from multiple SAS data sets

Reading from multiple SAS data sets is a snap. When multiple data sets are listed in the SET statement, each is processed in the order in which they are listed. Basically the data sets are in concatenated form. I recommend that, if this approach is used, you concatenate like data sets (that is, the same data and attributes) together—otherwise, missing values will be generated for observations containing columns that are not the same in each data set.

8 Starting at the nth observation

By default a SAS data set's observations are read starting at the first observation (unless a system option has overridden this default). To allow processing to begin at a specified observation other than the first one in a data set, SAS permits the assignment of a FIRSTOBS= option. This option can be specified at the global level (affecting all data sets) or at the local level (affecting only the data set it's specified for). The first example uses a FIRSTOBS= option in a global OPTIONS statement to start reading at observation 100. This approach applies the change to all data sets from that point on, or until it is modified or reset. The second example specifies a FIRSTOBS= data set option in a localized fashion to start reading observations from the specified data set at observation 100.

Code:

```
OPTIONS FIRSTOBS=100;
```

Code:

```
DATA FIRSTOBS;
  SET MOVIES (FIRSTOBS=100);
RUN;
```

9 Stopping at the nth observation

By default a SAS data set's observations are read until the end of file (unless a system option has overridden this default). To allow processing to end at a specified observation other than the last one in a data set, SAS permits the assignment of an OBS= option. This option can be specified at the global level (affecting all data sets) or at the local level (affecting only the data set it's specified for). The first example uses the OBS= option in a global OPTIONS statement to stop reading at observation 200. This approach applies the change to all data sets from that point on, or until it is modified or reset. The second example specifies the OBS= data set option in a localized fashion to stop reading observations from the specified data set at observation 200.

Code:

```
OPTIONS OBS=200;
```

Code:

```
DATA OBS;
  SET MOVIES (OBS=200);
RUN;
```

10 Setting a range for reading observations

The FIRSTOBS= and OBS= options can be specified together to establish a range of observations to read from a SAS data set (unless system options have been specified to override this default). The first example uses the FIRSTOBS= and OBS= options in a global OPTIONS statement to begin reading observations at 100 and stop reading at observation 200. This approach applies the change to all data sets from that point on, or until it is modified or reset. The second example specifies the FIRSTOBS= data set option to begin reading at observation 100 and the OBS= data set option to stop at observation 200.

Code:

```
OPTIONS FIRSTOBS=100 OBS=200;
```

Code:

```
DATA OBS;
  SET MOVIES (FIRSTOBS=100 OBS=200);
RUN;
```

11 Understanding the Program Data Vector (PDV)

A PDV serves as a type of temporary internal storage area (work area) for an observation. It's the area of memory where data values are either moved from an input buffer or created using SAS statements (such as LENGTH, assignment statements, and so on) for the purpose of building a SAS data set. Once the PDV record is built, it is written to a SAS data set as a single observation.

12 Understanding the difference between a subsetting IF and WHERE

Subsetting **IF** and **WHERE** statements are used to subset data. Although they produce identical results, each has very distinct differences in the way it processes and subsets data. A subsetting IF statement specified in a DATA step, is designed to select input records from an external input file and observations from a SAS data set. Each record from an external file is read into an input buffer where it is evaluated against a user-defined condition. Observations from a SAS data set, on the other hand, are evaluated while being read into the PDV. Based on the result of the evaluation, processing either continues with the current record, or the next record is read and the process is repeated.

In contrast to a subsetting IF, a WHERE statement can only subset observations from a SAS data set. Besides this distinct difference, a WHERE statement conserves on resources by first evaluating its expression prior to an observation being read into the PDV. This not only saves CPU, but also reduces I/O requirements as well. Another important distinction between the two statements is that a WHERE statement can be placed in a procedure to reduce the number of program steps while avoiding the creation of an extra SAS data set.

13 Subsetting observations with WHERE

The most flexible and efficient way to subset data set observations is with a WHERE statement or **WHERE=** data set option. This is the method of choice for SAS users in the know. A WHERE statement or WHERE= data set option can be specified to subset observations in either a DATA or PROC step.

To illustrate the application of a WHERE statement and WHERE= data set option, I present three examples, each producing the same results. When all things are equal, the choice of approaches is yours to make. But it's generally advisable to use the method that streamlines the code while minimizing the amount of resource requirements it takes during program execution. In the first example, "PG"-rated movies are selected from a SAS data set using a WHERE= data set option in a SET statement. Although this approach produces the same results as the next two examples, it does require the expenditure of considerably more I/O because data must be read and written not once, as in the next two examples, but twice.

Code:

```
DATA PG_MOVIES;
 SET MOVIES (WHERE=(RATING='PG'));
RUN;
PROC PRINT;
RUN;
```

In the second example, a subset of "PG"-rated movies is specified using a WHERE statement in the PRINT procedure.

Code:

```
PROC PRINT
        DATA=MOVIES
        NOOBS
        N;
   WHERE RATING = 'PG';
RUN;
```

In the third example, a WHERE= data set option is specified to subset "PG"-rated movies in the PRINT procedure.

Code:

```
PROC PRINT
        DATA=MOVIES (WHERE=(RATING='PG'))
        NOOBS
        N;
RUN;
```

14 Selecting variables

Selecting one or more variables for processing from a SAS data set is easy with the SAS System. It's accomplished by specifying a **KEEP** (or **DROP**) statement in a DATA step. Or for total compatibility in both DATA and PROC steps, a **KEEP=** (or **DROP=**) data set option can be specified. The first example retains the

TITLE and RATING variables by specifying a KEEP= data set option in a DATA step.

Code:

```
DATA PG_MOVIES;
 SET MOVIES (WHERE=(RATING='PG')
             KEEP=TITLE RATING);
RUN;
PROC PRINT;
RUN;
```

In the second example, a DROP= data set option is specified in the PRINT procedure to remove unwanted variables.

Code:

```
PROC PRINT
     DATA=MOVIES (WHERE=(RATING='PG')
       DROP=CATEGORY LENGTH STUDIO YEAR)
        NOOBS
        N;
RUN;
```

15 Renaming variables

Occasionally renaming one or more variables is necessary for processing reasons. When a variable needs to be renamed, SAS makes it easy with the **RENAME=** data set option. By providing complete compatibility in both DATA and PROC steps, a RENAME= data set option can be specified anywhere a SAS data set is referenced (for example, DATA or SET statement, DATA= or OUT= procedure keywords or parameters). To illustrate the application of a WHERE= data set option, I present two examples. The first example renames the TITLE variable to MOVIE_TITLE by specifying a RENAME= data set option in a SET statement of the DATA step.

Code:

```
DATA PG_MOVIES;
 SET MOVIES (WHERE=(RATING='PG')
             RENAME=(TITLE=MOVIE_TITLE));
RUN;
PROC PRINT;
RUN;
```

In the second example, a RENAME= data set option is specified in the **DATA=keyword** of the PRINT procedure.

Code:

```
PROC PRINT
     DATA=MOVIES (WHERE=(RATING='PG')
       RENAME=(TITLE=MOVIE_TITLE))
        NOOBS
        N;
RUN;
```

16 Understanding a WHERE expression's processing order

A WHERE expression executes immediately after all input data set options are applied, but before any other DATA step statements are executed. This ensures that data from an input data set must satisfy the conditions specified in the WHERE expression before being read into the PDV.

17 Executing WHERE expressions with BY groups

When WHERE and BY group processing occur in the same DATA or PROC step, each BY group is created after a WHERE expression is executed. As a result, the WHERE expression dictates what observations are selected as well as what the FIRST.variable and LAST.variable values will be, not the observations in the original input data set.

18 Creating an end-of-file indicator

Have you ever wanted to know when you've read the last observation from a SAS data set or list of data sets? SAS can be instructed to let you know when the last observation in one or more data sets is read. By specifying the **END=** option in the SET statement, a temporary variable is created that alerts you when the SET statement reads the last observation in the listed SAS data set(s). The temporary variable's value is initially assigned a value of 0, but is set to 1 when the last observation is read. SAS users frequently use this feature in their DATA steps to branch off to a routine that computes summary-level information that appears at the end of a report. The example uses the END= option to output summary-level information related to "PG"-rated movies to a data set called SUMMARY.

Code:

```
DATA PG_MOVIES(DROP=CTR_MOVIES)
     SUMMARY(KEEP=CTR_MOVIES);
  SET MOVIES(WHERE=(RATING="PG"))
         END=LAST_OBS;
  CTR_MOVIES + 1;
  OUTPUT PG_MOVIES;
  IF LAST_OBS THEN OUTPUT SUMMARY;
RUN;
PROC PRINT DATA=SUMMARY;
RUN;
```

Results:

```
         CTR_
Obs    MOVIES

 1        6
```

19 Determining the number of observations in an input data set

SAS can be instructed to let you know the number of observations in one or more data sets. By specifying the **NOBS=** option in the SET statement, a temporary variable is created that alerts you when the SET statement reads the last observation in the listed SAS data set(s). The temporary variable's value is the number of observations in the data set(s) listed in the SET statement. The example uses the NOBS= and END= options to output summary-level information related to "PG-rated" movies and the number of observations to a data set called COUNTERS.

Code:

```
DATA PG_MOVIES(DROP=CTR_OBS CTR_PG_MOVIES)
     COUNTERS(KEEP=CTR_OBS CTR_PG_MOVIES);
  SET MOVIES(WHERE=(RATING="PG"))
         NOBS=COUNTER END=LAST_OBS;
  CTR_PG_MOVIES + 1;
  CTR_OBS=COUNTER;
  OUTPUT PG_MOVIES;
  IF LAST_OBS THEN OUTPUT COUNTERS;
RUN;
PROC PRINT DATA=COUNTERS NOOBS;
RUN;
```

Results:

```
CTR_PG_
 MOVIES    CTR_OBS

    6         23
```

20 Reading SAS data sets directly

By default, every SAS data set is read sequentially. But what if the data you want resides at or near the end of a large data set? This can translate into longer and more costly runs due to the nature of a sequential read. SAS provides a more direct way to read data sets. Known as *random* or *direct access*, observations can be accessed without having to read each observation in a sequential manner.

You can access an observation directly by using the **POINT=** option of the SET statement. You'll need to know the observation number to use the POINT= option. Although it can't be used with a WHERE statement, a WHERE= data set option, or BY statement, it does allow direct access to an observation or group of observations easily. By specifying the NOBS= and POINT= options, the following example selects the odd numbered observations from the MOVIES data set using DO-loop processing.

Because a SAS data set is being read directly, a STOP statement is needed to prevent the endless looping of the DO-group loop.

Code:

```
DATA ALTERNATE_RECORDS;
  DO OBSNUM=1 TO TOTOBS BY 2;
    SET PATH.MOVIES
        NOBS=TOTOBS POINT=OBSNUM;
    OUTPUT;
  END;
  STOP;
RUN;
```

21 Reading a SAS data set into real memory

If you open and read a SAS data set multiple times during a session, and have sufficient real memory available, you may consider transferring data from disk (or some other storage medium) to memory. By specifying a **SASFILE** statement, the necessary buffers are automatically allocated to store the data in memory. Once data is read into real memory, the file remains open to accommodate other requests against the data until another SASFILE statement closes the file, or the program or session ends. By specifying the SASFILE statement, the following example opens and reads the MOVIES data set transferring observations from disk to memory.

Code:

```
SASFILE PATH.MOVIES OPEN;
DATA PG_MOVIES;
  SET MOVIES(WHERE=(RATING="PG"));
RUN;
SASFILE PATH.MOVIES CLOSE;
```

22 Specifying the number of buffers

Defining an adequate number of buffers (or holding areas) for data being sent to, or received from, disk is important when accessing and processing data. The default number of buffers for the **BUFNO=** option is 1, and the maximum is operating system-dependent. Under the Windows operating system, any number of buffers can be allocated because its value is based specifically on the amount of memory available. If uncertain about what value to assign the BUFNO= option, I recommend that users set BUFNO=MIN. This will assign a value of 0 and let SAS set a value best suited for the operating system. An alternative would be to specify the SASFILE statement to let SAS automatically allocate the necessary number of buffers.

23 Specifying a data set's level of access

Because more than one statement, procedure, window, or user can open a data set during a session, SAS provides a way to specify the level of shared access to a data set. By specifying the **CNTLLEV=MEM** data set option, you inform SAS that a data set should have the maximum level of data integrity protection by allowing multiple statements, procedures, windows, or users to read the data, but concurrent access to a single update is restricted. By specifying the **CNTLLEV=REC** data set option, a less restrictive level of protection is created allowing multiple updates to a data set while restricting concurrent updates to the same record.

24 Reading a generation data set (GENNUM=)

Reading multiple versions of a data set is made easy with the **GENNUM=** data set option. When a generation data set has been created with the GENMAX= data set option, SAS permits access to any of the generations (maximum of 1,000 archived generation data sets) by specifying the GENNUM= data set option with an integer number corresponding to the desired data set version. The PRINT procedure example shows the third-generation data set being accessed using the GENNUM=3 data set option.

Code:

```
PROC PRINT DATA=MOVIES(GENNUM=3);
RUN;
```

25 Accessing data from a view

The SAS System is designed to access data from a number of sources, including virtual tables known as *views*. Views don't actually contain data but consist of the instructions that are used in creating the view and accessing data from the underlying table or tables. Views can be accessed in the DATA step and in procedures as if they were SAS data sets. To better understand what views are available in a SAS library, review the results in the CONTENTS procedure output. You can also view the statements that make up the view. The example prints "PG"-rated movies from the view called VIEW_PG_MOVIES.

Code:

```
PROC PRINT DATA=VIEW_PG_MOVIES;
RUN;
```

26 Understanding dictionary views

Dictionary views provide users with the ability to monitor and manage their SAS environment. Available once a SAS session begins and found in the SASHELP libref, they offer information about libraries, catalogs, data sets, indexes, views, external files, SAS system option settings, data set variable attributes, macros, titles, footnotes, and much more.

27 Exploring the types of dictionary views

Currently 16 dictionary views are available in the SASHELP library. Their names and descriptions appear in Table 2-6.

Table 2-6. Dictionary Views

LIBNAME	MEMBER NAME	DESCRIPTION
SASHELP	VCATALG	Provides catalog information.
SASHELP	VCOLUMN	Provides column names and attribute information.
SASHELP	VEXTFL	Provides the FILREF, pathname, and engine for external files.
SASHELP	VINDEX	Provides data set index information for each libref.
SASHELP	VMACRO	Provides information about macro variables, their scope, and value.
SASHELP	VMEMBER	Provides SAS library information including member name and type, indexes, and path.
SASHELP	VOPTION	Provides SAS system option names and settings for your environment.
SASHELP	VSCATLG	Provides librefs and member name for allocated SAS catalogs.
SASHELP	VSLIB	Provides allocated librefs and paths.
SASHELP	VSTABLE	Provides librefs and member names for allocated SAS data sets.
SASHELP	VSTABVW	Provides librefs, member names, and member types for allocated SAS data sets.
SASHELP	VSTYLE	Provides librefs, template names, style names, and notes.
SASHELP	VSVIEW	Provides librefs and dictionary view names.
SASHELP	VTABLE	Provides librefs, member names and types, date created and modified, number of observations, observation length, number of variables, and performance tuning information.
SASHELP	VTITLE	Provides title location, title number, and title text.
SASHELP	VVIEW	Provides librefs, dictionary view names, member type, and engine name.

28 Accessing dictionary views

Accessing dictionary views stored in the SASHELP library is relatively easy. You'll need to know what kind of information you want and the name of the view (see tip #27 in this section) before you start. Once you've done this, you're ready to access the view in a DATA or PROC step. The first example accesses the VSLIB dictionary view in a DATA step and then prints the allocated librefs and paths.

Code:

```
DATA LIBREFS;
  SET SASHELP.VSLIB;
  WHERE UPCASE(LIBNAME)= 'PATH';
RUN;
PROC PRINT NOOBS;
RUN;
```

The second example accesses the VOPTION dictionary view to print SAS System options and settings.

Code:

```
PROC PRINT DATA=SASHELP.VOPTION NOOBS;
RUN;
```

29 Identifying the number of observations in a data set with VTABLE

Identifying the number of observations in any SAS data set is a snap with the VTABLE view. By specifying the view SASHELP.VTABLE in the SET statement, you can access the number of observations in any data set. The variables you'll want to keep are LIBNAME, MEMNAME, and NOBS. The following example selects all data sets for the library reference PATH keeping three variables: LIBNAME, MEMNAME, and NOBS.

Code:

```
DATA NOBS;
  SET SASHELP.VTABLE
        (KEEP=LIBNAME MEMNAME NOBS);
  WHERE UPCASE(LIBNAME)= 'PATH';
RUN;
PROC PRINT NOOBS;
RUN;
```

Results:

libname	memname	nobs
PATH	ACTORS	13
PATH	MOVIES	23

30 Reading catalog source files

Reading a SAS catalog source file into a SAS data set is easy. By specifying **CONTENTS OUT=libref** in the CATALOG procedure, you'll be able to write catalog source files to any data set. The following example writes the contents of the GAMES catalog in the SASHELP library.

Code:

```
PROC CATALOG CATALOG=SASHELP.GAMES;
  CONTENTS OUT=GAMES;
RUN;
QUIT;
PROC PRINT;
RUN;
```

Structured Query Language (SQL) Procedure

This section includes tips that will help you become familiar with one of the world's most versatile languages for data access, data manipulation, and data management. SQL is a Base SAS procedure that is powerful and, best of all, easy to use. You'll learn the basics of SQL syntax by example, how to construct simple data access queries, and perform a number of programming tasks quickly and easily.

1 Programming with SQL

SQL is a language that is used to communicate with libraries of data sets (or database tables). SQL is powerful because it's comprised of a set of commands or statements to enable reading, manipulating, and writing data.

2 Understanding ANSI SQL and PROC SQL extensions

The SAS Institute's PROC SQL implementation adheres to the guidelines imposed by the American National Standards Institute (ANSI) standards committee. It's in the best interest for software vendors including the SAS Institute to adhere to and support the standards related to ANSI SQL. But as can be expected, many software and database vendors extend the capabilities beyond the SQL standards (ANSI guidelines). In such cases, these extensions may be DBMS specific and are rarely supported by other vendors.

3 Bundling the SQL procedure with the Base-SAS product

The SAS System's SQL implementation is bundled with the base-product and invoked by running PROC SQL. Because it resides in the base-product, no additional licensing fees are required to take advantage of this powerful database language.

4 Remaining active until a QUIT; statement is issued

PROC SQL is designed as an *interactive procedure*—meaning that multiple statements (such as **CREATE TABLE** or **RUN** groups) can be processed without having to reissue the SQL procedure for each task. This is useful when more than one task is planned during a single session and can reduce the number of keystrokes. RUN groups are determined by specifying a semicolon (;) at the end of an SQL statement. A **QUIT;** statement is specified to terminate the procedure.

5 Processing with RUN groups and the handling of errors

Should the SAS System encounter a syntax error, the RUN group containing the error is not executed. Previous RUN groups are processed normally, though. For example, suppose the following statements are submitted as a group:

Code:

```
PROC SQL;
  CREATE TABLE G_RATED AS
    SELECT *
      FROM MOVIES
        WHERE RATING='G';
  SELECT *
    FROM G_RATED
      ODRER BY LENGTH;
QUIT;
```

In the previous example the first RUN group is executed, but a syntax error caused by the misspelling of the ORDER BY clause in the second RUN group prevents this step from being executed.

6 Storing separate pieces of information in a data set or table

A data set or table contains one or more pieces of information, similar to the cells of a spreadsheet. Each piece of information is referred to as a *column*. The reason for storing pieces of information separately as columns is to make data access, filtering, and sorting operations considerably easier. For example, storing city and state information as one column is technically-speaking correct, but it makes data-access operations more difficult. It is desirable to separate individual pieces of information into two or more columns.

7 Understanding columns and datatypes

By storing information as separate columns in a data set or table, each piece of information can be accessed, filtered, or sorted without the need to perform complex programming operations. Each column is assigned a *datatype* (character or numeric). By assigning a datatype, inappropriate data is prevented from being stored in the column. For example, if the column is to contain text (for example, a movie title) a character datatype is assigned. For columns containing numbers (movie length or admission price), a numeric datatype is used.

8 Understanding SQL statements and clauses

It is important to note that SQL statements and clauses are case insensitive. So, typing "SELECT" is the same as "Select" or "select." Although there are no established guidelines, many SQL programmers type statements and clauses in uppercase characters, and table and column names in lowercase characters, in an attempt to make program code more readable.

9 Ordering of columns and a column wildcard

When the column wildcard character asterisk (*) is specified in the SELECT statement, the order of selected columns is determined by the order in the table's descriptor record. In addition, all columns are selected.

10 Specifying criteria to subset and display values

The **WHERE** clause is used as part of the SELECT statement to restrict or subset row(s) of selected data. For example, the following query subsets and displays only those rows where the movie is rated as "PG".

Code:

```
PROC SQL;
  SELECT *
    FROM MOVIES
      WHERE RATING = "PG";
QUIT;
```

11 Understanding parentheses and order of evaluation in SQL

Any number of **AND** and **OR** operators can be used in a WHERE clause. Consequently, it is advisable to use parentheses to explicitly group operators, even if the default order of evaluation is the way you want it in the WHERE clause. Since parentheses have a higher order of evaluation than AND and OR, care should be exercised to construct correct WHERE clause operators.

To emphasize the importance of using parentheses, suppose you wanted to list "PG" and "PG-13" movies having a length less than 121 minutes. The first query shown next uses a WHERE clause without any parentheses, whereas the second query uses parentheses to group operators.

Code:

```
PROC SQL;
 SELECT TITLE, LENGTH
   FROM MOVIES
     WHERE RATING = "PG" OR
       RATING = "PG-13" AND
       LENGTH <= 120;
QUIT;
```

The results from this query shows that nine movies were selected, with three of them having a length greater than 120 minutes. Obviously the rows were not filtered as intended.

Results:

```
Title                          Length
Casablanca                        103
Jaws                              125
Rocky                             120
Star Wars                         124
Poltergeist                       115
The Hunt for Red October          135
National Lampoon's Vacation        98
Christmas Vacation                 97
Michael                           106
```

To fix the problem identified above, use parentheses to explicitly group related operators as follows.

Code:

```
PROC SQL;
  SELECT TITLE, LENGTH
    FROM MOVIES
    WHERE (RATING = "PG" OR
        RATING = "PG-13") AND
        LENGTH <= 120;
QUIT;
```

The results from this query shows that six movies were selected, and all have a length less than 121 minutes. This time the rows were filtered as intended.

Results:

```
Title                          Length
Casablanca                        103
Rocky                             120
Poltergeist                       115
National Lampoon's Vacation        98
Christmas Vacation                 97
Michael                           106
```

12 Understanding SELECT clause ordering

It's always useful to know the order of the various clauses on the **SELECT** statement. Table 2-7 identifies the order of each clause and whether the clause is required.

Table 2-7. Select Clause Ordering and Sequence

CLAUSE	REQUIRED
FROM	Yes
WHERE	No
GROUP BY	No
HAVING	No
ORDER BY	No

13 Using too many wildcards and processing time

Use caution when using wildcard characters for searching because they typically take longer to process than other types of searches. Try to avoid using wildcard characters at the beginning of a search pattern unless absolutely necessary.

14 Using caution in the placement of wildcard characters

Pay careful attention to the placement of wildcard characters since misplacement can frequently result in the wrong data being filtered.

15 Inserting a blank line between each row of output

When a query produces more output than can fit nicely across a page, SQL automatically flows output over to another line. This often makes output difficult to read. To enhance the readability of one or more "flowed" lines, the **DOUBLE** option can be specified on the PROC SQL statement.

Code:

```
PROC SQL DOUBLE;
  SELECT *
    FROM MOVIES;
QUIT;
```

16 Assigning clarity to column names with aliases

SQL supports the use of column aliases (or the assignment of an alternate name for a column or value). This handy feature enables ambiguous or easily misread (misinterpreted) column names in a table to be expanded or changed as needed. Aliases are assigned with the **AS** keyword. For the purpose of making the column headings more meaningful and self-documenting, the following example assigns the more descriptive column name of **Movie_Title** to the TITLE column.

Code:

```
PROC SQL;
  SELECT TITLE AS Movie_Title, RATING
    FROM MOVIES;
QUIT;
```

Results:

Movie_Title	Rating
Brave Heart	R
Casablanca	PG
Christmas Vacation	PG-13
Coming to America	R
Dracula	R
Dressed to Kill	R
Forrest Gump	PG-13
Ghost	PG-13
Jaws	PG
Jurassic Park	PG-13
Lethal Weapon	R
Michael	PG-13
National Lampoon's Vacation	PG-13
Poltergeist	PG
Rocky	PG
Scarface	R
Silence of the Lambs	R
Star Wars	PG
The Hunt for Red October	PG
The Terminator	R
The Wizard of Oz	G
Titanic	PG-13

17 Removing rows containing duplicate column values

When duplicate column values appear in two or more rows in a table, the DISTINCT keyword can be specified before the column name in a SELECT statement to remove the duplicates.

The next example removes rows containing duplicate movie ratings.

Code:

```
PROC SQL;
  SELECT DISTINCT RATING
    FROM MOVIES;
QUIT;
```

Results:

RATING
G
PG
PG-13
R

18 Sorting data by multiple columns

The differences between the way columns are specified in the **ORDER BY** clause in SQL and in the BY statement in the SORT procedure are worth mentioning. Most SAS programmers are aware that each column in a BY statement of PROC SORT is separated with one or more spaces. The next example shows the construct for specifying two columns in a BY statement in PROC SORT.

Code:

```
PROC SORT
   DATA=MOVIES;
  BY RATING LENGTH;
RUN;
```

In contrast, columns in the ORDER BY clause are separated with a comma (,) as the delimiter. The next example illustrates an ORDER BY clause in SQL.

Code:

```
PROC SQL;
  SELECT *
    FROM MOVIES
      ORDER BY RATING, LENGTH;
QUIT;
```

19 Sorting data in descending order in SQL

When rows of data need to be physically arranged in descending order, the ORDER BY clause is specified using the DESC keyword. In the following example, movies are arranged in ascending order (alphabetically) by their ratings and within each rating listed in descending order (longest to shortest) by their length.

The descending keyword DESC is specified after the column name, not before.

Code:

```
PROC SQL;
  SELECT TITLE,
         RATING,
         LENGTH
    FROM MOVIES
      ORDER BY RATING,
               LENGTH DESC;
QUIT;
```

20 Sorting by relative position in the select list

Sometimes it is more convenient to specify the column(s) to sort by in an ORDER BY clause with the *relative position* in the select list rather than by column name(s). The primary advantage of using this construct is to minimize the number of keystrokes. The next example shows the primary column RATING and the secondary column LENGTH being sorted in ascending order.

Code:

```
PROC SQL;
 SELECT TITLE,
        RATING,
        LENGTH
   FROM MOVIES
     ORDER BY 2, 3;
QUIT;
```

The downside of this approach is that it is all too easy to accidentally select the wrong column when columns are reordered in the select list.

21 Sorting columns not specified in a select list

It is perfectly legal and correct syntax to sort by one or more columns that are not part of a select list. The only exception to this rule is that when a column is specified by its relative position it must also be part of the select list.

22 Calculating statistics with summary functions

Frequently SQL is used to aggregate (or summarize) values directly from one or more tables, rather than presenting detailed information. Summary functions are designed to be very efficient, usually returning aggregated results far quicker than you could compute them yourself in a client application. See tip #26 in this section for a list of summary functions.

23 Using SQL to summarize data

Although the SQL procedure is frequently used to display or extract detailed information from tables in a database, it is also a wonderful tool for summarizing (or aggregating) data. By constructing simple queries, data can be summarized down rows (observations) as well as across columns (variables).

This flexibility gives SAS users an incredible range of power, and the ability to take advantage of several SAS-supplied (or built-in) summary functions. For example, it may be more interesting to see the average of some quantities rather than the set of all quantities. Without the ability to summarize data in SQL, users would be forced to write complicated formulas and/or routines, or even write and test DATA step programs to summarize data.

24 Summarizing data down rows

A common method of aggregating data in SQL is to summarize it down rows. The resulting aggregate is a single row (unless a GROUP BY clause is specified). For example, suppose you needed to know the average length of all "PG" and "PG-13" movies in our database table. The result from executing this query shows that the average movie length rounded to the hundredth position is 124.08 minutes.

Code:

```
PROC SQL;
  SELECT AVG(LENGTH)
         AS Average_Movie_Length
    FROM MOVIES
     WHERE RATING IN ("PG", "PG-13");
QUIT;
```

Results:

```
    Average_
 Movie_Length
     124.0769
```

25 Summarizing data across columns

As previously shown, SQL has the ability to aggregate data not only down rows but across columns. Being able to summarize data across columns often comes in handy, when a computation is required on two or more columns in each row. Suppose you wanted to know the difference in minutes between each "PG" and "PG-13" movie's running length with trailers (add-on specials for your viewing pleasure) and without trailers. This query computes the difference between the length of the movie and its trailer in minutes and once computed displays the range value for each row as Extra_Minutes.

Code:

```
PROC SQL;
  SELECT TITLE,
         RANGE(LENGTH_TRAIL, LENGTH)
         AS Extra_Minutes
    FROM MOVIES
     WHERE RATING IN ("PG", "PG-13");
QUIT;
```

Results:

Title	Extra_Minutes
Casablanca	0
Jaws	0
Rocky	0
Star Wars	0
Poltergeist	0
The Hunt for Red October	15
National Lampoon's Vacation	7
Christmas Vacation	6
Ghost	0
Jurassic Park	33
Forrest Gump	0
Michael	0
Titanic	36

26 Exploring summary functions

The SAS implementation of SQL provides a number of summary functions for users to take advantage of. Table 2-8 shows the functions that can be used to aggregate data.

Table 2-8. Available Summary Functions

SUMMARY FUNCTION	DESCRIPTION
AVG <or> **MEAN**	Determines the average or mean of values.
COUNT <or> **FREQ** <or> **N**	Determines the number of nonmissing values.
CSS	Determines the corrected sum of squares.
CV	Determines the coefficient of variation (percent).
MAX	Determines the largest value.
MIN	Determines the smallest value.
NMISS	Determines the number of missing values.
PRT	Determines the probability of a greater absolute value of Student's t.
RANGE	Determines the difference between the maximum and minimum values.
STD	Determines the standard deviation.
STDERR	Determines the standard error of the average (or mean).
SUM	Determines the sum of values.
SUMWGT	Determines the sum of the WEIGHT variable values.
T	Determines the Student's t value for testing the hypothesis that the population mean is zero.
USS	Determines the uncorrected sum of squares.
VAR	Determines the variance.

Summary

In this chapter, you learned the various ways to access data using Base SAS software. Whether your input data is blank-, comma-, or tab-delimited, fixed- or variable-length, or hierarchical, SAS has all right tool to get the job done quickly and, most importantly, correctly. You also learned the basics of the SQL procedure for accessing data from existing SAS data sets.

In the next chapter, "DATA Step Programming," you'll continue learning using a step-by-step approach about the DATA step programming language. Even if you're not a programmer, you'll find the tips and the many examples simple to understand.

CHAPTER 3
DATA Step Programming

THE DATA STEP programming language in the Base SAS software is a powerful and full-featured programming language. Whether you're a novice or advanced user, the tips covered in this chapter are designed to show you how to use it to your advantage. This chapter covers important keywords, structured coding techniques, date and time processing, operators and modifiers, SAS functions, program testing and debugging techniques, large file-processing techniques, and concepts such as observation loops, Program Data Vector (PDV), variable and value assignments, conditional processing, and logic branching—all to enable you to write better programs.

In this chapter, you'll learn how to

- Direct control to the top of an observation loop

- Retain values across observation loops

- Assign a variable's length

- Perform conditional logic

- Implement best practices coding standards

- Perform date and time processing

- Use date formats and informats

- Apply operators and modifiers and their order of evaluation

- Use arithmetic, character, date and time, and array functions as part of SAS statements

- Test and debug SAS program code

- Process large file efficiently and quickly

- Document and educate other users on complex processes, pieces of code, and other abstract coding constructs

The DATA Step Programming Language

This section includes tips that will show you how to get the most from the DATA step programming language. From understanding the DATA step's many features and capabilities to visualizing how the observation loop works, you'll find ways to take command of this powerful programming language. You'll also learn valuable techniques that can be applied to your own program code quickly and easily.

1 Understanding the DATA step language

The DATA step language is at the heart of the SAS System. It's a full-featured programming language designed to perform complex and powerful computing operations. In contrast to other compiled languages, a SAS program is structured in a top-down fashion. What this means is that a multi-step program is grouped into steps with each step running one step at a time, one after the next.

The DATA step language permits structured coding, algorithm, and data-processing constructs to be expressed using a style that is relatively easy to read and understand by other SAS users. An important feature of the DATA step language is that programs written on one machine are portable to other machines that fully support the SAS System (with the exception of operating system differences).

2 Understanding DATA step features and capabilities

The DATA step is a comprehensive, powerful, high-level language. As with all powerful languages, it possesses intrinsic features that enable it to be used for a variety of tasks and applications. The following list highlights some advantages of the DATA step.

- It has the ability to apply structured programming techniques, including the use of expressions and operators.

- It's a well-defined language that is free of ambiguities. It's considered self-documenting by some (a later section in this chapter presents useful tips to improve this important aspect of coding).

- It supports a variety of structures including strings, arrays, indexes, tables (formats), and more.

- It supports the ability to use a modular approach and can communicate with the calling program by way of parameters or global variables.

- It supports a variety of input-output access methods including sequential, fixed and variable length, delimited, hierarchical, random access, and third-party application (including MS-Word, Excel, and Access) files. SAS offers other licensed products that interface popular database products such as DB2, IMS, Oracle, and others.

- It is machine independent as well as portable.

- It quickly compiles and executes on machines where it is implemented.

- Its features and constructs are easily taught and learned without difficulty.

- It is useful in a wide range of programming applications and isn't designed for a narrow purpose or audience.

3 DATA step processing begins with the DATA statement

DATA step processing begins with the **DATA** statement. As the first statement in a user-written program, the DATA statement signals the beginning of a user-written step (as opposed to a canned procedure) and frequently also the creation of a SAS data set (unless a _NULL_ data set is specified). As the first executable DATA step statement, the DATA statement triggers the beginning of a DATA step and activates the DATA compiler. Once the step is successfully compiled it's automatically executed.

4 Understanding the observation loop

In programming terms a *loop* means a process or action that occurs repeatedly. It can repeat a specific number of times or until some condition has been met. Under certain circumstances a loop can also be controlled or manipulated by users (such as a DO loop or observation loop).

The observation loop in the SAS System meets this basic definition because data is read from one or more input files (such as an external file or SAS data set) one record or observation at a time. The observation loop and the statements in the step execute once for each input observation. Depending on the number of input files, the process continues a specified number of times until all the records have been read or some other condition has been met. Once all input observations have been read, the observation loop stops, passing control to the next step (if one exists). The flow diagram illustrated that follows shows a DATA step reading observations from a single input data set one at a time.

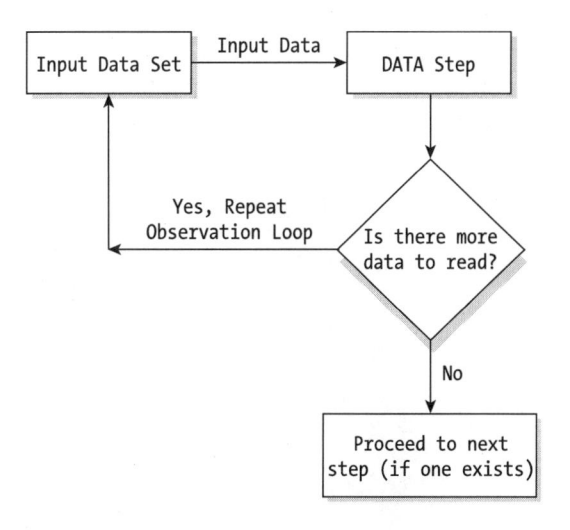

Figure 3-1. Observation loop flow diagram

5 Revisiting the Program Data Vector (PDV)

Although a tip was presented on the PDV in Chapter 2, it's an area that many users want to know more about as they write DATA steps. I've found over the years that as users expand their knowledge and understanding of the PDV, they are better equipped to control various aspects of data in memory. This is why I'm revisiting this important concept.

As you probably recall, the PDV serves as a temporary internal storage area, or working storage area (memory), for the values and attributes (such as size, type, label, and so on) of all variables in a DATA step. This fixed-length area of memory is automatically made available to each open data set and consists of data values that either have been moved from an input buffer (external file) or created using SAS statements (such as LENGTH, assignment statements, and so on) for the purpose of building a SAS data set. The PDV can be visualized as a multi-cell spreadsheet where each cell contains a piece of information or data. Once a PDV record is constructed, it's basically a single fixed-length observation that can be written to a data set, external output file, or used some other way.

6 Setting variables to missing at the top of an observation loop

Specific actions occur automatically at the top of each observation loop. Without a doubt, the most important action performed at the top of an observation loop is to set most or all variables stored in memory to missing values before each observation is read. This critical action causes data from the previous observation to be cleared before reading the next observation. This automatic action prevents data contamination from occurring.

7 Implying a RETURN to the top of an observation loop

After all statements in a DATA step are executed, and at the bottom of an observation loop an implied **RETURN** statement automatically directs control to the top of the observation loop. This enables the next observation to be read (if available) and processing within the step to continue, at least until all observations have been processed.

8 Stopping an observation loop

The SAS System makes it relatively easy to stop a DATA step before all the input observations are read and processed. A few simple and fairly common methods of stopping a program step are presented in Table 3-1.

Table 3-1. Stopping an Observation Loop

METHOD	DESCRIPTION
OBS= *n*	Specify the maximum number of observations to be read as input. This option can be used as a system option, INFILE option, and data set option.
_N_ used with STOP	Specify a value for the _N_ system variable in IF-THEN and STOP statements to stop processing after a certain observation, (as in IF _N_ > 100 THEN STOP;).
DO loop	Specify the maximum number of iterations that the SET statement will be performed in a DO loop.

9 Aborting a step

Occasionally it's necessary to include code that will not only stop a DATA step from processing but also will terminate a program, and possibly a session. Commonly used when a critical error condition is discovered in the data (or program), users can specify the **ABORT** statement in the DATA step to prevent a critical situation from developing. I've used this technique in applications where quality-control issues are of extreme importance requiring processes (for example, temperature and weld strength) to be within acceptable tolerances. When values exceed established QC requirements and guidelines, the process is immediately terminated so the cause of the problem can be determined before moving the data into production. The following example terminates the program step when the value for RATING is anything except "G," "PG," "PG-13," or "R."

Code:

```
DATA ACCEPTABLE_MOVIES;
  INFILE CARDS MISSOVER;
  INPUT @1 TITLE $15.
        @16 RATING $5.;
  IF RATING NOT IN ("G","PG"," PG-13"," R")
    THEN ABORT;
  CARDS;
Jaws            PG
Rocky           PG
Titanic         PG-13
Zoro
;
RUN;
```

Log Results:

```
25   DATA ACCEPTABLE_MOVIES;
26    INFILE CARDS MISSOVER;
27    INPUT @1 TITLE $15.
28        @16 RATING $5.;
IF RATING NOT IN ("G","PG","PG-13","R")
   THEN ABORT;
31    CARDS;

ERROR: Execution terminated by an ABORT
statement at line 29 column 50.
RULE:        ----+----1----+----2----+----3
----+----4----+----5----+----6----+----7
----+----8----+----9----+----0
34         Zoro
TITLE=Zoro RATING=  _ERROR_=1 _N_=4
NOTE: The SAS System stopped processing
this step because of errors.
WARNING: The data set
WORK.ACCEPTABLE_MOVIES may be
incomplete.  When this step was
stopped there were 3 observations and
2 variables.
WARNING: Data set WORK.ACCEPTABLE_MOVIES
was not replaced because this step was
stopped.
```

10 Branching at end-of-file

Users can instruct the SAS System to branch to one or more statements in the DATA step when all the records (external file) or observations (SAS data set) have been read. The ability to redirect process control in this way provides a method for users to compute summary totals, statistics, or some other end-of-file process. In the first example, data is read from an external file. The **EOF=** option is specified in the INFILE statement and a label of the same name is specified in the body of the code. In the second example, data is read from a SAS data set. The **END=** option is specified in the SET statement and an IF-THEN statement using the same name is specified.

✏️ *A RETURN statement is required for each label specified.*

Code:

```
DATA ACCEPTABLE_MOVIES;
 INFILE CARDS MISSOVER EOF=DONE;
 INPUT @1 TITLE $15.
     @16 RATING $5.;
 IF RATING NOT IN ("G","PG","PG-13","R")
    THEN ABORT;
 CTR_MOVIES+1;
RETURN;
DONE:
 PUT "Total # Movies: " CTR_MOVIES;
RETURN;
 CARDS;
Jaws         PG
Rocky        PG
Titanic      PG-13
;
RUN;
```

Code:

```
DATA ACCEPTABLE_MOVIES;
 SET MOVIES END=DONE;
 IF RATING NOT IN ("G","PG","PG-13","R")
    THEN ABORT;
 CTR_MOVIES+1;
 IF DONE THEN DO;
    PUT "Total # Movies: " CTR_MOVIES;
 END;
RUN;
```

11 Returning to the top of the observation loop

Certain implied conditions and SAS statements return process control to the top of the observation loop. In an earlier tip, we saw when control reaches the bottom of a DATA step, and at the bottom of an observation loop, an implied **RETURN** statement automatically directs control back to the top of the observation loop. But certain SAS statements are also available to redirect control to the top of the observation loop as well. Table 3-2 identifies other ways to redirect control to the top of the observation loop.

Table 3-2. Redirecting Control to the Top of an Observation Loop

SAS STATEMENT	DESCRIPTION
RETURN	Implied or explicit, the RETURN statement redirects control to the top of the observation loop.
DELETE	Deletes the current observation in memory and returns to the top of the observation loop.
LOSTCARD	Repositions the input pointer (external files) to he next input record and returns to the top of the observation loop.

12 Retaining values across observation loops

Under normal conditions variables are automatically assigned missing values at the top of the observation loop. An exception occurs when one or more variables are specified in a **RETAIN** statement. The RETAIN statement is a non-executable statement that can appear anywhere in a DATA step. When a RETAIN statement is specified, the variable is not reset to missing at the top of the observation loop. This permits a value from one observation to be retained to the next observation.

13 Preventing missing values from being assigned to a variable

Variables or members of an array specified in a RETAIN statement can be populated with an initial value other than missing during the first iteration of the observation loop. For example, the following RETAIN statement specifies an assignment of an initial value of 2002 to the YEAR_VIEWED variable in the DATA step shown here:

Code:

```
DATA _NULL_;
  RETAIN YEAR_VIEWED 2002;
  SET MOVIES;
  FILE PRINT;
  PUT @1 TITLE      $30.
      @33 CATEGORY  $20.
      @55 RATING    $5.
      @62 YEAR_VIEWED 4.;
RUN;
```

14 Assigning a variable's length with a LENGTH statement

A variable appearing for the first time can have its attributes, including its length and type, assigned to it automatically. For example, in the first coding example that follows, a variable DURATION is automatically assigned a character value (and hence its length) of "Short," "Medium," or "Long," based on the length of the first observation's movie. Because the variable DURATION is not predefined with a length or type, the first observation will assign the field's length and attributes. If the first observation is a movie with a length between 100 and 150 minutes (Medium), then the DURATION variable will be defined with sufficient length to store all possible values. Otherwise, data truncation will occur. Since there is no way to verify that the first observation will contain a movie of "Medium" length (without performing a specialized sort), the problem of truncation has a realistic chance of occurring.

Code:

```
DATA ASSIGN_LENGTH;
 SET MOVIES;
 IF LENGTH < 100 THEN
    DURATION = "Short";
 ELSE
 IF LENGTH > 150 THEN
    DURATION = "Long";
 ELSE
    DURATION = "Medium";
RUN;
```

To prevent the assignment of a variable too small to store all the possible ranges of values as in the previous example, a variable can have its length predefined before it's used. In the next example, a **LENGTH** statement is specified before the **IF-THEN/ELSE** statements to predefine the variable's attributes (length and type).

Code:

```
DATA ASSIGN_LENGTH;
 SET MOVIES;
 LENGTH DURATION $6.;
 IF LENGTH < 100 THEN
    DURATION = "Short";
 ELSE
 IF LENGTH > 150 THEN
    DURATION = "Long";
 ELSE
    DURATION = "Medium";
RUN;
```

15 Assigning a variable's attributes with the ATTRIB statement

Assigning a variable's attributes (including format, informat, label, or length) is easy with the **ATTRIB** statement. When assigned in a DATA step, the variable or variables in the descriptor record of the data set is permanently changed. For example, the **DURATION** variable is assigned a length and label in the code shown here.

Code:

```
DATA ATTRIB_EXAMPLE;
 SET MOVIES;
 ATTRIB DURATION
        LENGTH=$6 LABEL='Movie Length';
 IF LENGTH < 100 THEN
    DURATION = "Short";
 ELSE
 IF LENGTH > 150 THEN
    DURATION = "Long";
 ELSE
    DURATION = "Medium";
RUN;
```

16 Changing the length of an existing character variable

When the length of an existing character variable needs to be changed, use the **LENGTH** or **ATTRIB** statement as the *first statement* in a DATA step. The specified new length will be permanently changed in the descriptor record of the data set.

89

💣 *Use care to prevent data truncation from occurring when changing longer length variables to shorter lengths. For example, the ATTRIB statement is specified in the following DATA step to change the DURATION variable from 6 bytes to 7 bytes in length.*

✏️ *Even though the size of the variable was increased, the data content is unchanged.*

Code:

```
DATA ATTRIB_EXAMPLE;
 ATTRIB DURATION LENGTH=$7
  LABEL='Movie Length';
 SET ATTRIB_EXAMPLE;
RUN;
```

17 Executing WHEN conditions in a SELECT statement

As an alternative to a series of IF-THEN/ELSE statements, a **SELECT** statement with one or more **WHEN** conditions can be specified. The SELECT-WHEN statement enables a sequence of conditions to be constructed that when executed goes through the WHEN conditions until it finds one that satisfies the WHEN expression. Typically, a sequence of WHEN conditions are specified for a long series of conditions. The following example shows a variable DURATION being automatically assigned a character value of "Short," "Medium," or "Long" based on the mutually exclusive conditions specified in the WHEN and OTHERWISE conditions. Although not required, the OTHERWISE condition is useful to prevent missing values being assigned to DURATION.

Code:

```
DATA SELECT_EXAMPLE;
 SET MOVIES;
 LENGTH DURATION $5.;
 SELECT;
   WHEN (LENGTH < 100) DURATION = "Short";
   WHEN (LENGTH > 150) DURATION = "Long";
   OTHERWISE DURATION = "Medium";
 END;
RUN;
```

18 Counting with counters

Counters are used in programs to count everything from the number of widgets made to the number of observations read. SAS makes it easy to create a counter any time you need one. The simplest form of counter is one that is used without specifying any conditions. A counter is specified as variable+n and always results in a numeric value. For example, the following counter tallies the number of "G"-rated movies by incrementing the value of the counter by one for each "G"-rated movie.

✏️ *No RETAIN statement is necessary with counters unless an initial value other than missing period "." is required.*

Code:

```
DATA G_MOVIES;
 SET MOVIES;
 IF RATING = "G";
 CTR_MOVIES+1;
RUN;
```

19 Looping inside an observation loop

Looping inside the observation loop gives users a powerful way to repeat a process a number of times. By specifying a DO statement, users are provided three methods of constructing a loop inside a DATA step observation loop:

- Indexed DO loop

- DO WHILE loop

- DO UNTIL loop

20 Specifying an indexed DO loop

Indexed DO loops are coded inside an observation loop in a DATA step to iterate through a series of statements in a DO group. Essentially, the index value changes each time the DO group executes. Once the maximum value of the index value is reached, the DO loop stops after the last iteration.

21 Specifying a DO WHILE loop

Specifying a DO WHILE loop inside an observation loop permits a conditional block of code to be executed repeatedly. This allows the DO loop to continue running as long as the specified condition is true—otherwise it stops. Be advised that the condition is always evaluated at the top of the loop, and make sure that the condition is structured so that the loop can stop at some point. Otherwise, the DO WHILE loop could be an infinite loop and execute forever.

22 Specifying a DO UNTIL loop

Specifying a DO UNTIL loop inside an observation loop permits a conditional block of code to be executed repeatedly. The DO loop would continue running as long as the specified condition is true—otherwise it stops. Be advised that the DO UNTIL loop executes at least once because the condition is always evaluated at the bottom of the loop. Also make sure that the condition is structured so that the loop can stop at some point. Otherwise, the DO UNTIL loop could be an infinite loop and execute forever.

23 Best practices coding standards

Programmers and end-users have used the SAS software to develop programs and applications since the mid 1970s. Since then, many new versions and releases of the SAS software have been released. With each version and release, a variety of new products, user interfaces, windows, procedures, statements, options, format engines, output capabilities, templates, and an assortment of other tools and features far too numerous to list have been introduced. This means that many programs as well as chunks of code written in the 1970s, 1980s, and 1990s are still in operation today. It also means that best practices coding techniques (or the lack of) borrowed and used from programmers in the past have reappeared in various forms in code of the present.

Here are a number of simple suggestions and guidelines for applying best practice coding standards into existing as well as new program code. The following points have been successfully applied to bring a more manageable programming environment when using SAS software.

- After running a SAS program, immediately review the SAS Log for notes, warnings, and error messages (see the "Program Debugging" section later in this chapter for recommendations on how to turn on important information).

- Use the SQL procedure for code simplification. Because multiple processes can frequently be accomplished in a single SQL step, I/O may be reduced.

- When a DATA step or PROC can do the same job, use PROC whenever possible. Since procedures are tried-and-proven throughout the world's SAS installations, testing requirements are considerably fewer.

- Create user-defined format libraries to store formatted values in one place. This has the added advantage of making programs easier to maintain because formatted data values are not hard coded.

- Include RUN statements at the end of each DATA or PROC step (to separate step boundaries) to print benchmark statistics on the SAS Log immediately following each step.

- Document programs and routines with comments. In addition to comments that explain program logic, comments explaining why a particular piece of logic is in the program can be helpful too. This will minimize the maintenance time for other programmers and users.

- Assign descriptive and meaningful variable names. Besides improving the readability of program code, this practice acts as a form of documentation.

- Construct program header information to serve as program documentation for all programs. The following example illustrates the type of information that can be added so others have a useful documented history.

- Simplify and document complex code and operations. By splitting complex code into two or more programming statements, a program becomes easier to read as well as more maintainable.

- Always specify SAS data set names to prevent an incorrect data set from being processed.

- Utilize macros for redundant code and enable autocall processing by specifying the MAUTOSOURCE system option.

- Create Macro libraries to store common Macro routines in one place.

- Create permanent libraries containing information from daily, weekly, monthly, quarterly, and annual runs. The type of libraries will consist of scripts, SAS programs, SAS logs, output lists, and documentation consisting of instructions for others to follow when running programs.

- Create views based on user input to simplify and streamline complex or burdensome tasks. Any views that are created should be maintained and documented in a central view library.

- Code for unknown data values. This will prevent unassigned or null data values from falling through logic conditions.

- To minimize processing time, store informats, formats, and labels with the SAS data sets that use them. An important reason for using this technique is that many popular procedures use stored formats and labels as they produce output, eliminating the need to assign them in each individual step. This provides added incentives and value for programmers and users, especially since reporting requirements are usually time critical.

- Construct conditions that would render data unusable and abort (or end) the program. This prevents unwanted or harmful data from being processed or written to a data set.

- Test program code using "complete" test data, particularly if the data set is small or represents a random sample of a large data set.

- Set OBS=0 to test syntax and compile time errors without the risk of executing any observations through a DATA or PROC step.

- Use the VALIDATE clause to test syntax and compile time errors for PROC SQL code.

- Specify the NOREPLACE system option to prevent permanent SAS data sets from accidentally being overwritten while writing or testing a program.

- Take advantage of procedures that summarize large amounts of data by saving and using the results in order to avoid reading a large data set again.

- Add options that are frequently used into the SAS configuration file. This eliminates the time and keystrokes necessary to enter them during a SAS session.

- Add statements that are frequently used into the SAS autoexec file. This eliminates the time and keystrokes necessary to enter them during a SAS session.

- Specify SAS System options to turn on SAS log notes, messages, warnings, and included source code. The objective is to display any and all information that is available in a SAS session.

Date and Time Processing

This section includes valuable tips on processing date and time values. You'll learn how SAS handles and stores date and time values, how to access SAS-supplied date and time formats and informats, and how date formats and informats are applied.

1 Storing dates as a numeric value

In the SAS System, a numeric variable containing a SAS date value is stored as the number of days from the fixed date value of 01/01/1960 (January 1, 1960). The SAS date value for January 1, 1960 is represented as 0 (zero). A date earlier than this is represented as a negative number and a date later than this is represented as a positive number. This makes performing any date calculations easy.

2 Handling valid SAS dates

The SAS System handles leap year, century, and fourth-century adjustments automatically for date values beginning at 1582 A.D. through 20,000 A.D.

3 Storing time as a numeric value

In the SAS System, a numeric variable containing a SAS time value is stored as the number of seconds since midnight. The SAS time value for midnight is represented as 0 (zero). The SAS time value for 23:59:59.9 (or 11:59 p.m.) is 86399.9.

A SAS time value must always be a positive number.

4 Representing dates and time values with formats and informats

Because date and time values are stored and represented differently than we normally think of them, the SAS System provides a variety of date and time formats and informats. Without date and time formats and informats, handling date and time values would be somewhat difficult and awkward. Let's discuss what date/time formats and informats are.

A date format tells the SAS System how to display or write a date. Displaying a date value with a date format is accomplished with a **FORMAT** statement. Suppose, for example, that you wanted to display the date value 01/01/1960 using the month name, day, and year as follows: January 1, 1960. The following construct could be specified using a FORMAT statement:

Code:

```
DATA _NULL_;
 DATE=TODAY();
 FORMAT DATE WORDDATE18.;
 PUT DATE;
RUN;
```

5 Applying date and time formats

Date and time formats are applied (or associated) to variables in the following ways:

- Using a PUT statement
- Using a PUT function
- Using a FORMAT statement
- Using an ATTRIB statement
- Using a SELECT statement in the SQL procedure.

6 Applying a date format in a PUT statement

A format used with a **PUT** statement tells the SAS System how the displayed or printed value is supposed to look. Any character, numeric, and date/time formats can be used in a PUT statement. For example, a numeric variable containing a value of 15614 (or 10/01/2002) could be displayed or written in the form of MM/DD/YYYY using a PUT statement with the MMDDYYw. format as follows.

Code:

```
DATA _NULL_;
 DATE=MDY(10,01,2002);
 PUT DATE MMDDYY10.;
RUN;
```

Result:

10/01/2002

7 Applying a date format in a PUT function

A date format used in a **PUT** function converts a numeric variable to a formatted date value. Character, numeric, and date/time formats can be used in a PUT function. For example, a numeric variable containing a value of 15614 (or 10/01/2002) could be displayed or written in the form of MM/DD/YYYY using a PUT function with the MMDDYY10. format as follows.

The advantage of using a PUT function over other methods is that the new date format will be saved as a new character variable.

Code:

```
DATA _NULL_;
 DATE=MDY(10,01,2002);
 FORMAT_DATE = PUT(DATE,MMDDYY10.);
 PUT FORMAT_DATE;
RUN;
```

Result:

10/01/2002

8 Applying a date format with a FORMAT statement

A **FORMAT** statement may be specified in either a DATA or PROC step. When it's specified in a DATA step, and no stored format is saved for the variable in the data set, the date value is displayed with the format that is specified in a FORMAT statement (or an **ATTRIB** statement—see next tip). When a FORMAT statement is specified in a PROC step, the format is only applied for the duration of the step.

In the following PROC step example, a numeric variable of 15614 (or 10/01/2002) is stored in data set INFO. Since the variable DATE doesn't have a store format in the SAS data set, a FORMAT statement is used to display the date values in the form of MM/DD/YYYY.

Code:

```
PROC PRINT DATA=INFO;
 FORMAT DATE MMDDYY10.;
 VAR DATE;
RUN;
```

Result:

10/01/2002

In the following DATA step example, a numeric variable containing a value of 15614 (or 10/01/2002) is displayed or written in the form of MM/DD/YYYY with a FORMAT statement. It applies the specified format to the date value only for the duration of the step.

Code:

```
DATA INFO;
 DATE=MDY(10,01,2002);
 FORMAT DATE MMDDYY10.;
RUN;
```

Result:

10/01/2002

9 Applying a date format with an ATTRIB statement

An **ATTRIB** statement may be specified in either a DATA or PROC step. When it's specified in a DATA step, and a stored format isn't saved for the variable in the data set, the formatted date value can be displayed by specifying an

ATTRIB statement (or a FORMAT statement—see previous tip). When an ATTRIB statement is specified in a PROC step, the format is only applied for the duration of the step.

In the following PROC step example, a numeric variable of 15614 (or 10/01/2002) is stored in data set INFO. Because the variable DATE doesn't have a stored format defined in the SAS data set, an ATTRIB statement is used to display the date values in the form of MM/DD/YYYY.

Code:

```
PROC PRINT DATA=INFO;
 ATTRIB DATE FORMAT=MMDDYY10.;
 VAR DATE;
RUN;
```

Result:

10/01/2002

In the next DATA step example, a numeric variable containing a value of 15614 (or 10/01/2002) is displayed or written in the form of MM/DD/YYYY with an ATTRIB statement. It applies the specified format to the date value only for the duration of the DATA step.

Code:

```
DATA INFO;
 DATE=MDY(10,01,2002);
 ATTRIB DATE FORMAT=MMDDYY10.;
RUN;
```

Result:

10/01/2002

10 Applying a date format in an SQL SELECT statement

A format can be specified in an SQL **SELECT** statement. When it's specified in this way, and the format isn't stored as part of the data set, the date value can be displayed with a format that is specified in a SELECT statement.

In the following PROC SQL step example, a numeric variable of 15614 (or 10/01/2002) is stored in data set INFO. Since the variable DATE doesn't have a stored format in the SAS data set, a format modifier may be specified in a SELECT statement to display the date values in the form of MM/DD/YYYY as follows.

Code:

```
PROC SQL;
 SELECT DATE
  FORMAT=MMDDYY10.
   FROM MOVIES(OBS=1);
RUN;
```

Result:

10/01/2002

11 Defining a one-hundred-year period with the YEARCUTOFF= option

Occasionally date values are entered consisting of only a two-digit year. When this happens, the SAS System automatically determines which century (the 19th or 20th) to apply to a date value. The SAS System option that helps determine this is known as the **YEARCUTOFF=** option. On most systems, the default value for this option is YEARCUTOFF=1920. This informs the SAS System that 1920 is the first year of a one-hundred-year period. This means that any date containing a two-digit year (without the century) is considered to be between 1920 and 2019. To properly handle dates prior to 1920 or after 2019, a date value should contain the entire four-digit century and year.

12 Understanding date formats

Date formats (or output templates) convert SAS date values to a variety of character forms when representing dates. Table 3-3 shows four columns: 1) Format Name, 2) Form (how the date looks), 3) SAS statement and format example, and 4) Display Results (what the date looks like when it is displayed or printed after the format is applied).

Depending on the width specification (represented by w.), the printed date value may truncate or punctuate differently. Formatted date values generally right align, displaying or printing leading blanks when the number of characters is less than the specified width. Otherwise, when the formatted value is a word (as in WORDDATE20.), the value is left aligned and padded with trailing blanks. In Table 3-3, each example uses an actual date value of October 1, 2002, which represents a SAS date value of 15614.

Table 3-3. SAS Date Formats

FORMAT	FORM	STATEMENT	DISPLAY RESULTS
DATEw.	DDMMMYY	PUT DATE DATE7.;	01OCT02
	DDMMMYYYY	PUT DATE DATE9.;	01OCT2002
DDMMYYw.	DDMMYY	PUT DATE DDMMYY6.;	011002
	DD/MM/YY	PUT DATE DDMMYY8.;	01/10/02
	DD/MM/YYYY	PUT DATE DDMMYY10.;	01/10/2002
DOWNAMEw.	Day-of-week	PUT DATE DOWNAME.;	Tuesday
		PUT DATE DOWNAME3.;	Tue
JULDAYw.	DDD (Julian day of year)	PUT DATE JULDAY.;	274
JULIANw.	YYDDD	PUT DATE JULIAN.;	02274
	YYYYDDD	PUT DATE JULIAN7.;	2002274
MMDDYYw.	MMDDYY	PUT DATE MMDDYY6.;	100102
	MM/DD/YY	PUT DATE MMDDYY8.;	10/01/02
	MM/DD/YYYY	PUT DATE MMDDYY10.;	10/01/2002

Table 3-3. SAS Date Formats (Continued)

FORMAT	FORM	STATEMENT	DISPLAY RESULTS
MMYYxw.	MM/YY	PUT DATE MMYYS5.;	10/02
	MM/YYYY	PUT DATE MMYYS7.;	10/2002
MONNAMEw.	Month-name	PUT DATE MONNAME.;	October
	Mon	PUT DATE MONNAME3.;	Oct
MONTHw.	Month-of-year	PUT DATE MONTH.;	10
MONYYw.	MonYY	PUT DATE MONYY.;	Oct02
	MonYYYY	PUT DATE MONYY7.;	Oct2002
QTRw.	n (Quarter of year)	PUT DATE QTR.;	4
QTRRw.	Quarter-of-year (Roman)	PUT DATE QTRR.;	IV
WEEKDATEw.	Day-of-week	PUT DATE WEEKDATE9.;	Tuesday
	Day-of-week, MMM DD, YY	PUT DATE WEEKDATE15.;	Tue, Oct 1, 02
	Day-of-week, Month DD, YYYY	PUT DATE WEEKDATE.;	Tuesday, October 1, 2002
	Day-of-week, Month DD, YYYY	PUT DATE WEEKDATE29.;	Tuesday, October 1, 2002
WEEKDATXw.	Day-of-week	PUT DATE WEEKDATX9.;	Tuesday
	Day-of-week, DD MMM YY	PUT DATE WEEKDATX15.;	Tue, 1 Oct 02
	Day-of-week, DD Month YYYY	PUT DATE WEEKDATX.;	Tuesday, 1 October 2002
	Day-of-week, DD Month YYYY	PUT DATE WEEKDATX29.;	Tuesday, 1 October 2002
WEEKDAYw.	Day-of-week	PUT DATE WEEKDAY.;	3
WORDDATEw.	Mon	PUT DATE WORDDATE3.;	Oct
	Name-of-month	PUT DATE WORDDATE9.;	October
	Mon DD, YYYY	PUT DATE WORDDATE12.;	Oct 1, 2002
	Name-of-month DD, YYYY	PUT DATE WORDDATE.;	October 1, 2002
	Name-of-month DD, YYYY	PUT DATE WORDDATE18.;	October 1, 2002

Table 3-3. SAS Date Formats (Continued)

FORMAT	FORM	STATEMENT	DISPLAY RESULTS
WORDDATXw.	Mon	PUT DATE WORDDATX3.;	Oct
	Name-of-month	PUT DATE WORDDATX9.;	October
	DD Mon YYYY	PUT DATE WORDDATX12.;	1 Oct 2002
	DD Name-of-month YYYY	PUT DATE WORDDATX.;	1 October 2002
	DD Name-of-month YYYY	PUT DATE WORDDATX18.;	1 October 2002
YEARw.	YYYY	PUT DATE YEAR.;	2002
	YY	PUT DATE YEAR2.;	02
YYMMxw.	YYYY/MM	PUT DATE YYMMS.;	2002/10
YYMMDDw.	YYMMDD	PUT DATE YYMMDD6.;	021001
	YY/MM/DD	PUT DATE YYMMDD.;	02-10-01
	YYYY/MM/DD	PUT DATE YYMMDD10.;	2002-10-01
YYMONw.	YYYYMON	PUT DATE YYMON.;	2002OCT
YYQxw.	YYYY/4	PUT DATE YYQS.;	2002/4

13 Understanding date informats

Date informats (or input templates) provide instructions on how the SAS System is to read data values into a variable. To interpret date values correctly, it is important that a compatible informat be used. For example, if a numeric date informat were used to read a character date, a missing value would be assigned to the variable and an error message would be printed on the SAS Log. These kinds of unexpected results should be avoided if possible. Table 3-4 shows four columns: 1) Informat Name, 2) Form or the data value that is read with the informat, 3) Input Data (what date value looks like in input line), and 4) SAS statement and informat example.

A date value may be read or handled differently depending on the informat used and specified width (represented by w.). Unformatted date values may be left or right aligned and may contain trailing or leading blanks. The width specification tells the SAS System how many characters the unformatted date value is. In Table 3-4, each example uses an actual date value of October 1, 2002. The SAS variable will store the date value as 15614.

Table 3-4. SAS Date Informats

FORMAT	FORM	INPUT DATA	STATEMENT
DATEw.	DDMMMYY	1OCT02	INPUT DATE DATE7.;
	DD MMM YY	01 OCT 02	INPUT DATE DATE9.;
	DD-MMM-YY	01-OCT-02	INPUT DATE DATE9.;
	DMMMYYYY	1OCT2002	INPUT DATE DATE9.;
DDMMYYw.	DDMMYY	011002	INPUT DATE DDMMYY6.;
	DD/MM/YY	01/10/02	INPUT DATE DDMMYY8.;
	DD MM YY	01 10 02	INPUT DATE DDMMYY8.;
	DD/MM/YYYY	01/10/2002	INPUT DATE DDMMYY10.
JULIANw.	YYDDD	02274	INPUT DATE JULIAN.;
	YYYYDDD	2002274	INPUT DATE JULIAN7.;
MMDDYYw.	MMDDYY	100102	INPUT DATE MMDDYY.;
	MMDDYY	100102	INPUT DATE MMDDYY6.;
	MM/DD/YY	10/01/02	INPUT DATE MMDDYY8.;
	MM/DD/YYYY	10/01/2002	INPUT DATE MMDDYY10.;
MONYYw.	MonYY	Oct02	PUT DATE MONYY.;
	MonYYYY	Oct2002	INPUT DATE MONYY7.;
YYMMDDw.	YYMMDD	021001	INPUT DATE YYMMDD.;
	YYMMDD	021001	INPUT DATE YYMMDD6.;
	YY/MM/DD	02-10-01	INPUT DATE YYMMDD8.;
	YY MM DD	02 10 01	INPUT DATE YYMMDD8.;
	YYYY/MM/DD	2002-10-01	INPUT DATE YYMMDD10.;
YYQw.	YYQn	02Q4	INPUT DATE YYQ.;
	YYYYQn	2002Q4	INPUT DATE YYQ6.;

Operators and Modifiers

This section includes tips on how to use operators and modifiers such as Boolean, comparison, logical, and other SAS programming operators. You'll learn how to perform equality tests, conduct wildcard searching, compare variables or strings to one another, and complete a variety of common and necessary programming tasks.

1 Understanding operators and their order of evaluation

Operations are evaluated using a comprehensive set of Boolean and comparison operators. The operators and their order of evaluation are displayed in their order of evaluation in Table 3-5.

Table 3-5. Operators and Evaluation Order

ORDER	OPERATOR	DESCRIPTION
0	( )	Evaluates the expression enclosed in parentheses to be evaluated before all others.
1	**case-expression**	Selects result values when certain conditions are met.
2	**	Performs exponentiation (raises to a power).
	><	Selects minimum value from one or more operands.
	<>	Selects maximum value from one or more operands.
3	*	Performs multiplication.
	/	Performs division.
4	+	Performs addition.
	-	Performs subtraction.
5	||	Performs concatenation of operands.
6	<NOT> between-condition	Negates (excludes) one or more values between a range of values.
	<NOT> contains-condition	Negates one or more values in a list of values.
	<NOT> exists-condition	Negates one or more values described by a subquery.
	<NOT> in-condition	Negates one or more values found in a set condition.
	<NOT> like-condition	Negates one or more values to a pattern-matching condition.
	Is <NOT> condition	Negates one or more values not specified in the IS condition.
7	=	Specifies a value is equal to some other value.
	^=	Specifies a value does not equal some other value.

Table 3-5. Operators and Evaluation Order (Continued)

ORDER	OPERATOR	DESCRIPTION
7	>	Specifies a value is greater than some other value.
	<	Specifies a value is less than some other value.
	>=	Specifies a value greater than or equal to some other value.
	<=	Specifies a value less than or equal to some other value.
	=*	Specifies a sounds-like operation with character operands.
8	AND &	Specifies a logical AND condition.
9	OR |	Specifies a logical OR condition.
10	NOT ^	Specifies a logical NOT condition.

2 Understanding mathematical operators in SQL

SQL supports the identical set of mathematical operators that the DATA step language does. Table 3-6 describes the available mathematical operators and their order of evaluation.

Table 3-6. SQL Mathematical Operators

OPERATOR	DESCRIPTION
**	Exponentiation
*	Multiplication
/	Division
+	Addition
-	Subtraction

3 Combining comparison and logical operators

Comparison and *logical operators* can be combined to give queries the power to process multiple criteria. For example, the following subset selects "PG" and "PG-13" movies with a length less than 120 minutes.

Code:

```
DATA OPERATORS;
  SET MOVIES(WHERE=
    (RATING IN("PG","PG-13") AND
                 LENGTH < 120)
         KEEP=TITLE LENGTH RATING);
RUN;
```

Results:

```
Title                      Length   Rating

Casablanca                    103   PG
Poltergeist                   115   PG
Christmas Vacation             97   PG-13
Michael                       106   PG-13
National Lampoon's Vacation    98   PG-13
```

4 Negating a specified condition with the NOT operator

The **NOT** operator is used to negate whatever condition is specified. The NOT keyword is specified after the variable name. For example, the following subset selects all movies except "R" rated.

Code:

```
DATA OPERATORS;
  SET MOVIES(WHERE=(RATING NOT = "R")
             KEEP=TITLE RATING);
RUN;
```

Results:

Title	Rating
The Wizard of Oz	G
Casablanca	PG
Jaws	PG
Poltergeist	PG
Rocky	PG
Star Wars	PG
The Hunt for Red October	PG
Christmas Vacation	PG-13
Forrest Gump	PG-13
Ghost	PG-13
Jurassic Park	PG-13
Michael	PG-13
National Lampoon's Vacation	PG-13
Titanic	PG-13

5 Using the IN operator to group equality tests

The **IN** operator groups two or more equality tests together and operates as if an OR operator had been specified. It also reduces the number of keystrokes that have to be entered. For example, the following subset selects only "G" and "PG" movies.

Code:

```
DATA OPERATORS;
  SET MOVIES(WHERE=(RATING IN("G"," PG"))
             KEEP=TITLE LENGTH RATING);
RUN;
```

Results:

Title	Length	Rating
The Wizard of Oz	101	G
Casablanca	103	PG
Jaws	125	PG
Poltergeist	115	PG
Rocky	120	PG
Star Wars	124	PG
The Hunt for Red October	135	PG

6 Subsetting with the percent sign (%) wildcard and the LIKE operator

When part of a value is known and the rest is unknown, wildcard filtering can be used to search rows of data that match a certain search pattern. The **LIKE** operator combined with the percent sign (%) is used to match multiple characters in a search pattern. The following example creates a wildcard search pattern using the percent sign (%) by subsetting all movies that contain the word "The" as the first word in a movie title. This tells the DATA step to accept any number of characters after the text "The" in a movie title.

Code:

```
DATA OPERATORS;
  SET MOVIES(WHERE=(TITLE LIKE "The%")
             KEEP=TITLE LENGTH RATING);
RUN;
```

Results:

Title	Length	Rating
The Hunt for Red October	135	PG
The Terminator	108	R
The Wizard of Oz	101	G

7 Using multiple percent sign (%) wildcards in a search pattern

Sometimes it is useful to be able to combine two or more wildcard characters to broaden the search capabilities. The following example uses two wildcards, one at the beginning of the search pattern consisting of the text "the" and one at the end. To simplify the search even further, an UPCASE function is specified to convert all lowercase characters to uppercase.

Code:

```
DATA OPERATORS;
  SET MOVIES(WHERE=
      (UPCASE(TITLE) LIKE "%THE%")
          KEEP=TITLE LENGTH RATING);
RUN;
```

Results:

Title	Length	Rating
Silence of the Lambs	118	R
The Hunt for Red October	135	PG
The Terminator	108	R
The Wizard of Oz	101	G

8 Using the underscore (_) wildcard with the LIKE operator

Whereas the percent sign (%) matches multiple characters, the underscore (_) wildcard character matches just a single character. For example, the following subset selects movies based on a search pattern containing text followed by three underscores to subset all "PG" and "PG-13" movies.

Code:

```
DATA OPERATORS;
  SET MOVIES(WHERE=
      (UPCASE(RATING) LIKE "PG___")
          KEEP=TITLE LENGTH RATING);
RUN;
```

Results:

Title	Length	Rating
Casablanca	103	PG
Christmas Vacation	97	PG-13
Forrest Gump	142	PG-13
Ghost	127	PG-13
Jaws	125	PG
Jurassic Park	127	PG-13
Michael	106	PG-13
National Lampoon's Vacation	98	PG-13
Poltergeist	115	PG
Rocky	120	PG
Star Wars	124	PG
The Hunt for Red October	135	PG
Titanic	194	PG-13

9 Truncating and comparing strings with a colon (:) modifier

When comparing strings of different lengths, the string with the shorter length generally has its value padded with trailing blanks in order to make the comparison. This process can be overridden by using the colon (:) modifier with a comparison operator to truncate the longer string. The following example compares two different length strings using a colon (:) modifier. The longer string is truncated for the comparison.

Code:

```
DATA MOVIES;
  INFILE CARDS DSD;
  INPUT TITLE :$11.
        OLD_RATING $
        NEW_RATING $;
  IF OLD_RATING NE: NEW_RATING THEN
      OUTPUT;
  ELSE DELETE;
  CARDS;
Brave Heart,R,R
Jaws,PG,PG-13
Rocky,PG,PG
Titanic,PG-13,R
;
RUN;
PROC PRINT NOOBS N;
RUN;
```

Results:

TITLE	OLD_RATING	NEW_RATING
Jaws	PG	PG-13
Titanic	PG-13	R

N = 2

10 Reading input values with the n* informat modifier

You can read repetitive variables in a variable list using the same informat any time the need arises. This can reduce the number of keystrokes required when entering lengthier input lists. By specifying the **n*** modifier, you'll be able to repeat an assigned informat for a variable list as many times as necessary. For example, an input record containing three date variables, RENTED1, RENTED2, and RENTED3 could be read as follows. Each of these variables has the MMDDYY10. format applied to them.

Code:

```
DATA RENTALS;
 INFILE CARDS MISSOVER;
 INPUT (TITLE RENTED1-RENTED3)
         ($8. 3 * MMDDYY10.);
 FORMAT RENTED1-RENTED3 MMDDYY10.;
 CARDS;
Jaws    02/03/199804/15/199801/16/1999
Rocky   04/07/199011/18/1997
Titanic 05/14/199805/20/199810/01/2000
;
RUN;
```

Results:

TITLE	RENTED1	RENTED2	RENTED3
Jaws	02/03/1998	04/15/1998	01/16/1999
Rocky	04/07/1990	11/18/1997	.
Titanic	05/14/1998	05/20/1998	10/01/2000

11 Writing values with the n* format modifier

Here's a simple and quick method of writing a character string *n*-times that is sure to save you time. By specifying the **n*** modifier, you'll be able to repeat an assigned value as many times as necessary. Say you wanted to repeat the character value "+" 80 times. You could enter the value 80 times within quotes, or you could use the **n*** format modifier. The PUT statement writes 80 plus signs (+) across the SAS Log.

Code:

```
DATA RENTALS;
  SET MOVIES;
  IF _N_ = 1 THEN PUT 80*'+';
RUN;
```

SAS Log Results:

```
114  DATA RENTALS;
115    SET path.MOVIES;
116    IF _N_ = 1 THEN PUT 80*'+';
117  RUN;
++++++++++++++++++++++++++++++++++++++++
++++++++++++++++++++++++++++++++++++++++
NOTE: There were 22 observations read
from the data set PATH.MOVIES.
NOTE: The data set WORK.RENTALS has 22
observations and 6 variables.
```

SAS Functions

This section includes tips on how to use the numerous built-in functions to perform a variety of useful tasks. You'll learn how to apply functions in SAS statements, search a character variable for a desired value, use arithmetic functions to find the smallest or largest value in a list, convert a non-date value into a date value, use state and ZIP code functions to perform a variety of conversions from one type of code to another, and much more.

1 Using functions as part of a SAS statement

SAS functions offer a convenient way to perform numerous useful tasks. From arithmetic and statistical to character and date, functions can be specified as either data set options or in SAS statements. Two or more SAS functions can even be combined to perform common—and not so common—tasks. So the next time you're in the mood or just want to try something new, reach for one of these marvelous timesaving Base SAS functions and let it do the hard work for you quickly and easily.

2 Searching a character variable for a character string

Searching a variable for a character string is made easy with the **INDEX** function. By specifying it in a **WHERE=** data set option, WHERE statement, or subsetting IF statement, you can select those observations that satisfy the terms of the search. For example, selecting "PG" and "PG-13" movies from the RATING variable can easily be done using the INDEX function in a WHERE= data set option.

✏ *Using your online SAS documentation you can search on FUNCTIONS to see the list of SAS functions. When running interactively you can press F1 for help on functions.*

Code:

```
DATA INDEX;
  SET MOVIES(WHERE=(INDEX(RATING,'PG'))
             KEEP=TITLE RATING);
RUN;
```

Results:

```
Title                    Rating

Casablanca               PG
Christmas Vacation       PG-13
Forrest Gump             PG-13
Ghost                    PG-13
Jaws                     PG
Jurassic Park            PG-13
Michael                  PG-13
```

National Lampoon's Vacation	PG-13
Poltergeist	PG
Rocky	PG
Star Wars	PG
The Hunt for Red October	PG
Titanic	PG-13

3 Reversing a character-string value

Reversing a character-string value is easy with the **REVERSE** function. This function can be used as a means of safeguarding passwords and other critical information that is stored in data sets. For example, reversing the characters in RATING for "PG" and "PG-13" movies is accomplished with the REVERSE function.

Code:

```
DATA REVERSE;
 SET MOVIES(WHERE=
      (RATING IN("PG","PG-13"))
          KEEP=TITLE RATING);
 RATING=REVERSE(RATING);
RUN;
```

Results:

Title	Rating
Casablanca	GP
Jaws	GP
Poltergeist	GP
Rocky	GP
Star Wars	GP
The Hunt for Red October	GP
Christmas Vacation	31-GP
Forrest Gump	31-GP
Ghost	31-GP
Jurassic Park	31-GP
Michael	31-GP
National Lampoon's Vacation	31-GP
Titanic	31-GP

4 Exploring host operating system functions

Although the majority of functions require one or more arguments to be supplied, a few do not. Table 3-7 shows functions that receive their arguments from the host operating system and not as user-supplied values.

Table 3-7. Host Operating System Functions

FUNCTION	DESCRIPTION
DATE()	Returns current date as a SAS date value.
DATETIME()	Returns the current date and time of day.
TIME()	Returns the current time of day.
TODAY()	Returns the current date as a SAS date value.

5 Exploring arithmetic functions

SAS arithmetic functions provide users with a selection of basic tools to choose from. Table 3-8 shows a number of popular arithmetic functions and the tasks they perform.

6 Exploring array functions

Table 3-9 lists numerous array functions and describes the tasks they perform.

7 Exploring character functions

Character functions are typically used to modify character strings. Table 3-10 shows numerous character functions and gives a brief description of the tasks that each performs.

Table 3-8. SAS Arithmetic Functions

FUNCTION	DESCRIPTION
ABS(arg)	Returns an absolute value consisting of a nonnegative number.
MAX(arg1, arg2, ...)	Returns the largest of the nonmissing arguments using a minimum of two numeric values.
MIN(arg1, arg2, ...)	Returns the smallest of the nonmissing arguments using a minimum of two numeric values.
MOD(arg1, arg2)	Returns a numeric remainder value from dividing arg1 by arg2.
SIGN(arg)	Returns a value of –1 when arg is less than 0, 0 when arg is equal to 0, or 1 when arg is greater than 0.
SQRT(arg)	Returns a nonnegative numeric value consisting of the square root of a value.

Table 3-9. Array Functions

FUNCTION	DESCRIPTION
DIM <n> (array-name)	Returns the number of elements in a single-dimensional array.
DIM(array-name,bound)	Returns the number of elements in a specified dimension of a multi-dimensional array.
HBOUND <n> (array-name)	Returns the upper bound of a single-dimensional array.
HBOUND(array-name,bound)	Returns the upper bound in a specified dimension of a multi-dimensional array.
LBOUND <n> (array-name)	Returns the lower bound of a single-dimensional array.
LBOUND(array-name,bound)	Returns the lower bound in s specified dimension of a multi-dimensional array.

Table 3-10. Character Functions

FUNCTION	DESCRIPTION
BYTE(n)	Returns the nth character in the ASCII (values between 0 and 127) or EBCDIC (values between 0 and 255) collating sequence.
COLLATE(start-position<,end-position>) | (start-position<,,length>)	Returns an ASCII or EBCDIC collating sequence character string.
COMPBL(source)	Removes multiple blanks between words in a character string.

Table 3-10. Character Functions (Continued)

FUNCTION	DESCRIPTION
COMPRESS(source)	Removes blanks from a character string.
DEQUOTE(arg)	Removes quotation marks from a character value.
INDEX(source,arg)	Searches the source for the character or character string specified in the argument. A value of 0 is returned when no characters are found. Otherwise, a value corresponding to the position of the first character found is returned.
INDEXC(source,arg1<,...arg-n>)	Locates the first occurrence in the source (from left to right) for any character present in one or more of the arguments. A value of 0 is returned when no characters are found. Otherwise, a value corresponding to the position of the first character found is returned.
INDEXW(source,arg)	Searches the source for a specified word.
LEFT(arg)	Left aligns a character string expression.
LENGTH(arg)	Returns the length of a character string expression.
LOWCASE(arg)	Converts all characters in a character string expression to lowercase letters.
QUOTE(arg)	Inserts double quotation marks around a character string expression.
RANK(arg)	Returns the ASCII or EBCDIC collating sequence value corresponding to the position of a character.
REPEAT(arg,n)	Replicates a character string value the number of times indicated by n. The value of n cannot be a negative value.
REVERSE(arg)	Returns a character string value in reverse order.
RIGHT(arg)	Right aligns a character string expression.
SCAN(arg,n)	Searches a character string for words and returns the nth word.
SOUNDEX(arg)	Searches a character string for values that sound alike or have spelling variations.
SUBSTR(arg,position<,n>)= characters	Replaces a character string expression with the characters specified.
variable = SUBSTR(arg,position<,n>)	Extracts a portion of a character string expression from an argument.

Table 3-10. Character Functions (Continued)

FUNCTION	DESCRIPTION
TRANSLATE(source, exp1-to, exp2-from)	Replaces a portion of a character string expression with specific characters.
TRANWRD(source,target, replacement)	Replaces or removes all occurrences of a word in a character string expression.
TRIM(arg)	Removes trailing blanks from a character string expression.
TRIMN(arg)	Removes trailing blanks from a character string expression and assigns a null value if the expression is missing.
UPCASE(arg)	Converts all characters in a character string expression to uppercase letters.
VERIFY(source, arg)	Returns the first value in a character string expression (source) that is not present in the supplied argument.

8 Exploring date and time functions

SAS date and time functions provide an assortment of routines for providing a date and time value that can be in an expression. Table 3-11 shows numerous date and time functions with a brief description of the tasks that they perform.

9 Exploring financial functions

Financial functions consist of routines that are used to compute financial and accounting formulas related to payments and expenses. Table 3-12 shows numerous financial functions with a brief description of the tasks that each performs.

10 Exploring random number functions

Random number functions produce values that change based on a probability distribution. Table 3-13 shows numerous random number functions and gives a brief description of the tasks that each performs.

11 Exploring state and ZIP code functions

State and ZIP code functions convert state abbreviations, ZIP codes, FIPS codes, and other codes used to identify geographic regions, countries, and states into other values. Table 3-14 shows numerous state and ZIP code functions with a brief description of the tasks that each performs.

12 Exploring statistical functions

Statistical functions produce results based on a sample of data. Table 3-15 shows numerous statistical functions and offers a brief description of each.

13 Exploring trigonometric and hyperbolic functions

Trigonometric and hyperbolic functions produce measurements on circles, triangles, and other shapes. Table 3-16 shows numerous trigonometric and hyperbolic functions along with a brief description of the tasks that each performs.

Table 3-11. Date and Time Functions

FUNCTION	DESCRIPTION
DATEDIF(startdate, enddate, basis)	Returns the number of days between two dates.
DATE()	Returns the current date from the system as a SAS date value.
DATEJUL(arg)	Converts a Julian date to a SAS date value.
DATEPART(arg)	Extracts the date from a SAS datetime value.
DATETIME()	Returns the current date and time of day.
DAY(arg)	Returns the day of the month from a SAS date value.
DHMS(date,hour, min, sec)	Returns a SAS datetime value from date, hour, minute, and second values.
HMS(hour,minute,second)	Returns a SAS time value from hour, minute, and second values.
HOUR(arg)	Returns the hour from a SAS datetime or time value.
INTCK('interval',from,to)	Returns the number of time intervals in a specified time span.
JULDATE(arg)	Converts a SAS date value to a Julian date.
MDY(month,day,year)	Returns a SAS date value from month, day, and year values.
MINUTE(arg)	Returns the minute from a SAS date or datetime value.
MONTH(arg)	Returns a numeric month value (1 through 12) from a SAS date or datetime value.
QTR(arg)	Returns a numeric quarter value (1 through 4) from a SAS date or datetime value.
SECOND(arg)	Returns a numeric second value (0 through 59) from a SAS time value.
TIME()	Returns the current time of day from the system clock.
TIMEPART(arg)	Extracts a time value from a SAS datetime value.
TODAY()	Returns the current date from the system date as a SAS date value.
WEEKDAY(arg)	Returns a numeric day of the week value (1=Sunday, ...) from a SAS date or datetime value.
YEAR(arg)	Returns a numeric 4-digit year value from a SAS date value.
YRDIF(startdate,endate,basis)	Returns the difference in years from two SAS date values.
YYQ(year,quarter)	Returns a SAS date value from year and quarter values.

Table 3-12. Financial Functions

FUNCTION	DESCRIPTION
COMPOUND(amount, future, rate, period)	Computes and returns a compound interest calculation using three of the four arguments where amount is a numeric initial amount, future is a numeric future amount, rate is a numeric periodic interest rate expressed as a fraction, and periods represents the number related to compounding. The value for period is expressed as a numeric value, and represents a time frame such as 360 months.
CONVX(y, f, c)	Returns the enumerated cashflow convexity.
CONVXP(A, C, n, K)	Returns the enumerated cashflow stream convexity.
DACCDB(period, value, years, rate)	Returns the accumulated declining balance depreciation.
DACCDBSL(period, value, years, rate)	Returns the accumulated declining balance with conversion to a straight-line depreciation.
DACCSL(period, value, years)	Returns the accumulated straight-line depreciation.
DACCSYD(period, value, years)	Returns the accumulated sum-of-years-digits depreciation.
DACCTAB(period, value, t1,..., tn)	Returns the accumulated depreciation for each time period.
DEPDB(period, value, years, rate)	Returns the declining balance depreciation.
DEPDBSL(period, value, years, rate)	Returns the declining balance with conversion to a straight-line depreciation.
DEPSL(period, value, years)	Returns the straight-line depreciation.
DEPSYD(period, value, years)	Returns the sum-of-years-digits depreciation.
DEPTAB(period, value, t1, ..., tn)	Returns the depreciation from specified tables.
DUR(y, f, c1)	Returns the modified duration for an enumerated cashflow.
DURP(arg)	Returns the modified duration for a periodic cashflow stream.
INTRR(frequency, c0, c1, ..., cn)	Returns the fraction corresponding to the internal rate of return.
IRR(frequency, c0, c1, ..., cn)	Returns the percentage corresponding to the internal rate of return.

Table 3-12. Financial Functions (Continued)

FUNCTION	DESCRIPTION
MORT(amount, payment, rate, number)	Computes and returns the amortization calculation using three of the four arguments where amount is a numeric initial amount, future is a numeric future amount, rate is a numeric periodic interest rate expressed as a fraction, and period represents the number related to compounding.
NETPV(rate, frequency, c0, c1, ..., cn)	Returns net present value with rate represented as a fraction.
NPV(rate, frequency, c0, c1, ..., cn)	Returns net present value with rate represented as a percentage.
PVP(arg)	Returns the present value for a periodic cashflow stream.
SAVING(future, payment, rate, number)	Returns the future value of a periodic saving.
YIELD(A, C, n, K)	Returns the yield-to-maturity for a periodic cashflow stream.

Table 3-13. Random Number Functions

FUNCTION	DESCRIPTION
NORMAL(seed)	Returns a variate generated from a normal distribution using the Box-Muller transformation of RANUNI variates with a mean of 0 and variance of 1.
RANBIN(seed, n, p)	Returns a variate generated from a binomial distribution with a mean of np and a variance of np(1-p) where seed is an integer value $<2^{31}-1$, n is an integer number of independent Bernoulli trials value and is greater than 0 (zero), and p is a numeric probability of success value 0<p<1.
RANCAU(seed)	Returns a variate generated from a Cauchy distribution with location parameter 0 and scale parameter 1.
RANEXP(seed)	Returns a variate generated from an exponential distribution with parameter value of 1.
RANGAM(seed, ar)	Returns a variate generated from a gamma distribution with parameter ar where the seed is an integer value $<2^{31}-1$ and ar (acceptance-rejection) is a numeric shape pattern greater than 0 (zero).
RANNOR(seed)	Returns a variate generated from a normal distribution using the Box-Muller transformation of RANUNI variates with a mean of 0 (zero) and a variance of 1.

Table 3-13. Random Number Functions (Continued)

FUNCTION	DESCRIPTION
RANPOI(seed, m)	Returns a variate generated from a Poisson distribution with a mean value of m where seed is an integer value $<2^{31}-1$ and m is a numeric mean parameter greater than or equal to 0 (zero).
RANTBL(seed, p1, ..., pn)	Returns a variate generated from the probability mass function defined by p1 through pn where seed is an integer value $<2^{31}-1$ and pi is a numeric value between 0 and 1 inclusive.
RANTRI(seed, t)	Returns a variate generated from the triangular distribution with parameter t where seed is an integer value $<2^{31}-1$ and t is a numeric value with 0<t<1.
RANUNI(seed)	Returns a number generated from the uniform distribution on the interval (0,1) where the RANUNI function is the same as the UNIFORM function and the seed is an integer value $<2^{31}-1$.
UNIFORM(seed)	Returns a number generated from the uniform distribution on the interval (0,1) where UNIFORM function is the same as the RANUNI function and the seed is an integer value $<2^{31}-1$.

Table 3-14. State and ZIP Code Functions

FUNCTION	DESCRIPTION
FIPNAME(fips-code)	Returns a maximum of a 20-character uppercase state name corresponding to a numeric U.S. Federal Information Processing Standards (FIPS) code argument.
FIPNAMEL(fips-code)	Returns a maximum of a 20-character mixed uppercase and lowercase state name corresponding to a numeric U.S. Federal Information Processing Standards (FIPS) code argument.
FIPSTATE(fips-code)	Returns a two-character uppercase state postal code corresponding to a U.S. Federal Information Processing Standards (FIPS) code argument.
STFIPS(postal-code)	Returns a numeric U.S. Federal Information Processing Standards (FIPS) code from a two-character state postal code argument.
STNAME(postal-code)	Returns a maximum of a 20-character uppercase state name corresponding to a two-character state postal code argument.
STNAMEL(postal-code)	Returns a maximum of a 20-character mixed uppercase and lowercase state name corresponding to a two-character state postal code argument.
ZIPFIPS(zip-code)	Returns the two-digit U.S. Federal Information Processing Standards (FIPS) code corresponding to a five-digit ZIP code argument.

Table 3-14. State and ZIP Code Functions (Continued)

FUNCTION	DESCRIPTION
ZIPNAME(zip-code)	Returns a maximum of a 20-character uppercase state name corresponding to a five-digit ZIP code argument.
ZIPNAMEL(arg)	Returns a maximum of a 20-character mixed uppercase and lowercase state name corresponding to a five-digit ZIP code argument.
ZIPSTATE(arg)	Returns a two-character uppercase state postal code corresponding to a five-digit ZIP code argument.

Table 3-15. Statistical Functions

FUNCTION	DESCRIPTION
CSS(arg, arg, ...)	Returns the corrected sum of squares of the nonmissing arguments where a minimum of two numeric arguments are required. The keyword OF may be used to specify a variable list by preceding the list of arguments.
CV(arg, arg, ...)	Returns the coefficient of variation of the nonmissing arguments where a minimum of two numeric arguments are required. The keyword OF may be used to specify a variable list by preceding the list of arguments.
KURTOSIS(arg, arg, ...)	Returns the fourth moment of the nonmissing arguments using a minimum of four numeric arguments. The keyword OF may be used to specify a variable list by preceding the list of arguments.
MAX(arg, arg, ...)	Returns the largest of the nonmissing arguments using a minimum of two numeric arguments. The keyword OF may be used to specify a variable list by preceding the list of arguments.
MIN(arg, arg, ...)	Returns the smallest of the nonmissing arguments where a minimum of two numeric arguments are required. The keyword OF may be used to specify a variable list by preceding the list of arguments.
MEAN(arg, arg, ...)	Returns the average of the nonmissing arguments using a minimum of one numeric argument. The keyword OF may be used to specify a variable list by preceding the list of arguments.
MISSING(expression)	Returns a value that indicates whether the expression contains a missing.
N(arg, arg, ...)	Returns the number of nonmissing values in the list of arguments where a minimum of one argument is required. The keyword OF may be used to specify a variable list by preceding the list of arguments.

Table 3-15. Statistical Functions (Continued)

FUNCTION	DESCRIPTION
NMISS(arg, arg, ...)	Returns the number of missing values where a minimum of one numeric argument is required. The keyword OF may be used to specify a variable list by preceding the list of arguments.
ORDINAL(count, arg, arg, ...)	Returns the largest value from part of the list of arguments where a minimum of two numeric arguments are required. The count value indicates the number of arguments in the list. The keyword OF may be used to specify a variable list by preceding the list of arguments.
RANGE(arg, arg, ...)	Returns the difference between the largest and smallest nonmissing numeric arguments where a minimum of two numeric arguments are required. The keyword OF may be used to specify a variable list by preceding the list of arguments.
SKEWNESS(arg, arg, ...)	Returns the skewness (direction) statistic of the nonmissing arguments where a minimum of three numeric arguments are required. The keyword OF may be used to specify a variable list by preceding the list of arguments.
STD(arg, arg, ...)	Returns the square root of the arithmetic average of the squares of the deviations from the mean in a frequency distribution where a minimum of two numeric arguments are required. The keyword OF may be used to specify a variable list by preceding the list of arguments.
STDERR(arg, arg, ...)	Returns the standard error of the mean of nonmissing numeric arguments where a minimum of two arguments are required. The keyword OF may be used to specify a variable list by preceding the list of arguments.
SUM(arg, arg, ...)	Returns the result from adding nonmissing numbers together where a minimum of two arguments are required. The keyword OF may be used to specify a variable list by preceding the list of arguments.
USS(arg, arg, ...)	Returns the uncorrected sum of squares of nonmissing numeric arguments where a minimum of two arguments are required. The keyword OF may be used to specify a variable list by preceding the list of arguments.
VAR(arg, arg, ...)	Returns the square of the standard deviation (or variance) of nonmissing numeric arguments where a minimum of two arguments are required. The keyword OF may be used to specify a variable list by preceding the list of arguments.

Table 3-16. Trigonometric and Hyperbolic Functions

FUNCTION	DESCRIPTION
ARCOS(arg)	Returns the arccosine (inverse cosine) of a numeric argument in radians. The argument value must be between –1 and 1.
ARSIN(arg)	Returns the arcsine (inverse sine) of a numeric argument in radians. The argument value must be between –1 and 1.
ATAN(arg)	Returns the arctangent (inverse tangent) of a numeric argument in radians.
COS(arg)	Returns the cosine of a numeric argument where the argument is specified in radians.
COSH(arg)	Returns the hyperbolic cosine of a numeric argument.
SIN(arg)	Returns the sine of a numeric argument where the argument is specified in radians.
SINH(arg)	Returns the hyperbolic sine of a numeric argument.
TAN(arg)	Returns the tangent of a numeric argument where the argument is specified in Radians and is not an odd multiple of Π/2.
TANH(arg)	Returns the hyperbolic tangent of a numeric argument.

14 Exploring truncation functions

Truncation functions extract specific kinds of information from a numeric value. Table 3-17 shows several truncation functions with a brief description of each.

15 Exploring Web tool functions

Table 3-18 shows several Web tool functions and gives a brief description of the tasks each performs.

Table 3-17. Truncation Functions

FUNCTION	DESCRIPTION
CEIL(arg)	Returns the smallest integer that is greater than or equal to the numeric argument.
FLOOR(arg)	Returns the largest integer that is less than or equal to the numeric argument.
FUZZ(arg)	Returns the nearest integer if the numeric value is within 1E-12 of the integer. Otherwise it returns the argument.
INT(arg)	Returns the integer portion of a numeric argument truncating the decimal portion.
ROUND(arg,round-off)	Returns a nonnegative numeric value rounded to the nearest round-off unit where the default round-off unit (if omitted) is 1.
TRUNC(number,length)	Returns a truncated numeric value specified by length by padding the truncated value with 0s (zeros).

Table 3-18. Web Tool Functions

FUNCTION	DESCRIPTION
HTMLDECODE(arg)	Returns a decoded string using HTML numeric character references or HTML character entity references.
HTMLENCODE(arg)	Returns an encoded string using HTML character entity references.
URLDECODE(arg)	Returns a decoded string using the URL escape syntax.
URLENCODE(arg)	Returns an encoded string using the URL escape syntax.

Program Testing

This section includes tips on how to properly test SAS program code to help reduce the risks often associated with programs and computer systems. Because testing plays such an integral part in the development of a well-written program, every SAS user should take the necessary time to review these simple but essential tips. You'll learn the steps involved in a comprehensive testing process, who should be involved in the testing process, the various types of problems that can crop up during testing, and what type of test objectives and strategies should be considered.

Because program testing is frequently associated with debugging, users should also review the tips in the next section, "Program Debugging."

1 Understanding the program testing process

It goes without question that any program or piece of code needs to be tested. Without proper testing, there is a greater likelihood that a program will fail or not perform according to requirements. To abate the prospect of failure, Table 3-19 identifies the minimum steps to incorporate in a comprehensive testing process.

Table 3-19. Program Testing Process

ACTION	DESCRIPTION
Devise a plan	A *plan* begins with establishing clear and concise objectives about what it is you are trying to achieve. To provide a frame of reference for the test conditions, a plan should consist of a brief description of the inputs, outputs, and functions of the program or application being tested. It should also contain a description of each test, the rationale for performing the test, who will be responsible for carrying out each test, how each test will be performed and evaluated, and the methods of determining whether the test is a success or failure.
Execute the plan	Bring everyone up to speed in understanding the objectives of the plan, including conducting any necessary training. Then execute the plan.
Verify the results	Determine whether tests are progressing according to the plan and if the expected results are being achieved. Compare the results of the tests with the plan's objectives.
Take corrective action	If verification efforts reveal that results of tests are not what was expected, develop steps to take corrective action.

2 Testing participants

Every effort should be made to involve individuals critical to the application. The following participants should be involved in the testing process of major program—if not all programs.

- Designer
- Developer
- Programmer
- Tester
- Management
- End-user
- Customer and/or client
- Auditor

3 Programming errors and their causes

Numerous problems can result from programming-related errors. Some of the leading causes for programming errors include

- Incomplete or erroneous decision-making capabilities
- Program logic that does not conform to user specifications or requirements
- Incomplete or invalid edit check criteria causing observations (records) to be processed with incomplete data.

4 Understanding the purpose of testing

The purpose of testing is to identify potential problems (defects) in a program during the development process, validate that a program and/or application works according to user, customer, and organizational requirements, and correct any problems before they occur.

5 Exploring defects in programs

A program defect is caused by deviating from requirements and can result in user, customer, and/or organizational dissatisfaction. The most common types of defects built into a program include the following:

- Requirements specified by users incorrectly
- Requirements interpreted by IS incorrectly
- Program design does not achieve specified requirements
- Coding problem does not meet specifications
- Program instruction is miscoded or misused
- By correcting an error, the correction itself introduces additional defects
- The test detects an error in the program that is not an error or fails to detect an error when one exists.

6 Determining if a program defect will result in a failure

There are three categories of defects: wrong, missing, and extra. Defects associated with the *wrong* category involve specifications that have been implemented incorrectly. *Missing* defects involve a requirement that was desired but was not built into the completed program and/or application. *Extra* defects involve building a requirement into the program and/or application that was not specified or requested.

7 Exploring problems related to data

Data-related problems often result in problems for the program, application, customer or client, end-user, and technical staff. Because data is important to the decision-making process, its poor quality can severely affect computer-directed activities. The following items are things that should be watched for:

- Incomplete data used by programs.
- Missing values generated as a result of performing computations.
- Incorrect data used by programs.
- Outdated data being introduced and processed by programs.

8 Exploring the types of testing a program should endure

Several types of tests should be performed on a program before placing it in production. Table 3-20 identifies these tests.

9 Understanding test categories

There are several categories of tests: unit, integration, system, regression, and acceptance. *Unit* tests are designed to test a standalone program or unit of code. *Integration* tests are designed to test a group of programs to verify data and control are passed between programs correctly. *System* tests are designed to test whether the components of the system (combined programs) successfully function together. *Regression* tests are designed to test whether no unwanted changes were introduced during the change process. *Acceptance* tests are designed to ensure that the program and/or system meet the requirements of the user, customer, and organization.

10 Exploring test objectives and test strategies

A test strategy establishes the objectives for the test process and reduces the risks often associated with programs and computer systems. A comprehensive test strategy should involve determining the rankings of test objectives as well as which ones to use. In Table 3-21, representative samples of commonly used test objectives are identified.

Table 3-20. Types of Program Testing

ACTION	DESCRIPTION
Syntactical	Tests are designed to test whether organizational or departmental requirements (standards) have been used in the writing of program code.
Functional	Tests are designed to test the business requirements and determine that the program is doing what it was intended to do correctly.
Structural	Tests are designed to test the program and/or system architecture and determine that the program was implemented correctly.
Black-box	Tests are designed to test the data-driven capabilities of the program and are generally conducted without knowledge of how the program was constructed.
White-box	Tests are designed to test the program's logic and are conducted with knowledge of internal code and structure.

Table 3-21. Test Objectives and Test Strategies

TEST OBJECTIVE	DESCRIPTION
Access Control	Verify that program and application component resources are guarded against accidental and intentional misuse, modification, destruction, and disclosure.
Audit Trail	Verify that program and application components provide adequate and sufficient reports to substantiate processing accuracy, completeness, and timeliness.
Authorization	Assure that data is processed with intended purpose and no usage violation has occurred.
Compliance	Verify that program and application components are designed according to organizational policies, standards, and procedures.
Contingency	Assure that detailed step-by-step procedures are in place in the event of problems.
Correctness	Verify that the data being entered, processed, and output by program and application components is accurate and complete.
Data Integrity	Assure that program and application components use the correct input data and that the data is stored and retrieved correctly.
Ease of Use	Verify that manual and automated systems are easy to install, configure, and operate by anyone using the program and/or application.
Integration	Assure that program and application components can be integrated with other components in their processing environment.
Maintainability	Verify that program and application components can be located and fixed quickly.
Performance	Assure program and application components utilize optimal computing resources to perform its desired functions.
Portability	Verify that program and application components are transferable from one hardware and/or software environment to another.
Processing Continuity	Assure that necessary procedures and backup information are available to recover during periods of downtime.
Reliability	Verify that program and application components will perform their intended function over extended periods of time.
Service Levels	Verify that program and application components achieve their desired results within an acceptable time frame.

Program Debugging

This section includes tips on how to go about debugging a SAS program to help rid those pesky syntax, data, system, and logic-related problems that often occur during the development of a program. Because debugging plays such an integral part in the creation of a well-written program, every SAS user should take the necessary time to review these simple but essential tips. You'll learn the various types of errors that can occur in a program, how to check for and correct syntax errors, data, system, and logic errors, and much more.

Because program debugging is frequently associated with testing, users should also review the tips in the previous section, "Program Testing."

1 Reading the SAS Log to aid in error detection

The SAS Log displays important information about a program and the SAS environment. It assists in solving program-related problems by providing the following information:

- The program statements that were executed

- Important notes or information about a program

- The SAS data sets that were read and created

- The number of lines read from an external input file

- The number of observations and variables that were read and written

- Syntax, warning, and data messages

- The time and memory used by each program step.

2 Understanding SAS software usage errors

Usage errors, as you may be already aware, cause the SAS System to stop processing, produce warnings, or produce unexpected results. There are four types of usage errors: 1) Syntax, 2) Data, 3) System-related, and 4) Programming (Logic).

3 Violating syntax

Syntax errors are a result of violating one of the rules of syntax (discussed in Chapter 1, "The Basics"). The Supervisor stops processing the current program step, passing control to the following step or, if one does not exist, stops processing altogether. Common causes for this type of error are misspelled keywords, missing semi-colons, data set and/or variable names that are too long, or an invalid character as the first position.

4 Checking for syntax errors

It is a good idea to check for syntax errors before processing data in a program. To check for syntax, add the following OPTIONS statement to the first line of your program:

Code:

```
OPTIONS OBS=0 NOREPLACE;
```

The OBS=0 option tells the SAS System not to process any observations, and the NOREPLACE option prevents the replacement of SAS data sets with empty ones. Once your program's syntax is correct, you can change the preceding options statement to the following and run your program again:

Code:

```
OPTIONS OBS=MAX REPLACE;
```

The OBS=MAX option tells the SAS System to process the maximum number of observations, and the REPLACE option allows the replacement of SAS data sets with new ones.

5 Warnings, warnings, and more warnings

Warnings are less severe than syntax errors, because a program will continue to run with one or more warnings. Warnings are simply messages that something in your program (for example, statement spelling) is not quite right. The result is that the SAS System may have assumed something such as the spelling of a keyword that you may or may not have meant. Always verify each warning to ensure that the assumed action performed by the SAS System is the correct one.

6 Using the Enhanced Editor to alert you to coding problems

The Enhanced Editor combines the power of the Program Editor in the SAS Display Manager System with a set of visual aids to help write and debug SAS programs. The Enhanced Editor is only available when using the SAS System interactively. It identifies coding problems by color-coding program elements such as SAS keywords, numeric and character strings, dates, and a vast complement of other programming constructs.

7 Enabling and Disabling the Enhanced Editor

The Enhanced Editor can be activated by selecting **View▶Enhanced Editor** from the pull-down menus or by specifying the **WEDIT** command. Multiple instances of the Enhanced Editor can be opened at the same time by specifying the **WEDEIT** command the number of times needed.

To disable an open Enhanced Editor window, specify the **CLOSE** command or click the **Close** button located in the upper right-hand corner of the window.

8 Enabling the Enhanced Editor

The Enhanced Editor is enabled during a SAS session by specifying the option **ENHANCEDEDITOR** at SAS invocation or in the configuration file.

9 Checking for coding errors with the Enhanced Editor

The Enhanced Editor enables users to check program code for possible errors by color-coding program components. Color-coding provides a visual aid that makes finding coding problems easier. For example, if the keyword **RUN;** was misspelled as **RUM;**, the incorrect spelling would be color-coded as an error by applying a red font.

10 Opening the Enhanced Editor Options window

Before the Enhanced Editor Options window can be opened, make sure the Enhanced Editor window is the active window. Then select **Tools►Options►Enhanced Editor…** from the pull-down menus as illustrated in the following tips.

11 Customizing Enhanced Editor general options

Once the Enhanced Editor Options window is opened, two tabs are displayed: General and Appearance. **General** options control how the Enhanced Editor works.

12 Customizing Enhanced Editor Appearance options

Appearance options control the foreground and background colors, and font styles used by program components. Modify the settings you want to change and click the **OK** button when finished.

13 Opening Enhanced Editor Keyboard shortcuts

Before the Enhanced Editor Options window can be opened, make sure the Enhanced Editor window is the active window. Then, select **Tools►Options►Enhanced Editor Keys** from the pull-down menus. The Enhanced Editor navigation keyboard shortcuts are discussed in the next tip.

14 Exploring Enhanced Editor navigation keyboard shortcuts

The Enhanced Editor provides a number of shortcuts to help find coding errors in your programs. Table 3-22 illustrates many of these keyboard shortcuts.

Table 3-22. Enhanced Editor Navigation Keyboard Shortcuts

KEYBOARD SHORTCUT	DESCRIPTION
Ctrl + G	Go to line.
Arrow Down	Move cursor down.
Page Down	Move cursor down a page.
Arrow Left	Move cursor left.
Arrow Right	Move cursor right.
Ctrl + Home	Move cursor to beginning of document.
Home	Move cursor to beginning of line.
Ctrl + End	Move cursor to end of document.
End	Move cursor to end of line.
Ctrl + [<or > Ctrl +]	Move cursor to matching brace/parentheses.
Alt + Right	Move cursor to next case change.
Ctrl + Right	Move cursor to next word start.
Alt + Left	Move cursor to previous case change.
Ctrl + Left	Move cursor to previous word start.
Up	Move cursor up.
Page Up	Move cursor up a page.

Table 3-22. Enhanced Editor Navigation Keyboard Shortcuts (Continued)

KEYBOARD SHORTCUT	DESCRIPTION
Alt + Up	Move cursor to the first visible line.
Alt + Down	Move cursor to the last visible line.
Ctrl + Up	Scroll screen down.
Ctrl + Down	Scroll screen up.

15 Understanding data-related errors

Data errors are a result of defining a variable with incorrect attributes. Although processing continues in the current program step, the result may be the assignment of missing or null values. For example, if the Supervisor encounters character data when a variable has been defined as a numeric, it issues a warning message and sets the data value to missing. Data truncation or rounding frequently occurs when defining character data as a numeric variable or defining a variable with a length attribute smaller than the actual value.

16 Understanding system-related errors

System-related errors are a result of incorrectly specifying a SAS System option or not knowing your installation's default SAS System options. The Supervisor may or may not issue a warning message, depending on the type of error.

Leading causes for this type of error are the specification of an incorrect *pagesize* (vertical page length dimension), an incorrect *linesize* (horizontal page length dimension), or not realizing that the OBS=MAX system option has been hard-coded with a finite value. This problem gains greater importance as larger applications access data sets with hundreds of thousands or millions of observations.

17 Understanding programming (logic) errors

Programming (logic) errors are frequently a result of implementing "unsound" or "incorrect" logic conditions. This type of error is generated at time of execution and can be difficult to see, because Log messages related to the problem will be nonexistent. Leading causes can be from improper use of OR, AND, and NOT operators. Another cause, and often the most difficult to find, is not adhering to specifications correctly or not defining the requirements of a task in great enough detail.

18 Getting the SAS interpreter to recognize SAS statements

Has the SAS interpreter ever stopped responding to program steps that have been submitted? If you find yourself in this position, then the problem may be related to a coding error rather than a SAS product bug. Begin by checking your code for the presence of "unbalanced" single- or double-quotes, especially if you have used one or more TITLE or FOOTNOTE statements. The persistent "R" that is displayed at the bottom of the SAS Display Manager window may mean that the SAS interpreter is confused because it is stuck inside an unbalanced quoted string, comment, or Macro function. To resolve the problem you can try one of the following techniques:

- Submit the following sequence of characters: *))%*'"))*/;

- If that doesn't work, submit a **%MEND;** statement to close any open Macro definitions.

- If the problem still persists, submit a **QUIT;** statement to terminate any interactive procedures that may have been initiated.

- If all else fails, terminate the SAS session and start again.

Processing Large Files

This section includes tips on processing large files. Because of the potential abuse of system resources, including CPU, I/O, memory, and storage, users should be especially aware of available programming techniques while processing large files. You'll learn how to avoid the pitfalls associated with sorting: when to and when not to sort, efficiently create subsets, and when to create and use summary statistics.

Users interested in processing efficiencies should also review the tips in Chapter 7, "Efficiency and Performance."

1 Avoiding problems related to sorting

It's been said by many a SAS user that the SORT procedure is one of the easiest procedures to use and one of the most abused. This couldn't be truer. The trick to performing successful sorts is to first and foremost understand what your objective is. Then spend time planning how to best achieve those objectives while using the fewest possible resources. Here are a few guidelines to use whenever a sort process is involved:

- Determine whether the data in a large data set is already in sorted order. If it is, then a sort may not be necessary.

- Determine whether the data is in a particular sort order by specifying the BY statement in a DATA or PROC step (other than the SORT procedure). If the data isn't in the desired sort order specified in the BY statement, a runtime error is produced.

- Specify the NOTSORTED option when the observations with the same BY value are grouped but the observations within the group are in unsorted order.

- Determine whether any installation or resource constraints (for example, shortage of space) exist that could prevent a data set from being sorted.

- Understand the requirements of the DATA or PROC step that you plan to use as the input data set. Many procedures, including all of the summary procedures, don't need data in sorted order because they produce results in sorted order after summaries are produced anyway.

- Consider using a tag sort if a sort is needed. When a data set is too large to fit in memory, then tag sorting may be more efficient because it requires less temporary storage space and memory. Specify the TAGSORT option in the SORT procedure statement.

- Consider only sorting the observations and variables that are needed to satisfy the conditions of the analysis.

If the purpose of sorting is specifically subsetting, then I recommend that you consider other approaches to perform a subset, including using a WHERE= data set option in a SET statement.

2 Reversing the order of a data set without sorting

Occasionally a data set may be in the exact opposite order as needed. When this is the case, consider using the following DATA step logic to reverse the order of the observations without having to expend the resources to execute a SORT procedure.

Don't forget to code the STOP; statement—otherwise, your job will run forever.

Code:

```
DATA REVERSE_ORDER;
 DO I=NOBS TO 1 BY -1;
   SET MOVIES(KEEP=TITLE RATING)
       POINT=I NOBS=NOBS;
   OUTPUT;
 END;
 STOP;
RUN;
PROC PRINT NOOBS;
RUN;
```

Results:

Title	Rating
Titanic	PG-13
The Wizard of Oz	G
The Terminator	R
The Hunt for Red October	PG
Star Wars	PG
Silence of the Lambs	R
Scarface	R
Rocky	PG
Poltergeist	PG
National Lampoon's Vacation	PG-13
Michael	PG-13
Lethal Weapon	R
Jurassic Park	PG-13
Jaws	PG
Ghost	PG-13
Forrest Gump	PG-13
Dressed to Kill	R
Dracula	R
Coming to America	R
Christmas Vacation	PG-13
Casablanca	PG
Brave Heart	R

3 Creating subsets

When the number of observations and variables contained in a data set are excessively large, you may consider selectively sorting only the observations and variables that are needed to satisfy the conditions of the analysis. This will eliminate the expense associated with sorting unwanted observations and variables. Use the **WHERE=** and **KEEP=** data set options to reduce the size of a data set.

*Be sure to specify an **OUT=** data set with the SORT procedure to avoid accidentally writing over the "master" data set.*

4 Dividing data in BY-groups

Sorting large data sets can cause havoc on computer systems' available resources. When the creation of subsets still doesn't reduce the size of your data sets to a manageable size, consider dividing up your data in BY-groups using DATA step logic. This will enable you to create smaller subset data sets that can then be sorted individually and, once sorted in the order needed, concatenated back into the larger data set for processing.

5 Replacing subsetting IFs with WHEREs

Subsetting IF and WHERE statements are used to subset data. Although they produce identical results, each statement subsets data distinctively different from the other. A subsetting IF, when used with a data set, reads each observation into the PDV and then evaluates whether the user-defined condition or expression is true. This causes a considerable amount of additional I/O processing to occur.

The most flexible and efficient way to subset data set observations is with a WHERE statement or WHERE= data set option. Because it evaluates a user-defined condition before reading the observation into the PDV, it is the method of choice for SAS users in the know. A WHERE statement or WHERE= data set option can be specified to subset observations in either a DATA or PROC step.

To illustrate the application of a WHERE statement and WHERE= data set option, two examples, each producing the same results, follow. When all things are equal, the choice of approaches is yours to make. But it's generally advisable to use the method that streamlines the code while minimizing the amount of resource requirements it takes during program execution. In the first example, "PG"-rated movies are selected from a SAS data set using a WHERE= data set option in a SET statement. Although this approach produces the same results as the next two examples, it does require the expenditure of considerably more I/O because data must be read and written not once (as in the next two examples) but twice. In the second example, a WHERE= data set option is specified to subset "PG"-rated movies in the PRINT procedure.

Code:

```
DATA PG_MOVIES;
 SET MOVIES (WHERE=(RATING='PG'));
RUN;
PROC PRINT;
RUN;
```

Code:

```
PROC PRINT
       DATA=MOVIES (WHERE=(RATING='PG'))
       NOOBS
       N;
RUN;
```

6 Creating summary statistics

While data analysis can be performed from large data sets, I recommended you use, when possible, a small data set containing summary statistics instead. This will probably involve creating the summary data set, and from that the analysis be performed. This way, the large data set is processed only once in the creation of the data set containing the summary statistics.

When the type of information desired includes frequency counts, correlations, means, standard deviations, moments, and other numeric summaries, users can streamline a process many times by creating summary statistics and storing them in a smaller data set. The objective is to use the summary statistics in the smaller data set for further analysis. The first example, illustrated in Code Listing 3-1 with results shown in Results 3-1, uses the SUMMARY procedure to create summary statistics from a larger data set containing continuous numeric values. The second example, illustrated in Code Listing 3-2 with results shown in Results 3-2, uses the summary results from the SUMMARY procedure to subset "Comedy" movies.

Code Listing 3-1:

```
PROC SUMMARY DATA=MOVIES NWAY;
 VAR LENGTH;
 CLASS RATING CATEGORY;
 OUTPUT OUT=SUMMARY
        MEAN=LENGTH N=N_LENGTH;
RUN;
```

Results 3-1:

Rating	Category	_TYPE_	_FREQ_	LENGTH	N_LENGTH
G	Adventure	3	1	101.000	1
PG	Action Adventure	3	3	126.667	3
PG	Action Sci-Fi	3	1	124.000	1
PG	Drama	3	1	103.000	1
PG	Horror	3	1	115.000	1
PG-13	Action	3	1	127.000	1
PG-13	Comedy	3	2	97.500	2
PG-13	Drama	3	2	124.000	2
PG-13	Drama Romance	3	2	160.500	2
R	Action Adventure	3	1	177.000	1
R	Action Cops & Robber	3	2	140.000	2
R	Action Sci-Fi	3	1	108.000	1
R	Comedy	3	1	116.000	1
R	Drama Mysteries	3	1	105.000	1
R	Drama Suspense	3	1	118.000	1
R	Horror	3	1	130.000	1

Code Listing 3-2:

```
DATA ANALYSIS;
 SET SUMMARY;
 IF UPCASE(CATEGORY) = "COMEDY";
RUN;
PROC PRINT NOOBS;
RUN;
```

Results 3-2:

Rating	Category	_TYPE_	_FREQ_	LENGTH	N_LENGTH
G-13	Comedy	3	2	97.5	2
R	Comedy	3	1	116.0	1

Documentation

This section includes tips on developing documentation for SAS programs, pieces of code, and abstract coding constructs. Documentation serves an important function in programs. It provides valuable information about a program as well as its purpose and usage, including sample input and output. It also provides useful programmer and maintenance information, serving as a history of what has been added, changed, or deleted in the program.

1 Documenting a program with comments

Comments are a handy way of adding important documentation to a program. They provide valuable information for everyone that handles the program as well as a history related to its life. It provides a valuable service to IT and end-user departments everywhere describing the complexities of a process, a piece of code, or some other abstract coding construct that can be used to enhance its longevity and educate other users. Program comments come in three flavors:

- COMMENT statement

- Flower-box comment

- In-stream (delimited) comment

Each form of comment is illustrated in the next sections.

Comment statement

A comment statement begins with the word COMMENT and ends with a semicolon ";". Comments of this type cannot contain semicolons, unless the comment itself is enclosed within single- or double-quotes.

Code:

```
COMMENT MOVIES INFO;
```

Flower-box comment

A simple flower-box comment begins with an asterisk "*" and ends with a semicolon ";". Comments of this type cannot contain embedded semicolons.

Code:

```
* MOVIES INFORMATION;
```

A more elaborate flower-box comment, shown in Code Listing 3-3, is created to make code documentation easier to see and read (notice the resemblance to a flower-box.) Comments of this type cannot contain embedded semicolons.

Code Listing 3-3:

```
*************************************************************;
**** PROGRAM NAME..: MOVIES.SAS                         ****;
**** DESCRIPTION...: THIS PROGRAM READS A NON-SAS FILE  ****;
****                 CONTAINING MOVIE INFORMATION.      ****;
**** DATE WRITTEN..: 3-AUGUST-2002                      ****;
**** AUTHOR........: KIRK PAUL LAFLER                   ****;
****                 SOFTWARE INTELLIGENCE CORPORATION  ****;
**** MODIFICATIONS:                                     ****;
**** NONE.                                              ****;
*************************************************************;
```

In-stream comment

An in-stream comment can be written on a line by itself, or within statements. If semi-colons are used within a comment of this type, the SAS interpreter ignores them.

2 Using comments in a program

Any number of comments can be added to a program to help explain complex or tricky logic. SAS users aren't confined to using only one style (out of the three: COMMENT, flower-box, or in-stream) either—any combination of styles can and should be used.

3 Understanding that comments are non-executable

Comments are non-executable when placed in a program. A comment is a non-executable statement and therefore ignored by the SAS interpreter. This means the SAS System ignores during processing any text when properly used as a comment.

4 Inserting in-stream comments

When using in-stream comments, know the particulars of the host operating system you will be operating under. For example, on OS/MVS (mainframe) operating systems, a /* in column 1 and 2 is interpreted as the end of the SAS job. (This is a far cry from a non-executable in-stream comment!) So it is advisable to get into the habit of coding a /* beginning in columns 3 and 4. When in doubt, always consult the specific documentation of your host system for further information.

5 Saving labels and formats in SAS data sets

Programmers are always looking for ways to save time, especially during crunch-time. One technique that I've found useful is to assign variable labels and formats with all my SAS data sets. It's a fairly easy process, although it does require a little extra time initially to setup. But the rewards of having assigned them generally outweigh any initial time and cost in their creation. I like to think of it as part of the data preparation process—it's an approach that rewards over an over.

Sunil Gupta of Gupta Programming offers the following suggestions on using labels and formats: "Labels and formats are stored with many of our important SAS data sets to minimize processing time. A reason for using this technique is that many popular procedures use stored formats and labels as they produce output, eliminating the need to assign them in each individual step. This provides added incentives and value for programmers and end-users, especially since reporting requirements are usually time critical." The following example shows how a LABEL statement can be assigned to two variables in a data set.

Code:

```
DATA MOVIES;
 INFILE 'RAW-DATA-FILE' MISSOVER;
 INPUT @1 TITLE $15.
       @30 RENTED 10.;
 LABEL TITLE  = 'Movie Title'
       RENTED = 'Date Movie Rented';
RUN;
```

The following example illustrates how a FORMAT statement can be assigned to a numeric date value.

Code:

```
DATA MOVIES;
 INFILE 'RAW-DATA-FILE' MISSOVER;
 INPUT @30 RENTED MMDDYY10.;
 FORMAT RENTED MMDDYY10.;
RUN;
```

Summary

In this chapter, you learned a considerable number of valuable tips and techniques for gaining greater control over the many powerful features found in the DATA step programming language. As a full-featured programming language, it can be used for virtually any task or application. Novice, intermediate, and advanced users have a well-defined language that supports all the popular language constructs, such as string and logic processing, input-output access, arrays, indexes, tables, and so much more. You also learned tips and techniques for effectively testing and debugging programs, processing large files efficiently, and documenting program code or pieces of code.

In the next chapter, "Data Manipulation," you'll discover popular techniques for subsetting data, reshaping columns of data, and sending output to SAS data sets. Even if you're not a programmer, you'll find the tips and numerous examples simple to understand and to implement.

CHAPTER 4
Data Manipulation

THE ABILITY TO manipulate data in the Base SAS software plays a very important role in the preparation of data for data analysis. This chapter presents tips directly related to changing the way your data looks without changing the data itself. You'll learn essential techniques on the different ways of subsetting data, reshaping columns of data, and sending output to SAS data sets.

In this chapter, you'll learn how to

- Create new SAS data sets with a subsetting IF and WHERE
- Use SAS operators to subset data
- Use SAS statements such as IF-THEN/ELSE, DELETE, and SELECT to subset data
- Use System options to subset data
- Reshape columns of data with KEEP= / DROP= data set options
- Reshape data with a SET statement
- Reshape data by using the APPEND procedure
- Reshape data with multiple SET statements
- Reshape data by interleaving SAS data sets
- Reshape data by merging two or more SAS data sets
- Reshape data by joining in the SQL procedure
- Send output results to a SAS data set
- Use a variety of summary procedures to send output to a SAS data set

Subsetting Data

This section includes tips on how to subset data either by restricting the number of observations, variables, or both. You'll learn how to subset your data quickly and easily with these handy data manipulation tips.

1 Creating new data sets with a subset

New SAS data sets can be created from one or more external files or existing SAS data sets. When a data set is a subset, it contains part or all of the records or observations from the original external file or data set. Subsets generally contain fewer records or observations than the original external file or SAS data set they are derived from.

2 Subsetting IF

A subsetting **IF** statement is used to select one or more rows of data from an external raw data file or SAS data set. When a record from a raw data file is read into the input buffer (memory) or an observation from an existing SAS data set into the program data vector (PDV), the subsetting IF evaluates the user-defined condition to determine whether the record should be processed or not. In the following example, data is read from an external file into memory and saved as a subset in the G_RATED data set if it's a "G"-rated movie.

Code:

```
DATA G_RATED;
  INFILE "c:\movies.dat" MISSOVER;
  INPUT @1 TITLE  $15.
        @16 LENGTH 3.
        @19 RATING $5.;
  IF UPCASE(RATING)= "G";
RUN;
```

A subsetting IF statement can also be specified when processing existing SAS data sets. In the next example only "G"-rated movies are subset from an existing MOVIES data set and written to the G_RATED data set. Although this example produces the desirable results, it's not as efficient as using a WHERE statement, or a WHERE= data set option, in a DATA step.

Code:

```
DATA G_RATED;
  SET MOVIES;
  IF UPCASE(RATING)= "G";
RUN;
```

3 Subsetting observations with a WHERE= data set option

Using a **WHERE=** data set option is an efficient way to subset SAS data set observations. It evaluates whether a condition is true prior to reading an observation into memory (Program Data Vector—PDV for short). Unlike a subsetting IF statement, a WHERE= data set option can be specified in both a DATA and PROC step.

✎ Verify the number of opened and closed parentheses match before running program.

Code:

```
PROC PRINT
    DATA=MOVIES
            (WHERE=(UPCASE(RATING="G")))
    NOOBS
    N;
RUN;
```

4 Subsetting observations with operators

SAS *operators* can be specified for subsetting purposes. Comparison, logical, and arithmetic operations can be used with subsetting IF, WHERE statements, and WHERE= data set options. Comparison operators, illustrated in Table 4-1, evaluate whether a relationship exists between two values.

Table 4-1. Comparison Operators

OPERATOR	DEFINITION
=	equal to
^=	not equal to
>	greater than
<	less than
>=	greater than or equal to
<=	less than or equal to

The comparison operator > (greater than) can be used to subset movies with a length greater than 120 minutes as follows.

Code:

```
DATA LONG_MOVIES;
 SET MOVIES(WHERE=(LENGTH > 120));
RUN;
```

Logical operators, shown in Table 4-2, provide a way to link one or more comparisons together.

Table 4-2. Logical Operators

OPERATOR	DEFINITION
&	and
|	or
^	not

The logical operator & (AND) can be used to combine the two comparisons RATING="PG" and LENGTH>120 to form a subset of long-playing "PG"- rated movies. Note: Users may notice that the following example could also be consolidated into a single PROC PRINT step, thereby reducing I/O resources.

Code:

```
DATA LONG_PG_MOVIES;
 SET MOVIES(KEEP=TITLE LENGTH RATING
         WHERE=(UPCASE(RATING)=
             "PG" AND LENGTH > 120));
RUN;
PROC PRINT NOOBS;
RUN;
```

Results:

Title	Length	Rating
Jaws	125	PG
Star Wars	124	PG
The Hunt for Red October	135	PG

If the moviegoer only cared about one of the two conditions being true, the following example could be constructed using the | (OR) operator. The resulting subset would contain "PG"-rated movies or long-playing movies of 121 minutes or longer, or both.

Code:

```
DATA LONG_PG_MOVIES;
 SET MOVIES(KEEP=TITLE LENGTH RATING
         WHERE=(UPCASE(RATING) = "PG"
              OR LENGTH > 120));
RUN;
PROC PRINT NOOBS;
RUN;
```

Results:

Title	Length	Rating
Brave Heart	177	R
Casablanca	103	PG
Dracula	130	R
Forrest Gump	142	PG-13
Ghost	127	PG-13
Jaws	125	PG
Jurassic Park	127	PG-13
Poltergeist	115	PG
Rocky	120	PG
Scarface	170	R
Star Wars	124	PG
The Hunt for Red October	135	PG
Titanic	194	PG-13

5 Subsetting observations with a DELETE statement

A **DELETE** statement can be used as a way of subsetting observations. It is most often used to specify a condition for excluding observations such as in an IF statement with a THEN clause. Since the DELETE statement physically deletes observations, take care when using it. In the first example a DELETE statement is specified without a condition resulting in the MOVIES_SUBSET data set being empty.

💣 *To avoid deleting all observations in the subset data set, specify a subsetting IF statement or SELECT blocks to conditionally control what observations are kept, as well as those that aren't.*

Code:

```
DATA MOVIES_SUBSET;
 SET MOVIES;
 DELETE;
RUN;
```

The majority of the time a DELETE statement is used with a conditional subsetting IF or SELECT block. In these situations observations are deleted when the user-defined condition is true. In the next example, movies with a "PG" and "R" rating are deleted.

Code:

```
DATA MOVIES_SUBSET;
 SET MOVIES;
 IF UPCASE(RATING) IN ("PG","R")
        THEN DELETE;
RUN;
```

6 Subsetting observations with IF-THEN/ELSE and OUTPUT

IF-THEN/ELSE and **OUTPUT** statements can be used together to subset observations. Three subset data sets are created in the next example: G_RATED, PG_RATED, and PG13_RATED, using IF-THEN/ELSE logic with OUTPUT statements to direct what observations are subset, as well as to what data set.

Code:

```
DATA G_RATED
    PG_RATED
    PG13_RATED;
SET MOVIES;
IF UPCASE(RATING) = "G"
    THEN OUTPUT G_RATED;
ELSE
IF UPCASE(RATING) = "PG"
    THEN OUTPUT PG_RATED;
ELSE
IF UPCASE(RATING) = "PG-13"
    THEN OUTPUT PG13_RATED;
RUN;
```

A look at the SAS Log shows how the observations from the MOVIES data set are distributed to each of the subset data sets.

SAS Log Results:

```
24    DATA G_RATED
25        PG_RATED
26        PG13_RATED;
27      SET MOVIES;
IF UPCASE(RATING) = "G"
      THEN OUTPUT G_RATED;
29      ELSE
IF UPCASE(RATING) = "PG"
      THEN OUTPUT PG_RATED;
31      ELSE
IF UPCASE(RATING) = "PG-13"
      THEN OUTPUT PG13_RATED;
33    RUN;

NOTE: There were 22 observations read
from the data set MOVIES.
NOTE: The data set WORK.G_RATED has
1 observations and 6 variables.
NOTE: The data set WORK.PG_RATED has
6 observations and 6 variables.
NOTE: The data set WORK.PG13_RATED has
7 observations and 6 variables.
```

7 Subsetting observations with OBS= and FIRSTOBS= data set options

Occasionally, subsets of data are produced by setting the **OBS=** and/or **FIRSTOBS=** data set options. Each option can be used separately or together. When used together, the subset is based on a sequence of observations rather than the values of one or more variables. The default setting for each option is OBS=MAX and FIRSTOBS=1. To override these default settings, one could form a subset selecting the first 100 observations. By setting OBS= some value informs the SAS System to process up to and including that observation.

Code:

```
DATA SUBSET_100;
 SET MOVIES(OBS=100);
RUN;
```

Next we will see how the FIRSTOBS= option can be used to inform the SAS System to begin subsetting data starting at the tenth observation.

Code:

```
DATA SUBSET_10;
 SET MOVIES(FIRSTOBS=10);
RUN;
```

In the next example, the OBS= and FIRSTOBS= options are used together to begin subsetting observations beginning at 7 and ending at 10 resulting in 4 observations.

✏️ *The OBS= option doesn't specify the total number of observations; it specifies the last observation number to include.*

Code:

```
DATA SUBSET;
 SET MOVIES(FIRSTOBS=7 OBS=10);
RUN;
```

These options can also be used to subset observations in procedures. The advantage of using these options this way is to prevent the creation of an intermediate data set. The subsetting occurs at the procedure level.

Code:

```
PROC PRINT DATA=MOVIES(FIRSTOBS=7 OBS=10);
RUN;
```

8 Subsetting external input data with OBS= and FIRSTOBS= options

Records from external input files can be selected anywhere in the file by using the FIRSTOBS= and OBS= options in the INFILE statement. When these options are specified, the subset is based on a sequence of observations rather than the values of one or more variables. For example, setting FIRSTOBS=3 and OBS=4 selects the third and fourth records from the input file, and skips all the rest.

Code:

```
DATA EXTERNAL_INPUT;
 INFILE CARDS FIRSTOBS=3 OBS=4 MISSOVER;
 INPUT TITLE $ 1-11 RATING $ 13-17;
CARDS;
Brave Heart R
Jaws       PG
Rocky      PG
Titanic    PG-13
;
```

```
RUN;
PROC PRINT NOOBS;
RUN;
```

Results:

```
TITLE      RATING

Rocky      PG
Titanic    PG-13
```

9 Subsetting observations with SELECT blocks and OUTPUT

A SELECT block uses WHEN conditions to evaluate observations. Combined with an OUTPUT statement, observations can be subset quite easily. In the next example, three subset data sets are created G_RATED, PG_RATED, and PG13_RATED using a SELECT block, and WHEN conditions combined with OUTPUT statements to direct what observations are subset. The OTHERWISE condition deletes any input records that don't satisfy the user-defined WHEN conditions.

Code:

```
DATA G_RATED
     PG_RATED
     PG13_RATED;
 SET MOVIES;
 SELECT;
   WHEN(UPCASE(RATING) = "G")
       OUTPUT G_RATED;
   WHEN(UPCASE(RATING) = "PG")
       OUTPUT PG_RATED;
   WHEN(UPCASE(RATING) = "PG-13")
       OUTPUT PG13_RATED;
   OTHERWISE DELETE;
 END;
RUN;
```

SAS Log Results:

```
45    DATA G_RATED
46         PG_RATED
47         PG13_RATED;
48      SET MOVIES;
49      SELECT;
WHEN(UPCASE(RATING) = "G")
        OUTPUT G_RATED;
WHEN(UPCASE(RATING) = "PG")
        OUTPUT PG_RATED;
WHEN(UPCASE(RATING) = "PG-13")
        OUTPUT PG13_RATED;
53      OTHERWISE DELETE;
54      END;
55    RUN;
```

```
NOTE: There were 22 observations read
from the data set MOVIES.
NOTE: The data set WORK.G_RATED has
1 observations and 6 variables.
NOTE: The data set WORK.PG_RATED has
6 observations and 6 variables.
NOTE: The data set WORK.PG13_RATED has
7 observations and 6 variables.
```

Reshaping Columns of Data

This section includes tips on the various techniques that are used to reshape columns of data from external files and SAS data sets. You'll learn quick and easy ways to subset variables and records from external input files and from SAS data sets. These handy data manipulation tips will let you prepare your data to satisfy even the most demanding data-analysis requirements.

1 Understanding what reshaping data means

Reshaping is the process of adding/decreasing observations or variables from a SAS data set. New SAS data sets can be created from one or more external files or existing data sets. A new data set subset based on a larger original data set or external file can be considered reshaping. Because subset data sets generally contain fewer observations and/or variables than the original external file or SAS data set(s), it's classified as being reshaped. The concept of reshaping also applies when variables are added to or dropped from a data set.

2 Subsetting variables from external data

New SAS data sets can be created from one or more external files or existing data sets. When a data set is created this way, it contains a subset of the original external file or data set. Subsets generally contain fewer variables than the original external file or SAS data set they are derived from.

3 Subsetting variables in a DATA step

The **KEEP=** or **DROP=** data set options can be used in a DATA step to limit the number of variables (subset) being processed in the step. The KEEP= data set option instructs the SAS System to retain the variables TITLE and RATING from the MOVIES data set.

Code:

```
DATA FAMILY_MOVIES;
 SET MOVIES(WHERE=(UPCASE(RATING)= "G")
         KEEP=TITLE RATING);
 CTR_FAMILY_MOVIES+1;
RUN;
```

Occasionally the number of variables being kept is too numerous to specify in a KEEP= data set option. In these cases I recommend using a DROP= data set option as in the following example, to remove the YEAR (year movie was made) variable.

Code:

```
DATA FAMILY_MOVIES;
 SET MOVIES
       (WHERE=(UPCASE(RATING)= "G")
             DROP=YEAR);
 CTR_FAMILY_MOVIES+1;
RUN;
```

4 Subsetting variables in a PROC step

The KEEP= or DROP= data set options are used in a DATA or PROC step to limit the number of variables (subset) being processed in the step. The KEEP= data set option instructs the SAS System to keep the variables TITLE and RATING from the MOVIES data set. The advantage of using these options in this way is to prevent the creation of an intermediate data set. The reshaping occurs at the procedure level.

Code:

```
PROC PRINT
         DATA=MOVIES(KEEP=TITLE RATING);
RUN;
```

Occasionally the number of variables being kept is too numerous to specify in a KEEP= data set option. In these cases I recommend using a DROP= data set option, as in the following example, to remove the YEAR (year movie was made) variable.

Code:

```
PROC PRINT
         DATA=MOVIES(DROP=YEAR);
RUN;
```

5 Creating unique variable subsets for individual data sets

Reshaping columns of data can sometimes involve outputting unique variable subsets to individual data sets. The KEEP= (or DROP=) data set option combined with the power of computing summary statistics is the technique that will be illustrated. By using this technique, a unique list of variables can be kept for each data set. For example, creating two unique subsets, one containing detail information and the second containing summary information, from one pass of the MOVIES data set, is a task frequently performed by users around the world. The final piece to effectively creating both unique subsets is the **END=** option in the SET statement. The END= signals the end of the data set, enabling the summary observation to be written to the SUMMARY data set.

Code:

```
DATA DETAIL(KEEP=TITLE LENGTH RATING)
     SUMMARY(KEEP=CTR_G CTR_PG
         AVG_LENGTH_G AVG_LENGTH_PG);
 SET MOVIES END=EOF;
 SELECT;
   WHEN(UPCASE(RATING) = "G") THEN DO;
       CTR_G+1;
       TOT_G+LENGTH;
   END;
   WHEN(UPCASE(RATING) = "PG") THEN DO;
       CTR_PG+1;
       TOT_PG+LENGTH;
   END;
```

```
    OTHERWISE;
  END;
OUTPUT DETAIL;
  IF EOF THEN DO;
     AVG_LENGTH_G=TOT_G / CTR_G;
     AVG_LENGTH_PG=TOT_PG / CTR_PG;
     OUTPUT SUMMARY;
  END;
RUN;
```

DETAIL Output:

Title	Length	Rating
Brave Heart	177	R
Casablanca	103	PG
Christmas Vacation	97	PG-13
Coming to America	116	R
Dracula	130	R
Dressed to Kill	105	R
Forrest Gump	142	PG-13
Ghost	127	PG-13
Jaws	125	PG
Jurassic Park	127	PG-13
Lethal Weapon	110	R
Michael	106	PG-13
National Lampoon's Vacation	98	PG-13
Poltergeist	115	PG
Rocky	120	PG
Scarface	170	R
Silence of the Lambs	118	R
Star Wars	124	PG
The Hunt for Red October	135	PG
The Terminator	108	R
The Wizard of Oz	101	G
Titanic	194	PG-13

SUMMARY Output:

CTR_G	CTR_PG	AVG_LENGTH_G	AVG_LENGTH_PG
1	6	101	120.333

6 Concatenating SAS data sets in the DATA step

Concatenating SAS data sets is the process of storing one observation one after another until all the data sets and their observations have been combined. Currently, the SAS System allows a maximum of 50 data sets to be concatenated together. The following example concatenates three data sets ("G," "PG," and "PG-13" movies) together creating a combined single data set called **COMBINED**. Observations are read and concatenated from each data set one at a time, and in the order specified, to data set COMBINED.

Code:

```
DATA COMBINED;
  SET G_RATED PG_RATED PG13_RATED;
RUN;
```

7 Concatenating SAS data sets with the APPEND procedure

Although more users apply the concatenation process using a DATA step (see previous tip), there are good reasons for using the **APPEND** procedure (discussed in more detail in Chapter 7, "Efficiency and Performance"). The APPEND procedure is designed to let users specify data sets for the BASE= and DATA= options. The **BASE=** option identifies the data set that observations will be receiving and storing concatenated observations. The **DATA=** option identifies the data set that will be providing one or more observations to be concatenated. The following example concatenates a smaller data set G_RATED containing "G"-rated movies to the MOVIES data set.

Code:

```
PROC APPEND BASE=MOVIES
            DATA=G_RATED;
RUN;
```

SAS Log Results:

```
8    PROC APPEND BASE=MOVIES
9                DATA=G_RATED;
10   RUN;

NOTE: Appending WORK.G_RATED to WORK.MOVIES.
NOTE: There were 1 observations read from ↵
the data set WORK.G_RATED.
NOTE: 1 observations added.
NOTE: The data set WORK.MOVIES has 23 ↵
observations and 6 variables.
```

8 Specifying the BASE= option in APPEND procedure

For maximum efficiency and speed, specify the larger of the two SAS data sets as the BASE= data set. Put another way, the smaller data set should be referenced by the DATA= option. The **APPEND** procedure positions its record pointer at the end of the BASE= data set. It thereby avoids having to read observations individually as it does the observations specified by the DATA= data set.

9 Creating the BASE= data set in the APPEND procedure

If the data set referenced by the BASE= data set does not exist, the APPEND procedure automatically creates it in the library (libref) specified. This means that the data set referenced by the BASE= option does not have to already exist.

10 Understanding how the BASE= option works

When the BASE= data set exists, each observation in the DATA= data set is appended one observation at a time. When the BASE= data set doesn't exist, a new data set is created, and the observations are copied.

11 Omitting the BASE= or DATA= option with the APPEND procedure

Whenever a libref is omitted when specifying the BASE= or DATA= data sets, the default library can be assumed to be the WORK library.

12 Using the FORCE option

When one or more variables in the input data set (DATA=) are not present in the output data set (BASE=), the FORCE option must be specified as an option on the PROC statement to prevent a syntax error.

13 Missing values in the APPEND procedure

When a variable in the BASE= dataset does not exist in the DATA= dataset, the variable is assigned a missing value for all added observations.

14 Renaming a BASE= data set

There is more than one way to rename a data set in the SAS System. When a BASE= data set has to be renamed, users should refrain from using a DATA step to create a new data set with the desired name. This tends to be less efficient because the DATA – SET convention (see "Concatenating SAS data sets in the DATA step") must read and write every observation in

Data Manipulation

each data set. This expends additional CPU and I/O resources.

A more efficient approach to renaming a BASE= data set is to use the **DATASETS** procedure. In the following example, a base data set is renamed from MOVIES to MOVIES_MSTR using the RENAME statement of PROC DATASETS.

Code:

```
PROC DATASETS LIBRARY=work;
  RENAME MOVIES = MOVIES_MSTR;
RUN;
```

15 Reshaping data with two SET statements

When two SET statements are specified in a DATA step, the objective is to pair the observations. This is occasionally performed for the purpose of joining one observation from the first data set with the first observation in the second data set, and so on. Processing continues in this way until one or more of the data sets runs out of observations. In the next example, illustrated in Code Listing 4-1 with output shown in Results 4-1, two SET statements are used to join "PG" and "PG-13" movies together.

Code Listing 4-1:

```
DATA SET_JOIN;
 SET PG_RATING(KEEP=TITLE RATING
            RENAME=(TITLE=PG_TITLE
       RATING=PG_RATING));
 SET PG13_RATING(KEEP=TITLE RATING
            RENAME=(TITLE=PG13_TITLE
       RATING=PG13_RATING));
RUN;
```

Results 4-1:

```
PG13_
PG_TITLE                 PG_RATING    PG13_TITLE                   RATING

Casablanca               PG           Christmas Vacation           PG-13
Jaws                     PG           Forrest Gump                 PG-13
Poltergeist              PG           Ghost                        PG-13
Rocky                    PG           Jurassic Park                PG-13
Star Wars                PG           Michael                      PG-13
The Hunt for Red October PG           National Lampoon's Vacation  PG-13
```

The TITLE and RATING variables from the PG13_RATING data set were renamed to prevent the data from being overwritten.

16 Reshaping data with three SET statements

When three **SET** statements are specified in a DATA step, the objective is to pair the observations from each data set. The pairing of observations continues until one or more of the data sets run out of observations. In the next example, three SET statements are specified to join "PG," "PG-13," and "R" movies together.

If similar variables exist in any of the data sets, each variable needs to be renamed to prevent the data from being overwritten.

Code:

```
DATA SET_JOIN;
  SET PG_RATING(KEEP=TITLE RATING
             RENAME=(TITLE=PG_TITLE
      RATING=PG_RATING));
  SET PG13_RATING(KEEP=TITLE RATING
             RENAME=(TITLE=PG13_TITLE
      RATING=PG13_RATING));
  SET R_RATING(KEEP=TITLE RATING
             RENAME=(TITLE=R_TITLE
      RATING=R_RATING));
RUN;
```

17 Interleaving SAS data sets

The process of interleaving SAS data sets involves concatenating observations in sorted order. Before the data can be interleaved, it must first be verified that it is ordered by the BY variable. In the next example, "PG" and "PG-13" movies are interleaved in order of their length.

It's best to interleave data sets with similar data structures to prevent missing values from being assigned.

Code:

```
PROC SORT DATA=PG_RATING;
  BY LENGTH;
RUN;
PROC SORT DATA=PG13_RATING;
  BY LENGTH;
RUN;
DATA INTERLEAVE;
  SET PG_RATING(KEEP=TITLE LENGTH RATING)
    PG13_RATING(KEEP=TITLE LENGTH RATING);
  BY LENGTH;
RUN;
PROC PRINT NOOBS;
RUN;
```

Results:

Title	Length	Rating
Christmas Vacation	97	PG-13
National Lampoon's Vacation	98	PG-13
Casablanca	103	PG
Michael	106	PG-13
Poltergeist	115	PG
Rocky	120	PG
Star Wars	124	PG
Jaws	125	PG
Ghost	127	PG-13
Jurassic Park	127	PG-13
The Hunt for Red October	135	PG
Forrest Gump	142	PG-13
Titanic	194	PG-13

18 Overcoming the interleaving threshold

The maximum number of data sets that can be interleaved at one time is 50. Should you require more data sets to be interleaved, simply interleave the first 50 data sets as one group, the second 50 in a second group, and so on until all your groups have been processed. Then, using the group data sets, interleave these until you've successfully interleaved all data sets.

19 Using FIRST. and LAST. Variables

When a BY statement is specified, **FIRST.** and **LAST.** variables are temporarily created to inform you whether the first or last observation in the BY-group is being processed. In programming terms, users use these special system variables in DATA steps to perform special processing (for example, to write an observation to a data set or report, set counters to zero, or assign a value to a variable).

20 Outputting the values of FIRST. and LAST. variables to a data set

Because the FIRST. and LAST. variables are considered to be system (or automatic) variables, they are not automatically written to a SAS data set.

This is true for any system variable, but there is a way to get around this apparent limitation. Users can assign the value(s) of any system variable to a user-defined variable and then have the user-defined variable written to the SAS data set.

21 Combining data with one-to-one merging

Merging is the process of combining tables side-by-side, or horizontally, as illustrated in Figure 4-1. Similar to using two SET statements to combine observations, *one-to-one merging* combines the first observation from the first SAS data set with the first observation from the second SAS data set, the second observation from the first data set with the second observation from the second data set, and so on, until the observations in all data sets have been processed. In the next example, illustrated in Code Listing 4-2 with output shown in Results 4-2, a **MERGE** statement is specified to perform a one-to-one merge with PG_RATING and PG13-RATING data sets, creating a new data set in the process.

If similarly named variables exist in the data sets being combined, they need to be renamed to prevent the data from being overwritten.

```
Table One  <------>  Table Two
```

Figure 4-1. Merging tables side-by-side

Code Listing 4-2:

```
DATA ONE_TO_ONE_MERGE;
 MERGE PG_RATING(KEEP=TITLE RATING
                RENAME=(TITLE=PG_TITLE
         RATING=PG_RATING))
       PG13_RATING(KEEP=TITLE RATING
                RENAME=(TITLE=PG13_TITLE
         RATING=PG13_RATING));
RUN;
```

Results 4-2:

PG_TITLE	PG_RATING	PG13_TITLE	PG13_RATING
Casablanca	PG	Christmas Vacation	PG-13
Poltergeist	PG	National Lampoon's Vacation	PG-13
Rocky	PG	Michael	PG-13
Star Wars	PG	Ghost	PG-13
Jaws	PG	Jurassic Park	PG-13
The Hunt for Red October	PG	Forrest Gump	PG-13
		Titanic	PG-13

22 Applying caution when using one-to-one merges

Because a BY statement is not specified in a one-to-one merge, the observations in each data set are not matched but simply combined without any matching whatsoever. Specifically, a one-to-one merge places no importance on the relationship of the data sets being combined, because it just takes the first observation from the first data set and combines it with the first observation from the second data set, the second observation from the first data set and combines it with the second observation from the second data set, and so on and so forth. For this reason, users should exercise a certain level of care when using a one-to-one merge and know what their desired result should be before using this form of merge.

23 Combining data with match merging

Similar to a one-to-one merge, a *match merge* combines observations from two or more data sets into a single observation and stores the merged observations in a new data set. But this is where the similarities between the two types of merges end. Unlike a one-to-one merge, a match merge is more intelligent because it only combines observations in accordance with the values of a common variable. This key, and critical, difference is why many users choose a match merge over a one-to-one merge for their merging needs. In the next example, illustrated in Code Listing 4-3 with output shown in Results 4-3, two data sets are combined, MOVIES and ACTORS, using a common BY variable.

🖉 *Because this form of merge adheres to a common BY variable, each data set must be sorted, arranged, or indexed by the variable specified in the BY statement.*

🖉 *If required, you can merge by more than one variable in a BY statement.*

Code Listing 4-3:

```
DATA MATCH_MERGE;
 MERGE MOVIES(KEEP=TITLE LENGTH RATING)
       ACTORS(KEEP=TITLE ACTOR_LEADING);
 BY TITLE;
RUN;
```

Results 4-3:

Title	Length	Rating	Actor_Leading
Brave Heart	177	R	Mel Gibson
Casablanca	103	PG	
Christmas Vacation	97	PG-13	Chevy Chase
Coming to America	116	R	Eddie Murphy
Dracula	130	R	
Dressed to Kill	105	R	
Forrest Gump	142	PG-13	Tom Hanks
Ghost	127	PG-13	Patrick Swayze
Jaws	125	PG	
Jurassic Park	127	PG-13	
Lethal Weapon	110	R	Mel Gibson
Michael	106	PG-13	John Travolta
National Lampoon's Vacation	98	PG-13	Chevy Chase
Poltergeist	115	PG	
Rocky	120	PG	Sylvester Stallone
Scarface	170	R	
Silence of the Lambs	118	R	Anthony Hopkins
Star Wars	124	PG	
The Hunt for Red October	135	PG	Sean Connery
The Terminator	108	R	Arnold Schwarzenegger
The Wizard of Oz	101	G	
Titanic	194	PG-13	Leonardo DiCaprio

24 Understanding SAS and SQL terminology

As a way of communicating specific SQL concepts and terminology to SAS and SQL users, basic terminology equivalencies are presented. Table 4-3 presents important SAS terminology that SAS uses banter about in their daily lives along with their equivalent SQL terms.

Table 4-3. SAS and SQL Terminology

SAS TERM	SQL TERM
SAS Library	Database
SAS Data Set	Table
Observation	Row
Variable	Column
Merge	Join
Subset	Select Query

25 Understanding why joining is important

As relational database systems continue to grow in popularity, the need to access normalized data that has been stored in separate tables becomes increasingly important. By relating matching values in key columns in one table with key columns in two or more tables, information can be retrieved as if the data were stored in one huge file. Consequently, the process of joining data from two or more tables can provide new and exciting insights into data relationships.

26 Combining data with an SQL join

A *join* of two or more tables provides a means of gathering and manipulating data in a single SELECT statement. A common type of join in the SQL procedure is known as an *inner join*. Two or more tables are joined by specifying the names of each table in a WHERE clause of a SELECT statement. A comma separates each table specified in the WHERE clause.

Joins are specified on a minimum of two tables at a time, where a similar column from each table is used for the purpose of connecting the tables by defining relationships between them. This powerful feature allows disparate pieces of information to be combined together. Connecting columns should have similar values and the same datatype attributes since the join's success is dependent on these values. For example, the following SQL code, illustrated in Code Listing 4-4 with output shown in Results 4-4, references a join on two tables with TITLE specified as the connecting column (or common BY variable).

27 Creating a Cartesian Product join

When a **WHERE** clause is omitted in the join query, all possible combinations of rows and columns from each table is produced. This form of join is known as a *Cartesian Product*. Say, for example, that you join two tables with the first table consisting of 10 rows and the second table with 5 rows. The result of these two tables would consist of 50 rows. Very rarely is there a need to perform a join operation in SQL with a WHERE clause not specified. The primary importance of being aware of this form of join is to illustrate a base for all joins, since every join starts out as a Cartesian Product. As shown in Figure 4-2, the two tables would be combined without a corresponding WHERE clause. Consequently, no connection between common columns exists.

Code Listing 4-4:

```
PROC SQL;
 SELECT MOVIES.TITLE,
        RATING,
        ACTOR_LEADING
  FROM MOVIES(KEEP=TITLE RATING),
       ACTORS(KEEP=TITLE ACTOR_LEADING)
   WHERE MOVIES.TITLE = ACTORS.TITLE;
QUIT;
```

Results 4-4:

Title	Rating	Actor_Leading
Brave Heart	R	Mel Gibson
Christmas Vacation	PG-13	Chevy Chase
Coming to America	R	Eddie Murphy
Forrest Gump	PG-13	Tom Hanks
Ghost	PG-13	Patrick Swayze
Lethal Weapon	R	Mel Gibson
Michael	PG-13	John Travolta
National Lampoon's Vacation	PG-13	Chevy Chase
Rocky	PG	Sylvester Stallone
Silence of the Lambs	R	Anthony Hopkins
The Hunt for Red October	PG	Sean Connery
The Terminator	R	Arnold Schwarzenegger
Titanic	PG-13	Leonardo DiCaprio

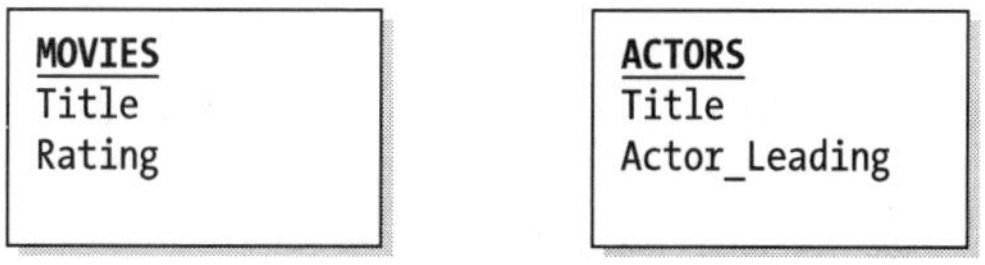

```
MOVIES
Title
Rating
```

```
ACTORS
Title
Actor_Leading
```

Figure 4-2. A Cartesian Product join

Code:

```
PROC SQL;
 SELECT MOVIES.TITLE,
        RATING,
        ACTOR_LEADING
  FROM MOVIES(KEEP=TITLE RATING),
       ACTORS(KEEP=TITLE ACTOR_LEADING);
QUIT;
```

28 Creating table aliases when joining

Table aliases provide a shortcut way to reference two or more tables within a join operation. Aliases are specified so that columns can be selected with a minimal number of keystrokes. To illustrate how table aliases in a join work, a two-table join is linked as illustrated in Figure 4-3. The example shows aliases defined for both tables in the FROM clause as well as in the SELECT statement and WHERE clause.

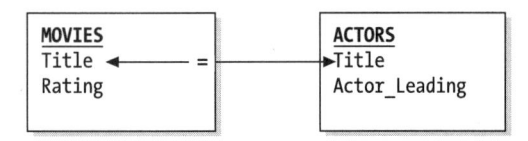

Figure 4-3. Creating and using table aliases

Code:

```
PROC SQL;
 SELECT M.MOVIE_NO,
        M.RATING,
        A.LEADING_ACTOR
  FROM MOVIES M, ACTORS A
   WHERE M.MOVIE_NO =
         A.MOVIE_NO;
QUIT;
```

29 Combining three or more tables with an SQL join

In an earlier tip, you saw where movie information was combined with the leading actor in each movie. You may also want to capture the customer account information of the renters who rented each movie. To do this, you will need to extract information from three different tables: CUSTOMERS, MOVIES, and ACTORS.

A three-table join follows the same rules as in a two-table join. Each table needs to be listed in the FROM clause with appropriate restrictions specified in the WHERE clause. Figure 4-4 illustrates how a three table join works.

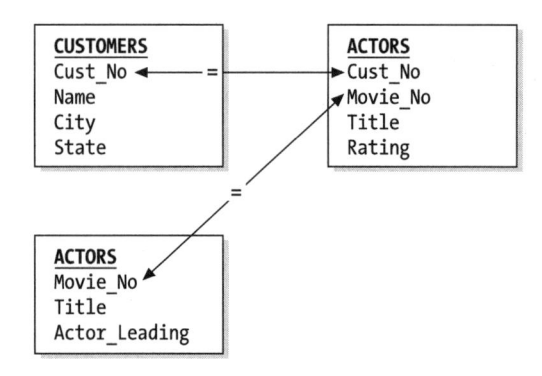

Figure 4-4. Creating a three-way table join

The following SQL code references a join with three tables specifying CUST_NO as the connecting column for the CUSTOMERS and MOVIES tables and MOVIE_NO as the connecting column for the MOVIES and ACTORS tables.

Code:

```
PROC SQL;
 SELECT C.CUST_NO,
        M.MOVIE_NO,
        M.RATING,
        M.CATEGORY,
        A.LEADING_ACTOR
  FROM CUSTOMERS C,
       MOVIES M,
       ACTORS A
   WHERE C.CUST_NO = M.CUST_NO AND
         M.MOVIE_NO = A.MOVIE_NO;
QUIT;
```

30 Understanding outer joins

Most often, joins are used to relate rows in one table with rows in another. But occasionally a join may be needed that includes rows from one or both tables as well as rows with no related rows. This concept, referred to as *row preservation*, is a feature offered by the outer join construct.

There are operational and syntax differences between inner (natural) and outer joins. First, the maximum number of tables that can be specified in an outer join is two (the maximum number of tables specified in an inner join is 32). Like an inner join, an outer join relates rows in both tables. But an outer join also includes rows with no related rows from one or both of the tables. This special handling of "matched" and "unmatched" rows of data is what differentiates an outer join from an inner join.

31 Exploring tasks with an outer join

An outer join can accomplish a variety of tasks that would require a great deal of effort using other methods. This is not to say that a process similar to an outer join could not be programmed—it would probably just require more work. Let's take a look at a few tasks that are possible with outer joins:

- List all customer accounts with rentals during the month, including customer accounts with no purchase activity.

- Compute the number of rentals placed by each customer, including customers who have not rented.

- Identify movie renters who rented a movie last month and those who did not.

Another obvious difference between an outer and inner join is the way the syntax is constructed. Outer joins use the LEFT JOIN, RIGHT JOIN, or FULL JOIN keywords, and have the WHERE clause replaced with an ON clause. These distinctions help identify outer joins from inner joins.

32 Deciding on a left or right outer join

Specifying a *left* or *right outer join* is a matter of choice. Either approach preserves the rows of data that didn't match the ON clause. Simply put, the only difference between a left and right join is the order of the tables the rows of data are related with. As such, you can construct an outer join using either approach as long as you use care when stating the ON clause.

33 Combining data with a left outer join

An outer join provides a means of gathering and manipulating data in a single SELECT statement. The way two tables are joined is by specifying the names of each table in an ON clause of a SELECT statement with the keyword **LEFT JOIN** or **RIGHT JOIN** specified for the type of join requested. No comma is used to separate the tables, as was used with an inner join.

Left outer joins are specified on a maximum of two tables at a time, and a column from each table is used for the purpose of connecting the two tables. This powerful feature allows disparate pieces of information to be combined together. Connecting columns should have similar values and the same datatype attributes since the join's success is dependent on these values. For example, the following left outer join, illustrated in Code Listing 4-5 with output shown in Results 4-5, references two tables MOVIES and ACTORS in the FROM clause with TITLE specified as the connecting column (or common BY variable) in the ON clause.

✎ *The resulting output displays all rows for which the SQL expression, referenced in the ON clause, matches both tables as well as the rows from the left table (MOVIES) that did not match any row in the right (ACTORS) table.*

Code Listing 4-5:

```
PROC SQL;
 SELECT MOVIES.TITLE,
        ACTOR_LEADING,
        RATING
   FROM MOVIES
   LEFT JOIN
        ACTORS
     ON MOVIES.TITLE = ACTORS.TITLE;
QUIT;
```

Results:

Title	Actor_Leading	Rating
Brave Heart	Mel Gibson	R
Casablanca		PG
Christmas Vacation	Chevy Chase	PG-13
Coming to America	Eddie Murphy	R
Dracula		R
Dressed to Kill		R
Forrest Gump	Tom Hanks	PG-13
Ghost	Patrick Swayze	PG-13
Jaws		PG
Jurassic Park		PG-13
Lethal Weapon	Mel Gibson	R
Michael	John Travolta	PG-13
Vacation	Chevy Chase	PG-13
Poltergeist		PG
Rocky	Sly Stallone	PG
Scarface		R
Silence of the Lambs	Anthony Hopkins	R
Star Wars		PG
Hunt for Red October	Sean Connery	PG
The Terminator	Arnold Schwarzenegger	R
The Wizard of Oz		G
Titanic	Leonardo DiCaprio	PG-13

34 Combining data with a right outer join

A right outer join is specified on a maximum of two tables at a time, and one or more columns from each table is used for the purpose of connecting the two tables. Connecting columns should have *"like"* values and the same datatype attributes, because the join's success is dependent on these values. For example, the following right outer join, illustrated in Code Listing 4-6 with output shown in Results 4-6, references two tables MOVIES and ACTORS in the FROM clause with TITLE specified as the connecting column (or common BY variable) in the ON clause.

🖉 *The resulting output displays all rows for which the SQL expression, referenced in the ON clause, matches both tables as well as the rows from the right table (ACTORS) that did not match any row in the left (MOVIES) table.*

Code Listing 4-6:

```
PROC SQL;
 SELECT MOVIES.TITLE,
        ACTOR_LEADING,
        RATING
   FROM MOVIES
     RIGHT JOIN
        ACTORS
     ON MOVIES.TITLE = ACTORS.TITLE;
QUIT;
```

Results 4-6:

Title	Actor_Leading	Rating
Brave Heart	Mel Gibson	R
Christmas Vacation	Chevy Chase	PG-13
Coming to America	Eddie Murphy	R
Forrest Gump	Tom Hanks	PG-13
Ghost	Patrick Swayze	PG-13
Lethal Weapon	Mel Gibson	R
Michael	John Travolta	PG-13
Vacation	Chevy Chase	PG-13
Rocky	Sly Stallone	PG
Silence of the Lambs	Anthony Hopkins	R
Hunt for Red October	Sean Connery	PG
The Terminator	Arnold Schwarzenegger	R
Titanic	Leonardo DiCaprio	PG-13

Chapter 4

Sending Output to SAS Data Sets

This section includes tips that show how data and output can be sent to SAS data sets. You'll learn proven techniques through effective examples on how the DATA step programming language and numerous summary-level procedures can produce output quickly and easily. These handy data manipulation tips will let you prepare your data to satisfy even the most demanding data-analysis requirements.

1 Sending output to a data set

Have you ever wondered how many ways there are to send output to a SAS data set? There may be more than you think. Here are some tips that will help make your programming experience more rewarding.

The SAS System provides users with many ways to send output to a SAS data set. You're probably familiar with some of them, and may have even used one or more techniques before. But are you aware of all the different methods? SAS users are constantly amazed at the number of ways output can be sent to a data set (that is, moved from a computer's memory to storage or other external device).

2 Creating an output data set with a subsetting IF statement

A common method of sending output to a data set is in a DATA step. When a single data set is the recipient of output, the use of an OUTPUT statement or implied OUTPUT (better known as implicit output) can be used.

In the case of implicit OUTPUT, the SAS System automatically writes the current observation to the data set as it encounters the last executable statement in the step. This action occurs as control is passed to the top of the DATA step or observation loop. The next example illustrates sending output to a single data set with a subsetting IF statement (and without an OUTPUT statement).

Code:

```
DATA RATING_PG;
 SET MOVIES;
 IF UPCASE(RATING)= "PG";
RUN;
```

3 Creating an output data with an IF-THEN/ELSE statement

To selectively control where output is sent, one or more OUTPUT statements can be specified. In the absence of an OUTPUT statement, the SAS System sends output to all specified data sets. When one or more OUTPUT statements are used, the current observation is directed to the specified data set. In the following example, the IF-THEN/ELSE statements control where output is sent.

Code:

```
DATA RATING_G
     RATING_PG
     RATING_PG13
     OTHER;
 SET MOVIES;
 IF RATING = "G" THEN
       OUTPUT RATING_G;
 ELSE
 IF RATING = "PG" THEN
       OUTPUT RATING_PG;
 ELSE
 IF RATING = "PG-13" THEN
       OUTPUT RATING_PG13;
 ELSE
 OUTPUT OTHER;
RUN;
```

4 Creating an output data set with WHEN conditions

One or more output data sets can be created using a series of OUTPUT statements in WHEN conditions. The following DATA step code illustrates a SELECT block with numerous WHEN conditions, and OUTPUT statements to create several output data sets.

> ✎ *It's recommended to always include an OTHERWISE clause in a SELECT group to process observations not meeting the other conditions.*

Code:

```
DATA RATING_G
     RATING_PG
     RATING_PG13
     OTHER;
  SET MOVIES;
  SELECT(RATING);
    WHEN ("G") OUTPUT RATING_G;
    WHEN ("PG") OUTPUT RATING_PG;
    WHEN ("PG-13") OUTPUT RATING_PG13;
    OTHERWISE OUTPUT OTHER;
  END;
RUN;
```

5 Creating an output data set with the CONTENTS procedure

The output from the **CONTENTS** procedure can be sent to a data set. The output data set describes each variable in the source data set. For example, the CONTENTS procedure appears in the next example. The CONTENTS procedure code produces a data set containing a single observation for each variable in the source data set and forty variables describing the data set, variables, and attributes.

Code:

```
PROC CONTENTS
     DATA=MOVIES
     OUT=CONTENTS;
RUN;
```

6 Exploring an output data set created with the CONTENTS procedure

We know that the output data set created by the CONTENTS procedure contains a single observation for each variable in the source data set. But what do the variables represent? The variables and their description are identified in Table 4-4.

Table 4-4. Output Data Set Variables

VARIABLE	DESCRIPTION
LIBNAME	Library name
MEMNAME	Library member name
MEMLABEL	Data set label
TYPEMEM	Data set type
NAME	Variable name
TYPE	Variable type
LENGTH	Variable length
VARNUM	Variable number
LABEL	Variable label
FORMAT	Variable format
FORMATL	Format length
FORMATD	Number of format decimals
INFORMAT	Variable informat
INFORML	Informat length
INFORMD	Number of informat decimals

Table 4-4. Output Data Set Variables (Continued)

VARIABLE	DESCRIPTION
JUST	Justification
NPOS	Position in buffer
NOBS	Observations in data set
ENGINE	Engine name
CRDATE	Create date
MODATE	Last modified date
DELOBS	Deleted observations in data set
IDXUSAGE	Use of variable in indexes
MEMTYPE	Library member type
IDXCOUNT	Number of indexes for data set
PROTECT	Password protection
FLAGS	Update flags
COMPRESS	Compression routine
REUSE	Reuse space
SORTED	Sorted indicator
SORTEDBY	Position of variable in sorted by clause
CHARSET	Host character set
COLLATE	Collating sequence
NODUPKEY	Sorting: no duplicate keys
NODUPREC	Sorting: no duplicate records
ENCRYPT	Encryption routine
POINTOBS	Point to observations
GENMAX	Maximum number of generations
GENNUM	Generation number
GENNEXT	Next generation number

7 Creating an output data set with the FREQ procedure

Descriptive statistics can be output to a data set with **PROC FREQ**. The output data set includes an output variable for each analysis variable and values for numerous statistics. For example, the following FREQ procedure sends output to a data set called FREQSTATS.

Code:

```
PROC FREQ DATA=MOVIES;
  OUTPUT OUT=FREQSTATS ALL;
  TABLES LENGTH / ALL;
RUN;
```

The FREQSTATS data set contains the analysis variable LENGTH (a numeric variable) and by default the values for N (Number of Subjects), Chi-Square, DF for Chi-Square, and P-value for Chi-Square are calculated and sent to the output data set, as shown in Figure 4-5.

8 Exploring the available statistics with the FREQ procedure

The FREQ procedure can be used to create a great number of statistics. The following list identifies the statistical keywords that can be sent to the output data set using the FREQ procedure.

- BINOMIAL
- CELLCHI2
- CHISQ
- CL
- CMH

- CMH1

- CMH2

- CUMCOL

- DEVIATION

- EXPECTED

- FISHER

- JT

- MEASURES

- OUTPCT

- PLCORR

- PRINTKWT

- RELRISK

- RISKDIFF

- SCORES=MODRIDIT | RANK | RIDIT | TABLE

- SCOROUT

- TOTPCT

- TREND

✎ *One or more keywords can be specified besides the output data set name in the OUTPUT OUT= statement.*

The FREQ Procedure

Length	Frequency	Percent	Cumulative Frequency	Cumulative Percent
97	1	4.55	1	4.55
98	1	4.55	2	9.09
101	1	4.55	3	13.64
103	1	4.55	4	18.18
105	1	4.55	5	22.73
106	1	4.55	6	27.27
108	1	4.55	7	31.82
110	1	4.55	8	36.36
115	1	4.55	9	40.91
116	1	4.55	10	45.45
118	1	4.55	11	50.00
120	1	4.55	12	54.55
124	1	4.55	13	59.09
125	1	4.55	14	63.64
127	2	9.09	16	72.73
130	1	4.55	17	77.27
135	1	4.55	18	81.82
142	1	4.55	19	86.36
170	1	4.55	20	90.91
177	1	4.55	21	95.45
194	1	4.55	22	100.00

Figure 4-5. Creating a data set with the FREQ procedure

9 Sending output to a data set with the MEANS procedure

Descriptive statistics can be output to a data set with PROC MEANS. The output data set includes an output variable for each analysis variable and values for N, MIN, MAX, MEAN, and STD (standard deviation). For example, the OUTPUT statement sends output to a data set called MEANSSTATS.

✎ *To prevent all variables from being selected, a VAR statement can be specified in the MEANS procedure.*

Code:

```
PROC MEANS DATA=MOVIES;
  OUTPUT OUT=MEANSSTATS;
RUN;
```

The MEANSSTATS data set contains the analysis variable is LENGTH (a numeric variable) and by default the values for N, MIN, MAX, MEAN, and STD are calculated and sent to the output data set, as shown in Figure 4-6.

TYPE	_FREQ_	_STAT_	Length	Year
0	22	N	22	22
0	22	MIN	97	1939
0	22	MAX	194	1997
0	22	MEAN	124.90909091	1982.9090909
0	22	STD	25.834471417	15.212492019

Figure 4-6. Creating a data set with the MEANS procedure

10 Exploring the available statistics with the MEANS procedure

The **MEANS** procedure can be used to create a number of statistics. The following list identifies the statistics that can be sent to the output data set using the MEANS procedure.

- CSS
- CV
- KURTOSIS
- LCLM
- MAX
- MEAN
- MIN
- N
- NMISS
- MEDIAN
- PROBT
- RANGE
- SKEWNESS
- STDDEV
- SUM
- SUMWGT
- UCLM
- USS
- VAR
- QRANGE
- T

✎ *One or more keywords can be specified besides the output data set name in the PROC MEANS statement.*

11 Sending output to a data set with the SUMMARY procedure

By default the **SUMMARY** procedure does not display any output but it does produce descriptive statistics that can be output to a data set. The output data set includes the variables _TYPE_, _FREQ_, and any statistics that have been specified. For example, output from the SUMMARY procedure is sent to a data set called SUMSTATS.

Code:

```
PROC SUMMARY DATA=MOVIES;
  VAR LENGTH;
  OUTPUT OUT=SUMSTATS
    N=N
    MIN=MIN
    MAX=MAX
    MEAN=MEAN
    STD=STD;
RUN;
```

The SUMSTATS data set contains a number of summarized variables as displayed in the data set shown in Figure 4-7.

12 Sending output to a data set with the UNIVARIATE procedure

Descriptive statistics can also be output to a data set with **PROC UNIVARIATE**. The output data set includes a variable for each analysis variable and values for the statistics that are requested. For example, output from the UNIVARIATE procedure is sent to a data set called UNIVSTATS.

Code:

```
PROC UNIVARIATE DATA=MOVIES;
  VAR LENGTH;
  OUTPUT OUT=UNIVSTATS
    N=n
    MIN=min
    MAX=max
    MEAN=mean
    STD=std ;
RUN;
```

The UNIVSTATS data set contains the analysis variable AGE (a numeric variable), and statistical values for N, MIN, MAX, MEAN, and STD (standard deviation), as shown in Figure 4-8.

	TYPE	_FREQ_	N	MIN	MAX	MEAN	STD
1	0	22	22	97	194	124.90909091	25.834471417

Figure 4-7. Creating a data set with the SUMMARY procedure

	number of nonmissing values, Length	the mean, Length	the standard deviation, Length	the largest value, Length	the smallest value, Length
1	22	124.90909091	25.834471417	194	97

Figure 4-8. Creating a data set with the UNIVARIATE procedure

13 Exploring the available statistics with the UNIVARIATE procedure

The UNIVARIATE procedure can be used to create a number of statistics. The lists that follow identify the statistics that can be sent to the output data set using the UNIVARIATE procedure.

> ✎ *One or more keywords can be specified besides the output data set name in the OUTPUT OUT= statement.*

Descriptive statistic keyword

- CSS
- CV
- KURTOSIS
- MAX
- MEAN
- MIN
- N
- NMISS
- MEDIAN
- MODE
- NMISS
- RANGE
- SKEWNESS
- STD
- STDMEAN
- SUM
- SUMWGT
- USS
- VAR

Quantile statistic keywords

- MEDIAN
- QRANGE

Hypothesis testing keywords

- MSIGN
- NORMAL
- PROBM
- PROBN
- PROBS
- PROBT
- SIGNRANK

14 Tracing output objects with ODS

Output Delivery System (ODS) provides another way to send a procedure's output to a SAS data set. But before you can successfully send a procedure's output to a SAS data set using ODS, you'll need to know two things: 1) how to identify an output object's name and 2) the naming conventions used in naming a SAS data set.

Identifying the names of output objects created in a procedure is relatively easy. For example, to identify the names of all the output objects created in the UNIVARIATE procedure for a data set containing "movie" data is accomplished by using the following code. The results of the trace are automatically displayed in the SAS Log. As can be seen from viewing the SAS Log, there are five output objects created by UNIVARIATE (Moments, BasicMeasures, TestsForLocation, Quantiles, and ExtremeObs). Once this is known, you're ready to send output to a SAS data set.

Code:

```
ODS TRACE ON;
   PROC UNIVARIATE DATA = MOVIES;
   RUN;
ODS TRACE OFF;
```

Log Results:

```
Output Added:
-------------
Name:   Moments
Label: Moments
Template: base.univariate.Moments
Path: Univariate.age.Moments
-------------
Output Added:
-------------
Name:   BasicMeasures
Label: Basic Measures of Location and ↵
Variability
Template: base.univariate.Measures
Path: Univariate.age.BasicMeasures
-------------
Output Added:
-------------
Name:   TestsForLocation
Label: Tests For Location
Template: base.univariate.Location
Path: Univariate.age.TestsForLocation
-------------
Output Added:
-------------
Name:   Quantiles
Label: Quantiles
Template: base.univariate.Quantiles
Path: Univariate.age.Quantiles
-------------
Output Added:
-------------
Name:   ExtremeObs
Label: Extreme Observations
Template: base.univariate.ExtObs
Path: Univariate.age.ExtremeObs
-------------
```

15 Sending output to a data set with ODS

We'll now see how data from any output-producing procedure can be sent to a data set using Output Delivery System (ODS). The advantage of using ODS to accomplish this is that the syntax remains consistent from procedure to procedure. There's no need to remember, as there was prior to ODS, the unique syntax requirements for each procedure.

The ability to send output, without using any fancy programming techniques, from any output-producing procedure to a SAS data set, is a feature many SAS users have wanted for along time. ODS provides users with a consistent way to output the results of any output-producing procedure to a SAS data set. Whether you use detail- or summary-level procedures, output from any output producing procedure can be sent to a SAS data set the same way. This not only saves time—it makes performing these types of tasks a simple matter.

The syntax used to send output to a SAS data set using ODS follows:

ODS OUTPUT
  output-object = SAS-dataset-name;

The ***output-object*** is the name assigned to the piece of information created by the specific procedure. The output-object name is identified by using the ODS TRACE ON statement (as shown previously). The ***SAS-dataset-name*** can be any valid user-supplied SAS name such as MOMENTS_RESULTS.

Continuing with the UNIVARIATE example, the results of just the MOMENTS output object can be sent to a SAS data set as follows:

Code:

```
ODS LISTING CLOSE;
ODS OUTPUT MOMENTS = MOMENTS_RESULTS;
  PROC UNIVARIATE DATA=MOVIES;
  RUN;
ODS OUTPUT CLOSE;
ODS LISTING;
```

In the preceding example, the Listing destination is closed (this prevents output from being sent to both the Listing and Output destinations). Then the desired output object is specified (as in MOMENTS) in the ODS OUTPUT statement and assigns a user-defined-SAS-dataset-name (as in MOMENTS_RESULTS). After the UNIVARIATE procedure sends the MOMENTS output to the user-defined data set, the Output destination is closed, and the Listing destination is reopened. The output is shown in Figure 4-9.

16 Converting observations into variables

Occasionally a data-manipulation problem requires turning observations into variables. When this is the case, **PROC TRANSPOSE** can be used to convert repeated observations to single observations. For example, each observation in data set MOVIES, shown in Figure 4-10, contains a movies rating and category (type of movie, as in Adventure, Comedy, and so on). The objective of the following code is to combine the four movie ratings into a single observation.

	VarName	Label1	cValue1	nValue1	Label2	cValue2	nValue2
1	Length	N	22	22.000000	Sum Weights	22	22.000000
2	Length	Mean	124.909091	124.909091	Sum Observations	2748	2748.000000
3	Length	Std Deviation	25.8344714	25.834471	Variance	667.419913	667.419913
4	Length	Skewness	1.45414494	1.454145	Kurtosis	1.71453814	1.714538
5	Length	Uncorrected SS	357266	357266	Corrected SS	14015.8182	14016
6	Length	Coeff Variation	20.682619	20.682619	Std Error Mean	5.50792781	5.507928
7	Year	N	22	22.000000	Sum Weights	22	22.000000
8	Year	Mean	1982.90909	1982.909091	Sum Observations	43624	43624
9	Year	Std Deviation	15.212492	15.212492	Variance	231.419913	231.419913
10	Year	Skewness	-2.1106473	-2.110647	Kurtosis	4.41807209	4.418072
11	Year	Uncorrected SS	86507286	86507286	Corrected SS	4859.81818	4859.818182
12	Year	Coeff Variation	0.76718051	0.767181	Std Error Mean	3.2433142	3.243314

Figure 4-9. Sending UNIVARIATE output to a data set

Code:

```
PROC SORT DATA=MOVIES
         OUT=SORTED_MOVIES;
 BY RATING TITLE;
RUN;
PROC TRANSPOSE DATA=SORTED_MOVIES
         OUT=TRANSPOSED_MOVIES_VARS;
 VAR TITLE;
 BY RATING;
RUN;
PROC PRINT NOOBS;
RUN;
```

Results can be seen in Figure 4-10.

Code:

```
PROC SORT DATA=MOVIES OUT=SORTED_MOVIES;
 BY RATING TITLE;
RUN;
PROC TRANSPOSE DATA=TRANSPOSED_MOVIES_VARS
         OUT=TRANSPOSED_MOVIES_OBS;
 VAR COL1-COL8;
 BY RATING;
RUN;
PROC PRINT NOOBS;
RUN;
```

Results can be seen in Figure 4-11.

17 Converting variables to observations

With observations converted to variables (see previous tip), you may want to name the transposed variable columns. The **TRANSPOSE** procedure lets you rename the columns to anything you like. For example, to rename the column names COL1-COL8, you could specify the TRANSPOSE procedures as follows.

	Rating	NAME OF FORMER VARIABLE	COL1	COL2	COL3	COL4	COL5	COL6	COL7	COL8
1	G	Title	The Wizard of Oz							
2	PG	Title	Casablanca	Jaws	Poltergeist	Rocky	Star Wars	The Hunt for Red October		
3	PG-13	Title	Christmas Vacation	Forrest Gump	Ghost	Jurassic Park	Michael	National Lampoon's Vacation	Titanic	
4	R	Title	Brave Heart	Coming to America	Dracula	Dressed to Kill	Lethal Weapon	Scarface	Silence of the Lambs	The Terminator

Figure 4-10. Data set view after being transposed into variables

	Rating	NAME OF FORMER VARIABLE	Title
1	G	COL1	The Wizard of Oz
2	G	COL2	
3	G	COL3	
4	G	COL4	
5	G	COL5	
6	G	COL6	
7	G	COL7	
8	G	COL8	
9	PG	COL1	Casablanca
10	PG	COL2	Jaws
11	PG	COL3	Poltergeist
12	PG	COL4	Rocky
13	PG	COL5	Star Wars
14	PG	COL6	The Hunt for Red October
15	PG	COL7	
16	PG	COL8	
17	PG-13	COL1	Christmas Vacation
18	PG-13	COL2	Forrest Gump
19	PG-13	COL3	Ghost
20	PG-13	COL4	Jurassic Park
21	PG-13	COL5	Michael
22	PG-13	COL6	National Lampoon's Vacation
23	PG-13	COL7	Titanic
24	PG-13	COL8	
25	R	COL1	Brave Heart
26	R	COL2	Coming to America
27	R	COL3	Dracula
28	R	COL4	Dressed to Kill
29	R	COL5	Lethal Weapon
30	R	COL6	Scarface
31	R	COL7	Silence of the Lambs
32	R	COL8	The Terminator

Figure 4-11. Data set view after being transposed into observations

Summary

In this chapter, you learned how to manipulate data in the Base SAS software. Each tip illustrated powerful techniques for reshaping the way your data looks without changing the actual data. You saw how to subset and reshape data using DATA step statements, options, and operators, as well through many popular summary procedures such as FREQ, MEANS, and UNIVARIATE. You also learned how to send output to SAS data sets using conventional DATA step programming methods, SAS procedures, and Output Delivery System (ODS). These techniques provide a unique set of powerful tools to help prepare your data for data analysis and other types of processing.

In the next chapter, "Data Management," you'll discover and explore popular techniques for copying data, concatenating data, describing data, sorting and indexing data, and managing data and your SAS data sets. Even if you're not a programmer, you'll find the tips and numerous examples simple to understand and to easy to implement.

CHAPTER 5

Data Management

MANAGING AND SAFEGUARDING data are principle objectives in data management. The Base SAS software provides all the essential tools for managing data and program resources. This chapter presents tips on copying, describing, sorting, and managing data. You'll learn essential techniques on a variety of useful data-management operations.

In this chapter, you'll learn how to

- Copy text files using a DATA step

- Use INFILE statement options to control the input record pointer

- Copy SAS data sets using a DATA step

- Use the COPY and DATASETS procedures to reproduce data sets and other file types

- Print a list of SAS library data sets

- Suppress printing individual files in SAS libraries

- Print an alphabetical list of variables

- Save sorted observations to a SAS data set

- Select observations to sort

- Store SAS libraries on disk and tape

- Modify a data set's attributes

- Update a SAS data set

- Age a SAS data set

- Concatenate a SAS data set

- Remove unwanted files from a SAS library

Copying Data

This section includes tips on how to copy data from a source location to a target location using a variety of DATA and PROC step approaches. You'll learn effective tips on managing your important data resources.

1 Copying data files

Copying files involves transferring a source file to a target file. Creating a SAS data set copy serves not only as a backup but also as a way to recover from disaster. Depending on the operating system used, one or more copy utilities are typically provided for users to choose from. When using the SAS System to copy, the source file is unchanged in the copy process, and the target file is created or replaced in the desired location.

2 Verifying FIRSTOBS= and OBS= System options are assigned

Before copying data sets, verify that the SAS System options **FIRSTOBS=** is set to 1 and **OBS=** is set to MAX. These settings permit all observations to be processed from start to finish.

3 Copying text files in a DATA step

Copying text files in a DATA step is a common task for SAS users. The DATA step is constructed to perform basic read and write operations for each record in the source file without modifying the records themselves. As each record is read from the source file, it is temporarily held in the input buffer before being written to the target file. The statements that are specified in the DATA step are **INFILE**, **INPUT**, **FILE**, and **PUT**. For example, copying the entire contents of a text file from one location to another could be coded as follows. The _INFILE_ option specified in the PUT statement writes the entire input buffer record to the target file.

Consult your operating system documentation for specific syntax for the INFILE and FILE statements.

Code:

```
DATA _NULL_;
 INFILE SOURCE;
 INPUT;
 FILE TARGET;
 PUT _INFILE_;
RUN;
```

4 Copying part of each record in a text file

The DATA step can be used to copy parts of a source file to a target file. This process involves controlling how much of each record is read into the input buffer. By specifying the **LENGTH=** option in the INFILE statement, users control what is copied, and essentially truncate the source record read into the input buffer. For example, when specifying a LENGTH= option, users are able to control what the maximum record length will be. The starting column position is 1. In the event the record length is longer than the value specified for the LENGTH= option, the source record on input is essentially truncated.

Code:

```
DATA _NULL_;
 INFILE CARDS LENGTH=RECLEN;
 INPUT;
 RECLEN=11;
 FILE TARGET;
 PUT _INFILE_;
 CARDS;
Brave Heart R
Jaws       PG
Rocky      PG
Titanic    PG-13
;
RUN;
```

Results

```
Brave Heart
Jaws
Rocky
Titanic
```

5 Copying text files starting in a designated record position

The DATA step can be used to copy a source file starting in a designated position in a text file. This process involves specifying a **START=** option in the INFILE statement to control the contents of each record read into the input buffer. By specifying the START= option in the INFILE statement, users can control the starting column position of what is read and copied. For example, when specifying a START= option, users are able to control what the starting column position in the source file should be—and ultimately control what text file data is read and copied.

Code:

```
DATA _NULL_;
 INFILE CARDS START=STARTPOS;
 INPUT;
 STARTPOS=13;
 FILE TARGET;
 PUT _INFILE_;
 CARDS;
Brave Heart  R
Jaws         PG
Rocky        PG
Titanic      PG-13
;
RUN;
```

Results:

```
R
PG
PG
PG-13
```

6 Specifying the LENGTH= and START= options when copying text files

To further control the process of copying text files, users can specify the LENGTH= and START= options together in a DATA step. By specifying the LENGTH= and START= options in the INFILE statement, further control is given over the contents of each record read into the input buffer. For example, when specifying the LENGTH= and START= options, users specify the starting column position and the length of the record read into the input buffer and ultimately control the extent of the text file data being copied.

Code:

```
DATA _NULL_;
 INFILE CARDS
        LENGTH=RECLEN
        START=STARTPOS;
 INPUT;
 RECLEN=15;
 STARTPOS=7;
 FILE TARGET;
 PUT _INFILE_;
 CARDS;
Brave Heart  R
Jaws         PG
Rocky        PG
Titanic      PG-13
;
RUN;
```

Results:

```
Heart  R
       PG
       PG
  c    PG-
```

7 Making multiple copies of text files

Making multiple copies of text files is just as easy as making a single copy. The only difference is that the DATA step contains multiple FILE and PUT statements, as the following example shows. For example, a single text file is copied from one location to three target files as follows:

Code:

```
DATA _NULL_;
 INFILE SOURCE;
 INPUT;
 FILE TARGET1;
 PUT _INFILE_;
 FILE TARGET2;
 PUT _INFILE_;
 FILE TARGET3;
 PUT _INFILE_;
RUN;
```

8 Copying SAS data sets in a DATA step

SAS users often need to copy or back up one or more SAS data sets. There are several ways to copy a data set. Unfortunately not all copy methods are the same and most definitely don't always produce the same results. Here's a tip that may prevent unexpected and unwanted surprises when copying data sets that have one or more indexes associated with them.

The SAS System provides several ways to copy a data set, but not all methods are designed to copy a data set with one or more indexes associated with it. A DATA step convention (DATA – SET statements) is often a first choice among SAS users when copying data sets. The coding is easy to construct, and the process is a simple one. In its simplest form, each observation is read into the Program Data Vector (PDV) and written to the specified data set, one observation at a time. Although this approach is convenient to use at times, it's not always the most efficient for making data set copies of data sets. More importantly, when a data set has one or more indexes associated with it, the DATA – SET convention has no way of knowing about, and hence, copying indexes. All it does is read and write, making copies of your data, not the data set indexes.

9 Exploring the advantages of DATA step copying

A real advantage for using a DATA step to copy source files is to be able to make copies of files within the same library. The reason this is possible is that the name of the target file can be changed. Using other methods, such as the COPY procedure, prohibits changing the name of the target file. Consequently, using the DATA step, a copied target file may have a different name than its source file.

10 Selecting data sets to copy

To selectively copy one or more SAS data sets from one location to another, specify the **IN=** library, an **OUT=** library, and a **SELECT** statement in the COPY procedure. Should the SELECT statement be omitted, all the SAS data sets (or other SAS files) in the IN= library are copied to the OUT= library destination. The following example illustrates two data sets, PG_RATING and PG13_RATING, being copied to a target location using the SELECT statement of the COPY procedure.

✏️ *The SELECT statement is optional and if specified instructs the SAS System what data sets, or files, to copy from the input location to the output location. If SELECT is omitted, the COPY procedure automatically copies all files, including indexes, from the input to output location.*

Code:

```
PROC COPY IN=WORK
          OUT=SAVE;
  SELECT
         PG_RATING
         PG13_RATING;
RUN;
```

11 Copying SAS files with the COPY procedure

A better and more efficient approach to copying data and other objects, including copying indexes, is to use the COPY procedure. Its purpose is to copy data sets as well as indexes quickly and completely. This method is designed to copy one or more SAS data sets (or other SAS members) from one library to another. It transfers a source file to a target location where the source file is unchanged, and the target file is created or replaced. For example, data sets can selectively be chosen for copying from a SAS library as follows:

Code:

```
PROC COPY IN=WORK
          OUT=SAVE
        MTYPE=(DATA
              PROGRAM);
  SELECT
         PG_RATING
         PG13_RATING;
RUN;
```

✏️ *This method of copying doesn't allow changing the name of the target file as it performs the copy.*

The IN= and OUT= parameters specify the input and output locations using the assigned librefs. The MTYPE= parameter, if specified, informs the SAS System to copy only data sets (and indexes) and not any other type of file that can be in a SAS data library. Other values that can be specified for MTYPE= include CATALOG for catalogs, PROGRAM for compiled DATA steps, and VIEW for views. See Note in the previous tip about using the SELECT statement.

12 Copying SAS Data sets – DATASETS Procedure syntax

SAS data sets can also be copied with the DATASETS procedure. The process works exactly the same as the COPY procedure, but the following syntax is used:

Code:

```
PROC DATASETS
     LIBRARY=libref;
  COPY OUT=libref;
   SELECT dataset;
QUIT;
```

13 Copying SAS data sets with the DATASETS procedure

Another way to copy data sets as well as indexes is by using the DATASETS procedure. Users provide the name of the SAS library to use as the input location with a **LIBRARY=** parameter. The **MTYPE=** parameter works the same as in the COPY procedure (see previous tip). The **COPY OUT=** statement specifies the output location using the assigned libref SAVE. The SELECT statement works the same as in the COPY procedure by selecting the desired data set or other SAS library member type. For example, the DATASETS procedure is used to copy data sets PG_RATING and PG13_RATING from a WORK library to a user-assigned library called SAVE.

Code:

```
PROC DATASETS
     LIBRARY=WORK
        MTYPE=DATA;
  COPY OUT=SAVE;
  SELECT
       PG_RATING
       PG13_RATING;
QUIT;
```

Describing Data

This section includes useful tips for capturing essential data-resource information. You'll learn quick and easy techniques of using the CONTENTS procedure to create file and variable lists and ordering variable lists. These handy data-management tips will help you prepare detailed data-resource repositories on all essential files in your organization.

🖉 *The output displayed in the figures in this section appears as Rich Text Format (RTF) and will look slightly different than output that you'll reproduce. For more on RTF, refer to Chapter 6, "Data Presentation."*

1 Exploring the CONTENTS procedure output

The **CONTENTS** procedure describes what is contained in one or more files and/or data sets in a specified library and includes the following information.

- Name of each data set
- Engine used to create the data set
- Date and time the data set was created
- Date and time the data set was last used
- Number of observations in the data set
- Number of variables in the data set
- Physical file location and name
- Alphabetical list of variables and attributes
- Alphabetical list of indexes and attributes

The basic syntax of the CONTENTS procedure code is illustrated in the following example, showing the ease with which it can be constructed. For self-documenting purposes, I recommend specifying the DATA= option. The result of running the CONTENTS procedure is the creation of a considerable amount of documentation—so much so that it can form the beginnings of a data-dictionary repository. The result of the CONTENTS procedure output is shown in Figure 5-1. (ODS and RTF are discussed in greater detail in Chapter 6, "Data Presentation.")

Data Management

2 Printing a list of SAS library data sets

It is often useful to print a list of the data sets and variables in a SAS library. This list (or directory) becomes increasingly more important as the number of data sets in a given library gets larger. The directory appears as the first page of output.

There are two methods of printing a library directory with the CONTENTS procedure. The first method prints a directory list with the **_ALL_** option of the CONTENTS procedure. The result of specifying the _ALL_ option provides the directory information, including LIBREF, Engine, Physical Name, File Name, File Size, and Last Modification Date.

Code:

```
ODS  LISTING CLOSE;
ODS RTF FILE='c:\CONTENTS.RTF';
  PROC CONTENTS DATA=PATH.MOVIES;
  RUN;
ODS RTF CLOSE;
ODS LISTING;
```

Results shown in Figure 5-1.

Code:

```
PROC CONTENTS DATA=PATH._ALL_;
RUN;
```

A second method of generating SAS library documentation is to specify the **DIRECTORY** and _ALL_ options. This will print all details related to the specified libref, as shown in Figures 5-2, 5-3, and 5-4. (ODS and RTF are discussed in greater detail in Chapter 6, "Data Presentation.")

Code:

```
ODS  LISTING CLOSE;
ODS RTF FILE='c:\CONTENTS-DIRECORY.RTF';
  PROC CONTENTS
       DATA=PATH._ALL_ DIRECTORY;
  RUN;
ODS RTF CLOSE;
ODS LISTING;
```

Figure 5-1. CONTENTS output

Results shown in Figures 5-2, 5-3, and 5-4.

Chapter 5

-----Directory-----	
Libref:	PATH
Engine:	V8
Physical Name:	C:\Books\Power SAS Tips (Apress L.P.)\Examples
File Name:	C:\Books\Power SAS Tips (Apress L.P.)\Examples

#	Name	Memtype	File Size	Last Modified
1	ACTORS	DATA	9216	10NOV1999:14:43:42
2	MOVIES	DATA	17408	17JUL2002:12:21:16
	MOVIES	INDEX	17408	17JUL2002:12:21:16

Figure 5-2. CONTENTS output with DIRECTORY option

Data Set Name:	PATH.ACTORS	Observations:	13
Member Type:	DATA	Variables:	3
Engine:	V8	Indexes:	0
Created:	13:15 Wednesday, November 10, 1999	Observation Length:	70
Last Modified:	14:43 Wednesday, November 10, 1999	Deleted Observations:	0
Protection:		Compressed:	NO
Data Set Type:		Sorted:	NO
Label:			

-----Engine/Host Dependent Information-----	
Data Set Page Size:	8192
Number of Data Set Pages:	1
First Data Page:	1
Max Obs per Page:	116
Obs in First Data Page:	13
Number of Data Set Repairs:	0
File Name:	C:\Books\Power SAS Tips (Apress L.P.)\Examples\actors.sas7bdat
Release Created:	8.0000M0
Host Created:	WIN_98

-----Alphabetic List of Variables and Attributes-----				
#	Variable	Type	Len	Pos
2	Actor_Leading	Char	20	30
3	Actor_Supporting	Char	20	50
1	Title	Char	30	0

Figure 5-3. CONTENTS output with DIRECTORY option (continued)

Data Set Name:	PATH.MOVIES	Observations:	22
Member Type:	DATA	Variables:	6
Engine:	V8	Indexes:	3
Created:	23:27 Friday, April 9, 1999	Observation Length:	88
Last Modified:	16:52 Tuesday, July 2, 2002	Deleted Observations:	1
Protection:		Compressed:	NO
Data Set Type:		Sorted:	NO
Label:			

-----Engine/Host Dependent Information-----	
Data Set Page Size:	8192
Number of Data Set Pages:	2
First Data Page:	1
Max Obs per Page:	92
Obs in First Data Page:	23
Index File Page Size:	4096
Number of Index File Pages:	4
Number of Data Set Repairs:	1
Last Repair:	16:52 Tuesday, July 2, 2002
File Name:	C:\Books\Power SAS Tips (Apress L.P.)\Examples\movies.sas7bdat
Release Created:	7.00.00P
Host Created:	WIN_95

-----Alphabetic List of Variables and Attributes-----				
#	Variable	Type	Len	Pos
3	Category	Char	20	34
2	Length	Num	3	84
6	Rating	Char	5	79
5	Studio	Char	25	54
1	Title	Char	30	4
4	Year	Num	4	0

-----Alphabetic List of Indexes and Attributes-----		
#	Index	# of Unique Values
1	Category	11
2	Rating	4
3	Title	22

Figure 5-4. CONTENTS output with DIRECTORY option (continued)

3 Suppressing the printing of individual files in SAS libraries

By default, the CONTENTS procedure prints a great deal of information—at times more than is needed. The CONTENTS output contains the library's directory, files (including data sets), variables, and variable attributes. You may wonder whether there is a way to suppress printing everything but the directory listing itself. An option exists to do just that.

Data Management

To suppress the printing of individual files in a library, use the **NODS** option in the CONTENTS procedure code. The result of the directory produced with the NODS option appears in Figure 5-5. (ODS and RTF are discussed in greater detail in Chapter 6, "Data Presentation.")

Code:

```
ODS LISTING CLOSE;
ODS RTF FILE='c:\CONTENTS-NODS.RTF';
  PROC CONTENTS
      DATA=PATH._ALL_
      NODS;
  RUN;
ODS RTF CLOSE;
ODS LISTING;
```

Results shown in Figure 5-5.

-----Directory-----	
Libref:	PATH
Engine:	V8
Physical Name:	C:\Books\Power SAS Tips (Apress L.P.)\Examples
File Name:	C:\Books\Power SAS Tips (Apress L.P.)\Examples

#	Name	Memtype	File Size	Last Modified
1	ACTORS	DATA	9216	10NOV1999:14:43:42
2	MOVIES	DATA	17408	17JUL2002:12:21:16
	MOVIES	INDEX	17408	17JUL2002:12:21:16

Figure 5-5. CONTENTS output with NODS option

4 Printing a contents "short" list

When you only need a listing of the variables, index information, sort information, and nothing else, use the **SHORT** option of PROC CONTENTS. A snapshot of the "short" list produced with the SHORT option appears below. The result of specifying the SHORT option appears in Figure 5-6. (ODS and RTF are discussed in greater detail in Chapter 6, "Data Presentation.")

Code:

```
ODS LISTING CLOSE;
ODS RTF FILE='c:\CONTENTS-SHORT.RTF';
PROC CONTENTS
    DATA=PATH._ALL_
    SHORT;
RUN;
ODS RTF CLOSE;
ODS LISTING;
```

Results shown in Figure 5-6.

-----Directory-----	
Libref:	PATH
Engine:	V8
Physical Name:	C:\Books\Power SAS Tips (Apress L.P.)\Examples
File Name:	C:\Books\Power SAS Tips (Apress L.P.)\Examples

#	Name	Memtype	File Size	Last Modified
1	ACTORS	DATA	9216	10NOV1999:14:43:42
2	MOVIES	DATA	17408	17JUL2002:12:21:16
	MOVIES	INDEX	17408	17JUL2002:12:21:16

-----Alphabetic List of Variables for PATH.ACTORS-----
Actor Leading Actor Supporting Title

-----Alphabetic List of Variables for PATH.MOVIES-----
Category Length Rating Studio Title Year

-----Alphabetic List of Indexes-----
Category Rating Title

Figure 5-6. CONTENTS output with SHORT option

5 Printing an alphabetical list of variables

By default, the CONTENTS procedure prints a data set's variables in position order (the order in which they were defined in the data set). This isn't always the easiest or best way to find variables, especially in large data sets. Sometimes it makes life a whole lot easier to view the variables in alphabetical order. By specifying the **POSITION** option, two sets of variable and attribute listings are printed: the first in alphabetical order and the second by position order. To display an alphabetical listing of variables, the POSITION option of PROC CONTENTS is specified. The results of the POSITION option appear in three separate figures, Figure 5-7, 5-8, and 5-9. (ODS and RTF are discussed in greater detail in Chapter 6, "Data Presentation.")

Code:

```
ODS  LISTING CLOSE;
ODS RTF FILE='c:\CONTENTS-POSITION.RTF';
  PROC CONTENTS DATA=PATH._ALL_ POSITION;
  RUN;
ODS RTF CLOSE;
ODS LISTING;
```

Results shown in Figures 5-7, 5-8, and 5-9.

-----Directory-----	
Libref:	PATH
Engine:	V8
Physical Name:	C:\Books\Power SAS Tips (Apress L.P.)\Examples
File Name:	C:\Books\Power SAS Tips (Apress L.P.)\Examples

#	Name	Memtype	File Size	Last Modified
1	ACTORS	DATA	9216	10NOV1999:14:43:42
2	MOVIES	DATA	17408	17JUL2002:12:21:16
	MOVIES	INDEX	17408	17JUL2002:12:21:16

Figure 5-7. CONTENTS output and the directory

Data Set Name:	PATH.MOVIES	Observations:	22
Member Type:	DATA	Variables:	6
Engine:	V8	Indexes:	3
Created:	23:27 Friday, April 9, 1999	Observation Length:	88
Last Modified:	16:52 Tuesday, July 2, 2002	Deleted Observations:	1
Protection:		Compressed:	NO
Data Set Type:		Sorted:	NO
Label:			

-----Engine/Host Dependent Information-----	
Data Set Page Size:	8192
Number of Data Set Pages:	2
First Data Page:	1
Max Obs per Page:	92
Obs in First Data Page:	23
Index File Page Size:	4096
Number of Index File Pages:	4
Number of Data Set Repairs:	1
Last Repair:	16:52 Tuesday, July 2, 2002
File Name:	C:\Books\Power SAS Tips (Apress L.P.)\Examples\movies.sas7bdat
Release Created:	7.00.00P
Host Created:	WIN_95

-----Alphabetic List of Variables and Attributes-----				
#	Variable	Type	Len	Pos
3	Category	Char	20	34
2	Length	Num	3	84
6	Rating	Char	5	79
5	Studio	Char	25	54
1	Title	Char	30	4
4	Year	Num	4	0

-----Variables Ordered by Position-----				
#	Variable	Type	Len	Pos
1	Title	Char	30	4
2	Length	Num	3	84
3	Category	Char	20	34
4	Year	Num	4	0
5	Studio	Char	25	54
6	Rating	Char	5	79

Figure 5-8. CONTENTS output with list of variables

-----Alphabetic List of Indexes and Attributes-----		
#	Index	# of Unique Values
1	Category	11
2	Rating	4
3	Title	22

Figure 5-9. CONTENTS output with index list

Sorting Data

This section includes tips that will help you more effectively order your data resources. You'll learn proven techniques on how to utilize the SORT procedure for best results. These handy data-management tips will help you order your data in the most efficient way to satisfy even the most demanding data-management requirements.

1   Returning sorted observations to the original SAS data set

The **SORT** procedure reads data from a source data set, sorts each observation in the source data set using the variable(s) specified in a **BY** statement, and produces SAS System Log messages. Sorted observations can be written back to the original data set when an OUT= option is omitted, or to a new data set when the OUT= option is specified. For example, sorted observations are returned to the original MOVIES data set in the following code.

Code:

```
PROC SORT DATA=MOVIES;
 BY TITLE;
RUN;
```

2   Saving sorted observations to a data set

Sorted observations can be saved to a new or existing data set when the OUT= option is specified. For example, sorted observations are saved to the SORTED_MOVIES data set in the following code.

Code:

```
PROC SORT
     DATA=MOVIES OUT=SORTED_MOVIES;
 BY TITLE;
RUN;
```

3   Understanding the sort order for numeric variables

The sorting order for numeric variables from smallest to largest are

- Missing values

- Negative numeric values

- Zero (0)

- Positive numeric values

4   Understanding the sort order for character variables

The sort order for character variables from smallest to largest depends on the operating system under which SORT is executed. The sort order for character variables appears in the following list.

EBCDIC order (CMS, MVS, VSE)

- blank . < (+ | & ! $ *) ; ^ - / , % _ ? ' : # @ = "

- a through z

- A through Z

- 0 through 9

ASCII order (AOS, MS-DOS, Windows, UNIX, VMS)

- blank ! " # $ % & ' ( ) * + , - . / 0 through 9 : ; < = > ? @
- A through Z [\ ] ^ _
- a through z { | } ~

5   Selecting observations to sort

Comparison and *logical* operators can be combined to subset observations prior to sorting. They give queries the power to process multiple criteria. For example, the following subset selects "PG" and "PG-13" movies with a length less than 120 minutes, sorts the subset observations by the movie title, and saves the sorted observations to the SORTED_MOVIES data set.

Code:

```
PROC SORT
        DATA=MOVIES(WHERE=
            (RATING IN("PG","PG-13") AND
                LENGTH < 120))
        OUT=SORTED_MOVIES
            (KEEP=TITLE CATEGORY RATING);
    BY TITLE;
RUN;
```

Results:

```
Title                        Category  Rating
Casablanca                   Drama     PG
Christmas Vacation           Comedy    PG-13
Michael                      Drama     PG-13
National Lampoon's Vacation  Comedy    PG-13
Poltergeist                  Horror    PG
```

Managing Data

This section includes tips on how to effectively store data on disk and tape, process multiple tape data sets, modify data set attributes, apply updates to important data sets, create a simulated generation data group, and manage all your data resources.

1   Accessing SAS data libraries

To read observations from or write observations to SAS data libraries, a **LIBNAME** statement is most frequently used. The LIBNAME statement creates a library reference to the data set that can then be specified in DATA and PROC steps.

Users create a SAS library reference by pressing the **CTRL+N** keys or by clicking the **Libraries** icon in the SAS Explorer window (for more details on using the SAS Explorer, refer to Chapter 1). Once the New library window is displayed, enter a name consisting of 1 to 8 alphanumeric characters (following valid SAS naming conventions). Then add the requested information in the Library Information area.

✏️ *If you are unsure of the file location, click the **Browse...** button for navigational assistance.*

Once the required information is entered and complete, click **OK** to create the library reference. With the library reference assigned to the current SAS session, users are able to reference existing and/or new data libraries.

2 Exploring SAS libraries

The SAS System automatically assigns four SAS libraries during invocation. Each library has a specific purpose, which is described in Table 5-1.

Table 5-1. SAS System Libraries

SAS LIBRARIES	DESCRIPTION
MAPS Library	The storage location of the external library that contains SAS error, warning, and informational messages.
SASHELP Library	The storage location of the SASHELP library containing Help files.
SASUSER Library	The storage location of the SASUSER library that contains the SAS-created user's profile catalog.
User-assigned Library	The external SAS library that is used when referencing user-assigned data sets.
WORK Library	The storage location containing WORK or temporary SAS data sets, and other SAS objects. When a data set is referenced with a one-level name, the library reference automatically points to the temporary WORK library.

3 Exploring SAS member types

The SAS System is able to store different types of file structures in a SAS library. These file structures are referred to as SAS *members*. Samples of the available SAS member types along with their descriptions appear in Table 5-2.

Table 5-2. SAS Member Types

SAS MEMBER TYPE	DESCRIPTION
ALL	Specifies all member types in a SAS library.
CAT	Specifies a SAS catalog (for example, SAS/AF program and Frame files).
DATA	Specifies a SAS data set.
FORMATC	Specifies a user-defined character format.
FORMATN	Specifies a user-defined numeric format.
GCAT	Specifies a graphic catalog (for example, SAS/GRAPH files).
INDEX	Specifies a simple or composite index structure associated with a data set.

4 Storing SAS libraries on disk

Storing SAS libraries on diskettes, hard drives, and CD-ROMs is relatively easy to do. For example, the following code stores a SAS data set called MOVIES to a SAS library directory on a hard drive.

Code:

```
LIBNAME DISK 'C:\EXAMPLES';
PROC COPY IN=WORK OUT=DISK;
  SELECT MOVIES;
QUIT;
```

5 Storing SAS libraries on tape

Storing SAS libraries on tape is a little different than storing them on disk. Tape storage stores computer data magnetically on a thin flexible material. Tapes make a great storage medium for backing up important SAS libraries, as well as for making the data portable, as in transport files. The drawback to tape storage is that it can take time to mount and access data stored on them. Also, tape storage is a sequential storage medium, so only one part of a tape can be accessed at a time. For example, the following code stores a SAS data set called MOVIES to a SAS library on tape. The libref WORK represents the source (or input) location and TAPE represents the target (or output) location.

🖉 *Many installations with data stored on tape require their access to be through Job Control Language (JCL). One or more DD (Data Definition) statements may be required for tape mounts, so consult your installation representative for details.*

🖉 *An additional consideration with tape media is that it degrades faster over time (seven years before needing to be re-copied), and could have a greater tendency to be lost or damaged.*

Code:

```
PROC COPY IN=WORK OUT=TAPE;
  SELECT MOVIES;
QUIT;
```

6 Reading data sets from two or more tapes

When data sets are stored on two or more tapes, it may be necessary to request multiple tape mounts to satisfy the request. For example, a COPY procedure can be specified to access the first data set on tape, and then a second COPY procedure would copy the second data set as shown in the following example.

🖉 *Another approach with reading data from two or more tapes is to concatenate the files in the JCL allocation controls.*

Code:

```
PROC COPY IN=TAPE1 OUT=WORK;
  SELECT MOVIES;
QUIT;
PROC COPY IN=TAPE2 OUT=WORK;
  SELECT ACTORS;
QUIT;
```

7 Renaming variables

Occasionally data set variables need to be renamed. Whether it's needed for a merge, or for anything else, users have a few choices when renaming variables. For example, the following code illustrates a temporary method of renaming a variable using a **RENAME=** data set option in the PRINT procedure.

Code:

```
PROC PRINT DATA=
    MOVIES(RENAME=(RATING=MOVIE_RATING))
    NOOBS
    N;
RUN;
```

The next method of renaming a variable is more permanent since the change is made to the permanent data set descriptor record using the DATASETS procedure, as follows.

Code:

```
PROC DATASETS LIBRARY=WORK;
  MODIFY MOVIES;
    RENAME RATING=MOVIE_RATING;
RUN;
```

SAS Log Results:

```
184  PROC DATASETS LIBRARY=work;
          -----Directory-----

Libref:         WORK
Engine:         V8
Physical Name:  C:\windows\TEMP\
SAS Temporary Files\_TD51779
File Name:      C:\windows\TEMP\
SAS Temporary Files\_TD51779

                      File
#  Name     Memtype  Size   Last Modified
1  MOVIES   DATA     17408  07JUL2002:16:26
   MOVIES   INDEX    17408  07JUL2002:16:26
2  SASGOPT  CATALOG  5120   07JUL2002:13:30
185    MODIFY MOVIES;
186    RENAME RATING=MOVIE_RATING;
NOTE: Renaming variable RATING to
MOVIE_RATING.
RUN;
```

8 Modifying a data set's attributes

Modifying a data set's attributes is really quite simple. By using the **MODIFY** statement of the DATASETS procedure, users are able to assign or change a data set label, type, and how the data set is sorted. In the following example, a more descriptive label is provided to the MOVIES data set for the CONTENTS procedure to display.

Code:

```
PROC DATASETS LIBRARY=WORK;
  MODIFY MOVIES
          (LABEL='My Favorite Movies');
RUN;
PROC CONTENTS;
RUN;
```

Results:

```
The CONTENTS Procedure

Data Set Name: WORK.MOVIES
Observations: 22
Member Type: DATA
Variables: 6
Engine: V8
Indexes: 3
Created: 16:26 Sunday, July 7, 2002
Observation Length: 88
Last Modified: 16:49 Sunday, July 7, 2002
Deleted Observations: 0
Protection:
Compressed: NO
Data Set Type:
Sorted: NO
Label: My Favorite Movies
```

9 Modifying a variable's label

Modifying a variable's attributes is really quite simple. By using the MODIFY and LABEL statements of the DATASETS procedure, users are able to assign or change a variable's label. For example, a more descriptive label is given to the TITLE variable in the MOVIES data set so when the CONTENTS and PRINT procedures are executed it will display a more descriptive heading.

Chapter 5

Code:

```
PROC DATASETS LIBRARY=WORK;
 MODIFY MOVIES;
  LABEL TITLE='My Favorite Movie';
RUN;
PROC PRINT
    DATA=MOVIES(KEEP=TITLE RATING)
    NOOBS
    LABEL;
RUN;
```

SAS Log Results:

```
NOTE: PROCEDURE DATASETS used:
      real time           19.72 seconds

227  PROC DATASETS LIBRARY=WORK;
              -----Directory-----

Libref:         WORK
Engine:         V8
Physical Name:  C:\windows\TEMP\
SAS Temporary Files\_TD51779
File Name:      C:\windows\TEMP\
SAS Temporary Files\_TD51779

                       File
# Name      Memtype  Size   Last Modified
1 MOVIES    DATA     17408  07JUL2002:17:05
  MOVIES    INDEX    17408  07JUL2002:17:05
2 SASGOPT   CATALOG  5120   07JUL2002:13:30
228    MODIFY MOVIES;
229    LABEL TITLE='My Favorite Movie';
230    RUN;

NOTE: PROCEDURE DATASETS used:
      real time            0.00 seconds

PROC PRINT
   DATA=MOVIES(KEEP=TITLE RATING)
   NOOBS
   LABEL;
232 RUN;

NOTE: There were 22 observations read
from the data set WORK.MOVIES.
```

Results

My Favorite Movie	RATING
Brave Heart	R
Casablanca	PG
Christmas Vacation	PG-13
Coming to America	R
Dracula	R
Dressed to Kill	R
Forrest Gump	PG-13
Ghost	PG-13
Jaws	PG
Jurassic Park	PG-13
Lethal Weapon	R
Michael	PG-13
National Lampoon's Vacation	PG-13
Poltergeist	PG
Rocky	PG
Scarface	R
Silence of the Lambs	R
Star Wars	PG
The Hunt for Red October	PG
The Terminator	R
The Wizard of Oz	G
Titanic	PG-13

10 Updating a SAS data set with the UPDATE statement

The **UPDATE** statement can be specified in a DATA step to apply corrections to individual observations within a SAS data set. By matching observations with a BY statement, the master data set has one or more observations applied from a new data set to existing observations. For example, to update the MOVIES data set by applying the observations in the data set NEW_MOVIES, we'll be able to apply the movie title "Rocky II" to the master data set as the following example shows. All of the original records in the MOVIES data set remain unchanged.

✏️ *The NEW_MOVIES data set structure should be similar to the MOVIES data set structure.*

Code:

```
PROC SORT DATA=MOVIES;
  BY TITLE;
RUN;
PROC SORT DATA=NEW_MOVIES;
  BY TITLE;
RUN;
DATA MOVIES_MSTR;
  UPDATE MOVIES NEW_MOVIES;
  BY TITLE;
RUN;
PROC PRINT
    DATA=MOVIES_MSTR(KEEP=TITLE RATING)
    NOOBS;
RUN;
```

Results:

Title	Rating
Brave Heart	R
Casablanca	PG
Christmas Vacation	PG-13
Coming to America	R
Dracula	R
Dressed to Kill	R
Forrest Gump	PG-13
Ghost	PG-13
Jaws	PG
Jurassic Park	PG-13
Lethal Weapon	R
Michael	PG-13
National Lampoon's Vacation	PG-13
Poltergeist	PG
Rocky	PG
Rocky II	**PG**
Scarface	R
Silence of the Lambs	R
Star Wars	PG
The Hunt for Red October	PG
The Terminator	R
The Wizard of Oz	G
Titanic	PG-13

11 Aging a SAS data set

Aging a SAS data set simulates creating a generation data group. Selected data sets are aged one-by-one, with the most current being the first generation and the oldest data set being the last generation in the data group. When the AGE statement is issued in the DATASETS procedure, each data set in the data group is renamed one generation older with the oldest data set being deleted from the data group. For example, creating a three-generation data group for MOVIES would be set up as follows.

✏️ *The advantage of using the AGE statement to back up is that you can easily maintain many versions of the same data set.*

Code:

```
PROC DATASETS LIBRARY=WORK;
  AGE MOVIES MOVIES1-MOVIES3;
QUIT;
```

12 Reading a generation data set (GENNUM=)

Reading multiple versions of a data set is made easy with the **GENNUM=** data set option. When a generation data set has been created with the GENMAX= data set option, SAS permits the access to any of the generations (maximum of 1,000 archived generation data sets) by specifying the GENNUM= data set option with an integer number corresponding to the desired data set version. The PRINT procedure example shows the third generation data set being accessed using the GENNUM=3 data set option. This would be the same MOVIES3 data set created in the previous tip.

Code:

```
PROC PRINT DATA=MOVIES(GENNUM=3);
RUN;
```

13 Managing SAS data sets with the APPEND procedure

The APPEND procedure is designed to concatenate observations from a smaller data set to a larger data set. For optimal data management, users would be well advised to concatenate data sets using the APPEND procedure rather than a DATA – SET statement convention.

As an alternative, users can leave the data as separate files and concatenate them using TSO (non-tape) or JCL.

14 Specifying the larger data set as the BASE= data set

For maximum efficiency and speed, specify the larger of the two SAS data sets as the **BASE=** dataset. Essentially the BASE= data set receives and stores the observations from the smaller data set. The smaller data set should be referenced specified as the DATA= option because it identifies the data set that will be providing one or more observations for appending. The APPEND procedure positions its record pointer at the end of the BASE= data set. It thereby avoids having to read observations individually as it does the observations specified by the DATA= data set.

15 Creating the BASE= data set automatically

If the data set referenced by the **BASE=** data set does not exist, the **APPEND** procedure automatically creates it in the same library (libref) as the BASE= data set. This means that the data set referenced by the BASE= option does not have to already exist. Any observations in the DATA= data set are appended one observation at a time to the BASE= data set.

16 Using the FORCE option

When one or more variables in the input data set (DATA=) are not present in the output data set (BASE=), the **FORCE** option must be specified as an option on the PROC statement to prevent a syntax error.

Missing values are assigned to the variables in the input data set not present in the output data set.

17 Exploring single-level data set names

When the libref is omitted when specifying the BASE= or DATA= data sets, the default library that is referenced is WORK.

18 Handling missing values in the APPEND procedure

When a variable in the BASE= dataset does not exist in the DATA= dataset, the variable is assigned a missing value for all added observations.

19 Concatenating two or more data sets with the APPEND procedure

When two or more data sets are to be concatenated, multiple APPEND procedures can be issued. The following syntax shows how two data sets (txn1, and txn2) are concatenated at the end of a base data set with the APPEND procedure.

Code:

```
PROC APPEND
    BASE=libref.master
    DATA=libref.txn1;
RUN;
PROC APPEND
    BASE=libref.master
    DATA=libref.txn2;
RUN;
```

20 Renaming a base data set

There is more than one way to rename a data set in the SAS System. When a data set has to be renamed, users should refrain from using a DATA step to create a new data set with the desired name. This tends to be less efficient because the DATA – SET statement convention (see tip #21, "Concatenating two or more data sets in a DATA step") must read and write every observation in the data set, which uses additional CPU and I/O resources.

A more efficient approach to renaming a data set, in this case a BASE= data set, is to use the DATASETS procedure. In the following example, the data set is renamed from ACCTXN to ACCTMSTR using the RENAME statement of PROC DATASETS.

Code:

```
PROC DATASETS LIBRARY=WORK;
   RENAME ACCTXN = ACCTMSTR;
RUN;
```

21 Concatenating two or more data sets in a DATA step

When concatenating two or more data sets, the DATA step is a logical approach to use. In fact, SAS users have been using the DATA - SET statements convention to concatenate two or more data sets since SAS software was first introduced. This is why so much legacy SAS code can be found using this convention, and not the APPEND procedure. Sometimes, old habits are difficult to break. For example, concatenating two data sets is a snap in the DATA step. Observations from the PG_RATING and PG13_RATING data sets are read one observation at a time and written to the new data set PG_PG13_RATINGS.

Code:

```
DATA PG_PG13_RATINGS;
  SET PG_RATING
      PG13_RATING;
RUN;
```

22 Removing all SAS files in a library

A quick way of removing all SAS files in a library would be to specify the **KILL** option in the DATASETS procedure. An optional **MEMTYPE=** option specifies the type of files to delete. If the MEMTYPE= option is omitted, all files are removed. In the example, all files are removed from the WORK library.

Chapter 5

🖉 *Use care when specifying the KILL option, because it doesn't ask permission before removing files.*

Code:

```
PROC DATASETS LIBRARY=WORK KILL;
RUN;
```

SAS Log Results:

```
PROC DATASETS LIBRARY=WORK KILL;
  -----Directory-----
Libref: WORK
Engine: V8
Physical Name: C:\windows\TEMP\
SAS Temporary Files\_TD72759
File Name:    C:\windows\TEMP\
SAS Temporary Files\_TD72759

                 File
# Name    Memtype Size  Last Modified
1 ACTORS  DATA    9216  19JUL2002:15:39
2 MOVIES  DATA    17408 19JUL2002:15:39
  MOVIES  INDEX   17408 19JUL2002:15:39
NOTE: Deleting WORK.ACTORS (memtype=DATA).
NOTE: Deleting WORK.MOVIES (memtype=DATA).
  RUN;
```

Summary

In this chapter, you learned a lot about managing and safeguarding your data. Each tip provided useful techniques for managing data resources using common DATA and PROC step methods. Using the Base SAS software, data management tasks are quick and easy to master.

In the next chapter, "Data Presentation," you'll discover an assortment of exciting and, more importantly, easy-to-use techniques to bring your data to life—including useful tips for quick and problem-free reporting using DATA and PROC step approaches. You'll also learn how to customize your output with a variety of built-in and ready-to-go formatting options. Finally, you'll discover how easy it is to format output for everyone to see using Web-ready techniques for viewing with a common Web browser.

CHAPTER 6

Data Presentation

DATA PRESENTATION IS a cornerstone of the Base SAS software. Reports display information in one of two ways: detail or summary form. SAS software provides numerous easy-to-use procedures to present the information you need, any time you need it. For a more custom look, you can create output presentations using the DATA step. This chapter presents a variety of tips on report-writing procedures, customizing reports with the DATA step, data presentation using ODS, and delivering online output using Web browser software.

In this chapter, you'll learn how to

- Take advantage of useful PROC PRINT reporting features

- Control orientation and labeling of column headers in PROC PRINT

- Suppress column headers in PROC PRINT

- Create custom-presentations with the DATA step

- Create two reports in a single DATA step

- Create two-, three-, and four-column output in the DATA step

- Format output with global ODS statements

- Create Rich Text Format (RTF) output

- Create PostScript output

- Integrate ODS into the DATA step

- Distribute content anywhere and anytime using ODS

- Create HTML output as an integrated Web application

- Combine output results using ODS

- Create Portable Document Format (PDF) output

- Create powerful drill-down applications using ODS

Report Writing and PROC PRINT

This section offers useful techniques when using PROC PRINT to better control the way the PRINT procedure formats output.

1 Suppressing the observation number in PROC PRINT output

By default, PROC PRINT automatically produces an observation number of output. Sometimes this can be a handy feature, but can also clutter the appearance of the report. By specifying the NOOBS option in the PROC PRINT statement, the observation number is suppressed.

Code:

```
PROC PRINT DATA=MOVIES
       (WHERE=(RATING='PG')
        KEEP=TITLE RATING) NOOBS;
RUN;
```

Results:

Title	Rating
Casablanca	PG
Jaws	PG
Poltergeist	PG
Rocky	PG
Star Wars	PG
The Hunt for Red October	PG

2 Writing a blank line between observations in PROC PRINT

When producing a report that contains more output than can fit nicely across a page, the PRINT procedure automatically flows output over to another line. This often makes output difficult to read. To enhance the readability of one or more "flowed" lines, the **DOUBLE** option can be specified on the PROC PRINT statement.

Code:

```
PROC PRINT DATA=MOVIES
       (WHERE=(RATING='PG')
        KEEP=TITLE RATING) DOUBLE NOOBS;
RUN;
```

Results:

Title	Rating
Casablanca	PG
Jaws	PG
Poltergeist	PG
Rocky	PG
Star Wars	PG
The Hunt for Red October	PG

3 Controlling the orientation of column headings in PROC PRINT

Users can control the orientation of column headings in the PRINT procedure by specifying the **HEADING=** option in the PROC PRINT statement. The valid values for the HEADING= option are **H** (Horizontal) or **V** (Vertical). For example, printing vertical headings requires the option V to be specified as follows.

Code:

```
PROC PRINT DATA=MOVIES
       (WHERE=(RATING='PG')
        KEEP=TITLE RATING) HEADING=V NOOBS;
RUN;
```

Results:

```
                    R
         T          a
         i          t
         t          i
         l          n
         e          g

Casablanca          PG
Jaws                PG
Poltergeist         PG
Rocky               PG
Star Wars           PG
The Hunt for Red October  PG
```

4 Printing labels as column headings in PROC PRINT

Users can print user-defined labels instead of variable names for column headings in the PRINT procedure. By specifying the **LABEL** option in the PROC PRINT statement, existing labels are printed, if available. Otherwise, users can define labels in the PRINT procedure.

✐ *Defining labels in the PRINT procedure means that the labels are temporary because they aren't permanently saved as part of the data set descriptor record.*

Code:

```
PROC PRINT DATA=MOVIES
       (WHERE=(RATING='PG')
        KEEP=TITLE RATING) LABEL NOOBS;
  LABEL TITLE='Movie Title'
        RATING='Movie Rating';
RUN;
```

Results:

```
                             Movie
Movie Title                  Rating

Casablanca                   PG
Jaws                         PG
Poltergeist                  PG
Rocky                        PG
Star Wars                    PG
The Hunt for Red October     PG
```

5 Breaking column headings

User-defined labels can be lengthy, causing output columns to be wider than necessary. The PRINT procedure lets users break a column heading so that it wraps to the next header line. This wrapping often gives the output a more professional and customized appearance. By specifying the **LABEL** and **SPLIT=** options in the PROC PRINT statement, labels are printed and split at the location of the split character.

✐ *Labels defined in the PRINT procedure are temporary and are not permanently saved as part of the data set descriptor record.*

Code:

```
PROC PRINT DATA=MOVIES
       (WHERE=(RATING='PG')
        KEEP=TITLE RATING)
        LABEL SPLIT='*' NOOBS;
  LABEL TITLE='Movie*Title'
        RATING='Movie*Rating';
RUN;
```

Results:

```
Movie                        Movie
Title                        Rating

Casablanca                   PG
Jaws                         PG
Poltergeist                  PG
Rocky                        PG
Star Wars                    PG
The Hunt for Red October     PG
```

6 Printing the number of observations at the end of a report

Occasionally it's useful to print a counter at the end of a report to alert users as to how many records have been printed. If the **N** option in the PROC PRINT statement is specified, the total number of observations printed appears at the end of a report.

Code:

```
PROC PRINT DATA=MOVIES
      (WHERE=(RATING='PG')
       KEEP=TITLE RATING) N NOOBS;
  LABEL TITLE='Movie Title';
RUN;
```

Results:

```
Movie Title                  Rating

Casablanca                   PG
Jaws                         PG
Poltergeist                  PG
Rocky                        PG
Star Wars                    PG
The Hunt for Red October     PG

N = 6
```

7 Printing the number of observations in BY group in a report

Occasionally it's useful to print the number of observations in a BY group in a report. This can provide valuable information to users. By specifying the N option in the PROC PRINT statement with a **BY** statement, the total number of observations in each BY group is printed in the report.

To use the BY statement, data must either be sorted or arranged in the desired order of the BY-variable.

Code:

```
PROC SORT DATA=MOVIES
          OUT=SORTED_MOVIES;
 BY RATING;
RUN;
PROC PRINT DATA=SORTED_MOVIES
      (KEEP=TITLE RATING) N NOOBS;
  LABEL TITLE='Movie Title'
        RATING='Movie Rating';
  BY RATING;
RUN;
```

Results:

```
Movie Rating=G

    Title
The Wizard of Oz

N = 1
```

Movie Rating=PG

Title
Casablanca
Jaws
Poltergeist
Rocky
Star Wars
The Hunt for Red October

N = 6

Movie Rating=PG-13

Title
Christmas Vacation
Forrest Gump
Ghost
Jurassic Park
Michael
National Lampoon's Vacation
Titanic

N = 7

Movie Rating=R

Title
Brave Heart
Coming to America
Dracula
Dressed to Kill
Lethal Weapon
Scarface
Silence of the Lambs
The Terminator

N = 8

8 Printing output consistently page-by-page

Users can have the PRINT procedure print variables consistently on each page of a multi-page report. By specifying the **UNIFORM** option in the PROC PRINT statement, SAS determines what the widest column width, or column-heading width, is for each variable and uses this information to print a consistent page column width for the entire report. The advantage of using the UNIFORM option is to enable a consistent width for an individual column from page to page in a multi-column report. This is particularly important for providing a consistent and uniform look to multi-page reports.

When the UNIFORM option isn't specified, a column's width can change from page to page when a variable containing varying data exists widths can shift from page to page, depending on the width of the widest column on the page.

Code:

```
PROC PRINT DATA=MOVIES NOOBS UNIFORM;
RUN;
```

9 Conserving CPU time with the FULL option

By specifying the **FULL** option in the PRINT procedure statement, you save CPU time. This becomes particularly more relevant when printing large multi-page reports. The reason is that SAS uses each variable's formatted widths as the column widths when printing each page of a report. Consequently, SAS doesn't need to expend any CPU determining what the largest, or smallest, columns for a printed page are.

10 Printing a blank column header

SAS lets you suppress a column header in a report anytime the need arises. All you have to do is specify a LABEL statement with the name of the variable you want the column header suppressed for, and provide a value of **'00'x** as follows.

> 🖉 *The LABEL option must be specified in the PROC PRINT statement for defined labels in the LABEL statement to appear.*

Code:

```
PROC PRINT DATA=MOVIES
      (WHERE=(RATING='PG')
       KEEP=TITLE RATING) NOOBS LABEL;
  LABEL TITLE='00'x;
RUN;
```

Results:

```
                              Rating

Casablanca                    PG
Jaws                          PG
Poltergeist                   PG
Rocky                         PG
Star Wars                     PG
The Hunt for Red October      PG
```

Custom Report Writing with the DATA Step

This section includes a number of useful techniques that can be used when using the DATA step to create and customize reports.

1 Understanding the advantages of "custom" report writing

Although SAS procedures are frequently used to produce detail and summary reports, requirements may demand a "custom" look that is not available from output-producing procedures. DATA step reporting provides greater flexibility, control, and the ability to design report output anyway that is needed—something that is not available with most procedures.

2 Specifying _NULL_

When a DATA step is needed to create an output file or report, but not a SAS data set, then the **DATA _NULL_** convention is typically used. This convention enables a DATA step to be used without wasting space for the storage of a data set.

3 Printing headings at the top of each page

User-defined headings are automatically written at the top of each page of output when a **HEADER=** option is specified. By specifying a HEADER= option in the FILE statement, users can instruct SAS to print headings at the top of each page. The heading text is coded as a subroutine and identified with a user-defined label within the DATA step. It automatically prints at the beginning of each new page. The header (identified by the label) H is printed at the top of each page of output, after which control returns to the detail-line PUT statement, as follows.

Code:

```
DATA _NULL_;
 SET MOVIES;
 FILE PRINT HEADER=H;
 PUT @1 TITLE $30.
    @35 RATING $5.;
RETURN;
H: PUT 'DETAIL REPORT';
RETURN;
RUN;
```

4 Suppressing the printing of the default SAS title

By default, the SAS title appears at the top of every page of output. Users can suppress the title by specifying the **NOTITLES** option in the FILE statement as follows.

Code:

```
DATA _NULL_;
 SET MOVIES;
 FILE PRINT NOTITLES HEADER=H;
 PUT @1 TITLE $30.
    @35 RATING $5.;
RETURN;
H: PUT 'DETAIL REPORT';
RETURN;
RUN;
```

5 Knowing when the end-of-file has occurred

Knowing when the end-of-file has occurred in the input SAS data set can be very helpful. By coding the **END=** option in the SET statement, users can test whether the end-of-file has occurred.

🖉 *When SAS reads the last observation from the input data set, it sets the end-of-file condition to a value of 1; otherwise, its value is 0.*

Code:

```
DATA _NULL_;
 SET MOVIES END=EOF;
 FILE PRINT NOTITLES HEADER=H;
 PUT @1 TITLE $30.
    @35 RATING $5.;
 IF EOF THEN PUT 'FINISHED!';
RETURN;
H: PUT 'DETAIL REPORT';
RETURN;
RUN;
```

6 Counting the number of lines left on a page

When designing a report that contains information that must be printed at the bottom of each page of output, the **LINESLEFT=** variable (or **LL=**) is a useful feature that users can use. Specified as an option in the FILE statement, the LINESLEFT= variable counts the number of lines left on a page. For example, before an observation is written to output, you may want to check whether there still is room at the bottom of the page to print the word 'FINISHED!'. If there isn't sufficient space to print at the bottom of the page, then it's printed on a new page.

Code:

```
DATA _NULL_;
 SET MOVIES END=EOF;
 FILE PRINT LINESLEFT=LEFT
          HEADER=H NOTITLES;
 IF LEFT < 3 THEN PUT _PAGE_;
```

```
     PUT @1 TITLE $30.
        @35 RATING $5.;
     IF EOF THEN PUT 'FINISHED!';
RETURN;
H: PUT 'DETAIL REPORT';
RETURN;
RUN;
```

7 Creating two reports in a single DATA step

When reporting requirements call for the creation of two reports from the same data, sometimes it is possible to create them both in a single DATA step. Typically this approach works best when one report contains detail information and the second report represents summary information. The primary advantage for creating two reports in a single step is to conserve on I/O resources (for more information, see Chapter 7, "Efficiency and Performance"). For example, two separate FILE statements and subroutines are coded, one for detail lines and the second for summary lines, as shown here.

Code:

```
DATA _NULL_;
  SET MOVIES END=EOF;
  FILE DETAIL LINESLEFT=LEFT
              HEADER=H NOTITLES;
  IF LEFT < 3 THEN PUT _PAGE_;
  PUT @1 TITLE $30.
      @35 RATING $5.;
  CTR_MOVIES+1;
  IF EOF THEN LINK SUMMARY;
RETURN;
H: PUT @15 'DETAIL REPORT';
RETURN;
SUMMARY:
  FILE SUMMARY NOTITLES;
  PUT @15 'SUMMARY REPORT'
```

```
      ///@12 'MY FAVORITE MOVIES'
      ////@12 'TOTAL MOVIES: ' CTR_MOVIES 3.;
RETURN;
RUN;
```

8 Creating two-column output in the DATA step

There are times when requirements call for output to be displayed in two columns. To accomplish this, a **FILE N=PS** (pagesize) option is specified to give the SAS System access to the entire page at a time. Then, two **DO loops** are used to control the positioning of output down rows and across columns. Next, within the DO loops, a **SET** statement is specified to control when the DATA step processes observations on input. Finally, a **PUT _PAGE_** statement is used to control printing the two columns of output per page.

The following example shows SAS code that first removes observations with duplicate BY values. It then prepares a two-column report similar to a two-column phone book. The maximum number of rows (controlled by the first DO loop) is set at 4 and the maximum number of columns (controlled by the second DO loop) is 16. Once the inner and outer DO groups are satisfied, the page is released with the PUT _PAGE_ statement.

Code:

```
PROC SORT DATA=MOVIES(KEEP=RATING)
          OUT=MOVIES_SORTED
          NODUPKEY;
  BY RATING;
RUN;
TITLE;
DATA _NULL_;
  FILE PRINT N=PS;
```

```
      DO ROW=1 TO 4;
        DO COL=1 TO 16 BY 8;
          SET MOVIES_SORTED;
          BY RATING;
          PUT #ROW @COL RATING $5.;
        END;
      END;
      PUT _PAGE_;
    RUN;
```

Results:

```
G        PG
PG-13    R
```

9 Creating three-column output in the DATA step

Producing three-column output is just as easy as creating two-column output. You begin by specifying a **FILE N=PS** (pagesize) option. This provides control over the entire page (as defined by the values set in the DO groups). Then, two **DO loops** are used to control the positioning of output down rows and across columns. Next, inside both DO loops, a **SET** statement (read) is specified to control when the DATA step processes observations on input. Finally, a **PUT _PAGE_** statement is used to control printing the output on each page.

The following example shows SAS code that prints a three-column report (similar to tip #8). The maximum number of rows (controlled by the first DO loop) is set at 4 and the maximum number of columns across the page (controlled by the second DO loop) is 24, in groups of three. Once each page is formatted, it's then released with the PUT _PAGE_ statement. The output consists of three columns.

Code:

```
PROC SORT DATA=MOVIES(KEEP=RATING)
          OUT=MOVIES_SORTED
          NODUPKEY;
  BY RATING;
RUN;
TITLE;
DATA _NULL_;
  FILE PRINT N=PS;
  DO ROW=1 TO 4;
    DO COL=1 TO 24 BY 8;
      SET MOVIES_SORTED;
      BY RATING;
      PUT #ROW @COL RATING  $5. @;
    END;
  END;
  PUT _PAGE_;
RUN;
```

Results:

```
G        PG        PG-13
R
```

10 Creating four-column report output in the DATA step

The following example shows SAS code that prints a four-column report. The maximum number of rows down a single page (controlled by the first DO loop) is set at 4 and the maximum number of columns across a page (controlled by the second DO loop) is 32, in groups of four. Once each page is formatted, it's released with the PUT _PAGE_ statement. The output consists of four columns.

Code:

```
PROC SORT DATA=MOVIES(KEEP=RATING)
     OUT=MOVIES_SORTED
     NODUPKEY;
  BY RATING;
RUN;
TITLE;
DATA _NULL_;
  FILE PRINT N=PS;
  DO ROW=1 TO 4;
    DO COL=1 TO 32 BY 8;
      SET MOVIES_SORTED;
      BY RATING;
      IF FIRST.RATING THEN
        PUT @COL RATING $5. @;
    END;
  END;
  PUT _PAGE_;
RUN;
```

Results:

```
G       PG      PG-13   R
```

Output Delivery System (ODS)

This section includes a number of popular tips for combining the power of ODS with various data presentation techniques. You'll learn how to integrate ODS in the DATA step, create RTF and HTML output, send output to a SAS data set, and create output only on the information you want.

1 Understanding the advantages of the Output Delivery System (ODS)

The SAS ODS provides many ways to format output. It controls the way output is accessed and formatted. Although ODS continues to support the creation of traditional SAS monospace output (that is, Listing), it provides many new output-formatting features and greater flexibility when working with output. Users have a powerful and easy way to create and access formatted procedure and DATA step output.

2 Using an earlier version of SAS software

First introduced in Version 6.12, ODS offers users the capability to format output to destinations other than traditional line printers. Although earlier versions don't offer the same capabilities as Version 8.2 or Version 9, they do enable the creation of "quality"-looking output without having to import output it into word processors such as Microsoft Word, or other third-party vendor software. The latest version of ODS includes the ability to create PostScript files, Rich Text Format (RTF) files, HyperText Markup Language (HTML), Portable Document Format (PDF), Extensible Markup Language (XML), as well as the ability to perform extensive output customizations.

3 Formatting output with global ODS statements

Users communicate output requirements by coding global ODS statements at the beginning and end of program steps in a SAS job. Each ODS statement is processed immediately by the SAS System. These embedded ODS statements control what format engine(s) are turned on, what output is selected, how output is handled, and what destination output is sent to. ODS is designed to manage and route output to several output destinations:

- Standard SAS listing (default)

- HTML code for web deployment

- Output SAS data set
- RTF
- PDF
- XML

By using global ODS statements, output is formatted and routed with simple precision to one or more of these output destinations, as shown in Figure 6-1. ODS improves the way system resources are utilized by permitting output to be routed to one or more output destinations at the same time. Specifying an ODS statement and destination at a particular point in a program is important, because output-producing PROC and DATA steps will respond by sending output to the open destination.

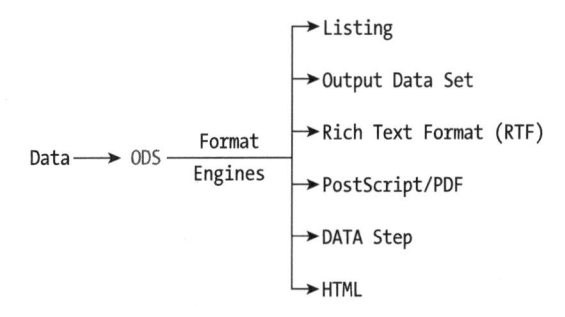

```
                          →Listing
                          →Output Data Set
                 Format   →Rich Text Format (RTF)
Data → ODS ──────────────
                 Engines  →PostScript/PDF
                          →DATA Step
                          →HTML
```

Figure 6-1. Available ODS destinations

4 Opening and closing destinations

The Listing destination is open by default at SAS invocation, whereas the other destinations are closed. If nothing is done to suppress output to the Listing destination, your SAS programs automatically produce Listing output, just as they always have in the SAS System. For example, **UNIVARIATE** output is sent to the Listing destination (or DMS Output window) as usual, as shown in the following program code. By closing the Listing destination after the UNIVARIATE procedure code, the SAS System will actually suppress output to the Listing destination until it is reopened.

Code:

```
ODS LISTING;
  PROC UNIVARIATE DATA=MOVIES;
  RUN;
ODS LISTING CLOSE;
```

5 Managing system resources

Multiple ODS destinations can be opened at the same time. ODS automatically sends output to any open output destinations. System resources are used when a destination is open. As a result, make sure any and all unwanted open destinations are closed when no longer needed to conserve system resources.

6 Understanding the difference between batch and interactive use

Many ODS features found in the interactive side of the SAS DMS can also be used in batch processing. ODS has been designed to make exciting new formatting options available to users. In a windowing environment, ODS can send output to the following destinations: the output window (DMS), the listing file, HTML, SAS data set, RTF, PostScript file, external output file (non-SAS file), or output device. The only exception for batch processing is having output sent to the output window.

7 Tracing procedure output

Output-producing procedures often create multiple pieces or tables of information. In order to discriminate between the various pieces of information, it's advantageous to know the names assigned to each piece of information. The ability to display the names of individual pieces of output information is called *tracing*. The ODS statement syntax **ODS trace ON / Listing** causes the SAS System to turn the trace feature on and print results to the SAS Listing destination.

Code:

```
ODS TRACE ON / LISTING;
   PROC UNIVARIATE DATA=MOVIES;
   RUN;
ODS TRACE OFF;
```

The trace record displays information about the data component, the table definition, and the output object. For example, the trace record displays the following output objects to the SAS Listing destination: 1) Moments, 2) BasicMeasures, 3) TestForLocation, 4) Quantiles, and 5) ExtremeObs. A sample trace record containing each output object's name, label, template, and path is displayed for the UNIVARIATE procedure.

✏️ *For each output object, the name, label, template, and path are displayed.*

SAS Log Results:

```
Output Added:
-------------
Name:       Moments
Label:      Moments
Template:   base.univariate.Moments
Path:       Univariate.age.Moments
-------------

Output Added:
-------------
Name:       BasicMeasures
Label:      Basic Measures of Location ↵
and Variability
Template:   base.univariate.Measures
Path:       Univariate.age.BasicMeasures
-------------

Output Added:
-------------
Name:       TestsForLocation
Label:      Tests For Location
Template:   base.univariate.Location
Path:       Univariate.age.TestsForLocation
-------------

Output Added:
-------------
Name:       Quantiles
Label:      Quantiles
Template:   base.univariate.Quantiles
Path:       Univariate.age.Quantiles
-------------

Output Added:
-------------
Name:       ExtremeObs
Label:      Extreme Observations
Template:   base.univariate.ExtObs
Path:       Univariate.age.ExtremeObs
-------------
```

8 Selecting output with ODS

A selection or exclusion list is created for each open ODS destination. Each list determines which output object(s) to send to ODS destinations. To accomplish this, ODS verifies whether an output object is included in a destination's selection, or exclusion, list. If it doesn't appear in this list, then the output object isn't sent to the ODS destination. If it's included in the list, ODS determines whether the object is included in the overall list. If the output object appears in the overall list, it's sent to the open destination(s). Otherwise, output isn't sent to the open ODS destination(s).

9 Selecting desired output objects

Once the individual names of each output object are known (from the **TRACE** option), the desired output object can be selected for reporting purposes. Selecting an output object is as easy as 1-2-3. Just specify an ODS SELECT statement and an *output-object* name. For example, the following code selects the single output object "Moments" from the UNIVARIATE procedure.

Code:

```
ODS SELECT MOMENTS;
  PROC UNIVARIATE DATA=MOVIES;
  RUN;
```

Results:

```
The UNIVARIATE Procedure
Variable:  Length

Moments

N  22
Sum Weights  22
Mean  124.909091
Sum Observations  2748
Std Deviation  25.8344714
Variance  667.419913
Skewness  1.45414494
Kurtosis  1.71453814
Uncorrected SS  357266
Corrected SS  14015.8182
Coeff Variation  20.682619
Std Error Mean  5.50792781
```

10 Deleting output from the Results window

The Results window identifies procedure output that has been produced, providing users with an improved way to manage their output. It is customarily a good thing to remove unwanted output displayed in this window to conserve on system resources. The Results window is opened by specifying the command **ODSRESULTS** on the DMS command line or by selecting **View Results** from the pull-down menu. To delete procedure output, follow these simple steps.

- Select the procedure folder you want to remove.

- Click the **Delete** button on the task bar.

- Select **Yes** to confirm the deletion of the procedure output folder.

11 Creating the standard "monospace" Listing file

The standard "monospace" Listing file is the default destination in the SAS System. To send output from any output-producing procedure or DATA step to the Output window (interactive SAS only), specify an ODS statement as follows.

Code:

```
ODS Listing;
```

Sending output to an external file requires specifying a **FILE=** parameter with the ODS statement. In the following example, output from the UNIVARIATE procedure is written to an external file located in the root directory of a PC hard drive.

Code:

```
ODS LISTING FILE='C:\Univariate-output.lis';
  PROC UNIVARIATE DATA=MOVIES;
  RUN;
```

12 Creating output data sets

Occasionally, output results must be sent to a SAS data set rather than to the Listing destination. Redirecting SAS procedure output to a data set is relatively simple with ODS. The syntax follows:

```
ODS output
  output-table-name =
  User-defined-table-name;
< SAS Code >
```

where *output-table-name* is the name of the desired output table (component) containing the information to be sent to a data set, such as *Moments* in the UNIVARIATE procedure. *User-defined-table-name* is the name you supply for the newly created data set. It can be defined as either a temporary or permanent data set. The first ODS statement closes the LISTING destination. Once an object is selected, it's sent to the output destination using the ODS OUTPUT statement. For example, the following code selects and sends the Moments from the UNIVARIATE procedure to a SAS data set in the following code. The final ODS statement reopens the LISTING destination at the end of the process.

Code:

```
ODS LISTING CLOSE;
ODS OUTPUT MOMENTS = MOVIE_MOMENTS;
  PROC UNIVARIATE DATA=MOVIES;
  RUN;
ODS LISTING;
```

13 Creating RTF

RTF is text consisting of formatting attributes codes, such as boldface, italics, underline, and so on. It is principally used to encapsulate text and formatting attributes during copy-and-paste operations. Word-processing programs such as Microsoft Word can readily handle RTF as input, making obsolete the need to reformat output.

For example, the first ODS statement selects the Moments output and assigns a name MOVIE_MOMENTS. The second ODS statement uses the RTF formatting engine to create an external file for the Moments output from the UNIVARIATE procedure. The

UNIVARIATE procedure is then executed. A final ODS statement closes the RTF destination. The results of the RTF output are displayed, as shown in Figure 6-2.

To create RTF output, the RTF extension is required as part of the filename.

Code:

```
ODS SELECT MOMENTS = MOVIE_MOMENTS;
ODS RTF FILE='ODS-RTF-UNIVARIATE.RTF';
  PROC UNIVARIATE DATA=MOVIES;
  RUN;
ODS RTF CLOSE;
```

Results shown in Figure 6-2:

The UNIVARIATE Procedure
Variable: Length

Moments			
N	22	Sum Weights	22
Mean	124.909091	Sum Observations	2748
Std Deviation	25.8344714	Variance	667.419913
Skewness	1.45414494	Kurtosis	1.71453814
Uncorrected SS	357266	Corrected SS	14015.8182
Coeff Variation	20.682619	Std Error Mean	5.50792781

Figure 6-2. Moments output displayed as an RTF file

14 Creating PostScript output

ODS enables the creation of a PostScript file from SAS output to help ensure that formatting and content are preserved while maintaining complete printer independence. The following example shows the creation of a PostScript file from the PRINT procedure output.

Code:

```
ODS LISTING CLOSE;
ODS PRINTER POSTSCRIPT;
  PROC PRINT DATA=MOVIES NOOBS N;
  RUN;
ODS PRINTER CLOSE;
ODS LISTING;
```

15 Assigning a default name to a PostScript file

Under Windows 98, when a PostScript file is created without assigning a filename, ODS assigns the name SASPRT.PS, and it is created in the directory C:\My Documents\My SAS Files\V8.

16 Specifying a PostScript name

To prevent ODS from assigning the SASPRT.PS default name to a PostScript file, a FILE= option with a user-assigned name can be specified in the ODS Printer statement. Consult your specific operating-system documentation for naming conventions. In the following code, the user-assigned name of EXAMPLE.PS is assigned to the PostScript output.

Code:

```
ODS LISTING CLOSE;
ODS PRINTER POSTSCRIPT FILE='EXAMPLE.PS';
  PROC PRINT DATA=MOVIES NOOBS N;
  RUN;
ODS PRINTER CLOSE;
ODS LISTING;
```

17 Integrating ODS into the DATA step

To provide improved custom output formatting capabilities, ODS is integrated into the DATA step. Two new options are necessary to take advantage of ODS in the DATA step: 1) the ODS option in the FILE statement, and 2) the _ODS_ option in the PUT statement. These two options are used to direct results of a DATA step to ODS. For example, the following code directs output from a DATA step through the RTF format engine to create an RTF file. The advantage of doing this is to enable greater control over the data presentation. The RTF file is displayed in Figure 6-3.

To create RTF output, the RTF extension is required as part of the filename.

Code:

```
ODS RTF FILE='ODS-DATA-STEP.RTF';
   DATA _NULL_;
     SET MOVIES(KEEP=TITLE RATING);
     FILE PRINT ODS;
     PUT _ODS_;
   RUN;
ODS RTF CLOSE;
```

Results shown in Figure 6-3.

Title	Rating
Brave Heart	R
Casablanca	PG
Christmas Vacation	PG-13
Coming to America	R
Dracula	R
Dressed to Kill	R
Forrest Gump	PG-13
Ghost	PG-13
Jaws	PG
Jurassic Park	PG-13
Lethal Weapon	R
Michael	PG-13
National Lampoon's Vacation	PG-13
Poltergeist	PG
Rocky	PG
Scarface	R
Silence of the Lambs	R
Star Wars	PG
The Hunt for Red October	PG
The Terminator	R
The Wizard of Oz	G
Titanic	PG-13

Figure 6-3. DATA step output displayed as an RTF file

18 Locating SAS-supplied format templates

SAS-supplied format templates are located in the SASHELP.TMPLMST library and consist of the following components:

- **Style definition**: Describes how output will appear for the entire SAS job. It is composed of one to many style elements.

- **Table definition**: Describes how output will appear for a single output object.

- **Style element**: Describes style attributes (such as default colors, fonts, and so on) to be used for a specific part of the output.

- **Table element**: Describes specific attributes about the data (for example, SAS formats) rather than the output appearance.

Output Delivery Goes Web

This section discusses exciting tips that will enable your output to be available anywhere and anytime. You'll learn how links and references are handled in HTML files created by ODS, how to combine output results from a variety of procedure sources, create PDF output, and build a drill-down user interface with minimal programming effort.

1 Distributing content anywhere and anytime

The Web is a dynamic medium capable of distributing content anywhere, anytime. The 24/7/365 model enables information to be refreshed and updated continuously as new material becomes available. A primary objective of Web publishers everywhere is to engage visitors with timely and interesting content that keeps bringing them back for more.

With huge appetites for information, organizations everywhere see the advantages of making information available on this exciting medium. What this means is that an organization's information resources are one of its most valuable assets. To take full advantage of these assets an organization must be able to utilize its information resources effectively to deliver that information to a wide variety of information channels.

Information access and delivery has been greatly improved with ODS. Output can be delivered to print, the Internet, an organization's intranet, as well as other mediums and information channels. ODS and its new Web-based HTML publishing feature makes the SAS System a potent tool for effective information delivery by being able to integrate information resources with visual representations.

2 Understanding HTML

HTML is used to format text for the Web. It is read and understood by any of the popular Web browsers such as Microsoft Internet Explorer or Netscape Navigator/Communicator.

Special instructions are formatted in HTML in *tags*. Tags provide important information about how text should be formatted and are frequently specified in pairs. Bear in mind, browsers may interpret tags differently. As a result, before deploying your output on the Web, verify that it is readable by the leading Web browsers (especially Internet Explorer and Navigator/Communicator).

HTML provides a way to modify tags through attributes. Specific attributes control text formats including font type, font size, and color, as well as provide important information about linking to other places in the same document or to another document anywhere on the Web.

An HTML link allows a browser to understand how to transfer control to other locations. As a browser sees each link, it usually highlights the associated text. Links are constructed using a pair of *anchor tags* to identify its destination. An anchor tag that links to a Uniform Resource Locator (URL) destination might look like the following example.

Code:

```
<A
href="http://www.apress.com">
</A>
```

The HREF attribute specifies what to link to and references a starting point for a link, in this case another URL. Once clicked, the corresponding home page for the URL is displayed. When using ODS, you will find that links and references are automatically created for you. To override any automatic link and reference features provided by ODS, you may need to make minimal changes to one or more HTML options. For further information about HTML, refer to a reference text on the subject.

3 Exploring links and references in ODS

The ODS statement controls how links and references are constructed between one or more HTML destination files. The basic syntax of the ODS statement follows:

Code:

```
ODS HTML ODS-action;
```

Or:

```
ODS HTML BODY=file-name < options >;
```

When an ODS-action is specified, one or more output objects are selected or excluded, or the HTML destination is closed. The available ODS-actions are 1) CLOSE, 2) EXCLUDE, 3) SELECT, and 4) SHOW. When an HTML file specification is specified, ODS routes one or more pieces of output to a designated file or files. The available ODS HTML options are identified in the following list.

ODS HTML Options

ANCHOR='anchor-name'

BASE='string'

GFOOTNOTE <or> NOGFOOTNOTE

GPATH=file-specification

GTITLE <or> NOGTITLE

HEADTEXT='HTML-document-head'

METATEXT='HTML-document-head'

NEWFILE=NONE <or> OUPUT <or> PAGE <or> PROC

PATH=file-specification

RECORD_SEPARATOR='string' <or> NONE

STYLE='style-definition'

TRANTAB='translation-table'

4 Exploring ODS HTML file types

Four types of files are produced with the ODS HTML destination: body, contents, page, and frame. Output is written to one or more of these files by substituting the specific option and filename in the ODS HTML statement. Figure 6-4 illustrates an integrated collection of HTML files with the BODY=, CONTENTS=, PAGE=, and FRAME= files. A brief explanation of each file is presented to describe their purpose and role in the integrated collection of HTML files.

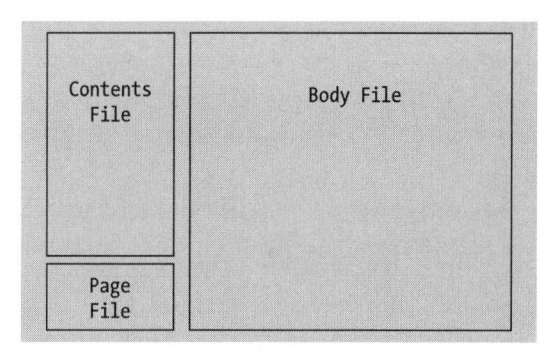

Figure 6-4. An integrated FRAME file within HTML

The body file

The body file consists of output created by your SAS job. When output is routed to the HTML destination, it is placed within one of three HTML tags 1) TABLE, 2) IMG, or 3) as an HTML table. The nature of the output object determines which of the three tags is used for displaying with a Web browser.

When creating the body file, ODS handles output objects differently depending on the nature of the output. If the output object consists of tabular data without any graphics, ODS places an object within TABLE tags. When the object contains a graphic image, it is placed within IMG tags. And when the object does not contain tabular data or any graphic images, it is tagged as an HTML table.

The contents file

The contents file consists of a link to each HTML table within the body file. Using an anchor tag, it permits linking to each table, making it easy to navigate to the desired output object. By using your browser software, you can view the contents file directly or as part of the frame file.

The page file

The page file consists of a link to each page of ODS created output. By using your browser, you can view the page file directly or as part of the frame file.

The frame file

The frame file integrates the body, contents, and page files into a cohesive Web page. The browser opens the FRAME file rather than the other three files separately.

5 Deploying output to the Web with ODS

ODS makes deploying standard SAS output to the Web a simple process. Syntactically correct HTML code is automatically produced and ready for you to deploy using your favorite Internet browser software. The ODS statement syntax appears here.

Code:

```
ODS HTML
 body='user-assigned-name';
  < SAS procedure code >;
ODS HTML Close;
```

6 Streaming (continuous) output with a BODY= file

When a **BODY=** file is specified without a contents, page, and frame file, the HTML destination creates a "streaming" or continuous-type of output by adding elevator bars (horizontal and vertical) as needed to ease navigation.

7 Viewing the frame file

The frame file integrates the body, contents, and page files, forming a familiar user interface, as displayed in Figure 6-5. Navigational bars (horizontal and vertical) are displayed as necessary for scrolling purposes.

When a CONTENTS= file is specified, ODS builds a linkable reference to each output object. The result is a selectable index called a *Table of Contents* with links to the body file for easier navigation through output.

When a PAGE= file is specified, ODS builds a linkable reference for each new page of output associated with each variable. The result is a selectable index called a *Table of Pages* with links to the body file for easier navigation through output.

Specifying the BODY=, CONTENTS=, and PAGE= options with the HTML destination, results in output objects being combined into a well-designed Web page known as a *frame*. A frame file enables output objects to be viewed simultaneously by integrating body, contents, and page files. The integrated look-and-feel enables output objects to be viewed without having to scroll through output sequentially.

8 Ignoring pagesize and linesize settings

The Options **PS=** (pagesize) and **LS=** (linesize) have no effect when used with the HTML destination (as opposed to most other output-producing steps that generate output to a print destination). If the PS= and LS= global system options are specified with the HTML destination, they are ignored.

9 Locating HTML files (Windows operating system)

The location of each HTML file (body, contents, page, and frame) created by the ODS HTML destination in the absence of a physical drive and directory specification is `C:\My Documents\My SAS Files\V8`.

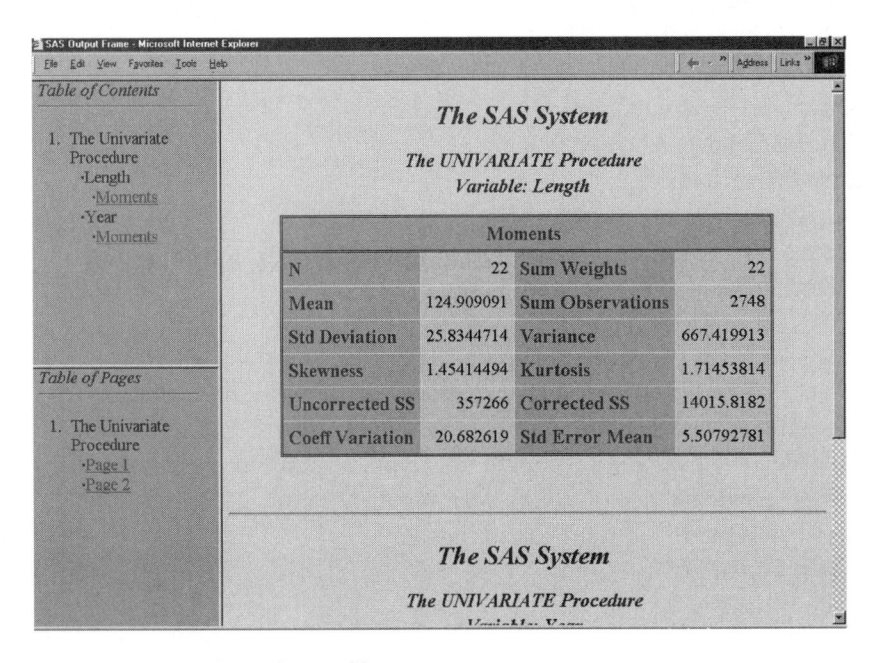

Figure 6-5. Viewing a frame file

🖉 *I recommend setting the PATH = option to save all HTML files in a single directory. See tip #12 in this section for an illustration of usage.*

10 Displaying PRINT procedure output in HTML format

To show how easy it is to create HTML-ready output from procedure output, the following ODS statements combined with PRINT procedure code will build a body file. Once the body file is created, it can be displayed using a standard Web browser, as shown in Figure 6-5.

Code:

```
ODS LISTING CLOSE;
ODS HTML BODY='C:\PRINT.HTML';
  PROC PRINT DATA=MOVIES
      (KEEP=TITLE RATING) NOOBS;
    TITLE 'Great Movies';
  RUN;
ODS HTML CLOSE;
ODS LISTING;
```

Results shown in Figure 6-6:

11 Specifying BODY=, CONTENTS=, PAGE=, and FRAME= files

Building an integrated Web-based page from UNIVARIATE procedure output is a snap with the HTML destination. In the following example, the Listing destination is suppressed, and the HTML format engine is specified using the BODY=, CONTENTS=, PAGE=, and FRAME= file options. Once the HTML output is generated, the HTML destination is closed, and the Listing destination reopened. After HTML output files are created, they can be displayed using a standard Web browser, as shown in Figure 6-7.

Great Movies

Title	Rating
Brave Heart	R
Casablanca	PG
Christmas Vacation	PG-13
Coming to America	R
Dracula	R
Dressed to Kill	R
Forrest Gump	PG-13
Ghost	PG-13
Jaws	PG
Jurassic Park	PG-13
Lethal Weapon	R
Michael	PG-13
National Lampoon's Vacation	PG-13
Poltergeist	PG
Rocky	PG
Scarface	R
Silence of the Lambs	R
Star Wars	PG
The Hunt for Red October	PG
The Terminator	R
The Wizard of Oz	G
Titanic	PG-13

Figure 6-6. PRINT procedure output displayed as an HTML file

Code:

```
ODS LISTING CLOSE;
ODS HTML
    BODY='ODS-BODY.HTML'
    CONTENTS='ODS-CONTENTS.HTML'
    PAGE='ODS-PAGE.HTML'
    FRAME='ODS-FRAME.HTML';
PROC UNIVARIATE
    DATA=MOVIES;
    TITLE 'Great Movies';
RUN;
ODS HTML CLOSE;
ODS LISTING;
```

Results shown in Figure 6-7.

12 Changing output labels

Specifying a PROCLABEL option lets you change the "default" label displayed on procedure output. For example, to change the label produced by the UNIVARIATE procedure from "The UNIVARIATE Procedure" to "Movie Classics Statistics," the following code is specified.

Code:

```
ODS HTML PATH='C:\SAS APP'
    BODY='ODS-BODY-LABEL.HTML'
    PAGE='ODS-PAGE-LABEL.HTML'
    CONTENTS='ODS-CONTENTS-LABEL.HTML'
    FRAME='ODS-FRAME-LABEL.HTML';
ODS PROCLABEL 'Great Movies';
PROC UNIVARIATE DATA=MOVIES;
    TITLE1 'Great Movies';
    TITLE2 'FRAME with Changed Labels';
RUN;
ODS HTML CLOSE;
```

13 Combining output results

With the streaming capabilities of HTML output, results can be combined that so they appear on the same screen (or page). This visual effect provides the perception that output is combined as one contiguous file. Rather than having output controlled by one or more page breaks, HTML automatically displays output without page boundaries. The following example code illustrates combining

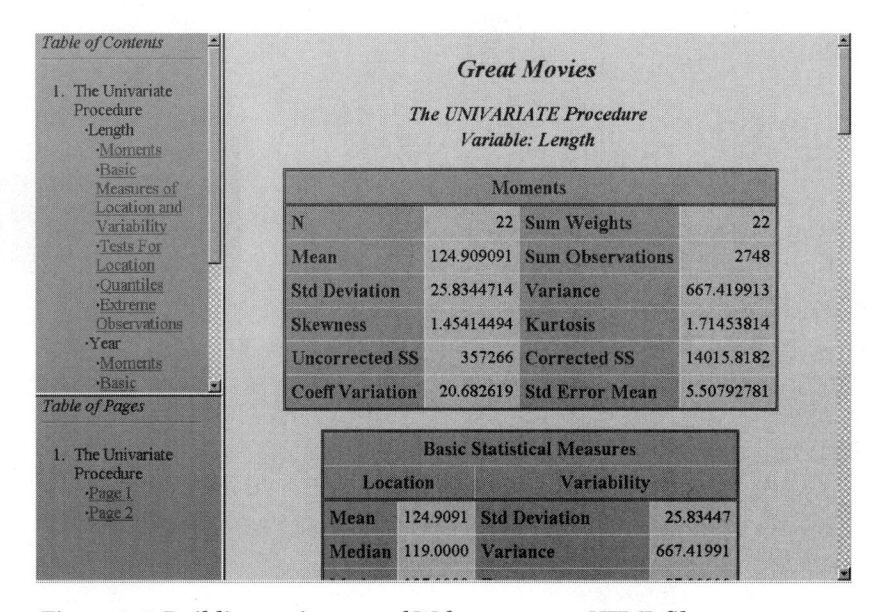

Figure 6-7. Building an integrated Web page as an HTML file

output from the PRINT and MEANS procedures. Output results from any SAS procedure can be used. The combined results are shown in Figure 6-8.

Code:

```
ODS HTML PATH='C:\SAS APP'
         BODY='ODS-BODY-COMBINED.HTML'
     CONTENTS='ODS-CONTENTS-COMBINED.HTML'
         PAGE='ODS-PAGE-COMBINED.HTML'
        FRAME='ODS-FRAME-COMBINED.HTML';
  PROC PRINT DATA=
       MOVIES(KEEP=TITLE RATING)
       NOOBS NOOBS N;
    TITLE1 'Great Movies';
    WHERE RATING IN ('G', 'PG');
  RUN;
  PROC MEANS DATA=MOVIES;
    TITLE1 'Summary of Greate Movies';
    CLASS RATING;
  RUN;
ODS HTML CLOSE;
```

Results shown in Figure 6-8.

14 Creating PDF output

Sharing output electronically is made simple with the ODS PDF format engine. Whether output is distributed to a single-workstation, a server, or the Internet, the PDF file format is a marvelous way to distribute output. This is because all display and printer dependencies are removed from the output. Essentially, a PDF file is a static representation or snapshot

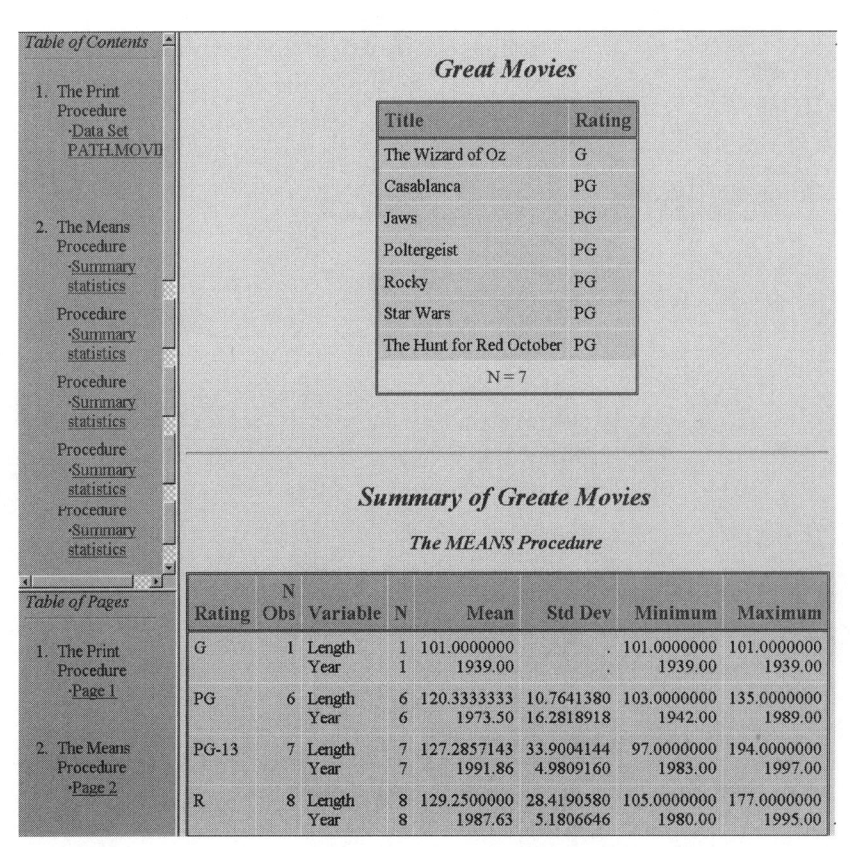

Figure 6-8. Combining ouput results as an HTML file

of your output at a specific time. As a result, output looks the same regardless of the display or printer being used.

Once PDF output is created, you'll need Adobe's Acrobat Reader software to view it. Acrobat Reader can be downloaded for free directly from Adobe's Web site at www.adobe.com. The benefit of using the ODS PDF destination is that output is rendered to look the same from one screen to the next as well as from printer to printer. The next example illustrates how PDF output is created from the results of the UNIVARIATE procedure. Output is sent to the user-defined file referenced by the FILE= option in the ODS PDF statement. The output appears in Figure 6-9.

Code:

```
ODS LISTING CLOSE;
ODS PDF FILE='ODS-UNIVARIATE.PDF';
  PROC UNIVARIATE DATA=MOVIES;
    TITLE1 'Creating PDF Output with ODS';
  RUN;
ODS PDF CLOSE;
ODS LISTING;
```

Results are shown in Figure 6-9.

15 Exploring the drill-down user interface

As a general rule, the best type of user-interface design for transaction-based applications is a drill-down user interface, as opposed to a character-based one. It's referred to as *drill-down* because users drill down through the data, layer by layer, until the desired information is found.

The key to building successful drill-down applications requires systems analysts and system designers to understand what users are trying to achieve with the data. These individuals must recognize the tasks users engage in while trying to access the desired information.

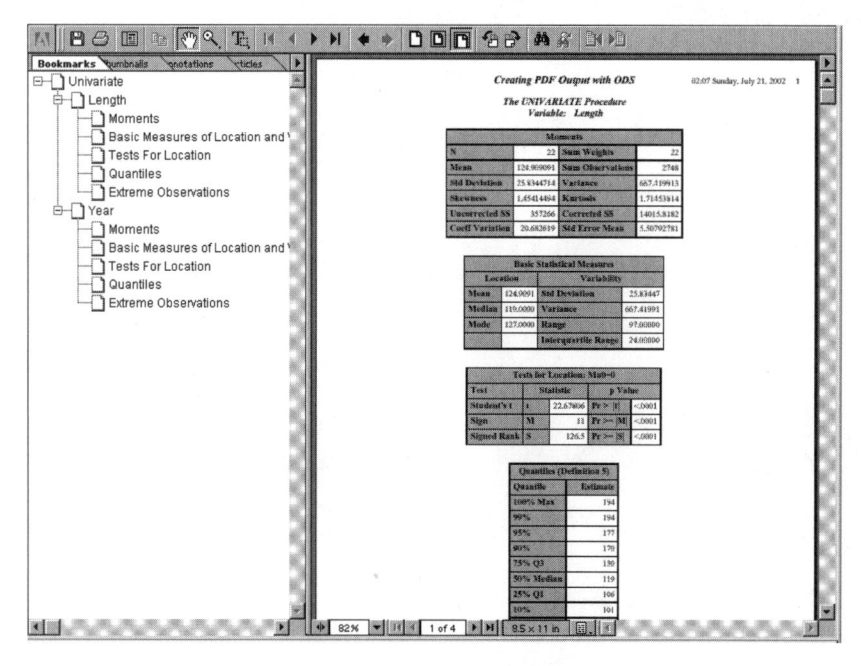

Figure 6-9. Sharing output electronically as a PDF file

These tasks are then translated into a series of selection criteria that users should be able to select from.

16 Building drill-down applications

To simplify the process of building a graphical drill-down application in the SAS System, five easy steps are presented.

1. Create a data set containing the location of the HTML link variable.

2. Create an HTML path with BODY and optional files.

3. Create a graph with SAS/GRAPH software using the HTML= option and link variable.

4. Create detail list drill-down pages.

5. Use a Web browser to navigate through resulting application.

17 Coding a drill-down application

To illustrate the type of coding necessary to build a drill-down application, a pie chart will display summary information on "G"-rated and "PG"-rated movies. A horizontal or vertical bar chart could also be used as the graphical-user interface. To display detailed information on a movie category, users would only need to click on the desired piece of the pie chart that they had an interest in, as shown in Figure 6-10. Control would then be passed, via hyperlinks, to the underlying detail output.

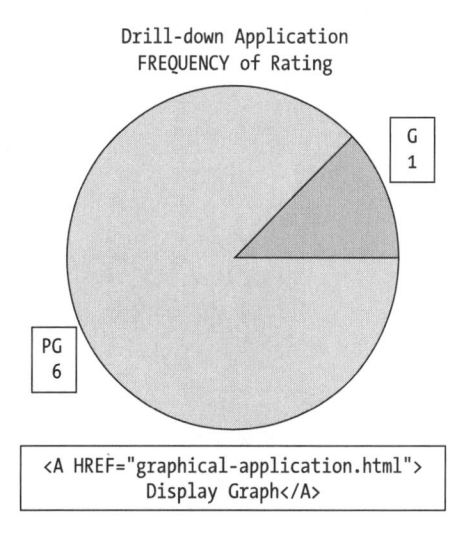

Figure 6-10. Viewing a pie chart as the drill-down application's user interface

An SAS coding technique used in building a drill-down application under the Windows platform is presented in the following example. In the first step, a variable called URLLINK is created and assigned a value equal to the appropriate drill-down HTML file. The second step creates a path to the HTML files so they can be stored in a single directory location. The third step creates a pie chart using the HTML= option to link the URLLINK variable created in step 1 above. Step 4a creates a "G"-rated drill-down HTML file and adds an optional footnote to link back to the main pie chart. Step 4b creates a "PG"-rated drill-down HTML file and adds an optional footnote to link back to the main pie chart. The drill-down UNIVARIATE list for "G"-rated movies appears in Figure 6-11, and the drill-down MEANS list for "PG"-rated movies appears in Figure 6-12.

A Drill-down Application

The UNIVARIATE Procedure
Variable: Length

Moments			
N	1	Sum Weights	1
Mean	101	Sum Observations	101
Std Deviation	.	Variance	.
Skewness	.	Kurtosis	.
Uncorrected SS	10201	Corrected SS	0
Coeff Variation	.	Std Error Mean	.

Basic Statistical Measures			
Location		Variability	
Mean	101.0000	Std Deviation	.
Median	101.0000	Variance	.
Mode	101.0000	Range	0
		Interquartile Range	0

Tests for Location: Mu0=0			
Test	Statistic		p Value
Student's t	t	.	Pr > |t|	.
Sign	M	0.5	Pr >= |M|	1.0000
Signed Rank	S	0.5	Pr >= |S|	1.0000

Quantiles (Definition 5)	
Quantile	Estimate
100% Max	101
99%	101
95%	101
90%	101
75% Q3	101
50% Median	101
25% Q1	101
10%	101
5%	101
1%	101
0% Min	101

Extreme Observations			
Lowest		Highest	
Value	Obs	Value	Obs
101	1	101	1

Display Graph

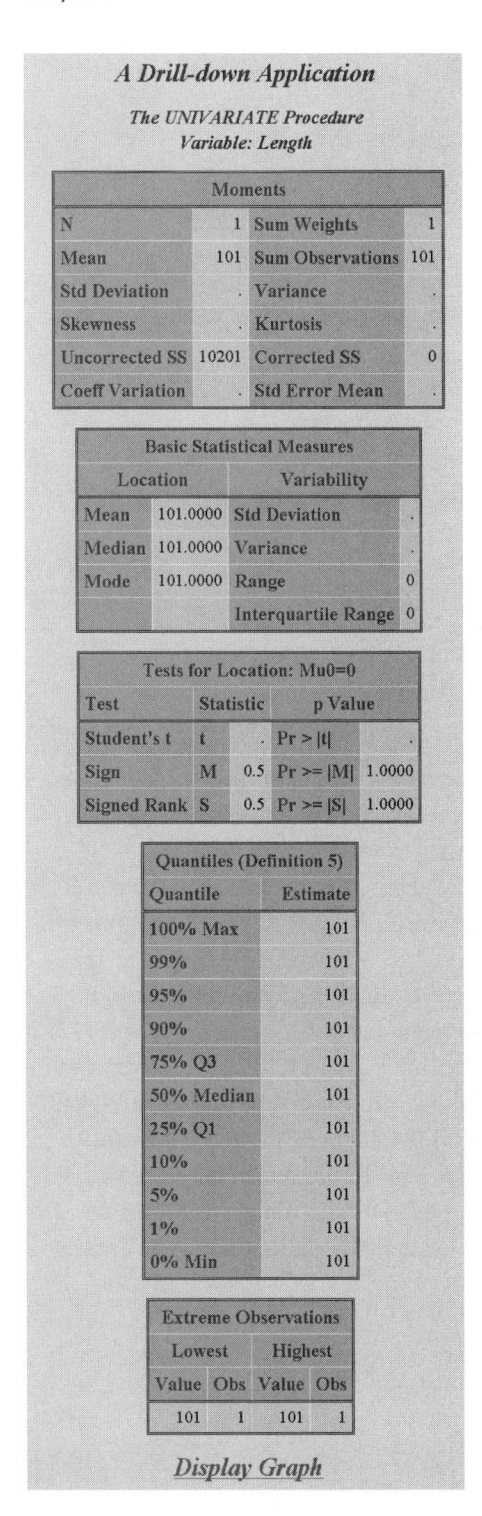

Figure 6-11. Drill-down list for "G"-rated movies

Code:

```
*STEP 1-Define data set & link variable;
DATA MOVIE_RATINGS_G_PG;
 SET MOVIES;
 LENGTH URLLINK $30.;
 IF UPCASE(RATING) = "G" THEN
    URLLINK="HREF=G-RATINGS-BODY.HTML";
 ELSE IF UPCASE(RATING) = "PG" THEN
    URLLINK="HREF=PG-RATINGS-BODY.HTML";
RUN;

*STEP 2-Create HTML path & BODY file;
ODS HTML
  PATH='C:\SAS APP'
  BODY='GRAPHICAL-APPLICATION.HTML';

*STEP 3-Create graph using HTML= option;
GOPTIONS DEVICE=GIF HSIZE=7IN VSIZE=4IN;
PROC GCHART DATA=MOVIE_RATINGS_G_PG;
 TITLE1 "Drill-down Application";
 PIE RATING / HTML=URLLINK;
 WHERE UPCASE(RATING) IN ('G', 'PG');
RUN;
QUIT;

*STEP 4a-Create G-rated drill-down list;
ODS LISTING CLOSE;
ODS HTML PATH='C:\SAS APP'
         BODY='G-RATINGS-BODY.HTML';
PROC UNIVARIATE DATA=MOVIE_RATINGS_G_PG ;
 TITLE1 'A Drill-down Application';
 FOOTNOTE1
    '<A HREF="graphical-application.html">
         Display Graph</A>';
 WHERE UPCASE(RATING)="G";
RUN ;
ODS HTML CLOSE;

*STEP 4b-Create PG-rated drill-down list;
ODS HTML PATH='C:\SAS APP'
         BODY='PG-RATINGS-BODY.HTML';
PROC MEANS DATA=MOVIE_RATINGS_G_PG ;
 TITLE1 'A Drill-down Application';
```

A Drill-down Application

The MEANS Procedure

Variable	N	Mean	Std Dev	Minimum	Maximum
Length	6	120.3333333	10.7641380	103.0000000	135.0000000
Year	6	1973.50	16.2818918	1942.00	1989.00

Display Graph

Figure 6-12. Drill-down list for "PG"-rated movies

```
FOOTNOTE1
  '<A HREF="graphical-application.html">
        Display Graph</A>';
WHERE UPCASE(RATING)="PG";
RUN ;
ODS HTML CLOSE;
ODS LISTING;
```

18 Testing Web output

Before deploying Web-based output to the Web or Intranet, it's important to visually inspect and test your output to see the behavior of each Web page. Web-validation services are also available for users to check Web pages for errors or inconsistencies.

> *Not all Web browsers handle HTML the same way. Microsoft Internet Explorer, as well as others, may display a Web page differently than Netscape Navigator/Communicator.*

19 Checking the Web deployment checklist

Before deploying Web output to an intranet, extranet, or Internet for others to see, it's recommended that a quality review be performed. This review will provide some assurance that the Web output is ready for others to view. The following recommendations should be considered and performed before deploying Web output.

- Check the spelling on each Web page before making it available on the Web.

- If possible, use a validation service to identify errors in your use of HTML.

- Test the Web pages to see how easy they are to access and browse through the information. You should verify that each Web page has a consistent design and layout.

- Turn off images to test how Web pages will look and what information is displayed when viewers use Web browsers that cannot display in pages or when they turn off images.

- Verify links to make sure each link takes you to the intended destination and that each link contains information of interest to your viewers.

- Enlist a test audience to check out your Web pages and to solicit their feedback. This feedback is very important because it will enable you to improve the way your Web pages look and operate. It is also important that you compare your test audience's feedback with your own objectives to determine which areas require more work.

- Test your Web pages with different Web browsers to evaluate how they will look. The two most popular Web browsers are Microsoft Internet Explorer and Netscape Navigator/Communicator.

- Test Web pages on different computers because they can look different when the content consists of graphics.

- Determine the speed of transferring Web page content. If the content is too image-rich, the excessive transfer times may cause viewers to tune out rather than tune in.

- View your Web pages at different resolutions to determine the amount of information a monitor can display.

Summary

In this chapter, you learned data presentation techniques using PROC PRINT, the DATA step, and ODS. Each tip provided insightful approaches for creating output any way it's needed. The Base SAS software, combined with other licensed SAS products (for example, SAS/GRAPH) can make your data presentation tasks easier than ever before.

In the next chapter, "Efficiency and Performance," you'll find a number of ways to make your programs run more efficiently while being more maintainable and easy to read. You'll learn useful tips that can be implemented quickly and easily to produce immediate results in the way your programs operate.

CHAPTER 7
Efficiency and Performance

EFFICIENCY AND PERFORMANCE are important concepts that involve improving the operation of the SAS software and your other programs. This chapter presents basic techniques on tuning a SAS program. You'll learn valuable tips on performance planning, CPU, I/O, memory, storage, and best-practices programming approaches to make your programs perform better. Space constraints prevent me from doing more than whetting your appetite on this topic—there are entire books written on the subject of tuning, and you should consult them for more minute details on this important aspect of running your software.

In this chapter, you'll learn how to

- Develop a basic planning checklist
- Apply basic CPU-performance techniques
- Avoid unnecessary sorting
- Determine whether an index is needed or not
- Use temporary arrays
- Apply basic I/O performance techniques
- Copy data sets with indexes
- Consolidate program steps
- Apply basic memory performance techniques
- Delete temporary WORK data sets
- Handle large data sets
- Apply basic storage performance techniques
- Assign lengths to numeric variables
- Compress SAS data sets
- Create user-defined formats for coded data
- Apply best-practices programming techniques
- Save labels and formats in SAS data sets
- Create views to reduce data redundancy
- Set system options to control messaging

Planning

This section offers valuable tips related to developing a plan for handling program design issues, constraints, and goals.

1 Planning is everything

It has been said that most people do not plan to fail—they just fail to plan. This adage could help millions of users throughout the world.

Much of a program's efficiency (or inefficiency) can be traced to the amount of planning that went into its development. Planning can make a world of difference in the operation and ultimate longevity of a program. Here's a basic planning checklist that can be used before coding your next program.

- Write down clearly what is expected of the new system, including input, processing, and output.

- Determine whether there are sufficient resources such as CPU time, memory, storage, work, and sort space. Shortages in any of these areas can cause a program to prematurely terminate or fail.

- Test programs with sample data. Test data sets also provide benchmarks for future enhancements and maintenance.

- Save intermediate data sets during processing. This prevents being forced to return to the beginning of a program.

- Read raw data only once and just what is needed.

2 Understanding what is meant by efficiency

Efficiency is a nebulous term that means many things to different people. To some it means how fast a program runs. To others it means how fast a program responds. And for still others, it means how efficiently a program uses available resources such as CPU, disk space (DASD), and memory. Efficiency can also refer to ease of code maintainability.

An efficient program gets the most from the existing hardware and software resources.

Efficiency describes how well a SAS program performs under varying conditions, such as during interactive use, as well as during shortages of specific resources including memory and storage. Efficiency involves taking a SAS program and seeing what can be done to improve its performance. Figure 7-1 illustrates the factors that can influence performance in a SAS environment.

3 Exploring the problem of competing resources

Tackling performance issues requires paying careful attention to each program's function in order to elaborate on performance criteria characteristics. There are numerous areas for consideration, so having an idea of what the current program's problems are before you start making modifications is very important. One way of accomplishing this is to solicit user participation. User participation can be crucial to understanding the requirements of a program as well as to successfully implementing efficiency techniques. When assessed early (preferably during the early phases of the program development process), user expectations help facilitate the measurement of resource utilization once the application is fully operational.

Once you gain a better understanding of the problem and where it is, you can begin working on a course of action. If the program is too demanding on available resources, then it is time to look into appropriate efficiency techniques to make it perform better. If the problem is isolated to overloaded operating systems or insufficient CPU, disk storage, or tape drive units, then operating system tuning, CPU capacity upgrades, or additional disk and tape drives may be necessary.

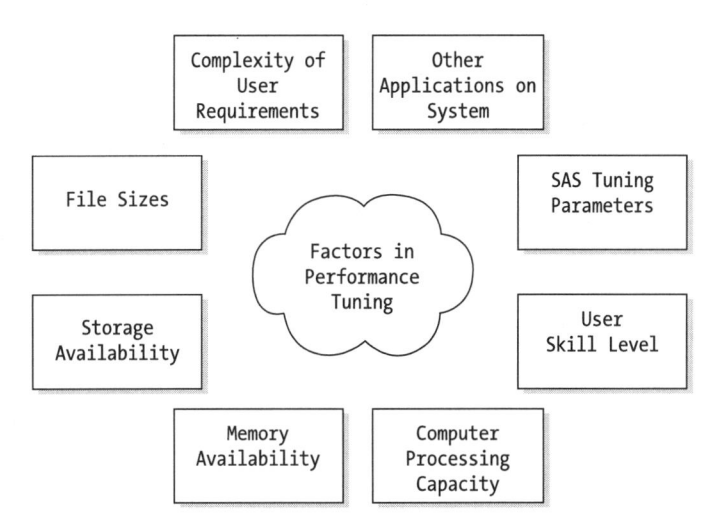

Figure 7-1. Factors affecting performance tuning

4 Developing a simple plan

You should develop a simple plan to handle program-design issues, constraints, and goals. Planning should include creating design objectives for input, processing, and output requirements. You should also develop design objectives for describing the scope of the task, the activities to be conducted, an assessment of impacts, efficiency improvement approaches, resource requirements, and schedules.

The plan should include an inventory of all SAS programs. In the review, analyze program components to determine resource- related issues that could impact organization goals. Conducting an inventory is an important step because it attempts to understand areas that could be vulnerable to one or more resource violations. You should use extreme care to ensure a comprehensive evaluation of all affected program areas.

One school of thought believes there is no better time than the present to deal with efficiency issues. You can use the following checklist as starting point for successfully tuning programs.

- Assess the load on the operating system, usually with the help of IT staff

- Develop a list of efficiency objectives

- Analyze the performance of key program components with the help of users

- Specific areas that should be analyzed include basic algorithms, Macro code, and data access

- Implement better coding techniques

The final steps in a plan should include

- Copies of programs that were made prior to any modifications in order to provide a way of recovering from inadvertent problems resulting from changes

- Description of how a program's components—including options, statements, and keywords—will be modified

- The method of conducting parallel and regression tests to determine effects of modifications

5 Applying simple strategies one at a time

Historically speaking, the first 90 percent of efficiency improvements can be gained relatively easily by applying simple techniques. It's often the final 10 percent that proves to be the challenge. Consequently, you will need to determine whether your application has reached "relative" optimal efficiency while maintaining a balance between time and cost. The rule of thumb in these cases is to

- Evaluate the program's performance
- Assess what efficiency technique may be warranted
- Apply the efficiency technique
- Conduct tests
- Evaluate the program's performance.

6 Striving for an "optimal" balance

Efficiency isn't a one-time proposition. Although it may be easier to implement efficiency techniques as early as possible (perhaps as early as the design phase), it is not always possible. For example, you may not know a program's performance or efficiency until after it has been completed and actually run. Another example in which it is impossible to implement efficiency techniques early on is the case of an inherited program. During times of customizations or enhancements, a program may still benefit from application of one or more efficiency techniques. As Russell R. Holmes of Synteract, Inc. explains, "Efficiency shouldn't be considered as a one-time activity. It's best to treat it as a continuing process of reaching an optimal balance between competing resources and activities."

CPU Techniques

This section includes a number of useful techniques that can be used to reduce the amount of CPU a program consumes while processing.

1 Treating CPU and elapsed time as baseline measurements

In a presentation on efficiency, Jeffrey A. Polzin of SAS Institute had this to say: "CPU and elapsed time are baseline measurements, since all the other measurements impact these in one way or another." This statement couldn't emphasize the importance of these two measurements any better, because virtually every efficiency problem can be attributed to these measurements in some way or another.

If a program is running at or near 100-percent utilization, and response-time problems exist, you may have an overloaded CPU. In these situations, check the percentage of time spent waiting for I/O operations to occur (disk-utilization problems). Possible ways to deal with this problem are to consider acquiring additional CPU capacity, to shift jobs to off-peak periods, or to tune the programs using one or more efficiency techniques. It is also a good idea to check with your system administrator for assistance.

Another problem area to check for is memory utilization. When the physical memory capacity is exceeded, data is transferred from physical memory to disk drives.

Then, when programs need data that is now stored on disk drives, the data has to be transferred or swapped back into memory. The result is a poor-performing program. As before, you should check with your system administrator for assistance.

2 Subsetting IF

Because so much of what SAS users do requires selecting samples of observations from an input source, the subsetting IF statement has been a widely used statement in the DATA step. Its introduction goes back to the earliest versions of SAS software, and it is designed to select input records from an external input file or observations from a SAS data set.

When reading a record from an external file, the SAS system reads it into a temporary internal storage area called an input buffer, where the record is then evaluated against a user-defined condition. Observations from a SAS data set are evaluated one at a time as well but are read into the Program Data Vector (PDV), another temporary storage area . Based on the result of the evaluation, processing either continues with the current record, or the next record is read and the process is repeated until the DATA step terminates. Because of the way the subsetting IF handles data, CPU costs are generally higher than with WHERE processing.

3 Understanding the efficiencies of WHERE processing

Prior to reading an observation into memory (PDV), WHERE processing determines whether a condition is true. Processing costs are often improved by using a WHERE statement, or WHERE= dataset option.

4 Using IF-THEN/ELSE

When nesting IF-THEN/ELSE statements, specify the conditions with the greatest likelihood of occurring first, followed by conditions with decreasing likelihood of occurrence in descending order. Once a true condition exists, the SAS System skips the remaining IF-THEN/ELSE statements. This is particularly important while working with large data sets because eliminating unnecessary logic can improve a program's performance by reducing CPU costs.

Code:

```
DATA MOVIES_LENGTH;
  SET MOVIES;
  LENGTH TYPE $14.;
  IF LENGTH < 90 THEN
      TYPE = 'Short Length';
  ELSE
  IF LENGTH BETWEEN 90 AND 120 THEN
      TYPE = 'Average Length';
  ELSE
  IF LENGTH > 120 THEN
      TYPE = 'Long Length';
RUN;
```

5 Using the IN operator

When processing multiple OR operators in subsetting IF or IF-THEN/ELSE conditions, consider using the IN operator. By doing so, CPU resources will most likely be saved. When an IN operator is specified, a comparison evaluating to true immediately stops processing the expression. In contrast, when multiple OR operators are specified, the evaluation continues to process the expression even when a comparison evaluates to true.

6 Concatenating SAS data sets

When concatenating data from one data set to another, use the APPEND procedure. Because processing only occurs for the transaction data set identified by the DATA= dataset option, the larger of the two data sets should be specified as the BASE= dataset option.

7 Turning off the Macro facility

Many installations automatically turn on the Macro facility at SAS invocation. This enables Macro and/or symbolic substitution to occur in each program executed. But if a program doesn't use the Macro facility, reference Macro variables, or perform Macro or symbolic substitution, then it may be more efficient to turn it off. By turning off the Macro facility, the SAS System avoids checking each line of code for Macro resolution, which means less work for the SAS System and thus more efficient CPU processing.

Whenever the macro facility is turned off, and the SAS System encounters a macro reference, an error message is issued to the SAS Log. The NOMACRO system option turns off the macro facility, as follows.

Code:

```
OPTIONS NOMACRO;
```

8 Avoiding unnecessary sorting

Unnecessary sorting is a significant problem in any programming language. The problem for the SAS System is magnified simply because the SORT procedure is so easy to use, and as a result is frequently abused. Over the years, I've reviewed countless programs containing one or more sorts before a PROC step—even PROCs whose sole purpose is to summarize data. I even overheard one user telling another, "if all else fails...just include a sort in your program." Although I was pretty sure the user was kidding, I began to wonder whether others hearing this unabashed comment would be swayed to try adding a PROC SORT the next time an unexplained error occurred in their code.

Sorting just for the sake of sorting is not the answer. Although legitimate reasons for sorting data do exist, the vast majority of requirements can be accomplished without the use of a sort routine at all. Here are a few suggestions to keep in mind the next time you're considering whether to use a PROC SORT.

- Determine what, if any, data arrangement is needed to satisfy data analysis or presentation requirements.

- Use a PROC CONTENTS to find out whether the data is already in a specific sort order.

- Specify the SORTEDBY= dataset option when the data is already sorted to prevent a sorted data set from being resorted a second time.

- If summary-level information is being generated from the data, then it's quite possible that sorting isn't needed at all.

- If memory resources are plentiful, choose a procedure that allows a CLASS statement to be specified.

- If a sort is necessary, sort in the most detailed order to consolidate the number of sorts.

- When data is grouped but not sorted, and you must use a BY statement, specify the NOTSORTED option in the BY statement.

- When storing permanent SAS data sets for use at a later time, consider what sort order will be useful for future analysis and presentation needs.

9 Controlling the amount of memory used for sorting

The SORTSIZE= option in the PROC SORT statement controls the amount of memory available for sorting. By limiting the virtual memory paging, the SORTSIZE= option can improve sort performance considerably. Valid values include MAX, *n* (bytes), *n*K (kilobytes), *n*M (megabytes), and *n*G (gigabytes).

10 Using a CLASS statement in procedures

Several procedures work quite well with unsorted data. Procedures such as FREQ, MEANS, SUMMARY, and UNIVARIATE are able to summarize unsorted data and present sorted results automatically. Where a procedure provides both BY and CLASS statements, and the data isn't already in the desired sort order, you should consider specifying the CLASS statement. This enables the type of analysis provided with a BY statement but avoids running the SORT procedure first. Of course, when the data is in the desired sort order, it's a good idea to use a BY statement.

11 Compressing and uncompressing data sets is CPU intensive

Using data-compression strategies may increase CPU resources while conserving storage requirements. Although compressing a data set may be perfectly acceptable for environments with abundant CPU resources, it can place unwanted strain on CPU-deprived installations. Therefore, determine whether data set compression will be a good or bad thing for you before you use this feature. When a data set is compressed, it must first be uncompressed, which requires additional CPU time.

12 Creating an index

You should create indexes when the data set is relatively large, when it is not updated frequently, and when any subset consists of less than 30 percent of the observations. You can create two types of indexes: *simple* and *composite* (composite indexes consist of two or more variables). You can create and index in the DATASETS procedure or in the SQL procedure.

The first of the following programs creates a simple index using the DATASETS procedure based on the variable RATING. The second one creates a composite index based on the variables RATING and CATEGORY.

Code:

```
PROC DATASETS LIBRARY=WORK;
 MODIFY MOVIES;
  INDEX CREATE RATING;
RUN;
```

Code:

```
PROC DATASETS LIBRARY=WORK;
 MODIFY MOVIES;
  INDEX CREATE INDEX=(RATING CATEGORY);
RUN;
```

13 Using LIBNAME engines

Use existing LIBNAME engines to read from and write to a DBMS object (such as an Oracle table) as if it were a SAS data set.

14 Using temporary arrays

Assigning constants to elements in _TEMPORARY_ arrays reduces CPU usage, as opposed to creating and dropping variables. This not only allows array elements to be accessed directly because they are stored contiguously in memory, it also conserves data storage space.

15 Using the Stored Program Facility

By using the Stored Program Facility for complex or long DATA steps, you eliminate the CPU time that would be spent compiling the DATA step code.

Be sure to store a copy of the DATA step source code.

I/O Techniques

This section offers a number of useful tips that can be used to reduce the amount of input/output (I/O) processes that a program performs.

1 Storing data as data sets

Store data as SAS data sets, not external files. A SAS data set is a very efficient form of storing data in the SAS System. When data is stored as an external file, it must first be read as raw data before each analysis. This generally increases I/O requirements and should be avoided.

2 Subsetting observations

Processing only the observations that are needed during the analysis reduces the amount of I/O resources required. This is accomplished by subsetting observations (records) that are processed with a subsetting IF statement when dealing with external data, a WHERE statement, or WHERE= dataset option when dealing with a SAS data set.

3 Creating subsets earlier than later

Performing subsets from large SAS data sets or external files as early as possible in a single DATA step and at one time can reduce I/O requirements.

4 Reducing the number of steps

Use a WHERE statement or WHERE= dataset option in procedures instead of creating a temporary subset data set in a DATA step and then running the procedure. This saves I/O by eliminating the DATA step used to create the subset.

5 Copying indexes

Using the DATASETS procedure COPY statement to copy data sets with indexes will save I/O and enable both the data sets and any indexes to be copied. In some legacy code, and prior to the advent of indexes, SAS data sets were frequently copied using a DATA – SET statement convention, which doesn't copy indexes.

6 Specifying the BASE= option in the APPEND procedure

Using the APPEND procedure to concatenate data from one data set to another reduces I/O requirements because processing is performed only on the transaction data set identified by the DATA= dataset option. Consequently, the larger of the two data sets should be specified as the BASE= dataset option.

7 Using SQL to consolidate steps

By using the SQL procedure, I/O can be saved because frequently you can accomplish multiple processes in a single SQL step. For example, the following SQL code sorts the observations by RATING and TITLE and then prints a simple report.

Code:

```
PROC SQL;
 SELECT TITLE, RATING
  FROM MOVIES
   ORDER BY RATING, TITLE;
QUIT;
```

8 Sorting only what is needed

Sorting only the variables and observations that are necessary to be processed can save on I/O. By specifying a WHERE statement or WHERE= dataset option and a KEEP (or DROP) statement or a KEEP= (or DROP=) dataset option, large deposits of unwanted data are eliminated before data is rearranged.

Memory Techniques

This section offers popular and effective memory-saving techniques that can be implemented into programs for improved performance.

1 Reading only data that is needed

Often programs read more variables than are required for the purposes of the analysis. To alleviate this type of problem, determine what variables are needed in the current or later step(s) and read just those variables. This can improve the way memory is used and the way your programs perform.

2 Using KEEP= or DROP= dataset options

Selecting only the variables needed for processing from a SAS data set can reduce memory requirements. You do this by specifying a KEEP (or DROP) statement in a DATA step. Or, for total compatibility in both DATA and PROC steps, you can specify a KEEP= (or DROP=) dataset option. The first of the following examples retains the TITLE and RATING variables by specifying a KEEP statement in a DATA step. In the second example, the DATA step is eliminated and a KEEP= dataset option is specified in the PRINT procedure to keep desired variables.

Code:

```
DATA PG_MOVIES;
   SET MOVIES;
   KEEP TITLE RATING;
RUN;
PROC PRINT;
RUN;
```

Code:

```
PROC PRINT DATA=MOVIES
      (KEEP=TITLE RATING)
         NOOBS
         N;
RUN;
```

3   Deleting WORK data sets

Temporary WORK data sets can use precious storage. Large, multi-step programs often create temporary data sets that are used once and never again. In these cases, the DELETE statement in the DATASETS procedure (see Chapter 5, "Data Management," for more information) is a handy way to perform general housekeeping by removing one or more unwanted data sets. In the first of the following examples, a single data set MOVIES is deleted from the WORK library. Removing multiple data sets from a SAS library is just as easy. In the second example, two data sets are deleted from the WORK library.

Code:

```
PROC DATASETS LIBRARY=WORK;
  DELETE MOVIES;
QUIT;
```

Code:

```
PROC DATASETS LIBRARY=WORK;
  DELETE MOVIES
         ACTORS;
QUIT;
```

4   Reducing memory requirements with WHERE processing

I discuss reducing memory requirements with WHERE processing in tip #3 in the "CPU Techniques" section.

5   Handling large data sets

When memory shortages are a problem or when you are dealing with very large data sets, divide the data set into smaller groups of observations by separating like (or similar) observations into smaller data sets. Once the observations are separated into smaller data sets, you can then concatenate the data sets in any order desired into a new data set, simulating a sort operation.

Storage Techniques

This section offers a number of performance-tuning tips that can be used to reduce the amount of storage consumed by SAS data sets and other program functions.

1   Using DATA _NULL_ to suppress the creation of a data set

When a DATA step is needed for programming reasons but you do not need to create a SAS data set, use DATA _NULL_. By using DATA _NULL_ you have all the advantages of the DATA step without the added expense of storing data in a data set. This technique not only saves storage space, it reduces the amount of CPU resources required to run a job.

2 Using KEEP= or DROP= dataset options

I discuss using KEEP= or DROP= dataset options in tip #2 in the "Memory Techniques" section.

3 Assigning lengths to numeric variables

By assigning a length to numeric variables with a LENGTH statement, you can substantially reduce storage requirements. Essentially, users can reduce a numeric variable's size and cut storage requirements without losing precision. This is especially useful for date variables because the default length of 8 bytes is twice as much space as is needed.

4 Compressing data sets

I discuss compressing data sets in tip #11 in the "CPU Techniques" section.

5 Creating user-defined formats for coded data

Create user-defined format libraries to store formatted values in one place. This has the added advantage of representing coded data with formats, as well as writing easier-to-maintain programs.

Programming Techniques

This section offers a number of useful tips that can be used to construct better and more efficient SAS programs. These valuable techniques illustrate the best-practices approach that every SAS user will benefit from.

1 Including RUN statements

Including RUN statements at the end of each DATA or PROC step (to separate step boundaries) permits the printing of benchmark statistics on the SAS log immediately following each step.

2 Assigning descriptive variable and data set names

Users should make every effort to assign descriptive and meaningful variable and data set names in programs. Esoteric abbreviations and naming conventions provide little help to users who are expected to understand the inner complexities of a program. Studies have shown that as a rule a program's complexities are greatly reduced with the use of descriptive names. To further enhance the self-documenting capabilities of a program, provide a list of variables and a short, one-line description in the standard documentation. Examples of acceptable abbreviations include AP for "Accounts Payable," MGR_ACCT for "Managerial Account," or SCI_METH for "Scientific Method." Assigning descriptive variable and data set names also provides a useful way of self-documenting a program.

3 Saving labels and formats in SAS data sets

Programmers are always looking for ways to save time, especially during crunch-time. One useful technique is to assign variable labels and formats with all SAS data sets. It's a fairly easy process, and even though it does require a little extra time to initially set up, the rewards of having assigned them generally outweigh any initial time and cost in their creation. I like to think of it as an approach that just keeps on giving.

Sunil Gupta of Gupta Programming offers these suggestions on using labels and formats, "Labels and formats are stored with many of our important SAS data sets to minimize processing time. A reason for using this technique is that many popular procedures use stored formats and labels as they produce output, eliminating the need to assign them in each individual step. This provides added incentives and value for programmers and end-users, especially since reporting requirements are usually time critical."

Descriptive variable information can be saved with any data set. In the first of the following examples, a LABEL statement assigns descriptive labels to two variables in the MOVIES data set. These labels are stored in the MOVIES data set's descriptor record, where they can be used in a later DATA or PROC step. Specific information related to how a variable's data should be read and displayed can also be saved with a data set. In the second example, an informat of MMDDYY10. and a format of MMDDYY10. are assigned to the RENTED variable in the MOVIES data set.

Code:

```
DATA MOVIES;
  INFILE 'RAW-DATA-FILE' MISSOVER;
  INPUT @1 TITLE   $25.
        @30 RATING $5.;
  LABEL TITLE = 'Movie Title'
        RATING= 'Movie Rating';
RUN;
```

Code:

```
DATA MOVIES;
  INFILE 'RAW-DATA-FILE' MISSOVER;
  INPUT @40 RENTED MMDDYY10.;
  FORMAT RENTED MMDDYY10.;
RUN;
```

4 Assigning a length to character variables

By using the LENGTH statement to set the length of character-assigned variables, you can prevent smaller values from assigning a variable's length.

5 Documenting programs and program code

SAS users should always document programs and routines with comments. Comments minimize the maintenance time for other programmers and users. Construct program header information to serve as program documentation for all programs. The flower-box comment, shown in Code Listing 7-1, provides the type of information that can make code easier to read and understand for other users. It also acts as a self-contained and permanent record of a program's documented history.

6 Storing data set informats, formats, and labels

An important reason for storing informats, formats, and labels with SAS data sets is that many popular procedures use stored formats and labels as they produce output, eliminating the need to assign them in each individual step. It also helps form the basis of a self-contained documentation library. This provides added incentives and value for programmers and users, especially because reporting requirements are usually time critical.

7 Creating views

Views based on user input and needs simplify and streamline complex or burdensome tasks. When designed properly, views can reduce the amount of data redundancy because they

Code Listing 7-1:

```
*************************************************************;
**** PROGRAM NAME..: MOVIES.SAS                          ****;
**** DESCRIPTION...: THIS PROGRAM READS A NON-SAS FILE   ****;
****                 CONTAINING MOVIE INFORMATION.       ****;
**** DATE WRITTEN..: 3-AUGUST-2002                       ****;
**** AUTHOR........: KIRK PAUL LAFLER                    ****;
****                 SOFTWARE INTELLIGENCE CORPORATION   ****;
**** MODIFICATIONS:                                      ****;
**** NONE.                                               ****;
*************************************************************;
```

point to the underlying data sets without duplicating them. They also can hide or shield complex logic processes from end-users. Any view that is created should be maintained and documented in a central view library.

8 Avoiding FORCE with indexes

When a SAS data set contains one or more user-defined indexes, avoid specifying the FORCE option in the PROC SORT statement. By default, PROC SORT doesn't sort and replace data sets containing an index, but if FORCE is specified it sorts and replaces sorted data and destroys any and all indexes in the process.

9 Coding for harmful data conditions

When unwanted or harmful data is being read or written, constructing conditions in IF-THEN, SELECT blocks, subsetting IF, user-defined informats and formats, and other statements would render the data unusable. This is considered a good programming practice because it essentially makes unusable or harmful data unavailable, and triggers the program to abort (or end).

10 Specifying NOREPLACE

Specifying the NOREPLACE system option prevents permanent SAS data sets from accidentally being overwritten while writing or testing a program.

11 Specifying SAS System options to control messaging

SAS System options can be specified to turn on SAS Log notes, messages, warnings, and included source code. The objective is to display any and all information that is available in a SAS session. Table 7-1 identifies a number of important options that, when specified, provide a considerable amount of control over a program's messaging capabilities.

Table 7-1. Messaging and SAS System Options

SAS OPTION	DESCRIPTION
DSNFERR	Processing automatically stops, and a message is printed to the SAS Log if a nonexistent SAS data set is referenced.
ERRORSABEND	When an error occurs, processing stops, as opposed to having a message printed on the SAS Log.
ERRORS=	Indicates the maximum number of observations for which detailed errors are displayed on the SAS Log. The default value for ERRORS= is 20.
FMTERR	An error message is printed on the SAS Log when a format or informat is referenced but can't be found.
MERROR	A warning message is printed on the SAS Log when a Macro-like name is referenced and does not match any defined Macro names that have been defined.
MSGLEVEL=	Controls how much information is printed to the SAS Log. The default value for MSGLEVEL= is N, which prints notes, warnings, and error messages.
NOTES	Specifies that notes will be printed to the SAS Log. Caution: Some users turn this option off by specifying NONOTES, so verify that this option is turned on when debugging a program.
SERROR	Displays a warning message when a reference to a Macro variable doesn't match an existing Macro variable.
SOURCE	Controls whether SAS source statements are printed to the SAS Log.
SOURCE2	Controls whether SAS include source statements (for example, %INCLUDE) are printed to the SAS Log.
VNFERR	When missing variables are encountered in a _NULL_ data set, this option prints a warning message on the SAS Log and sets the error flag _ERROR_=1.

Summary

In this chapter, you learned a variety of efficiency and performance-tuning techniques. Each tip can provide immediate performance gains. You'll need to determine what the specific needs of your hardware and software environment are. Then you can implement one or more performance-tuning techniques to make your programs perform better in those areas that have the greatest affect on CPU, I/O, memory, storage, and best-practices programming methods.

In the next chapter, "Configuration and Support," you'll find a number of installations and configurations to improve how the SAS software behaves. You'll also find out how to customize features to meet your specific needs. And you'll learn useful tips for accessing technical support, software and program downloads, and gaining access to a wealth of knowledge through user group participation.

CHAPTER 8

Configuration and Support

CONFIGURATION AND SUPPORT are areas that all too often don't get the attention they deserve. This chapter presents valuable tips to help you obtain answers to many important SAS System installation and configuration areas, and, once the software is up and running, find where to get ongoing technical support assistance. You'll learn techniques of controlling how SAS software behaves, as well as how it works. You'll also learn about the many services and the various ways SAS Technical Support can help answer your ongoing technical questions and needs.

In this chapter, you'll learn how to

- Install and remove Internet Explorer
- Change SAS System library locations
- Customize the SAS Configuration file
- Access SAS Institute's Service & Support Web site
- Perform searches for technical information
- Find and apply Hot Fixes
- Apply SAS System SETINITs
- Access a library of sample SAS programs and demos
- Exchange information and knowledge with other users with SAS-L
- Unsubscribe to SAS-L
- Share real-world experiences and expand your knowledge by attending user groups

Installation and Configuration

This section offers valuable tips related to the installation and configuration of the SAS System. You'll be able to enhance your SAS experience with customizable options and features.

1 Exploring Release 8.2 system requirements

Release 8.2 provides users with exciting new and enhanced capabilities. Before installing Release 8.2, you need to verify that your system hardware and software resources are adequate. For complete details about the system requirements for Release 8.2 under a variety of different operating environments, see the following Web sites.

To view these documents, you'll need Adobe Acrobat Reader, which is a free download from www.adobe.com.

MVS, OS/390, mainframe

http://www.sas.com/service/admin/admindoc/system_req/mvs82m0.pdf

CMS, mainframe

http://www.sas.com/service/admin/admindoc/system_req/cms82m0.pdf

Microsoft Windows NT, Windows 2000, and Windows X

http://www.sas.com/service/admin/admindoc/system_req/win82m0.pdf

OS/2

http://www.sas.com/service/admin/admindoc/system_req/os282m0.pdf

ABI+ for Intel architecture

http://www.sas.com/service/admin/admindoc/system_req/iabi82m0.pdf

Compaq Tru64 UNIX

http://www.sas.com/service/admin/admindoc/system_req/dgunix82m0.pdf

HP-UX 64-bit enabled

http://www.sas.com/service/admin/admindoc/system_req/hppa82m0_64.pdf

AIX 64-bit enabled

http://www.sas.com/service/admin/admindoc/system_req/aix82m0_64.pdf

Open VMS VAX

http://www.sas.com/service/admin/admindoc/system_req/vmsvax82m0.pdf

Solaris 64-bit enabled

http://www.sas.com/service/admin/admindoc/system_req/sol82m0_64.pdf

IRIX

http://www.sas.com/service/admin/admindoc/system_req/irix82m0.pdf

Linux

http://www.sas.com/service/admin/admindoc/system_req/linux82m0.pdf

2 Installing Internet Explorer 5 in SAS Release 8.2 for Windows

To take advantage of many wonderful features available in Release 8.2, you'll want to install Internet Explorer 5 (IE5), unless it's already installed. IE5 permits the viewing of HTML output created with ODS within the SAS System. This offers a significant advantage by eliminating the need to view output with an external browser.

Installing IE5 doesn't override your default Web browser or alter your Web browser settings.

3 Removing Internet Explorer 5 in SAS Release 8.2 for Windows

If you decide that you just don't like Internet Explorer 5, you can remove it at any time. Just follow these simple instructions:

- Click the **Start** button on the Windows desktop and select **Control Panel** from the **Settings** drop-down list.

- Click **Add/Remove Programs** from the Control panel.

- Select the version of Internet Explorer you want to remove and click the **Add/Remove** button.

4 Launching the SAS System installation process

Before launching the SAS System installation process, make sure all nonessential Windows applications (such as Microsoft Word, screen savers, and so on) are closed. Then, insert the Setup Disk (CD-ROM) into the source drive to initiate the AutoPlay feature, assuming AutoPlay is enabled on your computer. If the installation process doesn't automatically begin, click the **Start** button on the Windows desktop and select the **Run** menu option and enter the following command.

Code:

```
c:\SETUP
```

5 Changing SAS System library locations

Installation creates the SAS System libraries WORK and SASUSER. By default, they are each assigned a specific location on your hard drive under Windows 95, 98, and NT (for personal or client use). If you do nothing to alter these settings, the installation process automatically assigns them to a unique directory. But, as a user-initiated selection, the installation process does permit changing the location of these important libraries. At the specified prompt, just enter an alternative directory or navigate to the desired directory. The following default folders are used for the WORK and SASUSER libraries.

SASUSER Library: Windows 95 and Windows 98

<My Documents folder>\My SAS Files\V8

SASUSER Library: Windows NT

<Windows NT folder>\Profiles\<userid>\Personal\My SAS Files\V8

WORK Library: Windows 95 and Windows 98

C:\Windows\Temp\SAS Temporary Files\

WORK Library: Windows NT

%TEMP\SAS Temporary Files

6 Choosing between different installation configurations

As a licensed SAS site, you can choose which type of installation you want. The SAS Setup permits three types of installation configurations for Personal or Client use.

- **Complete**: Installs all components that have been registered by your SAS site.

- **Custom**: Installs only those components that you select and that have been registered by your SAS site.

- **Client**: Installs all components that have been registered by your SAS site to a network location allowing local machines to access the network version.

7 Invoking the SAS System

Once the SAS System is successfully installed, you're ready to invoke it for the first time. Here's how it's done.

1. Click the **Start** button on the Windows desktop, select **Programs**, and choose **The SAS System**.

2. Click The SAS System for Windows Release x.x to invoke the SAS System.

8 Discovering the SAS System's Configuration startup file

When the SAS System initializes, it processes a startup file called the Configuration file (SASV8.CFG). This file establishes important system options that control how the SAS System behaves. Options are available to control such things as communications, environment control, files, input control, graphics, log and procedure output control, Macro, sort, and system administration settings. For example, settings for linesize and pagesize, turning the DMS on or off, size of SAS work and sort space, number of buffers, printer options, location of SASUSER and WORK libraries, YEARCUTOFF value, and more can be specified here.

Under the Windows operating system, the SASV8.CFG file is located in the folder C:\Program Files\SAS Institute\SAS\V8. It's an ASCII file, so it can be opened and viewed with any editor that can handle and save ASCII files (for example, WordPad). The file is shown in Figure 8-1.

9 Customizing the SAS Configuration file

The SAS Configuration file is customizable, meaning you can modify specific settings. Using an ASCII editor (such as WordPad), users may modify the Configuration file to satisfy specific needs. You can specify two types of options: ones with a value assigned to them and ones that toggle between on and off.

Customizing the SAS Configuration file isn't difficult. You need to make your edits above the Warning box in the SASV8.CFG file. Before changing anything, though, you should be aware of the options specific to your operating system (see the following tip for a list of options under the Windows operating system). These can be found in the Help facility by entering "SAS System options."

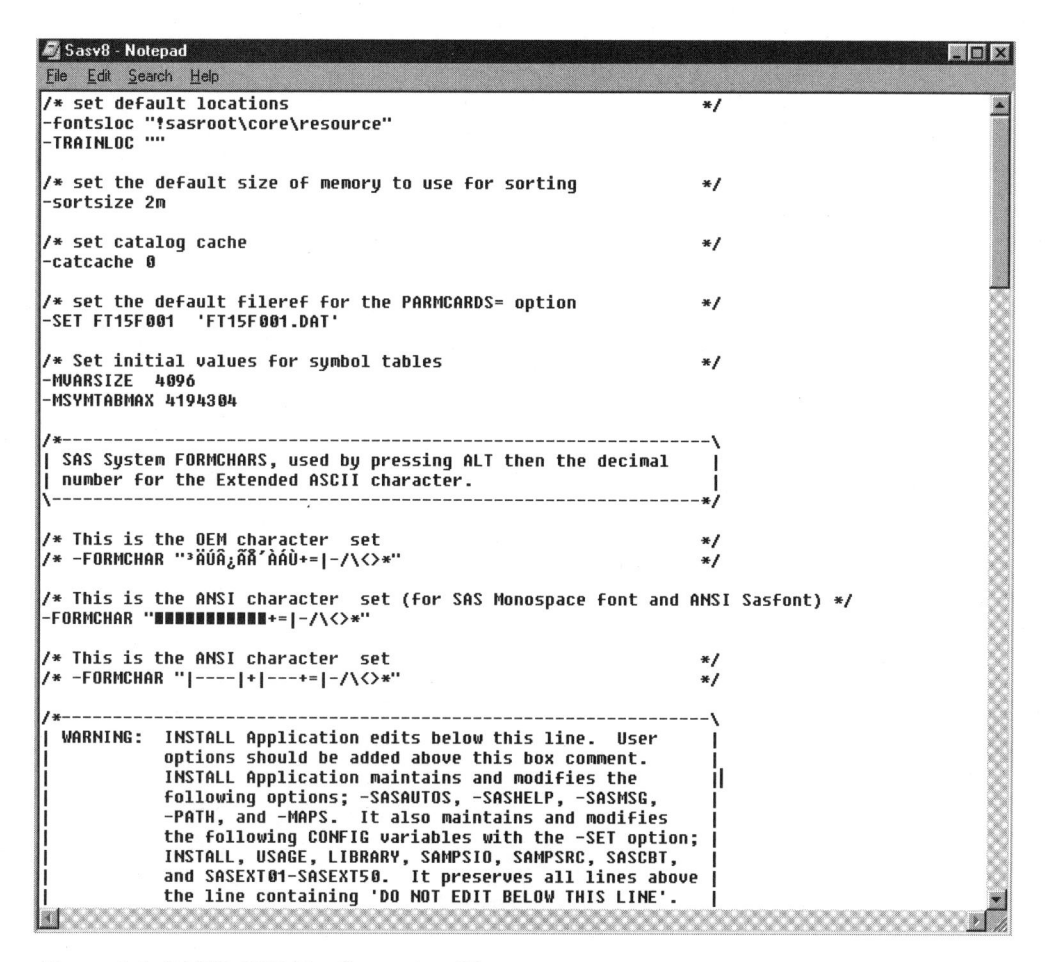

Figure 8-1. SASV8.CFG Configuration file

A couple of examples can illustrate how easy it is to customize the Configuration file. To turn centering off (by default it is on), you specify **–NOCENTER**. And to change the default value for the OBS= option from MAX to 1,000, you specify **–OBS 1000**.

Options that have a value assigned do not have an equal sign (=) specified—instead a blank is used. Once your changes are made save the file as ASCII text.

10 Listing of System options under the Windows operating system

The System options available under Windows are numerous indeed. The alphabetical list that follows was derived from the information in the SAS Help facility. For a more detailed understanding of each option and their values, consult the descriptions listed under "SAS System options" in the Help facility or the appropriate technical documentation for your operating system.

SAS System options (Windows)

ALTLOG	ENHANCEDEDITOR	NLSCOMPATMODE	SET
ALTPRINT	FILTERLIST	NUMKEYS	SGIO
AUTHSERVER	FONT	NUMMOUSEKEYS	SHORTFILEEXT
AUTOEXEC	FONTALIAS	OBS	SORTPGM
AWSCONTROL	FONTSLOC	OPLIST	SORTSIZE
AWSDEF	FORMCHAR	PAGENO	SPLASH
AWSMENU	FULLSTIMER	PAGESIZE	SPLASHLOC
AWSMENUMERGE	GISMAPS	PATH	STIMEFMT
AWSTITLE	HELPEXT	PFKEY	STIMER
BLKSIZE	HELPLOC	PRINT	SYSIN
BUFNO	HELPREGISTER	PROCLEAVE	SYSLEAVE
BUFSIZE	HOSTPRINT	PRTABORTDLGS	SYSPARM
CATCACHE	ICON	PRTSETFORMS	SYSPRINT
CLEANUP	LINESIZE	REALMEMSIZE	SYSPRINTFONT
COMDEF	LOADMEMSIZE	REGISTER	TOOLDEF
CONFIG	LOCALE	RESOURCESLOC	UNBUFLOG
DBCS	LOG	RSASUSER	USER
DBCSLANG	MAPS	RTRACE	USERICON
DBCSTYPE	MAXMEMQUERY	RTRACELOC	VERBOSE
DEVICE	MEMCACHE	S	WEBUI
ECHO	MEMLIB	S2	WINDOWSMENU
EMAILDLG	MEMSIZE	SASAUTOS	WORK
EMAILID	MSG	SASCONTROL	XCMD
EMAILPW	MSGCASE	SASHELP	XMIN
EMAILSYS	MSYMTABMAX	SASINITIALFOLDER	XSYNC
ENCODING	MVARSIZE	SASUSER	XWAIT
ENGINE	NEWS	SCROLLBARFLASH	

The Service & Support Web Site

This section includes a number of useful tips to help you with many service and support questions. You'll get helpful tips on using SAS Institute's 24/7 Service & Support Web site, as well as other educational resources.

1 Accessing the Service & Support Web site

The SAS Service & Support Web site covers such areas as Technical Support, Administrator Resources, Contacts Support, Demos and Downloads, Users Groups to Training, Certification, SAS Publishing, Library of White Papers and Newsletters, and a number of SAS communities. The URL is `http://www.sas.com/service/index.html`, shown in Figure 8-2.

2 Searching techniques

Searching the SAS Institute Web site is the quickest way to find the most likely sources of information. Results are automatically ranked so that the documents most relevant to your search appear first. To get the most out of searching, keep the following in mind.

- Read the instructions on the site about using SAS Search most effectively and become familiar with the search engine's features and capabilities

- Be specific: use multiple keywords that aren't likely to appear on irrelevant pages

- Specify search keywords in uppercase to indicate an exact match (**SQL**)—this only returns documents with the word spelled in uppercase characters.

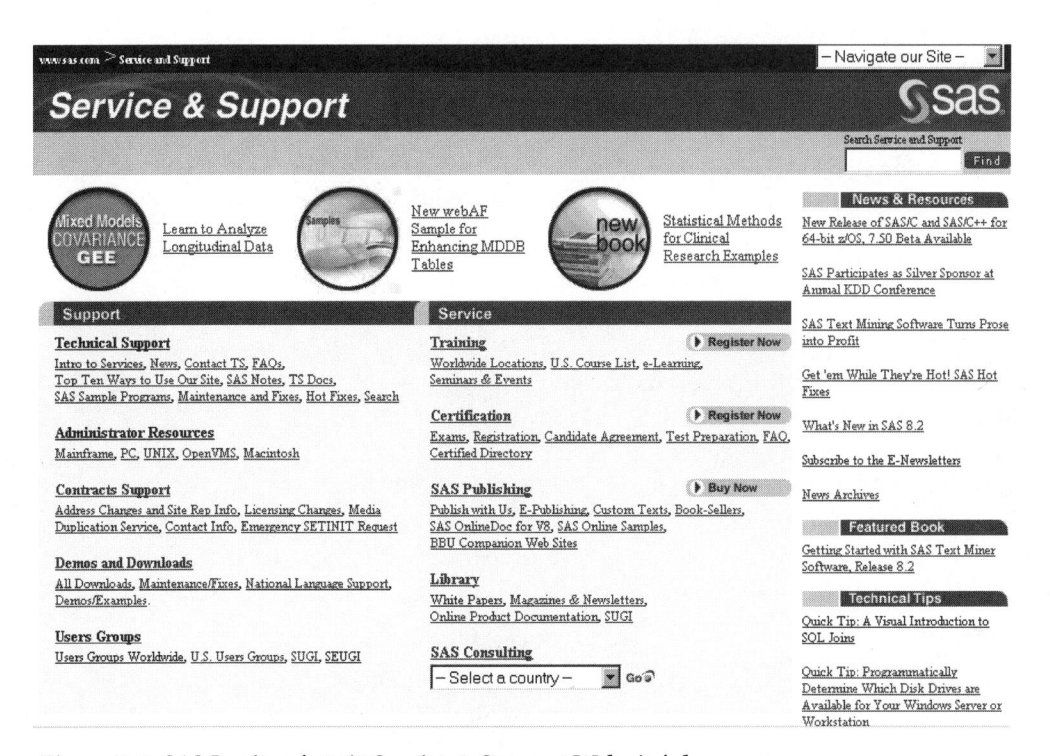

Figure 8-2. SAS Institute's 24/7 Service & Support Web site's home page

- Use lowercase characters for a much broader search (**sql**)—this returns documents containing the keywords sql, sQl, sqL, SqL, SQl, and SQL.

- Use quotation marks (" ") around phrases to find an exact match of the phrase (**"SQL joins"**)—this returns documents containing the exact phrase (the words must appear in the exact order that they are specified)

- Use commas to separate keywords or phrases

- Use + or – signs to indicate that the keyword or phrase is required or excluded (**"Goodnight, +James"**)—this finds documents containing references to the CEO of SAS Institute, and (**SQL -"version 6.12"**) finds documents referencing SQL in versions other than Version 6.12.

3 Narrowing your search results with Boolean search operators

If you've tried the suggestions in the previous tip and are still getting way too many useless or irrelevant results, it's time to try Boolean operators. The term *Boolean operator* is a fancy way of saying AND, OR, and NOT. Here's how each operator works.

- **AND**: Searches for all the keywords or search terms. For example, **SQL AND joins** finds documents on which both words appear. If you leave a space between keywords, the Search automatically adds an AND.

- **OR**: Searches any keywords or search terms. For example, **SQL OR joins** finds documents that contain either **SQL** or **joins** but not necessarily both.

- **NOT**: Excludes keywords or search terms. For example, **SQL NOT joins** finds documents that contain **SQL** but that don't contain **joins**.

4 Searching by search categories

SAS's Search Web page provides a number of search categories. These are best used when you're able to identify the topic area of your search. For example, if you were looking for information on **Base SAS**, you'd probably concentrate your search in the **Products** category. Here's a list of the different search categories SAS Search provides:

SAS search categories

Our Company
Administrative Resources
Certification
Communities
Contact Us
Consulting
Contracts Support
Demos and Downloads
Employment
Intelligence Solutions
Library
News and Events
Partners
Products
Publications
SAS Publishing
Service and Support
Software
Subscriptions
Success Stories
Technical Support
Training
Users Groups
Worldwide Offices

5 Contacting SAS technical support

You can contact SAS Institute's technical support for SAS user sites located in the U.S. and Canada by calling 1-919-677-8008 between 9 a.m. and 5 p.m. Eastern time, Monday through Friday. You'll need your site license number to utilize this service. Or you can send a detailed email describing your question or problem to Support@SAS.com.

6 Searching technical notes for programming problems

As a means of providing comprehensive support services for users, a library of technical support documents is available including product documentation for Base SAS Procedures, Macros, Windows, Maintenance Bug Fixes, and many more documents. To access this large selection of technical support documents, follow these simple steps.

- From the Service & Support Web site, click **TS Docs** under the **Technical Support** heading.

- Click the **Indexed by Category** link. Note: A second link is provided: **Indexed by Number**.

- Enter a keyword or document name in the **Search all technical documents for:** field and click the **Search** button, as shown in Figure 8-3.

- In the Results window, shown in Figure 8-4, click the document(s) of interest.

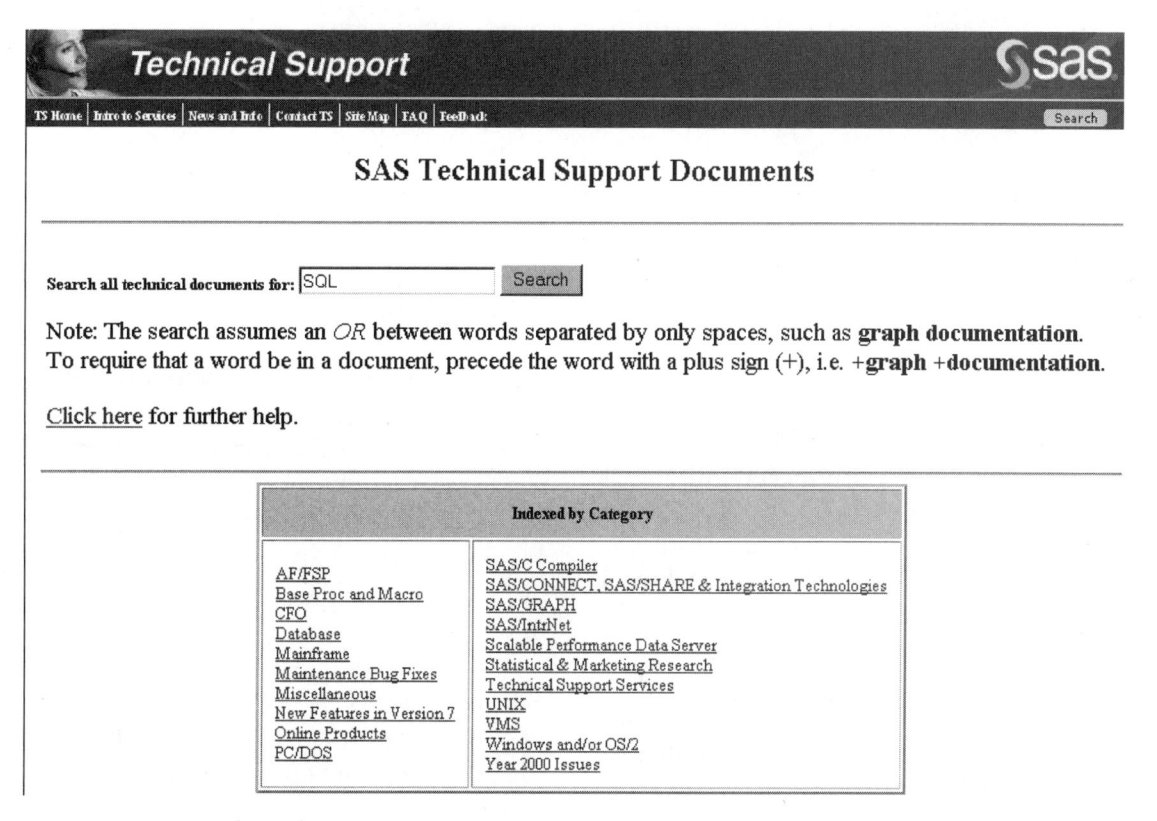

Figure 8-3. SAS Technical Support Documents Search window

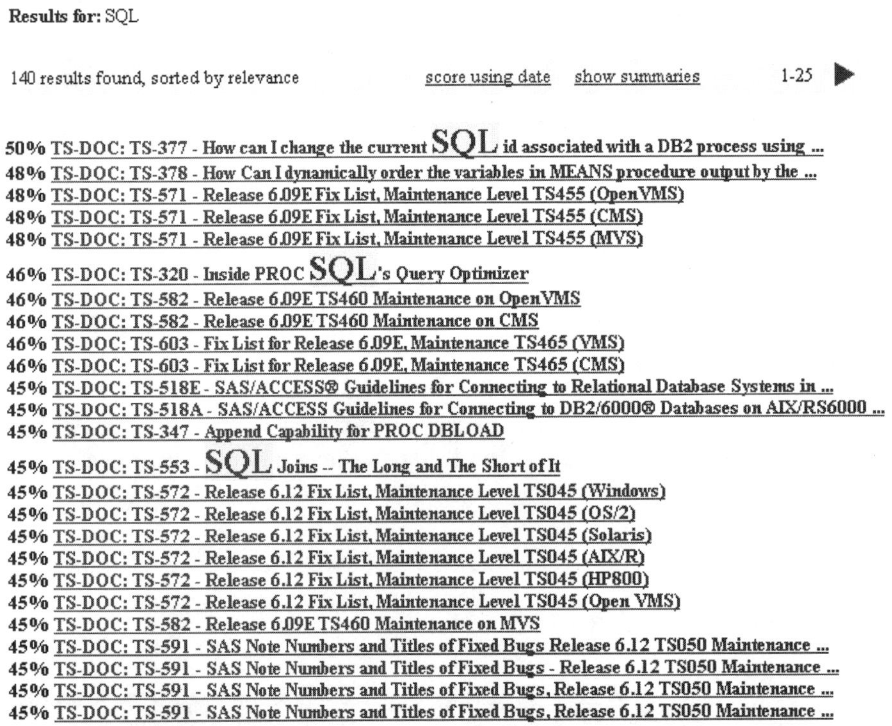

Results for: SQL

140 results found, sorted by relevance   score using date   show summaries   1-25 ▶

50% TS-DOC: TS-377 - How can I change the current SQL id associated with a DB2 process using ...
48% TS-DOC: TS-378 - How Can I dynamically order the variables in MEANS procedure output by the ...
48% TS-DOC: TS-571 - Release 6.09E Fix List, Maintenance Level TS455 (OpenVMS)
48% TS-DOC: TS-571 - Release 6.09E Fix List, Maintenance Level TS455 (CMS)
48% TS-DOC: TS-571 - Release 6.09E Fix List, Maintenance Level TS455 (MVS)
46% TS-DOC: TS-320 - Inside PROC SQL's Query Optimizer
46% TS-DOC: TS-582 - Release 6.09E TS460 Maintenance on OpenVMS
46% TS-DOC: TS-582 - Release 6.09E TS460 Maintenance on CMS
46% TS-DOC: TS-603 - Fix List for Release 6.09E, Maintenance TS465 (VMS)
46% TS-DOC: TS-603 - Fix List for Release 6.09E, Maintenance TS465 (CMS)
45% TS-DOC: TS-518E - SAS/ACCESS® Guidelines for Connecting to Relational Database Systems in ...
45% TS-DOC: TS-518A - SAS/ACCESS Guidelines for Connecting to DB2/6000® Databases on AIX/RS6000 ...
45% TS-DOC: TS-347 - Append Capability for PROC DBLOAD
45% TS-DOC: TS-553 - SQL Joins -- The Long and The Short of It
45% TS-DOC: TS-572 - Release 6.12 Fix List, Maintenance Level TS045 (Windows)
45% TS-DOC: TS-572 - Release 6.12 Fix List, Maintenance Level TS045 (OS/2)
45% TS-DOC: TS-572 - Release 6.12 Fix List, Maintenance Level TS045 (Solaris)
45% TS-DOC: TS-572 - Release 6.12 Fix List, Maintenance Level TS045 (AIX/R)
45% TS-DOC: TS-572 - Release 6.12 Fix List, Maintenance Level TS045 (HP800)
45% TS-DOC: TS-572 - Release 6.12 Fix List, Maintenance Level TS045 (Open VMS)
45% TS-DOC: TS-582 - Release 6.09E TS460 Maintenance on MVS
45% TS-DOC: TS-591 - SAS Note Numbers and Titles of Fixed Bugs Release 6.12 TS050 Maintenance ...
45% TS-DOC: TS-591 - SAS Note Numbers and Titles of Fixed Bugs - Release 6.12 TS050 Maintenance ...
45% TS-DOC: TS-591 - SAS Note Numbers and Titles of Fixed Bugs, Release 6.12 TS050 Maintenance ...
45% TS-DOC: TS-591 - SAS Note Numbers and Titles of Fixed Bugs, Release 6.12 TS050 Maintenance ...

Figure 8-4. Search Results window

7 Accessing Maintenance Bug Fix documentation

Have you ever wondered if documentation for a particular bug exists? SAS provides detailed documentation on how to deal with a variety of known bugs. Documentation exists for Release 6.09E, 6.12, 8.1, and 8.2. Follow these steps to access Maintenance Bug Fixes in HTML format.

- From the Service & Support Web site, click **Maintenance and Fixes** under the **Technical Support** heading.

- Enter a keyword or topic in the **Search all technical documents for:** field and click the **Search** button. An alternative to entering a topic is to click the link corresponding to the TS-nn number that is listed.

- In the Results window, click the document(s) of interest.

8 Finding Hot Fixes

Hot Fixes are designed to repair a customer application when it experiences a problem. Each is specific to certain operating systems and releases, so take care not to download one that doesn't match what you're running. For a complete list of Hot Fixes by operating system, by product, by bundle, or by release, follow these steps.

1. From the Service & Support Web site, click **Hot Fixes** under the **Technical Support** heading.

2. After reviewing the list of Hot Fixes, click the link that matches your operating system and release of SAS.

3. Click the product link that you'd like to download a Hot Fix for (for example, Base SAS).

4. Click the download button corresponding to the hot fix needed.

You can download SAS System Hot Fixes from http://ftp.sas.com/techsup/download/hotfix/hotfix.html.

9 Upgrading SAS Release 8.1 to 8.2 under Windows and Hot Fixes

SAS technical support issued an Alert for Windows 8.1/8.2 SAS users stating that any Release 8.1 Hot Fixes that were applied before April 19, 2001 will not automatically be replaced with Release 8.2. Hot fixes installed on a PC will have an audit file, identified with an .AUD file extension, in folder !SASROOT\core\sasinst\hotfix. If the date associated with the Hot Fix is on or after April 19, 2001, then upgrading from 8.1 to 8.2 should work properly. But if the Hot Fix was applied before this date, then prior to upgrading to Release 8.2, users have to download and reapply affected Hot Fixes or uninstall Release 8.1 (using Windows Add/Remove Programs utility) and then manually remove any remaining files still residing in the Release 8.1 directory—or contact SAS technical support at 1-919-677-8008.

For complete details, read the Alert in its entirety at http://ftp.sas.com/service/techsup/tsnews-1/0145.html.

10 Applying the SAS System Version 8 SETINIT under Windows

Authorization to use the SAS System is based on an annual license. At the end of the annual license cycle, SAS Institute provides an authorization code to the SAS Installation Representative. This authorization code is contained in a file called SETINIT.SAS (prior to Release 8.2) or SETINIT.SSS (Release 8.2) and must be applied in order to run the software. For complete details about applying the SAS System Version 8 SETINIT under Windows, see http://www.sas.com/service/admin/admindoc/setinit/win8.3.pdf.

11 Handling SETINIT problems during SAS Release 8.2 installation

During the installation of SAS Release 8.2, you may encounter a problem in which the "Enter location of new setinit" dialog box appears repeatedly. If this occurs, the problem could be related to a hidden extension of .txt being appended to SETINIT.SSS (the setinit file). To correct it, you'll need to open the setinit file using Notepad, save it to any directory using the filename "setinit.sss" (enclosed in double-quotes), and then exit Notepad.

For complete details about the problem and its remedy, refer to SN006691 or visit http://www.sas.com/service/techsup/unotes/SN/006/006691.html.

12 Applying a SETINIT when the SAS System has expired

If your SAS System has expired, the only way to apply a SETINIT is to run the SETNAME SAS program by specifying the following SETINIT SAS option.

Code:

```
SAS SETNAME (SETINIT)
```

13 Accessing a library of sample SAS programs

Do you find that you learn best by seeing how other users write SAS programs? SAS provides a library of sample SAS programs for just this purpose. You'll be able to access and view samples from a variety of topics including Base SAS, SAS/CONNECT, SAS/GRAPH, and SAS/STAT, to name just a few. Here's how it's done.

1. From the Service & Support Web site, click **SAS Sample Programs** under the **Technical Support** heading.

2. Enter a keyword or topic in the **Search samples for:** field and click the **Search Samples for** button, as shown in Figure 8-5. An alternative to entering a topic is to click the link corresponding to the product that is listed.

3. In the Results window, click the document(s) of interest.

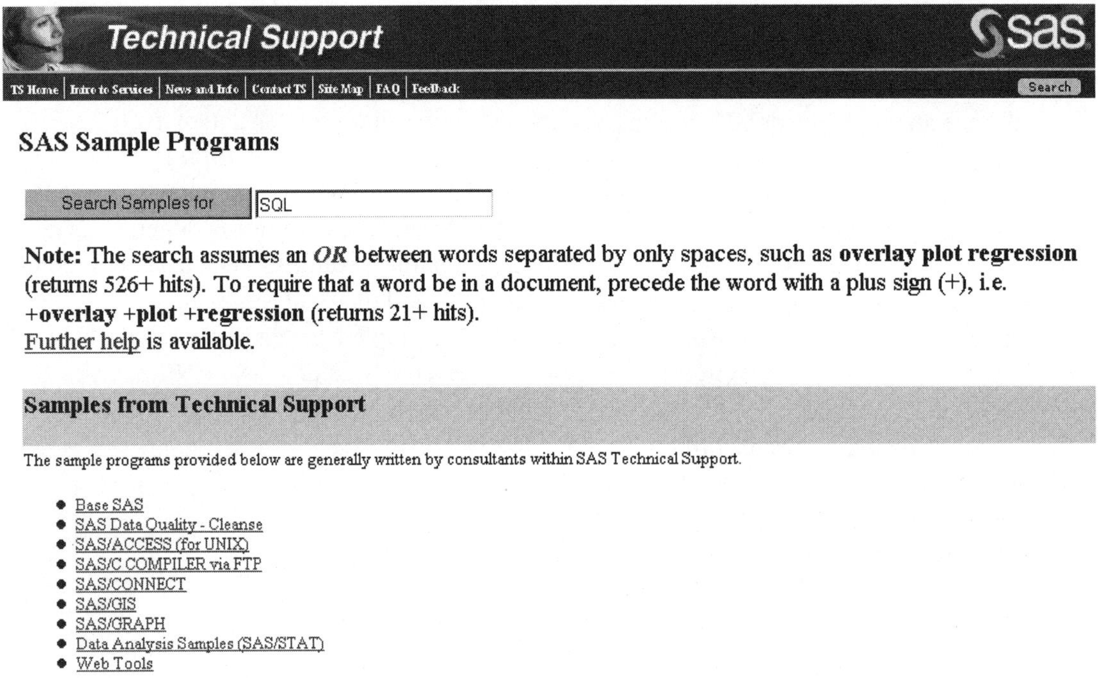

Figure 8-5. Library of SAS Sample Programs Search window

14 Downloading demos and examples

A variety of demos and examples are available for download. Users can access informative content covering products such as Enterprise Reporter, SAS/GRAPH, SAS/OR, SAS/GIS, SAS/IntrNet, DataFlux, StatView, and JMP. Here's how.

1. From the Service & Support Web site, click **Demos/Examples** under the **Demos and Downloads** heading.

2. Click the link you'd like to download from (for example, **Enterprise Reporter**, **SAS/GRAPH**, and so on).

3. Click the version of SAS demos/examples you'd like to download (for example, Versions 6, 8, or 9).

4. Choose from PDF or txt README formats and click the **Request Download** button corresponding to the examples needed.

15 Subscribing to the SAS-L email list

Exchanging information, knowledge, and experiences about SAS Software with users from around the world is only a free subscription away. SAS-L is an Internet destination that all SAS users should know about. This terrific resource is a user-run Internet email list. Charles Shipp, a SAS and JMP consultant and trainer, shares his experiences on how effective Internet communication can be: "SAS-L and JMP-L provide valuable and timely information for programmers and users alike. For those with programming interests these list servers are wonderful links to the global SAS user community at large. Information is shared by other 'like-minded' programmers and users freely and openly."

Charles Shipp has found the SAS-L to be a very useful tool indeed. He frequently reads the many posts from other SAS professionals to enhance his knowledge in important technical areas. And if you have a technical question of your own, he says, "You can put up your question before you go home from work at 5 p.m. and have several answers when you return at 7 a.m. in the morning." SAS-L offers a very productive and timely approach to getting many of your technical support questions answered.

Users wanting to access or participate on SAS-L only need to subscribe by sending an e-mail message to LISTSERV@uga.cc.uga.edu with the subject line "SUBSCRIBE SAS-L" and <your_full_name> in the body of the message. Once you've subscribed, the list server will send you a message explaining the standard controls you can use and how to use the Help and Archive features. Then, be prepared to receive posts on virtually any SAS topic from this engaging email list.

You can also send questions to SAS-L@LISTSERV.UGA.EDU *and ask for a reply to your address, without being a subscriber.*

16 Participating in SAS-L

To participate in the SAS-L discussion group you'll need to use two email addresses. The first one, LISTSERV@listserv.uga.edu, as discussed in the previous tip, is for you to talk to the Listserv. You can send "HELP" or "INFO REFCARD" in the body of a message to the Listserv, and it will reply with a list of commands you can send it, such as the ones you use when you leave for and return from vacation.

Vacation settings

- **SET SAS-L nomail**: Send this when you go on vacation.

- **SET SAS-L mail**: Send this when you return from vacation.

The second email address to be aware of is the one you use to send questions and comments to the group: SAS-L@listserv.uga.edu. Messages sent to this address are automatically sent to everyone on the list. For this reason, you'll want to be very considerate of what you send. You shouldn't send Listserv commands to this address, and you may want to first listen and read the messages before you begin participating. You'll be able to tell by reading the Subject lines of email messages which ones you want to read and which to discard.

🖉 *Remember also that* support@sas.com *is another address for assistance with your SAS programming questions.*

17 Unsubscribing from SAS-L

You can unsubscribe from SAS-L any time you like by simply sending an email message to listserv@uga.cc.uga.edu with the Subject line "UNSUBSCRIBE SAS-L" and <your_full_name> in the body of the message.

18 Exploring the world of SAS user groups

SAS user groups provide users with a vehicle for learning, training, and sharing ideas. "Strong (user) groups have certain elements in common. They have a mechanism for bringing in new leadership and talent. These groups offer strong programs that meet the needs and interests of a variety of users," states Sally A. Roberson of SAS Institute Inc. Each user group reinforces the techniques of sharing real-world experiences and expanding knowledge through presentations, demos, hands-on workshops, and interactions with other users.

Several types of user groups exist within the SAS user community.

- International (SUGI, SEUGI)

- Regional (MWSUG, NESUG, WUSS)

- City (SANDS, SCSUG)

- Corporate (City of Dallas, Northrop)

- Special-Interest (Consultants, JMP)

19 Attending SUGI—the event no SAS user should miss

SAS User Group International (better known as SUGI) is an annual event for all SAS users. Thousands gather from around the world to hear and see exciting presentations, exchange ideas and experiences, view SAS Institute demonstrations, learn from other users, and meet old and new acquaintances. For more information about SUGI events and conferences, visit http://www.sugi.com.

Summary

In this chapter, you learned a number of ways of customizing your SAS installation and configuration, as well as ways of accessing a treasure trove of online technical-support services.

In the next chapter, "New Version 9 Features," you'll find a number of great new features available in Version 9. You'll learn new features in the DATA step, the output-delivery system (ODS), the SAS Macro Facility, and much more.

CHAPTER 9

New Version 9 Features

THE RELEASE OF VERSION 9 introduces many new and exciting features, further enhancing SAS' reputation and reach in the fast growing business-intelligence software marketplace.Introduced as Project Mercury at the 27th annual SAS Users Group International Conference in the spring of 2002, Version 9 boasts unprecedented performance and scalability. This chapter presents tips on a number of the new features introduced in Version 9. With a focus on creating open and adaptable technologies, as well as reducing IT costs, SAS is committed to improving its support in the area of Web services by providing software that can be integrated into all IT environments.

In this chapter, you'll learn many new Version 9 features, including

- DATA step Perl Regular Expressions (PRXs) for performing faster searches

- Text search, retrieval, and replacement capabilities with regular expressions

- Output Delivery System (ODS) features

- ODS MARKUP destination capabilities for creating Web content

- HTML and XML options used with the ODS MARKUP destination

- Macro statements and options

- The SAS Learning Edition

The DATA Step

This section provides an early look at the number of useful new DATA step features found in Version 9.

1 Performing faster searches and text replacement with Perl Regular Expressions (PRXs)

Performing text operations related to matching, changing, or translating a string of characters is popular in text-processing applications. *Perl Regular Expressions* (PRXs) enable users to perform complex word matching and text replacement where a set of characters determines a pattern found in the text. UNIX users have used regular expressions for some time, and now many new functions such as PRXPARSE, PRXMATCH, PRXPARSE, PRXPOSN, PRXCHANGE and more are available in Version 9 of the SAS System.

2 Describing PRXs and metacharacters

If you need to know something or want to identify patterns in text, PRXs provide the tools to get the job done. They provide a powerful way to search and match strings and retrieve and validate data. Although unique in their syntax, regular expressions are essentially a string of characters and special characters called *metacharacters* (for example,

/text-string/, \d). The advantage of using metacharacters lies in their ability to search, match, and replace data faster than other methods, and in requiring fewer steps than other methods.

3 Getting started with a simple match

Let's start with the simplest of examples. Suppose you wanted to search a string for the word "sas" using lowercase characters—your regular expression would simply be "sas". The words "sas", "sassy", "sassafras", "sasquatch", and "Manassas" would also match the regular expression. If the various derivations from your simple search were acceptable, then you could stop the search right there. But by expanding your knowledge of PRX, and specifically with other SAS functions, you can restrict the number of matches many fold, reducing the number of non-matches and leaving you with results that are more specific to your needs.

4 Performing another simple match with PRX

Although the syntax requirements for PRX are rather unique, SAS users, and especially Perl users, will find that they're not too difficult to master. Mastering them is well worth the investment in time, especially learning to improve the way searches, matches, and replaces are performed. For example, to perform a simple match operation, the regular expression /sas/ looks for the characters "sas" in a text string. The slashes "/" surrounding the regular expression act as delimiters.

5 Parsing data with regular expressions

Version 9's new DATA step function PRXPARSE parses data using a set of rules defined in the metacharacters. The PRXPARSE function uses the metacharacters to identify patterns in data.

For example, the following SAS program assigns a series of metacharacters to the REGEXP variable using the PRXPARSE function. The MOVIE_CODE adheres to a format or template of *xx-xxxx* where the first two positions represent the movie studio where the movie was made and the remaining four positions represent the unique movie number (serial number). The metacharacters being passed to PRXPARSE consist of a first and last slash to represent a delimiter for the regular expression. The \d notation represents the three digits, followed by a dash, and then four more digits.

Code:

```
DATA _NULL_;
  LENGTH TITLE $30.
         RATING $5.
         MOVIE_CODE $7.;
  INPUT TITLE $
        RATING $
        MOVIE_CODE $;
  REGEXP=
    PRXPARSE("/[0-9]{2}\-[0-9]{4}/");
  CARDS;
Jaws PG 01-1234
Rocky PG 07-5555
Titanic PG-13 15-4321
;
RUN;
```

6 Finding data with regular expressions

The PRXMATCH function's purpose is to see if a match occurs using the pattern specified in the PRXPARSE function. When a match is found, a value representing the column position where the pattern matched the value is returned; otherwise, a zero is returned when a match isn't found. Common applications for using PRXMATCH include validating telephone numbers, ZIP/postal codes, and email addresses against a lookup table. Other uses include verifying that telephone numbers are stored in an acceptable format as well as finding and substituting text characters (searching and replacing).

7 Retrieving text with regular expressions

You can combine Version 9's PRXPOSN function with regular expressions to enable the retrieval of the position and length of a data value. This approach comes in handy when processing telephone numbers or ZIP/postal codes to verify for correctness.

8 Searching and replacing text

Frequently, search and replace operations are needed when working with text data. Version 9's PRXCHANGE function is available, along with PRXPARSE, for making text replacements. PRXPARSE uses the pattern-identification number, the number of times a match should be replaced, and a character variable to perform the replacement on.

9 Exploring other PRX functions

Version 9 provides a few other PRX functions for use in the DATA step. Table 9-1 lists these little wonders, each of which makes text-processing a bit more powerful.

Table 9-1. Other PRX Functions

PRX FUNCTION	DESCRIPTION
PRXDEBUG	Routes Perl debug information to the SAS Log.
PRXFREE	Releases memory allocated to parsed regular expressions.
PRXNEXT	Specifies that regular expression text matches be repeated.
PRXPAREN	Revisits the most recent match found.
PRXSUBSTR	Determines the position and length of a match.

Output Delivery System (ODS)

This section discusses a number of new and enhanced Version 9 ODS features.

1 Understanding ODS MARKUP

With Version 9, ODS MARKUP enters the production world. Its ability to create a variety of file types—including comma-separated values (CSV), HyperText Markup Language (HTML), Extensible Markup Language (XML), Wireless Markup Language (WML), compact HTML (CHTML), typesetting languages such as LaTeX and Troff, and others—makes ODS MARKUP flexible and popular for creating exciting Web content. You use the same syntax for ODS MARKUP as you do for the ODS HTML destination, with the one exception of specifying a **TAGSET=** option to indicate the type of markup language to send output to.

2 Exploring ODS MARKUP file types

You write output to one or more files by substituting the specific option and filename in the ODS MARKUP statement. Here is a brief list of the purpose of each file, followed by more detailed information. You can specify the following types of files with the ODS MARKUP destination:

- Body= file
- Contents= file
- Page= file
- Frame= file
- Code= XSL (Extensible Stylesheet Language)
- Stylesheet= option

The body file

The body file consists of output created by your SAS job. It takes on the characteristics of whatever tagset was specified (such as HTML, XML, and so on). When output is routed to the HTML destination, it is placed within one of three HTML tags:

- TABLE
- IMG
- As an HTML table

The nature of the output object determines which of the three tags is used for displaying with a Web browser. When creating the body file, ODS handles output objects differently depending on the nature of the output. If the output object consists of tabular data without any graphics, ODS inserts the object within TABLE tags. When the object contains a graphic image, ODS places it within IMG tags. And when the object does not contain tabular data or a graphic image, ODS tags it as an HTML table.

The contents file

The contents file consists of a link to each output object in the body file. It uses an anchor tag to link to each table. With your browser, you can view the contents file directly or as part of the frame file.

The page file

The page file consists of a link to each page of output in the body file. With your browser, you can view the page file directly or as part of the frame file.

The frame file

The frame file integrates the body, contents, and page files into a cohesive Web page when you specify the HTML tagset.

3 Obtaining a list of tagset names

The SAS System lets you request a list of the various tagsets stored in the read-only SASHELP.TMPLMST library and, if available, the SASUSER.TEMPLAT library. To obtain a list of tagset names, run the following TEMPLATE procedure. The results illustrate a partial listing of the available tagset names.

Code:

```
PROC TEMPLATE;
  LIST TAGSETS;
RUN;
```

Results:

```
Listing of: SASHELP.TMPLMST
Path Filter is: Tagsets
Sort by: PATH/ASCENDING

Obs  Path                 Type
 1   Tagsets              Dir
 2   Tagsets.Chtml        Tagset
 3   Tagsets.Colorlatex   Tagset
 4   Tagsets.Csv          Tagset
 5   Tagsets.Csvall       Tagset
 6   Tagsets.Default      Tagset
 7   Tagsets.Docbook      Tagset
 8   Tagsets.Event_map    Tagset
 9   Tagsets.Graph        Tagset
10   Tagsets.Htmlcss      Tagset
11   Tagsets.Imode        Tagset
12   Tagsets.Latex        Tagset
13   Tagsets.Phtml        Tagset
14   Tagsets.Pyx          Tagset
15   Tagsets.Sasxmog      Tagset
16   Tagsets.Sasxmoh      Tagset
17   Tagsets.Sasxmoim     Tagset
18   Tagsets.Sasxmor      Tagset
19   Tagsets.Troff        Tagset
20   Tagsets.Wml          Tagset
21   Tagsets.Wmlolist     Tagset
22   Tagsets.sasXML       Tagset
23   Tagsets.sasioXML     Tagset
```

4 Creating HTML output with MARKUP

Building an integrated Web-based page from UNIVARIATE procedure output is a snap with the MARKUP destination. The following example suppresses the Listing destination and specifies the TAGSET= PHTML (basic HTML) format engine using the BODY=, CONTENTS=, PAGE=, and FRAME= file options. Once the output is generated, the MARKUP destination is closed, and the Listing destination reopened. After output files are created, you can display the frame file in a standard Web browser, as shown in Figure 9-1.

Code:

```
ODS LISTING CLOSE;
ODS SELECT MOMENTS;
ODS MARKUP
     BODY='ODS-BODY.HTM'
  CONTENTS='ODS-CONTENTS.HTM'
     PAGE='ODS-PAGE.HTM'
    FRAME='ODS-FRAME.HTM'
   TAGSET=PHTML;
  PROC UNIVARIATE
     DATA=MOVIES
        (KEEP=TITLE RATING LENGTH);
    TITLE 'Creating MARKUP Output';
  RUN;
ODS MARKUP CLOSE;
ODS LISTING;
```

Results shown in Figure 9-1.

5 Creating XML output with MARKUP

Creating generic XML markup from UNIVARIATE procedure output is a snap with the MARKUP destination. The following example suppresses the Listing destination, specifies the BODY= file option, and omits the TAGSET= option (default tagset is ODSXML). Once the output is generated, the MARKUP destination is closed and the Listing destination reopened. After output files are created, you can display the body file in a standard Web browser.

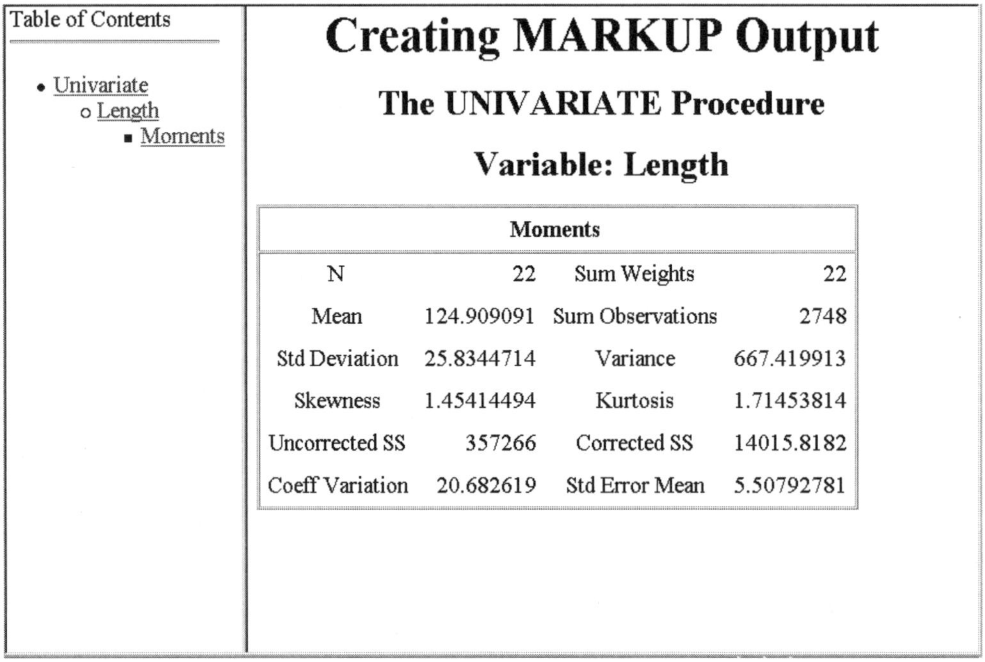

Creating MARKUP Output

The UNIVARIATE Procedure

Variable: Length

Table of Contents

- Univariate
  - Length
    - Moments

Moments			
N	22	Sum Weights	22
Mean	124.909091	Sum Observations	2748
Std Deviation	25.8344714	Variance	667.419913
Skewness	1.45414494	Kurtosis	1.71453814
Uncorrected SS	357266	Corrected SS	14015.8182
Coeff Variation	20.682619	Std Error Mean	5.50792781

Figure 9-1. HTML output created with the ODS MARKUP destination

Code:

```
ODS LISTING CLOSE;
ODS MARKUP BODY='SASXML-BODY.XML';
  PROC UNIVARIATE
     DATA=MOVIES
        (KEEP=TITLE RATING LENGTH);
     TITLE 'Creating XML Output';
  RUN;
ODS MARKUP CLOSE;
ODS LISTING;
```

6 Understanding Document Type Definitions (DTDs)

The XML specification is founded on the ability to share or exchange information freely to anywhere. Achieving this objective requires development and enforcement of standards. This way, not only information is shared, but the rules that control *how* the information will be shared is shared. Conceptually, XML consists of five parts:

- Content definition

- Structure definition

- Human and machine convergence

- Separation of content from relationships

- Separation of structure from presentation

Documents and their content are designed to share information. You accomplish this sharing in two parts: XML document and XML *document type definitions* (DTDs). A DTD establishes the rules that control the order, structure, and attributes of a document and its use of tags. Essentially, when a user accesses a document, the DTD, as the arbitrator, interprets its rules and processes the document.

7 Creating an XML output and DTD with MARKUP

Creating generic XML markup with a DTD from UNIVARIATE procedure output is easy with the MARKUP destination. The following example suppresses the Listing destination and specifies a body file and a frame, along with the TAGSET= assigned as DEFAULT. Once the output is generated, the MARKUP destination is closed and the Listing destination reopened. After output files are created, you can access the frame file for interpretation and processing the document. You can access the XML markup file in a common Web browser.

The file extension used on the body file is XML, whereas the frame file uses the DTD extension.

Code:

```
ODS LISTING CLOSE;
ODS MARKUP BODY='SASXML-BODY.XML'
        FRAME='SASXML-FRAME.DTD'
        TAGSET=DEFAULT;
  PROC UNIVARIATE
      DATA=MOVIES
          (KEEP=TITLE RATING LENGTH);
    TITLE 'Creating XML Output';
  RUN;
ODS MARKUP CLOSE;
ODS LISTING;
```

8 Combining MARKUP output

Combining MARKUP output requires using two ODS statements: one for the XML document and the other for the destination of your choice. The following example combines an XML document with an HTML document using the CHTML destination (compact HTML, meaning no style information) from UNIVARIATE output.

Code:

```
ODS LISTING CLOSE;
ODS MARKUP BODY='SASXML-BODY.XML';
ODS CHTML BODY='SASHTML-BODY.HTML';
  PROC UNIVARIATE
      DATA=MOVIES
          (KEEP=TITLE RATING LENGTH);
    TITLE 'Combining XML and HTML Output';
  RUN;
ODS MARKUP CLOSE;
ODS CHTML CLOSE;
ODS LISTING;
```

9 Using ODS to get "page xx of yy" page numbering

Although limited to just PostScript (PS) output, SAS Version 9 provides a way to produce "page xx of yy" page numbering in output. Using the ODS PS statement, users can apply the macros developed by Tom Abernathy of Pfizer, Inc. Once the PS file is generated, you can convert it to PDF with Adobe's Acrobat Distiller or the shareware ps2pdf. These Macros can be downloaded from the SAS Institute Web site. To find them, search for "Pageof macros."

SAS Macro Facility

This section introduces several new Version 9 Macro statements and options.

1 Exploring new Version 9 Macro statements

Version 9 has two new macro statements. Table 9-2 describes each of them.

2 Exploring new Version 9 Macro options

Version 9 has four new Macro options. Table 9-3 describes each of them.

One More Tip

Here's an important tip on acquiring a personal copy of the SAS Learning Edition.

1 Learning made easy with the SAS Learning Edition

Acquiring skills in data management, statistical analysis, graphics, business forecasting, quality improvement, and an assortment of other products is easy with the SAS Learning Edition. Designed for students and business professionals, this PC-based business intelligence software provides users with a way to expand

Table 9-2. New Version 9 Macro Statements

MACRO STATEMENT	DESCRIPTION
%ABORT	Similar to the ABORT statement in the DATA step, the %ABORT statement is used inside a Macro to stop executing the current Macro. The available options with the %ABORT statement are ABEND or RETURN.
%RETURN;	Allows the current Macro to successfully terminate processing. The %RETURN Macro statement directs control to a label located just before the %MEND statement.

Table 9-3. New Version 9 Macro Options

MACRO OPTION	DESCRIPTION
MAUTOLOCDISPLAY	This toggle displays the location of the source code and where it's obtained to compile an autocall Macro on the SAS Log. The information displayed on the SAS Log is similar to the MLOGIC option. The default setting is NOMAUTOLOCDISPLAY. Note: If both the MAUTOLOCDISPLAY and MLOGIC options are set, the MAUTOLOCDISPLAY information will not display.
MCOMPILNOTE	Displays a note on the SAS Log when a Macro has completed compilation. The available values with this option are: NONE (default), NOAUTOCALL, and ALL.
MLOGICNEST	This toggle displays additional nesting information on the SAS Log. The default setting is NOMLOGICNEST.
MPRINTNEST	This toggle prints additional information to the SAS Log when the MPRINT option is specified. The default setting is NOMPRINTTEST.

their SAS knowledge through hands-on experience. You can request more information or obtain your own personal copy of this groundbreaking new software directly from SAS Institute, or through any good bookstore, such as Borders Books and Music or Amazon.com.

Summary

This chapter gave you a brief overview of a number of new Version 9 features. SAS software not only empowers users with the "Power to Know" but also provides a powerful set of open and adaptable technology solutions. The outlook for SAS users everywhere has never looked brighter.

APPENDIX
SAS System Options

THE FOLLOWING TABLE lists the SAS system options. The first setting in each table entry is usually the default setting (on most operating systems).

SYSTEM OPTION	DESCRIPTION
ALTLOG=destination	Specifies an external file location or device where a copy of the SAS Log is to be written. It's specified at SAS invocation, or in the configuration file.
ALTPRINT=destination	Specifies an external file location or device where a copy of the SAS procedure output is to be written. It's specified at SAS invocation, or in the configuration file.
**BATCH	NOBATCH**	Specifies whether the default system option settings CLEANUP, LINESIZE=, OVP, PAGESIZE=, SOURCE, and SPOOL will be affected when the SAS System is initiated. It's specified at SAS invocation, or in the configuration file
BINDING=DEFAULTEDGE |	Specifies what binding edge to use for duplex printing. The following arguments are available: **LONGEDGE	SHORTEDGE DEFAULTEDGE** specifies the default edge as the binding edge for duplex printing. **LONGEDGE** specifies the long edge as the binding edge for duplex printing. **SHORTEDGE** specifies the short edge as the binding edge for duplex printing. The BINDING= system option is specified in an OPTIONS statement, in the OPTIONS window, at SAS invocation, or in the configuration file.
BOTTOMMARGIN=margin-size	Specifies what the size of the bottom margin on the printed page will be. By default, the margin-size unit argument is in inches. This option is specified in an OPTIONS statement, in the OPTIONS window, at SAS invocation, or in the configuration file.

SYSTEM OPTION	DESCRIPTION
BUFNO=*n* | MIN | MAX	Specifies the number of buffers to use for SAS data sets in the current SAS session. Users can control how many buffers are available for data sets opened for input, output, or update. The following arguments are available: **BUFNO=n** specifies a user-defined number ranging in value from 0 to the largest 4-byte integer available on your operating system. **BUFNO=MIN** specifies that the number of buffers is to be set at zero. **BUFNO=MAX** specifies that that the largest 4-byte integer available on the operating system be used. This option is specified at SAS invocation, or in the configuration file.
BUFSIZE=number-of-buffers	Specifies the number of buffers to be allocated during input, output, or update activities in a SAS data set. It's specified in an OPTIONS statement, in the OPTIONS window, at SAS invocation, or in the configuration file.
BUFSIZE=number-of-bytes	Specifies the size (in bytes) of input/output buffers used for SAS data sets. It's specified in an OPTIONS statement, in the OPTIONS window, at SAS invocation, or in the configuration file.
BYERR | NOBYERR	Specifies whether the SAS System sets the error flag and issues an error message when a null data set is input to the SORT procedure. The BYERR | NOBYERR system option is specified at SAS invocation or in the configuration file.
BYLINE | NOBYLINE	Specifies whether each by group has a by-line printed above it., The BYLINE | NOBYLINE system option is specified in an OPTIONS statement, in the OPTIONS window, at SAS invocation, or in the configuration file.
CAPS | NOCAPS	Specifies whether lowercase characters that are read from input sources, CARDS, CARDS4, and PARMCARDS statements are converted to uppercase. It's specified in an OPTIONS statement, in the OPTIONS window, at SAS invocation, or in the configuration file.
CARDIMAGE | NOCARDIMAGE	Generally used on MVS, CMS, and VSE host systems, this system option specifies whether the SAS System should process source and data lines as an 80-byte (Hollerith) card image. It's specified in an OPTIONS statement, in the OPTIONS window, at SAS invocation, or in the configuration file.

SYSTEM OPTION	DESCRIPTION
CATCACHE=n	Specifies how many SAS catalogs to keep open at a time to avoid excessive overhead of repeatedly opening and closing the same catalogs. It's specified at SAS invocation or in the configuration file.
CHARCODE | NOCHARCODE	Specifies whether users can substitute a combination of characters for special characters and is entered in an OPTIONS statement, in the OPTIONS window, at SAS invocation, or in the configuration file. This system option is primarily used when one or more special characters are not available on a keyboard.
CLEANUP | NOCLEANUP	Specifies how the SAS System is to handle out-of-resource conditions (e.g., such as memory, disk, etc.) associated with nonessential resources and is entered in an OPTIONS statement, in the OPTIONS window, at SAS invocation, or in the configuration file.
CMPOPT | NOCMPOPT	Specifies whether SAS program code is optimized for more efficient execution. By default, the **CMPOPT** system option is specified at SAS invocation. In contrast, the **NOCMPOPT** option is specified when efficiency is secondary to displaying error messages associated with debugging.
COMAMID=access-method-id	Specifies a communication access method identifier to use with products such as SAS/SHARE and SAS/CONNECT software and is entered in an OPTIONS statement, at SAS invocation, or in the configuration file.
CONNECTREMOTE=session-id	Specifies the remote session ID used by SAS/CONNECT software. This option is specified in an OPTIONS statement, in the OPTIONS window, at SAS invocation, or in the configuration file.
CONNECTSTATUS | NOCONNECTSTATUS	Specifies whether to display the transfer window in SAS/CONNECT software. This option is specified in an OPTIONS statement, in the OPTIONS window, at SAS invocation, or in the configuration file.
CONNECTWAIT | NOCONNECTWAIT	Specifies whether to wait for a remote submit statement to complete before control returns to the local session in SAS/CONNECT software. This option is specified in an OPTIONS statement, in the OPTIONS window, at SAS invocation, or in the configuration file.

SYSTEM OPTION	DESCRIPTION
**CPUID	NOCPUID**	Specifies whether the CPU information is written to the SAS Log following the licensing information. Specifying the **CPUID** system option writes the information to the SAS Log, while **NOCPUID** suppresses the information from appearing in the SAS Log. This option is specified at SAS invocation or in the configuration file.
**DBCS	NODBCS**	Specifies whether double-byte character sets should be recognized by the SAS System and is entered at SAS invocation or in the configuration file. This option is specified when 2 bytes are used for each character set such as when lowercase characters read from an input source are converted to uppercase, and to support foreign languages such as Chinese, Japanese, Korean, and Taiwanese.
DBCSLANG=language	Specifies the double-byte character set (DBCS) language to use and is entered at SAS invocation or in the configuration file. The following language arguments can be specified: CHINESE, JAPANESE, KOREAN, TAIWANESE, or UNKNOWN.
DBCSTYPE=encoding-method	Specifies the type of encoding method used for the double-byte character set (DBCS) and is entered at SAS invocation or in the configuration file. The following encoding methods are available: DEC, DG, EUC (Extended UNIX Code), FACOM (Fujitsu), HITAC (Hitachi), HP15, IBM, PCIBM, PRIME, and SJIS.
**DETAILS	NODETAILS**	Specifies whether to display additional directory list information in a data library. This option is specified in an OPTIONS statement, in the OPTIONS window, at SAS invocation, or in the configuration file.
DEVICE=driver-name	Specifies the terminal device driver for SAS/GRAPH software. It's specified in an OPTIONS statement, in the OPTIONS window, at SAS invocation, or in the configuration file.
**DMR	NODMR**	Specifies whether a remote SAS session is enabled so SAS/CONNECT software can be run. It's specified at SAS invocation, or in the configuration file.
**DMS	NODMS**	Specifies whether the SAS Display Manager System is active during the SAS session. It's specified at SAS invocation, or in the configuration file.

SYSTEM OPTION	DESCRIPTION
**DSNFERR	NODSNFERR**	Specifies whether an error message is generated by the SAS System when a program that references an input or update SAS data set cannot be found. It is specified in an OPTIONS statement, in the OPTIONS window, at SAS invocation, or in the configuration file.
**DUPLEX	NODUPLEX**	Specifies whether output is printed using the printer controls specified in the BINDING= system option. By default, the **NODUPLEX** system option specifies that duplex printing is not to be performed. When the **DUPLEX** system option is specified, output is printed using the argument set in the BINDING= option. This option is specified in an OPTIONS statement, OPTIONS window, at SAS invocation, or in the configuration file.
**ECHOAUTO	NOECHOAUTO**	Specifies whether the SAS source lines of code read from the autoexec file are printed (echoing feature) to the SAS Log. It's specified at SAS invocation, or in the configuration file.
ENGINE=engine-name	Specifies the default engine name to be associated with a SAS library. It's specified at SAS invocation, or in the configuration file.
FORMCHAR='formatting-characters'	Specifies the default output formatting characters to use in constructing tabular output outliers and dividers for the FREQ and TABULATE procedures. The string of formatting characters can be up to 64 bytes long, and anything less than 64 bytes is automatically padded with blanks. The option and formatting characters are specified in an OPTIONS statement, in the OPTIONS window, at SAS invocation, or in the configuration file.
FORMDLIM='delimit-character'	Specifies a character to use for printing page break delimiters in SAS System output. It is specified in an OPTIONS statement, in the OPTIONS window, at SAS invocation, or in the configuration file.
FORMS=form-name	Specifies the form that was created with FSFORMS to customize the appearance of output generated by interactive windowing procedures. It's specified in an OPTIONS statement, in the OPTIONS window, at SAS invocation, or in the configuration file.
**GWINDOW	NOGWINDOW**	Specifies whether SAS/GRAPH output can be displayed in the GRAPH window of SAS Display Manager System. It's specified in an OPTIONS statement, in the OPTIONS window, at SAS invocation, or in the configuration file.

SYSTEM OPTION	DESCRIPTION
IMPLMAC | NOIMPLMAC	Specifies whether the macro processor will examine the first word of every statement to determine if that word is a statement-style Macro call. This has no effect on the ability to call a Macro using name-style macro invocation. It's specified in an OPTIONS statement, in the OPTIONS window, at SAS invocation, or in the configuration file.
LEFTMARGIN=margin-size	Specifies what the size of the left margin on the printed page will be. By default, the margin-size unit argument is in inches. This option is specified in an OPTIONS statement, in the OPTIONS window, at SAS invocation, or in the configuration file.
MAUTOSOURCE | NOMAUTOSOURCE	Specifies whether the Macro autocall feature is enabled. It's specified in an OPTIONS statement, in the OPTIONS window, at SAS invocation, or in the configuration file.
MERROR | NOMERROR	Specifies whether the Macro language compiler is to issue warning messages when the Macro processor cannot match a Macro-like name to a Macro keyword. It's specified in an OPTIONS statement, in the OPTIONS window, at SAS invocation, or in the configuration file.
MLOGIC | NOMLOGIC	Specifies whether the Macro processor is used as a debugging tool by tracing Macro execution and writing any trace information to the SAS Log. It's specified in an OPTIONS statement, in the OPTIONS window, at SAS invocation, or in the configuration file.
MPRINT | NOMPRINT	Specifies whether any Macro-generated statements from Macro execution are written to the SAS Log. It's specified in an OPTIONS statement, in the OPTIONS window, at SAS invocation, or in the configuration file.
MRECALL | NOMRECALL	Specifies whether the autocall libraries are searched each time a Macro is invoked for an undefined Macro name, even though an earlier search could not find it. It's specified in an OPTIONS statement, in the OPTIONS window, at SAS invocation, or in the configuration file.
MSTORED | NOMSTORED	Specifies whether the Macro facility searches the SASMACR catalog as referenced by the SASMSTORE= option for a stored compiled Macro. This option is specified at SAS invocation or in the configuration file.

SYSTEM OPTION	DESCRIPTION
MVARSIZE=*n* **| MIN | MAX**	Specifies the maximum size of Macro variables stored in memory. The following arguments are available: **MVARSIZE=***n* specifies a user-defined number ranging in value from 0 to the largest 4-byte integer available on your operating system. **MVARSIZE=MIN** specifies that the value be set at zero and all Macro variables be written out to disk. **MVARSIZE=MAX** specifies that the largest 4-byte integer available on your operating system be used. This option is specified at SAS invocation, or in the configuration file.
NEWS=file-specification	Specifies an external file containing installation- or user-defined messages that are written to the SAS Log. It's specified at SAS invocation, or in the configuration file.
NOTES | NONOTES	Specifies whether SAS System notes are written to the SAS Log. Note: Warning and error messages are printed to the SAS Log even when NONOTES is specified. It's specified in an OPTIONS statement, in the OPTIONS window, at SAS invocation, or in the configuration file.
OVP | NOOVP	Specifies whether overprinting will be allowed for output lines produced by the SAS System. When the OVP option is specified, it generally refers to the ability to print underscores (_) directly below a word, as opposed to a dash on a separate line below a word when NOOVP is specified. It's specified in an OPTIONS statement, in the OPTIONS window, at SAS invocation, or in the configuration file.
PAPERSIZE=LETTER	Specifies the size of the paper to use when printing. By default, LETTER is used. Refer to the Registry Editor for a listing of other available paper size arguments. This option is specified in an OPTIONS statement, in the OPTIONS window, at SAS invocation, or in the configuration file.
PARM='string'	Specifies a character-string that can be passed to an external program. It's specified in an OPTIONS statement, in the OPTIONS window, at SAS invocation, or in the configuration file.
PRINT=destination	Specifies an external file or device to write the SAS output file when a program executes in non-interactive display manager mode. The PRINT= option is specified at SAS invocation, or in the configuration file.

SYSTEM OPTION	DESCRIPTION
	Specifies the number of significant digits used in calculating p-values for some statistical procedures. It's specified in an OPTIONS statement, in the OPTIONS window, at SAS invocation, or in the configuration file.
PROCLEAVE=value	Specifies how much memory to leave unallocated so any memory-intensive procedures can terminate normally should the error recovery be initiated. The amount of memory specified can be bytes, kilobytes, or megabytes and can range in value from 0 to the maximum amount of available space (refer to your specific host system documentation for details). It's specified in an OPTIONS statement, at SAS invocation, or in the configuration file.
REMOTE=session-id	Specifies a host-specific remote session identifier to run SAS/CONNECT software. It's specified in an OPTIONS statement, in the OPTIONS window, at SAS invocation, or in the configuration file.
RIGHTMARGIN=margin-size	Specifies what the size of the right margin on the printed page will be. By default, the margin-size unit argument is in inches. This option is specified in an OPTIONS statement, in the OPTIONS window, at SAS invocation, or in the configuration file.
S=n | MAX	Specifies the length of program statements and data on lines, exclusive of sequence numbers, following a CARDS statement (used to process in-stream data). Fixed- or variable-length records can be input with this option where n represents a length from 0 to the largest signed, host-specific 4-byte integer and **MAX** represents the largest signed, 4-byte host-specific integer. It's specified in an OPTIONS statement, in the OPTIONS window, at SAS invocation, or in the configuration file.
SASAUTOS=library | (library1, library2, ... libraryn)	Specifies the storage location of the autocall library or libraries containing definitions of SAS Macros. It's specified in an OPTIONS statement, in the OPTIONS window, at SAS invocation, or in the configuration file.
SASHELP=library	Specifies the storage location of the SASHELP library containing Help files. It's specified at SAS invocation, or in the configuration file.
SASMSG=library	Specifies the storage location of the external library that contains SAS error, warning, and informational messages. It's specified at SAS invocation, or in the configuration file.

SYSTEM OPTION	DESCRIPTION
SASMSTORE=libref	Specifies the libref associated with the library (cannot be WORK) containing the catalog of compiled stored SAS macros. This option is specified in an OPTIONS statement, in the OPTIONS window, at SAS invocation, or in the configuration file.
SASUSER=library	Specifies the storage location of the SASUSER library that contains the SAS-created user's profile catalog. It's specified at SAS invocation, or in the configuration file.
SEQ=n	Specifies the number of numeric characters in a sequence field. By default, the SAS System assumes an eight numeric character sequence field. Because some editors place one or more alphabetic characters in the beginning of a sequence field (e.g.for example, ABC00001), the **SEQ=** system option is specified to indicate the starting position the numeric portion begins. The value specified for n represents the number of digits that are right justified in the sequence field. For example, if the sequence field contains a value of ABC00001, then a value of SEQ=5 would be specified. It's specified in an OPTIONS statement, in the OPTIONS window, at SAS invocation, or in the configuration file.
SERROR | NOSERROR	Specifies whether a warning message is issued when a Macro variable reference cannot be matched with an equivalent Macro variable. The causes for this type of warning include misspelling the name in a macro variable reference, referencing a variable before it is defined, enclosing an ampersand (&) by itself in double quotes, and specifying an ampersand (&) followed by a string without a blank between the ampersand and the string. The SERROR | NOSERROR system option is specified in an OPTIONS statement, in the OPTIONS window, at SAS invocation, or in the configuration file.
SETINIT | NOSETINIT	Specifies whether the site licensing information can be changed after the installation process has occurred. It's specified at SAS invocation, or in the configuration file.
SITEINFO=file-specification	Specifies an external file location containing site-specific information. When the SITEINFO= system option and the SITEINFO display manager command are specified, site-specific information is displayed in the SITEINFO window. The SITEINFO= option is specified at SAS invocation, or in the configuration file.

SYSTEM OPTION	DESCRIPTION
SKIP=*n* | MIN | MAX	Specifies the number of lines to skip at the top of each page of output before the first line is printed. Users can control at what line output is to begin printing by specifying the following system option arguments: **SKIP**=*n* specifies a user-defined number ranging in value from 0 to 20. **SKIP=MIN** specifies that zero lines will be skipped at the top of each page before printing. **SKIP=MAX** specifies that 20 lines will automatically be skipped at the top of each page before printing the first line of output. This option is specified in an OPTIONS statement, in the OPTIONS window, at SAS invocation, or in the configuration file.
SOLUTIONS | NOSOLUTIONS	Specifies whether all SAS windows will contain the SOLUTIONS menu choice and whether the SAS Explorer will display the SOLUTIONS folder. This option is specified at SAS invocation, or in the configuration file.
SPOOL | NOSPOOL	Specifies whether SAS statements are written to a WORK library data set so the statements can be later resubmitted with a %INCLUDE or redisplayed with a %LIST statement. It's specified in an OPTIONS statement, in the OPTIONS window, at SAS invocation, or in the configuration file.
SYMBOLGEN | NOSYMBOLGEN	Specifies whether the Macro processor displays the resolution of macro variable references. It's specified in an OPTIONS statement, in the OPTIONS window, at SAS invocation, or in the configuration file.
SYSLEAVE=value	Specifies how much memory to leave unallocated so the SAS System can terminate normally should the error recovery be initiated. The amount of memory specified can be bytes, kilobytes, or megabytes and can range in value from 0 to the maximum amount of available space (refer to you specific host system documentation for details). It's specified in an OPTIONS statement, at SAS invocation, or in the configuration file.
SYSPARM='characters'	Specifies a character string that can be passed to other SAS programs including a DATA step using the SYSPARM() function or by using the automatic macro variable reference &SYSPARM. The character string value can be a maximum length of 200 characters. The SYSPARM= system option can be specified in an OPTIONS statement, in the OPTIONS window, at SAS invocation, or in the configuration file.

SYSTEM OPTION	DESCRIPTION
S2=S | *n*	Specifies the length of secondary source (program) statements that comes from a %INCLUDE statement, an AUTOEXEC file, or an autocall Macro file. When the S2=S system option is specified, the current value of the S= system option is used to compute the record length. Otherwise, when the S2=*n* option is specified, the *n* value is used to compute the record length. The S2=S | *n* system option is specified in an OPTIONS statement, in the OPTIONS window, at SAS invocation, or in the configuration file.
TAPECLOSE=REREAD | LEAVE | REWIND | DISP	Specifies a default CLOSE volume disposition to be executed when a SAS data library on tape is closed. The following arguments are valid with the TAPECLOSE= system option: **REREAD** positions the tape volume at the tapemark preceding the file just closed. **LEAVE** positions the tape volume at the tapemark following the file just closed. **REWIND** rewinds the tape volume to the beginning of the tape. **DISP** positions the tape volume corresponding to the disposition specified in the host system's control language. The TAPECLOSE= system option is specified in an OPTIONS statement, in the OPTIONS window, at SAS invocation, or in the configuration file.
TERMINAL | NOTERMINAL	Specifies whether a terminal is attached at SAS invocation. When the TERMINAL system option is specified, it is assumed that the current SAS session is being invoked in foreground. Otherwise, when the NOTERMINAL option is specified the terminal is not attached and the current SAS session is being invoked in background (or batch). It's specified at SAS invocation or in the configuration file.
TOPMARGIN=margin-size	Specifies what the size of the top margin on the printed page will be. By default, the margin-size unit argument is in inches. This option is specified in an OPTIONS statement, in the OPTIONS window, at SAS invocation, or in the configuration file.
TRAINLOC="train-location"	Specifies the location of SAS online training courses. This option is specified at SAS invocation or in the configuration file.

SYSTEM OPTION	DESCRIPTION
USER=library	Specifies the name of the default external SAS library that is used when referencing one-level names (e.g.,such as data set names). This system option can be specified to reduce the number of keystrokes associated with referencing SAS library members. However, if WORK is specified as the argument with the USER= system option, any member names (e.g.for example, data sets) referenced with one-level names refers to the temporary WORK library. The USER= system option is specified in an OPTIONS statement, in the OPTIONS window, at SAS invocation, or in the configuration file.
VALIDVARNAME=V7 | V6 | UPCASE	Specifies what type of variable names can be created during a SAS session. The valid arguments include the following: **V7**: Default argument used to create a variable name consisting of a combination of 32 mixed-case, alphanumeric characters where the first character can only be alpha or an underscore (_) and the remaining positions can be alpha, underscore (_), or numeric. **V6**: Used to create Version 6 variable names consisting of a combination of 8 mixed-case, alphanumeric characters where the first character can only be alpha or an underscore (_) and the remaining positions can be alpha, underscore (_), or numeric. **UPCASE**: Used to create a variable name consisting of a combination of alphanumeric characters where the first character can only be alpha or an underscore (_) and the remaining positions can be alpha, underscore (_), or numeric.
VNFERR | NOVNFERR	Specifies whether a warning is issued, an error flag (_ERROR_=1) is set, and/or processing stopped due to a missing variable being encountered when a MERGE statement is specified in a DATA _NULL_ step as when the VNFERR system option is set. However, if NOVNFERR is specified, the SAS System does not set _ERROR_=1 or stop processing when a variable not found, but issues a warning. The VNFERR | NOVNFERR system option is specified in an OPTIONS statement, in the OPTIONS window, at SAS invocation, or in the configuration file.

INDEX

Symbols

% (percent sign wildcard)
    multiple wildcards in search pattern, 104
    subsetting with LIKE operator and, 103
%INCLUDE statement, 13
: (colon modifier), 104–105
; (semicolon)
    ending statements with, 3
    marking end of data containing, 5
_ (underscore wildcard), 104

A

aborting DATA step, 86–87
accessing
    data from other applications with DDE, 62
    DDE triplet from Excel, 62–63
    dictionary views, 72–73
    EFI, 58
    libraries, 176
    Service & Support Web site, 233
    windows with commands, 28, 29–30
anchor tags, 201
ANSI SQL extensions, 74
Appearance options for Enhanced Editor, 124
APPEND procedure
    concatenating data sets with, 141–142, 183
    creating BASE= data set in, 142
    data set management with, 182
    handling missing values in, 182
    missing values in, 142
    omitting BASE= or DATA= option with, 142
    specifying BASE= option in, 142, 221
applying SETINIT, 237–238
arithmetic functions, 107, 108
array functions, 107, 108
ATTRIB statement
    applying date format with, 95–96
    assigning variable attributes with, 89
AUTOEXEC= system option, 11
AUTOEXEC file, 11
autosave preferences for DMS, 22

B

BASE= option
    about, 142
    creating data set automatically with, 182
    renaming, 143
    specifying
        in APPEND procedure, 142, 221
        larger data set as BASE= data set, 182
Base SAS, 74
batch mode
    batch use of ODS features, 195
    interactive mode vs., 7
best practices coding standards, 91–93
blank-delimited data, 44–45
body file
    in ODS MARKUP, 244
    specifying, 205–206
    streaming output with, 203
Boolean search operators, 234
Browse... button (SAS Explorer), 34
buffers
    clearing, 26
    input, 44
    sharing input and output, 57
    specifying number of, 70–71
BY groups
    dividing data in, 127
    executing WHERE expressions with, 68
    printing number of observations in, 188–189

C

CARDS statement, 5, 44
carriage-control characters, 54
Cartesian Product join, 148–149
case insensitivity of SQL statements, 75
catalog
    reading source files for, 73
    viewing contents of, 37–38
character functions, 107, 108–110

character string functions
    reversing character-string value, 107
    searching character variable in, 106–107
character variables
    assigning length to, 224
    changing length of existing, 89–90
    searching character string for, 106–107
    sort order for, 175–176
CLASS statement, 219
CLEAR command, 27
CLEAR LOG command, 27
CLEAR OUTPUT command, 27
CLEAR PGM command, 26
CLEAR RECALL command, 26
CLEAR TAB command, 27
clearing
    buffer, 26
    contents of window, 27
    Log window, 27
    Output window, 27
    Program Editor window, 26
    tab settings, 27
colon (:) modifier, 104–105
column headings
    breaking, 187–188
    orienting, 186–187
    printing
        blank column header, 190
        labels as, 187
column pointers
    formatted-style input for, 52
    types of, 52
columns. *See also* column headings; variables
    breaking column headings, 187–188
    datatypes for SQL procedures, 75
    defined, 74
    maintaining width of, 189
    multiple column reports
        two-column output, 192–193
        three-column output, 193
        four-column output, 193–194
    ordering of and column wildcard, 75
    reshaping, 139–153
        BASE= option in APPEND procedure, 142
        Cartesian Product join, 148–149

combining data with SQL join, 148
combining three or more tables, 150
concatenating data sets, 141–142, 183
creating BASE= data set in APPEND procedure, 142
creating unique variable subsets for individual data sets, 140–141
defined, 139
FIRST. and LAST. variables, 145
FORCE option for, 142
importance of joining, 148
interleaving data sets, 144–145
match merging, 146–147
missing values in APPEND procedure, 142
one-to-one merging, 145–146
outer joins, 151–153
renaming BASE= data set, 142–143
SAS and SQL terminology equivalents, 148
SET statements for, 143–144
subsetting variables, 139–140
table aliases and joining, 149–150
resizing detail, 37
sorting
    by multiple, 78
    columns not specified in select list, 79
summarizing data across, 80
using aliases for, 77
comma-delimited input files
    quoted values in, 46
    reading, 45
        input containing missing values, 45–46
        with modified-list-input, 48–49
command line, replacing with PMENU Facility, 27
commands
    for accessing DMS windows, 28, 29–30
    Editor line, 28, 33
    Output Manager, 21–22
    SAS Explorer keyboard, 40–41
    setting number of saved, 25
    using, 28, 30–31
    X, 18
COMMENT statement, 130
comparison operators, 102, 135

COMPRESS=YES|NO option, 16
compressing data sets
    performance and, 219
    as storage advantage, 15–16, 223
    tracking and reusing free space, 16
    uncompressing observations, 16
concatenating
    data sets
        in APPEND procedure, 141–142, 183
        CPU performance and, 218
        in DATA step, 141
    multiple input files, 55–56
Configuration file
    customizing, 230–231
    locating, 230
    specifying options in, 10
contents file
    as ODS HTML file type, 203
    in ODS MARKUP, 244
    specifying, 205–206
CONTENTS procedure
    printing
        alphabetical list of variables, 174
        list of library data sets, 171–172
        short list, 173
        suppressing for individual files in libraries, 172–173
    sending output to data sets with, 155–156
    syntax of, 170–171
control flow, 7–8
controls
    column pointer, 52
    line-hold, 53
    line-pointer, 53
COPY procedure, 169
copying data, 165–170
    data files, 165
    data sets, 168–170
    file copying, 35, 169
    text files, 166–168
    verifying FIRSTOBS= and OBS= options are assigned, 166
counters, 90
counting lines left on page, 191–192
CPU performance, 216–220
    avoiding unnecessary sorting, 218–219
    baseline measurements for, 216–217
    concatenating data sets, 218
    controlling memory used for sorting, 219
    data set compression and performance, 219
    efficiencies of WHERE processing, 217
    indexing large data sets, 219
    nesting IF...THEN/ELSE statements, 217
    saving resources with IN operator, 217
    specifying CLASS statement in procedures, 219
    Stored Program Facility, 220
    subsetting IF and CPU costs, 217
    temporary arrays, 220
    turning off Macro facility, 17, 218
    using LIBNAME engines, 220
custom report writing, 190–194
    counting lines left on page, 191–192
    creating two reports with single DATA step, 192
    DATA_NULL_ convention for, 190
    multiple column output
        two-column output, 192–193
        three-column output, 193
        four-column, 193–194
    overview, 190
    printing headings at top of page, 190–191
    setting end-of-file, 191
    suppressing printing of default title, 191

D

DATA= option, 142
data access, 43–81
    external data, 43–63
        accessing EFI, 58
        accessing with DDE, 62–63
        assigning error condition to missing values, 54
        assigning missing values with MISSOVER option, 49–50
        coding INFILE statement with in-stream data, 44
        concatenating and reading multiple files, 55–56

data access *(continued)*
    conditionally executing files, 56–57
    formatted-style input, 50–51, 52–53
    holding input record, 53–54
    identifying, 44
    importing delimited files with EFI, 58–62
    input buffer, 44
    last record in file, 56
    logical record length, 57
    mixing input styles with named-input data, 48
    reading blank-delimited data with list input, 44–45
    reading carriage-control characters from input file, 54
    reading comma-delimited input files, 45–46, 48–49
    reading data with column-style of input, 50
    reading hierarchical files, 57–58
    reading multiple input files with EOF option, 56
    reading named-input data, 47–48
    reading next input record with FLOWOVER option, 54–55
    reading records padded with blanks, 57
    reading tab-delimited input, 46–47
    reading varying length records, 49, 90
    SAS file compatibility, 43–44
    sharing input and output buffers, 57
    specifying first records to read, 51
    specifying maximum number of records to read, 51
    specifying number of lines available to input pointer, 52
  overview, 43
  SAS data objects, 63–73
    accessing data from view, 71–73
    associating libref with library, 63
    creating end-of-file indicator, 69
    determining number of observations in input data set, 69
    dictionary views, 71–73
    executing WHERE expressions with BY groups, 68
    listing librefs defined in session, 63–64
    PDV, 66
    processing order for WHERE expression, 68
    reading catalog source files, 73
    reading data sets, 65–66, 70, 71, 181–182
    referencing data sets without listing libref, 63
    renaming variables, 68
    SAS engines available under Windows, 64
    SAS/ACCESS engine names, 64–65
    selecting variables for processing from data set, 67–68
    setting range for reading observations, 66
    specifying data set's level of access, 71
    specifying number of buffers, 70–71
    subsetting IF and WHERE statements, 66–67
    subsetting observations with WHERE statements, 67
    VTABLE view, 73
SQL procedure, 73–81
  ANSI SQL and PROC SQL extensions, 74
  available summary functions, 80–81
  bundled with Base-SAS product, 74
  calculating statistics with summary functions, 79
  column aliases, 77
  columns and datatypes, 75
  inserting blank lines between rows, 77
  ordering of columns and column wildcard, 75
  overview, 73
  parentheses and evaluation order in, 75–76
  placing wildcard characters, 77
  processing performance with wildcard searches, 76
  processing with RUN groups and error handling, 74
  programming in SQL, 73
  removing rows containing duplicate column values, 77–78
  SELECT clause ordering, 76
  sorting, 78–79

Index

specifying criteria to subset and display values, 75
statements and clauses, 75
storing information in data set, 74
summarizing data, 79–80
terminating, 74

data management tips. *See also* managing data
   accessing libraries, 176
   aging a data set, 181
   concatenating data sets, 183
   creating BASE= data set automatically, 182
   data set management, 182
   FORCE option, 182
   handling missing values, 182
   modifying
      data set's attributes, 179
      variable's label, 179–180
   reading
      data sets from two or more tapes, 178
      generation data set, 71, 181–182
   removing all files in library, 183–184
   renaming
      base data sets, 183
      variables, 178–179
   single-level data set names, 182
   specifying larger data set as BASE= data set, 182
   storing libraries on tape, 178
   types
      of libraries, 177
      of members, 177
   updating data set, 180–181

data manipulation, 133–164
   reshaping data columns, 139–153
      BASE= option and, 142
      Cartesian Product join, 148–149
      combining data with SQL join, 148
      combining three or more tables with SQL join, 150
      concatenating data sets, 141–142
      creating BASE= data set in APPEND procedure, 142
      creating unique variable subsets for individual data sets, 140–141
      defined, 139
      FIRST. and LAST. variables, 145
      FORCE option for, 142
      interleaving data sets, 144–145
      joins, 148
      match merging, 146–147
      missing values in APPEND procedure, 142
      with multiple SET statements, 144
      omitting BASE= or DATA= option with APPEND procedure, 142
      one-to-one merging, 145–146
      outer joins, 151–153
      renaming BASE= data set, 142–143
      SAS and SQL terminology equivalents, 148
      specifying BASE= option in APPEND procedure, 142
      subsetting variables, 139–140
      table aliases created when joining, 149–150
   sending output to data sets, 154–163
      CONTENTS procedure for, 155–156
      converting observations into variables, 162–163
      converting variables to observations, 163
      creating statistics with UNIVARIATE procedure, 160
      FREQ procedure for, 156–157
      IF...THEN/ELSE statement for, 154
      with MEANS procedure, 157–158
      ODS for, 161–162
      overview, 154
      subsetting IF statement for, 154
      SUMMARY procedure for, 158–159
      tracing output, 160–161, 196
      with UNIVARIATE procedure, 159–160, 162
      with WHEN conditions, 155
   subsetting, 133–139
      creating new data sets with, 133
      external input data with OBS= and FIRSTOBS= options, 138
      IF statement, 134
      observations, 134–139

data objects, 63–73
  accessing
    data from view, 71
    dictionary views, 72–73
  associating libref with library, 63
  creating end-of-file indicator, 69
  determining number of observations in input data set, 69
  dictionary views, 71–72
  executing WHERE expressions with BY groups, 68
  listing librefs defined in session, 63–64
  PDV, 66
  processing order for WHERE expression, 68
  reading catalog source files, 73
  reading data sets
    directly, 70
    into real memory, 70
    reading from multiple data sets, 65
    reading generation data set, 71, 181–182
    sequentially, 65
    starting/stopping at nth observation, 65–66
  referencing permanent data sets without specifying libref, 63
  renaming variables, 68
  SAS engines available under Windows, 64
  selecting variables for processing from data set, 67–68
  setting range for reading observations, 66
  specifying
    data set's level of access, 71
    number of buffers, 70–71
  subsetting
    IF and WHERE statements, 66–67
    observations with WHERE statements, 67
  VTABLE view, 73
data presentation, 185–212
  custom report writing with DATA step, 190–194
    coding END= option to set end-of-file, 191
    counting lines left on page, 191–192
    DATA_NULL_ convention for, 190
    multiple column output, 192–194
    overview, 190
    printing headings at top of page, 190–191
    suppressing printing of default SAS title, 191
    two reports in single DATA step, 192
  ODS, 194–201
    about, 194
    creating output data sets, 198
    creating standard "monospace" Listing file, 198
    deleting output from Results window, 197
    features for interactive and batch use, 195
    format templates, 200–201
    formatting output with global statements, 194–195
    integrating into DATA step, 200
    opening and closing destinations, 195
    in PostScript, 199
    in RTF, 198–199, 200
    selecting desired output objects, 197
    tracing output, 160–161, 196
  output to Web, 201–212
    about HTML, 201–202
    changing output labels, 206
    checking deployment checklist, 211–212
    combining output results, 206–207
    creating PDF output, 207–208
    deploying with ODS, 203
    displaying PRINT procedure output in HTML, 205
    drill-down user interface and applications, 208–211
    ignoring pagesize and linesize settings, 204
    links and references in ODS, 202
    locating HTML files in Windows, 204–205
    ODS HTML file types, 202–203
    overview, 201
    specifying BODY=, CONTENTS=, PAGE=, and FRAME= files, 205–206

streaming output with BODY= file, 203
testing, 211
viewing frame file, 204
report writing and PROC print, 185–190
  column headings, 186–188
  conserving CPU time with FULL
      option, 189
  printing blank column header, 190
  printing number of observations,
      188–189
  printing output consistently, 189
  suppressing observation number in
      output, 185–186
  writing blank line between
      observations, 186
data sets. *See also* subsetting
  aging, 181
  avoiding deleting all observations in, 136
  BASE=, 142
  compressing
    for performance, 219
    for storage advantage, 15–16, 223
    tracking and reusing free space, 16
  concatenating
    in APPEND procedure, 141–142, 183
    CPU performance and, 218
    in DATA step, 141, 183
  copying
    in DATA step, 168
    with DATASETS procedure, 169–170
    selecting to copy, 168–169
  deleting WORK, 222
  determining number of observations in, 69
  indexing large, 219
  interleaving, 144–145
  KEEP= or DROP= data set options, 221–222
  managing, 182
  memory techniques for large, 222
  modifying attributes of, 179
  names of single-level, 182
  naming, 3, 5, 182, 223
  output, 198
  preventing accidental replacement of, 15
  printing list of library, 171–172
  processing observations in middle of, 15

reading
  directly, 70
  generation, 71, 181–182
  into real memory, 70
  most recently created, 14–15
  from multiple, 65
  sequentially, 65
  from two or more tapes, 178
referencing without specifying libref, 63
renaming base, 142–143, 183
reversing order without sorting, 127
saving
  labels and formats in, 131–132, 223–224
  sorted observations to, 175
selecting variables for processing from,
    67–68
sending output to, 154–163
  with CONTENTS procedure, 155–156
  converting observations into variables,
      162–163
  converting variables to observations,
      163
  for FIRST. and LAST. variables, 145
  with FREQ procedure, 156–157
  with IF...THEN/ELSE statement, 154
  with MEANS procedure, 157–158
  ODS for, 161–162
  overview, 154
  with subsetting IF statement, 154
  with SUMMARY procedure, 158–159
  tracing output, 160–161, 196
  with UNIVARIATE procedure, 159–160,
      162
  with WHEN conditions, 155
sorting unindexed, 36
specifying
  larger data set as BASE= data set, 182
  level of access, 71
  observations for starting/stopping
      reading, 65–66
storing
  data as, 220
  informats, formats, and labels, 224
  separate pieces of SQL information in,
      74

data sets *(continued)*
  structure of, 3
  uncompressing observations for, 16
  updating, 180–181
  variable subsets as unique, 140–141
  view of imported data as, 62
DATA statement
  about, 3
  beginning DATA step programming with, 84
  writing observations with, 6
DATA step programming, 83–132
  aborting DATA step, 86–87
  about, 83–84
  assigning variable's attributes and length, 88–89
  best practices coding standards, 91–93
  branching at end-of-file, 87
  changing length of existing character variable, 89–90
  checking syntax in, 15
  concatenating data sets in, 141, 183
  copying
    data sets, 168
    text files in, 166
  counting with counters, 90
  custom report writing, 190–194
    coding END= option to set end-of-file, 191
    counting lines left on page, 191–192
    DATA_NULL_ convention for, 190
    four-column output, 193–194
    overview, 190
    printing headings at top of page, 190–191
    suppressing printing of default SAS title, 191
    three-column output, 193
    two reports created in single DATA step programming, 192
    two-column output, 192–193
  DATA statement, 84
  date and time processing, 93–100
    applying date and time formats, 94
    applying date format, 95–96
    date format tables, 97–99
    date informat tables, 99–100
    defining one-hundred-year period, 96–97
    handling valid SAS dates, 93
    representing dates and time values with formats and informats, 94
    storing dates as numeric value, 93
    storing time as numeric value, 94
  DO UNTIL loop, 91
  DO WHILE loop, 91
  documentation, 130–132
    with comments, 130–131
    inserting in-stream comments, 131
    saving labels and formats in data sets, 131–132
  executing WHEN conditions in SELECT statement, 90
  functions, 106–118
    arithmetic, 107, 108
    array, 107, 108
    character, 107, 108–110
    date and time, 110, 111
    financial, 110, 112–113
    host operating system, 107
    random number, 110, 113–114
    reversing character-string value, 107
    searching character variable in character string, 106–107
    state and zip code, 110, 114–115
    in statement, 106
    statistical, 110, 115–116
    trigonometric and hyperbolic, 110, 117
    truncation, 117
    Web tool, 117, 118
  implying RETURN to top of observation loop, 86
  indexed DO loop, 91
  integrating ODS into, 200
  looping inside observation loops, 91
  observation loop, 85
  operators and modifiers, 101–106
    combining comparison and logical operators, 102
    grouping equality tests with IN operator, 103
    multiple percent sign wildcards in search pattern, 104
    negating specified condition with NOT operator, 102–103

operators and evaluation order, 101–102
reading input values with n* informat modifier, 105
SQL mathematical operators, 102
subsetting with percent sign wildcard and LIKE operator, 103
truncating and comparing strings with colon modifier, 104–105
underscore wildcard with LIKE operator, 104
writing values with n* informat modifier, 105–106
overview, 83
PDV and, 85
preventing missing values from being assigned to variables, 88
processing large files, 126–129
    avoiding sorting problems, 126
    creating subsets, 127
    creating summary statistics, 128–129
    dividing data in BY-groups, 127
    replacing subsetting IFs with WHEREs, 128
    reversing data set order without sorting, 127
program debugging, 122–126
    data-related errors, 125
    detecting errors in SAS Log, 122
    in Enhanced Editor, 123–125
    getting SAS interpreter to recognize statements, 125–126
    programming (logic) errors, 125
    syntax errors, 122–123
    system-related errors, 125
    usage errors, 122
    warnings, 123
program testing, 118–121
    determining if defects result in failures, 119
    exploring program defects, 119
    problems related to data, 119–120
    process in, 118
    programming errors and causes, 119
    test categories, 120, 121
    test objectives and test strategies, 120
    testing participants, 119
    types of, 120
    understanding purpose of, 119
    retaining values across observation loops, 88
    returning to top of observation loop, 87–88
    searching with PRXs, 241–243
    setting variables to missing values at top of observation loop, 85
    stopping observation loop, 86
    subsetting variables in, 139–140
    techniques, 83–93
    using Stored Program Facility for CPU performance, 220
data truncation
    avoiding when reading varying length records, 49, 90
    truncating strings with colon with colon modifier, 104–105
databases. *See also* libraries
    SAS and non-SAS terms for, 2–3
DATALINES statements, 44
DATA_NULL_
    custom report writing and, 190
    suppressing data set creation with, 222
data-related errors, 125
DATASETS procedure, 169–170
date and time, 93–100
    date and time formats, 94
    date formats
        about, 97
        applying, 95–96
        tables, 97–99
    date informat tables, 99–100
    defining one-hundred-year period, 96–97
    displaying at top of printed page, 12
    handling valid SAS dates, 93
    representing dates and time values with formats and informats, 94
    storing dates as numeric value, 93
    storing time as numeric value, 94
date and time functions, 110, 111
date formats
    about, 97
    applying, 95–96
    tables, 97–99

date informat tables, 99–100
DDE (Dynamic Data Exchange)
    accessing DDE triplet from Excel, 62–63
    accessing external data from other applications, 62
debugging. *See* program debugging
Delete Confirmation dialog box, 36
DELETE statement, 136
deleting
    files from library, 35–36
    ODS output, 197
    output from Results window, 197
deployment checklist for Web development, 211–212
describing data, 170–174
    CONTENTS procedure output for, 170–171
    printing
        alphabetical list of variables, 174
        list of library data sets, 171–172
        short list, 173
    suppressing printing of individual files in libraries, 172–173
destinations
    available ODS, 195
    opening and closing, 195
dictionary views, 71–72
    accessing, 72–73
    defined, 71
    types of, 71–72
DIRECTORY option of CONTENTS procedure, 171, 172
disabling
    Enhanced Editor, 123
    Macro language, 17
    PMENU Facility, 27
Display Manager. *See* SAS Display Manager System
DO loop, indexed, 91
DO UNTIL loop, 91
Document Type Definitions (DTDs), 246–247
documentation, 130–132
    with comments, 130–131
    documenting programs and program code, 224
    inserting in-stream comments, 131
    SAS library of technical support documents, 235–236
    saving labels and formats in data sets, 131–132
downloading SAS demos and examples, 239
drill-down applications, 208–211
    about, 208–209
    building, 209
    coding, 209–211
DROP= data set options, 221–222
DSD option of INFILE statement, 45
DTDs (Document Type Definitions), 246–247
duplicating files, 35
Dynamic Data Exchange. *See* DDE

E

Editor. *See* SAS Editor
efficiency and performance
    CPU techniques, 216–220
        avoiding unnecessary sorting, 218–219
        baseline measurements for performance, 216–217
        concatenating data sets, 218
        controlling memory used for sorting, 219
        data set compression and performance, 219
        efficiencies of WHERE processing, 217
        indexing large data sets, 219
        nesting IF...THEN/ELSE statements, 217
        saving resources with IN operator, 217
        specifying CLASS statement in procedures, 219
        Stored Program Facility, 220
        subsetting IF and CPU costs, 217
        temporary arrays, 220
        turning off Macro facility, 17, 218
        using LIBNAME engines, 220
    I/O techniques, 220–221
        consolidating steps in SQL, 221
        copying indexes, 220
        creating subsets earlier, 220
        reducing number of steps, 220
        sorting only what is needed, 221
        specifying BASE= option in APPEND procedure, 221
        storing data as data sets, 220
        subsetting observations, 220

memory techniques, 221–222
  delete WORK data sets, 222
  KEEP= or DROP= data set options, 221–222
  for large data sets, 222
  reading only data needed, 221
  WHERE processing and reduced memory requirements, 222
planning, 213–216
  advantages of, 213–214
  applying simple strategies one at a time, 216
  competing resources and, 214
  developing plan, 215–216
  efficiency defined, 214, 215
programming techniques, 223–226
  assigning descriptive variable and data set names, 223
  assigning length to character variables, 224
  avoiding FORCE option with indexes, 225
  coding for harmful data conditions, 225
  controlling messaging with system options, 225–226
  creating views, 224–225
  documenting programs and program code, 224
  RUN statements, 223
  saving labels and formats in data sets, 223–224
  specifying NOREPLACE system option, 225
  storing data set informats, formats, and labels, 224
storage techniques, 222–223
  assigning lengths to numeric values, 223
  compressing data sets, 223
  creating user-defined formats for coded data, 223
  suppressing data set creation with DATA_NULL_, 222
EFI (External File Interface)
  accessing, 58
  importing delimited files with, 58–62
  enabling Enhanced Editor, 123
END= option
  setting report end-of-file with, 191
  variables created with, 56
end-of-file indicator, 69
Enhanced Editor
  customizing General and Appearance options, 124
  enabling/disabling, 123
  identifying coding problems in, 123
  navigation keyboard shortcuts, 124–125
  opening
    General keyboard shortcuts, 124
    Options window, 124
EOF option, 56
erasing WORK library files, 11
error handling
  assigning error condition to missing input data values, 54
  controlling printing of error messages for data errors, 16
  generating error messages when format not found, 18
  for RUN groups, 74
errors
  data-related, 125
  detecting in SAS Log, 122
  programming, 119, 125
  syntax, 122–123
  system-related, 125
  usage, 122
evaluation order
  of operators, 101–102
  in parentheses, 75–76
exiting system, 9
eXtensible Markup Language. *See* XML
external data, 43–63
  accessing
    data from other applications with DDE, 62
    DDE triplet from Excel, 62–63
    EFI, 58
  assigning
    error condition to missing input data values, 54

external data *(continued)*
- missing values with MISSOVER option, 49–50
- avoiding truncation when reading varying length records, 49
- coding INFILE statement with in-stream data, 44
- column pointers with formatted-style input, 52
- concatenating and reading multiple input files, 55–56
- conditionally executing input files, 56–57
- holding input record, 53–54
- identifying, 44
  - last record in file, 56
- importing delimited files with EFI, 58–62
- input buffer, 44
- in-stream data vs., 5–6
- line pointers with formatted-style input, 52–53
- mixing other styles of input with named-input data, 48
- reading
  - blank-delimited data with list input, 44–45
  - carriage-control characters from input file, 54
  - comma-delimited data with modified-list-input, 48–49
  - comma-delimited input containing quoted values, 46
  - comma-delimited input files, 45
  - comma-delimited input files containing missing values, 45–46
  - data with column-style of input, 50
  - data with formatted-style of input, 50–51
  - hierarchical files, 57–58
  - multiple input files with EOF option, 56
  - named-input data, 47–48
  - next input record with FLOWOVER option, 54–55
  - records padded with blanks, 57
  - tab-delimited input, 46–47
- SAS file compatibility, 43–44
- sharing input and output buffers, 57
- specifying
  - first input records to read, 51
  - logical record length, 57
  - maximum number of input records to read, 51
  - number of lines available to input pointer, 52
- subsetting variables from, 139

External File Interface. *See* EFI

F

files. *See also* processing large files
- concatenating and reading multiple input, 55–56
- Configuration, 10, 230–231
- contents, 203, 205–206, 244
- copying
  - with COPY procedure, 169
  - and moving between libraries, 35
- creating
  - PDF, 207–208
  - PostScript, 199
  - RTF, 198–199, 200
  - standard "monospace" Listing, 198
  - subsets of large, 127
- deleting from library, 35–36
- displaying details and, 40
- duplicating, 35
- end-of-file indicator, 69
- identifying last record in, 56
- large icons displayed for, 38
- locating HTML, 204–205
- ODS HTML, 202–203
- processing large, 126–129
- reading hierarchical, 57–58
- refreshing order of sorted, 36
- removing all in library, 183–184
- renaming, 35
- SAS file compatibility, 43–44
- showing in list, 39
- small icons displayed for, 39
- sorting, 36
- specifying BODY=, CONTENTS=, PAGE=, and FRAME=, 205–206
- storage format for system, 6

suppressing printing of individual library, 172–173
viewing properties of, 34–35
financial functions, 110, 112–113
Find dialog box, 22–23
FIRST. variable, 145
FIRSTOBS= option
    assigning when copying data, 166
    reassigning to first observation, 14
    subsetting
        external input data with OBS= and, 138
        observations with, 137–138
    using, 14
flower-box comment, 130–131
FLOWOVER option, 54–55
FORCE option
    avoiding with indexes, 225
    missing values and, 182
    reshaping data columns with, 142
FORMAT function, 95
FORMAT statement, 94
formatting
    format templates, 200–201
    output with global ODS statements, 194–195
    storing formats, 224
frame file
    as ODS HTML file type, 203
    in ODS MARKUP, 244
    specifying, 205–206
    viewing, 204
"free format" style for statements, 3–4
FREQ procedure, 156–157
FULL option, 189
FULLSTIMER system option, 14
Function Keys
    browsing, modifying, and saving settings for DMS, 23–24
    shortcuts for, 27–28
    window, 25
functions, 106–118
    arithmetic, 107, 108
    array, 107, 108
    character, 107, 108–110
    date and time, 110, 111
    financial, 110, 112–113
    host operating system, 107

PRX, 243
random number, 110, 113–114
reversing character-string value, 107
searching character variable in character string, 106–107
state and zip code, 110, 114–115
in statement, 106
statistical, 110, 115–116
summary, 79, 80–81
trigonometric and hyperbolic, 110, 117
truncation, 117
Web tool, 117, 118

G

General options for Enhanced Editor, 124
General Properties window, 34
GENNUM= data set, 71, 181–182
getting started, 1–9
    avoiding reserved names for data set and variable names, 5
    coding statements in "free format" style, 3–4
    comparison of SAS and non-SAS terms, 2–3
    control flow of standard and macro programs, 7–8
    data set structure, 3
    exiting system, 9
    getting system help, 9
    in-stream vs. external input data, 5–6
    interactive vs. batch mode, 7
    naming data sets and variables, 3
    observations, 5
    overview of SAS System software, 1–2
    proprietary storage format, 6
    role of SAS Supervisor, 4
    statement syntax, 3
    step boundaries, 8–9
    turning off SAS Display Manager System, 7
    variables, 4
    writing observations
        with DATA statement, 6
        with OUTPUT statement, 6
        with RETURN statement, 6
        with SQL procedures, 6

H

help
    for Display Manager System, 23
    getting system, 9
host operating system functions, 107
hot fixes, 236–237
HTML (HyperText Markup Language)
    about, 201–202
    creating output with ODS MARKUP in, 245, 246
    displaying PRINT procedure output in, 205
    ignoring ODS pagesize and linesize settings, 204
    links and references in ODS, 202
    locating files in Windows, 204–205
    ODS HTML file types, 202–203

I

I/O performance techniques, 220–221
    consolidating steps in SQL, 221
    copying indexes, 220
    creating subsets earlier, 220
    measuring elapsed time for I/O, 216–217
    reducing number of steps, 220
    sorting only what is needed, 221
    specifying BASE= option in APPEND procedure, 221
    storing data as data sets, 220
    subsetting observations, 220
icons
    displaying large icons for files, 38
    displaying small icons for files, 39
IF...THEN/ELSE statement
    nesting, 217
    sending output to data sets, 154
    subsetting with, 136–137
IF statement
    replacing subsetting IFs with WHEREs, 128
    replacing with WHEREs to process large files, 128
    subsetting, 66–67, 134
        CPU costs and, 217
        output to data sets, 154
IN operator, 103, 217

indexes
    avoiding FORCE option with, 225
    copying for improved I/O performance, 220
    for large data sets, 219
INFILE statement, 44, 45
informats
    date informat tables, 99–100
    n* informat modifier, 105–106
    representing dates and time values with, 94
    storing, 224
input. *See also* external data
    holding records in buffer, 53
    line pointers with formatted-style, 52–53
    mixing with named-input data, 48
input buffers, 44, 57
input files
    assigning error condition to missing data values, 54
    comma-delimited, 45–46, 48–49
    concatenating and reading multiple, 55–56
    conditionally executing, 56–57
    entering delimited, 60
    holding input record, 53–54
    identifying last record in file, 56
    reading
        carriage-control characters from, 54
        multiple files with EOF option, 56
        next record with FLOWOVER option, 54–55
    tab-delimited, 46–47
input pointer
    number of lines available to, 52
    specifying number of lines available to, 52
installing and configuring SAS System, 227–232
    changing library locations, 229–230
    customizing Configuration file, 230–231
    Internet Explorer 5 in Release 8.2, 228
    invoking SAS System, 230
    launching SAS System installation, 229
    locating Configuration file, 230
    Release 8.2 system requirements, 227–228

System options available under Windows, 231–232
types of installation configurations, 230
in-stream data
coding INFILE statement with, 44
external input data vs., 5–6
in-stream comments, 131
marking end of data containing semicolons, 5
interactive mode
batch mode vs., 7
ODS features and, 195
interleaving data sets, 144–145
Internet Explorer 5, 228
invoking SAS Explorer, 34

J

joins, 148–153. *See also* merging
combining
data with SQL, 148
three or more tables with SQL, 150
creating
Cartesian Product, 148–149
table aliases, 149–150
importance of, 148
outer, 151
combining data with left, 151–152
combining data with right, 153
specifying left or right, 151

K

KEEP= data set options, 221–222
keyboard shortcuts
for Enhanced Editor navigation, 124–125
Function Key shortcuts for DMS, 27–28
opening Enhanced Editor General, 124
for SAS Explorer, 40
keywords
beginning statements with, 3
FREQ statistical, 157
MEANS statistical, 158
specifying in OUTPUT OUT= statement, 157
UNIVARIATE statistical, 160
KILL option, 183–184

L

labels
adding to procedures, 12
changing Web output, 206
modifying variable's, 179–180
printing as column headings, 187
saving in data sets, 131–132, 223–224
storing, 224
LAST. variable, 145
LENGTH statement, 88–89
LIBNAME engines, 220
libraries. *See also* librefs
accessing, 176
associating libref with, 63
changing locations of, 229–230
copying and moving files between, 35
deleting files from, 35–36
member types in, 177
printing list of data sets in, 171–172
removing all files in, 183–184
storing
on disk, 177
on tape, 178
suppressing printing of individual files in, 172–173
types of, 177
library reference, 34
librefs
associating with library, 63
listing session, 63–64
referencing permanent data sets without specifying, 63
LIKE operator, 103
line commands for SAS Editor, 28, 33
line pointers
formatted-style input for, 52–53
types of, 53
line-hold controls, 53
Listing destination, 195
Listing file, 198
log. *See* SAS Log
Log window, 19
logical operators, 102, 135

Index

loops. *See also* observation loops
    defined, 85
    DO UNTIL, 91
    DO WHILE, 91
    indexed DO loop, 91
    looping inside observation, 91
LRECL= option, 57

M

Macro facility. *See* SAS Macro facility
maintenance bug fix documentation, 236
managing data, 165–184
    copying, 165–170
        copying part of record in text file, 166
        data files, 165
        data sets, 168, 169–170
        file copying with COPY procedure, 169
        making multiple copies of text files, 168
        selecting data sets to copy, 168–169
        specifying LENGTH= and START=
            options when copying text files, 167
        text files, 166, 167
        verifying FIRSTOBS= and OBS= options are assigned, 166
    data management tips, 176–184
        accessing libraries, 176
        aging a data set, 181
        concatenating data sets, 183
        creating BASE= data set automatically, 182
        data set management with APPEND procedure, 182
        FORCE option, 182
        handling missing values in APPEND procedure, 182
        modifying data set's attributes, 179
        modifying variable's label, 179–180
        reading data sets from two or more tapes, 178
        reading generation data set, 71, 181–182
        removing all files in library, 183–184
        renaming base data sets, 183
        renaming variables, 178–179
        single-level data set names, 182
        specifying larger data set as BASE= data set, 182
        storing libraries, 177, 178
        types of libraries, 177
        types of members, 177
        updating data set with UPDATE statement, 180–181
    describing data, 170–174
        CONTENTS procedure output, 170–171
        printing list of library data sets, 171–172
        printing list of variables, 174
        printing short list, 173
        suppressing printing of individual files in libraries, 172–173
    sorting data, 175–176
match merging, 146–147
mathematical operators, 102
MEANS procedure, 157–158
memory performance techniques, 221–222
    controlling amount used for sorting, 219
    delete WORK data sets, 222
    KEEP= or DROP= data set options, 221–222
    for large data sets, 222
    reading only data needed, 221
    WHERE processing and reduced memory requirements, 222
merging
    match, 146–147
    one-to-one, 145–146
messaging in SAS, 225–226
metacharacters, 241–242
Microsoft Internet Explorer 5, 228
Microsoft Windows
    applying SETINIT, 237
    System options available under, 231–232
MISSING='character' option, 12
missing values
    in APPEND procedure, 142
    assigning error condition to, 54
    comma-delimited input files containing, 45–46
    handling in APPEND procedure, 182
    preventing assignment to variables, 88
    setting to variables at top of observation loop, 85
MISSOVER option, 49–50

modifiers
   reading input values with n* informat, 105
   truncating and comparing strings with colon, 104–105
   writing values with n* informat, 105–106
MODIFY statement, 179–180
moving files between libraries, 35

N

named-input data
   mixing other styles of input with, 48
   reading, 47–48
naming
   avoiding reserved names for data sets and variables, 5
   data sets, 3, 5, 182, 223
   variables, 3
navigating
   Browse... button for assistance, 34
   between DMS windows, 22
   Enhanced Editor keyboard shortcuts for, 124–125
nesting IF...THEN/ELSE statements, 217
NODS option in CONTENTS procedure, 173
NOFULLSTIMER system option, 14
NOREPLACE system option, 225
NOSTIMER system option, 14
NOT operators, 102–103
numeric value lengths, 223
numeric variable sort order, 175

O

OBS= option
   assigning when copying data, 166
   subsetting external input data with FIRSTOBS= and, 138
   subsetting observations with, 137–138
OBS=0 option, checking syntax in DATA or PROC step, 15
OBS=MAX system option
   processing maximum number of observations with, 15
   specifying with WHERE option, 15
observation loops. *See also* loops
   implying RETURN to top of, 86
   about, 85
   retaining values across, 88
   returning to top of, 87–88
   setting variables to missing values at top of, 85
   stopping, 86
observations
   converting
      into variables, 162–163
      variables to, 163–164
   creating, 5
   DATA statement for writing, 6
   determining number of in data set, 69
   identifying number of in data set, 73
   OUTPUT statement for writing, 6
   printing number of
      in BY group, 188–189
      at report end, 188
   processing
      maximum number with OBS=MAX, 15
      in middle of data set, 15
   reading data sets starting/stopping at nth observation, 65–66
   reassigning FIRSTOBS= option to first, 14
   RETURN statement for writing, 6
   returning to original data set after sorting, 175
   setting range for reading, 66
   sorting unindexed, 36
   specifying read order in data set, 14–15
   SQL procedures for writing, 6
   subsetting
      with DELETE statement, 136
      for I/O performance, 220
      with IF...THEN/ELSE and OUTPUT statements, 136–137
      with OBS= and FIRSTOBS= data set options, 137–138
      with operators, 134–136
      with SELECT blocks and OUTPUT, 138–139
      with WHERE= data set option, 134
      with WHERE statements, 67
   suppressing number in PROC PRINT output, 185–186
   uncompressing for data sets, 16
   writing blank line between, 186

Index

ODS (Output Delivery System), 194–201
  about, 194
  creating
    output data sets, 198
    PostScript output, 199
    RTF output, 198–199, 200
    standard "monospace" Listing file, 198
  deleting output from Results window, 197
  features of Version 9, 243–247
    combining MARKUP output, 247
    creating HTML and XML output with MARKUP, 245–246
    creating XML output and DTDs, 247
    DTDs, 246–247
    obtaining list of tagset names, 244–245
    ODS MARKUP, 243–244
    "page xx of by" page numbering, 247
  format templates, 200–201
  formatting output with global statements, 194–195
  integrating into DATA step, 200
  interactive and batch use features, 195
  opening and closing destinations, 195
  output to Web, 201–212
    about HTML, 201–202
    changing output labels, 206
    checking deployment checklist, 211–212
    combining output results, 206–207
    creating PDF output, 207–208
    deploying, 203
    displaying PRINT procedure output in HTML, 205
    drill-down user interface and applications, 208–211
    ignoring pagesize and linesize settings, 204
    links and references in ODS, 202
    locating HTML files in Windows, 204–205
    ODS HTML file types, 202–203
    overview, 201
    specifying BODY=, CONTENTS=, PAGE=, and FRAME= files, 205–206
    streaming output with BODY= file, 203
    testing, 211
    viewing frame file, 204
  selecting desired output objects, 197
  sending output to data sets, 161–162
  tracing output, 160–161, 196
ODS MARKUP, 243–244
  about, 243
  combining output, 247
  creating HTML and XML output with, 245–246
  file types in, 244
  obtaining list of tagset names, 244–245
one-to-one merging, 145–146
opening and closing ODS destinations, 195
operators
  combining comparison and logical, 102
  comparison and logical, 135
  evaluation order of, 101–102
  grouping equality tests with IN, 103
  multiple percent sign wildcards in search pattern, 104
  negating specified condition with NOT, 102–103
  SQL mathematical, 102
  subsetting with percent sign wildcard and LIKE, 103
  underscore wildcard with LIKE, 104
options, 9–18. *See also specific options by name*
  adding labels to procedures, 12
  arguments for SORTPGM=, 18
  AUTOEXEC= system, 11
  centering procedure output, 12
  changing settings for, 10
  checking syntax in DATA or PROC step, 15
  compressing data set size, 15–16
  controlling
    error-message printing for data errors, 16
    session performance, 10
    system initialization with, 10–11
  designating printer line width and number of lines, 12
  determining settings at SAS invocation, 10
  disabling Macro, 17
  displaying settings for, 10
  entering values for YEARCUTOFF= system, 11–12

erasing WORK library files at invocation and end of session, 11
executing statements after AUTOEXEC file, 11
generating error message when format not found, 18
MISSING='character,' 12
overview, 9–10
preventing accidental replacement of data sets, 15
printing
    displaying date and time at top of page, 12
    multiple output pages on same page, 17
    output in color, 17
    page number at top of printed page, 13
    specifying number of copies, 17
problem detection and resolution with SOURCE2 system, 14
processing
    maximum number of observations with OBS=MAX, 15
    observations in middle of data set, 15
reassigning FIRSTOBS= option to first observation, 14
resetting page numbers, 13
running program in batch or non-interactive mode, 11
selecting most recently created data set for read operation, 14–15
sorting data, 18
SOURCE system option for problem detection and resolution, 13
specifying
    last observation to process, 15
    OBS=MAX with WHERE, 15
    observation to begin reading in data set, 14
    options in Configuration file, 10
system
    available under Windows, 231–232
    listing of SAS software, 251–262
terminating program with abend, 16–17
tracking and reusing free space in compressed data set, 16
uncompressing data set's observations, 16
value for invalid numeric data, 13
Version 9 macro, 248
viewing and changing DMS, 23
writing
    performance statistics and subsets to SAS Log, 14
    source files included with statement to SAS Log, 13
    source statements to SAS Log, 13
    X command for opening application in minimized window, 18
OUT= data set, specifying with SORT procedure, 127
output. *See also* ODS
    formatting with global ODS statements, 194–195
    sending to data sets, 154–163
        CONTENTS procedure for, 155–156
        converting observations into variables, 162–163
        converting variables to observations, 163
        for FIRST. and LAST. variables, 145
        FREQ procedure for, 156–157
        IF...THEN/ELSE statement for, 154
        MEANS procedure for, 157–158
        ODS for, 161–162
        overview, 154
        subsetting IF statement, 154
        SUMMARY procedure for, 158–159
        tracing output, 160–161, 196
        UNIVARIATE procedure for, 159–160, 162
        WHEN conditions for, 155
    Web, 201–212
        about HTML, 201–202
        changing output labels, 206
        checking deployment checklist, 211–212
        combining output results, 206–207
        creating PDF output, 207–208
        deploying with ODS, 203
        displaying PRINT procedure output in HTML, 205
        drill-down user interface and applications, 208–211

Web *(continued)*
  ignoring pagesize and linesize settings, 204
  links and references in ODS, 202
  locating HTML files in Windows, 204–205
  ODS HTML file types, 202–203
  overview, 201
  specifying BODY=, CONTENTS=, PAGE=, and FRAME= files, 205–206
  streaming output with BODY= file, 203
  testing, 211
  viewing frame file, 204
output buffers, 57
Output Delivery System. *See* ODS
Output Manager, 21–22
output objects
  deleting from Results window, 197
  selecting desired, 197
  tracing, 160–161, 196
OUTPUT statement
  subsetting observations with SELECT blocks and, 138–139
  subsetting with, 136–137
  writing observations with, 6
Output window, 20

P

page file
  as ODS HTML file type, 202–203
  in ODS MARKUP, 244
  specifying, 205–206
page numbers
  "page *xx* of *by*", 247
  resetting, 13
parentheses and order of evaluation in SQL procedures, 75–76
PDF files, 207–208
PDV (Program Data Vector)
  DATA steps and, 85
  defined, 66
percent sign (%) wildcard
  multiple wildcards in search pattern, 104
  subsetting with LIKE operator and, 103
performance. *See* efficiency and performance
Perl Regular Expressions. *See* PRXs

planning for performance, 213–214
  applying simple strategies one at a time, 216
  competing resources and, 214
  developing plan, 215–216
  efficiency defined, 214, 215
PMENU Facility, 27
PostScript output, 199
PRINT procedure, 205
printing
  alphabetical list of variables, 174
  controlling error-message printing for data errors, 16
  designating printer line width and number of lines, 12
  displaying
    date and time at top of page, 12
    page number at top of page, 13
  list of library data sets, 171–172
  multiple output pages on same page, 17
  number of observations
    in BY group, 188–189
    at report end, 188
  output
    in color, 17
    consistently, 189
  report headings at top of page, 190–191
  report labels as column headings, 187
  short list of variables, 173
  specifying number of copies printed, 17
  suppressing
    default SAS title, 191
    for individual library files, 172–173
problem detection and resolution, 13
PROC print
  breaking column headings, 187–188
  conserving CPU time with FULL option, 189
  orienting column headings, 186–187
  printing
    blank column header, 190
    labels as column headings, 187
    number of observations at report end, 188
    number of observations in BY group, 188–189
    output consistently, 189

suppressing observation number in PROC PRINT output, 185–186
writing blank line between observations, 186
PROC SQL
  about, 74
  as interactive procedure, 74
PROC statement, 3
PROC step
  checking syntax in, 15
  subsetting variables in, 140
PROC TRANSPOSE procedure, 162–163
processing large files, 126–129
  avoiding sorting problems, 126
  creating subsets, 127
  creating summary statistics, 128–129
  dividing data in BY-groups, 127
  replacing subsetting IFs with WHEREs, 128
  reversing data set order without sorting, 127
Program Data Vector (PDV), 66, 85
program debugging, 122–126
  DATA step programming, 123–125
  data-related errors, 125
  detecting errors in SAS Log, 122
  in Enhanced Editor
    customizing General and Appearance options, 124
    enabling/disabling, 123
    identifying coding problems, 123
    navigation keyboard shortcuts, 124–125
    opening General keyboard shortcuts, 124
    opening Options window, 124
  getting SAS interpreter to recognize statements, 125–126
  programming (logic) errors, 125
  syntax errors, 122–123
  system-related errors, 125
  usage errors, 122
  warnings, 123
Program Editor window, 19
program testing, 118–121
  determining if defects result in failures, 119
  exploring program defects, 119
  problems related to data, 119–120
  process in, 118
  programming errors and causes, 119
  test categories, 120, 121
  test objectives and test strategies, 120
  testing
    participants, 119
    Web output, 211
  types of, 120
  understanding purpose of, 119
programming
  identifying coding problems in Enhanced Editor, 123
  for performance, 223–226
    assigning descriptive variable and data set names, 223
    assigning length to character variables, 224
    avoiding FORCE option with indexes, 225
    coding for harmful data conditions, 225
    controlling messaging with system options, 225–226
    creating views, 224–225
    documenting programs and program code, 224
    RUN statements, 223
    saving labels and formats in data sets, 131–132, 223–224
    specifying NOREPLACE system option, 225
    storing data set informats, formats, and labels, 224
  programming (logic) errors, 125
  in SQL, 73
  terminating programs with abend, 16–17
proprietary storage format, 6
PRXs (Perl Regular Expressions), 241–243
  about, 241–242
  finding, parsing, and retrieving data, 242–243
  functions of, 243
  searching and replacing text, 243
  simple matches with, 242
PUT function, 95
PUT statement, 94

R

random number functions, 110, 113–114
reading
    catalog source files, 73
    data sets
        directly, 70
        into real memory, 70
        multiple data sets, 65
        sequentially, 65
        setting range for reading observations, 66
        starting/stopping at nth observation, 65–66
        from two or more tapes, 178
    external data
        avoiding truncation with varying length records, 49
        blank-delimited data with list input, 44–45
        carriage-control characters from input file, 54
        column-style input, 50
        comma-delimited data with modified-list-input, 48–49
        comma-delimited input containing quoted values, 46
        comma-delimited input files, 45
        comma-delimited input files containing missing values, 45–46
        concatenating and reading multiple input files, 55–56
        first input records to read, 51
        formatted-style input, 50–51
        hierarchical files, 57–58
        maximum number of input records to read, 51
        multiple input files with EOF option, 56
        named-input data, 47–48
        next input record with FLOWOVER option, 54–55
        records padded with blanks, 57
        tab-delimited input, 46–47
    generation data set, 71, 181–182
    input values with n* informat modifier, 105
    only data needed, 221
records
    copying
        data text files from designated position, 167
        part of, 166
    holding in buffer, 53
    logical record length, 57
    padded with blanks, 57
    reading varying length, 49, 90
    specifying
        first input records to read, 51
        logical length, 57
        maximum number to read, 51
refreshing order of sorted files, 36
regular expressions. *See* PRXs
Release 8.2 system requirements, 227–228
removing Internet Explorer 5 in Release 8.2, 228
Rename dialog box, 35
renaming
    base data sets, 142–143, 183
    files, 35
    variables, 68, 178–179
report writing, 185–190
    breaking column headings, 187–188
    conserving CPU time with FULL option, 189
    customizing with DATA step, 190–194
    orienting column headings, 186–187
    printing
        blank column header, 190
        labels as column headings, 187
        number of observations at report end, 188
        number of observations in BY group, 188–189
        output consistently, 189
    suppressing observation number in PROC PRINT output, 185–186
    writing blank line between observations, 186
reshaping data columns, 139–153
    concatenating data sets
        in APPEND procedure, 141–142, 183
        in DATA step, 141

creating
  BASE= data set in APPEND procedure, 142
  unique variable subsets for individual data sets, 140–141
defined, 139
FIRST. and LAST. variables, 145
FORCE option for, 142
how BASE= option works, 142
interleaving data sets, 144–145
joins
  combining data with SQL, 148
  combining three or more tables with, 150
  creating Cartesian Product, 148–149
  creating table aliases, 149–150
  importance of, 148
merging
  match, 146–147
  one-to-one, 145–146
missing values in APPEND procedure, 142
omitting BASE= or DATA= option with APPEND procedure, 142
outer joins, 151–153
renaming BASE= data set, 142–143
SAS and SQL terminology equivalents, 148
SET statements for, 144
specifying BASE= option in APPEND procedure, 142
subsetting variables
  in DATA step, 139–140
  from external data, 139
  in PROC step, 140
resizing detail columns, 37
resource competition, 214
Results window, 20, 21, 197
RETAIN statement, 90
RETURN statement, 6, 86, 87
rows. *See also* observations
  inserting blank lines between output, 77
  removing duplicate column values, 77–78
  specifying criteria to subset and display values, 75
  summarizing data down, 79–80
RTF output, 198–199, 200
RUN groups, 74
RUN statements, 223

S

SAS Display Manager System, 18–33
  adjusting Editor settings, 25–26
  browsing, modifying, and saving function key settings, 23–24
  checking program text for spelling errors, 26
  clearing
    buffer with CLEAR RECALL command, 26
    contents of window with CLEAR command, 27
    Log window with CLEAR LOG command, 27
    Output window with CLEAR OUTPUT command, 27
    Program Editor window with CLEAR PGM command, 26
    tab settings with CLEAR TAB command, 27
  commands
    for accessing windows in, 28, 29–30
    line commands for SAS Editor, 28, 33
    for Output Manager, 21–22
    setting number saved, 25
    using, 28, 30–31
  customizing toolbar button settings, 24
  disabling PMENU Facility, 27
  exploring toolbar buttons, 24
  Function Key shortcuts, 27–28
  help for, 23
  replacing command line with PMENU Facility, 27
  SAS Editor commands, 28, 31–33
  saving work, 22
  searching with Find dialog box, 22–23
  setting autosave preferences for, 22
  turning on/off, 7
    Enhanced Editor, 22
  viewing and changing options for, 23
  windows
    clearing, 26, 27
    commands for accessing, 28, 29–30
    Function Keys, 25
    invoking, 23
    Log, 19
    navigating between, 22

285

SAS Display Manager System *(continued)*
 Output, 20
 Output Manager, 20–21
 Program Editor, 19
 Results, 20
 SAS System Options, 24
SAS Editor
 adjusting settings for, 25–26
 commands for, 28, 31–33
 line commands for, 28, 33
 turning on Enhanced Editor, 22
SAS engines
 available under Windows, 64
 SAS/ACCESS engine names, 64–65
SAS Explorer, 34–41
 copying files from one library to another, 35
 creating new library reference, 34
 deleting files from library, 35–36
 displaying files
  all details, 40
  as large icons, 38
  in list, 39
  as small icons, 39
 duplicating files, 35
 illustrated, 36
 invoking, 34
 keyboard commands, 40–41
 keyboard shortcuts for, 40
 moving files from one library to another, 35
 overview, 34
 refreshing file order of sorted files, 36
 renaming files, 35
 resizing detail columns, 37
 sorting files, 36
 toggling Show Tree on/off, 37
 viewing
  contents of catalog, 37–38
  file properties, 34–35
SAS Import/Export Wizard
 Destination window, 61
 entering delimited input file in Select File window, 60
 entering filename to create PROC IMPORT statements, 61
 illustrated, 59
 selecting delimited file from, 59
SAS Learning Edition, 248–249
SAS Log
 detecting errors in, 122
 displaying date and time at top of page, 12
 writing
  all performance statistics to, 14
  source files included with statement to, 13
  source statements to, 13
  subset of performance statistics to, 14
SAS Macro facility
 control flow of, 8
 turning off, 17, 218
 in Version 9, 248
SAS Supervisor role, 4
SAS System. *See also* SAS System support; versions
 about, 1–2
 applying SETINIT, 237–238
 best practices coding standards, 91–93
 comments as non-executable in, 131
 comparison of SAS and non-SAS terms, 2–3
 Configuration file, 10, 230–231
 contacting technical support, 235
 controlling messaging in, 225–226
 determining settings when invoking, 10
 displaying option settings, 10
 downloading demos and examples, 239
 exiting, 9
 features of Version 9, 241–249
  in DATA step, 241–242
  in ODS, 243–247
  SAS Learning Edition, 248–249
  SAS Macro facility, 248
 hot fixes, 236–237
 improved quality of output, 194
 information on known bugs, 236
 invoking, 230
 launching installation for, 229
 library
  of sample programs, 238
  of technical support documents, 235–236
 overview of, 1–2

286

Release 8.2 system requirements, 227–228
terminology equivalents for SQL and, 148
types
    of libraries, 177
    of members, 177
types of installation configurations, 230
upgrading from 8.1 to 8.2, 237
user groups, 240
valid dates in, 93
SAS System Options window, 24
SAS System support, 227–240
    installation and configuration, 227–232
        changing library locations, 229–230
        customizing Configuration file, 230–231
        installing or removing Internet Explorer 5 in Release 8.2, 228
        invoking SAS System, 230
        launching SAS System installation, 229
        locating Configuration file, 230
        Release 8.2 system requirements, 227–228
        System options available under Windows, 231–232
        types of installation configurations, 230
    Service & Support Web site, 233–240
        accessing, 233
        applying SETINIT, 237–238
        attending SUGI, 240
        contacting technical support, 235
        downloading demos and examples, 239
        hot fixes, 236–237
        illustrated, 233
        information on known bugs, 236
        sample SAS programs on, 238
        SAS user groups, 240
        searching techniques, 233–234
        subscribing and participating in SAS-L email list, 239–240
        technical support documents on, 235–236
        upgrading from 8.1 to 8.2, 237
SAS User Group International (SUGI), 240
SAS-L email list, 239–240
saving
    CPU resources with IN operator, 217
    labels and formats in data sets, 131–132, 223–224
    sorted observations to data set, 175
    work in DMS, 22
search categories for Service & Support Web site, 233–234
searching
    with Find dialog box, 22–23
    processing SQL wildcard searches, 76
    with PRXs, 241
        finding, parsing, and retrieving data, 242–243
        PRXs functions, 243
        searching and replacing text, 243
        simple matches with, 242
    on Service & Support Web site, 233–234
SELECT blocks, 138–139
Select Delimited File Options dialog box, 60
SELECT statement
    clause ordering in, 76
    executing WHEN conditions in, 90
    omitting in copying procedure, 169
selecting
    desired output objects, 197
    output with ODS, 197
semicolons (;)
    ending statements with, 3
    marking end of data containing, 5
Service & Support Web site, 233–240
    accessing, 233
    applying SETINIT, 237–238
    attending SUGI, 240
    contacting technical support, 235
    downloading demos and examples, 239
    hot fixes, 236–237
    illustrated, 233
    information on known bugs, 236
    library
        of sample SAS programs, 238
        of technical support documents, 235–236
    SAS user groups, 240
    searching techniques, 233–234
    subscribing and participating in SAS-L email list, 239–240
    upgrading from 8.1 to 8.2, 237

session performance, controlling, 10
SET statements
    reshaping data columns with three, 144
    reshaping data columns with two, 143–144
SETINIT, 237–238
SHORT option in CONTENTS procedure, 173
Show Tree view, 37
sorting
    to achieve subsetting, 126
    avoiding
        problems with large files, 126
        unnecessary, 218–219
    by relative position in select list, 79
    columns not specified in select list, 79
    controlling amount of memory used, 219
    data, 18
    files, 36
    I/O performance and, 221
    refreshing file order of sorted files, 36
    returning observations to original data set after, 175
    reversing data set order without, 127
    saving sorted observations to data set, 175
    selecting observations for, 176
    sort order for numeric and character variables, 175–176
    SQL data, 78
SORTPGM= option, 18
SORTSIZE= option, 219
SOURCE2 option, 14
SOURCE option, 13
spelling checks, 26
SQL (Structured Query Language), 73–81
    ANSI SQL and PROC SQL extensions, 74
    available summary functions, 80–81
    bundled with Base-SAS product, 74
    calculating statistics with summary functions, 79
    column aliases, 77
    columns and datatypes, 75
    consolidating steps to improve I/O performance, 221
    inserting blank lines between row output, 77
    ordering of columns and column wildcard, 75
    overview, 73
    parentheses and order of evaluation in, 75–76
    placing wildcard characters, 77
    processing
        performance with wildcard searches, 76
        with RUN groups and error handling, 74
    programming in SQL, 73
    removing rows containing duplicate column values, 77–78
    SELECT clause ordering, 76
    sorting
        by multiple columns, 78
        by relative position in select list, 79
        columns not specified in select list, 79
        data in descending order, 78
    specifying criteria to subset and display values, 75
    statements and clauses, 75
    storing separate pieces of information in data set, 74
    summarizing data
        across columns, 80
        down rows, 79–80
        with, 79
    terminating, 74
    terminology equivalents for SAS and, 148
    writing observations with, 6
SQL SELECT statement, 96
state and zip code functions, 110, 114–115
statements. *See also specific statements by name*
    beginning and ending, 3
    coding in "free format" style, 3–4
    executing after AUTOEXEC file, 11
    functions in, 106
    getting SAS interpreter to recognize, 125–126
    SQL clauses and, 75
    subsetting IF and WHERE, 66–67
    syntax for, 3
    Version 9 macro, 248
statistical functions, 110, 115–116
statistics
    created with MEANS procedure, 158
    created with UNIVARIATE procedure, 160
step boundaries, 8–9

STIMER system option, 14
STOP; statement, 127
storage format, 6
storage techniques, 222–223
    assigning lengths to numeric values, 223
    compressing data sets, 223
    creating user-defined formats for coded data, 223
    suppressing data set creation with DATA_NULL_, 222
Stored Program Facility, 220
storing libraries
    on disk, 177
    on tape, 178
streaming Web output, 203
strings
    reversing character-string value, 107
    searching character variable in character, 106–107
    truncating and comparing with colon modifier, 104–105
subsetting, 133–139
    creating new data sets with subset, 133
    external input data with OBS= and FIRSTOBS= options, 138
    I/O performance and, 220
    IF and WHERE statements, 66–67
    IF statement, 134
    with LIKE operator and percent sign wildcard, 103
    observations with
        DELETE statement, 136
        IF...THEN/ELSE and OUTPUT statements, 136–137
        OBS= and FIRSTOBS= data set options, 137–138
        operators, 134–136
        SELECT blocks and OUTPUT, 138–139
        WHERE= data set option, 134
        WHERE statements, 67
    replacing IFs with WHEREs to process large files, 128
    sorting to achieve, 126
    variables
        in DATA step, 139–140
        from external data, 139
        in PROC step, 140

SUGI (SAS User Group International), 240
summarizing data
    across columns, 80
    by down rows, 79–80
    SQL procedure for, 79
summary functions, 79, 80–81
    available, 80–81
    calculating statistics with, 79
SUMMARY procedure, 158–159
summary statistics, 128–129
syntax
    checking in DATA or PROC step, 15
    of CONTENTS procedure, 170–171
    DATASETS procedure, 169
    errors in, 122–123
    of ODS statement, 202
    statement, 3
    for tracing ODS output, 196
system initialization, 10–11
system options
    available under Windows, 231–232
    listing of SAS System, 251–262
system-related errors, 125

T

tab settings, 27
tab-delimited input, 46–47
table. *See* data sets
table aliases, 149–150
tags, 201
technical support. *See also* Service & Support Web site
    contacting, 235
    email address for, 240
    searching technical notes, 235–236
temporary arrays, 220
testing. *See* program testing
text file copying
    in DATA step, 166
    from designated record position, 167
    making multiple copies of, 168
    part of record in, 166
    specifying LENGTH= and START= options, 167

time
- applying date and time formats, 94
- displaying at top of printed page, 12
- representing values with formats and informats, 94
- storing as numeric value, 94
- time functions, 110, 111

toolbar buttons
- customizing settings, 24
- exploring, 24

tracing output, 160–161, 196
TRANSPOSE procedure, 162–163
trigonometric and hyperbolic functions, 110, 117
truncation functions, 117
turning on/off
- Enhanced Editor, 22
- Macro facility, 17, 218
- SAS Display Manager System, 7
- Show Tree view, 37

U

underscore (_) wildcard, 104
UNIFORM option, 189
UNIVARIATE procedure
- creating data sets with, 159–160, 162
- statistical keywords for, 160

unsubscribing from SAS-L, 240
UPDATE statement, updating data sets with, 180–181
usage errors, 122
user groups, 240
user-defined formats for coded data, 223

V

vacation settings for SAS-L, 240
values for invalid numeric data, 13
variables
- applying date and time formats to, 94
- assigning
  - attributes with ATTRIB statement, 89
  - descriptive names, 223
  - length to character, 224
  - length with LENGTH statement, 88–89
- avoiding reserved names for, 5
- changing length of existing character, 89–90
- converting
  - to observations, 163–164
  - observations into, 162–163
- created with END= option, 56
- creating, 4
- FIRST. and LAST., 145
- modifying label of, 179–180
- naming conventions for, 3
- output data set, 155–156
- preventing missing values from being assigned to, 88
- printing list of, 173, 174
- renaming, 68, 178–179
- searching character string for character, 106–107
- selecting for processing from data set, 67–68
- sort order for numeric and character, 175–176
- specifying in MEANS procedure, 158
- subsetting
  - in DATA step, 139–140
  - from external data, 139
  - in PROC step, 140

versions
- improved quality of output, 194
- Internet Explorer 5 in Release 8.2, 228
- Release 8.2 system requirements, 227–228
- upgrading from Release 8.1 to 8.2, 237

viewing
- contents of catalog, 37–38
- file properties, 34–35
- frame file, 204

views
- accessing data from, 71
- creating, 224–225
- dictionary, 71–72
- VTABLE, 73

W

warnings, 123
Web output, 201–212
    about HTML, 201–202
    changing output labels, 206
    checking deployment checklist, 211–212
    combining output results, 206–207
    creating PDF output, 207–208
    deploying with ODS, 203
    displaying PRINT procedure output in HTML, 205
    drill-down user interface and applications, 208–211
    ignoring pagesize and linesize settings, 204
    links and references in ODS, 202
    locating HTML files in Windows, 204–205
    ODS HTML file types, 202–203
    overview, 201
    specifying BODY=, CONTENTS=, PAGE=, and FRAME= files, 205–206
    streaming output with BODY= file, 203
    testing, 211
    viewing frame file, 204
Web sites, accessing Service & Support, 233
Web tool functions, 117, 118
WHEN conditions
    executing in SELECT statement, 90
    sending output to data sets, 155
WHERE= option, 15, 134
WHERE expressions, 68
WHERE statements
    CPU efficiency of, 217
    processing large files by replacing IFs with, 128
    reduced memory requirements and, 222
    replacing subsetting IFs with, 128
    subsetting, 66–67
wildcard characters
    multiple percent sign wildcards in search pattern, 104
    ordering of columns and column wildcard, 75
    placing in SQL statements, 77
    processing performance with wildcard searches, 76
    subsetting with LIKE operator and percent sign wildcard, 103
    underscore wildcard with LIKE operator, 104
Windows. *See* Microsoft Windows
windows
    clearing, 26, 27
    commands for accessing DMS, 28, 29–30
    invoking anytime in DMS, 23
    Log, 19, 27
    navigating between DMS, 22
    opening application in minimized, 18
    Output, 20–21, 27
    Program Editor, 19, 26
    Results, 20
    SAS System Options, 24
    searching in selected, 23
WORK data sets, 222
WORK library files, 11
writing
    all performance statistics to SAS Log, 14
    source files included with statement to SAS Log, 13
    source statements to SAS Log, 13
    subset of performance statistics to SAS Log, 14

X

X command, 18
XML (eXtensible Markup Language)
    creating output and DTDs in ODS MARKUP, 247
    creating output with ODS MARKUP in, 245–246
    DTDs, 246–247

Y

YEARCUTOFF= option
    defining, 96–97
    entering values for, 11–12

Apress Titles

ISBN	PRICE	AUTHOR	TITLE
1-893115-73-9	$34.95	Abbott	Voice Enabling Web Applications: VoiceXML and Beyond
1-893115-01-1	$39.95	Appleman	Dan Appleman's Win32 API Puzzle Book and Tutorial for Visual Basic Programmers
1-893115-23-2	$29.95	Appleman	How Computer Programming Works
1-893115-97-6	$39.95	Appleman	Moving to VB .NET: Strategies, Concepts, and Code
1-59059-023-6	$39.95	Baker	Adobe Acrobat 5: The Professional User's Guide
1-59059-039-2	$49.95	Barnaby	Distributed .NET Programming in C#
1-59059-068-6	$49.95	Barnaby	Distributed .NET Programming in VB .NET
1-893115-09-7	$29.95	Baum	Dave Baum's Definitive Guide to LEGO MINDSTORMS
1-893115-84-4	$29.95	Baum, Gasperi, Hempel, and Villa	Extreme MINDSTORMS: An Advanced Guide to LEGO MINDSTORMS
1-893115-82-8	$59.95	Ben-Gan/Moreau	Advanced Transact-SQL for SQL Server 2000
1-893115-91-7	$39.95	Birmingham/Perry	Software Development on a Leash
1-893115-48-8	$29.95	Bischof	The .NET Languages: A Quick Translation Guide
1-59059-041-4	$49.95	Bock	CIL Programming: Under the Hood of .NET
1-59059-053-8	$44.95	Bock/Stromquist/Fischer/Smith	.NET Security
1-893115-67-4	$49.95	Borge	Managing Enterprise Systems with the Windows Script Host
1-59059-019-8	$49.95	Cagle	SVG Programming: The Graphical Web
1-893115-28-3	$44.95	Challa/Laksberg	Essential Guide to Managed Extensions for C++
1-893115-39-9	$44.95	Chand	A Programmer's Guide to ADO.NET in C#
1-59059-015-5	$39.95	Clark	An Introduction to Object Oriented Programming with Visual Basic .NET
1-893115-44-5	$29.95	Cook	Robot Building for Beginners
1-893115-99-2	$39.95	Cornell/Morrison	Programming VB .NET: A Guide for Experienced Programmers
1-893115-72-0	$39.95	Curtin	Developing Trust: Online Privacy and Security
1-59059-014-7	$44.95	Drol	Object-Oriented Macromedia Flash MX
1-59059-008-2	$29.95	Duncan	The Career Programmer: Guerilla Tactics for an Imperfect World
1-893115-71-2	$39.95	Ferguson	Mobile .NET
1-893115-90-9	$49.95	Finsel	The Handbook for Reluctant Database Administrators
1-59059-024-4	$49.95	Fraser	Real World ASP.NET: Building a Content Management System
1-893115-42-9	$44.95	Foo/Lee	XML Programming Using the Microsoft XML Parser
1-893115-55-0	$34.95	Frenz	Visual Basic and Visual Basic .NET for Scientists and Engineers
1-59059-038-4	$49.95	Gibbons	.NET Development for Java Programmers
1-893115-85-2	$34.95	Gilmore	A Programmer's Introduction to PHP 4.0
1-893115-36-4	$34.95	Goodwill	Apache Jakarta-Tomcat
1-893115-17-8	$59.95	Gross	A Programmer's Introduction to Windows DNA
1-893115-62-3	$39.95	Gunnerson	A Programmer's Introduction to C#, Second Edition

ISBN	PRICE	AUTHOR	TITLE
1-59059-030-9	$49.95	Habibi/Patterson/Camerlengo	The Sun Certified Java Developer Exam with J2SE 1.4
1-893115-30-5	$49.95	Harkins/Reid	SQL: Access to SQL Server
1-59059-009-0	$49.95	Harris/Macdonald	Moving to ASP.NET: Web Development with VB .NET
1-59059-006-6	$39.95	Hetland	Practical Python
1-893115-10-0	$34.95	Holub	Taming Java Threads
1-893115-04-6	$34.95	Hyman/Vaddadi	Mike and Phani's Essential C++ Techniques
1-893115-96-8	$59.95	Jorelid	J2EE FrontEnd Technologies: A Programmer's Guide to Servlets, JavaServer Pages, and Enterprise JavaBeans
1-893115-49-6	$39.95	Kilburn	Palm Programming in Basic
1-893115-50-X	$34.95	Knudsen	Wireless Java: Developing with Java 2, Micro Edition
1-893115-79-8	$49.95	Kofler	Definitive Guide to Excel VBA
1-893115-57-7	$39.95	Kofler	MySQL
1-893115-87-9	$39.95	Kurata	Doing Web Development: Client-Side Techniques
1-893115-75-5	$44.95	Kurniawan	Internet Programming with Visual Basic
1-893115-38-0	$24.95	Lafler	Power AOL: A Survival Guide
1-893115-46-1	$36.95	Lathrop	Linux in Small Business: A Practical User's Guide
1-893115-19-4	$49.95	Macdonald	Serious ADO: Universal Data Access with Visual Basic
1-59059-044-9	$49.95	MacDonald	User Interfaces in VB .NET: Windows Forms and Custom Controls
1-893115-06-2	$39.95	Marquis/Smith	A Visual Basic 6.0 Programmer's Toolkit
1-893115-22-4	$27.95	McCarter	David McCarter's VB Tips and Techniques
1-59059-021-X	$34.95	Moore	Karl Moore's Visual Basic .NET: The Tutorials
1-893115-27-5	$44.95	Morrill	Tuning and Customizing a Linux System
1-893115-76-3	$49.95	Morrison	C++ For VB Programmers
1-59059-003-1	$44.95	Nakhimovsky/Meyers	XML Programming: Web Applications and Web Services with JSP and ASP
1-893115-80-1	$39.95	Newmarch	A Programmer's Guide to Jini Technology
1-893115-58-5	$49.95	Oellermann	Architecting Web Services
1-59059-020-1	$44.95	Patzer	JSP Examples and Best Practices
1-893115-81-X	$39.95	Pike	SQL Server: Common Problems, Tested Solutions
1-59059-017-1	$34.95	Rainwater	Herding Cats: A Primer for Programmers Who Lead Programmers
1-59059-025-2	$49.95	Rammer	Advanced .NET Remoting (C# Edition)
1-59059-062-7	$49.95	Rammer	Advanced .NET Remoting in VB .NET
1-893115-20-8	$34.95	Rischpater	Wireless Web Development
1-59059-028-7	$39.95	Rischpater	Wireless Web Development, Second Edition
1-893115-93-3	$34.95	Rischpater	Wireless Web Development with PHP and WAP
1-893115-89-5	$59.95	Shemitz	Kylix: The Professional Developer's Guide and Reference
1-893115-40-2	$39.95	Sill	The qmail Handbook
1-893115-24-0	$49.95	Sinclair	From Access to SQL Server
1-59059-026-0	$49.95	Smith	Writing Add-ins for Visual Studio .NET
1-893115-94-1	$29.95	Spolsky	User Interface Design for Programmers
1-893115-53-4	$44.95	Sweeney	Visual Basic for Testers

ISBN	PRICE	AUTHOR	TITLE
1-59059-035-X	$59.95	Symmonds	GDI+ Programming in C# and VB .NET
1-59059-002-3	$44.95	Symmonds	Internationalization and Localization Using Microsoft .NET
1-59059-010-4	$54.95	Thomsen	Database Programming with C#
1-893115-29-1	$44.95	Thomsen	Database Programming with Visual Basic .NET
1-893115-65-8	$39.95	Tiffany	Pocket PC Database Development with eMbedded Visual Basic
1-59059-027-9	$59.95	Torkelson/Petersen/Torkelson	Programming the Web with Visual Basic .NET
1-59059-018-X	$34.95	Tregar	Writing Perl Modules for CPAN
1-893115-59-3	$59.95	Troelsen	C# and the .NET Platform
1-59059-011-2	$59.95	Troelsen	COM and .NET Interoperability
1-893115-26-7	$59.95	Troelsen	Visual Basic .NET and the .NET Platform: An Advanced Guide
1-893115-54-2	$49.95	Trueblood/Lovett	Data Mining and Statistical Analysis Using SQL
1-893115-68-2	$54.95	Vaughn	ADO.NET and ADO Examples and Best Practices for VB Programmers, Second Edition
1-59059-012-0	$49.95	Vaughn/Blackburn	ADO.NET Examples and Best Practices for C# Programmers
1-893115-83-6	$44.95	Wells	Code Centric: T-SQL Programming with Stored Procedures and Triggers
1-893115-95-X	$49.95	Welschenbach	Cryptography in C and C++
1-893115-05-4	$39.95	Williamson	Writing Cross-Browser Dynamic HTML
1-59059-060-0	$39.95	Wright	ADO.NET: From Novice to Pro, Visual Basic .NET Edition
1-893115-78-X	$49.95	Zukowski	Definitive Guide to Swing for Java 2, Second Edition
1-893115-92-5	$49.95	Zukowski	Java Collections
1-893115-98-4	$54.95	Zukowski	Learn Java with JBuilder 6

Available at bookstores nationwide or from Springer Verlag New York, Inc. at 1-800-777-4643; fax 1-212-533-3503. Contact us for more information at sales@apress.com.

Apress Titles Publishing SOON!

ISBN	AUTHOR	TITLE
1-59059-022-8	Alapati/Reid	Expert Oracle 9i Database Administration
1-59059-000-7	Cornell	Programming C#
1-59059-033-3	Fraser	Managed C++ and .NET Development
1-893115-74-7	Millar	Enterprise Development: A Programmer's Handbook
1-893115-43-7	Stephenson	Standard VB: An Enterprise Developer's Reference for VB 6 and VB .NET
1-59059-032-5	Thomsen	Database Programming with Visual Basic .NET, Second Edition
1-59059-007-4	Thomsen	Building Web Services with VB .NET

Available at bookstores nationwide or from Springer Verlag New York, Inc. at 1-800-777-4643; fax 1-212-533-3503. Contact us for more information at sales@apress.com.

About Apress

Apress, located in Berkeley, CA, is a fast-growing, innovative publishing company devoted to meeting the needs of existing and potential programming professionals. Simply put, the "A" in Apress stands for *"The Author's Press™"* and its books have *"The Expert's Voice™"*. Apress' unique approach to publishing grew out of conversations between its founders Gary Cornell and Dan Appleman, authors of numerous best-selling, highly regarded books for programming professionals. In 1998 they set out to create a publishing company that emphasized quality above all else. Gary and Dan's vision has resulted in the publication of over 50 titles by leading software professionals, all of which have *The Expert's Voice*™.

Do You Have What It Takes to Write for Apress?

Apress is rapidly expanding its publishing program. If you can write and refuse to compromise on the quality of your work, if you believe in doing more than rehashing existing documentation, and if you're looking for opportunities and rewards that go far beyond those offered by traditional publishing houses, we want to hear from you!

Consider these innovations that we offer all of our authors:

- **Top royalties with *no* hidden switch statements**
  Authors typically only receive half of their normal royalty rate on foreign sales. In contrast, Apress' royalty rate remains the same for both foreign and domestic sales.

- **A mechanism for authors to obtain equity in Apress**
  Unlike the software industry, where stock options are essential to motivate and retain software professionals, the publishing industry has adhered to an outdated compensation model based on royalties alone. In the spirit of most software companies, Apress reserves a significant portion of its equity for authors.

- **Serious treatment of the technical review process**
  Each Apress book has a technical reviewing team whose remuneration depends in part on the success of the book since they too receive royalties.

Moreover, through a partnership with Springer-Verlag, New York, Inc., one of the world's major publishing houses, Apress has significant venture capital behind it. Thus, we have the resources to produce the highest quality books *and* market them aggressively.

If you fit the model of the Apress author who can write a book that gives the "professional what he or she needs to know™," then please contact one of our Editorial Directors, Dan Appleman (dan_appleman@apress.com), Gary Cornell (gary_cornell@apress.com), Jason Gilmore (jason_gilmore@apress.com), Simon Hayes (simon_hayes@apress.com), Karen Watterson (karen_watterson@apress.com), or John Zukowski (john_zukowski@apress.com) for more information.

THE EDGAR
BEDSIDE CO

THE EDGAR ALLAN POE BEDSIDE COMPANION

Morgue and Mystery Tales

edited by

PETER HAINING

LONDON
VICTOR GOLLANCZ LTD
1980

© Seventh Zenith Ltd 1980

ISBN 0 575 02908 0

Printed in Great Britain by
St Edmundsbury Press, Bury St Edmunds, Suffolk

CONTENTS

INTRODUCTION	7
THE DEAD ALIVE Anonymous	21
THE MAN IN THE BELL William Maginn	25
THE DEAD DAUGHTER Henry Glassford Bell	32
A DREAM Edgar Allan Poe	40
THE JOURNAL OF JULIUS RODMAN Edgar Allan Poe	44
WHO IS THE MURDERER? Edgar Allan Poe	105
THE FIRE-FIEND Charles D. Gardette	149
THE LIGHTHOUSE Edgar Allan Poe & Robert Bloch	155
THE MAD TRIST Edgar Allan Poe & Robert Haining	171

— were never finished before Poe died

ACKNOWLEDGEMENTS

The Editor is deeply grateful to those who helped him in the research of this book, in particular the staff at the British Museum, the New York Public Library, and the London Library. Thanks also to Bill Lofts for assistance, Robert Haining for his contribution, and A. M. Heath Literary Agency for permission to reprint the Poe story, "The Lighthouse", completed by Robert Bloch.

INTRODUCTION

The Pioneer of Mystery

IN THE YEAR 1835, Edgar Allan Poe, struggling hard to make his impact on American literature, confided in a letter to a friend the methods he was using in the creation of the short stories he hoped might someday secure him a reputation. "The ludicrous," he said, "is heightened into the grotesque; the fearful coloured into the horrible; the witty exaggerated into the burlesque; the singular wrought out into the strange and the mystical."

Today, almost a century and a half later, it may seem surprising that a man of such unquestioned genius could have failed to receive the instant acknowledgement to which he was entitled. Yet, as we also know, while his times treated him badly, history has subsequently lauded his name and his works, seeing him clearly as a great pioneer of mystery fiction.

The Creator of the Modern Horror Story. The Developer of Science Fiction. The Father of Detective Fiction. Such laurels can, with every justification, be attached to Poe's name. Even The Most Read Fantasy Writer of the Twentieth Century is not beyond him—for despite all the brilliant authors that have emerged during the past three quarters of a century, his stories remain in print year after year in virtually every language, and the best of them are anthologized repeatedly. Time has done nothing to age this work, or deprive it of the bright spark of magic that makes it immediately appealing to each new generation.

Nor has time played the trick on Poe that it has done on other great writers in the Fantasy genre: Mary Shelley (*Frankenstein*) and Bram Stoker (*Dracula*), for instance, have become overshadowed by their monstrous creations, yet Poe remains a colossus, the variety of his work defying any such simple association. Indeed, his name has become synonymous with all that is best in the genre, and no modern writer could hope for higher praise than to be compared with him.

There are many explanations that can, and have been, offered to explain Poe's success. His originality, his style, and the masterful way he handles atmosphere and characterization have all been singled out for praise. For my part—and I can claim to have been reading and studying Poe since childhood—it is his diversity that sets him above all others. His stories take us through such a wide range of subjects, places and times; they tell us about men from different backgrounds in many extraordinary situations and transport us from the bowels of the earth to the far reaches of space. There is hardly a topic which did not attract Poe at some time during his life, and which, after he had embraced it in his fiction, was ever quite the same again. From his own sad life too, he extracted the power of his emotions to give us stories and poems that are, quite simply, unforgettable.

I have tried to reflect his diversity of talent in this anthology, which has the distinction of containing several previously uncollected items by Poe (an achievement of which, as an editor, I am naturally proud considering the multitude of editions of his works and the innumerable studies of his life), as well as a small group of stories which were directly influential on some of his best-known tales. For though his originality of conception is never in question, Poe—like any great writer—found inspiration from other sources, as Professor Burton R. Pollin has remarked in his notable study, *Discoveries in Poe* (1970). "Almost every masterpiece of literature," he writes, "reflects a variety of sources, recent and remote, major and minor, all absorbed and held by the creative spirit in a state of dynamic but subliminal flux, until the moment of conception."

The Edgar Allan Poe Bedside Companion consists of three specific groups of stories. The first section contains three short tales which Poe acknowledged reading and which later inspired important stories of his own. In the second part I have returned to print three stories by Poe which have not appeared in his Collected Works and have consequently been unavailable to readers since the last century. And thirdly, by way of rounding out the picture, I have included three items directly inspired by Poe: a famous hoax poem "The Fire-Fiend"; "The Lighthouse", a story he left unfinished at his death and which has now been completed by one of his most distinguished literary heirs, Robert Bloch; and, finally, a completely new story never published elsewhere, "The Mad Trist", based on a fascinating idea contained in perhaps the most popular of all his works. Together, I believe, this group of nine stories throws new light on the diversity of his talent as well as adding some important items to the library of Poe material. They are all splendid reading into the bargain!

However, before you begin, let me offer a little information about the background to the stories which will, I hope, enhance your appreciation and enjoyment of them.

Poe was, by his own admission, an avid reader of newspapers and magazines throughout his life, and few periodicals gave him greater pleasure than the British monthly, *Blackwood's Magazine*, to which he tried to contribute for some years and praised in a revealing essay entitled "The Psyche Zenobia" first published in the *American Museum*, November 1838. (The story was later re-titled "How to Write a Blackwood Article" and has remained under that title ever since.)

Blackwood's Magazine was founded in 1817 by an Edinburgh bookseller-turned-publisher, William Blackwood (1776–1834) and was almost certainly the first periodical in English to publish stories and poems. The excellent taste of its various editors over the years has enabled it to flourish to this day. It seems likely that Poe began reading the magazine in his childhood, for his foster father, John Allan, imported books and magazines as well as other merchandise from Britain. What is certain is that it sparked his youthful imagination and sowed the seeds which were later to flower into several remarkable stories. Two items from *Blackwood's* which in his essay about the magazine Poe specifically mentions having read, and which we can clearly see as being influential on his work, begin this collection. They are "The Buried Alive" and "The Man in the Bell".

"The Buried Alive" appeared in the October 1821 issue of *Blackwood's* and this is how Poe described the effect the story had on him in his later essay (Poe misquotes the title, but there is no doubt it is the story he has in mind): "There was 'The Dead Alive' a capital thing!—the record of a gentleman's sensations when entombed before the breath was out of his body—full of taste, terror, sentiment, metaphysics and erudition. You would have sworn that the writer had been born and brought up in a coffin."

No author is credited with "The Buried Alive" and subsequent research has failed to identify any possible writer. That Poe should have been so attracted to the story comes as no surprise, for as a child he had always been frightened of the dark, and had heard of at least two instances of premature burial. The direct result was his story "The Premature Burial", also a first-person account, which he wrote in 1844 and which has subsequently been reprinted countless times as well as being impressively filmed with Ray Milland in 1962.

Next, in his *Blackwood's* essay, Poe turns to "The Man in the Bell" which was published in the following month's issue (November 1821):

> And then there was "The Man in the Bell", a paper by-the-by which I cannot sufficiently recommend to your attention. It is the history of a young person who goes to sleep under the clapper of a church bell and is awakened by its tolling for a funeral. The sound drives him mad and, accordingly, pulling out his tablets, he gives a record of his sensations. Sensations are the great things after all!

The impression this story had on Poe is further underlined by the fact that he mentioned it again in a letter to Thomas White dated 30 April 1835. Although, once again, no author's name appears on the story, it has been established that it was written by William Maginn (1794–1842) a prolific contributor to the magazine, who was born in Cork and moved to London, where he wrote stories and essays for several of the leading publications of the day.

Maginn's story inspired two important Poe works, "The Devil in the Belfry", his grotesque little yarn published in 1839, and "The Pit and the Pendulum" (1842), the popular and quite terrifying story which has never been out of print and was filmed twice, in 1912 and 1961, the later version starring Vincent Price.

The third story in this first section also comes from a Scottish magazine and aside from its direct inspiration of a Poe story, must have done much to nurture the American's obsession with doomed heroines. The story called "The Dead Daughter" was written by Henry Glassford Bell (1803–1874) and appeared in the magazine he edited, *The Edinburgh Literary Journal,* for 1 January 1831.

Bell, who has been referred to as "The Last of the Literary Sheriffs", was initially a writer and editor, but then turned to the law, ultimately becoming Sheriff of Glasgow, so denying the world of letters a rare talent. In studying the small group of stories that Bell wrote during the three year period he ran the Journal (1828–1831), I think it is possible to see that he was one of the single most important influences on Poe, and indeed in the *Dictionary of National Biography* (1885), two of his stories, "The Dead Daughter" and "The Living Mummy" are specifically cited in this context, with the remark that from them "Edgar Poe seems to have taken the hint for two of his most famous fantasies." The Poe stories are, of course, "Morella" (1835), perhaps the most tragic of his ill-fated ladies, and the grimly humorous "Some Words with a Mummy" (1845).

The second section of the anthology includes three previously uncollected stories by Poe: "A Dream", "The Journal of Julius Rodman" and "Who is the Murderer?". While the first is just a brief, imaginative fantasy—nonetheless important—the other two are novella length: a story of travel and high adventure in unexplored regions, and the exposition of a baffling murder mystery.

"A Dream" was first recorded by Professor Killis Campbell while researching Poe and his life, but although he mentions the story in his book, *The Mind of Poe* (1933), it is not reprinted. The fantasy originally appeared in the Philadelphia *Saturday Evening Post* of 13 August 1831, and although not the earliest of his stories, is certainly one of his first attempts at fantasy fiction. It has been suggested that an eclipse of the moon on 12 February 1831, which Poe observed, may have inspired him to write the tale; but what is certain is that the employment of a dream as the basis of the fantasy was a technique he was to use again during his career.

"The Journal of Julius Rodman" shows us a completely different side of Poe's genius: that of travelogue writer. The story was written as a serial in 1840 for *Burton's Magazine*, and remains unfinished because Poe apparently quarrelled with his employer and was discharged from his job before he could complete it. Edward H. Davidson is one of the few Poe scholars to have pointed out the significance of the tale in his *Poe: a Critical Study* (1957):

> Only twice did Poe try his hand at a sustained narrative, first in "The Narrative of A. Gordon Pym" (in two instalments in the *Southern Literary Messenger* for January and February 1837, and separately as a "finished" book in 1838) and, second, in "The Journal of Julius Rodman" published serially in *Burton's Gentleman's Magazine* from January through June 1840. *The latter has never been printed separately or gathered among his tales.* [My italics.]
>
> In a way one narrative is a commentary on the other; both begin at the same place in the creative imagination—with the facts of a voyage or a journey to unexplored lands. One remains earthbound and text-confined to its sources, which Poe quite ruthlessly copied, extracted or revised; the other, "Pym", takes off from its sources, comes back to them for supporting details, and then transforms and makes them into art.
>
> In their way both are hoaxes; they presume to recount adventures with a complete, an almost deadly seriousness,

and base the separate incidents on undoubted facts which science and exploration could confirm. For "Rodman" Poe relied almost entirely on Washington Irving's *Astoria*, itself a derivation from other narratives, and on the journals of Lewis and Clark . . .

Poe calls the "Journal", "a journey beyond the extreme bounds of civilization" and goes on to add:

Within the limits of the United States there is very little ground which has not, of late years, been traversed by men of science, or the adventurer. But in those wide and desolate regions which lie north of our territory, and to the westward of Mackenzie's River, the foot of no civilized man, with the exception of Mr Rodman and his very small party, has ever been known to tread.

The central character of the story, Julius Rodman, is a typical Poe hero, a man of morbid sensibilities driven to the wilds to avoid the rest of mankind. He is said to belong to a family who had emigrated from England, lives a hermit-like existence in Kentucky, and sets off in 1791 on the expedition which is detailed in the Journal. Poe claims that the manuscript on which the account is based was "always supposed to have been lost" but has lately been rediscovered "in a secret drawer of a bureau which had belonged to Mr Julius Rodman".

The only disappointing fact about this remarkable novella, with its colourful and descriptive account of life in the American wilds —complete with dramatic encounters with dangerous animals and war-like Red Indians—is that Poe never returned to the task of completing it. This said, it still makes fascinating reading, and I am delighted to be returning it to print after such a long absence.

The last story in the section, "Who is the Murderer?", is the subject of some controversy as to whether Poe actually wrote it. The renowned Poe scholar Mary E. Phillips, in her book *Edgar Allan Poe: the Man* (1926) has no doubt in assigning it to him, and believes it was one of the articles which he said he had written for British magazines in the early 1840s. It appeared anonymously in *Blackwood's* of May 1842—the magazine we know Poe admired and to which he always wanted to contribute.

If this claim is correct (and I find the evidence convincing) then Poe wrote "Who is the Murderer?" not long after his pioneer detective story, "The Murders in the Rue Morgue" (1841), and before "The Mystery of Marie Roget", which was published between November 1842 and February 1843. This fact established, it appeared at a time when Poe was deeply absorbed with the art of "ratiocination" (as he called detective work), and the style of presentation, with the witnesses giving their testimony one by one, is very like that adopted in "The Murders in the Rue Morgue". The entire story also has much of Poe's circumstantiality, and I am sure the reader will be fascinated by the mystery whether or not he has doubts about its authorship.

In the last section of the book I have included three items inspired by Poe. Two of these are stories, but the first is a poem, "The Fire-Fiend", for of course Poe also left his mark on poetry with such marvellous verses as "The City in the Sea", "The Bells" and his immortal "The Raven".

"The Fire-Fiend" was first published some ten years after Poe's death in the *New York Saturday Press* on 19 November 1859, announced as "a recently discovered Poe manuscript". It was however prefaced by these remarks from the Editor: "We postpone several articles this week to make place for the following communication, which we print with the single remark that we 'don't see it.' " Such was the public acclaim which greeted the poem that the editor's undoubted scepticism about the authenticity of the work was ignored, and it was soon being republished in both magazine and book form as "an unpublished manuscript of the late Edgar A. Poe".

The most extraordinary part of the drama was still to be played out. For when a young Philadelphian named Charles Desmarais Gardette (1830–1884) came forward to confess that the editor's misgivings had been fully justified and that he had written the poem, hardly anyone took any notice! He had created "The Fire-Fiend", Gardette said, to prove to a friend that it was possible to imitate Poe's style and he had taken "The Raven" as his model. The subsequent widespread republication of the hoax poem only proved how right he had been.

In 1864, Gardette felt compelled to publish a booklet explaining just how he had written the poem, thereby hoping to quash once and for all the stories that it was genuine. He concluded the work with these remarks:

> "The Fire-Fiend", then, was written as a hoax, published as hoax with an editorial remark sufficiently indicating the fact to any reader of fair perspicacity; and, as no money was asked, nor received for or by its publication, and no efforts whatever made to disseminate or perpetuate the hoax, either by its publisher or author, I feel no hesitation in pronouncing it, and in believing that my readers will pronounce it, to have been a venial and harmless literary joke, instead of an "unjustifiable fraud", "forgery" and a "great wrong" as some have declared it to be.

Even after such an unqualified admission, it is still the fact that over the intervening years there have been other writers and scholars who have suggested that "The Fire-Fiend" was, after all, a genuine piece by Poe. The reader will easily appreciate how this fine poem can engender such a viewpoint—but the fact remains that it *is* a fraud!

"The Lighthouse", the story which follows the poem, is undeniably partly the work of Poe, for the manuscript which was left unfinished at the time of his death still exists, and following its rediscovery was completed by Robert Bloch in 1953. The rediscovery was made by the leading Poe scholar, Professor T. O. Mabbott, who reprinted the fragment in the antiquarian journal, *Notes & Queries* of 25 April 1942. He described the work as "probably the last story Poe wrote", consisting of four pages of manuscript "written in the very neat hand characteristic of Poe's last years'' (See the sample lines at the foot of this page). Of the story itself, Professor Mabbott writes:

> Obviously the story is a typical one, finding a close parallel in theme to "The Descent into the Maelstrom" which also concerns an adventure with perils of the sea. The theme of loneliness is one frequent in Poe's poems and tales. Even the name of the big dog, Neptune, Poe had used for a canine character before, in his "Julius Rodman". And the tale was obviously to be of mood, the mood of terror. The question remains, however, which is always asked of an unfinished story. Can we guess how it would come out?

Professor Mabbott decided to invite Robert Bloch, an acknowledged master of macabre fiction and an admirer of Poe, to write his own version of the ending based on the clues existing in the manuscript. What he produced is reprinted here, and when I sought Bob's agreement to the use of the story in this collection, he re-emphasized how he had tried to retain the style and intentions of Poe's original, disguising as much as possible where he

Jan 1 — 1796. This day — my first on the light-house — I make this entry in my Diary, as agreed on with De Grät. As regularly as I can keep the journal, I will — but there is no telling what may happen to a man all alone as I am — I may get sick, or worse . . . . .

had taken over. I invite you, therefore, to try and see if you can spot where the pens changed hands before all is revealed at the end of the story. "The Lighthouse" is surely a most remarkable work by two masters of the genre whose collaboration spans the grave and almost one hundred years of time!

Collaboration is also a factor in the final story in the collection, "The Mad Trist". It was inspired by "The Fall of the House of Usher", which is widely considered to be Poe's finest short story —and also happens to be my favourite. It was while re-reading the tale recently that I had the idea for the story which my brother, Robert Haining, has worked out as "The Mad Trist".

What intrigued me once again was the reference to the "antique volume" called *The Mad Trist* by Sir Launcelot Canning which is found on the shelves in Roderick Usher's library. Passages from this book form part of the narrative of the tale, and at first reading it is easy enough to believe the work might be genuine. In fact, it is an imaginary book created by Poe, although the author is surely meant to be related to the famous William Canynge (1399–1474) the Mayor of Bristol and hero of Thomas Chatterton's Rowley Poems, which Poe so loved. Another interesting point about this Launcelot Canning is that Poe also used his name as the "author" of a piece of poetry he was going to use as the motto for a magazine *The Stylus* which he and Thomas Cottrell Clarke tried to launch in 1843. (Sadly, the plan never came to fruition.) Poe himself designed the front cover of the magazine— illustrated overleaf—as well as the motto which ran:

> —unbending that all men
> Of thy firm TRUTH may say—"Lo! this is writ
> With the antique iron pen."
> Launcelot Canning

It was as a result of this, that the names of Poe and Canning and *The Mad Trist* began to swirl around in my mind until the plot of a story took shape, inspired by Poe's invention. Once I had worked out the intriguing possibilities of the concept, I asked my brother, an accomplished writer in the fantasy field, to put some flesh on my skeleton and give it a life of its own. I hope you will agree after reading "The Mad Trist" that he has produced a story Poe himself would have approved of; read in conjunction with "The Fall of the House of Usher" it becomes doubly effective.

These, then, are my "Morgue and Mystery Tales" as Poe might have called them. Each, I think, brings us a little closer to understanding the enigma that was Edgar Allan Poe. But it is, perhaps, his destiny to be always out there in the darkness of the imagination. For should we ever find him and learn his great secret, would any fascination remain in stories such as these?

PETER HAINING
FEBRUARY, 1980

THE

STYLUS

A

Monthly Journal of Literature Proper
The Fine Arts And The Drama.

Aureus aliquando STYLUS, ferreus, aliquando.
                                    Paullus Jovius.

EDITED BY
EDGAR A. POE

THE DEAD ALIVE

Anonymous

I HAD BEEN for some time ill of a low and lingering fever. My strength gradually wasted, but the sense of life seemed to become more and more acute as my corporeal powers became weaker. I could see by the looks of the doctor that he despaired of my recovery; and the soft and whispering sorrow of my friends taught me that I had nothing to hope.

One day towards the evening, the crisis took place. I was seized with a strange and indescribable quivering—a rushing sound was in my ears—I saw around my couch innumerable strange faces; they were bright and visionary, and without bodies. There was light, and solemnity, and I tried to move, but could not. For a short time a terrible confusion overwhelmed me, and when it passed off, all my recollection returned with the most perfect distinctness, but the power of motion had departed. I heard the sound of weeping at my pillow—and the voice of the nurse say, "He is dead." I cannot describe what I felt at these words. I exerted my utmost power of volition to stir myself, but I could not move even an eyelid. After a short pause my friend drew near; and sobbing, and convulsed with grief, drew his hand over my face, and closed my eyes. The world was then darkened, but I still could hear, and feel, and suffer.

When my eyes were closed, I heard by the attendants that my friend had left the room and, I soon after found, the undertakers were preparing to habit me in the garments of the grave. Their thoughtlessness was more awful than the grief of my friends. They laughed at one another as they turned me from side to side, and treated what they believed a corpse, with the most appalling ribaldry.

When they had laid me out, these wretches retired, and the

degrading formality of affected mourning commenced. For three days, a number of friends called to see me. I heard them, in low accents, speak of what I was; and more than one touched me with his finger. On the third day, some of them talked of the smell of corruption in the room.

The coffin was procured—I was lifted and laid in. My friend placed my head on what was deemed its last pillow, and I felt his tears drop on my face.

When all who had any peculiar interest in me, had for a short time looked at me in the coffin, I heard them retire; and the undertaker's men placed the lid on the coffin, and screwed it down. There were two of them present—one had occasion to go away before the task was done. I heard the fellow who was left begin to whistle as he turned the screw-nails; but he checked himself, and completed the work in silence.

I was then left alone—everyone shunned the room. I knew, however, that I was not yet buried; and though darkened and motionless, I had still hope; but this was not permitted long. The day of interment arrived—I felt the coffin lifted and borne away —I heard and felt it placed in the hearse. There was a crowd of people around; some of them spoke sorrowfully of me. The hearse began to move—I knew that it carried me to the grave. It halted, and the coffin was taken out. I felt myself carried on shoulders of men, by the inequality of the motion. A pause ensued —I heard the cords of the coffin moved—I felt it swing as dependent by them. It was lowered, and rested on the bottom of the grave—the cords were dropped upon the lid—I heard them fall. Dreadful was the effort I then made to exert the power of action, but my whole frame was immovable.

Soon after, a few handfuls of earth were thrown upon the coffin. Then there was another pause—after which the shovel was employed, and the sound of the rattling mould, as it covered me, was far more tremendous than thunder. But I could make no effort. The sound gradually became less and less, and by a surging reverberation in the coffin, I knew that the grave was filled up, and that the sexton was treading in the earth, slapping the grave with the flat of his spade. This too ceased, and then all was silent.

I had no means of knowing the lapse of time; and the silence continued. This is death, thought I, and I am doomed to remain in the earth till the resurrection. Presently the body will fall into corruption, and the epicurean worm, that is only satisfied with the flesh of man, will come to partake of the banquet that has been prepared for him with so much solicitude and care. In the contemplation of this hideous thought, I heard a low and undersound in the earth over me, and I fancied that the worms and the reptiles of death were coming—that the mole and the rat of the grave would soon be upon me. The sound continued to grow louder and nearer. Can it be possible, I thought, that my friends suspect they have buried me too soon? The hope was truly like light bursting through the gloom of death.

The sound ceased, and presently I felt the hands of some dreadful being working about my throat. They dragged me out of the coffin by the head. I felt again the living air, but it was piercingly cold; and I was carried swiftly away—I thought to judgment, perhaps perdition.

When borne to some distance, I was then thrown down like a clod—it was not upon the ground. A moment after I found myself on a carriage; and, by the interchange of two or three brief sentences, I discovered that I was in the hands of two of those robbers who live by plundering the grave, and selling the bodies of parents, and children, and friends. One of the men sung snatches and scraps of obscene songs, as the cart rattled over the pavement of the streets.

When it halted, I was lifted out, and I soon perceived, by the closeness of the air, and the change of temperature, that I was carried into a room; and, being rudely stripped of my shroud, was placed naked on a table. By the conversation of the two fellows with the servant who admitted them, I learnt that I was that night to be dissected.

My eyes were still shut, I saw nothing; but in a short time I heard, by the bustle in the room, that the students of anatomy were assembling. Some of them came round the table, and examined me minutely. They were pleased to find that so good a subject had been procured. The demonstrator himself at last came in.

Previous to beginning the dissection, he proposed to try on me some galvanic experiment—and an apparatus was arranged for that purpose. The first shock vibrated through all my nerves: they rung and jangled like the strings of a harp. The students expressed their admiration at the convulsive effect. The second shock threw my eyes open, and the first person I saw was the doctor who had attended me. But still I was as dead: I could, however, discover among the students the faces of many with whom I was familiar; and when my eyes were opened, I heard my name pronounced by several of the students, with an accent of awe and compassion, and a wish that it had been some other subject.

When they had satisfied themselves with the galvanic phenomena, the demonstrator took the knife, and pierced me on the bosom with the point. I felt a dreadful crackling, as it were, throughout my whole frame—a convulsive shuddering instantly followed, and a shriek of horror rose from all present. The ice of death was broken up—my trance ended. The utmost exertions were made to restore me, and in the course of an hour I was in the full possession of all my faculties.

THE MAN IN THE BELL

William Maginn

IN MY YOUNGER days, bell-ringing was much more in fashion among the young men of ——, than it is now. Nobody, I believe, practises it there at present except the servants of the church, and the melody has been much injured in consequence. Some fifty years ago, about twenty of us who dwelt in the vicinity of the Cathedral, formed a club, which used to ring every peal that was called for; and, from continual practice and a rivalry which arose between us and a club attached to another steeple, and which tended considerably to sharpen our zeal, we became very Mozarts on our favourite instruments. But my bell-ringing practice was shortened by a singular accident, which not only stopped my performance, but made even the sound of a bell terrible to my ears.

One Sunday, I went with another into the belfry to ring for noon prayers, but the second stroke we had pulled showed us that the clapper of the bell we were at was muffled. Someone had been buried that morning, and it had been prepared, of course, to ring a mournful note. We did not know of this, but the remedy was easy. "Jack," said my companion, "step up to the loft, and cut off the hat," for the way we had of muffling was by tying a piece of an old hat, or of cloth (the former was preferred) to one side of the clapper, which deadened every second toll. I complied, and mounting into the belfry, crept as usual into the bell, where I began to cut away. The hat had been tied on in some more complicated manner than usual, and I was perhaps three or four minutes in getting it off; during which time my companion below was hastily called away, by a message from his sweetheart I believe, but that is not material to my story. The person who called him was a brother of the club who, knowing that the time had come for ringing for service, and not thinking that anyone was above, began to pull. At this moment I was just getting out, when I felt the bell moving; I guessed the reason at once—it was a moment of terror; but by a hasty, and almost convulsive effort, I succeeded in jumping down, and throwing myself on the flat of my back under the bell.

The room in which it was, was little more than sufficient to contain it, the bottom of the bell coming within a couple of feet of the floor of lath. At that time I certainly was not so bulky as I am now, but as I lay it was within an inch of my face. I had not laid myself down a second, when the ringing began—it was a dreadful situation. Over me swung an immense mass of metal, one touch of which would have crushed me to pieces; the floor under me was principally composed of crazy laths, and if they gave way, I was precipitated to the distance of about fifty feet upon a loft, which would, in all probability, have sunk under the impulse of my fall, and sent me to be dashed to atoms upon the marble floor of the chancel, an hundred feet below. I remembered—for fear is quick in recollection—how a common clockwright, about a month before, had fallen, and bursting through the floors of the steeple, driven in the ceilings of the porch, and even broken into the marble tombstone of a bishop who slept beneath. This was my first terror, but the ringing had not continued a minute, before a more awful and immediate dread came on me. The deafening sound of the bell smote into my ears with a thunder which made me fear their drums would crack. There was not a fibre of my body it did not thrill through: it entered my very soul; thought and reflection were almost utterly banished; I only retained the sensation of agonizing terror. Every moment I saw the bell sweep within an inch of my face; and my eyes—I could not close them, though to look at the object was bitter as death—followed it instinctively in its oscillating progress until it came back again. It was in vain I said to myself that it could come no nearer at any future swing than it did at first; every time it descended, I endeavoured to shrink into the very floor to avoid being buried under the down-sweeping mass; and then reflecting on the danger of pressing too weightily on my frail

THE MAN IN THE BELL

support, would cower up again as far as I dared.

At first my fears were mere matter of fact. I was afraid the pulleys above would give way, and let the bell plunge on me. At another time, the possibility of the clapper being shot out in some sweep, and dashing through my body, as I had seen a ramrod glide through a door, flitted across my mind. The dread also, as I have already mentioned, of the crazy floor tormented me, but these soon gave way to fears not more unfounded, but more visionary, and of course more tremendous. The roaring of the bell confused my intellect, and my fancy soon began to teem with all sorts of strange and terrifying ideas. The bell pealing above, and opening its jaws with a hideous clamour, seemed to me at one time a ravening monster, raging to devour me; at another, a whirlpool ready to suck me into its bellowing abyss. As I gazed on it, it assumed all shapes; it was a flying eagle, or rather a roc of the Arabian story-tellers, clapping its wings and screaming over me. As I looked upward into it, it would appear sometimes to lengthen into indefinite extent, or to be twisted at the end into the spiral folds of the tail of a flying-dragon. Nor was the flaming breath, or fiery glance of that fabled animal, wanting to complete the picture. My eyes inflamed, bloodshot and glaring, invested the supposed monster with a full proportion of unholy light.

It would be endless were I to merely hint at all the fancies that possessed my mind. Every object that was hideous and roaring presented itself to my imagination. I often thought that I was in a hurricane at sea, and that the vessel in which I was embarked tossed under me with the most furious vehemence. The air, set in motion by the swinging of the bell, blew over me, nearly with the violence, and more than the thunder of a tempest; and the floor seemed to reel under me, as under a drunken man. But the most awful of all the ideas that seized on me were drawn from the supernatural. In the vast cavern of the bell hideous faces appeared, and glared down on me with terrifying frowns, or with grinning mockery, still more appalling. At last, the devil himself, accoutred, as in the common description of the evil spirit, with hoof, horn, and tail, and eyes of infernal lustre, made his appearance, and called on me to curse God and worship him, who was powerful to save me. This dread suggestion he uttered with the full-toned clangour of the bell. I had him within an inch of me, and I thought on the fate of the Santon Barsisa. Strenuously and desperately I defied him, and bade him be gone. Reason, then, for a moment, resumed her sway, but it was only to fill me with fresh terror, just as the lightning dispels the gloom that surrounds the benighted mariner, but to show him that his vessel is driving on a rock, where she must inevitably be dashed to pieces. I found I was becoming delirious, and trembled lest reason should utterly desert me. This is at all times an agonizing thought, but it smote me then with tenfold agony. I feared lest, when utterly deprived of my senses, I should rise, to do which I was every moment tempted by that strange feeling which calls on a man, whose head is dizzy from standing on the battlement of a lofty castle, to precipitate himself from it, and then death would be instant and tremendous. When I thought of this, I became desperate. I caught the floor with a grasp which drove the blood from my nails; and I yelled with the cry of despair. I called for help, I prayed, I shouted, but all the efforts of my voice were, of course, drowned in the bell. As it passed over my mouth, it occasionally echoed my cries, which mixed not with its own sound, but preserved their distinct character. Perhaps this was but fancy. To me, I know, they then sounded as if they were the shouting, howling, or laughing of the fiends with which my imagination had peopled the gloomy cave which swung over me.

You may accuse me of exaggerating my feelings; but I am not. Many a scene of dread have I since passed through, but they are nothing to the self-inflicted terrors of this half hour. The ancients have doomed one of the damned, in their Tartarus, to lie under a rock, which every moment seems to be descending to annihilate him—and an awful punishment it would be. But if to this you add a clamour as loud as if ten thousand furies were howling about you—a deafening uproar banishing reason, and

THE MAN IN THE BELL

driving you to madness—you must allow that the bitterness of the pang was rendered more terrible. There is no man, firm as his nerves may be, who could retain his courage in this situation.

In twenty minutes the ringing was done. Half of that time passed over me without power of computation—the other half appeared an age. When it ceased, I became gradually more quiet, but a new fear retained me. I knew that five minutes would elapse without ringing but, at the end of that short time, the bell would be rung a second time, for five minutes more. I could not calculate time. A minute and an hour were of equal duration. I feared to rise, lest the five minutes should have elapsed, and the ringing be again commenced, in which case I should be crushed, before I could escape, against the walls or framework of the bell. I therefore still continued to lie down, cautiously shifting myself, however, with a careful gliding, so that my eye no longer looked into the hollow. This was of itself a considerable relief. The cessation of the noise had, in a great measure, the effect of stupefying me, for my attention, being no longer occupied by the chimeras I had conjured up, began to flag. All that now distressed me was the constant expectation of the second ringing, for which, however, I settled myself with a kind of stupid resolution. I closed my eyes, and clenched my teeth as firmly as if they were screwed in a vice. At last the dreaded moment came, and the first swing of the bell extorted a groan from me, as they say the most resolute victim screams at the sight of the rack, to which he is for a second time destined. After this, however, I lay silent and lethargic, without a thought. Wrapped in the defensive armour of stupidity, I defied the bell and its intonations. When it ceased, I was roused a little by the hope of escape. I did not, however, decide on this step hastily but, putting up my hand with the utmost caution, I touched the rim. Though the ringing had ceased, it still was tremulous from the sound, and shook under my hand, which instantly recoiled as from an electric jar. A quarter of an hour probably elapsed before I again dared to make the experiment, and then I found it at rest. I determined to lose no time, fearing that I might have lain then already too long, and that the bell for evening service would catch me. This dread stimulated me, and I slipped out with the utmost rapidity, and arose. I stood, I suppose, for a minute, looking with silly wonder on the place of my imprisonment, penetrated with joy at escaping, but then rushed down the stony and irregular stair with the velocity of lightning, and arrived in the bellringer's room. This was the last act I had power to accomplish. I leant against the wall, motionless and deprived of thought, in which posture my companions found me when, in the course of a couple of hours, they returned to their occupation.

They were shocked, as well they might be, at the figure before them. The wind of the bell had excoriated my face, and my dim and stupefied eyes were fixed with a lack-lustre gaze in my raw eyelids. My hands were torn and bleeding, my hair dishevelled, and my clothes tattered. They spoke to me, but I gave no answer. They shook me, but I remained insensible. They then became alarmed, and hastened to remove me. He who had first gone up with me in the forenoon, met them as they carried me through the churchyard, and through him, who was shocked at having, in some measure, occasioned the accident, the cause of my misfortune was discovered. I was put to bed at home, and remained for three days delirious, but gradually recovered my senses. You may be sure the bell formed a prominent topic of my ravings, and if I heard a peal, they were instantly increased to the utmost violence. Even when the delirium abated, my sleep was continually disturbed by imagined ringings, and my dreams were haunted by the fancies which almost maddened me while in the steeple. My friends removed me to a house in the country, which was sufficiently distant from any place of worship, to save me from the apprehensions of hearing the church-going bell; for what Alexander Selkirk, in Cowper's poem, complained of as a misfortune, was then to me as a blessing. Here I recovered; but, even long after recovery, if a gale wafted the notes of a peal towards me, I started with nervous apprehension. I felt a Mahometan hatred to all the bell tribe, and envied the subjects of the Commander of the Faithful the sonorous voice of their

Muezzin. Time cured this, as it does the most of our follies; but, even at the present day, if, by chance, my nerves be unstrung, some particular tones of the cathedral bell have power to surprise me into a momentary start.

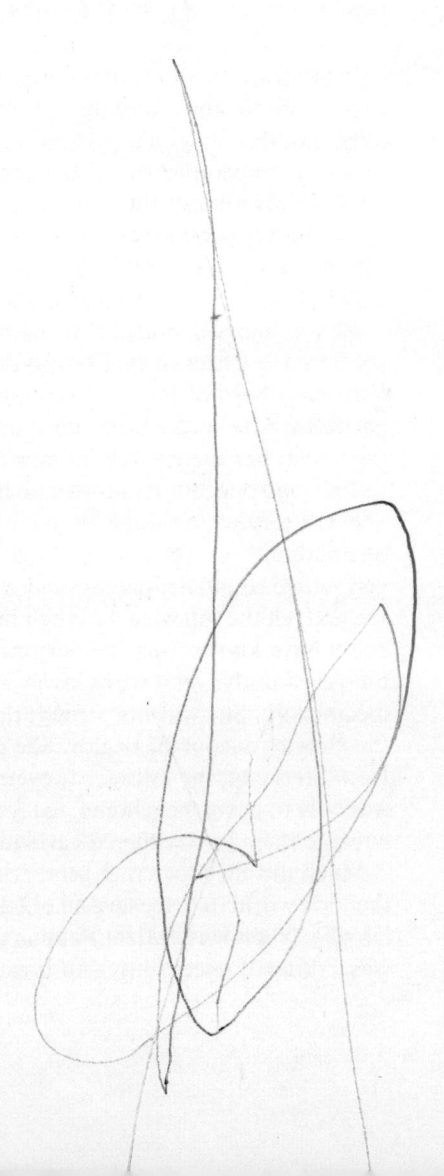

THE DEAD DAUGHTER

Henry Glassford Bell

THE BUILDING WAS a solitary one, and had a cold and forbidding aspect. Its tenant, Adolphus Walstein, was a man whom few liked: not that they charged him with any crime, but he was of an unsocial temperament; and ever since he came to the neighbourhood, thinly inhabited as it was, he had contracted no friendship, formed no acquaintance. He seemed fond of wandering among the mountains; and his house stood far up in one of the wild valleys formed by the Rhaetian Alps, which intersect Bohemia.

He was married, and his wife had once been beautiful. She even yet bore the traces of that beauty, though somewhat faded. She must have been of high birth too, for her features and gait were patrician. She spoke little; but you could not look on her and fancy that her silence was for lack of thought.

They had one only child—a daughter—a pale but beautiful girl. She was very young—not yet in her teens—but the natural mirth of childhood characterized her not. It seemed as if the gloom that had settled round her parents had affected her too; it seemed as if she had felt the full weight of their misfortunes, almost before she could have known what misfortune was. She smiled sometimes, but very faintly; yet it was a lovely smile—more lovely that it was melancholy. She was not strong; there was in her limbs none of the glowing vigour of health. She cared not for sporting in the fresh breeze on the hillside. If ever she gathered wild flowers, it was only to bring them home, to lay them in her mother's lap, and wreathe them into withered garlands.

Much did they love that gentle child: they had nothing else in the wide world to love, save an old domestic, and a huge Hungarian dog. Yet it was evident Paulina could not live; at least her life was a thing of uncertainty—of breathless hope and fear. She was

THE DEAD DAUGHTER

tall beyond her years; but she was fragile as the stalk of the white-crowned lily. She was very like her mother; though there was at times a shade upon her brow that reminded you strongly of the darker countenance of her father. It was said, that when he took his gun, and went out all day in search of the red deer, far up among the rocky heights, he would forget his purpose for hours, and seating himself upon some Alpine promontory, would gaze upon his lonely house in the valley below, till the sun went down in the stormy west; and as evening drew on, and a single light faintly glimmered from one of the windows of his mansion, he has brushed a hot tear from his eye, and started into recollection. It was dark ere he came home, and the winds howled drearily. In their sitting room—a room but barely furnished—he found his wife plying her needle beside the lamp, and at a little distance the dying flame of the wood fire threw its ghastly flickerings on the pale face of his daughter. He stood at the door, and leant upon his gun in silence. They knew his mood, and were silent also. His eye was fixed upon his daughter; she would have fascinated yours too. *It was no common countenance.* Not that any individual feature could have been singled out as peculiar, but the general expression was such as, once seen, haunted the memory for ever. Perhaps it was the black eye—blacker than the ebon hair—contrasted with the deadly paleness of her white-rose cheek. It was deep sunk, too, under her brow. But it is needless to form conjectures: none knew in what that expression originated—there was a mystery in it. She had a long thin arm, and tapering fingers, and a hand crossed by many a blue vein. Its touch was in general thrillingly cold, yet at times it was feverishly hot. Her mother had borne many a child, but all died in early infancy. Yet her father's fondest wish was to see a son rising by his side into manhood; nor did he despair of having the wish gratified. It was said his dying commands would have given that son much to do.

Paulina was now thirteen; but the canker was busy within, and even her mother saw at last that she, too, was to be taken from her. It was a stern dispensation; the only child of her heart—the only one whom her sleepless care had been able to fence in from the grasp of the spoiler—her meditation and her dream for thirteen years—the one only sad sunbeam whose watery and uncertain ray lighted up their solitude. But evil had followed them as a doom, nor was that doom yet completed.

She died upon an autumn evening. She had been growing weaker for many a day, and they saw it, but spoke not of it. Nor did she; it seemed almost a pain for her to speak; and when she did, it was in a low soft tone, inaudible almost to all but the ear of affection. Yet was the mind within her busy with all the restless activity of feverish reverie. She had strange daydreams; and life and the distant world often flashed upon her in far more than the brightness of reality. Often, too, all faded away; and though her eyes were still open, darkness fell around her, and she dwelt among the mysteries and immaterial shapes of some shadowy realm. It would be fearful to know all that passed in the depth of that lonely girl's spirit. It was an autumn evening—sunny, but not beautiful—silent, but not serene. She had walked to the brook that came down the mountains, and which formed a pool and babbling cascade not a stone-cast from the door. Perhaps she grew suddenly faint; for her mother, who stood at the window, saw her coming more hastily than usual across the field. She went to meet her; she was within arm's length, when her daughter gave a faint moan, and, falling forward, twined her cold arms round her mother's neck, and looked up into her face with a look of agony. It was only for a moment; her dark eye became fixed—it grew white with the whiteness of death, and the mother carried her child's body into its desolate home.

If her father wept—it was at night when there was no eye to see. The Hungarian dog howled over the dead body of its young mistress, and the old domestic sat by the unkindled hearth, and wept as for her own firstborn; but the father loaded his gun, as was his wont, and went away among the mountains.

The priests came, and the coffin, and a few of the simple peasants. She was carried forth from her chamber, and her father followed. The procession winded down the valley. The tinkling of the holy bell mingled sadly with the funeral chant. At last the little train disappeared; for the churchyard was among the hills, some miles distant. The mother was left alone. She fell upon her knees, and lifted up her eyes and her clasped hands to her God, and prayed—fervently prayed, from the depths of her soul—that he might never curse her with another child. The prayer was almost impious; but she was frantic in her deep despair, and we dare not judge her.

A year has passed away, and that lonely house is still in the Bohemian valley, and its friendless inmates haunt it still. Walstein's wife bears him another child, and hope almost beats again in his bosom, as he asks, with somewhat of a father's pride, if he has now a son. But the child was a daughter, and his hopes were left unfulfilled. They christened the infant Paulina; and many a long day and dreary night did its mother hang over its cradle, and shed tears of bitterness, as she thought of her who lay unconscious in the churchyard away among the hills. The babe grew, but not in the rosiness of health. Yet it seldom suffered from acute pain; and when it wept, it was with a kind of suppressed grief, that seemed almost unnatural to one so young. It was long ere it could walk; when at last it did, it was without any previous effort.

Time passed on without change and without incident. Paulina was ten years old. Often had Philippa, with maternal fondness, pointed out to her husband the resemblance which she alleged existed between their surviving child and her whom they had laid in the grave. Walstein, as he listened to his wife, fixed his dark penetrating eye upon his daughter, and spoke not. The resemblance was, indeed, a striking one—it was almost supernatural. She was the same tall pale girl, with black, deep sunk eyes, and long dark ebon hair. Her arms and hands were precisely of the same mould, and they had the same thrilling coldness in their touch. Her manners, too, her disposition, the sound of her voice, her motions, her habits, and, above all, her expression of countenance—that characteristic and indescribable expression—were the very same. Her mother loved to dwell upon this resemblance; but her father, though he gazed and gazed upon her, yet ever and anon started, and walked with hasty strides across the room, and sometimes, even at night, rushed out into the darkness, as one oppressed with wild and fearful fancies.

They had few of the comforts, and none of the luxuries of life, in that Bohemian valley. Philippa had carefully laid aside all the clothes that belonged to her dead daughter; and now that the last child of her age was growing up, and was so like her that was gone, she loved to dress her sometimes in her sister's dress; and the pale child wore the clothes, and talked of the lost Paulina, almost as if she had known her.

One night her mother plied her needle beside her lamp, and at a little distance her daughter, in a simple white dress, which had once been another's, sat musing over the red embers of a dying fire. A thunderstorm was gathering, and the rain was already falling heavily. Walstein entered; his eye rested on his daughter, and he almost shrieked; but he recovered himself, and with a quivering lip sat down in a distant corner of the room. His Hungarian dog was with him; it seemed to have caught the direction of his master's eye, and as its own rested keenly on Paulina, the animal uttered a low growl. It was strange that the dog never seemed to love the child. It is probable that she was hardly aware of her father's entrance, for she appeared absorbed in her own thoughts. As the blue and flickering flame fell upon her face, she smiled faintly.

"O God! it is! it is!" cried Walstein, and fell senseless on the floor.

His wife and daughter hurried to his assistance, and he recovered; but he pointed to Paulina, and said falteringly, "Philippa! send *her* to bed." With a quiet step, his daughter moved across the room; at the door, she was about to kiss her mother, but Walstein thundered out, "Forbear!" and rising, closed the door with trembling violence. Philippa had often seen her husband in his wilder moods, but seldom thus strangely agitated; yet, had she known the conviction that had arisen in his mind, she would have ceased to wonder.

He had watched long and narrowly, and now he was unable to

conceal longer from himself the fearful truth. It was not in her wan beauty alone that she resembled her sister—it was not merely in the external development of her form; he knew, he felt, that the second Paulina, born after her sister's death, was *the same Paulina as she whom he had laid in the grave.* There was horror in the idea, yet could it not be resisted. But even now he breathed it not to his wife, and silently they passed to their chamber. The secret of his soul, however, which he would never have told her by day and awake, the wretched Philippa gathered from him in his unconscious mutterings in the dead watches of the night. When the thought came upon her, it fell upon her heart like a weight of lead. Her maternal affection struggled with it, and with the thousand proofs that came crowding of themselves into her memory, to strengthen and to rivet it, and the struggle almost overturned her reason.

The Paulina, in whom her heart was wrapped up twelve years ago, had frequently dreams of a mysterious meaning, which she used to repeat to her mother when no one else was by. A few days after the occurrences of the evening to which we have alluded, the living child, who had come in the place of the dead, told Philippa she had dreamt a dream. She recited it, and Philippa shuddered to hear an exact repetition of one she well remembered listening to long ago, and which she had ever since locked up in her own bosom. Even in sleep, it seemed that, by some awful mystery, Paulina was living over again.

Time still passed on, and the pale child shot up into a girl. She was thirteen; though a stranger would have thought her some years older. It was manifest that she, too, was dying. (There was a dismal doubt haunted her father's mind whether she had ever lived.) She never spoke of her deceased sister; indeed, she seldom spoke at all; but when they asked if she were well, she shook her head, and stretched an arm towards the churchyard.

To that churchyard her father went one moonlight night. It was a wild fancy, yet he resolved to open his daughter's grave, and look once more upon her mouldering remains. He had a reason for his curiosity, which he scarcely dared own even to himself. He told the sexton of his purpose; and, though the old man guessed not his object, he took his spade and his pickaxe, and speedily commenced his task. It was an uncertain night. The wind came in gusts, and sometimes died away into strange silence. The dim moonlight fell upon the white tomb-stones, and the shadows of the passing clouds glided over them like spirits. The sexton pursued his work, and had already dug deep. Walstein stood by his side.

"I have not come to the coffin yet," said the old man, in a tone bordering upon wonder; "yet I could tell the very spot blindfold in which I put it with these hands thirteen years ago."

"Dig on, for the love of Heaven!" said Walstein, and his heart began to beat audibly. There was a short pause.

"My digging is of no use," said the sexton. "I am past the place where I laid the coffin; and may the Holy Virgin protect me, for there is not a vestige either of it or the body left."

Walstein groaned convulsively, and leapt into the grave, but in vain; the sexton had reported truly. He had just stepped up again into the moonlight, when a cold hand was laid upon his shoulder. He started, and turning round, saw that his daughter stood beside him.

"Paulina! Just Heaven! what can have brought you so far from home? at night, too, and weak as you are? it will be your destruction."

She took no notice of the question, but fixing her quiet look upon the grave, she said, "Father, I shall soon lie there."

It was the thirteenth anniversary of Paulina's death, and the swollen brook was brawling hoarsely down the mountains, for a tempestuous autumn had already anticipated winter. The shutters of the upper chamber were closed, and Philippa sat by the sickbed of her last child. The sufferer raised her pale and languid head, and whilst her dark eye appeared to wander in the delirium of fever, she said, with a struggle, "Mother, is it not a mysterious imagination—but I feel as if I had lived before, and that my thoughts were happier and better than they are now?" Philippa shuddered, and gazed almost with terror upon her child. "It is a dream, Paulina; one of the waking dreams of over-watchfulness. Be still, sweet girl; an hour's sleep will refresh you." As she spoke, Paulina *did* sleep, but there was little to refresh in such slumber. Her whole frame was agitated convulsively; her bosom heaved with unnatural beating; her hands alternately grasped the coverlet, as if to tear it into shreds, and were ever and anon lifted up to her head, where her fingers twined themselves among the tresses of her ebon hair; her lips moved incessantly; her teeth chattered; her breath came short and thick, as if it would have made itself palpable to the senses. Terrible gibberings succeeded, and her poor mother knew that the moment of dissolution was at hand. In an instant all was still—the grasp of the hand was relaxed—the heaving and the beating ceased—the lips were open, but the breath of life that had ebbed and flowed between them had finished its task, and was gone; a damp distillation stood upon the brow—it was the last sign of agony which expiring nature gave.

That night Walstein dreamed a dream. Paulina, wrapped in her winding sheet, stood opposite his couch. Her face was pale and beautiful as in life, but under the folds of her shroud he discovered the hideous form of a skeleton. The vision became double: a grave opened as if spontaneously, and another Paulina burst the cerements asunder, and looked with her dead eye full upon her father. Walstein trembled, and awoke. A strange light glanced under his chamber door. Who was there stirring at that dead hour of night? He threw the curtains aside. The moon was still up; an indescribable impulse urged him to rush towards the room in which the body of his daughter lay. He passed along the lobby; the door of the chamber was open; the Hungarian dog lay dead at the threshold; *the corpse was gone.*

A DREAM

Edgar Allan Poe

A FEW EVENINGS since, I laid myself down for my night's repose. It has been a custom with me, for years past, to peruse a portion of the Scriptures before I close my eyes in the slumbers of night. I did so in the present instance. By chance, I fell upon the spot where inspiration has recorded the dying agonies of the God of Nature. Thoughts of these, and the scenes which followed his giving up the ghost, pursued me as I slept.

There is certainly something mysterious and incomprehensible in the manner in which the wild vagaries of the imagination often arrange themselves; but the solution of this belongs to the physiologist rather than the reckless dreamer.

It seemed that I was some Pharisee, returning from the scene of death. I had assisted in driving the sharpest nails through the palms of Him who hung on the cross, a spectacle of the bitterest woe that mortality ever felt. I could hear the groan that ran through his soul, as the rough iron grated on the bones when I drove it through.

I retired a few steps from the place of execution, and turned round to look at my bitterest enemy. The Nazarene was not yet dead: the life lingered in the mantle of clay, as if it shuddered to walk alone through the valley of death. I thought I could see the cold damp that settles on the brow of the dying, now standing in large drops on His. I could see each muscle quiver—the eye, that began to lose its lustre, in the hollow stare of the corpse. I could hear the low gurgle in his throat. A moment—and the chain of existence was broken, and a link dropped into eternity.

I turned away, and wandered listlessly on, till I came to the centre of Jerusalem. At a short distance rose the lofty turrets of the Temple, its golden roof reflected rays as bright as the source from which they emanated. A feeling of conscious pride stole over me, as I looked over the broad fields and lofty mountains which surrounded this pride of the eastern world. On my right rose Mount Olivet, covered with shrubbery and vineyards; beyond that, and bounding the skirts of mortal vision, appeared mountains piled on mountains; on the left were the lovely plains of Judea; and I thought it was a bright picture of human existence, as I saw the little brook Cedron speeding its way through the meadows, to the distant lake. I could hear the gay song of the beauteous maiden, as she gleaned in the distant harvest field; and, mingling with the echoes of the mountain, was heard the shrill whistle of the shepherd's pipe, as he called the wandering lamb to its fold. A perfect loveliness had thrown itself over animated nature.

But "a change soon came o'er the spirit of my dream." I felt a sudden coldness creeping over me. I instinctively turned towards the sun, and saw a hand slowly drawing a mantle of crape over it. I looked for stars, but each one had ceased to twinkle—for the same hand had enveloped them in the badge of mourning. The silver light of the moon did not dawn on the sluggish waves of the Dead Sea, as they sang the hoarse requiem of the Cities of the Plain; but she hid her face, as if shuddering to look on what was doing on the earth. I heard a muttered groan, as the spirit of darkness spread his pinions over an astonished world.

Unutterable despair now seized me. I could feel the flood of life slowly rolling back to its fountain, as the fearful thought stole over me, that the day of retribution had come.

Suddenly, I stood before the Temple. The veil, which had hid its secrets from unhallowed gaze, was now rent. I looked for a moment: the priest was standing by the altar, offering up the expiatory sacrifice. The fire, which was to kindle the mangled limbs of the victim, gleamed for a moment on the distant walls, and then was lost in utter darkness. He turned around, to rekindle it from the living fire of the candlestick; but that, too, was gone. It was still as the sepulchre.

I turned and rushed into the street. The street was vacant. No sound broke the stillness, except the yell of the wild dog, who revelled on the half-burnt corpse in the Valley of Hinnom. I saw a light stream from a distant window, and made my way towards it. I looked in at the open door. A widow was preparing the last morsel she could glean for her dying babe. She had kindled a little fire; and I saw with what utter hopelessness of heart she beheld the flame sink away, like her own dying hopes.

Darkness covered the universe. Nature mourned, for its parent had died. The earth had enrobed herself in the habiliments of sorrow, and the heavens were clothed in the sables of mourning. I now roamed in restlessness, and heeded not whither I went. At once there appeared a light in the east. A column of light shot athwart the gloom, like the light-shot gleams on the darkness of the midnight of the pit, and illuminated the sober murkiness that surrounded me. There was an opening in the vast arch of heaven's broad expanse. With wondering eyes, I turned towards it.

Far into the wilderness of space, and at a distance that can only be meted by a "line running parallel with eternity", but still awfully plain and distinct, appeared the same person whom I had clothed with the mock purple of royalty. He was now garmented in the robe of the King of Kings. He sat on his throne: but it was not one of whiteness. There was mourning in heaven; for, as each angel knelt before him, I saw that the wreath of immortal amaranth which circled his brow was changed for one of cypress.

I turned to see whither I had wandered. I had come to the burial ground of the monarchs of Israel. I gazed with trembling limbs, as I saw the clods which covered the mouldering bones of some tyrant begin to move. I looked at where the last monarch had been laid, in all the splendour and pageantry of death, and the sculptured monument began to tremble. Soon it was overturned, and from it issued the tenant of the grave. It was a hideous, unearthly form, such as Dante, in his wildest flights of terrified fancy, never conjured up. I could not move, for terror had tied up volition. It approached me.

I saw the grave-worm twining itself amongst the matted locks which in part covered the rotten skull. The bones creaked on each other as they moved on the hinges, for its flesh was gone. I listened to their horrid music, as this parody on poor mortality stalked along. He came up to me; and, as he passed, he breathed the cold damps of the lonely, narrow house directly in my face.

The chasm in the heavens closed; and, with a convulsive shudder, I awoke.

THE JOURNAL OF JULIUS RODMAN
Being an Account of the First Passage across the Rocky Mountains of North America ever Achieved by Civilised Man

Edgar Allan Poe

I

AFTER THE DEATH of my father, and both sisters, I took no further interest in our plantation at the Point, and sold it, at a complete sacrifice, to M. Junôt. I had often thought of trapping up the Missouri, and resolved now to go on an expedition up that river, and try to procure peltries, which I was sure of being able to sell at Petite Côte to the private agents of the Northwest Fur Company. I believed that much more property might be acquired in this way, with a little enterprise and courage, than I could make by any other means. I had always been fond, too, of hunting and trapping, although I had never made a business of either, and I had a great desire to explore some portion of our western country, about which Pierre Junôt had often spoken to me. He was the eldest son of the neighbour who bought me out, and was a man of strange manners and somewhat eccentric turn of mind, but still one of the best-hearted fellows in the world, and certainly as courageous a man as ever drew breath, although of no great bodily strength. He was of Canadian descent, and having gone, once or twice, on short excursions for the Fur Company, in which he had acted as *voyageur*, was fond of calling himself one, and of talking about his trips. My father had been very fond of Pierre, and I thought a good deal of him myself; he was a great favourite, too, with my younger sister, Jane, and I believe they would have been married had it been God's will to have spared her.

When Pierre discovered that I had not entirely made up my

THE JOURNAL OF JULIUS RODMAN

mind what course to pursue after my father's death, he urged me to fit out a small expedition for the river, in which he would accompany me; and he had no difficulty in bringing me over to his wishes. We agreed to push up the Missouri as long as we found it possible, hunting and trapping as we went, and not to return until we had secured as many peltries as would be a fortune for us both. His father made no objection and gave him about three hundred dollars; then we proceeded to Petite Côte for the purpose of getting our equipments, and raising as many men as we could for the voyage.

Petite Côte* is a small place on the north bank of the Missouri, about twenty miles from its junction with the Mississippi. It lies at the foot of a range of low hills, and upon a sort of ledge, high enough above the river to be out of the reach of the June freshets. There are not more than five or six houses, and these of wood, in the upper part of the place; but, nearer to the east, there is a chapel and twelve or fifteen good dwellings, running parallel with the river. There are about a hundred inhabitants, mostly Creoles of Canadian descent. They are extremely indolent, and make no attempt at cultivating the country around them, which is a rich soil, except now and then when a little is done in the way of gardening. They live principally by hunting, and trading with the Indians for peltries, which they sell again to the Northwest Company's agents. We expected to meet with no difficulty here in getting recruits for our journey, or equipments, but were disappointed in both particulars; for the place was too poor in every respect to furnish all that we wanted, so as to render our voyage safe and efficient.

We designed to pass through the heart of a country infested with Indian tribes, of whom we knew nothing except by vague report, and whom we had every reason to believe ferocious and treacherous. It was therefore particularly necessary that we should go well provided with arms and ammunition, as well as in some force as regards numbers; and if our voyage was to be

*Now St Charles.

a source of profit, we must take with us canoes of sufficient capacity to bring home what peltries we might collect. It was the middle of March when we first reached Petite Côte, and we did not succeed in getting ready until the last of May. We had to send twice down the river to the Point for men and supplies, and neither could be obtained except at great cost. We should have failed at last in getting many things absolutely requisite, if it had not so happened that Pierre met with a party on its return from a trip up the Mississippi, and engaged six of its best men, besides a canoe, or piroque, purchasing, at the same time, most of the surplus stores and ammunition.

This seasonable aid enabled us to get fairly ready for the voyage before the first of June. On the third of this month (1791) we bade adieu to our friends at Petite Côte, and started on our expedition. Our party consisted in all of fifteen persons. Of these, five were Canadians from Petite Côte, and had all been on short excursions up the river. They were good boatmen, and excellent companions, as far as singing French songs went, and drinking, at which they were pre-eminent; although, in truth, it was a rare thing to see any of them so far the worse for liquor as to be incapable of attending to duty. They were always in a good humour, and always ready to work; but as hunters I did not think them worth much, and as fighting men I soon discovered they were not to be depended upon. There were two of these five Canadians who engaged to act as interpreters for the first five or six hundred miles up the river (should we proceed so far), and then we hoped to procure an Indian occasionally to interpret, should it be necessary; but we had resolved to avoid, as far as possible, any meetings with the Indians, and rather to trap ourselves than run the great risk of trading, with so small a party as we numbered. It was our policy to proceed with the greatest caution, and expose ourselves to notice only when we could not avoid it.

The six men whom Pierre had engaged from aboard the return Mississippi boat were as different a set from the Canadians as could well be imagined. Five of them were brothers, by the name of Greely (John, Robert, Meredith, Frank and Poindexter), and bolder or finer looking persons it would have been difficult to find. John Greely was the eldest and stoutest of the five, and had the reputation of being the strongest man, as well as best shot, in Kentucky, from which State they all came. He was full six feet in height, and of most extraordinary breadth across the shoulders, with large strongly-knit limbs. Like most men of great physical strength, he was exceedingly good-tempered, and on this account was greatly beloved by us all. The other four brothers were all strong, well-built men too, although not to be compared with John. Poindexter was as tall, but very gaunt, and of a singularly fierce appearance; but, like his elder brother, he was of peaceable demeanour. All of them were experienced hunters and capital shots. They had gladly accepted Pierre's offer to go with us, and we made an arrangement with them which ensured them an equal share with Pierre and myself in the profits of the enterprise; that is to say, we divided the proceeds into three parts, one of which was to be mine, one Pierre's, and one shared among the five brothers.

The sixth man whom we enlisted from the return boat was also a good recruit. His name was Alexander Wormley, a Virginian, and a very strange character. He had originally been a preacher of the gospel, and had afterwards fancied himself a prophet, going about the country with a long beard and hair, and in his bare feet, haranguing everyone he met. This hallucination was now diverted into another channel, and he thought of nothing else than of finding gold mines in some of the fastnesses of the country. Upon this subject he was as entirely mad as any man could well be; but upon all others was remarkably sensible and even acute. He was a good boatman and a good hunter, and as brave a fellow as ever stepped, besides being of great bodily strength and swiftness of foot. I counted much upon this recruit, on account of his enthusiastic character, and in the end I was not deceived, as will appear.

Our other two recruits were a negro belonging to Pierre Junôt, named Toby, and a stranger whom we had picked up in the woods near Mill's Point, and who joined our expedition upon the instant as soon as we mentioned our design. His name was Andrew Thornton, also a Virginian, and I believe of excellent family, belonging to the Thorntons of the northern part of the State. He had been from Virginia about three years; during the whole of which time he had been rambling about the western country, with no other companion than a large dog of the Newfoundland species. He had collected no peltries, and did not seem to have any object in view, more than the gratification of a roving and adventurous propensity. He frequently amused us, when sitting around our camp fires at night, with the relation of his adventures and hardships in the wilderness, recounting them with a straightforward earnestness which left us no room to doubt their truth; although, indeed, many of them had a marvellous air. Experience afterwards taught us that the dangers and difficulties of the solitary hunter can scarcely be exaggerated, and that the real task is to depict them to the hearer in sufficiently distinct colours. I took a great liking to Thornton, from the first hour in which I saw him.

I have only said a few words respecting Toby; but he was not the least important personage of our party. He had been in old M. Junôt's family for a great number of years, and had proved himself a faithful negro. He was rather too old to accompany such an expedition as ours; but Pierre was not willing to leave him. He was an able-bodied man, however, and still capable of enduring great fatigue. Pierre himself was probably the feeblest of our whole company, as regards bodily strength, but he possessed great sagacity, and a courage which nothing could daunt. His manners were sometimes extravagant and boisterous, which led him to get into frequent quarrels, and had once or twice seriously endangered the success of our expedition; but he was a true friend, and in that one point I considered him invaluable.

I have now given a brief account of all our party, as it was when we left Petite Côte.* To carry ourselves and accoutrements, as

---

*Mr Rodman has not given any description of himself; and the account of his party is by no means complete without a portraiture of its leader. "He was about twenty-five years of age," says Mr James Rodman in a memorandum now before us, "when he started up the river. He was a remarkably vigorous and active man,

well as to bring home what peltries might be obtained, we had two large boats. The smallest of these was a piroque made of birch bark, sewed together with the fibres of the roots of the spruce tree, the seams payed with pine resin, and the whole so light that six men could carry it with ease. It was twenty feet long, and could be rowed with from four to twelve oars; drawing about eighteen inches water when loaded to the gunwale and, when empty, not more than ten. The other was a keel-boat which we had made at Petite Côte (the canoe having been purchased by Pierre from the Mississippi party). It was thirty feet long, and, when loaded to the gunwale, drew two feet of water. It had a deck twenty feet of its length forward, forming a cuddy-cabin, with a strong door, and of sufficient dimensions to contain our whole party with close crowding, as the boat was very broad. This part of it was bullet-proof, being wadded with oakum between two coatings of oak-plank; and in several positions we had small holes bored, through which we could fire upon an enemy in case of attack, as well as observe their movements; these holes, at the same time, gave us air and light, when we closed the door; and we had secure plugs to fit them when necessary. The remaining ten feet of the length was open, and here we could use as many as six oars; but our main dependence was upon poles which we employed by walking along the deck. We had also a short mast, easily shipped and unshipped, which was stepped about seven feet from the bow, and upon which we set a large square sail when the wind was fair, taking in mast and all when it was ahead.

In a division made in the bow, under the deck, we deposited ten kegs of good powder, and as much lead as we considered proportionate, one tenth ready moulded in rifle bullets. We had also stowed away here a small brass cannon and carriage, dismounted and taken to pieces, so as to lie in little compass, thinking that such a means of defence might possibly come into play at some period of our expedition. This cannon was one of three which

---

but short in stature, not being more than five feet three or four inches high; strongly built, with legs somewhat bowed. His physiognomy was of a Jewish cast, his lips thin, and his complexion saturnine."

had been brought down the Missouri by the Spaniards two years previously, and lost overboard from a piroque, some miles above Petite Côte. A sand bar had so far altered the channel at the place where the canoe capsized that an Indian discovered one of the guns, and procured assistance to carry it down to the settlement, where he sold it for a gallon of whiskey. The people at Petite Côte then went up and procured the other two. They were very small guns, but of good metal and beautiful workmanship, being carved and ornamented with serpents like some of the French fieldpieces. Fifty iron balls were found with the guns, and these we procured. I mention the way in which we obtained this cannon, because it performed an important part in some of our operations, as will be found hereafter. Besides it, we had fifteen spare rifles, boxed up, and deposited forward with the other heavy goods. We put the weight here, to sink our bows well in the water, which is the best method, on account of the snags and sawyers in the river.

In the way of other arms we were sufficiently provided; each man having a stout hatchet and knife, besides his ordinary rifle and ammunition. Each boat was provided with a camp kettle, three large axes, a towing line, two oilcloths to cover the goods when necessary, and two large sponges for bailing. The piroque had also a small mast and sail (which I omitted to mention), and carried a quantity of gum, birchbark and watape, to make repairs with. She also had in charge all the Indian goods which we had thought necessary to bring with us, and which we purchased from the Mississippi boat. It was not our design to trade with the Indians; but these goods were offered us at a low rate, and we thought it better to take them, as they might prove of service. They consisted of silk and cotton handkerchiefs; thread, lines, and twine; hats, shoes, and hose; small cutlery and ironmongery; calicoes and printed cottons; Manchester goods; twist and carrot tobacco; milled blankets; and glass toys, beads, etc., etc. All these were done up in small packages, three of which were a man's load. The provisions were also put up so as to be easily handled; and a part was deposited in each boat. We had, altogether, two hundredweight of pork, six hundredweight of biscuit, and six hundredweight of pemmican. This we had made at Petite Côte, by the Canadians, who told us that it is used by the Northwest Fur Company in all their long voyages, when it is feared that game may not prove abundant. It is manufactured in a singular manner. The lean parts of the flesh of the larger animals is cut into thin slices, and placed on a wooden grate over a slow fire, or exposed to the sun (as ours was), or sometimes to the frost. When it is sufficiently dried in this way, it is pounded between two heavy stones, and will then keep for years. If, however, much of it is kept together, it ferments upon the breaking up of the frost in the spring and, if not well exposed to the air, soon decays. The inside fat, with that of the rump, is melted down and mixed, in a boiling state, with the pounded meat, half and half; it is then squeezed into bags, and is ready to eat without any further cooking, being very palatable without salt or vegetables. The best pemmican is made with the addition of marrow and dried berries, and is a capital article of food.* Our whiskey was in carboys, of five gallons each, and we had twenty of these, a hundred gallons in all.

When everything was well on board, with our whole company, including Thornton's dog, we found that there was but little room to spare, except in the big cabin, which we wished to preserve free of goods, as a sleeping place in bad weather; we had nothing in here except arms and ammunition, with some beaver traps and a carpet of bearskins. Our crowded state suggested an expedient which ought to have been adopted at all events: that of detaching four hunters from the party, to course along the river banks, and

---

*The pemmican here described by Mr Rodman is altogether new to us, and is very different from that with which our readers have no doubt been familiarized in the journals of Parry, Ross, Back, and other Northern voyagers. This, if we remember, was prepared by long continued boiling of the lean meat (carefully excluding fat) until the soup was reduced to a very small proportion of its original bulk, and assumed a pulpy consistency. To this residue, many spices and much salt were added, and great nutriment was supposed to be contained in the little bulk. The positive experience of an American surgeon, however, who had an opportunity of witnessing, and experimenting upon, the digestive process through an open wound in the stomach of a patient, has demonstrated that *bulk* is, in itself, an essential in this process, and that consequently the condensation of the nutritive property of food involves, in a great measure, a paradox.

keep us in game, as well as to act in capacity of scouts, to warn us of the approach of Indians. With this object we procured two good horses, giving one of them in charge of Robert and Meredith Greely, who were to keep upon the south bank; and the other in charge of Frank and Poindexter Greely, who were to course along the north side. By means of the horses they could bring in what game was shot.

This arrangement relieved our boats very considerably, lessening our number to eleven. In the small boat were two of the men from Petite Côte, with Toby and Pierre Junôt. In the large one were the Prophet (as we called him), or Alexander Wormley, John Greely, Andrew Thornton, three of the Petite Côte men, and myself, with Thornton's dog.

Our mode of proceeding was sometimes with oars, but not generally; we most frequently pulled ourselves along by the limbs of trees on shore; or, where the ground permitted it, we used a tow-line, which is the easiest way, some of us being on shore to haul, while some remained on board, to set the boat off shore with poles. Very often we poled together. In this method (which is a good one when the bottom is not too muddy, or full of quicksands, and when the depth of water is not too great) the Canadians are very expert, as well as at rowing. They use long, stiff and light poles, pointed with iron; with these they proceed to the bow of the boat, an equal number of men at each side; the face is then turned to the stern, and the pole inserted in the river, reaching the bottom; a firm hold being thus taken, the boatmen apply the heads of the poles to the shoulder, which is protected by a cushion, and, pushing in this manner, while they walk along the gunwale, the boat is urged forward with great force. There is no necessity for any steersman, while using the pole; for the poles direct the vessel with wonderful accuracy.

In these various modes of getting along, now and then varied with the necessity of wading, and dragging our vessels by hand, in rapid currents or through shallow water, we commenced our eventful voyage up the Missouri River. The skins, which were considered as the leading objects of the expedition, were to be obtained, principally, by hunting and trapping, as privately as possible, and without direct trade with the Indians, whom we had long learned to know as in the main a treacherous race, not to be dealt with safely in so small a party as ours. The furs usually collected by previous adventurers upon our contemplated route included beaver, otter, marten, lynx, mink, musquash, bear, fox, kitt-fox, wolverine, raccoon, fisher, wolf, buffalo, deer, and elk; but we proposed to confine ourselves to the more costly kinds.

The morning on which we set out from Petite Côte was one of the most inspiring and delicious; and nothing could exceed the hilarity of our whole party. The summer had hardly yet commenced, and the wind, which blew a strong breeze against us at first starting, had all the voluptuous softness of spring. The sun shone clearly, but with no great heat. The ice had disappeared from the river, and the current, which was pretty full, concealed all those marshy and ragged alluvia which disfigure the borders of the Missouri at low water. It had now the most majestic appearance, washing up among the willows and cottonwood on one side, and rushing, with a bold volume, by the sharp cliffs on the other. As I looked up the stream (which here stretched away to the westward, until the waters apparently met the sky in the great distance) and reflected on the immensity of territory through which those waters had probably passed, a territory as yet altogether unknown to white people, and perhaps abounding in the magnificent works of God, I felt an excitement of soul such as I had never before experienced, and secretly resolved that it should be no slight obstacle which should prevent my pushing up this noble river farther than any previous adventurer had done. At that moment I seemed possessed of an energy more than human, and my animal spirits rose to so high a degree that I could with difficulty content myself in the narrow limits of the boat. I longed to be with the Greelys on the bank, that I might give full vent to the feelings which inspired me, by leaping and running on the prairie. In these feelings Thornton participated strongly, evincing a deep interest in our expedition, and an admiration of the beautiful scenery around us, which rendered him from that moment a particular favourite with myself. I never, at any period of my life, felt so keenly as I then did, the want of some friend to whom I could converse freely and without danger of being misunderstood. The sudden loss of all my relatives by death had saddened, but not depressed, my spirits, which appeared to seek relief in a contemplation of the wild scenes of nature; and these scenes, and the reflections which they encouraged, could not, I found, be thoroughly enjoyed, without the society of some one person of reciprocal sentiments. Thornton was precisely the kind of individual to whom I could unburden my full heart, and unburden it of all its extravagant emotion, without fear of incurring a shadow of ridicule, and even in the certainty of finding a listener as impassioned as myself. I never, before or since, met with any one who so fully entered into my own notions respecting natural scenery; and this circumstance alone was sufficient to bind him to me in a firm friendship. We were as intimate, during our whole expedition, as brothers could possibly be, and I took no steps without consulting him. Pierre and myself were also friends, but there was not the tie of reciprocal thought between us, that strongest of all mortal bonds. His nature, although sensitive, was too volatile to comprehend all the devotional fervour of my own.

The incidents of the first day of our voyage had nothing remarkable in them; except that we had some difficulty in forcing our way, towards nightfall, by the mouth of a large cave on the south side of the river. This cave had a very dismal appearance as we passed it, being situated at the foot of a lofty bluff, full two hundred feet high, and jutting somewhat over the stream. We could not distinctly perceive the depth of the cavern, but it was about sixteen or seventeen feet high, and at least fifty in width.*

---

*The cave here mentioned is that called the "Tavern" by the traders and boatmen. Some grotesque images are painted on the cliffs, and commanded, at one period, great respect from the Indians. In speaking of this cavern, Captain Lewis says that it is 120 feet wide, 20 feet high, and 40 deep, and that the bluffs overhanging it are nearly 300 feet high. We wish to call attention to the circumstance that, in every point, Mr Rodman's account falls short of Captain Lewis's. With all his evident enthusiasm, our traveller is never prone to the exaggeration of facts. In a great variety of instances like the present, it will be found that his statements respecting quantity (in the full sense of the term) always fall within the truth, as this truth is since ascertained. We regard this as a remarkable trait in his

The current ran past it with great velocity and, as from the nature of the cliff we could now tow, it required the utmost exertion to make our way by it; which we at length effected by getting all of us, with the exception of one man, into the large boat. This one remained in the piroque, and anchored it below the cave. By uniting our force, then, in rowing, we brought the large boat up beyond the difficult pass, paying out a line to the piroque as we proceeded, and by this line hauling it up after us, when we had fairly ascended. We passed, during the day, Bonhomme, and Osage Femme rivers, with two small creeks and several islands of little extent. We made about twenty-five miles, notwithstanding the head wind, and encamped at night on the north bank, and at the foot of a rapid called Diable.

June 4. Early this morning, Frank and Poindexter Greely came into our camp with a fat buck, upon which we all breakfasted in high glee, and afterwards pushed on with spirit. At the Diable rapid, the current sets with much force against some rocks which jut out from the south, and render the navigation difficult. A short distance above this we met with several quicksand bars, which put us to trouble; the banks of the river here fall in continually, and, in the process of time, must greatly alter the bed. At eight o'clock we had a fine fresh wind from the eastward, and, with its assistance, made rapid progress, so that by night we had gone perhaps thirty miles, or more. We passed, on the north, the river Du Bois, a creek called Charité,* and several small islands. The river was rising fast as we came to, at night, under a group of cottonwood trees, there being no ground near at hand upon

---

mind; and it is assuredly one which would entitle his observations to the highest credit, when they concern regions about which we know nothing beyond these observations. In all points which relate to effects, on the contrary, Mr Rodman's peculiar temperament leads him into excess. For example, he speaks of the cavern now in question as of a "dismal appearance", and the colouring of his narrative respecting it is derived principally from the sombre hue of his own spirit, at the time of passing the rock. It will be as well to bear these distinctions in mind, as we read his Journal. His facts are never heightened; his impressions from these facts must have, to ordinary perceptions, a tone of exaggeration. Yet there is no falsity in this exaggeration, except in view of a general sentiment upon the thing seen and described. As regards his own mind, the apparent gaudiness of colour is the absolute and only true tint.

*La Charette? Du Bois is no doubt Wood River.

which we were disposed to encamp. It was beautiful weather, and I felt too much excited to sleep; so, asking Thornton to accompany me, I took a stroll into the country, and did not return until nearly daylight. The rest of our crew occupied the cabin, for the first time, and found it quite roomy enough for five or six more persons. They had been disturbed, in the night, by a strange noise overhead, on deck, the origin of which they had not been able to ascertain; as, when some of the party rushed out to see, the disturber had disappeared. From the account given of the noise, I concluded that it must have proceeded from an Indian dog, who had scented our fresh provisions (the buck of yesterday) and was endeavouring to make off with a portion. In this view I felt perfectly satisfied; but the occurrence suggested the great risk we ran in not posting a regular watch at night, and it was agreed to do so for the future.

[Having thus given, in Mr Rodman's own words, the incidents of the two first days of the voyage, we forbear to follow him minutely in his passage up the Missouri to the mouth of the Platte, at which he arrived on the 10th of August. The character of the river throughout this extent is so well known, and has been so frequently described, that any further account of it is unnecessary; and the Journal takes note of little else, at this portion of the tour, than the natural features of the country, together with the ordinary boating and hunting occurrences. The party made three several halts for the purpose of trapping, but met with no great success; and finally concluded to push farther into the heart of the country, before making any regular attempts at collecting peltries. Only two events of moment are recorded, for the two months which we omit. One of these was the death of a Canadian, Jacques Lauzanne, by the bite of a rattlesnake; the other was the encountering of a Spanish commission sent to intercept and turn the party back, by order of the commandant of the province. The officer in charge of the detachment, however, was so much interested in the expedition, and took so great a fancy to Mr Rodman, that our travellers were permitted to proceed. Many small bodies of Osage and Kanzas Indians hovered occasionally about the boats, but evinced nothing of hostility. We leave the voyagers for the present, therefore, at the mouth of the river Platte, on the 10th of August 1791, their number having been reduced to fourteen.]

II

[HAVING REACHED the mouth of the river Platte, our voyagers encamped for three days, during which they were busily occupied in drying and airing their goods and provisions, making new oars and poles, and repairing the birch canoe, which had sustained material injury. The hunters brought in an abundance of game, with which the boats were loaded to repletion. Deer was had for the asking, and turkeys and fat grouse were met with in great plenty. The party, moreover, regaled on several species of fish, and, at a short distance from the river banks, found an exquisite kind of wild grape. No Indians had been seen for better than a fortnight, as this was the hunting season, and they were doubtless engaged in the prairies, taking buffalo. After perfectly recruiting, the voyagers broke up their encampment, and pushed on up the Missouri. We resume the words of the Journal.]

August 14. We started with a delightful breeze from the S.E., and kept along by the southern shore, taking advantage of the eddy, and going at a great rate, notwithstanding the current, which, in the middle, was unusually full and strong. At noon, we stopped to examine some remarkable mounds on the south-western shore, at a spot where the ground seems to have sunk considerably to an extent of three hundred acres or more. A large pond is in the vicinity, and appears to have drained the low tract. This is covered with mounds of various sizes and shapes, all formed of sand and mud, the highest being nearest the river. I could not make up my mind whether these hillocks were of natural or artificial construction. I should have supposed them made by the Indians, but for the general appearance of the soil, which had apparently been subjected to the violent action of water.* We stayed at this spot the rest of the day, having made altogether twenty miles.

August 15. Today we had a heavy, disagreeable head wind, and made only fifteen miles, with great labour; encamping at night beneath a bluff on the north shore, this being the first bluff on that side which we had seen since leaving the Nodaway River. In the night it came on to rain in torrents, and the Greelÿs brought in their horses, and ensconced themselves in the cabin. Robert swam the river with his horse from the south shore, and then took the canoe across for Meredith. He appeared to think nothing of either of these feats, although the night was one of the darkest and most boisterous I ever saw, and the river was much swollen. We all sat in the cabin very comfortably, for the weather was quite cool, and were kept awake for a long time by the anecdotes of Thornton, who told story after story of his adventures with the Indians on the Mississippi. His huge dog appeared to listen with profound attention to every word that was said. Whenever any particularly incredible circumstance was related, Thornton would gravely refer to him as a witness. "Nep," he would say, "don't you remember that time?" or "Nep can swear to the truth of that —can't you, Nep?" when the animal would roll up his eyes immediately, loll out his monstrous tongue, and wag his great head up and down, as much as to say: "Oh, it's every bit as true as the Bible." Although we all knew that this trick had been taught the dog, yet for our lives we could not forbear shouting with laughter, whenever Thornton would appeal to him.

August 16. Early this morning passed an island, and a creek about fifteen yards wide, and, at a farther distance of twelve miles, a large island in the middle of the river. We had now, generally, high prairie and timbered hills on the north, with low ground on the south, covered with cottonwood. The river was excessively crooked, but not so rapid as before we passed the

---

*These mounds are now well understood to indicate the position of the ancient village of the Ottoes, who were once a very powerful tribe. Being reduced by continual hostilities, they sought protection of the Pawnees, and migrated to the south of the Platte, about thirty miles from its mouth.

Platte. Altogether there is less timber than formerly; what there is, is mostly elm, cottonwood, hickory, and walnut, with some oak. Had a strong wind nearly all day, and by means of the eddy and this, we made twenty-five miles before night. Our encampment was on the south, upon a large plain, covered with high grass, and bearing a great number of plum trees and currant bushes. In our rear was a steep woody ridge, ascending which we found another prairie extending back for about a mile, and stopped again by a similar woody ridge, followed by another vast prairie, going off into the distance as far as the eye can reach. From the cliffs just above us we had one of the most beautiful prospects in the world.*

August 17. We remained at the encampment all day, and occupied ourselves in various employments. Getting Thornton, with his dog, to accompany me, I strolled to some distance to the southward, and was enchanted with the voluptuous beauty of the country. The prairies exceeded in beauty anything told in the tales of the *Arabian Nights*. On the edges of the creeks there was a wild mass of flowers which looked more like art than nature, so profusely and fantastically were their vivid colours blended together. Their rich odour was almost oppressive. Every now and then we came to a kind of green island of trees, placed amid an ocean of purple, blue, orange and crimson blossoms, all waving to and fro in the wind. These islands consisted of the most majestic forest oaks, and, beneath them, the grass resembled a robe of the softest green velvet, while up their huge stems there clambered generally a profusion of grapevines, laden with delicious ripe fruit. The Missouri in the distance presented the most majestic appearance; and many of the real islands with which it was studded were entirely covered with plum bushes, or other shrubbery, except where crossed in various directions by narrow, mazy paths, like the alleys in an English flower-garden; and in these alleys we could always see either elks or antelopes, who had no doubt made them. We returned, at sunset, to the

---

*The Council Bluffs.

encampment, delighted with our excursion. The night was warm, and we were excessively annoyed by mosquitoes.

August 18. Today passed through a narrow part of the river, not more than two hundred yards wide, with a rapid channel, much obstructed with logs and driftwood. Ran the large boat on a sawyer, and half filled her with water before we could extricate her from the difficulty. We were obliged to halt, in consequence, and overhaul our things. Some of the biscuit was injured, but none of the powder. Remained all day, having only made five miles.

August 19. We started early this morning and made great headway. The weather was cool and cloudy, and at noon we had a drenching shower. Passed a creek on the south, the mouth of which is nearly concealed by a large sand island of singular appearance. Went about fifteen miles beyond this. The highlands now recede from the river, and are probably from ten to twenty miles apart. On the north is a good deal of fine timber, but on the south very little. Near the river are beautiful prairies, and along the banks we procured four or five different species of grape, all of good flavour and quite ripe; one is a large purple grape of excellent quality. The hunters came into camp at night from both sides of the river, and brought us more game than we well knew what to do with—grouse, turkeys, two deer, an antelope and a quantity of yellow birds with black striped wings; these latter proved delicious eating. We made about twenty miles during the day.

August 20. The river, this morning, was full of sand bars and other obstructions; but we proceeded with spirit, and reached the mouth of a pretty large creek, before night, at a distance of twenty miles from our last encampment. The creek comes in from the north, and has a large island opposite its mouth. Here we made our camp, with the resolution of remaining four or five days to trap beaver, as we saw great signs of them in the neighbourhood. This island was one of the most fairy-looking situations in the world, and filled my mind with the most delightful and novel emotions. The whole scenery rather resembled what I had dreamed of when a boy than an actual reality. The banks sloped down very gradually into the water, and were carpeted with a soft grass of a brilliant green hue, which was visible under the surface of the stream for some distance from the shore; especially on the north side, where the clear creek fell into the river. All round the island, which was probably about twenty acres in extent, was a complete fringe of cottonwood, the trunks loaded with grapevines in full fruit, and so closely interlocking with each other that we could scarcely get a glimpse of the river between the leaves. Within this circle the grass was somewhat higher, and of a coarser texture, with a pale yellow or white streak down the middle of each blade, and giving out a remarkably delicious perfume, resembling that of the vanilla bean, but much stronger, so that the whole atmosphere was loaded with it. The common English sweet grass is no doubt of the same genus, but greatly inferior in beauty and fragrance. Interspersed among it in every direction, were myriads of the most brilliant flowers, in full bloom, and most of them of fine odour—blue, pure white, bright yellow, purple, crimson, gaudy scarlet, and some with streaked leaves like tulips. Little knots of cherry trees and plum bushes grew in various directions about, and there were many narrow winding paths which circled the island, and which had been made by elks or antelopes. Nearly in the centre was a spring of sweet and clear water, which bubbled up from among a cluster of steep rocks, covered from head to foot with moss and flowering vines. The whole bore a wonderful resemblance to an artificial flower-garden, but was infinitely more beautiful, looking rather like some of those scenes of enchantment which we read of in old books. We were all in ecstasy with the spot, and prepared our camp in the highest glee, amid its wilderness of sweets.

[The party remained here a week, during which time, the neighbouring country to the north was explored in many directions, and some peltries obtained, especially upon the creek mentioned. The weather was fine, and the enjoyment of the voyagers suffered no alloy, in their terrestrial Paradise. Mr Rodman, however, omitted no necessary precautions, and sentries were regularly posted every night, when all hands assembled at camp, and made merry. Such feasting and drinking were never before known, the Canadians proving themselves the very best fellows in the world at a song or over a flagon. They did nothing but eat, and cook, and dance, and shout French carols at the top of their voice. During the day they were chiefly entrusted with the charge of the encampment, while the steadier members of the party were absent upon hunting or trapping expeditions. In one of these Mr Rodman enjoyed an excellent opportunity of observing the habits of the beaver; and his account of this singular animal is highly interesting; the more so as it differs materially, in some points, from the ordinary descriptions.

He was attended, as usual, by Thornton and his dog, and had traced up a small creek to its source in the highlands about ten miles from the river. The party came at length to a place where a large swamp had been made by the beavers, in damming up the creek. A thick grove of willows occupied one extremity of the swamp, some of them overhanging the water at a spot where several of the animals were observed. Our adventurers crept stealthily round to these willows, and, making Neptune lie down at a little distance, succeeded in climbing, unobserved, into a large and thick tree, where they could look immediately down upon all that was going on.

The beavers were repairing a portion of their dam, and every step of their progress was distinctly seen. One by one the architects were perceived to approach the edge of the swamp, each with a small branch in his mouth. With this he proceeded to the dam, and placed it carefully, and longitudinally, on the part which had given way. Having done this, he dived immediately, and in a few seconds reappeared above the surface with a quantity of stiff mud, which he first squeezed so as to drain it of its moisture in a great degree, and then applied with his feet and tail (using the latter as a trowel) to the branch which he had just laid upon the breach. He then made off among the trees, and was quickly succeeded by another of the community, who went through precisely the same operation.

In this way the damage sustained by the dam was in a fair way of being soon repaired. Messieurs Rodman and Thornton observed the progress of the work for more than two hours, and bear testimony to the exquisite skill of the artisans. But as soon as a beaver left the edge of the swamp in search of a branch, he was lost sight of among the willows, much to the chagrin of the observers, who were anxious to watch his further operations. By clambering a little higher up in the tree, however, they discovered everything. A small sycamore had been felled, apparently, and was now nearly denuded of all its fine branches, a few beavers still nibbling off some that remained, and proceeding with them to the dam. In the meantime a great number of the animals surrounded a much older and larger tree, which they were busily occupied in cutting down. There were as many as fifty or sixty of the creatures around the trunk, of which number six or seven would work at once, leaving off one by one, as each became weary, a fresh one stepping into the vacated place. When our travellers first observed the sycamore, it had been already cut through to a great extent, but only on the side nearest the swamp, upon the edge of which it grew. The incision was nearly a foot wide, and as cleanly made as if done with an axe; and the ground at the bottom of the tree was covered with fine longitudinal slips, like straws, which had been nibbled out, and not eaten; as it appears that these animals only use the bark for food. When at work some sat upon the hind legs, in the posture so common with squirrels, and gnawed at the wood, their forefeet resting upon the edge of the cut, and their heads thrust far into the aperture. Two of them, however, were entirely within the incision; lying at length, and working with great eagerness for a short time, when they were relieved by their companions.

Although the position of our voyagers was anything but comfortable, so great was their curiosity to witness the felling of the sycamore that they resolutely maintained their post until sunset, an interval of eight hours from the time of ascending. Their chief embarrassment was on Neptune's account, who could with difficulty be kept from plunging into the swamp after the plasterers who were repairing the dam. The noise he made had several times disturbed the nibblers at the tree, who would every now and then start, as if all actuated by one mind, and listen attentively for many minutes. As evening approached, however, the dog gave over his freaks, and lay quiet; while the beavers went on uninterruptedly with their labour.

Just as the sun began to set, a sudden commotion was observed among the woodcutters, who all started from the tree, and flew round to the side which was untouched. In an instant afterwards it was seen to settle down gradually on the gnawed side, till the lips of the incision met; but still it did not fall, being sustained partially by the unsundered bark. This was now attacked with zeal by as many nibblers as could find room to work at it, and very quickly severed; when the huge tree, to which the proper inclination had already been so ingeniously given, fell with a tremendous crash, and spread a great portion of its topmost branches over the surface of the swamp. This matter accomplished, the whole community seemed to think a holiday was deserved and, ceasing work at once, began to chase each other about in the water, diving, and slapping the surface with their tails.

The account here given of the method employed by the beaver in its woodcutting operations is more circumstantial than any we have yet seen, and seems to be conclusive in regard to the question of design on the animal's part. The intention of making the tree fall towards the water appears here to be obvious. Captain Bonneville, it will be remembered, discredits the alleged sagacity of the animal in this respect, and thinks it has no further aim than to get the tree down, without any subtle calculation in respect to its mode of descent. This attribute, he thinks, has been ascribed to it from the circumstance that trees in general, which grow near the margin of water, either lean bodily towards the stream, or stretch their most ponderous limbs in that direction, in search of the light, space and air which are there usually found. The beaver, he says, attacks, of course, those trees which are nearest at hand, and on the banks of the stream or pond, and these, when cut through, naturally preponderate towards the water. This suggestion is well-timed, but by no means conclusive against the design of the beaver whose sagacity, at best, is far beneath that which is positively ascertained in respect to many classes of inferior animals, infinitely below that of the lion-ant, of the bee, and of the coralliferi. The probability is that, were two trees offered to the choice of the beaver, one of which preponderated to the water, and the other did not, he would, in felling the first, omit, as unnecessary, the precautions just described, but observe them in felling the second.

In a subsequent portion of the Journal other particulars are given respecting the habits of the singular animal in question, and of the mode of trapping it employed by the party, and we give them here for the sake of continuity. The principal food of the beavers is bark, and of this they put by regularly a large store for winter provision, selecting the proper kind with care and deliberation. A whole tribe, consisting sometimes of two or three hundred, will set out together upon a foraging expedition, and pass through groves of trees all apparently similar, until a particular one suits their fancy. This they cut down, and, breaking off its most tender branches, divide them into short slips of equal length, and divest these slips of their bark, which they carry to the nearest stream leading to their village, thence floating it home. Occasionally the slips are stored away for the winter without being stripped of the bark; and, in this event, they are careful to remove the refuse wood from their dwellings, as soon as they have eaten the rind, taking the sticks to some distance. During the spring of the year the males are never found with the tribe at home, but always by themselves, either singly, or in parties of two or three, when they appear to lose their usual habits of sagacity, and fall an easy prey to the arts of the trapper. In summer they return home, and busy themselves, with the females, in making provision for winter. They are described as exceedingly ferocious animals when irritated.

Now and then they may be caught upon shore; especially the males in spring, who are then fond of roving to some distance from the water in search of food. When thus caught, they are easily killed with a blow from a stick; but the most certain and efficacious mode of taking them is by means of the trap. This is simply constructed to catch the foot of the animal. The trapper places it usually in some position near the shore, and just below the surface of the water, fastening it by a small chain to a pole stuck in the mud. In the mouth of the machine is placed one end of a small branch, the other end rising above the surface, and well soaked in the liquid bait whose odour is found to be attractive to the beaver. As soon as the animal scents it, he rubs his nose against the twig, and in so doing steps upon the trap, springs it, and is caught. The trap is made very light, for the convenience of portage, and the prey would easily swim off with it but for its being fastened to the pole by a chain; no other species of fastening could resist his teeth. The experienced trapper readily detects the presence of beaver in any pond or stream, discovering them by a thousand appearances which would afford no indication to the unpractised observer.

Many of the identical woodcutters whom the two *voyageurs* had watched so narrowly from the treetop fell afterwards a victim to trap, and their fine furs became a prey to the spoilers, who made sad havoc in the lodge at the swamp. Other waters in the neighbourhood also afforded the travellers much sport; and they long remembered the island at the creek's mouth, by the name of Beaver Island, in consequence. They left this little paradise in high spirits on the twenty-seventh of the month and, pursuing their hitherto somewhat uneventful voyage up the river, arrived, by the first of September, without any incident of note, at the mouth of a large river on the south, to which they gave the name of Currant River, from some berries abounding upon its margin, but which was, beyond doubt, the Quicourre. The principal objects of which the Journal takes notice in this interval are the numerous herds of buffalo which darkened the prairies in every direction, and the remains of a fortification on the south shore of the river, nearly opposite the upper extremity of what has been since called Bonhomme Island. Of these remains a minute description is given, which tallies in every important particular with that of Captains Lewis and Clarke. The travellers had passed the Little Sioux, Floyd's, the Great Sioux, White Stone and Jacques rivers on the north; with Wawandysenche Creek and White Paint River on the south, but at neither of these streams did they stop to trap for any long period. They had also passed the great village of the Omahas, of which the Journal takes no notice whatever. This village, at the time, consisted of full three hundred houses, and was inhabited by a numerous and powerful tribe; but it is not immediately upon the banks of the Missouri, and the boats probably went by it during the night, for the party had begun to adopt this mode of progress, through fear of the Sioux. We resume the narrative of Mr Rodman, with the second of September.]

September 2. We had now reached a part of the river where, according to all report, a great deal of danger was to be apprehended from the Indians, and we became extremely cautious in our movements. This was the region inhabited by the Sioux, a warlike and ferocious tribe, who had, upon several occasions, evinced hostility to the whites, and were known to be constantly at war with all the neighbouring tribes. The Canadians had many incidents to relate respecting their savage propensities, and I had much apprehension lest those cowardly creatures should take an opportunity of deserting, and retracing their way to the Mississippi. To lessen the chances of this, I removed one of them from the piroque, and supplied his place by Poindexter Greely. All the Greelys came in from the shore, turning loose the horses. Our arrangement was now as follows: in the piroque, Poindexter Greely, Pierre Junôt, Toby, and one Canadian; in the large boat, myself, Thornton, Wormley; John, Frank, Robert, and Meredith Greely; and three Canadians, with the dog. We set sail about dusk, and, having a brisk wind from the south, made good headway, although as night came on we were greatly embarrassed by the shoals. We continued our course without interruption, however, until a short time before daybreak, when we ran into the mouth of a creek, and concealed the boats among the underwood.

September 3 and 4. During both of these days it rained and blew with excessive violence, so that we did not leave our retreat at all. The weather depressed our spirits very much, and the narratives of the Canadians about the terrible Sioux did not serve to raise them. We all congregated in the cabin of the large boat, and held a council in regard to our future movements. The Greelys were for a bold push through the dangerous country, maintaining that the stories of the *voyageurs* were mere exaggerations, and that the Sioux would only be a little troublesome, without proceeding to hostility. Wormley and Thornton, however, as well as Pierre (all of whom had much experience in the Indian character) thought that our present policy was the best, although it would necessarily detain us much longer on our voyage than would otherwise be the case. My own opinion coincided with theirs; in our present course we might escape any collision with the Sioux, and I did not regard the delay as a matter of consequence.

September 5. We set off at night, and proceeded for about ten miles, when the day began to appear, and we hid the boats as before, in a narrow creek, which was well adapted to the purpose, as its mouth was almost blocked up by a thickly-wooded island. It again came on to rain furiously, and we were all drenched to the skin before we could arrange matters for turning in, in the cabin. Our spirits were much depressed by the bad weather, and the Canadians especially were in a miserable state of dejection. We had now come to a narrow part of the river where the current was strong, and the cliffs on both sides overhung the water, and were thickly wooded with lynn, oak, black walnut, ash, and chestnut. Through such a gorge we knew it would be exceedingly difficult to pass without observation, even at night, and our apprehensions of attack were greatly increased. We resolved not to recommence our journey until late, and then to proceed with the most stealthy caution. In the meantime we posted a sentry on shore and one in the piroque, while the rest of us busied ourselves in overhauling the arms and ammunition, and preparing for the worst.

About ten o'clock we were getting ready to start, when the dog gave a low growl, which made us all fly to our rifles; but the cause of the disturbance proved to be a single Indian of the Ponca tribe,

THE JOURNAL OF JULIUS RODMAN   69

who came up frankly to our sentry on shore, and extended his hand. We brought him on board, and gave him whiskey, when he became very communicative, and told us that his tribe, who lived some miles lower down the river, had been watching our movements for several days past, but that the Poncas were friends and would not molest the whites, and would trade with us upon our return. They had sent him now to caution the whites against the Sioux, who were great robbers, and who were lying in wait for the party at a bend in the river, twenty miles farther up. There were three bands of them, he said, and it was their intention to kill us all, in revenge for an insult sustained by one of their chiefs, many years previously, at the hands of a French trapper.

III

[WE LEFT OUR travellers, on the fifth of September, apprehending a present attack from the Sioux. Exaggerated accounts of the ferocity of this tribe had inspired the party with an earnest wish to avoid them; but the tale told by the friendly Ponca made it evident that a collision must take place. The night voyages were therefore abandoned as impolitic, and it was resolved to put a bold face upon the matter, and try what could be effected by blustering. The remainder of the night of the fifth was spent in warlike demonstration. The large boat was cleared for action as well as possible, and the fiercest aspect assumed which the nature of the case would permit. Among other preparations for defence, the cannon was got out from below, and placed forward upon the cuddy deck, with a load of bullets, by way of canister shot. Just before sunrise the adventurers started up the river in high bravado, aided by a heavy wind. That the enemy might perceive no semblance of fear or mistrust, the whole party joined the Canadians in an uproarious boat song at the top of their voices, making the woods reverberate, and the buffaloes stare.

The Sioux, indeed, appear to have been Mr Rodman's bugbears *par excellence,* and he dwells upon them and their exploits with peculiar emphasis. The narrative embodies a detailed account of the tribe, an account which we can only follow in such portions as appear to possess novelty, or other important interest. "Sioux" is the French term for the Indians in question; the English have corrupted it into "Sues". Their primitive name is said to be "Darcotas". Their original seats were on the Mississippi, but they had gradually extended their dominions, and, at the date of the Journal, occupied almost the whole of that vast territory circumscribed by the Mississippi, the Saskatchawine, the Missouri, and the Red River of Lake Winnipeg. They were subdivided into numerous clans. The Darcotas proper were the Winowacants, called the Gens du Lac by the French, consisting of about five hundred warriors, and living on both sides of the Mississippi, in the vicinity of the Falls of St Anthony. Neighbours of the Winowacants, and residing north of them on the river St Peter's, were the Wappatomies, about two hundred men. Still farther up the St Peter's lived a band of one hundred, called the Wappytooties, among themselves, and by the French the Gens des Feuilles. Higher up the river yet, and near its source, resided the Sissytoonies, in number two hundred or thereabouts. On the Missouri dwelt the Yanktons and the Tetons. Of the first tribe there were two branches, the northern and southern, of which the former led an Arab life in the plains at the sources of the Red, Sioux and Jacques rivers, being in number about five hundred. The southern branch kept possession of the tract lying between the river Des Moines on the one hand, and the rivers Jacques and Sioux on the other. But the Sioux most renowned for deeds of violence are the Tetons; and of these there were four tribes: the Saonies, the Minnakenozzies, the Okydandies, and the Bois-Brulés. These last, a body of whom were now lying in wait to intercept the *voyageurs,* were the most savage and formidable of the whole race, numbering about two hundred men, and residing on both sides of the Missouri near the rivers called by Captains Lewis and Clarke, the White and Teton. Just below the Chayenne River were the Okydandies, one hundred and fifty. The Minnakenozzies, two hundred and fifty, occupied a tract between the Chayenne and the Watarhoo; and the Saonies, the largest of the Teton bands, counting as many as three hundred warriors, were found in the vicinity of the Warreconne.

Besides these four divisions (the regular Sioux) there were five tribes of seceders called Assiniboins; the Menatopae Assiniboins, two hundred, on Mouse River, between the Assiniboin and the Missouri; the Gens de Feuilles Assiniboins, two hundred and fifty, occupying both sides of White River; the Big Devils, four hundred and fifty, wandering about the heads of Porcupine and Milk rivers; with two other bands whose names are not mentioned, but who roved on the Saskatchawine, and numbered together about seven hundred men. These seceders were often at war with the parent or original Sioux.

In person, the Sioux generally are an ugly, ill-made race, their limbs being much too small for the trunk, according to our ideas of the human form; their cheekbones are high, and their eyes protruding and dull. The heads of the men are shaved, with the exception of a small spot on the crown, whence a long tuft is permitted to fall in plaits upon the shoulders; this tuft is an object of scrupulous care, but is now and then cut off, upon an occasion of grief or solemnity. A full-dressed Sioux chief presents a striking appearance. The whole surface of the body is painted with grease and coal. A shirt of skins is worn as far down as the waist, while round the middle is a girdle of the same material, and sometimes of cloth, about an inch in width; this supports a piece of blanket or fur passing between the thighs. Over the shoulders is a white-dressed buffalo mantle, the hair of which is worn next the skin in fair weather, but turned outwards in wet. This robe is large enough to envelop the whole body, and is frequently ornamented with porcupine quills (which make a rattling noise as the warrior moves), as well as with a great variety of rudely painted figures, emblematical of the wearer's military character. Fastened to the top of the head is worn a hawk's feather, adorned with porcupine quills. Leggings of dressed antelope skin serve the purpose of pantaloons, and have seams at the sides about two inches wide, and bespotted here and there with small tufts of human hair, the trophies of some scalping excursion. The moccasins are of elk or buffalo skin, the hair worn inwards; on great occasions the chief is seen with the skin of a polecat dangling at the heel of each boot. The Sioux are indeed partial to this noisome animal, whose fur is in high favour for tobacco pouches and other appendages.

The dress of a chieftain's squaw is also remarkable. Her hair is suffered to grow long, is parted across the forehead, and hangs loosely behind, or is collected into a kind of net. Her moccasins do not differ from her husband's; but her leggings extend upwards only as far as the knee, where they are met by an awkward shirt of elk skin depending to the ankles, and supported above by a string going over the shoulders. This shirt is usually confined to the waist by a girdle, and over all is thrown a buffalo mantle like that of the men. The tents of the Teton Sioux are described as of neat construction, being formed of white-dressed buffalo hide, well secured and supported by poles.

The region infested by the tribe in question extends along the banks of the Missouri for some hundred and fifty miles or more, and is chiefly prairie land, but is occasionally diversified by hills. These latter are always deeply cut by gorges or ravines, which in the middle of summer are dry, but form the channels of muddy and impetuous torrents during the season of rain. Their edges are fringed with thick woods, as well at top as at bottom; but the prevalent aspect of the country is that of a bleak lowland, with rank herbage, and without trees. The soil is strongly impregnated with mineral substances in great variety; among others with glauber salts, copperas, sulphur and alum, which tinge the water of the river and impart to it a nauseous odour and taste. The wild animals most usual are the buffalo, deer, elk, and antelope. We again resume the words of the Journal.]

September 6. The country was open, and the day remarkably pleasant: so that we were all in pretty good spirits notwithstanding the expectation of attack. So far, we had not caught even a glimpse of an Indian, and we were making rapid way through their dreaded territory. I was too well aware, however, of the savage tactics to suppose that we were not narrowly watched, and had made up my mind that we should hear something of the Tetons at the first gorge which would afford them a convenient lurking-place.

About noon a Canadian bawled out, "The Sioux! the Sioux!" and directed attention to a long narrow ravine which intersected the prairie on our left, extending from the banks of the Missouri as far as the eye could reach, in a southwardly course. This gully was the bed of a creek, but its waters were now low, and the sides rose up like huge regular walls on each side. By the aid of a spyglass I perceived at once the cause of the alarm given by the *voyageur*. A large party of mounted savages were coming down the gorge in Indian file, with the evident intention of taking us unawares. Their calumet feathers had been the means of their detection; for every now and then we could see some of these bobbing up above the edge of the gully, as the bed of the ravine forced the wearer to rise higher than usual. We could tell that they were on horseback by the motion of these feathers. The party was coming upon us with great rapidity; and I gave the word to pull on with all haste so as to pass the mouth of the creek before they reached it. As soon as the Indians perceived by our increased speed that they were discovered, they immediately raised a yell, scrambled out of the gorge, and galloped down upon us, to the number of about one hundred.

Our situation was now somewhat alarming. At almost any other part of the Missouri which we had passed during the day, I should not have cared so much for these freebooters; but, just here, the banks were remarkably steep and high, partaking of the character of the creek banks, and the savages were enabled to overlook us completely, while the cannon, upon which we had placed so much reliance, could not be brought to bear upon them at all. What added to our difficulty was that the current in the middle of the river was so turbulent and strong that we could make no headway against it except by dropping arms, and employing our whole force at the oars. The water near the northern shore was too shallow even for the piroque, and our only mode of proceeding, if we designed to proceed at all, was by pushing in within a moderate stone's throw of the left or southern bank, where we were completely at the mercy of the Sioux, but where we could make good headway by means of our poles and the wind, aided by the eddy. Had the savages attacked us at this juncture I cannot see how we could have escaped them. They were all well provided with bows and arrows, and small round shields, presenting a very noble and picturesque appearance. Some of the chiefs had spears, with fanciful flags attached, and were really gallant-looking men.

Either good luck upon our own parts, or great stupidity on the parts of the Indians, relieved us very unexpectedly from the dilemma. The savages, having galloped up to the edge of the cliff just above us, set up another yell, and commenced a variety of gesticulations, whose meaning we at once knew to be that we should stop and come on shore. I had expected this demand, and had made up my mind that it would be most prudent to pay no attention to it at all, but proceed on our course. My refusal to stop had at least one good effect, for it appeared to mystify the Indians most wonderfully, who could not be brought to understand the measure in the least, and stared at us, as we kept on our way without answering them, in the most ludicrous amazement. Presently they commenced an agitated conversation among themselves, and at last finding that nothing could be made of us, fairly turned their horses' heads to the southward and galloped out of sight, leaving us as much surprised as rejoiced at their departure.

In the meantime we made the most of the opportunity, and pushed on with might and main, in order to get out of the region of steep banks before the anticipated return of our foes. In about two hours we again saw them in the south, at a great distance, and their number much augmented. They came on at full gallop, and were soon at the river; but our position was now much more advantageous, for the banks were sloping, and there were no trees to shelter the savages from our shot. The current, moreover, was not so rapid as before, and we were enabled to keep in mid-channel. The party, it seems, had only retreated to procure an interpreter, who now appeared upon a large grey horse, and, coming into the river as far as he could without swimming, called out to us in bad French to stop, and come on shore. To this I made one of the Canadians reply that, to oblige our friends the Sioux, we would willingly stop for a short time, and converse, but that it was inconvenient for us to come on shore, as we could not do so without incommoding our great Medicine (here the Canadian pointed to the cannon), who was anxious to proceed on his voyage, and whom we were afraid to disobey.

At this they began again their agitated whisperings and gesticulations among themselves, and seemed quite at a loss what to do. In the meantime the boats had been brought to anchor in a favourable position, and I was resolved to fight now, if necessary, and endeavour to give the freebooters so warm a reception as would inspire them with wholesome dread for the future. I reflected that it was nearly impossible to keep on good terms with these Sioux, who were our enemies at heart, and who could only be restrained from pillaging and murdering us by a conviction of our prowess. Should we comply with their present demands, go on shore, and even succeed in purchasing a temporary safety by concessions and donations, such conduct would not avail us in the end, and would be rather a palliation than a radical cure of the evil. They would be sure to glut their vengeance sooner or later, and, if they suffered us to go on our way now, might hereafter attack us at a disadvantage, when it might be as much as we could do to repel them, to say nothing of inspiring them with awe. Situated as we were here, it was in our power to give them a lesson they would be apt to remember; and we might never be in so good a situation again. Thinking thus, and all except the Canadians agreeing with me in opinion, I determined to assume a bold stand, and rather provoke hostilities than avoid them. This was our true policy. The savages had no firearms which we could discover, except an old carbine carried by one of the chiefs; and their arrows would not prove very effective weapons when employed at so great a distance as that now between us. In regard to their number, we did not care much for that. Their position was one which would expose them to the full sweep of our cannon.

When Jules (the Canadian) had finished his speech about incommoding our great Medicine, and when the consequent agitation had somewhat subsided among the savages, the interpreter spoke again and propounded three queries. He wished to know, first, whether we had any tobacco, or whiskey, or fireguns; secondly, whether we did not wish the aid of the Sioux in rowing our large boat up the Missouri as far as the country of the Ricarees, who were great rascals; and, thirdly, whether our great Medicine was not a very large and strong green grasshopper.

To these questions, propounded with profound gravity, Jules replied, by my directions, as follows: first, that we had plenty of whiskey, as well as tobacco, with an inexhaustible supply of fireguns and powder; but that our great Medicine had just told us that the Tetons were greater rascals than the Ricarees; that they were our enemies; that they had been lying in wait to intercept and kill us for many days past; that we must give them nothing at all, and hold no intercourse with them whatever; we should therefore be afraid to give them anything, even if so disposed, for fear of the anger of the great Medicine, who was not to be trifled with. Secondly, that, after the character just given the Sioux Tetons, we could not think of employing them to row our boat; and, thirdly, that it was a good thing for them (the Sioux) that our great Medicine had not overheard their last query, respecting the "large green grasshopper"; for, in that case, it might have gone very hard with them (the Sioux). Our great Medicine was anything but a large green grasshopper, and *that* they should soon see, to their cost, if they did not immediately go, the whole of them, about their business.

Notwithstanding the imminent danger in which we were all placed, we could scarcely keep our countenances in beholding the air of profound admiration and astonishment with which the savages listened to these replies; and I believe that they would have immediately dispersed, and left us to proceed on our voyage, had it not been for the unfortunate words in which I informed them that they were greater rascals than the Ricarees. This was, apparently, an insult of the last atrocity, and excited them to an

THE JOURNAL OF JULIUS RODMAN

uncontrollable degree of fury. We heard the words "Ricaree! Ricaree!" repeated, every now and then, with the utmost emphasis and excitement; and the whole band, as well as we could judge, seemed to be divided into two factions; the one urging the immense power of the great Medicine, and the other the outrageous insult of being called greater rascals than the Ricarees. While matters stood thus, we retained our position in the middle of the stream, firmly resolved to give the villains a dose of our canistershot, upon the first indignity which should be offered us.

Presently, the interpreter on the grey horse came again into the river, and said that he believed we were no better than we should be; that all the palefaces who had previously gone up the river had been friends of the Sioux, and had made them large presents; that they, the Tetons, were determined not to let us proceed another step unless we came on shore and gave up all our fire-guns and whiskey, with half of our tobacco; that it was plain that we were allies of the Ricarees (who were now at war with the Sioux), and that our design was to carry them supplies, which we should not do; lastly, that they did not think very much of our great Medicine, for he had told us a lie in relation to the designs of the Tetons, and was positively nothing but a great green grasshopper, in spite of all that we thought to the contrary. These latter words, about the great green grasshopper, were taken up by the whole assemblage as the interpreter uttered them, and shouted out at the top of the voice, that the great Medicine himself might be sure to hear the taunt. At the same time, they all broke into wild disorder, galloping their horses furiously in short circles, using contemptuous and indecent gesticulations, brandishing their spears, and drawing their arrows to the head.

I knew that the next thing would be an attack, and so determined to anticipate it at once, before any of our party were wounded by the discharge of their weapons; there was nothing to be gained by delay, and everything by prompt and resolute action. As soon as a good opportunity presented itself, the word was given to fire, and instantly obeyed. The effect of the discharge was very severe, and answered all our purposes to the full. Six of the Indians were killed, and perhaps three times as many badly wounded. The rest were thrown into the greatest terror and confusion and made off into the prairie at full speed, as we drew up our anchors, after reloading the gun, and pulled boldly in for the shore. By the time we had reached it, there was not an unwounded Teton within sight.

I now left John Greely, with three Canadians, in charge of the boats, landed with the rest of the men, and, approaching a savage who was severely but not dangerously wounded, held a conversation with him, by means of Jules. I told him that the whites were well disposed to the Sioux, and to all the Indian nations; that our sole object in visiting his country was to trap beaver, and see the beautiful region which had been given the red men by the Great Spirit; that when we had procured as many furs as we wished, and seen all we came to see, we should return home; that we had heard that the Sioux, and especially the Tetons, were a quarrelsome race, and that therefore we had brought with us our great Medicine for protection; that he was now much exasperated with the Tetons on account of their intolerable insult in calling him a green grasshopper (which he was not); that I had had great difficulty in restraining him from a pursuit of the warriors who had fled, and from sacrificing the wounded who now lay around us; and that I had only succeeded in pacifying him by becoming personally responsible for the future good behaviour of the savages. At this portion of my discourse the poor fellow appeared much relieved, and extended his hand in token of amity. I took it, and assured him and his friends of my protection as long as we were unmolested, following up this promise by a present of twenty carrots of tobacco, some small hardware, beads, and red flannel, for himself and the rest of the wounded.

While all this was going on, we kept a sharp lookout for the fugitive Sioux. As I concluded making the presents, several gangs of these were observable in the distance, and were evidently seen by the disabled savage; but I thought it best to pretend not to perceive them, and shortly afterwards returned to the boats. The whole interruption had detained us full three hours, and it was after three o'clock when we once more started on our route. We made extraordinary haste, as I was anxious to get as far as possible from the scene of action before night. We had a strong wind at our back, and the current diminished in strength as we proceeded, owing to the widening of the stream. We therefore made great way, and by nine o'clock had reached a large and thickly wooded island, near the northern bank, and close by the mouth of a creek. Here we resolved to encamp, and had scarcely set foot on shore, when one of the Greelys shot and secured a fine buffalo, many of which were upon the place. After posting our sentries for the night, we had the hump for supper, with as much whiskey as was good for us. Our exploit of the day was then freely discussed, and by most of the men was treated as an excellent joke; but I could by no means enter into any merriment upon the subject. Human blood had never, before this epoch, been shed at my hands; and although reason urged that I had taken the wisest, and what would no doubt prove in the end the most merciful course, still conscience, refusing to hearken even to reason herself, whispered pertinaciously within my ear: "It is human blood which thou hast shed." The hours wore away slowly; I found it impossible to sleep. At length the morning dawned, and with its fresh dews, its fresher breezes, and smiling flowers, there came a new courage and a bolder tone of thought, which enabled me to look more steadily upon what had been done, and to regard in its only proper point of view the urgent necessity of the deed.

September 7. Started early and made great way, with a strong cold wind from the east. Arrived about noon at the upper gorge of what is called the Great Bend, a place where the river performs a circuit of full thirty miles, while by land the direct distance is not more than fifteen hundred yards. Six miles beyond this is a creek about thirty-five yards wide, coming in from the south. The country here is of peculiar character; on each side of the river the shore is strewed thickly with round stones washed from the bluffs, and presenting a remarkable appearance for miles. The channel is very shallow, and much interrupted with sand bars. Cedar is here met with more frequently than any other species of timber, and the prairies are covered with a stiff kind of prickly pear, over which our men found it no easy matter to walk in their moccasins.

About sunset, in endeavouring to avoid a rapid channel, we had the misfortune to run the larboard side of the large boat on the edge of a sand bar, which so heeled us over that we were very near getting filled with water, in spite of the greatest exertion. As it was, much damage was done to the loose powder, and the Indian goods were all more or less injured. As soon as we found the boat careening, we all jumped into the water, which was here up to our armpits, and by main force held the sinking side up. But we were still in a dilemma, for all our exertions were barely sufficient to keep from capsizing, and we could not spare a man to do anything towards pushing off. We were relieved, very unexpectedly, by the sinking of the whole sand bar from under the boat, just as we were upon the point of despair. The bed of the river in this neighbourhood is much obstructed by these shifting sands, which frequently change situations with great rapidity, and without apparent cause. The material of the bars is a fine hard yellow sand, which, when dry, is of a brilliant glass-like appearance, and almost impalpable.

September 8. We were still in the heart of the Teton country, and kept a sharp lookout, stopping as seldom as possible, and then only upon the islands, which abounded with game in great variety —buffaloes, elk, deer, goats, black-tailed deer, and antelopes, with plover and brant of many kinds. The goats are uncommonly tame, and have no beard. Fish is not so abundant here as lower down the river. A white wolf was killed by John Greely in a ravine upon one of the smaller islands. Owing to the difficult navigation, and the frequent necessity of employing the tow-line, we did not make great progress this day.

September 9. Weather growing sensibly colder, which made us all anxious of pushing our way through the Sioux country, as it would be highly dangerous to form our winter encampment in their vicinity. We aroused ourselves to exertion, and proceeded rapidly, the Canadians singing and shouting as we went. Now and then we saw, in the extreme distance, a solitary Teton, but no attempt was made to molest us, and we began to gather courage from this circumstance. Made twenty-eight miles during the day, and encamped at night, in high glee, on a large island well-stocked with game, and thickly covered with cottonwood.

[We omit the adventures of Mr Rodman from this period until the tenth of April. By the last of October, nothing of importance happening in the interval, the party made their way to a small creek which they designated as Otter Creek; and, proceeding up this about a mile to an island well adapted for their purpose, built a log fort and took up their quarters for the winter. The location is just above the old Ricara villages. Several parties of these Indians visited the *voyageurs,* and behaved with perfect friendliness; they had heard of the skirmish with the Tetons, the result of which hugely pleased them. No further trouble was experienced from any of the Sioux. The winter wore away pleasantly, and without accident of note. On the tenth of April the party resumed their voyage.]

IV

April 10, 1792. The weather was now again most delicious, and revived our spirits exceedingly. The sun began to have power, and the river was quite free of ice, so the Indians assured us, for a hundred miles ahead. We bade adieu to Little Snake [a chief of the Ricarees who had shown the *voyageurs* many evidences of friendship during the winter] and his band, with unfeigned regret, and set out, after breakfast, on our voyage. Perrine (an agent of the Hudson Bay Fur Company on his way to Petite Côte) accompanied us with three Indians for the first ten miles, when he took leave of us and made his way back to the village, where (as we afterwards heard) he met with a violent death from the hands of a squaw, to whom he offered some insult. Upon parting with the agent, we pushed on vigorously up the river, and made great way, notwithstanding a rapid current. In the afternoon, Thornton, who had been complaining for some days past, was taken seriously ill; so much so that I urged the return of the whole party to the hut, there to wait until he should get better; but he resisted this offer so strongly that I was forced to yield. We made him a comfortable bed in the cabin, and paid him every attention; but he had a raging fever, with occasional delirium, and I was much afraid that we should lose him. In the meantime we still pushed ahead with resolution, and by night had made twenty miles, an excellent day's work.

April 11. Still beautiful weather. We started early, and had a good wind, which aided us greatly; so that, but for Thornton's illness, we should all have been in fine spirits. He seemed to grow much worse, and I scarcely knew how to act. Everything was done for his comfort which could be done; Jules, the Canadian, made him some tea, from prairie herbs, which had the effect of inducing perspiration, and allayed the fever very sensibly. We stopped at night on the mainland to the north, and three hunters went out into the prairie by moonlight, returning at one in the morning, without their rifles, and with a fat antelope.

They related that, having proceeded many miles across the country, they reached the banks of a beautiful rivulet, where they were much surprised and alarmed at discovering a large war-party of the Saonie Sioux, who immediately took them prisoners, and carried them a mile on the other side of the stream to a kind of park, or enclosure, walled with mud and sticks, in which was a large herd of antelopes. These animals were still coming into the park, the gates of which were so contrived as to prevent escape. This was an annual practice of the Indians. In the autumn, the antelopes retire for food and shelter from the prairie to the mountainous regions on the south of the river. In the spring they recross it in great numbers, and are then easily taken by being enticed into a strong enclosure as above described.

The hunters (John Greely, the Prophet, and a Canadian) had scarcely any hope of escape from the clutches of the Indians (who numbered as many as fifty), and had well-nigh made up their minds to die. Greely and the Prophet were disarmed and tied hand

and foot; the Canadian, however, was suffered, for some reason not perfectly understood, to remain unbound, and was only deprived of his rifle, the savages leaving him in possession of his hunter's knife (which, possibly, they did not perceive, as it was worn in a sort of sheath in the side of his legging), and treating him otherwise with a marked difference from their demeanour to the others. This circumstance proved the source of the party's deliverance.

It was, perhaps, nine o'clock at night when they were first taken. The moon was bright but, as the air was unusually cool for the season, the savages had kindled two large fires at a sufficient distance from the park not to frighten the antelopes, who were still pouring into it continually. At these fires they were occupied in cooking their game when the hunters so unexpectedly came upon them from round a clump of trees. Greely and the Prophet, after being disarmed and bound with strong thongs of buffalo hide, were thrown down under a tree at some distance from the blaze; while the Canadian was permitted to seat himself, in charge of two savages, by one of the fires, the rest of the Indians forming a circle round the other and larger one. In this arrangement, the time wore away slowly, and the hunters were in momentary expectation of death; the cords of the two who were bound caused them, also, infinite pain, from the tightness with which they were fastened. The Canadian had endeavoured to hold a conversation with his guards, in the hope of bribing them to release him, but could not make himself understood. About midnight, the congregation around the large fire were suddenly disturbed by the dash of several large antelopes in succession through the midst of the blaze. These animals had burst through a portion of the mud wall which confined them, and, mad with rage and affright, had made for the light of the fire, as is the habit of insects at night in like circumstances. It seems, however, that the Saonies had never heard of any similar feat, of these usually timid creatures, for they were in great terror at the unexpected interruption, and their alarm increased to perfect dismay, as the whole captured herd came rushing and bounding upon them, after the lapse of a minute or so from the outbreak of the first few. The hunters described the scene as one of the most singular nature. The beasts were apparently frantic, and the velocity and impetuosity with which they flew, rather than leaped through the flames, and through the midst of the terrified savages, was said by Greely (a man not in the least prone to exaggerate) to have been not only an imposing but even a terrible spectacle. They carried everything before them in their first plunges; but, having cleared the large fire, they immediately dashed at the small one, scattering the brands and blazing wood about; then returned, as if bewildered, to the large one, and so backwards and forwards until the decline of the fires, when, in small parties, they scampered off like lightning to the woods.

Many of the Indians were knocked down in this furious mêlée, and there is no doubt that some of them were seriously, if not mortally, wounded by the sharp hoofs of the agile antelopes. Some threw themselves flat on the ground, and so avoided injury. The Prophet and Greely, not being near the fires, were in no danger. The Canadian was prostrated at the first onset by a kick which rendered him senseless for some minutes. When he came to himself he was nearly in darkness; for the moon had gone behind a heavy thunder-cloud, and the fires were almost out, or only existed in brands scattered hither and thither. He saw no Indians near him, and instantly arousing himself to escape, made, as well as he could, for the tree where his two comrades were lying. Their thongs were soon cut, and the three set off at full speed in the direction of the river, without stopping to think of their rifles, or of anything beyond present security. Having run for some miles, and finding no one in pursuit, they slackened their pace, and made their way to a spring for a draught of water. Here it was they met with the antelope which, as I mentioned before, they brought with them to the boats. The poor creature lay panting, and unable to move, by the border of the spring. One of its legs was broken, and it bore evident traces of fire. It was no doubt one of the herd which had been the means of deliverance. Had there been even a chance of its recovery the hunters would have spared it in token of

THE JOURNAL OF JULIUS RODMAN 85

their gratitude, but it was miserably injured, so they put it at once out of its misery, and brought it home to the boats, where we made an excellent breakfast upon it next morning.

April 12, 13, 14, and 15. During these four days we kept on our course without any adventure of note. The weather was very pleasant during the middle of the day, but the nights and mornings were exceedingly cold, and we had sharp frosts. Game was abundant. Thornton still continued ill, and his sickness perplexed and grieved me beyond measure. I missed his society very much, and now found that he was almost the only member of our party in whom I could strictly confide. By this I merely mean that he was almost the only one to whom I could, or would, freely unburden my heart, with its wild hopes and fantastic wishes—not that any individual among us was unworthy of implicit faith. On the contrary, we were all like brothers, and a dispute, of any importance, never occurred. One interest seemed to bind all; or rather we appeared to be a band of *voyageurs* without interest in view, mere travellers for pleasure. What ideas the Canadians might have held upon this subject I cannot, indeed, exactly say. These fellows talked a great deal, to be sure, about the profits of the enterprise, and especially about their expected share of it; yet I can scarcely think they cared much for these points, for they were the most simple-minded, and certainly the most obliging set of beings upon the face of the earth. As for the rest of the crew, I have no doubt in the world that the pecuniary benefit to be afforded by the expedition was the last thing upon which they speculated. Some singular evidences of the feeling which more or less pervaded us all occurred during the prosecution of the voyage. Interests, which, in the settlements, would have been looked upon as of the highest importance, were here treated as matters unworthy of a serious word, and neglected, or totally discarded upon the most frivolous pretext. Men who had travelled thousands of miles through a howling wilderness, beset by horrible dangers, and enduring the most heartrending privations for the ostensible purpose of collecting peltries, would seldom take the trouble to secure them when obtained, and would leave behind them without a sigh an entire *cache* of fine beaver skins rather than forego the pleasure of pushing up some romantic-looking river, or penetrating into some craggy and dangerous cavern, for minerals whose use they knew nothing about, and which they threw aside as lumber at the first decent opportunity.

In all this my own heart was very much with the rest of the party; and I am free to say that, as we proceeded on our journey, I found myself less and less interested in the main business of the expedition, and more and more willing to turn aside in pursuit of idle amusement, if indeed I am right in calling by so feeble a name as amusement that deep and most intense excitement with which I surveyed the wonders and majestic beauties of the wilderness. No sooner had I examined one region than I was possessed with an irresistible desire to push forward and explore another. As yet, however, I felt as if in too close proximity to the settlements for the full enjoyment of my burning love of nature and of the unknown. I could not help being aware that some civilized footsteps, although few, had preceded me in my journey; that some eyes before my own had been enraptured with the scenes around me. But for this sentiment, ever obtruding itself, I should no doubt have loitered more frequently on the way, turning aside to survey the features of the region bordering upon the river, and perhaps penetrating deeply, at times, into the heart of the country to the north and south of our route. But I was anxious to go on; to get, if possible, beyond the extreme bounds of civilization; to gaze, if I could, upon those gigantic mountains of which the existence had been made known to us only by the vague accounts of the Indians. These ulterior hopes and views I communicated fully to no one of our party save Thornton. He participated in all my most visionary projects, and entered completely into the spirit of the romantic enterprise which pervaded my soul. I therefore felt his illness as a bitter evil. He grew worse daily, while it was out of our power to render him any effectual assistance.

April 16. Today we had a cold rain with a high wind from the north, obliging us to come to anchor until late in the afternoon. At four o'clock p.m. we proceeded, and made five miles by night. Thornton was much worse.

April 17 and 18. During both these days we had a continuance of raw, unpleasant weather, with the same cold wind from the north. We observed many large masses of ice in the river, which was much swollen and very muddy. The time passed unpleasantly, and we made no way. Thornton appeared to be dying, and I now resolved to encamp at the first convenient spot, and remain until his illness should terminate. We accordingly, at noon this day, drew the boats up a large creek coming in from the south and formed an encampment on the mainland.

April 25. We remained at the creek until this morning, when, to the great joy of us all, Thornton was sufficiently recovered to go on. The weather was fine, and we proceeded gaily through a most lovely portion of the country, without encountering a single Indian, or meeting with any adventure out of the usual course until the last of the month, when we reached the country of the Mandans, or rather of the Mandans, the Minnetarees, and the Ahnahaways; for these three tribes all live in the near vicinity of each other, occupying five villages. Not a great many years ago the Mandans were settled in nine villages, about eighty miles below, the ruins of which we passed without knowing what they were—seven on the west and two on the east of the river; but they were thinned off by the smallpox and their old enemies the Sioux, until reduced to a mere handful, when they ascended to their present position. [Mr R. gives here a tolerably full account of the Minnetarees and Ahnahaways or Wassatoons; but we omit it, as differing in no important particular from the ordinary statements respecting these nations.] The Mandans received us with perfect friendliness, and we remained in their neighbourhood three days, during which we overhauled and repaired the piroque, and otherwise refitted. We also obtained a good supply of hard corn, of a mixed colour, which the savages had preserved through the winter in holes near the front of their lodges. While with the Mandans we were visited by a Minnetaree chief, called Wauke-rassah, who behaved with much civility, and was of service to us in many respects. The son of this chief we engaged to accompany us as interpreter as far as the great fork. We made the father several presents, with which he was greatly pleased.* On the first of May we bade adieu to the Mandans, and went on our way.

May 1. The weather was mild, and the surrounding country began to assume a lovely appearance with the opening vegetation, which was now much advanced. The cottonwood leaves were quite as large as a crown, and many flowers were full blown. The low grounds began to spread out here more than usual, and were well supplied with timber. The cottonwood and common willow, as well as red willow, abounded; with rose bushes in great plenty. Beyond the low grounds on the river, the country extended in one immense plain without wood of any kind. The soil was remarkably rich. The game was more abundant than we had ever yet seen it. We kept a hunter ahead of us on each bank, and today they brought in an elk, a goat, five beavers, and a great number of plovers. The beavers were very tame and easily taken. This animal is quite a *bonne bouche* as an article of food; especially the tail, which is of a somewhat glutinous nature, like the fins of the halibut. A beaver tail will suffice for a plentiful dinner for three men. We made twenty miles before night.

May 2. We had a fine wind this morning, and used our sails until noon, when it became rather too much for us, and we stopped for the day. Our hunters went out and shortly returned with an immense elk whom Neptune had pulled down after a long chase, the animal having been only slightly wounded by a buckshot. He measured six feet in height. An antelope was also caught about dusk. As soon as the creature saw our men, it flew off with the greatest velocity, but after a few minutes stopped, and returned on its steps, apparently through curiosity, then bounded away again. This conduct was repeated frequently, each time the game coming nearer and nearer, until at length it ventured within rifle distance, when a shot from the Prophet brought it down. It was lean and with young. These animals, although of incredible swiftness of foot, are still bad swimmers, and thus frequently fall

---

*The chief Waukerassah is mentioned by Captains Lewis and Clarke, whom he also visited.

a victim to the wolves, in their attempts to cross a stream. Today made twelve miles.

May 3. This morning we made great headway, and by night had accomplished full thirty miles. The game continued to be abundant. Buffaloes, in vast numbers, lay dead along the shore, and we saw many wolves devouring the carcasses. They fled always at our approach. We were much at a loss to account for the death of the buffaloes, but some weeks afterwards the mystery was cleared up. Arriving at a pass of the river where the bluffs were steep and the water deep at their base, we observed a large herd of the huge beasts swimming across, and stopped to watch their motions. They came in a sidelong manner down the current, and had apparently entered the water from a gorge, about half a mile above, where the bank sloped into the stream. Upon reaching the land on the west side of the river they found it impossible to ascend the cliffs, and the water was beyond their depth. After struggling for some time, and endeavouring in vain to set a foothold in the steep and slippery clay, they turned and swam to the eastern shore, where the same kind of inaccessible precipices presented themselves, and where the ineffectual struggle to ascend was repeated. They now turned a second time, a third, a fourth, and a fifth, always making the shore at very nearly the same places. Instead of suffering themselves to go down with the current in search of a more favourable landing (which might have been found a quarter of a mile below), they seemed bent upon maintaining their position, and, for this purpose, swam with their breasts at an acute angle to the stream, and used violent exertions to prevent being borne down. At the fifth time of crossing, the poor beasts were so entirely exhausted that it was evident they could do no more. They now struggled fearfully to scramble up the bank, and one or two of them had nearly succeeded when, to our great distress (for we could not witness their noble efforts without commiseration), the whole mass of loose earth above caved in, and buried several of them in its fall, without leaving the cliff in better condition for ascent. Upon this the rest of the herd commenced a lamentable kind of lowing or moaning, a sound conveying more of a dismal sorrow and despair than anything which it is possible to imagine, I shall never get it out of my head. Some of the beasts made another attempt to swim the river, struggled a few minutes, and sank, the waves above them being dyed with the red blood that gushed from their nostrils in the death agony. But the greater part, after the moaning described, seemed to yield supinely to their fate, rolled over on their backs, and disappeared. The whole herd was drowned; not a buffalo escaped. Their carcasses were thrown up in half an hour afterwards upon the flat grounds a short distance below, where, but for their ignorant obstinacy, they might so easily have landed in safety.

May 4. The weather was delightful, and, with a fair warm wind from the south, we made twenty-five miles before night. Today Thornton was sufficiently recovered to assist in the duties of the boat. In the afternoon he went out with me into the prairie on the west, where we saw a great number of early spring flowers of a kind never seen in the settlements. Many of them were of a rare beauty and delicious perfume. We saw also game in great variety, but shot none, as we were sure the hunters would bring in more than was wanted for use, and I was averse to the wanton destruction of life. On our way home we came upon two Indians of the Assiniboin nation, who accompanied us to the boats. They had evinced nothing like distrust on the way, but, on the contrary, had been frank and bold in demeanour; we were therefore much surprised to see them, upon coming within a stone's throw of the piroque, turn, both of them, suddenly round, and make off into the prairie at full speed. Upon getting a good distance from us, they stopped and, ascended a knoll which commanded a view of the river. Here they lay on their bellies, and, resting their chins on their hands, seemed to regard us with the deepest astonishment. By the aid of a spyglass I could minutely observe their countenances, which bore evidence of both amazement and terror. They continued watching us for a long time. At length, as if struck with a sudden thought, they arose hurriedly and commenced a rapid flight in the direction from which we had seen them issue at first.

May 5. As we were getting under way very early this morning, a large party of Assiniboins suddenly rushed upon the boats, and succeeded in taking possession of the piroque before we could make any effectual resistance. No one was in it at the time except Jules, who escaped by throwing himself into the river, and swimming to the large boat, which we had pushed out into the stream. These Indians had been brought upon us by the two who had visited us the day before, and the party must have approached us in the most stealthy manner imaginable, as we had our sentries regularly posted, and even Neptune failed to give any token of their vicinity.

We were preparing to fire upon the enemy when Misquash (the new interpreter—son of Waukerassah) gave us to understand that the Assiniboins were friends and were now making signals of amity. Although we could not help thinking that the highway robbery of our boat was but an indifferent way of evincing friendship, still we were willing to see what these people had to say, and desired Misquash to ask them why they had behaved as they did. They replied with many protestations of regard; and we at length found that they really had no intention of molesting us any further than to satisfy an ardent curiosity which consumed them, and which they now entreated us to appease. It appeared that the two Indians of the day before, whose singular conduct had so surprised us, had been struck with sudden amazement at the sooty appearance of our negro, Toby. They had never before seen or heard of a blackamoor, and it must therefore be confessed that their astonishment was not altogether causeless. Toby, moreover, was as ugly an old gentleman as ever spoke, having all the peculiar features of his race—the swollen lips, large white protruding eyes, flat nose, long ears, double head, pot belly and bow legs. Upon relating their adventure to their companions, the two savages could obtain no credit for the wonderful story, and were about losing caste forever, as liars and double-dealers, when they proposed to conduct the whole band to the boats by way of vindicating their veracity. The sudden attack seemed to have been the mere result of impatience on the part of the still incredulous Assiniboins; for they never afterwards evinced the slightest hostility, and yielded up the piroque as soon as we made them understand that we would let them have a good look at old Toby. The latter personage took the matter as a very good joke, and went ashore at once, *in naturalibus,* that the inquisitive savages might observe the whole extent of the question. Their astonishment and satisfaction were profound and complete. At first they doubted the evidence of their own eyes, spitting upon their fingers and rubbing the skin of the negro to be sure that it was not painted. The wool on the head elicited repeated shouts of applause, and the bandy legs were the subject of unqualified admiration. A jig dance on the part of our ugly friend brought matters to a climax. Wonder was now at its height. Approbation could go no further. Had Toby but possessed a single spark of ambition he might then have made his fortune forever by ascending the throne of the Assiniboins, and reigning as King Toby the First.

This incident detained us until late in the day. After interchanging some civilities and presents with the savages, we accepted the aid of six of the band in rowing us about five miles on our route, a very acceptable assistance, and one for which we did not fail to thank Toby. We made, today, only twelve miles, and encamped at night on a beautiful island which we long remembered for the delicious fish and fowl which its vicinity afforded us. We stayed at this pleasant spot two days, during which we feasted and made merry, with very little care for the morrow, and with very little regard to the numerous beaver which disported around us. We might have taken at this island one or two hundred skins without difficulty. As it was, we collected about twenty. The island is at the mouth of a tolerably large river coming in from the south, and at a point where the Missouri strikes off in a due westerly direction. The latitude is about 48 degrees.

May 8. We proceeded with fair winds and fine weather, and after making twenty or twenty-five miles, reached a large river coming in from the north. Where it debouches, however, it is very narrow, not more than a dozen yards wide, and appears to be quite choked up with mud. Upon ascending it a short distance, a fine bold stream is seen, seventy or eighty yards wide, and very deep, passing through a beautiful valley, abounding in game. Our new guide told us the name of this river, but I have no memorandum of it.* Robert Greely shot here some geese which build their nests upon trees.

May 9. In many places a little distant from the river banks, today, we observed the ground encrusted with a white substance which proved to be a strong salt. We made only fifteen miles, owing to several petty hindrances, and encamped at night on the mainland, among some clumps of cottonwood and rabbit-berry bushes.

May 10. Today the weather was cold, and the wind strong, but fair. We made great headway. The hills in this vicinity are rough and jagged, showing irregular broken masses of rock, some of which tower to a great height, and appear to have been subject to the action of water. We picked up several pieces of petrified wood and bone; and coal was scattered about in every direction. The river gets very crooked.

May 11. Detained the greater part of the day by squalls and rain. Towards evening it cleared up beautifully with a fair wind, of which we took advantage, making ten miles before encamping. Several fat beavers were caught, and a wolf was shot upon the bank. He seemed to have strayed from a large herd which were prowling about us.

May 12. Landed today at noon, after making ten miles, upon a small steep island, for the purpose of overhauling some of our things. As we were about taking our departure, one of the Canadians, who led the van of the party and was several yards in advance, suddenly disappeared from our view with a loud scream. We all ran forward immediately, and laughed heartily upon finding that our man had only tumbled into an empty *cache,* from which we soon extricated him. Had he been alone, however, there is much room for question if he would have got out at all. We

---

*Probably White-Earth River.

examined the hole carefully, but found nothing in it beyond a few empty bottles; we did not even see anything serving to show whether French, British, or Americans had concealed their goods there; and we felt some curiosity upon this point.

May 13. Arrived at the junction of the Yellowstone with the Missouri, after making twenty-five miles during the day. Misquash here left us, and returned home.

V

THE CHARACTER OF the country through which we had passed for the last two or three days was cheerless in comparison with that to which we had been accustomed. In general it was more level; the timber being more abundant on the skirts of the stream, with little or none at all in the distance. Wherever bluffs appeared upon the margin we descried indications of coal, and we saw one extensive bed of a thick bituminous nature which very much discoloured the water for some hundred yards below it. The current is more gentle than hitherto, the water clearer, and the rocky points and shoals fewer, although such as we had to pass were as difficult as ever. We had rain incessantly, which rendered the banks so slippery that the men who had the towing lines could scarcely walk. The air, too, was disagreeably chilly, and upon ascending some low hills near the river we observed no small quantity of snow lying in the clefts and ridges. In the extreme distance on our right we had perceived several Indian encampments which had the appearance of being temporary, and had been only lately abandoned. This region gives no indication of any permanent settlement, but appears to be a favourite hunting ground with the tribes in the vicinity, a fact rendered evident by the frequent traces of the hunt, which we came across in every direction. The Minnetarees of the Missouri, it is well known, extend their excursions in pursuit of game as high as the great fork, on the south side; while the Assiniboins go up still higher. Misquash informed us that between our present encampment and the Rocky Mountains we should meet with no lodges except those of the Minnetarees that reside on the lower or south side of the Saskatchawine.

The game had been exceedingly abundant, and in great variety: elk, buffalo, big-horn, mule-deer, bears, foxes, beaver, etc., etc., with wild fowl innumerable. Fish was also plentiful. The width of the stream varied considerably from two hundred and fifty yards to passes where the current rushed between bluffs not more than a hundred feet apart. The face of these bluffs generally was composed of a light yellowish freestone intermingled with burnt earth, pumice stone, and mineral salts. At one point the aspect of the country underwent a remarkable change, the hills retiring on both sides to a great distance from the river, which was thickly interspersed with small and beautiful islands, covered with cottonwood. The low grounds appeared to be very fertile; those on the north wide and low, and opening into three extensive valleys. Here seemed to be the extreme northern termination of the range of mountains through which the Missouri had been passing for so long a time, and which are called the Black Hills by the savages. The change from the mountainous region to the level was indicated by the atmosphere, which now became dry and pure; so much so indeed that we perceived its effects upon the seams of our boats, and our few mathematical instruments.

As we made immediate approach to the forks it came on to rain very hard, and the obstructions in the river were harassing in the extreme. The banks in some places were so slippery, and the clay so soft and stiff, that the men were obliged to go barefooted, as they could not keep on their moccasins. The shores also were full of pools of stagnant water, through which we were obliged to wade, sometimes up to our armpits. Then again we had to scramble over enormous shoals of sharp-pointed flints, which appeared to be the wreck of cliffs that had fallen down *en masse*. Occasionally we came to a precipitous gorge or gully, which it would put us to the greatest labour to pass; and in attempting to push by one of these the rope of the large boat (being old and much worn) gave way and permitted her to be swung round by the current upon a ledge of rock in the middle of the stream, where the water was so deep that we could only work in getting her off by the aid of the piroque, and so were a full six hours in effecting it.

At one period we arrived at a high wall of black rock on the south, towering above the ordinary cliffs for about a quarter of a mile along the stream; after which there was an open plain, and about three miles beyond this again, another wall of a light colour, on the same side, fully two hundred feet high; then another plain or valley, and then still another wall of the most singular appearance arises on the north, soaring in height probably two hundred and fifty feet, and being in thickness about twelve feet, with a very regular artificial character. These cliffs present indeed the most extraordinary aspect, rising perpendicularly from the water. The last mentioned are composed of very white soft sandstone, which readily receives the impression of the water. In the upper portion of them appears a sort of frieze or cornice formed by the intervention of several thin horizontal strata of a white freestone, hard, and unaffected by the rains. Above them is a dark rich soil, sloping gradually back from the water to the extent of a mile or thereabouts, when other hills spring up abruptly to the height of full five hundred feet more.

The face of these remarkable cliffs, as might be supposed, is chequered with a variety of lines formed by the trickling of the rains upon the soft material, so that a fertile fancy might easily imagine them to be gigantic monuments reared by human art, and carved over with hieroglyphical devices. Sometimes there are complete niches (like those we see for statues in common temples) formed by the dropping out bodily of large fragments of the sandstone; and there are several points where staircases and long corridors appear, as accidental fractures in the freestone cornice happen to let the rain trickle down uniformly upon the softer material below. We passed these singular bluffs in a bright moonlight, and their effect upon my imagination I shall never forget. They had all the air of enchanted structures (such as I have dreamed of), and the twittering of myriads of martins, which have built their nests in the holes that everywhere perforate the mass, aided this conception not a little. Besides the main walls there are, at intervals, inferior ones, of from twenty to a hundred feet high, and from one to twelve or fifteen feet thick, perfectly regular in shape, and perpendicular. These are formed of a succession of large black-looking stones, apparently made up of loam, sand, and quartz, and absolutely symmetrical in figure, although of various sizes. They are usually square, but sometimes oblong (always parallelipedal), and are lying one above the other as exactly and with as perfect regularity as if placed there by some mortal mason; each upper stone covering and securing the point of junction between two lower ones, just as bricks are laid in a wall. Sometimes these singular erections run in parallel lines, as many as four abreast; sometimes they leave the river and go back until lost amid the hills; sometimes they cross each other at right angles, seeming to enclose large artificial gardens, the vegetation within which is often of a character to preserve the illusion. Where the walls are thinnest, there the bricks are less in size, and the converse. We regarded the scenery presented to our view at this portion of the Missouri as altogether the most surprising, if not the most beautiful, which we had yet seen. It left upon my own mind an impression of novelty, of singularity, which can never be effaced.

Shortly after reaching the fork we came to a pretty large island on the northern side, one mile and a quarter from which is a low ground on the south very thickly covered with fine timber. After this there were several small islands, at each of which we touched for a few minutes as we passed. Then we came to a very black-looking bluff on the north, and then to two other small islands, about which we observed nothing remarkable. Going a few miles farther we reached a tolerably large island situated near the point of a steep promontory, afterwards passing two others, smaller. All these islands are well timbered. It was at night, on the 13th of May, that we were shown by Misquash the mouth of the large river, which in the settlement goes by the name of the Yellow

Stone, but by the Indians is called the Ahmateaza.* We made our camp on the south shore in a beautiful plain covered with cottonwood.

May 14. This morning we were awake and stirring at an early hour, as the point we had now reached was one of great importance, and it was requisite that, before proceeding any farther, we should make some survey by way of ascertaining which of the two large streams in view would afford us the best passage onward. It seemed to be the general wish of the party to push up one of these rivers as far as practicable, with a view of reaching the Rocky Mountains, when we might perhaps hit upon the head waters of the large stream Aregan, described by all the Indians with whom we had conversed upon the subject, as running into the great Pacific Ocean. I was also anxious to attain this object, which opened to my fancy a world of exciting adventure, but I foresaw many difficulties which we must necessarily encounter if we made the attempt with our present limited information in respect to the region we should have to traverse, and the savages who occupied it; about which latter we only knew indeed that they were generally the most ferocious of the North American Indians. I was afraid, too, that we might get into the wrong stream, and involve ourselves in an endless labyrinth of troubles which would dishearten the men. These thoughts, however, did not give me any long uneasiness, and I set to work at once to explore the neighbourhood; sending some of the party up the banks of each stream to estimate the comparative volume of water in each, while I myself, with Thornton and John Greely, proceeded to ascend the high grounds in the fork, whence an extensive prospect of the surrounding region might be attained. We saw here an immense and magnificent country spreading out on every side into a vast plain, waving with glorious verdure, and alive with countless herds of buffaloes and wolves, intermingled with occasional elk and antelope. To

---

*There appears to be some discrepancy here which we have not thought it worth while to alter as, after all, Mr Rodman may not be in the wrong. The Amateaza (according to the narrative of Lewis and Clarke) is the name given by the Minnetarees not to the Yellow Stone, but to the Missouri itself.

the south the prospect was interrupted by a range of high, snow-capped mountains, stretching from southeast to northwest, and terminating abruptly. Behind these again was a higher range, extending to the very horizon in the northwest. The two rivers presented the most enchanting appearance as they wound away their long snake-like lengths in the distance, growing thinner and thinner until they looked like mere faint threads of silver as they vanished in the shadowy mists of the sky. We could glean nothing, from their direction so far, as regards their ultimate course, and so descended from our position much at a loss what to do.

The examination of the two currents gave us but little more satisfaction. The north stream was found to be the deeper, but the south was the wider, and the volume of water differed but little. The first had all the colour of the Missouri, but the latter had the peculiar round gravelly bed which distinguishes a river that issues from a mountainous region. We were finally determined by the easier navigation of the north branch to pursue this course, although from the rapidly increasing shallowness we found that in a few days, at farthest, we should have to dispense with the large boat. We spent three days at our encampment, during which we collected a great many fine skins, and deposited them, with our whole stock on hand, in a well-constructed *cache* on a small island in the river a mile below the junction.* We also brought in a great quantity of game, and especially of deer, some haunches of which we pickled or corned for future use. We found great

---

Caches are holes very frequently dug by the trappers and fur traders, in which to deposit their furs or other goods during a temporary absence. A dry and retired situation is first selected. A circle about two feet in diameter is then described; the sod within this carefully removed and laid by. A hole is now sunk perpendicularly to the depth of a foot, and afterwards gradually widened until the excavation becomes eight or ten feet deep, and six or seven feet wide. As the earth is dug up, it is cautiously placed on a skin, so as to prevent any traces upon the grass, and, when all is completed, is thrown into the nearest river, or otherwise effectually concealed. This *cache* is lined throughout with dried sticks and hay, or with skins, and within it almost any species of backwoods property may be safely and soundly kept for years. When the goods are in, and well covered with buffalo hide, earth is thrown upon the whole, and stamped firmly down. Afterwards the sod is replaced, and a private mark made upon the neighbouring trees, or elsewhere, indicating the precise location of the depôt.

abundance of the prickly pear in this vicinity, as well as chokeberries in great plenty upon the low grounds and ravines. There were also many yellow and red currants (not ripe), with gooseberries. Wild roses were just beginning to open their buds in the most wonderful profusion. We left our encampment in fine spirits on the morning of May 18.

May 18. The day was pleasant, and we proceeded merrily, notwithstanding the constant interruptions occasioned by the shoals and jutting points with which the stream abounds. The men, one and all, were enthusiastic in their determination to persevere, and the Rocky Mountains were the sole theme of conversation. In leaving our peltries behind us, we had considerably lightened the boats, and we found much less difficulty in getting them forward through the rapid currents than would otherwise have been the case. The river was crowded with islands, at nearly all of which we touched. At night we reached a deserted Indian encampment, near bluffs of a blackish clay. Rattlesnakes disturbed us very much, and before morning we had a heavy rain.

May 19. We had not proceeded far before we found the character of the stream materially altered, and very much obstructed by sand bars, or rather ridges of small stones, so that it was with the greatest difficulty we could force a passage for the larger boat. Sending two men ahead to reconnoitre, they returned with an account of a wider and deeper channel above, and once again we felt encouraged to persevere. We pushed on for ten miles and encamped on a small island for the night. We observed a peculiar mountain in the distance to the south, of a conical form, isolated, and entirely covered with snow.

May 20. We now entered into a better channel, and pursued our course with little interruption for sixteen miles, through a clayey country of peculiar character, and nearly destitute of vegetation. At night we encamped on a very large island, covered with tall trees, many of which were new to us. We remained at this spot for five days to make some repairs in the piroque.

During our sojourn here an incident of note occurred. The banks of the Missouri in this neighbourhood are precipitous, and formed of a peculiar blue clay, which becomes excessively slippery after rain. The cliffs, from the bed of the stream back to the distance of a hundred yards, or thereabouts, form a succession of steep terraces of this clay, intersected in numerous directions by deep and narrow ravines, so sharply worn by the action of water at some remote period of time as to have the appearance of artificial channels. The mouths of these ravines, where they debouche upon the river, have a very remarkable appearance, and look from the opposite bank, by moonlight, like gigantic columns standing erect upon the shore. To an observer from the uppermost terrace the whole descent towards the stream has an indescribably chaotic and dreary air. No vegetation of any kind is seen.

John Greely, the Prophet, the interpreter Jules, and myself started out after breakfast one morning to ascend to the topmost terrace on the south shore for the purpose of looking around us; in short, to see what could be seen. With great labour, and by using scrupulous caution, we succeeded in reaching the level grounds at the summit opposite our encampment. The prairie here differs from the general character of that kind of land in being thickly overgrown for many miles back with cottonwood, rose bushes, red willow, and broad-leaved willow; the soil being unsteady, and at times swampy, like that of the ordinary low grounds; it consists of a black-looking loam, one third sand, and when a handful of it is thrown into water, it dissolves in the manner of sugar, with strong bubbles. In several spots we observed deep incrustations of common salt, some of which we collected and used.

Upon reaching these level grounds we all sat down to rest, and had scarcely done so when we were alarmed by a loud growl immediately in our rear, proceeding from the thick underwood. We started to our feet at once in great terror, for we had left our rifles at the island, that we might be unencumbered in the scramble up the cliffs, and the only arms we had were pistols and knives. We had scarcely time to say a word to each other before two enormous brown bears (the first we had yet encountered during the voyage) came rushing at us open-mouthed from a clump of rose bushes. These animals are much dreaded by the Indians, and with reason, for they are indeed formidable creatures, possessing prodigious strength, with untameable ferocity, and the most wonderful tenacity of life. There is scarcely any way of killing them by a bullet, unless the shot be through the brains, and these are defended by two large muscles covering the side of the forehead, as well as by a projection of a thick frontal bone. They have been known to live for days with half a dozen balls through the lungs, and even with very severe injuries in the heart. So far we had never met with a brown bear, although often with its tracks in the mud or sand, and these we had seen nearly a foot in length, exclusive of the claws, and full eight inches in width.

What to do was now the question. To stand and fight, with such weapons as we possessed, was madness; and it was folly to think of escape by flight in the direction of the prairie; for not only were the bears running towards us from that quarter, but, at a very short distance back from the cliffs, the underwood of brier bushes, dwarf willow, etc., was so thick that we could not have made our way through it at all, and if we kept our course along the river between the underwood and the top of the cliff, the animals would catch us in an instant; for as the ground was boggy we could make no progress upon it, while the large flat foot of the bear would enable him to travel with ease. It seemed as if these reflections (which it takes some time to embody in words) flashed all of them through the minds of all of us in an instant; for every man sprang at once to the cliffs, without sufficiently thinking of the hazard that lay there.

The first descent was some thirty or forty feet, and not very precipitous; the clay here also partook in a slight degree of the loam of the upper soil; so that we scrambled down with no great difficulty to the first terrace, the bears plunging after us with headlong fury. Arrived here, we had not a moment for hesitation. There was nothing left for us now but to encounter the enraged beasts upon the narrow platform where we stood, or to go over the second precipice. This was nearly perpendicular, sixty or seventy feet deep, and composed entirely of the blue clay which was now saturated with late rains, and as slippery as glass itself. The Canadian, frightened out of his senses, leaped to the edge at once, slid with the greatest velocity down the cliff, and was hurled over the third descent by the impetus of his course. We then lost sight of him, and of course supposed him killed; for we could have no doubt that his terrific slide would be continued from precipice to precipice until it terminated with a plunge over the last into the river, a fall of more than a hundred and fifty feet.

Had Jules not gone in this way it is more than probable that we should all have decided, in our extremity, upon attempting the descent; but his fate caused us to waver, and in the meantime the monsters were upon us. This was the first time in all my life I had ever been brought to close quarters with a wild animal of any strength or ferocity, and I have no scruple to acknowledge that my nerves were completely unstrung. For some moments I felt as if about to swoon, but a loud scream from Greely, who had been seized by the foremost bear, had the effect of arousing me to exertion, and when once fairly aroused I experienced a kind of wild and savage pleasure from the conflict.

One of the beasts, upon reaching the narrow ledge where we stood, had made an immediate rush at Greely, and had borne him to the earth, where he stood over him, holding him with his huge teeth lodged in the breast of his overcoat, which, by the greatest good fortune, he had worn, the wind being chilly. The other, rolling rather than scrambling down the cliff, was under so much headway when he reached our station that he could not stop himself until the one half of his body hung over the precipice; he staggered in a sidelong manner, and his right legs went over while he held on in an awkward way with his two left. While thus situated he seized Wormley by the heel with his mouth, and for an instant I feared the worst, for in his efforts to free himself from the grasp, the terrified struggler aided the bear to regain his footing. While I stood helpless, as above described, through terror, and watching the event without ability to render the slightest aid, the shoe and moccasin of Wormley were torn off in the grasp of the animal, who now tumbled headlong down to the next terrace, but stopped himself, by means of his huge claws, from sliding farther. It was now that Greely screamed for aid, and the Prophet and myself rushed to his assistance. We both fired our pistols at the bear's head; and my own ball, I am sure, must have gone through some portion of his skull, for I held the weapon close to his ear. He seemed more angry, however, than hurt; the only good effect of the discharge was in his quitting his hold of Greely (who had sustained no injury) and making at us. We had nothing but our knives to depend upon, and even the refuge of the terrace below was cut off from us by the presence of another bear there. We had our backs to the cliff, and were preparing for a deadly contest, not dreaming of help from Greely (whom we supposed mortally injured) when we heard a shot, and the huge beast fell at our feet, just when we felt his hot and horribly fetid breath in our faces. Our deliverer, who had fought many a bear in his lifetime, had put his pistol deliberately to the eye of the monster, and the contents had entered the brain.

Looking now downwards, we discovered the fallen bruin making ineffectual efforts to scramble up to us, the soft clay yielding to his claws, and he fell repeatedly and heavily. We tried him with several shots, but did no harm, and resolved to leave him where he was for the crows. I do not see how he could ever have made his escape from the spot. We crawled along the ledge on which we stood for nearly half a mile before we found a practicable path to the prairie above us, and did not get into camp until late in the night. Jules was there all alive, but cruelly bruised; so much so, indeed, that he had been unable to give any intelligible account of his accident or of our whereabouts. He had lodged in one of the ravines upon the third terrace, and had made his way down its bed to the river shore.

WHO IS THE MURDERER?

Edgar Allan Poe

IN THE SUMMER of the year 1830, there lived at a place called Eaglescliffe, near Yarm, in the North Riding of Yorkshire, a man of the name of William Huntley. He was one of the sons of a respectable farmer who had died about ten years before, leaving behind him a widow and several children, and considerable property to be divided between them; but his will was so imperfect and obscure as to have led to a Chancery suit, in order to determine the true distribution of the property according to his intention—which was, to leave his widow the interest of a certain sum for her life, and considerable legacies to each of his children, payable as they became of age. His son William was, in the year 1830, about thirty-four years of age, and married, but lived apart from his wife, with whom he had quarrelled. Owing to his being so long kept out of his little property, he became a weaver in order to support himself—and was, in fact, in very humble circumstances. In point of personal appearance—a matter to which I call your particular attention—he was of middling stature; he had a broad, squat face; his head was very large behind; his forehead a retreating one, with rather a deep indentation between the eyebrows; and he was pitted with the smallpox. But there was one peculiarity in his face—a very prominent tooth on the left side of the under-jaw—which caught everyone's eye on first looking at him. It occasioned him to have a sort of "twist of the mouth"—for which he had been always known and ridiculed by his companions, even at school.

The solicitor who had the management of the affairs in Chancery was a Mr Garbutt, residing at Yarm, and still living. He had occasionally assisted the family, and, amongst them, William Huntley, by small advances during the time of their being kept out of their property. At length, on *Thursday, 22nd July 1830*—I also beg your attention to dates—Mr Garbutt was enabled to pay over to him the money due under the will; and on that day gave him a sum of £85.16s.4d.—the balance due after deducting the above-mentioned advances—in seventeen £5 banknotes of the bank of Messrs Backhouse and Company, bankers at Stockton-upon-Tees, and the remainder in silver and copper. He was also entitled to receive other money, which Mr Garbutt had received instructions from him to endeavour to obtain; and I believe that he would have been entitled to a still further sum on his mother's death.

As I have already mentioned, Huntley at this time resided at Eaglescliffe, but was in the constant habit of coming over to a small village at a few miles' distance, called Hutton Rudby, where his mother lived, and also an intimate friend of his, one Robert Goldsborough, whose house, on such occasions, he was in the habit of making his own—always passing the night there. Goldsborough was about Huntley's age; was a widower, with a couple of children, and in very destitute circumstances, having even been in the receipt of parish relief down to within a very few months of the period at which this narrative commences. On the day of Huntley's receiving his money, viz. Thursday, the 22nd July, he went over to Hutton Rudby, and stayed there one or two days, principally in company with his friend Goldsborough. There is some reason to believe that Huntley was desirous of preventing two or three creditors of his from knowing that he had received so considerable a sum of money; and also that he had, about the time in question, intimated to one or two persons a wish to go to America.

He appears to have gone very frequently to and fro, between Hutton Rudby and Eaglescliffe, during the ensuing week. At an early hour, five o'clock, on the morning of *Friday, the 30th July,* he was seen coming to Goldsborough's house; again, about three o'clock in the afternoon of that day, walking on the high road, in company with Goldsborough, and a man named Garbutt; a third time, at eight o'clock in the evening of the same day, sitting

WHO IS THE MURDERER?

in Goldsborough's house; and about ten o'clock that night, he, Goldsborough, and Garbutt, were observed walking together in a cheerful and friendly manner—Goldsborough with a gun in his hand—all apparently bending their steps towards Crathorne Wood, which was close by, on a poaching errand. From that moment to the present, Huntley has never once been seen or heard of.

The circumstance of his disappearance was noticed as soon as six on the ensuing day, Saturday—and his continued absence rapidly increased the suspicion and alarm of the neighbourhood. A quantity of stale-looking blood being seen on the side of the high road, on the ensuing Monday morning, very near the spot where he had been last seen walking with Goldsborough and Garbutt—and also a man's recollecting that, between eleven and twelve o'clock on Friday night, he had heard the report of a gun in Crathorne Wood, added to the circumstance of Huntley's having been seen so frequently in Goldsborough's company, down even to the moment of his sudden disappearance, naturally pointed suspicion at Goldsborough, and anxious enquiries were at once made of him by many persons, to know what had become of Huntley. To one person, a creditor of Huntley's, Goldsborough said, with an easy confident air, that he had set Huntley on the road to Whitby, where he was going to take ship for America. To Whitby instantly went several persons in quest of the missing man, but in vain; no such person had been seen or heard of in that direction, nor was there—nor had there been for some time —in that port any vessel bound for America. The disappointed enquirers returned to Goldsborough, to announce the fruitlessness of their search, when he gave another account of Huntley's movements; namely, that he had set Huntley on the way to Liverpool, there to take ship for America; and a short time afterwards, to another class of enquirers, he told an entirely different story, that he had set Huntley on his way to Bidsdale, to see some friends of his residing there.

All this kindled still more vivid suspicion against him. Constables and others searched his house, and found in it a watch, and various articles of clothing, belonging to Huntley, but none of which he made the least attempt to conceal. When asked to account for his possession of them, he gave inconsistent answers. First, he said that Huntley had given them to him; but, on being reminded how improbable it was that a man so covetous as Huntley should have done so, he said that the fact was that he had lent Huntley money, and, on his going off to America, he had left the articles in question as a security for the repayment of what he owed. In short, Goldsborough was universally supposed to have murdered Huntley. On one occasion he said, without any embarrassment of manner, when taunted on the subject, "You'll all see, by and by, whether he's been murdered!" On another occasion, after following to his door a person who had just quitted it, he said to a man standing near, "That gentleman has been here asking after Huntley, but he'll neither find him at my house, nor at Whitby, nor nowhere else." Confident that the missing man had been murdered, the neighbours, and also the constables, searched far and wide after his body. To a party thus engaged, he once went up and said, impatiently, "You fools! it's no use searching there! Only you give up, and I'll bring Huntley to you in a fortnight!" From some cause or other, these efforts were shortly afterwards discontinued.

Some week or ten days after Huntley's disappearance, Goldsborough was observed sitting opposite a very large fire in his house, reading; and a strong smell was perceived as of woollen burning. "Dear me," said a person to him, "you've a large fire for summer time?" He said he could not sleep, so he was sitting up reading. To another person mentioning the smell of woollen burning, he replied that he had been burning only some old things which he had pulled from under the stairs. At times he appeared disconsolate, and agitated, and very reserved. Again, he was found suddenly in possession of a considerable sum of money—in banknotes, gold and silver—which he rather exhibited with some ostentation than concealed, and this as early as within a day or two after Huntley's disappearance: offering to lend to some persons, and making various purchases for himself. He remained at his house till towards the close of the autumn, when, wearied with the perpetual suspicions and ill-feeling exhibited towards him, he removed to the town of Barnsley, about thirty or forty miles off, and hired a loom of a man, at whose house he took up his abode. When asked what his name was, he replied, "Touch me lightly." He brought with him a good stock of clothes—many of them Huntley's—two watches, and plenty of money, with which he was very liberal. He complained of being out of health, and did no work—his chief amusement being the going out to shoot small birds. Some weeks afterwards he went away, and returned in company with a woman, whom he said he had married —and that she had brought him a sum of £80 for her fortune. On being asked whence he had come, he replied, "from Darlington" —and passed under the name of Robert Towers.

This mysterious disappearance of Huntley, connected as it was with the circumstances above related with reference to Goldsborough, gradually ceased to be the subject of gossip and speculation. But it may be asked, Why were not the startling facts of the case made the subject of a formal judicial enquiry? Let me ask another question, however, What proof was there that Huntley had been murdered at all, or that he was even dead? Was it impossible—or very improbable—that Goldsborough's account of the matter might be a true one, viz. that Huntley had gone to America, and that Goldsborough was purposely giving contradictory accounts of Huntley's movements, to enable him to elude discovery? There was, in fact, no *corpus delicti*—the very first step failed. No lawyer, on the above facts only, would feel himself warranted in recommending the prosecution of Goldsborough for murder, with so serious a chance of an acquittal: in which case, he could never have been again tried as the murderer, however conclusive might be evidence subsequently discovered. "However strong and luminous may be the circumstances, the coincidence of which tends to indicate guilt," observes a distinguished writer on the law of evidence, Mr Starkie, "they avail nothing, unless the *corpus delicti—the fact that the crime has been actually perpetrated*—shall have been first established. So long as the least doubt exists as to *the act*, there can be no certainty as to the criminal agent."

Thus, then, matters rested for a period of eleven years—that is, till the 21st June 1841—when a number of workmen were employed by a respectable farmer, a Quaker, named Nellist, in making some alteration in the sides of a *stell*, i.e. a brook or rivulet, dividing a place called Stokesley from another called Seymour. While one of the labouring men, named Robinson, was engaged in cutting into one of the sides of the stell, at a spot where there was a curve or bend in the stream, called Stokesley Beck, and which was about five miles distant from the spot where Huntley, Garbutt, and Goldsborough had been last seen walking together, after turning up two cattle bones, he discovered one belonging to a human body —a shin bone; and presently, within a space of about a yard and a quarter, "the bones of a Christian", as he expressed it; in fact, a complete skeleton, with the exception of the feet. The head lay at a distance of a yard from the shin bone. Deeming this rather a curious circumstance, he took out the bones very carefully, and laid them out at length on the side of the stell. They had lain at a depth of about three feet from the surface; and had evidently not been deposited there by digging a hole down from the surface, like a grave, but by hollowing out, or digging a hole in the stell-side, and then thrusting in the body, "back-side first, and doubled up," to use the words of the witness. The soil was tough and clayey; and the spot lay at a distance of about a hundred yards from the high road. This stell was, in fact, not an inconsiderable stream, sometimes subject to overflows; and there was a wooden footbridge over it, a good way higher up the stream. The skull was removed from the earth very carefully by hand. It was filled with earth, and the lower back part of it appeared to have been broken off. The bones having been thus carefully laid out, on Robinson's master, Nr Nellist, arriving at the spot in the evening, he saw them with not a little surprise; and on looking at the skull and jaw bone, particularly noticed *a long projecting tooth on the left side of the lower jaw*. With the exception of two or three, all the teeth were in their sockets, and remained in them till the bones, which had been very damp when first discovered, began to dry, when some of the teeth fell out, and, amongst others, the remarkable and all important tooth in question. Before this had occurred, however, Mr Nellist took home with him, on the same evening, the skull and jaw bone, and kept them, together with the loose teeth, in a pail. They were shortly afterwards, but before the prominent tooth in question had dropped out, seen by various persons; several of whom, on noticing the tooth, at once said that the skull was Huntley's, whom they had known. Mr Nellist committed the skull and teeth, a day or two afterwards, to the care of one Gernon, a constable, who put them into a basket; and having heard of the former suspicions against Goldsborough, whom he also ascertained to be then living under another name at Barnsley, set off of his own accord, carrying with him the bones, to take Goldsborough into custody.

On the evening of the 23rd June, he found Goldsborough sitting in his house alone, without his coat, which hung over a chairback. "I have come," said the constable abruptly, "to take you into custody for the murder of William Huntley, eleven years ago"—on which Goldsborough appeared dreadfully agitated. "Look at this," continued the officer, taking out the shattered skull, and showing it to Goldsborough, "and tell me if it isn't the remains of Huntley?" Goldsborough could not look at it, but his eyes wandered round the room; and with increasing trepidation, and bursting into tears, he exclaimed, "I'm innocent! They may swear my life away if they please, but I never had any clothes, or a watch [the constable had asked him if he had not a watch belonging to Huntley], or anything belonging to Huntley! The last time I ever saw him was on Thursday!" The constable then took him into custody, but released him the next morning, considering the evidence against him not sufficient to warrant his detention, especially as he had arrested Goldsborough on his own responsibility only.

The whole matter was soon, however, brought under the notice of the magistrates, and steps were taken at once to obtain any evidence that might throw light on this long-hidden transaction

—a reward of one hundred pounds being offered, in the usual terms, to anyone who should give such evidence as would lead to the discovery and conviction of the murderer of William Huntley. Shortly afterwards a man of the name of Thomas Groundy was heard making such observations as led to his being taken into custody, and on the 10th of August Goldsborough also was again arrested—having continued ever since in the same house in which he had formerly been seized, at Barnsley—on the charge of having murdered William Huntley; Thomas Groundy being charged as an accessory after the fact. The magistrates having heard all the evidence which had been collected, were of opinion that it was expedient for the ends of justice to permit Groundy to turn king's evidence, as it is called—i.e. to be relieved from the charge against himself, in order to give evidence impeaching his fellow-prisoner. That was done; and the following is a verbatim copy of his deposition—every syllable of which is worthy of notice, in consequence of an extraordinary circumstance which occurred shortly after it had been taken:

Thomas Groundy, being charged before us as an accessory after the fact to the murder by Robert Goldsborough of William Huntley, and being, after the hearing of all the evidence on the part of the prosecution, in the exercise of our discretion, admitted by us at this stage of the proceedings to give evidence against the said Robert Goldsborough, on his oath, saith:

On the Wednesday after William Huntley was missing, Robert Goldsborough came to me, and asked me if I would help him with a bag to Stokesley—he was going to America; and I told him I would go, and we went by Neville's hind house, and then we kept no road, and we went down to yon wood beside the stone bridge. He took me to a bag which was laid upon the ground in the wood, and I laid hold of it, and I found like a man's head, and I asked him what it was—and he stopped about five minutes before he spoke, and he then said, "It is a bad job, it is Huntley—as he was walking by me, I shot

WHO IS THE MURDERER?

him." Then I felt frightened, and wanted to go home, and Goldsborough said, "If you mention it, I'll give you as much." And I said I would not mention it, and I wanted to make off, and I made off. That body was in the wood, within two or three hundred yards from the bridge. It is quite a lonely place. It was a rough place in the wood. Goldsborough never said anything more to me about it, and I was frightened, and durst not mention it to him. It was about hay-time. I knew William Huntley. He had a long tooth, and used to twist his mouth.

Sworn, &c., 14th August 1841.

The mark of
THOMAS + GROUNDY.

Two or three hours afterwards, Groundy hanged himself! He had been placed in a room in York Castle, only to await the arrival of his sureties, who were to be bound with him for his appearance to give evidence at the trial, and had not been left above half an hour before he was found suspended by his neckerchief and braces to one of the iron bars of the window, his knees resting on the floor, and quite dead. He had been in good health and spirits, and perfectly sober, up to the last moment of his being seen alive; having observed, in answer to enquiries, that what he had just been swearing to he had mentioned to two or three persons, whom he named, shortly after the facts had happened. An inquest was held on his body, and a verdict returned of *felo de se*. To return, however—Goldsborough, having heard the whole of the evidence thus adduced against him, including, of course, that of Groundy, voluntarily made and signed the following statement, which also I shall present to you *verbatim*:

On Thursday the 22nd July 1830, William Huntley came to my house, and stopped and talked a while, and asked me to take a walk with him. We took a walk down over the bridge, and through Sir William Foulis's plantation. We sat down on the side of the footpath, in the plantation; and he says, "I want you to look at some papers I have;" and so he pulled them out of his inside coat pocket, one a largish paper, which he had got from Mr Garbutt, and he says, "I have been drawing my money," and said he had drawn £85.16s., and he said, "what is the reason of all this money kept back?" I looked at the paper, and told him what the sums were for. He said he did not want it mentioned to every person, for Dalkin, Robert Moon, and some others, who wanted money of him, would be at him. I told him I had nothing to do with it—I should say nothing about it—so we came home together, and he was backwards and forwards out of our house, and other houses in the town, all the day. He laid with me all night, as he generally used to do when he came to the town. He was backwards and forwards all the next day, and he hired a cart and brought a loom down from Robert Moon's, and sold it to George Farnaby that day, and he stopped all night again, and slept with me, and then he came to Stokesley on the Saturday, and tried me several times to go to America with him. I went with him to Stokesley. We were together awhile at Stokesley on that day, and then we parted, and I never saw him any more until the Thursday following, and he came down to me at Farnaby's shop at Hutton, and called of me out, and pushed me sadly to go to America with him, and I told him I had two children, and I should not leave them, as I was both father and mother to them. So he stopped awhile, and he said if I would not go, he could not force me; but if I would go, I should share with him as long as he had a halfpenny. I refused, and he stopped on a while, and we went out, and I set him down a few yards from the door, and left him. We shaked hands and parted; and he said, if Mr Garbutt did not put it out about his money, he would stop a few days longer, if people did not get to know about it. I have no more to say about it. That was the very last time I clapped my eyes upon him. If it was the last words I had to speak, I never was in Crathorne Woods, nor Weary Bank Woods, with Thomas Groundy. You may think it's a lie; but if it were the last words I had to speak, I never was with him.

ROBERT GOLDSBOROUGH.

He was then committed to York Castle, to take his trial at the next spring assizes for Yorkshire—an occasion looked forward to with universal interest by the inhabitants of that great county. Accordingly, at nine o'clock on Wednesday morning, the 9th of March 1842, he made his appearance at the bar of the Crown Court, before Mr Baron Rolfe—than whom a more patient, acute, and clear-headed judge could not have been selected to try such a case—to meet the fearful charge now made against him, of the "wilful murder of William Huntley, by discharging at him a loaded gun, and thereby giving him a mortal wound, of which he instantly died."

"Put up Robert Goldsborough," said the clerk of arraigns to the governor of the castle, as soon as Mr Baron Rolfe had taken his seat; and in a few moments' time a man was led along to the bar of the court, whose appearance instantly excited in me a mixed feeling of pity and suspicion—the latter, however, predominating. He was forty-seven years of age, of average make and height, wearing an old but decent-looking drab greatcoat, a printed cotton neckerchief, clean shirt-collar, and a pair of somewhat tarnished doeskin gloves. His hair and whiskers were of a dull sandy colour; his face rather long and thin; his eyes grey, heavy and slow in their movements, and with a sad expression; his upper lip long and heavy; his mouth compressed, with a certain indication of sullenness and determination. In short, his features were altogether of a rigid cast and a phlegmatic character, wearing an expression of great anxiety and depression. Whatever inward emotion he might be experiencing, he preserved an external composure of manner. On being placed at the bar, he rested his arms on the iron bar, with his hands clasped together—never removing the gloves he wore. This was the attitude which he preserved, with scarce any variation, during the whole of his two days' trial. He pleaded "Not Guilty" with an air of modest firmness and sadness—eyeing each of his jurymen as they were sworn, and also the judge in his imposing ermine robes, and the counsel immediately beneath him, with anxious attention. He appeared to me a man of firm nerves, or rather perhaps of slow feeling, who had made up his mind to the worst. Was he not an object of profound interest? Had he really done the deed which now, after so many years' concealment, was to be dragged into the light of day? Had he shot dead the companion walking beside him in unsuspicious sociality, rifled the bleeding body, and then thrust it, in the dead of the night, into the earth? Or was he standing there as innocent of the crime imputed to him as the judge who was to try him, yet long blighted by unjust suspicion, and now despairing of a fair trial—the miserable victim of blind and cruel prejudice—to be convicted, within a few days hanged, his body buried within the precincts of the prison; and presently afterwards William Huntley to appear again, alive and well!

The counsel for the prosecution opened the case with candour and judgment, giving a very clear account of the facts he expected to be able to establish; and in one of his observations the judge subsequently expressed his anxious concurrence, namely, the necessity there was for the jury to be on their guard against a certain air of romance which seemed shed over the case, and against a secret notion that the guilt of a long-hidden murder was *destined*, by some sort of special providence, to be brought home against the person now charged with it. I shall now proceed to give you a condensed and accurate account of all the *material* facts proved—you keeping your eye, all the while, on any points of coincidence or contradiction that may strike you; and I shall add such observations on the demeanour and character of the witnesses, as may possibly enable you the better to appreciate the value of their evidence. You are already supplied with a key to it, in the brief narrative I have given you in the former part of this article.

At the instance of the prisoner's counsel, all the witnesses were ordered out of court before the counsel opened the case for the prosecution. The following, then, was the evidence adduced to prove, first, that William Huntley *had been* murdered; and secondly, by Robert Goldsborough, the prisoner at the bar.

William Garbutt, a solicitor, proved the facts stated, at the commencement of the narrative, as to the family, the property,

WHO IS THE MURDERER?

the person of William Huntley; particularly the prominent tooth, the payment to him of £85. 16s. 4d. on Thursday the 22nd July 1830. He had examined the skull which had been found, and, from his recollection of the form of Huntley's countenance, believed it to have been his. He had never heard Huntley talk of going to America. A warrant had been issued against Garbutt in 1830, but unsuccessfully, as he had then absconded, and never since been heard of.

George Farnaby had known both Huntley and Goldsborough well. They were very intimate; and the last time he had seen them together was on *Thursday*, 29th July 1830. He saw Goldsborough enter his house (which was in the same yard as the witness's house) about 3 p.m. the next day (*Friday*), with a sort of sack, but could not guess what it contained, nor whether it was light or heavy. On the next evening (*Sunday*), Goldsborough stood at his window, and pressed the witness to accompany him to Yarm fair the next morning, saying, that a man there owed him £5; which sum Goldsborough offered to lend to the witness. Goldsborough went to the fair, and bought a cow there, and put it into a field belonging to witness. A week afterwards I was at Goldsborough's, when Dalkin called to enquire after Huntley. Goldsborough said, Huntley had gone to Whitby to sail for America. The witness had himself heard Huntley speak, at different times, of going to America.

Robert Braithwaite saw Huntley come to Goldsborough's door, knock, and be admitted, about *five o'clock in the morning of Friday, 30th July 1830*. He had a particular tooth in his under jaw, which pushed his lips out. Witness had seen the skull and jaw bone; and the tooth in it corresponded exactly with that of Huntley. Just before his disappearance, witness (a tailor) had made him a dark green coat with yellow roundish buttons, raised in the middle; a yellowish striped waistcoat with yellow buttons; and a pair of patent cord trousers, with a yellow sandy cast, and a broadish rib; and he distinctly observed that Huntley wore those trousers when he called at Goldsborough's, at five o'clock on the Friday morning. Witness had known Goldsborough all his life.

He was always very poor, and unable to pay witness for his clothes without the greatest difficulty.

James Gears was sitting smoking his pipe on the roadside, (where he was engaged breaking stones) at Hutton Rudby, *between three and four o'clock in the afternoon of Friday, 30th July 1830*. Huntley, Goldsborough, and Garbutt came up together, lit their pipes at mine, and then went down the lane, northward, towards Middleton. That was the last time he ever saw Huntley. On *Wednesday, 4th August* 1830, Goldsborough and I were walking together towards some potato fields, and he pulled a quantity of silver out of his left-hand pocket, and four or five £5 banknotes out of his righthand pocket. I knew them by the stamp to be £5 notes. He told me they were Bank of England notes. I said, "Robert, thou's well off—much better than I. I work hard for my family, and yet never have a penny to call my own." He said he had got the money out of the Stockton-on-Tees bank, where he could draw money whenever he wanted it, for he dealt in poultry. He had always till then been very poor; having many times occasion to borrow a little meal and a little flour from the witness. The witness had mentioned the circumstance of the three men lighting their pipes from his, to Bewick the constable, on Monday the 2nd August 1830. [If that were so, he must have then had his suspicions against Goldsborough; and it is rather odd that two days afterwards he should be walking so familiarly with Goldsborough, and should not have challenged him more strictly as to his suddenly acquired wealth. As singular is it that Goldsborough, if guilty, should have so stupidly exhibited it to one who well knew his previous poverty; and that, too, at the very time when everybody was beginning to suspect him as Huntley's murderer.]

James Braithwaite: The last time he ever saw Huntley was about *eight o'clock in the evening of Friday, 30th July 1830*, sitting on a box near the fire-place in Goldsborough's house. His face was full towards witness, who saw him quite plainly. On Monday, 2nd August 1830, was Yarm fair day; and on witness passing along the high road, about nine o'clock in the evening, he observed a pool of blood about fifty yards from the bridge, which

WHO IS THE MURDERER?

is a little below Foxton Bank, on the road from Yarm to Rudby. He mentioned the circumstance the same day to Brigham, the constable. About ten days afterwards, in passing Goldsborough's house about ten o'clock one night, he observed a large fire, and went in, and told Goldsborough that there was a strong smell of woollen burning. He replied that he had been burning some old rags. The witness soon after reminded him that it was bed time, and said, "Aren't you going to bed?" He replied "No; I can't sleep."

James Maw [By far the most important witness in the case. A violent attempt was made to impeach his credit; but in my opinion, and in that of all I conversed with, quite unsuccessfully. He was about forty years old, very calm and collected—with a sort of quaint frankness of manner, and gave his evidence in a fair, straightforward way.]: The last time he had ever seen Huntley was *about nine o'clock on the night of Friday, 30th July 1830*, near the bridle road leading to Crathorne Wood, in company with Goldsborough, who carried a new gun, and Garbutt—all three of whom the witness had long known well. Huntley wore a dark green coat, a yellow neckcloth, (that the witness particularly noticed), and darkish trousers and waistcoat. He spoke to witness, and said, "Where hast thou been, thou caffy dog? [which was a common expression of Huntley's] Wilt go along with us?" "No," replied the witness, "you'll be getting into mischief with your poaching!" "*Do* thou go with us," said Huntley; "we're going to try a new gun, and, if we catch a hare, we'll go to Crathorne, have it stewed, and get some ale." He then pulled out of his pockets some notes, showed them to the witness, and said, "I've plenty of money—I've been to Mr Garbutt's, and drawn part of my fortune." On this, Goldsborough said, "Put up thy money, thou fool; why art exposing it that way?" and then he added (but the witness was not sure whether to Huntley or Garbutt), "We'll have nobody with us." They then went on through the gate on to Crathorne bridle road, and the witness went home, which he reached about ten o'clock. [I shall give the remainder of his evidence in his own words.] "On Saturday, 7th August, Bewick the constable and I went to the shop of Hall, a butcher at Hutton Rudby, and there we had some talk about Huntley's being missing; and we and several others went that night to Goldsborough's house. Bewick said, 'Goldy, there are strange reports about Huntley; what hast thou *really* done with him?' Goldsborough was very much agitated, making no answer for some time; then said he had set Huntley on the Whitby road as far as Easley Bridge, to take ship for America. But I said *that* was very unlikely, for there had been no ship advertised to go to America. Shortly afterwards, he said he had set Huntley on the Tontine road, to take coach for Liverpool—which was in the opposite direction to Whitby. I asked if Huntley had booked at the Tontine? Goldsborough said no, he had got on the coach beyond the Tontine. On this we all told him these were two opposite tales. I forget what his answer was, but he seemed very much agitated—so much so, that he quite shook, and required to use both his hands to put his hat on. Bewick and I at another time went to call on him, and found him walking up and down before some houses near his own. Bewick said, 'Now, really tell us, what hast thou done with Huntley?' He answered and said [that was the formal style in which much of the witness's evidence was given] 'I set him up Carlton Bank, to go into Bilsdale, to see some friends of his.' We said that was again another different story; but I forget his answer. The same evening, I and four other men (some of them constables), who all died of the cholera when it was here, went to Goldsborough's house to search it—he not objecting to it. We found a pair of woollen corded trousers, an old waistcoat, and an old coat. I could almost have sworn they were all Huntley's. We also found six new shirts, marked 'W. H. 1', 'W. H. 2', 'W. H. 3', 'W. H. 4', 'W. H. 5', 'W. H. 6', in an old-fashioned piece of furniture, like a box or press, upstairs; not in the room where one Hannah Best was engaged washing. The shirts had been made by one Hannah Butterwick; she was then there, and is now living, but I know not where. We asked Goldsborough how he explained all these things; and he said that Huntley had given the things to him. We said, 'No, no; he's too greedy a man for that,' on which

Goldsborough said he had lent Huntley money, and he had left these things in part payment. There was a watch, seemingly of silver, with 'W. H.' engraved on the back, hanging up over the fireplace. We took it down, and examined it. There were two papers inside, one with the name of 'Mr Needham', the other 'Mr Stephenson, watch and clock-maker, Stokesley'. Goldsborough gave the same account of the watch as he had given of the clothes and shirts. There was a gun up the stairs, like the one I had observed in his hand when I last saw him with Huntley: it was new-looking. His sister-in-law pointed to it, crying and saying, 'Oh, Robert, this is the thing thou'st either killed or hurt Huntley with.' He replied, 'Hold thy tongue, thou fool!' and was much agitated. I afterwards was one of those who went to search for Huntley's body. About fifty yards from that part of the road where the blood was found, near Foxton Bridge, I recollect seeing a place, in a potato ground, where the earth seemed to have been *newly dug*. [It certainly seems most unaccountable that, if this circumstance really had been observed at that time, a spot so challenging suspicion should not have been instantly examined.] After we had been searching some time, we met Goldsborough, who said, 'Where have you been searching to-day?' Several persons replied 'In Foxton Beck, Foxton Woods, and Middleton and Crathorne Woods.' Goldsborough answered, 'He's far more likely to be found in Stokesley Beck.' " [*The very place where the skeleton was found.*] The witness then described Huntley's face, particularly his projecting tooth; and said he had seen the skull and jaw bone, with the projecting tooth in it, just in the same place as Huntley's was, and projecting in the same way.

John Sanderson lived in a house 200 yards from Crathorne Wood, and well recollected hearing, about eleven or twelve o'clock on the night of Friday, 30th July 1830 (the Friday before Yarm fair), a shot fired in the wood; and a second within about a minute afterwards. It seemed about a quarter of a mile off. He got up and listened; but heard nothing more. There was game in the wood, and there *were* sometimes poachers.

Bartholomew Goldsborough: On going on Monday morning,

2nd August 1830, to Yarm fair, saw a pool of stale-looking blood, about one and a half feet in diameter, lying on the high road (which was not much frequented), a little on the Crathorne side of the road, and in a slanting direction towards the gate leading into Crathorne Wood. He had noticed this blood before he had heard that Huntley was missing. The place where the blood lay was from four to six miles' distance from Stokesley Beck, where the skeleton was found.

Thomas Richardson had sold Goldsborough a single-barrelled gun, on Monday, 26th July 1830, for 8s. It was an old one, but cleaned and polished up so as to look like a new one. He did not pay for it, saying, he would take it on trial. A day or two after Yarm Fair (which was on Monday, 2nd August 1830), the witness called on him for payment. Goldsborough said he would return it—he did not want it, and had not used it. The witness thrust his finger down the muzzle, and when he drew it out it was dirty with the mark of powder. The witness showed him the finger, and told him he *had* used the gun; which the witness then took away. When the witness entered Goldsborough's house, the latter was engaged at a chest, in which were some clothes; he particularly recollected seeing a pair of woollen cord trousers, broad striped, and a yellow cast with them; a yellow waistcoat with a dark stripe, with gilt buttons. There were other clothes of a dark colour. The trousers and waistcoat were Huntley's—for the witness had seen him wear them. He had also seen Huntley wearing a green coat with brass buttons, having a nob on them. [This witness gave his evidence in a satisfactory manner; and admitted, on cross examination, having been once or twice, some time before, imprisoned for poaching, and once for having stolen some goslings; of which, however, he strenuously declared that he had not been guilty. Mr Baron Rolfe, in summing up, seemed to attach no weight to these circumstances as impeaching the value of his evidence.]

Joseph Dalkin: Heard on Sunday, 1st August 1830, of Huntley's disappearance, and went on that day to Goldsborough's, to enquire after him. Goldsborough said he had set Huntley along Stokesley Lane—that he was going to sail for America from

Whitby, at four o'clock on the next morning (Monday.) Witness said he would go and stop him, for he owed witness £4 for a suit of clothes. Goldsborough said, "Huntley and I have had all that matter talked over about his owing thee money; he never intends paying thee—and it's of no use thy going after him." The witness, however, did go immediately to Whitby (a distance of thirty miles) and searched the whole town for Huntley, but in vain: nor was there any vessel going to America. When the witness measured Huntley, he wore a pair of patent cord trousers, with broad rib, and yellowish cast. He had pressed Huntley several times, in vain, to pay his bill.

George Bewick, a linen manufacturer, and also, in 1830, a constable. He had known Huntley, and recollected his disappearance. In consequence of hearing of it, he went soon after to Hall's (the butcher's) shop, where were Goldsborough and several others; but he did not then recollect whether the witness Maw was also there. Huntley's wife also accompanied witness, and he said to Goldsborough, "There's a report that Huntley is missing; and, as I hear you were last with him, I thought you the likeliest person to ask about him." He replied that "Huntley had some relations at Bilsdale, and had gone there to see them." "Why then," asked the witness, "did you tell Joe Dalkin he had gone to Whitby, and thereby give him a sixty miles' journey for nought?" He made some unsatisfactory answer; but what it was the witness did not recollect. He was agitated, and trembled. The witness then said to him, "I understand thou hast Huntley's five shirts: how did'st thou come by them?" He answered that he had bought them of Huntley: to which the witness replied, "I understand you and Huntley bought a web from George Farnaby between you, which made you five shirts each; and it was not likely that either you could buy or he would sell you his five shirts; and here's his wife says he was badly off for shirts—having only a bad one on, and a worse one off!" His answer to this the witness had forgotten. He proceeded to give the same description of Huntley's person which had been given by the other witnesses; adding, "Huntley had something more remarkable about his appearance than most men," and that he had seen and examined the skull and jaw bone, and believed it to be Huntley's. [This was an important witness; of respectable character and appearance; and corroborating the evidence of Maw in several most material particulars. No attempt even was made to shake him by cross-examination.]

Anthony Wiles, till within the last seven years, had lived next door to his stepsister, who kept a chandler's shop at Hutton Rudby; and where he had often seen Huntley go in to change his money into half-crown pieces, for which he always seemed to have a peculiar fancy. Witness knew Goldsborough well; and recollected the time of Yarm fair, on Monday, 2nd August 1830. On the Saturday before (31st July) recollected seeing Goldsborough, *Thomas Groundy*, and two others, in a public house drinking, in the front kitchen; they came in about twelve o'clock at night, and remained there till four o'clock in the morning. They had at least thirteen pints of ale; and Goldsborough paid for all—giving half-crowns, and getting change for them every second or third pint. The witness was one of those who had searched for Huntley's body on the Friday or Saturday after he was missing. After having been home to get some refreshment, they returned to their task; and while at a hay stack, which was near about two miles from the place where the bones were found, Goldsborough came up, anxious and breathless, and said, "What are you doing there?—a lot of fools! If you'll only wait, I'll bring him forward in a fortnight!"

Then was adduced the evidence of the discovery of the bones, and the locality where they were found, of which I have already given some account. The "Stell" in question seemed to be a sort of tributary stream to the river Leven, two or three yards deep, though not very broad, and was occasionally subject to floods, when its water would run very rapidly down, past the spot where the bones were found, which was in a sort of small bend or curve of the stream, where the current had in a manner undermined the bank, which it left considerably overhanging. As I understood it, this hollowed part must have been still further excavated, for the purpose of receiving the body, which was supposed to have been

WHO IS THE MURDERER?

thrust in "backside foremost", leaving the skull at one angle, and the feet at the opposite one of the base of the triangle. The soil was, I believe, alluvial. The spot in question was a very secluded one, being the property of a Colonel——, who had once or twice been seen fishing in it. There was a footbridge, but at a very considerable distance, higher up the stream. The whole of a human skeleton was found except the feet, the small bones of which might have been exposed to the action of the current, and from time to time washed away. All the bones, and particularly the skull, were removed most carefully by the hand, so that no injury might be inflicted by spade or pickaxe. When first discovered, it would appear certain that there was a very prominent tooth on the left of the lower jaw, which arrested the attention of all those who saw it; but soon afterwards, owing to the inconceivable carelessness and stupidity of those entrusted with the custody of such all-important articles, and who permitted every idle visitor to have free access to them, the tooth in question—alas!—was lost! I confess I have seldom experienced such a rising of indignation, as when this disgraceful deficiency of evidence was thus accounted for; and had I been the judge, the very least symptom of my displeasure would have been the disallowance of the costs of any witness in whose custody the bones had been placed when the tooth in question was with them. But to return—it was now nearly five o'clock in the afternoon, and as the case for the crown must inevitably close very shortly, it was very properly determined upon to produce the bones during the broad daylight, to enable the jury, judge and witnesses, to see them distinctly. As soon as I heard a whispered suggestion to that effect, I fixed my eyes closely on the prisoner. As soon as he heard the order given to produce the bones, I perceived that he slightly changed colour; and turning his head a little towards the witness box, where he expected them to be produced, he directed quick furtive glances, while a new square deal box was brought forward, and unlocked. To the eye of a close observer, the prisoner's countenance now evidenced the miserable and almost overpowering agitation he was experiencing—and that, withal, he was nerving himself up, so to speak, to a great effort. I perceived his breast twice or thrice heave heavily; and, though conscious of being watched closely by those around him, he could not keep his eyes for more than a moment away from the box, with whose mysterious contents he was to be so quickly confronted. At length a dark brown skull, the hinder part appearing to have been broken off, was lifted out of the box: the prisoner's under lip drooped a little, and perceptibly quivered for a moment or two—and after one or two glances at the skull, he looked in another direction, his eyes—if I know any thing of human expression—full of suppressed agony and terror. Yet again—and again—he glanced at the dumb but fearful witness produced against him; and from a certain tremulous motion of the ends of his neckerchief, I could perceive that his heart was beating violently. Still he never moved from the position which he had occupied since the morning; though I learnt from one of the turnkeys who stood near him in the dock, that at the period I am mentioning, and also at several other periods of the day, he trembled so violently, and his knees seemed so near giving way, that they almost thought he would have fallen.

In these observations concerning the prisoner's demeanour, I am happy to find myself corroborated by a learned friend, himself a very close observer, who was engaged in the case, and made a point of watching the prisoner closely at the moment which I also had selected for so doing. He tells me that he had also observed another little circumstance—that the prisoner listened with comparative unconcern to those portions of the evidence relating to the blood found on the road, the sound of the gun shot heard in the wood, his possession of the clothes of Huntley, and his conflicting accounts concerning them and the movements of Huntley; but whenever there was any allusion to the disposal of the body, the carrying of it, and depositing it at Stokesley Beck, he became evidently painfully absorbed by what was said—agitated and apprehensive—always, however, striving to conceal his emotion.

For what reason I know not, but no other portions of the skeleton were produced in court than the skull, the jaw bone, the teeth, and a portion of the pelvis. I examined them all very carefully. They were of a dark brown colour, with no appearance of decay —on the contrary, they seemed strong and compact. Most of the teeth were so loose as to fall out of the sockets, unless held in them while the jaw bone and skull were being examined. None of the teeth were decayed, but were just such as might have been expected in a healthy adult, who had at all events never had diseased teeth. I examined very minutely the socket which had contained, when the bones were first discovered, the prominent tooth—the first molar tooth on the left side of the lower jaw—subsequently so strangely lost. There was little *apparent* difference between it and its corresponding socket on the other side of the lower jaw; than which, however, it was a trifle deeper, and the outside edge projected a little, and only a very little, more outwards. But even had they both been precisely similar, I conceive it yet quite possible that the tooth may, in life, have been a larger one than usual above the gum, and inclining a little outwards, so as to cause a perceptible protrusion of the under lip. As far as my own impression goes, I should certainly have felt the greatest difficulty in pronouncing, from the mere appearance of the socket, that the tooth it had contained must have been such a prominent and projecting one, as to give the living individual a remarkable peculiarity of countenance. But it must be borne in mind that a very striking prominent tooth that socket actually did contain when first removed from the earth, unless all the witnesses who said they observed it, Mr Strother the surgeon included, are perjured, or labouring under an inconceivable delusion on the subject. The skull was dark, and of compact texture; but the first thing that struck you was, that a great portion of the lower hinder part was wanting, and seemed to have been broken off. It had no appearance of having decayed or mouldered away, but of having been fractured, broken off; but whether before or after death, I cannot venture to offer an opinion. The edge was rough and abrupt—I mean not smooth and uniform, but strong and well defined. In short, the missing part *must* have been broken off. I observed no traces whatever of shot marks in any part of the skull or jaw. About two-thirds of the back part of the skull were missing. If one may be allowed to speculate in such a matter, I should say that, if a loaded gun or pistol had been discharged during lifetime at the person to whom that skull had belonged, say with the muzzle pointed at or near either ear, in a direction parallel, or nearly so, with the other; or if, even, it had been discharged from behind, but in a somewhat upward direction; or if the person had been felled by a heavy blow from behind, and subsequently repeated till death ensued; or if, having been in the first instance shot, the back of the head had been battered in by blows from any heavy instrument, whether before or after death —in any of these cases, I should have expected the skull, after lying ten or twelve years in the ground, without having ever been in any coffin, to present the appearance exhibited by the skull in question, while I was handling and examining it in court. But I could by no means say that such an appearance could not also have been occasioned by any violent injury suffered by the skull five, eight, ten, or twelve years after death. It will be observed that the skull in question was found in a tough clayey soil, near a stream, where it may have lain for twelve years, or more, without probably having ever been touched or disturbed since first deposited there; and, when first discovered, was carefully removed by the hand only of him who first saw it. What inference is to be drawn from the fact that the skull was found full of earth, but not the sockets of the eyes, nor the mouth, I know not. As to judging from the mere skull of the general form of the countenance during life, it is obviously a matter of infinite difficulty. Who, for instance, can tell whether the party's face was a fat or a lean one? All I can say is, that having heard the same account given by so many of the witnesses of Huntley's face and head, and without regarding their further statement that the skull, in their opinion, had belonged to him, I thought it very probable that such was the fact. The skull was large, particularly towards the back part; the forehead narrow, and rather retreating; there was some sinking between the eyebrows; and from the bones of the nose, I should think it must have been a flat spreading nose.

WHO IS THE MURDERER?

The only professional witness called, was a respectable surgeon who lived in the neighbourhood where the bones were found. He swore that when he first saw the jaw bone, a day or two after it had been discovered, it contained the remarkable projecting tooth in question; and from the form of the skull, and of the pelvis, he was confident that they had been those of an adult male. He also said, that from the form of the socket, it must have contained such a tooth as would have given Huntley the appearance described by the witnesses. "It is," said he, holding the skull and jaw bone together in his hand, "the skull of a person who had a short round face, a low forehead sloping back, a broad flat nose, and a depression at the top of it." The bones, he continued, appeared to have been in the ground nine or ten years: they *might* have lain there as long even as twenty years; and though certainly much would depend, with reference to such a point, upon the nature of the soil where they had lain, he had not made any chemical examination of it. From the broken appearance of the skull, he pronounced a confident opinion that the person to whom it had belonged had died a violent death. In answer to a pointed question from the judge, the witness repeated that the tooth in question, when he saw it in the jaw, projected a good deal more than such a tooth generally did. So much for the bones.

There was offered in evidence the deposition of Thomas Groundy, and the prisoner's counsel strongly urged that it was inadmissible. The contrary, however, was clear; and Mr Baron Rolfe so held. Groundy had been admitted by the magistrates to give evidence, having been himself thereby exonerated from the charge against him; that evidence had been given on oath, voluntarily, and in the presence of the prisoner, who might have put to him any questions he might have thought proper; the witness was since dead; and his deposition fell within the ordinary rule—being *admissible* in evidence; but what *credit* was due to it, was, of course, quite another matter. The governor of the castle was then sworn, and he proved the fact of Groundy's having been found dead in the manner already described; and then the deposition was formally read in evidence by the officer of the Court.

Mr Garbutt (the first witness, and who was also the clerk to the magistrates) then proved, that as soon as the above deposition had been made, he, accompanied by a police-officer, went to Crathorne Wood, and they found places in it exactly corresponding with those named in the deposition. At the insistance of the prisoner's counsel, Gernon, the officer to whose care the bones had been first committed, was recalled, and produced a flat button which had been found near the bones, and which was of a different description from the buttons which had been spoken of by the witnesses as worn by Huntley—for the purpose, of course, of weakening the evidence of identity. The prisoner's own statement before, on being committed for trial, was then formally put in and read. This closed the case against the prisoner; and it being nearly seven o'clock in the evening, the Court adjourned—the jury being accommodated during the night in the Castle, so that they might enter into conversation with no persons whatever on any pretence.

When the prisoner was placed again at the bar, at nine o'clock on the ensuing morning, his countenance bore marks of the anxiety and agitation he must have endured in the interval, and looked worn and haggard indeed. His counsel then rose, and addressed the jury for three hours, often with considerable force and ingenuity. He impugned the credibility of almost all the witnesses—especially those who had given the strongest evidence. He denied that there was a tittle of evidence to show that Huntley was not at this moment alive and well—and ridiculed the idea of the skull produced being that of Huntley, commenting with just severity on the absence of the tooth—the great point of the pretended identity. His opinion, he said, was, that the bones had belonged to a female; and his "hypothesis" that some drunken person had fallen from the bridge into the stream, been drowned, and the body carried down by the current, and forced into the bend of the stream, where they had been found. He proceeded to argue, at great length and with much vehemence; that the prisoner's possession of Huntley's clothes and property—which he denied to be the fact, for the witnesses "lied"—was consistent

WHO IS THE MURDERER?

with a scheme between him and Huntley to enable the latter to go to America. He said the evidence was a tissue of exaggerations, misrepresentations, and perjuries—the legitimate produce of the "blood money" which had been had recourse to. If Huntley were murdered, again, might it not have been by Garbutt? or Groundy—who had, immediately after his false evidence, gone and hanged himself, like Judas?

He sat down, urging on the jury that it was infinitely better that ten guilty persons should escape, than that one innocent person should be condemned; and Mr Baron Rolfe immediately proceeded to discharge his very responsible and difficult duty of summing up the whole case to the jury. I took no notes of it; and do not, consequently, feel myself warranted in giving any detailed account of so critical a matter, from mere recollection. None of the newspapers have rendered me, in this dilemma, the slightest assistance: for, after giving at great length the speech of the prisoner's counsel (who, of course, must take only one view of the case), the view taken by the judge—the able, experienced, and *impartial* person, on whose view, in nine cases out of ten, adopted by the jury, the prisoner's fate almost exclusively depends in capital charges—is thus summarily dismissed: "Mr Baron Rolfe then proceeded to sum up, commenting on the evidence as he proceeded, and pointing out such facts as bore for or against the prisoner"—but what those facts were, or how dealt with by the judge, the reader of the paper has not the slightest glimmering notion afforded him. If anything said by me could have the least weight with the gentlemen who perform the honourable and responsible duties of reporting cases of law, especially in great criminal trials in the newspapers, I would recommend them to give the *evidence* fully, and also a careful account of the judge's summing up to the jury.

Mr Baron Rolfe's summing up was decidedly adverse to a conviction. He first read over to the jury the whole of the evidence which had been adduced in the case; and then gave a very lucid statement of the principles by which the law required him to be governed, in estimating the value of that evidence. He left it fairly to them to judge whether sufficient had been done to satisfy them, beyond all *reasonable* doubt, that the bones produced were those of Huntley; but accompanied by a strong expression of his own opinion, that the evidence was of a very unsatisfactory nature. Unless they were satisfied on *that* head, there was an end of the case, for the very first step failed, viz. proving that Huntley was dead. If, however, on the whole of the facts, they should feel satisfied in the affirmative, then came the other great question in the case—had Huntley been murdered by the prisoner at the bar? Was the evidence strong enough to bring home the charge to him? His lordship advised them to place little or no reliance on the evidence contained in Groundy's deposition; and then proceeded to analyse the *viva voce* evidence which had been given. Even if the whole of it were believed by the jury, still it was not *absolutely* inconsistent with the fact of the prisoner's innocence of having murdered Huntley, and with the truth of his story that he had assisted Huntley in going off secretly to America. Without impugning the general character of the witnesses, his lordship pointed out how unconsciously liable persons were, in cases like these, to fit facts to preconceived notions, giving them a complexion and a connection not warrantable by the reality—and all this without *intending* to state what they believed to be untrue. Many of the facts spoken to were utterly irreconcilable with the supposition of the prisoner's conscious guilt; while others again were certainly difficult to be accounted for on the supposition of his innocence. Some were highly improbable, and others inconsistent; while in one or two instances there were material discrepancies between the witnesses: for instance, Maw spoke positively to seeing *six* shirts, numbered accordingly, up to "W. H. 6", whereas Bewick proves that there were only *five*—that Huntley and the prisoner had bought a web sufficient to make them five shirts apiece. Again, the time and place where the blood was found—if found it had been—and the two reports of a gun in the wood, were, especially when coupled with the great distance at which the bones were found, circumstances very difficult to

WHO IS THE MURDERER?

connect with the death of Huntley, in the manner suggested by the prosecution. The case, in fact, was distinguished by many singular circumstances—and the duty which thus devolved on the jury was a serious and difficult one, requiring of them calm and unprejudiced consideration. They were to remember that it was for the prosecutor to satisfy them of the guilt of the prisoner—beyond all *reasonable* doubt. If, however, they did entertain serious doubts, then it was their duty to consider the case as *not proved*, or—to use a phrase of which his lordship did not approve—"to give the prisoner *the benefit* of the doubt." Finally, they had sworn to give their verdict *according to the evidence*, and that only. It was their solemn duty to do so, and entirely to disregard any consequences that might follow in their verdict.

The jury then retired from court, attended, as usual, by a sworn bailiff, and taking with them the bones which had been produced in evidence. The prisoner eyed them as they went with deep anxiety, and was then removed from the bar, to await the agitating moment of their return. While he is sitting alone in this frightful suspense, and the jury are engaged in their solemn deliberation, let us endeavour ourselves to deal with this extraordinary case, by considering the principles which our law brings to bear upon such an enquiry—the various solutions of which the facts are susceptible, and which of those solutions we should ourselves be inclined to adopt.

First, then, said the law in this case, in the autumn of 1830—let me be assured of the fact that a murder has been committed—that the missing person is really dead. Melancholy experience warrants the anxiety of the law on this score, namely, to obtain evidence that the missing person is actually dead. The great Lord Hale would never allow a conviction for murder, unless proof were first given of the death of the party charged to have been murdered, by either direct evidence of the fact, or the actual finding of the body; " and this," says he (2 Hale, 290), " for the sake of two cases—the first, one mentioned by my Lord Coke: 'The niece of a gentleman had been heard to cry out, *Good uncle, do not kill me!* and soon afterwards disappeared. He, being presently suspected of having destroyed her for the sake of her property, was required to produce her before the justices of assize. She, however, had absconded, whereby he was unable to produce her; but, thinking to avert suspicion, procured another girl resembling his niece, and produced her as his niece. The fraud was detected, and, together with other circumstances, appeared so strongly to prove the guilt of the uncle, that he was convicted and executed for the supposed murder of his niece, who, as it afterwards turned out, was still living!' " "The second case," continues Lord Hale, "happened within my own remembrance in Staffordshire, where one A was long missing; and, upon strong presumptions, B was supposed to have murdered him, and to have consumed him to ashes in an oven, that he might never be found; and upon this, B was indicted for murder, convicted, and executed. Within one year afterwards, A returned, having been indeed sent beyond seas against his will by B, who had thus been innocent of the offence for which he suffered." But by far the most remarkable case of this kind on record is that of Ambrose Gwynne, who, on evidence which really appeared conclusive and irresistible, was condemned for murder, hanged and gibbeted; yet, in consequence of a series of singular circumstances, he survived his supposed execution—escaped to a foreign country, and there actually saw and conversed with the very person for the murder of whom he had been condemned to die! Surely the frightful possibility of the recurrence of such cases as these, warrants the law in requiring full and decisive evidence of the death of the party missing. By this, however, is not meant that actual proof of the finding and identifying of the body is absolutely essential. "To lay down a strict rule to such an extent," justly observes Mr Starkie, "might be productive of the most horrible consequences." Accordingly, in Hindmarch's case (2 Leach, 571), a mariner being indicted for the murder of his captain at sea, and a witness swearing that he saw the prisoner throw the captain overboard, and he was never seen or heard of afterwards, it was left to the jury to say whether the deceased had not been killed by the prisoner before being thrown into the sea. The jury found him guilty—with the subsequent unanimous approbation of the twelve judges to whom the case was referred, and the prisoner was executed. It is indeed easy to imagine cases in which the bodies of murdered persons, especially infants, might be removed at once, and for ever, by the murderers, beyond the reach of discovery.

But, to return to the case before us. Where was, in 1830, the *corpus delicti* proof of the fact that a murder had been actually committed? The grounds of *suspicion* were extraordinarily strong; but our law will not convict upon mere suspicion. Then how far was this essential deficiency supplied in 1841, by the discovery of the skeleton, coupled with the additional evidence which that event enabled those engaged in the investigation to collect? First, was that skeleton the skeleton of Huntley? It was a very singular place for a skeleton to have been found in; the position of the bones was curious, to say the least, strongly favouring the notion of the body to which they had belonged having been hastily doubled up and thrust into the earth in the way suggested; the prominent tooth was a most signal token of identity, and as a *fact*, spoken to by several credible witnesses; the general appearance of the skull certainly suited the descriptions of Huntley's countenance and head given by many witnesses; and its battered, broken appearance behind, was, to say the least, a singular circumstance in the case. But I can add nothing to what I have already presented to the reader on this part of the case—and he must judge for himself.

To come next to the testimony of the witnesses. Let me first advert to the circumstance of the reward of one hundred pounds offered for the production of such evidence as should lead to a conviction. Whether or not such a procedure be a politic one? whether calculated to assist or obstruct the progress of justice?— in the one case, by stimulating persons who would otherwise be indifferent, into ferreting out real facts; in the other case, by tempting to the fabrication of false evidence for the sake of gain—I shall not stay to enquire. It is in my opinion a question of importance and difficulty; but one thing is clear—the practice affords a constant topic, under the name of "blood money", for vituperative declamation on the behalf of the most guilty prisoner, and is calculated too often to turn the scale the wrong way—to incline a candid, but anxious juryman, to a distrust of evidence really of the most satisfactory description. Of course, I can speak for myself only; but I believed that all the witnesses intended to speak the truth. I think Mr Baron Rolfe was also of that opinion, though he seemed to suspect that one or two of the witnesses, by long brooding over the matter, had got to put things together which ought not to have been, and even to suppose one or two matters to have happened, which had not. There were certainly discrepancies—but none of a very material description; and could it be otherwise, when such a large body of witnesses came to speak to so many different circumstances, which had happened so long before? An entire concord, in things great and small, would have been a most palpable badge of fraud and falsehood. The circumstance of Huntley's sudden disappearance only the day but one before a particular day, viz. Monday, 2nd August, on which Yarm fair was held, will account for a tolerably minute recollection of what happened about that period; and above all, the attention of the whole neighbourhood was directed, *at the time,* to the circumstances attending so remarkable a disappearance of one of their neighbours and companions. Several of the principal witnesses, moreover, answered promptly in the affirmative to questions put by the prisoner's counsel, manifestly for his advantage—for instance, as to their having heard Huntley talk of going to America, and the absence of all concealment by the prisoner of the clothes, &c., belonging to Huntley. As to the discrepancy with reference to the six shirts spoken of so distinctly and specifically by Maw, while Bewick, whom he described to have been with him at the time, spoke of their being only *five*, and gave a decisive reason for it, with great deference to the judge, I think it deserving of very little consideration. Bewick *corroborates* Maw up to *five* of the shirts, leaving it plain that Maw is under a *bona fide* mistake—after such a lapse of time—as to there having been a sixth. Thus the important fact of the prisoner's being in possession of *five* new shirts belonging to Huntley, is clearly established.

Let me first direct your attention to the *prisoner's own statement*—a matter which, especially when the statement is made deliberately, is always worthy of attention. "In criminal cases," observes the distinguished writer on the Law of Evidence, from whom I have already quoted, "the statement made by the accused is of essential importance in some points of view. Such is the complexity of human affairs, and so infinite the combinations of circumstances, that the true hypothesis which is capable of explaining and reuniting all the apparently conflicting circumstances of the case, may escape the acutest penetration—but the prisoner, so far as he alone is concerned, can always afford a clue to them; and though he may be unable to support his statement by evidence, his account of the transaction is, for this purpose, always most material and important. The effect may be, on the one hand, to suggest a view which consists with the innocence of the accused, and might otherwise have escaped observation; while, on the other hand, its effect may be to narrow the question to the consideration whether that statement be or be not excluded by the evidence." Now, in the present case, the prisoner's statement corroborates a considerable portion of the evidence. He admits a full knowledge, on Thursday, the 22nd July 1830, of Huntley's possession of £85. 16s. 4d., and that Thursday, 29th July 1830, was "the very last time he clapped eyes on" Huntley. Nevertheless, four witnesses speak decisively to the fact of their having seen him in Huntley's company at four different periods of the ensuing memorable day, Friday—viz. 5 o'clock, a.m.; 3 or 4 o'clock, p.m.; 8 o'clock, p.m.; and 9 or 10 o'clock, p.m. —on the last of which occasions, the prisoner (having a gun in his hand), Huntley, and Garbutt being together, and going towards Crathorne Wood, to which they were then very near. Was this a mere error of recollection, or a wilful falsehood of the prisoner's? Or are all the four witnesses contradicting him—each speaking to a different period of the day, and to a different place—in error, or conspirators and perjurers? If they be speaking the truth, it is next to impossible to believe that Goldsborough could have *forgotten* the circumstance of his having been so much in Huntley's company, up even to within an hour or two of his being so mysteriously missing—knowing that his movements in connection with Huntley had immediately become the subject of keen enquiry, and most vehement suspicion. If, then, he deliberately falsified the fact, what are we at liberty to infer from that circumstance, as to his object and motives? Again, before he made the statement, he had heard all the evidence against him read over—and a very essential part of it was that respecting his having been, so very soon after Huntley's disappearance, in possession of his clothes, and also of a large sum of money. Yet he makes no allusion to these matters—neither denies nor accounts for them in any way whatever: and it must not be forgotten that, when arrested by Gernon in June 1841, he denied having ever had any of Huntley's clothes, or his watch. He makes no attempt to account for his sudden possession of so much money between the period of Huntley's disappearance and the spring of 1831—though he did state, *then*, that he had married a wife with *eighty* pounds! Nor does he offer any explanation of the contradictory accounts he had given as to Huntley's having gone to America, and his—the prisoner's —possession of the clothes, &c.; nor re-affirm any of them. In short, his statement appears as remarkable for what it does *not* contain, as it is important for what it *does*. I also consider it characterized by no little tact and circumspection, on the supposition of his guilt: he frankly admits a great deal which he felt he might be contradicted in, if he were to deny it—viz. his knowledge of Huntley's receipt of the exact sum (within a few pence) on the day of his actually receiving it; suggesting a motive for his absconding to America, and for his so frequently being in the prisoner's company—asserting that he finally parted openly with Huntley at the shop door of Farnaby, in the town of Hutton Rudby; and contenting himself with a brief but solemn denial of the truth of Groundy's statement.

That statement, and its author's suicide immediately after making it, invest the whole facts of the case with an air of extraordinary mystery. It contains on the face of it surely a glaring improbability—namely, that the prisoner should have been so insane as to commit himself gratuitously and irretrievably to one who he knew might immediately have caused his apprehension, and secured incontestable proof of his guilt in the murdered body. Stranger still, perhaps, is it, that if Groundy really had no further part in the business than he represents in that statement, he should not have disclosed the guilt of Goldsborough at once, instead of continuing ever after burdened with such a guilty secret, and for no adequate motive. It is to be observed that one of the witnesses, Anthony Wiles, disclosed *incidentally* (for his evidence was called with another view) a circumstance worthy of attention—viz. that one of the men with whom the prisoner was drinking on the Saturday night after Huntley's disappearance, was *Groundy*: yet the prisoner says, "if it was the last words I had to speak, I never was with him." At all events, a faint ray of light is thrown on the case, by the fact that Groundy was actually acquainted with the prisoner, and in his company about the very time of the transaction deposed to. Again, the truth of his description of the localities, is confirmed by those who went to examine them. The prisoner asks him nothing: *was it because he dared not?*

Let us now follow the course of events. I take it to be proved beyond all reasonable doubt, that, contrary to the deliberate signed statement of the prisoner, he was seen with a gun about ten o'clock at night on Friday, 30th July 1830, in company with Huntley and Garbutt, near a lane or bridle road leading to Crathorne Wood. That gun he had purchased only a few days previously, but after his knowledge of the fact of Huntley's receipt of his money. The report of a gun is heard from the wood within an hour or an hour and a half afterwards; Huntley is never seen or heard of any more; and between twelve and one o'clock that night, the prisoner is observed stealing out of his house, to go and listen at the constable's house, and, after being so occupied for a minute or two, return to his own. The next time that he is seen, is when drinking in company with Groundy late on Saturday night. But, on returning for a moment to the wood—it is certainly an embarrassing fact that the witness spoke to having heard *two* reports within half a minute of each other; whereas the prisoner's was a single-barrelled gun. If the witness's recollections were accurate—which I saw no reason whatever to doubt—how is the fact to be accounted for? If the prisoner's was the only gun, it is next to impossible that he could have so rapidly reloaded and fired again, especially under the horrid circumstances supposed. Was there, then, a second gun, which had been unobserved by them, and in Garbutt's hand?—or concealed, in readiness, in the wood?—or had he or the prisoner a *pistol* also, with which to repair an ineffectual first shot?—or was one of the shots fired by a poacher in another part of the wood? However wide of the mark may be all these speculations, there was one fact in evidence respecting this gun which I do not recollect Mr Baron Rolfe commenting upon to the jury. A day or two after the disappearance of Huntley, Richardson called on the prisoner for payment of this gun, when the prisoner refused, and returned it, saying that he did not want it, *and had not used it*: on which, Richardson put his finger down the muzzle to try it, and drew it back all blackened with discharged powder, and thus convicted him of a falsehood. What inference is to be drawn from this?

Then, as to the blood found on the road, a fact spoken to by two credible witnesses at the trial, one of them having also named it to the constable the same day on which he observed it—was it human blood? If so, it was lying very near the spot where Huntley had last been seen; and, if his blood, it must have been lying there, moreover, two days and two nights—i.e. from Friday midnight, till nine o'clock a.m. on Monday morning. The blood was described as *"stale* looking", and the weather had been fair and dry, but the road was not a much frequented one. It was spoken of by one witness as a "pool"; but if so, it could not have lain there since the Friday night; blood then shed, would have become a dark coagulated mass, possibly covered with dust. Again, on the supposition of its having been Huntley's blood, he must have been murdered on the high road; was that a probable thing, when they were close by the secret shades of Crathorne Wood, to which they were all seen going? May they have gone into the wood? May Huntley have become alarmed at their conduct—made his way out of the wood into the high road, and there received the murderous fire of his assailants? But the spot where the blood lay was, moreover, from four to six miles' distance from Stokesley Beck, where the bones were found. When and by whom was Huntley's body taken to Stokesley Beck? It could not have been taken the same night, at least; it is very highly improbable that such would be the fact, for the prisoner was at his own house between twelve and one o'clock that night; and, according to Groundy's account, the body of Huntley was lying in the wood on Wednesday the 4th August. Where then had it lain between the Friday night and the Wednesday following? In a secret part of the wood, covered up? or had it been buried on the Friday night temporarily, in the potato garth, where Maw said he saw some earth that looked newly dug? I own that I am not satisfied with the last piece of Maw's evidence; for it is hard to believe, that had he really witnessed so suspicious an appearance, at such a spot, after such a supposed tragedy, and when actually in quest of the body, he must have called attention to it, and dug it up. I ought to mention, however, that it did not appear that Maw was then aware of the circumstance of the blood on the road.

Here let me put together two little circumstances in the case, which may suggest a not unimportant inference. It would appear highly probable, assuming the bones to have been Huntley's, that for obvious reasons his body would have been stripped of its clothing, to lessen any subsequent chances of detection. Now, there were no vestiges of clothing found with the bones, and eleven years was not, I should think, a sufficiently long space of time to admit of woollen clothes decaying or mouldering away so entirely, as to leave no trace of them—not even buttons of bone or metal—with the exception of one large flat button, which was found at or near the spot, and not answering to the description of any belonging to Huntley, and possibly there by mere accident. If Huntley had been shot, his clothes must have been stained and steeped in blood, and the safety of the murderers would require the destruction of such evidences of their guilt. Now, several witnesses speak to the fact of Goldsborough's being seen alone a day or two after Huntley's disappearance, in his house, late at night, with a large fire (in the first week of August) burning something that gave out a strong *"smell of woollen burning"*. May these have been the bloody clothes of Huntley?

To proceed. The prisoner, seen in Huntley's company up to within a few hours of his sudden and total disappearance, is seen, the day but one after, laying out £7 in the purchase of a cow, and in possession of both banknotes and gold—having been, up to a very short time before, in the most abject poverty, and even destitution—and, moreover, in possession of a large quantity of clothes belonging, unquestionably, to the missing man. This of itself, unexplained, is sufficient to raise a violent presumption of the prisoner's guilt. But here also great caution is necessary. "If a horse be stolen from A," says Lord Hale, "and the same day B be found on him, it is a strong presumption that B stole him. Yet I do recollect that, before a very learned and wary judge, in such an instance B was condemned, and executed, at Oxford assizes: and yet, within two assizes afterwards, C being apprehended for another robbery, upon his judgment and execution confessed that *he* had been the man who stole the horse, and that, being closely pursued, he desired B, a stranger, to walk his horse for him, while he turned aside, as he said, for a necessary occasion, and escaped, and B was apprehended with the horse, and died innocently."

Now, in the present case, here is a man suddenly missing, known to have been possessed of a considerable sum of money—the prisoner to have been aware of it—to have been seen in his company up to almost the last moment before his disappearance—to become suddenly enriched, having previously been a pauper—and in possession of very many articles of clothing belonging to the missing man. All these circumstances point one way; but then, on the other hand, no attempt is made to conceal his possession of either money or clothes, nor to escape or quit the neighbourhood during the time when suspicion was hottest. Then he gives certainly contradictory answers concerning the way in which he became possessed of these matters—but all *may* be reconciled with the story he tells, that the missing man has gone to America, and that he (the prisoner) assisted him, and still seeks to baffle the pursuit of his absent friend. But if the latter story be true, is it probable, is it credible, that Huntley, meditating such an expedition, would first strip himself of all his newly purchased clothes, leave them behind him, and never afterwards come or send to claim them? But all the facts of the case, as fairly and as accurately stated as I know, are now laid before you; and is not this indeed a striking specimen of the importance of, and the difficulties attending, circumstantial evidence?

I shall proceed to propose several hypotheses for your consideration, in order to see whether any of them will reconcile all the circumstances, or which of them will reconcile most of them, and in the most natural manner. "The force of circumstantial evidence, being exclusive in its nature, and the mere coincidence of the hypothesis with the circumstances being, in the abstract, insufficient, unless they exclude every other supposition, it is essential to enquire, with the most scrupulous attention, what other hypotheses there may be agreeing wholly or partially with the facts in evidence. Those which agree even partially with the circumstances are not unworthy of examination, because they lead to a more accurate examination of those facts with which, at first, they might appear to be inconsistent; and it is possible that on a more accurate examination of these facts, their authenticity may be rendered doubtful, or even altogether disproved." The same able writer from whom this passage is quoted, Mr Starkie, has another observation, which also I wish you to take along with you in dealing with the facts of this case.

"To *acquit,* on light, trivial and fanciful suppositions, and remote conjectures, is a virtual violation of the juror's oath; while, on the other hand, he ought not to *condemn*, unless the evidence exclude from his mind all *reasonable* doubt as to the guilt of the accused, and *unless he be so convinced by the evidence, that he would venture to act upon that conviction, in matters of the highest concern and importance to his own interest.*"

First Hypothesis: Huntley really did go off in the way alleged, to America or elsewhere, to avoid his creditors, and also his wife, and be relieved from the burden of supporting her. He may have since died a natural—an accidental—or a violent death, under circumstances depriving him of the opportunity of disposing by will of what he knew was coming to him; and this death may have happened very shortly after his departure. He left the more valuable portions of his clothes and property, and a great portion of his money, in Goldsborough's hands, to be forwarded to him; and Goldsborough acted dishonestly by him, in disposing of the clothes and spending the money. Huntley may be now alive, and meditating a return home.

Second Hypothesis: Huntley is dead, and was murdered by Garbutt, in whose company he had been left by Goldsborough. Garbutt being also pursued by the officers of justice for other offences, hastily absconded, and may now be dead, or abroad.

Third Hypothesis: Groundy was the actual murderer, possibly instigated by Goldsborough; or Goldsborough only subsequently informed by Groundy of the murder, and insisting on receiving a great portion of the money, as the price of his silence. He committed suicide from fear lest his guilt should come out in court, at the trial—through his being unable to stand solemn and public questioning upon the subject. He may have been also partly influenced by remorse at having wrongfully sworn away the life of Goldsborough.

Fourth Hypothesis: Groundy, Garbutt, and Goldsborough, or Groundy and Goldsborough, were all concerned as principals in the murder. The second gun was Groundy's, who joined them in the wood.

Lastly: With reference to the prisoner at the bar, let us enquire more fully, whether his guilt or innocence is more consistent with the proved facts of the case.

If *innocent*, he must stand or fall by his story of Huntley's having left him on his way to America, after in vain pressing Goldsborough to accompany him. It certainly does appear that Huntley had contemplated such a step, and there are other circumstances favouring the notion that Goldsborough and Huntley had been busily concerting a scheme for Huntley's going off privately to America. He was, during the whole of the time between the 22nd and 30th July, incessantly coming over to Goldsborough, and remaining in his company. At five o'clock in the morning of the day of his disappearance, he was seen coming to Goldsborough's house, where he was immediately admitted. They may have arranged that Goldsborough should go and fetch Huntley's things, the same day, from Huntley's to Goldsborough's house, to keep for, or send after, Huntley; in pursuance of which Goldsborough went, and returned with the articles in question in a sack, during the afternoon of the same day. It may have been a part of the arrangement, that Huntley should leave a considerable portion of his money in Goldsborough's hands, for safety's sake—to be remitted as Huntley might want it. Or Goldsborough might have promised and intended to follow him shortly afterwards; but fondness for his children may have kept him back— and he may have determined on playing Huntley false, and appropriating the money and property left with him to his own use, relying on Huntley's not venturing to return, lest he should be saddled with the support of his wife; but if he should return, then resolving to impose on him as much difficulty as possible in claiming his own, by converting his money and articles of furniture, and of farming purchases. His contradictory accounts of Huntley's movements are consistent with his wish to baffle the pursuers of Huntley, by putting them on false scents; and this may serve to explain his light jocular tone in speaking of Huntley's absence, "You'll all see, by and by, whether he's murdered or not." In this view of the case, the blood on the road, the gun shot in the wood, and the burning of clothes soon afterwards, if such facts really happened, have no true connection with each other; and the skull and bones produced, were not the skull and bones of Huntley. Let it, moreover, be borne in mind, that Goldsborough did not attempt any concealment of property or money, or escape —neither after nor before suspicion had settled on him—not even when set at liberty after his arrest in the month of July 1841.

But if the prisoner be *guilty*, let us imagine that, from the time of learning that Huntley had become possessed of so considerable a sum of money, the prisoner had conceived the idea of destroying him in order to obtain that money, and in such a manner as to warrant the belief of the neighbourhood that he had only carried into effect his previously expressed intention of going off to America. That in pursuance of such an intention, Huntley had sent his clothes, &c., on the Friday, to the prisoner's house—that, in short, they formed the contents of the bag, or sack, which the prisoner was seen carrying into his house on the Friday afternoon. That, either alone, or in company with Garbutt or Groundy, he allured Huntley into Crathorne Wood, under the pretext of shooting a hare, and enjoying a pleasant supper together; which Huntley—who might have become loquacious through previous drinking with the prisoner, and possibly Garbutt and Groundy, or one of them—mentioned to Maw, in a merry humour, on meeting him on the road, as described by Maw. That he may have been shot, either in the wood, or on the high road, where the blood was found; and his body buried for a while, or concealed in the wood till it could be permanently disposed of. That the prisoner then returned to his own house, and having been, possibly, alarmed by some noise into the suspicion that his motions had been watched, slipped out, shortly afterwards, to ascertain whether there were any gounds for his fears. That he then cleansed himself from any marks of the deed in which he had been engaged, and resolved on the course he should pursue—namely, to give out that he had set Huntley on his way to America. That, finding the current of suspicion setting in more strongly against him than he had anticipated, he resolved, on due deliberation, distrusting the chance of escaping by flight, to stay and brave it out by a bold and consistent adherence to the fiction of Huntley's having gone off secretly to America. That if neither Garbutt nor Groundy had been originally parties to the murder, the prisoner may have taken both, or either, subsequently, into his confidence, to secure his or their assistance in successfully disposing of the body; rewarding him or them by a sum of money, which he might have represented as

WHO IS THE MURDERER?

being the greater portion of what he had found on the person of Huntley. That the prisoner, either alone, or assisted by one or both of these men, afterwards disinterred the body, if temporarily buried, or removed it from any place where it had lain hid, and carried it to Stokesley Beck, at night-time, and thrust it, naked, into a hole they dug into the bank of the Beck, as a place distant, secluded, and to escape suspicion—bringing home the bloody clothes, and burning them as soon as possible. That, subsequently, he became agitated, silent, and reserved—tormented by his own reflections, and terrified by the continued strength of public suspicion, and the search after Huntley's body. That his object being to divert the searchers, if possible, from proceeding towards Stokesley Beck, he conceived himself likely to attain that end by himself suggesting that the body might be found there—a bold and desperate expedient, founded on the belief that any suggestion of that sort by *him*, would certainly be disregarded. That, finding the search at length abandoned, and the vehemence of public suspicion to be abating, but yet rendering his continuance at Hutton Rudby troublesome and dangerous, he resolved to transfer his residence, under a forged name, to Barnsley. That when, so many years afterwards, so abruptly challenged as the murderer of Huntley, he was thrown off his guard, so as to forget the notoriety of his having possessed the clothes and property of Huntley, and denied that fact to the officer who took him into custody. That he was dismayed by the appearance of Groundy against him, and dared not ask him any questions, lest he should thereby reveal more of the transaction; and, consequently, felt compelled to content himself with a general denial of Groundy's statements. That he inwardly shrunk from the frightful spectacle of the shattered skull, knowing it to be that of Huntley—and that HORROR looked up at him from these eyeless sockets.

But stay! A sudden stir announces the return, after a long absence, of the jury; and the crowded court is quickly hushed into agitated silence, as the jury enter—the foreman carrying with him the skull and bones; and the prisoner is re-placed at the bar to hear his doom. The judge has in readiness, but concealed, the black cap, should it become, within a few moments, his dreadful duty to pronounce sentence of death upon the prisoner. The names of the jury are called over one by one, and the prisoner eyes them with unutterable feelings. Then comes the fearful moment.

Clerk of Arraigns: Gentlemen of the Jury, are you agreed upon your verdict? Do you say that Robert Goldsborough, the prisoner at the bar, is guilty of the murder and felony with which he stands charged, or not guilty?

Foreman: NOT GUILTY.

Clerk of Arraigns: Gentlemen of the Jury, you say that the prisoner at the bar, Robert Goldsborough, is not guilty. That is your verdict; and so you say all? (To the Governor of the Castle) Remove the prisoner from the bar.

The verdict did not seem wholly unexpected by the audience; and it was received in blank silence. The prisoner exhibited no symptoms of satisfaction or exultation on hearing the verdict pronounced; but maintained the same phlegmatic *oppressed* air which he had exhibited throughout. As soon, however, as he was removed from the bar, and before he had quitted the dock, he whispered, with tremulous eagerness, in the ear of the officer, "*Can they try me again, lad?*" "No; thou's clear of it now, altogether," was the reply: on which Goldsborough heaved a very deep sigh, and said, "If they'd put me on my trial in 1830, I could have got plenty to come forward and clear me." Within half an hour afterwards, he was seen dressed as he had appeared at the bar of the court, only that he had his hat on, and carried a small bundle of clothes tied up in a blue and white cotton handkerchief under his arm, walking quietly out of the frowning gates of York Castle, once more a free man, to go whithersoever he chose. He was quickly joined by two mean-looking men; and spent the next hour or so in walking about the town, and looking in to the various shop windows, occasionally followed by a little crowd of boys and others who had recognised him.

How, now, say you candid and attentive reader? Had you been upon the jury, should you have said—*Guilty* or *Not Guilty*?

THE FIRE-FIEND
A Nightmare

Charles D. Gardette

I

In the deepest dearth of midnight,
    while the sad and solemn swell
Still was floating, faintly echoed
    from the forest chapel bell—
Faintly, falteringly floating o'er the sable
    waves of air
That were thro' the midnight rolling, chafed
    and billowy with the tolling—
In my chamber I lay dreaming, by the fire-
    light's fitful gleaming,
And my dreams were dreams foredoomed to care!

II

As the last, long, lingering echo of the
    midnight's mystic chime,
Lifting through the sable billows of the
    thither shore of Time—
Leaving on the starless silence not a token
    nor a trace—
In a quivering sigh departed; from my
    couch in fear I started—

Started to my feet in terror, for my dream's
    phantasmal error
Painted in the fitful fire a frightful,
    fiendish, flaming face!

III

On the red hearth's reddest centre,
    from a blazing knot of oak,
Seemed to gibe and grin this
    phantom when in terror I awoke;
And my slumberous eyelids straining as I
    staggered to the floor,
Still in that dread vision seeming, turned
    my gaze toward the gleaming
Hearth and there—Oh, God! I saw it; and
    from its flaming jaw it
Spat a ceaseless, seething, hissing,
    bubbling, gurgling stream of gore!

IV

Speechless struck with stony silence,
    frozen to the floor I stood,
Till methought my brain was hissing with
    that hissing, bubbling blood;
Till I felt my life stream oozing, oozing
    from those lambent lips;
Till the demon seemed to name me—then
    a wondrous calm o'ercame me,

And my brow grew cold and dewy, with a
    death damp stiff and gluey,
And I fell back on my pillow, in apparent
    soul eclipse.

V

Then as in death's seeming shadow,
    in the icy fall of fear
I lay stricken, came a hoarse and
    hideous murmur to my ear;
Came a murmur like the murmur of
    assassins in their sleep—
Muttering: "Higher! higher! higher! I
    am demon of the Fire!
I am Arch-Fiend of the Fire! and each
    blazing roof's my pyre,
And my sweetest incense is the blood and
    tears my victims weep!

VI

"How I revel on the prairie! how I roar
    among the pines!
How I laugh when from the village o'er
    the snow the red flame shines,
And I hear the shrieks of terror with a life
    in every breath!
How I scream with lambent laughter, as I
    hurl each crackling rafter

Down the fell abyss of fire—until higher!
    higher! higher!
Leap the high priests of my altar, in their
    merry dance of death!

VII

"I am Monarch of the Fire! I am Vassal
    King of Death!
World enriching, with the shadow
    of its doom upon my breath!
With the symbol of Hereafter flaming from
    my fatal face!
I command the Eternal Fire! Higher!
    higher! higher! higher!
Leap my ministering demons, like the
    phantasmagoric lemans
Hugging Universal Nature in their
    hideous embrace!"

VIII

Then a sombre silence shut me in a
    solemn, shrouded sleep,
And I slumbered like an infant in the
    'Cradle of the Deep';
Till the belfry in the forest quivered with
    the matin stroke,
And the martins from the edges of its
    lichen-lidded ledges,

Skimmered through the russet arches,
    where the light in torn files marches,
Like a routed army struggling through the
    serried ranks of oak.

IX

Thro' my ivy-fretted casements,
    filtered in a tremulous note,
From the tall and stately linden
    where the robin swelled his throat—
Querulous, quaker-breasted robin, calling
    quaintly for his mate!
Then I started up unbidden from my
    slumber, nightmare ridden,
With the memory of that dire demon in my
    central fire,
On my eye's interior mirror like the
    shadow of a fate!

X

Ah! the fiendish fire had smouldered to a
    white and formless heap.
And no knot of oak was flaming as it
    flamed upon my sleep;
But around its very centre, where the
    demon face had shone,
Forked shadows seemed to linger, pointing,
    as with spectral anger,

To a Bible, massive, golden, on a table
　carved and olden;
And I bowed and said, "All power is of
　God—of God alone!"

THE LIGHTHOUSE

Edgar Allan Poe & Robert Bloch

January 1, 1796. This day—my first on the lighthouse—I make this entry in my Diary, as agreed on with De Grät. As regularly as I *can* keep the journal, I will—but there is no telling what may happen to a man all alone as I am—I may get sick or worse. . .

So far well! The cutter had a narrow escape—but why dwell on that, since I am *here*, all safe? My spirits are beginning to revive already, at the mere thought of being—for once in my life at least—thoroughly *alone*; for of course Neptune, large as he is, is not to be taken into consideration as "society". Would to Heaven I had ever found in "society" one half as much *faith* as in this poor dog; in such case I and "society" might never have parted—even for a year. . .

What most surprises me, is the difficulty De Grät had in getting me the appointment—and I a noble of the realm! It could not be that the Consistory had any doubt of my ability to manage the light. *One* man has attended it before now—and got on quite as well as the three that are usually put in. The duty is a mere nothing; and the printed instructions are as plain as possible. It would never have done to let Orndoff accompany me. I should never have made any way with my book as long as he was within reach of me, with his intolerable gossip—not to mention that everlasting meerschaum. Besides, I wish to be *alone*. . .

It is strange that I never observed, until this moment, how dreary a sound that word has—"alone"! I could half fancy there was some peculiarity in the echo of these cylindrical walls—but oh, no!—that is all nonsense. I do believe I am going to get nervous about my insulation. *That* will never do. I have not forgotten De Grät's prophecy. Now for a scramble to the lantern and a good look around to "see what I can see". . . To see what I can see indeed!—not very much. The swell is subsiding a little, I think—but the cutter will have a rough passage home, nevertheless. She will hardly get within sight of the Norland before noon tomorrow—and yet it can hardly be more than 190 or 200 miles.

January 2. I have passed this day in a species of ecstasy that I find it impossible to describe. My passion for solitude could scarcely have been more thoroughly gratified. I do not say *satisfied*; for I believe I should never be satiated with such delight as I have experienced today. . .

The wind lulled after daybreak, and by the afternoon the sea had gone down materially. . . Nothing to be seen with the telescope even, but ocean and sky, with an occasional gull.

January 3. A dead calm all day. Towards evening, the sea looked very much like glass. A few seaweeds came in sight; but besides them absolutely *nothing* all day—not even the slightest speck of cloud. . . Occupied myself in exploring the lighthouse. . . It is a very lofty one—as I find to my cost when I have to ascend its interminable stairs—not quite 160 feet, I should say, from the low-water mark to the top of the lantern. From the bottom *inside* the shaft, however, the distance to the summit is 180 feet at least: thus the floor is 20 feet below the surface of the sea, even at low tide. . .

It seems to me that the hollow interior at the bottom should have been filled in with solid masonry. Undoubtedly the whole would have been thus rendered more *safe*—but what am I thinking about? A structure such as this is safe enough under any circumstances. I should feel myself secure in it during the fiercest hurricane that ever raged—and yet I have heard seamen say that, occasionally, with a wind at South-West, the sea has been known to run higher here than anywhere, with the single exception of the Western opening of the Straits of Magellan.

No mere sea, though, could accomplish anything with this solid iron-riveted wall—which, at 50 feet from high-water mark, is four feet thick, if one inch. The basis on which the structure rests seems to me to be chalk...

January 4. I am now prepared to resume work on my book, having spent this day in familiarizing myself with a regular routine.

My actual duties will be, I perceive, absurdly simple—the light requires little tending beyond a periodic replenishment of the oil for the six-wick burner. As to my own needs, they are easily satisfied, and the exertion of an occasional trip down the stairs is all I must anticipate.

At the base of the stairs is the entrance room; beneath that is twenty feet of empty shaft. Above the entrance room, at the next turn of the circular iron staircase, is my store room which contains the casks of fresh water and the food supplies, plus linens and other daily needs. Above that—again another spiral of those interminable stairs!—is the oil room, completely filled with the tanks from which I must feed the wicks. Fortunately, I perceive that I can limit my descent to the store room to once a week if I choose, for it is possible for me to carry sufficient provisions in one load to supply both myself and Neptune for such a period. As to the oil supply, I need only to bring up two drums every three days and thus insure a constant illumination. If I choose, I can place a dozen or more spare drums on the platform near the light and thus provide for several weeks to come.

So it is that in my daily existence I can limit my movements to the upper half of the lighthouse; that is to say, the three spirals opening on the topmost three levels. The lowest is my "living room"—and it is here, of course, that Neptune is confined the greater part of the day; here, too, that I plan to write at a desk near the wall-slit that affords a view of the sea without. The second highest level is my bedroom and kitchen combined. Here the weekly rations of food and water are contained in cupboards for that purpose; here, too, is the ingenious stove fed by the selfsame oil that lights the beacon above. The topmost level is the service room giving access to the light itself and to the platform surrounding it. Since the light is fixed, and its reflectors set, there is no need for me ever to ascend to the platform save when replenishing the oil supply or making a repair or adjustment as per the written instructions—a circumstance which may well never arise during my stay here.

Already I have carried enough oil, water and provender to the upper levels to last me for an entire month—I need stir from my two rooms only to replenish the wicks.

For the rest, I am free! utterly free—my time is my own, and in this lofty realm I rule as King. Although Neptune is my only living subject I can well imagine that I am sovereign o'er all I see—ocean below and stars above. I am master of the sun that rises in rubicund radiance from the sea at dawn, emperor of wind and monarch of the gale, sultan of the waves that sport or roar in roiling torrents about the base of my palace pinnacle. I command the moon in the heavens, and the very ebb and flow of the tide does homage to my reign.

But enough of fancies—De Grät warned me to refrain from morbid or from grandiose speculation—now I shall take up in all earnestness the task that lies before me. Yet this night, as I sit before the window in the starlight, the tides sweeping against these lofty walls can only echo my exultation; I am free—and, at last, alone!

January 11. A week has passed since my last entry in this diary, and as I read it over, I can scarce comprehend that it was I who penned those words.

Something has happened—the nature of which lies unfathomed. I have worked, eaten, slept, replenished the wicks twice. My outward existence has been placid. I can ascribe the alteration in my feelings to naught but some inner alchemy; enough to say that a disturbing change has taken place.

Alone! I, who breathed the word as if it were some mystic incantation bestowing peace, have come—I realize it now—to loathe the very sound of the syllables. And the ghastliness of meaning I know full well.

THE LIGHTHOUSE

It is a dismaying, it is a dreadful thing, to be alone. Truly alone, as I am, with only Neptune to exist beside me and by his breathing presence remind me that I am not the sole inhabitant of a blind and senseless universe. The sun and stars that wheel overhead in their endless cycle seem to rush across the horizon unheeding—and, of late, unheeded, for I cannot fix my mind upon them with normal constancy. The sea that swirls or ripples below me is naught but a purposeless chaos of utter emptiness.

I thought myself to be a man of singular self-sufficiency, beyond the petty needs of a boring and banal society. How wrong I was!—for I find myself longing for the sight of another face, the sound of another voice, the touch of other hands whether they offer caresses or blows. Anything, anything for reassurement that my dreams are indeed false and that I am *not*, actually, alone.

And yet I *am*. I am, and I will be. The world is two hundred miles away; I will not know it again for an entire year. And it in turn—but no more! I cannot put down my thoughts while in the grip of this morbid mood.

January 13. Two more days—two more centuries!—have passed. Can it be less than two weeks since I was immured in this prison tower? I mount the turret of my dungeon and gaze at the horizon; I am not hemmed in by bars of steel but by columns and pillars and webs of wild and raging water. The sea has changed; grey skies have wrought a wizardry so that I stand surrounded by a tumult that threatens to become a tempest.

I turn away, for I can bear no more, and descend to my room. I seek to write—the book is bravely begun, but of late I can bring myself to do nothing constructive or creative—and in a moment I fling aside my pen and rise to pace. To endlessly pace the narrow, circular confines of my tower of torment.

Wild words, these? And yet I am not alone in my affliction—Neptune, Neptune the loyal, the calm, the placid—feels it too.

Perhaps it is but the approach of the storm that agitates him so—for Nature bears closer kinship with the beast. He stays constantly at my side, whining now, and the muffled roaring of the waves without our prison causes him to tremble. There is a chill in the air that our stove cannot dissipate, but it is not cold that oppresses him. . .

I have just mounted to the platform and gazed out at the spectacle of gathering storm. The waves are fantastically high; they sweep against the lighthouse in titanic tumult. These solid walls of stone shudder rhythmically with each onslaught. The churning sea is grey no longer—the water is black, black as basalt and as heavy. The sky's hue has deepened so that at the moment no horizon is visible. I am surrounded by a billowing blackness thundering against me. . .

Back below now, as lightning flickers. The storm will break soon, and Neptune howls piteously. I stroke his quivering flanks, but the poor animal shrinks away. It seems that he fears even my presence; can it be that my own features betray an equal agitation? I do not know—I only feel that I am helpless, trapped here and awaiting the mercy of the storm. I cannot write much longer.

And yet I will set down a further statement. I must, if only to prove to myself that reason again prevails. In writing of my venture up to the platform—my viewing of the sea and sky—I omitted to mention the meaning of a single moment. There came upon me, as I gazed down at the black and boiling madness of the waters below, a wild and wilful craving to become one with it. But why should I disguise the naked truth?—I felt an insane impulse to hurl myself into the sea!

It has passed now; passed, I pray, forever. I did not yield to this perverse prompting and I am back here in my quarters, writing calmly once again. Yet the fact remains—the hideous urge to destroy myself came suddenly, and with the force of one of those monstrous waves.

And what—I force myself to realize—was the meaning of my demented desire? It was that I sought escape, escape from loneliness. It was as if by mingling with the sea and the storm I would no longer be *alone*.

But I defy the elements. I defy the powers of the earth and of the heavens. Alone I am, alone I *must* be—and come what may,

I shall survive! My laughter rises above all your thunder!

So—ye spirits of the storm—blow, howl, rage, hurl your watery weight against my fortress—I am greater than you in all your powers. But wait! Neptune. . .something has happened to the creature—I must attend him.

January 16. The storm is abated. I am back at my desk now, alone—truly alone. I have locked poor Neptune in the store-room below; the unfortunate beast seems driven out of his wits by the forces of the storm. When last I wrote he was worked into a frenzy, whining and pawing and wheeling in circles. He was incapable of responding to my commands and I had no choice but to literally drag him down the stairs by the scruff of his neck and incarcerate him in the store-room where he could not come to harm. I own that concern for *my* safety was involved—the possibility of being imprisoned in this lighthouse with a mad dog must be avoided.

His howls, throughout the storm, were pitiable indeed, but now he is silent. When last I ventured to gaze into the room I perceived him sleeping, and I trust that rest and calm will restore him to my full companionship as before.

Companionship!

How shall I describe the horrors of the storm I faced *alone*?

In this diary entry I have prefaced a date—January 16—but that is merely a guess. The storm has swept away all track of Time. Did it last a day, two days, three—as I now surmise—a week, or a century? I do *not* know.

I know only an endless raging of waters that threatened, time and again, to engulf the very pinnacle of the lighthouse. I know only an eternity of ebony, an aeon of billowing black composed of sea and sky commingled. I only know that there were times when my own voice outroared the storm—but how can I convey the cause of *that*? There was a time, perhaps a full day, perhaps much longer, when I could not bear to rise from my couch but lay with my face buried in the pillows, weeping like a child. But mine were not the pure tears of childhood innocence—call them, rather, the tears of Lucifer upon the realization of his eternal fall from grace. It seemed to me that I was truly the victim of an endless damnation; condemned forever to remain a prisoner in a world of thunderous chaos.

There is no need to write of the fancies and fantasies which assailed me through those unhallowed hours. At times I felt that the lighthouse was giving way and that I would be swept into the sea. At times I knew myself to be a victim of a colossal plot—I cursed De Grät for sending me, knowingly, to my doom. At times (and these were the worst moments of all) I felt the full force of loneliness, crashing down upon me in waves higher than those wrought by water.

But all has passed, and the sea—and myself—are calm again. A peculiar calmness, this; as I gaze out upon the water there are certain phenomena I was not aware of until this very moment.

Before setting down my observations, let me reassure myself that I am, indeed, *quite* calm; no trace of my former tremors or agitation yet remains. The transient madness induced by the storm has departed and my brain is free of phantasms—indeed, my perceptive faculties seem to be sharpened to an unusual acuity.

It is almost as though I find myself in possession of an additional sense, an ability to analyze and penetrate beyond former limitations superimposed by Nature.

The water on which I gaze is placid once more. The sky is only lightly leaden in hue. But wait—low on the horizon creeps a sudden flame! It is the sun, the Arctic sun in sullen splendour, emerging momentarily from the pall to incarnadine the ocean. Sun and sky, sea and air about me, turn to blood.

Can it be I who but a moment ago wrote of returned, regained sanity? I, who have just shrieked aloud, "Alone!" —and half-rising from my chair, heard the muffled booming echo reverberate through the lonely lighthouse, its sepulchral accent intoning "*Alone!*" in answer? It may be that I am, despite all resolution, going mad; if so, I pray the end comes soon.

THE LIGHTHOUSE

January 18. There will be no end! I have conceived a notion, a theory which my heightened faculties soon will test. I shall embark upon an experiment...

January 26. A week has passed here in my solitary prison. Solitary?—perhaps, but not for long. The experiment is proceeding. I must set down what has occurred.

The sound of the echo set me to thinking. One sends out one's voice and it comes back. One sends out one's thoughts and— can it be that there is a response? Sounds, as we know, travels in waves and patterns. The emanations of the brain, perhaps, travel similarly. And they are not confined by physical laws of time, space, or *duration*.

Can one's thoughts produce a reply that *materializes*, just as one's voice produces an echo? An echo is a product of a certain vacuum. A thought...

Concentration is the key. I have been concentrating. My supplies are replenished, and Neptune—visited during my venture below—seems rational enough, although he shrinks away when I approach him. I have left him below and spent the past week here. Concentration, I repeat, is the key to my experiment.

Concentration, by its very nature, is a difficult task: I addressed myself to it with no little trepidation. Strive but to remain seated quietly with a mind "empty" of all thought, and one finds in the space of a very few minutes that the errant body is engaged in all manner of distracting movement—foot tapping, finger twisting, facial grimacing.

This I managed to overcome after a matter of many hours—my first three days were virtually exhausted in an effort to rid myself of nervous agitation and assume the inner and outer tranquillity of the Indian fakir. Then came the task of "filling" the empty consciousness—filling it completely with *one* intense and concentrated effort of will.

What echo would I bring forth from nothingness? What companionship would I seek here in my loneliness? What was the sign or symbol I desired? What symbolized to me the whole absent world of life and light?

De Grät would laugh me to scorn if he but knew the concept that I chose. Yet I, the cynical, the jaded, the decadent, searched my soul, plumbed my longing, and found that which I most desired—a simple sign, a token of all the earth removed: a fresh and growing flower, a *rose*!

Yes, a simple rose is what I have sought—a rose, torn from its living stem, perfumed with the sweet incarnation of life itself. Seated here before the window I have dreamed, I have mused, I have then concentrated with every fibre of my being upon a *rose*.

My mind was filled with redness—not the redness of the sun upon the sea, or the redness of blood, but the rich and radiant redness of the rose. My soul was suffused with the scent of a rose: as I brought my faculties to bear exclusively upon the image, these walls fell away, the walls of my very flesh fell away, and I seemed to merge in the texture, the odour, the colour, the actual *essence* of a rose.

Shall I write of this, the seventh day, when seated at the window as the sun emerged from the sea, I felt the commanding of my consciousness? Shall I write of rising, descending the stairs, opening the iron door at the base of the lighthouse and peering out at the billows that swirled at my very feet? Shall I write of stooping, of grasping, of holding?

Shall I write that I have indeed descended those iron stairs and returned here with my wave-borne trophy—*that this very day, from waters two hundred miles distant from any shore, I have reached down and plucked a fresh rose?*

January 28. It has not withered! I keep it before me constantly in a vase on this table, and it is a priceless ruby plucked from dreams. It is real—as real as the howls of poor Neptune, who senses that something odd is afoot. His frantic barking does not disturb me; nothing disturbs me, for I am master of a power greater than earth or space or time. And I shall use this power, now, to bring me the final boon. Here in my tower I have become quite the philosopher: I have learned my lesson well and realize that I do not desire wealth, or fame, or the trinkets of society. My need is simply this—companionship. And now, with the power that is mine to control, I shall have it!

Soon, quite soon, I shall no longer be alone!

January 30. The storm has returned, but I pay it no heed; nor do I mark the howlings of Neptune, although the beast is now literally dashing himself against the door of the store room. One might fancy that his efforts are responsible for the shuddering of the very lighthouse itself, but no; it is the fury of the Northern gale. I pay it no heed, as I say, but I fully realize that this storm surpasses in extent and intensity anything I could imagine as witness to its predecessor.

Yet it is unimportant; even though the light above me flickers and threatens to be extinguished by the sheer velocity of wind that seeps through these stout walls; even though the ocean sweeps against the foundations with a force that makes solid stone seem flimsy as straw; even though the sky is a single black roaring mouth that yawns low upon the horizon to engulf me.

These things I sense but dimly, as I address myself to the appointed task. I pause now only for food and a brief respite—and scribble down these words to mark the progress of resolution towards an inevitable goal.

For the past several days I have bent my faculties to my will, concentrating utterly and to the uttermost upon the summoning of a Companion.

This Companion will be—I confess it!—a woman; a woman far surpassing the limitations of common mortality. For she is, and must be fashioned, of dreams and longing, of desire and delight beyond the bounds of flesh.

She is the woman of whom I have always dreamed, the One I have sought in vain through what I once presumed, in my ignorance, was the world of reality. It seems to me now that I have always known her, that my soul has contained her presence forever. I can visualize her perfectly—I know her hair, each strand more precious than a miser's gold; the riches of her ivory and alabaster brow, the perfection of her face and form are etched forever in my consciousness. De Grät would scoff that she is but the figment of a dream—but De Grät did not see the rose.

The rose—I hesitate to speak of it—has gone. It was the rose which I set before me when first I composed myself to this new effort of will. I gazed at it intently until vision faded, senses stilled, and I lost myself in the attempt of conjuring up my vision of a Companion.

Hours later, the sound of rising waters from without aroused me. I gazed about, my eyes sought the reassurance of the rose and rested only upon a *foulness*. Where the rose had risen proudly in its vase, red crest rampant upon a living stem, I now perceived only a noxious, utterly detestable strand of ichorous decay. No rose this, but only seaweed; rotted, noisome and putrescent. I flung it away, but for long moments I could not banish a wild presentiment—was it true that I had deceived myself? Was it a weed, and only a weed I plucked from the ocean's breast? Did the force of my thought momentarily invest it with the attributes of a rose? Would anything I called up from the depths—the depths of sea or the depths of consciousness—be *truly* real?

The blessed image of the Companion came to soothe these fevered speculations, and I knew myself saved. There *was* a rose; perhaps my thought had created it and nourished it—only when my entire concentration turned to other things did it depart, or resume another shape. And with my Companion, there will be no need for focussing my faculties elsewhere. She, and she alone, will be the recipient of everything my mind, my heart, my soul possesses. If will, if sentiment, if love are needed to preserve her, these things she shall have in entirety. So there is nothing to fear. Nothing to fear. . .

Once again now I shall lay my pen aside and return to the great task—the task of "creation", if you will—and I shall not fail. The fear (I admit it!) of loneliness is enough to drive me forward to unimaginable brinks. She, and she alone, can save me, shall save

THE LIGHTHOUSE

me, *must* save me! I can see her now—the golden glitter of her—and my consciousness calls to her to rise, to appear before me in radiant reality. Somewhere upon these storm-tossed seas she *exists*, I know it—and wherever she may be, my call will come to her and she will respond.

January 31. The command came at midnight. Roused from the depths of the most profound innermost communion by a thunder-clap, I rose as though in the grip of somnambulistic compulsion and moved down the spiral stairs.

The lantern I bore trembled in my hand; its light wavered in the wind, and the very iron treads beneath my feet shook with the furious force of the storm. The booming of the waves as they struck the lighthouse walls seemed to place me within the centre of a maelstrom of ear-shattering sound, yet over the demoniacal din I could detect the frenzied howls of poor Neptune as I passed the door behind which he was confined. The door shook with the combined force of the wind and of his still desperate efforts to free himself—but I hastened on my way, descending to the iron door at the base of the lighthouse.

To open it required the use of both hands, and I set the lantern down at one side. To open it, moreover, required the summoning of a resolution I scarcely possessed—for beyond that door was the force and fury of the wildest storm that ever shrieked across these seething seas. A sudden wave might dash me from the doorway, or, conversely, enter and inundate the lighthouse itself.

But consciousness prevailed; consciousness drove me forward.

I *knew*, I thrilled to the certainty that *she* was without the iron portal—I unbolted the door with the urgency of one who rushes into the arms of his beloved.

The door swung open—blew open—roared open—and the storm burst upon me; a ravening monster of black-mouthed waves capped with white fangs. The sea and sky surged forward as if to attack, and I stood enveloped in Chaos. A flash of lightning revealed the immensity of utter Nightmare.

I saw it not, for the same flash illumined the form, the

lineaments of *she* whom I sought.

Lightning and lantern were unneeded—her golden glory outshone all as she stood there, pale and trembling, a goddess arisen from the depths of the sea!

Hallucination, vision, apparition? My trembling fingers sought, and found, their answer. Her flesh was real—cold as the icy waters from whence she came, but palpable and permanent. I thought of the storm, of doomed ships and drowning men, of a girl cast upon the waters and struggling towards the succour of the lighthouse beacon. I thought of a thousand explanations, a thousand miracles, a thousand riddles or reasons beyond rationality. Yet only one thing mattered—my Companion was here, and I had but to step forward and take her in my arms.

No word was spoken, nor could one be heard in all that Inferno. No word was needed, for she smiled. Pale lips parted as I held out my arms, and she moved closer. Pale lips parted—and I saw the pointed teeth, set in rows like those of a shark. Her eyes, fishlike and staring, swam closer. As I recoiled, her arms came up to cling, and they were cold as the waters beneath, cold as the storm, cold as death.

In one monstrous moment I *knew*, knew with uttermost certainty, that the power of my will had indeed summoned, the call of my consciousness *had* been answered. But the answer came not from the living, for nothing lived in this storm. I had sent my will out over the waters, but the will penetrates all dimensions, and my answer had come from *below* the waters. *She* was from below, where the drowned dead lie dreaming, and I had awakened her with a horrid life. A life that thirsted, and must drink. . .

I think I shrieked, then, but I heard no sound. Certainly, I did not hear the howls from Neptune as the beast, burst from his prison, bounded down the stairs and flung himself upon the creature from the sea.

His furry form bore her back and obscured my vision; in an instant she was falling backwards, away, into the sea that spawned her. Then, and only then, did I catch a glimpse of the final moment of animation in that which my consciousness had summoned. Lightning seared the sight inexorably upon my soul—the sight of the ultimate blasphemy I had created in my pride. The rose had wilted. . .

The rose had wilted and become seaweed. And now, the golden one was gone and in its place was the bloated, swollen obscenity of a thing long-drowned and dead, risen from the slime and to that slime returning.

Only a moment, and then the waves overwhelmed it, bore it back into the blackness. Only a moment, and the door was slammed shut. Only a moment, and I raced up the iron stairs, Neptune yammering at my heels. Only a moment, and I reached the safety of this sanctuary.

Safety? There is no safety in the universe for me, no safety in a consciousness that could create such horror. And there is no safety here—the wrath of the waves increases with every moment, the anger of the sea and its creatures rises to an inevitable crescendo.

Mad or sane, it does not matter, for the end is the same in either case. I know now that the lighthouse will shatter and fall. I am already shattered, and must fall with it.

There is time only to gather these notes, strap them securely in a cylinder and attach it to Neptune's collar. It may be that he can swim, or cling to a fragment of debris. It may be that a ship, passing by this toppling beacon, may stay and search the waters for a sign—and thus find and rescue the gallant beast.

That ship shall not find me. I go with the lighthouse and go willingly, down to the dark depths. Perhaps—is it but perverted poetry?—I shall join my Companion there forever. Perhaps. . .

The lighthouse is trembling. The beacon flickers above my head and I hear the rush of waters in their final onslaught. There is—yes—a wave, bearing down upon me. It is higher than the tower, it blots out the sky itself, everything. . .

Editor's note: Edgar Allan Poe's original manuscript of "The

Lighthouse" *covered four handwritten pages and ended with the notation for January 3. "I took over from there," Robert Bloch says, "and it gave me no end of satisfaction to help give new life to the very last story from the pen of Poe."*

THE MAD TRIST

Robert Haining
Based on an idea by Edgar Allan Poe

I HAD TAKEN up a position some twenty yards away, next to a small yew tree near the edge of the graveyard. From this vantage point I could observe the service, detached from it and the small group of close relatives whose company I felt unable to share, yet close enough to it to be able to offer my respects to the man with whom I have been so closely involved during his last months. In view of all that he had strived for in life, it seemed a sad tribute that his parting should be marked by such a humble and forlorn gathering. The sense of emptiness pervaded even the words of the priest as his droning voice echoed through the tiny churchyard.

The atmosphere of that solemn occasion absorbed me, and wrapped in my imagined solitude, I began recalling the strange and terrifying events of recent weeks that had brought us both to this dismal place. Yet even as I did so, thinking myself, as I said, to be quite alone, I suddenly realized that someone was standing behind me. I felt a cold breath against my cheek and a gentle nudge as if I had been stalked by a friend who had found amusement in my serious contemplations. I turned quickly.

"Good afternoon," he said solemnly and his eyes, after first focusing on me with some intensity, relaxed and gazed across at the same group of figures that had been holding my attention. "A melancholy hour," he went on, "the moment when all our dreams of immortality are laid to rest."

I smiled at his choice of words. He was a small man, but one of distinguished bearing. I thought that perhaps he too had some connection with the deceased. I turned back to look at the service.

"What brings you to witness this sad event?" It seemed he was not interested in a passing conversation.

"I knew him once," I replied, somewhat irritated by his inquisitiveness.

"But not well enough. Or do you have some reason for being only a distant observer?"

I did not feel inclined to answer his question at that moment, and in any case I did not want to give him any reason to delay his departure, but as I turned to make some appropriate response he whispered,

"Please! I did not wish to interrupt you. It is a moment that will not return. Forgive me."

I thought that as he had now realized the indelicacy of his earlier remarks, he would choose to be on his way. As it was, we stood together in silence, I expecting him to go at any moment, and becoming increasingly irritated by his stubborn refusal to leave me in peace.

Yet the longer the man stayed the more my feelings toward him seemed to mellow. Once again I found myself reflecting on the previous weeks, and on the events that had brought both me and indeed the poor unfortunate, who was the object of this late afternoon ceremony, to this place. The happenings of the last few weeks had weighed heavily upon me before but never more so than now. Was it for that reason I began to think of my companion almost as a Father Confessor? His anonymous, perhaps fleeting presence, offered in some strange way an opportunity for me to unburden my thoughts, to exorcize those spirits that so often plagued me. My solitary life offered few such chances in the normal way. The service was still continuing as I said:

"I suppose in a way I feel partly responsible."

"For the fate of this poor fellow?"

I nodded.

"It was a chance remark, you see. How could I have known that it would have, for him, such dire consequences?"

"Have you met Mr Canning, Roger?"

It was at one of Simon's parties where we first met. I had accepted, after many earlier refusals, an invitation to attend one

THE MAD TRIST

of Simon Montague's literary parties, which he threw regularly in his large Victorian house near the centre of Bristol. After only half an hour I was feeling ill at ease for I seemed to know nobody, and my conversation, as so often seemed to be the case at such occasions, was proving unable to hold the attention of any of the other guests with whom I had become casually paired.

Sensing my boredom, yet determined not to let me slip quietly away, Simon was trying one last throw.

"William Canning is one of our distinguished local authors on the supernatural. Roger here," he said, presenting my literary credentials to the elderly, distinguished man who was now before me, "is something of an expert on. . .er. . .Edgar Allan Poe, is it, Roger? He's written some articles. You two should have a lot in common."

Simon's voice carried a certain condescension, as if he was barely able to accept that such writing was truly literary. For a moment I almost felt as if the two of us were being isolated from the rest of the gathering and that in due course we might be expected to reveal some aspect of a freakish personality that would explain the source of our curious interests. Such an attitude, if in any sense a true reflection of what Simon was thinking, would however have been quite unworthy of this quiet dignified man, whose white hair and slender build lent an almost aristocratic quality to his appearance.

The introductions made, Simon disappeared and the two of us were suddenly alone, neither quite sure of what to make of the other. As a rule, I had found other writers of the supernatural no more companionable than any other type of author. But I had heard of William Canning and had read one or two of his short stories, stories that had struck me as both intelligent and sensitive, far removed from the normal pattern followed by work of that kind. I knew also that he had not enjoyed great financial success from his writing and that his stylistic appeal was very much restricted to a narrow group of devotees for whom he was something of a cult figure. His mode of life was comfortable if not extravagant; he lived for example in an old house on the outskirts of Bristol near the Clifton Gorge, a house that had remained in the Canning family for many years.

We talked for some time about a new book he was trying to write. Although it was not his first, he was finding the project a difficult one to start, partly he claimed because of its scope and partly because of his age and growing infirmity. It was, in his own words, his "last quest for immortality", a last attempt to attain a goal that, he admitted, had been responsible for first luring him into writing. It seemed a naive confession from a man of his age. As a younger man, I too had dreamed of writing the great novel that would ensure my fame. Like him, it had eluded me and now even the very urge seemed irrelevant or at least unattainable. But with William Canning, the instinct had been reborn (perhaps it had never died) and with his life now drawing surely to a close, I could see it had reached a disturbing intensity. But there was more—the folly of a jealous comparison with an earlier member of the family who had attained just that immortality he craved.

On a sudden impulse, as if to emphasize his point, he began talking about one of his ancestors—William Canynges—one of the great men of Bristol, who in the early fifteenth century had been a famous merchant. From these beginnings, Canynges had gone on to become five times mayor of the city and later its MP. To crown his achievements, he had been instrumental in rebuilding the church of St Mary Redcliffe, one of the most famous churches in the West of England. Here was an ancestor worthy of respect, his achievements within the city, as laudable as they had become immortal. Would that he, William Canning, could also find some work, however humble in comparison, that would ensure that his name lived on.

I listened with interest to his description of William Canynges, though as he returned to his theme of immortality I became increasingly embarrassed once more. But my interest stemmed not so much from the historical details as from a half-forgotten reference to that famous name.

"Canynges!" I said deliberately when he paused, spelling the name as I now recalled where I had seen it before. "Have you ever read 'The Fall of the House of Usher' by Poe?"

Canning was somewhat surprised by the sudden change of conversation.

"I must have read it once," he replied, somewhat bemused.

"There's a reference in that story to a book, *The Mad Trist*, written by a Sir Launcelot Canning. The reference to it, and readings from it, form part of the climax to the story."

My mention of it had been partly casual, a process of thinking out loud once I had discovered the answer to my problem. Now that I thought about it more I remembered from earlier researches on the topic that a number of experts had believed there to be a connection between the mythical Sir Launcelot and William Canynges of Bristol. I found it quite fascinating to be making the acquaintance of a descendant of one who, quite unwittingly, had become part of the Poe legend.

William Canning's own reaction seemed less good-humoured. Perhaps it was because here was yet another aspect of his ancestor's immortality to add to what he already found a depressingly long list. He stood silently as I explained the connection, emphasizing mainly for his benefit the common view, which at the time I shared: the book was purely mythical, an invention of Poe's imagination for the purpose of building up tension in his famous story.

When I had finished William Canning remained silent. He seemed to have become deeply engrossed in his thoughts as if he were recalling some distant event. Then he looked at me.

"*The Mad Trist*. Yes, of course. I had almost forgotten. So long ago."

I did not understand what he meant that night, and he was not willing to elaborate further. Shortly afterwards he left the party, passing me in the corridor as I took my coat to leave. On the steps of Simon Montague's house, only half listening to Simon's garrulous banter, I watched Canning's shuffling figure as it disappeared along the darkly lit street. I wondered then what strange thoughts I had resurrected in him. It was to be several weeks however before I was to get an answer.

*

I did not see him again for some time, not, in fact, until he paid me a call late one evening. He came unannounced and it was so late that I felt sure, as I let him in, that it had to be on the most urgent business. In the event it proved to be a matter that could well have waited, and the meeting served only to confirm in my mind earlier reports of his eccentricity.

He was anxious to know from me the names and addresses of some Poe experts in this country and the United States. At first he would say nothing except that he was researching a short story, but in view of our last meeting I was suspicious. I offered him a drink and was pleased when he finally took off his coat and sat down in front of the fire.

We talked rather casually for a while. I enquired about his book but he seemed to have made no further progress with it. Indeed from his manner it seemed as if he had abandoned it.

After several further drinks, his attitude becoming a good deal more mellow in the process, he mentioned in passing the name of his ancestor William Canynges again. I seized upon it, referring once more to the Poe story, for I felt sure that his enquiry and his famous forebear were linked in some way.

After a short pause during which he seemed to be trying, unsuccessfully as it turned out, to curb his inclination to tell me what he knew, he finally said:

"This life of my illustrious forebear is not quite as honourable as might appear from a superficial account." He paused. "Perhaps I should ask you to keep what I say to yourself, for it is a family legend, you see, that towards the end of his life William Canynges dabbled in the occult. Participating in pagan ceremonies, even founding a clandestine devil-worshipping sect as a result of experiments he had carried out taking drugs. As the legend goes, he was so horrified by what he discovered that he became deeply religious, giving up all secular matters to concentrate his mind on atoning for his blasphemous experiments. That was why he became a monk, shunning all social life until his death in 1474." He paused again. "I remember my father once telling me, goodness that was a long time ago, I had quite forgotten. . .

he once told me that William Canynges had written his experiences down. . .or so it was imagined."

Canning paused to swallow his drink. I was anxious that he should not leave before he had finished telling me what he knew.

"How is this known?" I said, topping up his glass.

"Thank you. Oh, it's just handed down the generations. It's a family story."

For a moment he looked down into his glass. Canning had never married, he had no heirs.

"But what evidence is there of him having written down his experiences? It's a matter of speculation amongst some art historians that drugs were used to induce hypnotic trances, and these visions then provided ideas for some Renaissance painters. There's Hieronymus Bosch, for example. But the paintings exist. Was any manuscript ever found?"

Canning smiled.

"It's true," he went on, "that no trace of a book or even a manuscript was ever found amongst Canynges's papers and possessions. But that's not quite the end of the matter."

Canning leant forward, lowering his voice as if afraid that his words might be overheard by some unseen but malevolent force.

"On his deathbed, Canynges is supposed to have given the book to one of the monks. Apparently his illness was sudden and in his dying moments he pleaded with the man to destroy the book. Now, for one reason or another, the monk is supposed not to have obeyed these instructions. Maybe he read it and would not take the responsibility for burning it. Whatever the reason, he kept it in his possession for over a quarter of a century and then in his turn entrusted it to another priest who was sailing from Bristol to America with John Cabot. Perhaps in some way he felt he was fulfilling his pledge to William, for he must have thought that once in America it would be lost forever."

Canning sat back in his chair as if the effort of recounting the tale had exhausted him. He stared at me, and I can still recall those haunting eyes, for he was like a man who had sensed his mission in life. A current of excitement ran through everything he said.

"The book did reach America, according to the family story, but what happened to it after that no one knows." He paused, continuing with a note of triumph in his voice. "The book remained lost until Poe himself saw it."

"Poe!" I exclaimed. It took me a second to realize what he was saying. "You mean that book, the one William Canynges wrote of his experiences, was *The Mad Trist* in 'The Fall of the House of Usher?' "

"Exactly!" said Canning. "I believe that there was such a book, and that it is no chance that the names of Sir Launcelot Canning and William Canynges are linked. They are one and the same!"

"But the book is mythical," I protested.

"Correction. It is believed to be mythical. I tell you that such a book was written, and I believe Poe saw a copy of it and used it in his story."

I was amazed by his suggestion. Coming from anyone else I would have dismissed it as mere idle speculation, but coming from a descendant of the man, it had to be taken seriously even though it ran counter to everything that was known about Poe's reference to *The Mad Trist*. Indeed the revelation—if it were true—threw a new and fascinating light not only on the story, but also on Poe's life itself. Was it possible, for example, that the depravities supposedly contained therein had been partly to blame for Poe's own disintegration of mind and his own descent into alcohol and drugs? Was it possible that the terrors described in the Canynges manuscript, only hinted at in 'The Fall of the House of Usher', really existed in some lost manuscript? What an incredible discovery it would make! What a sensation it would create in literary and occult circles! What immortality it would create for the man who discovered the manuscript!

Immortality! I looked up at him and realized that the very idea had occurred to him. Why else would he have given up work on his novel? Now he was standing and his words carried a deep and disturbing conviction:

"And now, if you please, I would be obliged if you would give

THE MAD TRIST

me those addresses, for I have work to do. I hope I can trust to your discretion in this matter. It would not do to reveal any of this until more definite proof can be presented."

And there the matter rested for several weeks, at least as far as I was concerned. I must confess that the thought of discovering such a rare and important document fascinated me even then, but I did nothing, nor could I discover what progress Canning was making. I did not see him, and though I passed his house on several occasions it always seemed deserted.

As it happened I met him again, quite by chance, one Friday night. I had gone to a little restaurant near the dockland section of Bristol. It is my habit to dine out once a week to escape the monotony of my own cooking. As fate would have it on that occasion he was there and though he seemed none too pleased, I managed to invite myself to his table.

It took little effort on my part to turn the conversation towards his quest for *The Mad Trist* though as before he seemed reluctant to go into detail. Remembering our earlier conversation and the lubricating effect liquor seemed to have upon him I ordered a bottle of wine and duly began to ply the man. Yet for all he said that night it seemed to me at the time that he had made little progress. Little did I realize that, in a way, the discoveries he had already made had sealed his terrible fate.

"I cannot help wondering if there is a clue in the life of this gentleman."

Canning had been visiting the church of St Mary Redcliffe, his ancestor's crowning achievement. From conversations he had had, he had made a connection between his illustrious forebear and the celebrated Bristol poet Thomas Chatterton. The connection could hardly have been more bizarre.

Canning explained that Chatterton had lived some three hundred years after William Canynges. Moreover, whereas Canynges had found status and distinction in his time, Chatterton's brief life—a mere eighteen years—had been marked as much by scandal as by any honourable recognition. He had indulged in literary fraud, fabricating "antique" verses and plays. He had gained further notoriety by satirizing leading figures of Bristol. Partly because of this he had left Bristol in 1770 and come to London, lodging first in Shoreditch later in Holborn. Although he had some further literary success, it provided insufficient reward to prevent him from descending into the ranks of the penniless and starving. Finally, in despair, he committed suicide, so ending his days in a pauper's grave attached to the Shoe Lane Workhouse. Not until after his death did collections of his work appear in print.

I could not imagine how the lives of two such different men could in any way be connected. Canning however was obviously enjoying my confusion and he savoured the explanation like a detective confronting a murderer with the weight of damning evidence.

"Chatterton claimed in 1768 to have found a manuscript written by Canynges. It was entitled 'Elinour and Juga', but, and this is the real point. . .he claimed to have found the manuscript in Canynges's coffin in St Mary Redcliffe."

Canning sat back to observe my reaction. In the event I must have disappointed him.

"Claimed?" I queried. "What do you mean? Does this manuscript exist?"

Canning seemed offended by my question and after a rather lengthy silence he replied testily, "Well, the manuscript was probably a forgery. Chatterton is thought to have written it himself."

I said nothing in reply and his manner became more indignant. But how could I react otherwise? It seemed to me he was behaving irrationally. In the absence of any solid evidence he was grabbing at anything. If the manuscript was a forgery, whether Chatterton claimed it came from Canynges's coffer was of little significance. If the "Elinour and Juga" manuscript was genuine, did he seriously believe that *The Mad Trist* or a copy of it might lie in the same place in Canynges's tomb? Surely if it did exist, the notorious Chatterton would have taken that manuscript too. And yet, I reflected, there was the young poet's suicide to consider. Was it possible that the text was so horrific that he had returned it to the tomb? Was it possible that what the book revealed played some part in Chatterton's eventual suicide, as perhaps it did in Poe's own death? The coincidence was striking.

I was about to ask him whether that was his belief but the chance was lost as he said,

"And there's this as well." His voice carried an undercurrent of hostility now. He was finding my attitude tedious.

He took out of his pocket a letter that had come from America. Presumably one of my American contacts had been able to give him something. He unfolded a small piece of paper and handed it across to me. It was a photocopy of a page from an old newspaper, *The Saturday Museum*. Poe had been associated with it in 1843, but the piece here made yet another reference to the mysterious Sir Launcelot Canning. The story referred to a publication Poe had been planning to start called *The Stylus*. For his motto, Poe had planned to use a quote signed with the name Launcelot Canning. I read it, and then re-read it, making little sense of its message:

> —— unbending that all men
> Of thy firm TRUTH may say—"Lo! this is writ
> With the antique *iron* pen."

I handed it back to him, shrugging my shoulders in a display of incomprehension.

"I had hoped you would have been more. . .open minded."

Canning was obviously offended. He had mistaken my gesture for a form of ridicule. It had not been intended as such, simply a sign that I did not understand the importance of these fragmented pieces of information. It was too late however to undo the damage and he looked at me fiercely as he stood up to leave.

"I am sorry that you consider my efforts wasted and the results of my research nothing more than meaningless bits of gibberish."

I could feel in his voice all the hurt pride of a man who had suffered countless rejections from others he took to be less talented or less worthy than himself. He pulled on his coat hurriedly. There was no arrogance in his movements, no sense of inner conviction that could not be destroyed by an indifferent world. His manner was more transparent than that. He was like a hurt child whose first faltering efforts had met a stern rebuke. He wanted to be away from me and any attempt on my part to repair the damage would only have added insult to the wreck of our brief confidence.

In the distance the small group of mourners had begun to move away from the graveside. I stood upright now, no longer leaning against the yew tree. I wanted to walk over to the grave, but I felt a hand rest on my shoulder.

"Please go on," whispered my companion. "I am sure you have more to tell me."

The story was nearly told, but the most important pieces were still missing. Now that I had started, it was only right to finish.

In the days that followed I became obsessed by what Canning had told me. Nothing of what he had said had really made sense, and yet nor was I able to dismiss his words from my mind. Perhaps his own intensity had something to do with it, the evident fervour with which he was pursuing his enquiries. Looking back, perhaps that was the only thread that ran through this whole business, but it was enough to draw me one day down to the church of St Mary Redcliffe—that and a phone call I had just had from Simon Montague, telling me that Canning had been making regular visits to the church, spending long hours in silent contemplation near Canynges's tomb. I was reminded of course of our last conversation. Here surely was the answer to the question I had been unable to put to him. Canning really did believe that some part of the mystery had its solution in the tomb of William Canynges. Was it concern for his safety or some less honourable motive that encouraged me to find out more about what he was doing?

On my first visit I managed to speak to one of the wardens of the church. He had, in fact, noticed Canning, his attention having been drawn by a number of sudden outbursts. Canning, it seemed, on more than one occasion, had ended his vigil in a state of some agitation, roaring incoherently at his ancestor's tomb before storming out of the church in a fury.

I made no reference to any of the conversations I had had with Canning. I certainly could not be sure he was about to make some dramatic move, and yet on an impulse I described myself to the warden as a close friend. I suggested to him that if Canning began acting strangely again that he might care to let me know. I told him that the old man had no close relations and rather than let the police deal with any odd behaviour, I would do my best to intercede. I indicated to him that his behaviour was just one aspect of encroaching senility. I left him with my telephone number.

Two weeks passed and nothing happened. Then late one evening, whilst I was at home working, the phone rang. It was a call from the church warden of St Mary Redcliffe. He sounded anxious and begged me to come immediately; if not, his only recourse would be to call in the police. William Canning had somehow got into the muniment room where his ancestor's remains lay buried and had now barricaded himself in. Strange noises were coming from the room. I told the warden I would be there immediately, yet even as I hurried to make the appointment I could not in any way imagine the reason for William Canning's strange turn of behaviour.

I arrived to find the warden waiting for me at the North Porch and we went immediately to the door of the muniment room. Even as we approached the solid oak door, we could both hear the strange incantations issuing from within. The words were incoherent, but the strangely guttural tones had a pagan quality. I thought of desecration, for it was as if the very presence of these sounds was offensive, an abomination to the surroundings in which they were uttered.

"Mr Canning." The warden beat on the oak door, as if to

demonstrate the nature of his earlier efforts. It was clear that such exertion was futile.

"What could he be using," I asked, "to barricade himself in?"

"There are some chairs in there, and a table. Nothing else except a visitor's book and pen."

"Then should we push? Perhaps if we both try we might get in."

Judging by the sounds coming from within it seemed imperative that we act quickly.

The warden nodded and we both leant our weight hard against the door. But even as we did so, the sounds from within seemed to rise to a new and terrifying crescendo. We pushed harder and felt something behind the door slip. As the door gave an inch a thin stream of light cut the cloistered gloom and the sounds rose to yet a new climax. A thin column of incense curled out through the slit in the door. Even in that poor light I could see that the interior was heavily laden with smoke.

"More!" I shouted and we heaved again. The door gave another inch and through the murk I could see a figure moving slowly about the room, his arms held up aloft whilst strange inhuman sounds seemed to pour from his barely opened mouth.

"Canning!" I shouted, for in that instant I feared for his life. What was it that made me predict so accurately that within that terrible place, Canning was stirring up forces far beyond his capacity to contain? Was it perhaps that I sensed Canning was not alone?

I shouted to him again as we moved the obstruction further back, but still I could not gain access and now it seemed as if he were screaming the words. Yet why did his lips not move? It was as if he were possessed, not the master of the rites he was performing, but in some strange way the sacrificial victim.

"Canning! Stop before it is too late!"

We pushed again, harder still, and yet with every slight movement of the door it seemed as if Canning's figure was retreating further into the thick smoke at the far end of the room. The smoke descended like a shroud and a shrill scream broke the air.

THE MAD TRIST

Was it Canning's voice? His figure was now lost.

"Canning, for God's sake!"

In that instant the obstruction gave and we staggered into the room. Canning was before us, half enveloped in the gloom, his body now seeming to be above us, as if elevated by some giant hand.

"The tomb! The tomb!"

Canning, his face transfixed, seemed to be pointing at his ancestor's tomb. Had he made the discovery? Had he found out where the manuscript lay? But as he moved towards me I could see that his hand was clutching his heart. He staggered, his foot catching a large book that lay open on the floor near the centre of the room.

I rushed towards him, grabbing him as he fell and then laying him gently on the ground. As I did so I saw that the stone flags were covered with strange symbols.

But in that moment I realized Canning was dead and as I moved his hand I could see that he had been clutching a pen—an ancient rusted iron pen that had been driven into his body.

"The visitor's pen," gasped the warden.

"The antique iron pen!" Now words that had seemed so incomprehensible before returned to my mind. They were no more comprehensible now and yet they carried a bitter irony:

> —— unbending that all men
> Of thy firm TRUTH may say—"Lo! this is writ
> With the antique *iron* pen."

I looked up at the warden. I made no mention of what I knew, but instead recalled an earlier sensation just before we had entered the muniment room.

"There is no one in this room except you and I. But look!"

I showed him how deeply the lethal point had been driven into Canning's body, and then added: "Could he possibly have done this himself?"

In that moment I saw the book that Canning had tripped on.

I pulled it towards me across the floor and after scanning the text turned to the title page.

"The book," I said to my companion, "was by the necromancer Dr John Dee. Canning had been using one of his occult books to resurrect the ghost of his ancestor either to point the way conclusively to the tomb where he believed the book to be, or else to tell him where it did lie. If he discovered anything, then his message died with him."

My companion said nothing, but I felt his presence behind me as I walked slowly towards the freshly dug grave. The gravedigger was near by, preparing to do his work.

"I cannot help but wonder," I continued, "whether in the end Canning was right."

"What do you mean?" he asked.

"His last words, his last gestures were to point to the tomb. I cannot help wondering if in the end the old man was right—the manuscript, or some copy of it, does lie in the tomb."

The idea had been preying on my mind ever since the night of Canning's ceremony.

We were standing beside the grave of William Canning now, and as I took a small handful of dirt and sprinkled it onto the wooden coffin, I added:

"Immortality. It is a futile quest of itself, but when the fruit is there for the picking. . ."

"So you too are fascinated by the same possibility?"

I sensed that my companion's voice had changed. . .had stiffened. For the first time he walked past me and stood staring at me from the far side of the grave, his eyes almost luminous in the gloom that had now descended on the graveyard. A cold wind was rising, gusting about me yet somehow not disturbing the stillness that had also suddenly fallen.

I looked away, unable to return his remorseless gaze. The gravedigger, who was standing near us, seemed transfixed, his hand upon the spade. In the distance the mourners were motionless. It was as if time itself had stopped.

Immediately I looked back at my companion, whose head was now bowed as if in silent supplication. His appearance had changed too. Now he was standing before me in monk's habit so that even as he raised his head, the long cowl hid every feature of his face. Even before he spoke I now knew who my companion was. Canning's ceremony had not failed in its intended purpose. I had not been deceived in those moments before entering the muniment room.

"Why do you crave immortality at my expense? You must pursue this matter no further!"

His voice was threatening and as he spoke he held out his fist, as if he were holding a knife, and then brought it down with a sudden jabbing motion. The gesture could only have been a re-enactment of how that murderous antique iron pen had been driven into Canning's heart. As I had first suspected, that fatal wound had not been self-inflicted, and now before me stood Canning's murderer.

"Then tell me where it is? Where is *The Mad Trist*?"

At last I spoke the words. Even if this were to be my final hour and the knowledge of that book to be the instrument of my destruction, yet still, like Canning before me, I wanted to know. Like one who wishes to know the profoundest mysteries of the universe, in that instant I would have sacrificed my life for a moment of truth.

The sounds echoed through the stillness of the graveyard as I repeated:

"Tell me where the book is to be found and I swear to God I will say nothing. Is it in the tomb?"

He started to move away now, melting into the darkness, but then paused as if he could not decide whether to give me an answer. I begged him again and he turned to face me.

"Is it in the tomb?" I repeated. "Tell me!"

"You are correct, for where else could it be. . ." His words were barely audible, as if they were addressed as much to himself as to me. I sensed a riddle in what he said and as he spoke he lowered his cowl so that for the first time I saw his face.

In that moment before he was lost to my sight I understood his meaning more clearly than if it had been inscribed on parchment and set before me. For was not every page of that "book" etched upon his tortured face? Was not every word reflected in his haunted eyes? Here was the true object of that fatal quest, as perhaps Canning had realized in his last seconds of life. For me Canynges's message stretched out through time to speak more eloquently than any text, indeed it was a message that Poe himself would have understood well: What need have they of a book— those who have spoken with the Devil.